05/07

Capital Affairs

Capital Affairs

London and the Making of the Permissive Society

Frank Mort

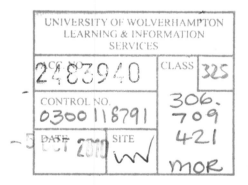
Yale University Press
New Haven and London

Designed by Emily Angus

Printed in China

Library of Congress Cataloging-in-Publication Data

Mort, Frank.

Capital affairs : London and the making of the permissive society / Frank Mort.

p. cm.

Includes bibliographical references and index.

ISBN 978-0-300-11879-7 (alk. paper)

1. Sex–England–London–History–20th century.

2. Sex scandals–England–London–History–20th century.

3. London (Eng.)–Social conditions. I. Title.

HQ18.G7M67 2010

306.7709421'09045dc22

2010005259

For Daniel

Contents

Acknowledgements

This book has had a lengthy and somewhat curious intellectual gestation. It started life when I was a postgraduate student in the Centre for Cultural Studies at the University of Birmingham. Encouraged by the expansion of academic interest in the history of sexuality, I proposed writing a thesis on the permissive legislation of the 1950s and 1960s. In fact, what I produced was a very different work, a history of medico-moral politics in England, which became my first book, *Dangerous Sexualities*. Since then many other projects have intervened and times and historical perspectives have changed, but my interest in the genesis of liberal sexual morality has remained. This work is the outcome, and Gillian Malpass, my editor at Yale University Press, has sustained the project from the outset with her enormous enthusiasm, care, and patience.

Let me also begin by thanking those grant agencies and institutions that supported my research and writing. I am extremely grateful to the Arts and Humanities Research Council for their research leave grant in 1999–2000 (Metropolitan Culture and Moral Change no. APN 9195) which provided valuable time to develop the book. An American fellowship at the National Humanities Center in 2001–2, generously financed by the Benjamin Duke Fellowship and the Andrew W. Mellon Foundation, enabled me to extend its original scope. Subsequently, a fellowship at the Shelby Cullom Davis Center for Historical Studies in the History Department at Princeton University provided very important support at a critical juncture. In the final stage, my stay in the History Department at Johns Hopkins University as John Hinckley Visiting Professor gave me time and space to revise the manuscript.

I have worked at two institutions since 1998 when the book was conceived. The research advisory committee in the School of Cultural and Innovation Studies at the University of East London generously underwrote my work through its sabbatical leave policy. Since 2004, the School of Arts, Histories and Cultures at the University of Manchester has provided me with an exciting intellectual environment to complete the project. I am grateful to both institutions for making it possible for me to research and write.

Libraries and librarians have loomed large in my work. I would like to thank the staff at the Bishopsgate Library, Bodleian Library, University of Oxford, British Film Institute Library, British Library and the National Sound Archive, British Newspaper Library, British Library of Political and Economic Science, Columbia University Libraries, Duke University Libraries, Guildhall Library, Jewish Museum London, Kensington and Chelsea Libraries, The Kinsey Institute for Research in Sex, Gender, and Reproduction, London Metropolitan Archives, The National Archives, The New York Public Library, Princeton University Library, The Sheridan Libraries of The Johns Hopkins University, Theatre Museum London, University College London Library, University of North Carolina Libraries, University of Reading Library, Victoria and Albert Museum Archive of Art and Design, Wellcome Library, Westminster City Archives, and The Women's Library.

Over more than a decade this project has been my calling card to seminars and colloquia in Britain, the rest of Europe, and the United States, all of which have contributed in important ways to the development of my ideas. The meetings of the Economic and Social Research Council's funded seminar programme, Transforming London: Rethinking Regeneration through Commerce, Planning, and Art (Grant A2612), helped to concentrate my thoughts about capital city culture. My thanks to Alison Blunt, Michael Keith, Miles Ogborn, David Pinder, Rob Stone, and Sophie Watson. Miles Ogborn also commented on my manuscript as part of our collaborative editorial discussions for a special issue of the *Journal of British Studies* on Transforming Metropolitan London (2004), as did James Epstein. Contributors to the Raphael Samuel History Centre's Researching the Metropolis programme at the University of East London and the Bishopsgate Institute, when I was the Centre's Director, also provided a sounding board for my ideas, and I am grateful to John Marriott for his support. Fellows and staff at the Davis Center and members of the History Department at Princeton, especially Gyan Prakash, Peter Brown, Sheila Crane, David Frisby, Kevin Kruse, Pamela Long, Martin Murray, Jordan Sand, Sarah Schrank, and Christine Stansell made my year there an especially productive one as a member of the Cities: Space, Society, and History programme. More recently, a three-year seminar series focused on the Urban Atlantic and funded by the British Academy's International Networks Scheme also helped me think about London in a wider comparative international context. In New York as well as at home, George Chauncey, Jane Jacobs, Harvey Molotch, Andrew Ross, Richard Sennett, and Daniel Walkowitz were particularly important in this dialogue. Discussions with Frank Trentmann and members of the ESRC and AHRC funded Cultures of Consumption research programme provided a stimulating context for me to revise my ideas about post-war consumerism. At the University of Manchester, my three years spent as Director of the Centre for Interdisciplinary Research in the Arts provided a fresh forum for thinking about sexuality and urban culture, and I am very grateful to Janet Wolff, Ana Carden-Coyne, and Atreyee Sen for their support.

Many individuals have been extremely generous with their time and advice when I pressed them for specific information about the post-war period. I am indebted to the late Jean Graham Hall and the late Patrick Trevor-Roper, both of whom shared their recollections of the Wolfenden committee, while Michael Burn told me about Guy Burgess. Joanna Marschner, Curator, Historic Royal Palaces, Kensington Palace, provided guidance on the complexities of British court dress, Maggie Bird, Head of the Metropolitan Police Historic Collection, and Alan Moss helped me with questions about police administration, Clive Elmsley responded to my ideas on the Profumo affair, Jane Chippindale at the *Yorkshire Post* helped with information about John Wolfenden, while Tony Dunn remembered Paul Raymond. Kathryn Johnson, Curator of Modern Drama Collections at the British Library, generously shared a preliminary draft of her article on the Lord Chamberlain's Office with me.

Friends and colleagues offered acute readings of different parts of the text at various stages of its evolution. My thanks to Lucy Bland, Charlotte Brunsdon, Harry Cocks, Martin Francis, Susan Glenn, Max Jones, Tom Lacqueur, Angus McLaren, Sean Nixon, James Vernon, and Chris Waters. I am also grateful for incisive comments and advice from Sally Alexander, Peter Bailey, Chris Breward, Becky Conekin, Laura Doan, Geoff Eley, Geoff Field, Peter Gatrell, Till Geiger, David Gilbert, Lesley Hall, Nick Harrigan, Matt Houlbrook, Kali Israel, Patrick Joyce, Tony McElligott, Adrian Rifkin, George Robb, Mike Savage, Bill Schwarz, Penny Summerfield, and Chris Weedon. Pat Thane and an anonymous reviewer took time out of their year to read the manuscript for Yale, and I have acted on much of their good advice. My students have been among my best critics: first and foremost my PhD students past and present and the members of my Sexuality, Gender, and Urban Culture graduate class at Manchester. My stay as Visiting Professor of Modern British History at Columbia University in 2004 gave me an opportunity to teach the history of London in a different national context; I would like to thank Victoria de Grazia for inviting me and for her intellectual support and friendship.

Various parts of the book were first tried out at seminars and international conferences, and I thank collectively convenors, commentators, and audiences alike for helping me to focus my ideas at the University of California Berkeley, Cambridge Historical Society, Cardiff University, Centre for Interdisciplinary Research Bielefeld University, Einstein Forum Potsdam, Fawcett Society, Fordham University, German Historical Institute London, Johns Hopkins University, University of Limerick, University of Michigan, New York University, Royal College of Art, The Royal Society, Victoria and Albert Museum, University of York, Annual Conference of the Royal Geographical Society and the Institute of British Geographers, Annual Meeting of the American Historical Association, Centre for Contemporary British History Summer Conference, European Social Science History Conference, North American Conference on British Studies, and the Social History Society Annual Conference.

Since the book has been a while in the making some parts of the material have been published in earlier versions. Parts of Chapter 3 appeared as 'Scandalous Events: Metropolitan Culture and Moral Change in Post-Second World War London', *Representations* 93 (Winter 2006): 106–37 (Berkeley: University of California Press), and I acknowledge the Regents of the University of California for permission to publish. This chapter also drew on my 'Fantasies of Metropolitan Life: Planning London in the 1940s', *Journal of British Studies* 42, no. 1 (January 2004): 120–51 (Chicago: University of Chicago Press). A version of Chapter 5 originally appeared as 'Striptease, the Erotic Female Moving Body and Live Sexual Entertainment in Mid-Twentieth-Century London', *Social History* 32, no. 1 (February 2007): 27–53 (Abingdon: Taylor & Francis), and I acknowledge Taylor & Francis for permission to reprint this material. Quotations from the Mass Observation Archive, University of Sussex, are reproduced with the permission of Curtis Brown Group Ltd, London, on behalf of the Trustees of the Mass Observation Archive, Copyright The Trustees of the Mass Observation Archive. My deep appreciation to the Trustees of the Harold Macmillan Book Trust for permission to quote from the diaries of Harold Macmillan, as well as to the Bodleian Library, University of Oxford, as holders of the archive.

Finishing the book I was aided by Michelle Johansen and Ethan Miller. Robert Kincaid was both meticulous and highly creative in checking the text and assisting with picture research and the index. Nancy Marten was a superb copy editor, while the editorial team at Yale, and especially Emily Angus, gave constant practical help and advice. Lynn Nead has shared an ongoing interdisciplinary conversation about urban culture and has commented on many of my ideas. In a very different way my mother Lilian Mort has been there throughout as a source of support, giving me her own memories of the 1950s. I owe an enormous debt to Judith Walkowitz's scholarship and friendship. She has been my London interlocutor throughout the research, giving me fine comments on the manuscript over a number of years; her exemplary approach to cultural history has been so important for my own thinking. My final thanks go to Daniel Virgili, who has lived with me and with this project since its inception. He has given excellent editorial advice, intellectual help, and constant practical and personal support. The book is dedicated to him with love and gratitude.

Illustrations

11 'Social and Functional Analysis of the Central Area', Arthur Ling, in J. H. Forshaw and Patrick Abercrombie, *County of London Plan* (London: Macmillan, 1943), Plate VI, 2. Reproduced by kind permission of the Corporation of London and London Metropolitan Archives.

12 'Eye level view of St Paul's Cathedral from the south side of Cannon Streeet (widened on north side) at corner of Friday Street', perspective by J. D. M. Harvey, no. 4a, Corporation of London, Court of Common Council, *Report to the Right Honourable the Lord Mayor etc. on the Preliminary Draft Proposals for Post War Reconstruction in the City of London* (London: Batsford, 1944), p. 17. Reproduced by kind permission of London Metropolitan Archives.

13 Neighbours chatting while police guard number 10 Rillington Place, 25 March 1953, photographer unknown. Popperfoto/Getty Images.

14 Family snapshot of John Christie, undated, in Criminal Cases: Christie, John Reginald Halliday (1949–1953), TNA PRO HO 291/228. The National Archives, reproduced by kind permission of the Metropolitan Police Authority.

15 Kitchen of 10 Rillington Place showing the body of one of the murdered women, 1953, photographer Chief Inspector Percy Law, Photographic Department Scotland Yard, in Criminal Cases: Christie, John Reginald Halliday (1949–1953), TNA PRO HO 291/228. The National Archives, reproduced by kind permission of the Metropolitan Police Authority.

16 Front room of 10 Rillington Place showing the body of Mrs Ethel Christie, 1953, photographer Chief Inspector Percy Law, Photographic Department Scotland Yard, in Criminal Cases: Christie, John Reginald Halliday (1949–1953), TNA PRO HO 291/228. The National Archives, reproduced by kind permission of the Metropolitan Police Authority.

Between pages 134 and 135

17 Restored interior of the grand hall of the Central Criminal Courts, known as the Old Bailey, 8 September 1952, photographer Central Press/Stringer. Getty Images.

18 Kathleen Maloney, undated, photographer unknown, in Criminal Cases: Christie, John Reginald Halliday (1949–1953), TNA PRO HO 291/228. The National Archives, reproduced by kind permission of the Metropolitan Police Authority.

Every effort has been made to trace copyright holders of the illustrations. In the event of any queries please contact Yale University Press, London

Introduction

When Alfred Kinsey arrived in London in the autumn of 1955 he came looking for sex. The English capital was the second leg of the American sexologist's seven-week tour that took him from the vice squads and transvestites of Copenhagen, through the cruising grounds of Rome and the 'whorehouses' of Naples, to the strict Catholic prohibitions of Madrid.[1] Wherever he went in Europe Kinsey was feted as an international celebrity. Fresh from the publication of his massive survey of female sexuality at home and driven by his enthusiasm for finding new sexual information across the Atlantic, he planned a full schedule.

Once settled in London Kinsey busied himself with his research. He began work on the British Museum's extensive collection of erotica; he lunched with Oscar Wilde's son Vyvyan, whom he found to be a 'rather sober and dullish businessman'.[2] He also spent a day at Wormwood Scrubs, the vast Victorian prison in west London, where he witnessed the glaring contradictions of the English penal system at first hand. Kinsey was amazed to discover that 30 per cent of the men were there for sex crimes.[3] A dedicated team of psychiatrists and social workers impressed him enormously, but the Scrubs still carried out a vicious regime of corporal punishment; prisoners could be flogged with up to twenty lashes on their bare back.[4] Scandalous incidents of this sort confirmed his belief that sadomasochism was rife in England. They were encouraged by the eccentricities of the public school system and clearly evident from the calling cards for whipping and domination that were everywhere in newsagents' windows across the West End.[5] Kinsey's lecture to the Maudsley Hospital was given a standing ovation when he called for the wholesale reform of the sex laws because they were archaic and inhumane.[6]

Kinsey's research was in the best traditions of Anglo-Saxon empiricism; his sexual naturalism, with its commitment to the power of statistics and a distrust of 'Continental' theorizing, guaranteed him a warm welcome in many parts of London's public and intellectual culture. But Kinsey's reputation rested on more than his status as a number cruncher; he was equally famous as an ethnographer of sex. Keen to get to new fieldwork, he immediately asked to see the capital's red-light district. With the Assistant Keeper of the British Library as their guide, Kinsey and his wife Clara set off one Saturday evening on a sex tour of the West End, tracking across the dense network of narrow streets and cross routes that led north from Piccadilly Circus and Leicester Square into Soho.

Kinsey was astounded by the sheer amount of sexual activity on public display in London. In streets bordering onto the West End's fashionable entertainment district, which was the gathering place for the social elites, commercial sex was rife. Soho was the backstage for exotic cultural and sexual encounters of all kinds. Just around the corner from elegant restaurants and glamorous nightclubs he encountered the most blatant soliciting by prostitutes of both sexes; at two and three in the morning they 'were letting their hands dribble across the crotch of passer[s] by'.[7] Police activity was at best haphazard and at worst downright corrupt; arrests were purely random and officers turned a blind eye to the way 'queers' were beaten up by male prostitutes. Young guardsmen were particularly aggressive predators, and Kinsey christened them 'dare devils' who would go 'all out for sex' by parading themselves in 'skin-tight uniforms'.[8] As for the women, most of the streetwalkers around Piccadilly were 'trim and neat', but when Kinsey and his party ventured deep into Soho they met the bedraggled 'worn out hags' familiar from his research on American cities.[9]

Fresh from his night-time observations, Kinsey appeared at the Home Office, where he was interviewed by John Wolfenden's government inquiry set up to examine homosexuality and prostitution. His graphic evidence caused a stir when he likened soliciting in London to its visibility in Central America; Kinsey reported that he had 'never seen such . . . prostitution . . . except in Havana'.[10] His uncomfortable comparison was meant to shock, with its suggestion of Latino-style excess in the heart of the nation's capital. For Kinsey, the seemingly insatiable demand for commercial sex was a clear sign that England was a repressed society. Taking an American view of this sexual legacy, he concluded: 'I am quite convinced . . . that we have inherited a lot of attitudes from our English forebears.'[11]

Kinsey's fieldwork celebrated the traditional rights of privileged men to move easily across the whole of the city and experience its diversity. He tracked between the venues of professional society, national government, and the low-life sexual haunts that were close to the centres of power. His claims to urban spectatorship carried a strong erotic charge.[12] Like many earlier generations of experts who had explored the West End's subcultures, Kinsey was not just a disinterested observer. A powerful streak of voyeurism marked his encounters with sexual London, energizing his ethnography in unpredictable ways. Despite his hostility to abstract theorizing, Kinsey was not averse to making generalizations about sex and the English on the basis of his one-off tour of Soho. This esoteric district north of Piccadilly Circus had the capacity to stimulate powerful ideas about national life and sexual character.

Alfred Kinsey's observations were not unique. London's sexual notoriety was obsessively dissected throughout the 1950s when anxieties about public and private vice pressed hard on national politics. Purity campaigners were outraged, men-of-the-world delighted, and foreign visitors like Kinsey were astounded by the city's sexual cultures. Sex erupted onto the agenda of successive Conservative governments; Churchill's Cabinet nervously discussed homosexuality and prostitution three times during the winter of 1953, and ten years later metropolitan scandal almost brought down Harold Macmillan's administration in the fallout from the Profumo affair, which commanded world attention. This is the story of London's capital affairs.

My book is a cultural history of London in the decade that begins in the early 1950s and climaxes with the Profumo scandal. I use London as the urban prism to focus the dynamic changes to sex and personal life taking place during this period, changes that historians have regularly addressed via the idea of the permissive society. But permissiveness is a slippery term that conceals as much as it reveals about contemporary sexuality and urban culture. My book challenges a number of its foundational myths and offers a new interpretation of the shifting attitudes to sex, politics and society in England during these years.

Capital Affairs takes issue with the progressive version of the 1960s. This argument stresses that the rise of the permissive society was a linear and directed force that erupted in the late 1950s and ran its course through the decade that followed, modernizing sexual behaviour in ways that were socially beneficial and qualitatively different from the system of public morality that preceded it. As one historian has put it, the period witnessed a positive 'revolution in . . . lifestyles, family relationships and personal freedoms for the vast majority of ordinary people'; it was a moment of 'outstanding historical significance'.[13] Centre stage in this liberal narrative of the 1960s are professional experts like Kinsey and go-ahead commercial entrepreneurs, who together pioneered changes in public attitudes to homosexuality, pornography and female sexuality as test cases of permissiveness. In this version of events, rising material affluence and the expanding welfare state are seen to provide the infrastructure for the new sexual culture.[14] On the major themes that historians have used to identify the permissive moment, I outline a different chronology and an alternative interpretation of events. Four interrelated issues focus my disagreements with established accounts. They centre on questions of periodization, the social consequences of the permissive society, its key protagonists, and the connections between sex and wider cultural and economic processes.

My account parts company with histories of the 1960s that see the decade as a watershed break with earlier attitudes to sex and social morality. Indeed, a major challenge in writing the book was to identify precisely what was new about post-war culture and what was part of longer transformations. Contemporary changes to sexuality did not originate exclusively in this decade, nor in the post-war years alone; they were the product of much broader histories. Writing from inside the culture of the period, Christopher Booker was one of the first to recognize that many of the shifts in English life conventionally associated with this moment had an extensive genesis, an argument confirmed by the work of recent historians.[15]

This book has pushed the issues of continuity and discontinuity still further; I show how Victorian social policies and value systems remained a strong presence in public and private life in the years after 1945. The Wolfenden committee's agenda on homosexuality and prostitution was set by a legal framework inherited from late nineteenth-century sexual politics, while Victorian ideas about the moral rectitude expected from men holding high office continued to influence the activities of leading characters in the Profumo affair. Social purity campaigners, backed by the organized churches and endorsed by prominent politicians, also remained a significant force at moments of national scandal. Seen from these vantage points, the permissive society was neither a revolution in English social life nor a radical break with the sexual cultures that preceded it; rather it was an extremely uneven acceleration of shifts that had a much longer period of incubation.

In short, I am making a strong case for the *longue durée* of sexual and social relations and their transformation during the post-war years. This awareness of the past in the present has implications for the way the book is organized. Like all historians I am concerned with change over time, but my perspective on London life is not simply longitudinal. I disrupt linear chronologies by casting key moments of nineteenth- and early twentieth-century urban history as the deep context for many of the changes to sex and morality in the years after 1945. *Capital Affairs* has resisted providing closure to some chapters, emphasizing that cultural change generated inconclusive outcomes that were the product of unresolved business between different social and sexual actors.

Events and characters contained in the book profoundly question the idea that the sexual regime of the 1960s was progressive. To be sure, self-consciously liberal champions of enlightened moral influence were hard at work in post-war London, but their ambitions were checked by men and women who were driven by very different motives. Predatory sexual rakes, sophisticated pimps and manipulative young women who sold themselves for cash and lucrative publicity were equally important players in this metropolitan world, and casualties and sexual victims abounded. Whiggish accounts of the 1960s have ignored this reprobate and shady cast of characters. The appearance of libertines and modern seductresses in my London story challenges liberal readings of the period because they draw attention to the ongoing connections between sex and social power. Feminists were among the first to question the value of permissiveness for women, while Michel Foucault's counter-history has confronted evolutionary accounts of modern sexuality, with their optimistic belief in progress from nineteenth-century repression to contemporary emancipation.[16]

Capital Affairs does not present the sexual history of the post-war period as a story of the inexorable triumph of professional society. My book challenges the world view of the experts with a less familiar but equally influential grouping who remade sexuality after the war. The upper-class leaders of London's fashionable society competed for space and attention in public debate about sex, and they significantly reshaped social attitudes through their own idiosyncratic styles of behaviour. Historians have conventionally defined the years after 1945 as witnessing the near-terminal decline of the English social elites, yet in the linked areas of sexuality and culture their influence was far from over. Professionals like Kinsey generated sexual knowledge as a prelude to social action, whereas aristocratic and gentry figures wielded power through the aura of their personalities, centred on the rituals of etiquette and display in the capital city. In the metropolitan social scene of the 1950s the man-about-town and related feminine celebrities were the focus of widespread sexual interest, especially via their reported affairs and complex entanglements with London's underworld. Sociologists worried that their patrician culture was regressive, part of the seductions of the past that prevented the country from embarking on a much-needed programme of modernization.[17] Yet the popular media advertised the foibles of the metropolitan elite as dynamic and even forward-looking. The ongoing cultural influence of the upper class is one of the neglected themes of post-war English history.

Capital Affairs is sex-centred but it is not sex obsessed. To be sure, my story identifies the two sexual cultures singled out by Kinsey, sex between men and the wide variety of commercially organized forms of female prostitution, as the focus of enormous national anxiety in the 1950s. But I situate these sexual practices in a much broader and longer history of London's pleasure economy, which provided leisure and entertainment for very different groups of consumers. Analysing sex as part of these wider networks of consumption, rather than as a tightly circumscribed field of sexual acts, delivers a number of benefits. It makes it easier to trace connections between sexual markets and adjacent forms of commercial culture, especially in the compressed urban spaces of London's central area. By the middle of the decade when rationing finally ended and West End shops announced the advent of material abundance, sex, food and leisure were promoted as the capital's major attractions. In a single evening, privileged men moved rapidly between different amusements which included dining out and sophisticated entertainment as well as sex. The expansion of each of these markets had important consequences for the development of the others, as entrepreneurs stimulated the cultural and sexual appetites of consumers across different sectors of London's night-time economy.

Viewing consumer culture in this way has the potential to recast post-war accounts of the relationship between sex and material affluence. Rather than viewing changes to sexuality as a product of changing economic conditions, which is the traditional way that the story of permissiveness has been told, sex is seen as an intrinsic part of the shifting economics of consumer demand. Advertising, marketing and retailing – the triple engines of domestic consumption – played a major role in restructuring sexual attitudes and personal life, while an intense focus on individualized, eroticized pleasure became central to the consumer tastes of younger women and affluent men. The political economy of modern sexuality is yet to be written, but *Capital Affairs* begins to map some of its defining post-war features.

The 'capital' of my title is deliberately meant to suggest the London-centredness of so many of these developments, but unlike historians who see the city's dominance as natural or obvious, I understand it as a specific product of the mid-twentieth century. From the Second World War through to the early 1960s London was repositioned as central to national and world affairs, and this renaissance had a major impact on sexuality not just in the capital but across the country. A dizzying and contradictory mixture of social policies, political anxieties and media fantasies advertised the city's moral problems and its erotic allure for very different audiences.

Part of London's revival was encouraged by the war itself and its aftermath. The conflict had produced powerful ideas about the metropolis as the heroic rallying point for the free world: the only European capital not to fall to Fascist or Communist regimes. Blitzkrieg on the home front inspired leaders of the planning profession to lay out an ambitious programme for rebuilding the city that would be 'worthy of London's fortitude, and of a new renaissance'.[18] By the time Kinsey arrived in the mid-1950s, these state-led schemes were being eclipsed by a much more familiar facet of London's growth. Government and the City of London rushed to reposition the metropolis as the hub of finance and world trade, while a clutch of property developers and architects became the spokesmen for what Peter Ackroyd, following Dickens, has called that monstrous, voracious and intensely commercial London.[19]

Alongside London's commercial revival, and sometimes partly linked to it, was the capital's renaissance as a centre of patrician social life. Monarchy, the royal family and the metropolitan gentry reinvented themselves and were reinvented in the early 1950s; their energetic activities partly transformed London from a city overshadowed by the destruction of war and the drabness of austerity to a place of glamorous display. Elite metropolitan spectacle received a major fillip from the year-long flurry of activity that accompanied the coronation of Elizabeth II in 1953. But coronation London also focused public disquiet on the seedy underside of the royal capital. Kinsey was one of many commentators who noted the worrying proximity of monarchy and high society to the West End's dubious sexual playgrounds.

Post-war London also remained a metropolis in the imperial sense of the term, albeit on a diminished scale given Indian independence and the formal winding up of empire in 1947. Yet the Colonial Office in Whitehall still administered Crown colonies in large areas of eastern and southern Africa, while the invented idea of the Commonwealth as a looser substitute for empire, with London as its centre and the Queen as its head, preserved the myth of an imperial foreign policy. It was matched by London's changing role as a city of immigrants, especially for men and women arriving from the Caribbean, India and Pakistan. New Commonwealth migration marked the first stage of the capital's post-colonial transformation, after a period between the wars when London had become less foreign. Its impact had far-reaching consequences not only for the city's demography but also for many Londoners' sense of themselves as white and English.

Taken together these flows of power, wealth and cultural authority highlighted sexuality as a significant feature of public policy and moral anxiety during the 1950s. Escalating concern about transgressive sex revealed how and why London occupied a paradigmatic role in national debates about public morality. Purity campaigners insisted that official or landmark London demanded special protection from the threat posed by unruly or dangerous sexualities, and the presence of monarchy as well as government bolstered their arguments. Leading editors in Fleet Street's newspaper industry endorsed the view that though London was a special case, immorality in the capital set trends that affected beliefs and behaviour across the whole country. London's sexual exceptionalism and its potentially expansive and invasive moral influence were the two themes that dominated successive moral panics about vice during the post-war years. Politicians and civil servants overwhelmingly took London as the reference point in their frequent public pronouncements about the nation's morals, while Kinsey used his Soho fieldwork to make much broader generalizations about the sexual character of English society. Most significantly of all, when public intellectuals at the Home Office sought to reform the laws on homosexuality and prostitution, they followed an extraordinary process of policy making in miniature, where concern about central London's streets formed the basis for nationwide legislation.

In the West End's public spaces and in Soho's intimate nightclubs, as well as in the courtroom and in the pages of the national press, the official world of Establishment London collided with the city's sexually wayward and unruly characters, who included young West Indian men as

well as street women, pimps, and men who loved other men. Social investigators like Kinsey relished the suggestive sexual possibilities generated
by his midnight meetings with the capital's *demi-monde*, but these encounters were much more than esoteric incidents provided for the amusement
of professional men-about-town. They played a major role in reshaping
attitudes to homosexuality and prostitution as well as in influencing much
wider gendered and racialized understandings of normal and deviant
behaviour. Homosexual *causes célèbres*, such as the trial of Lord Montagu
of Beaulieu and his friends for indecency with two young airmen in 1954,
macabre sexual murders like those committed by the serial killer John
Christie at Rillington Place the previous year, and scandals like the
Profumo affair, which compromised leading politicians in a web of
intrigue and Cold War espionage, were all high-profile events that dominated public life during the post-war years. The notion of 'affairs' in the
book's title is meant to capture their dramatic moral conflicts, as public
figures were brought into close and disturbing contact with opposing
sexual worlds.

All these episodes had different origins, but they were linked by the
mutual dependence of high and low cultures that were promiscuously
interrelated both in the official sphere of Westminster and Whitehall and
in the world of West End leisure and entertainment. All of them pushed
together competing beliefs about transgressive and pleasure-seeking forms
of male and female sexuality, set against the traditions of marriage and
the family. They also highlighted anxieties about the capital's cosmopolitan cultures, especially the way London was being transformed by West
Indian migration. These scandals preserved some of the features of nineteenth-century urban encounters between overworld and underworld.
Many of them evoked images from the Victorian city, or more precisely
what was perceived to be Victorian in the 1950s, which was in reality an
eclectic pastiche of images and experiences drawn from the nineteenth-
and early twentieth-century past. Many of them, too, reproduced the
tropes of 'Eros and altruism' characteristic of urban slumming, a tradition
which, as Seth Koven has argued, implicated metropolitan reformers in
complex personal and sexual dialogues with London's low life well into
the twentieth century.[20]

Historians have tended to view these scandals as backward-looking in
their social obsessions, reproducing the structures and strictures of nineteenth-century morality that were supposedly swept away by the
permissive moment of the 1960s.[21] Such a reading not only substantially

underplays their impact in favour of the more familiar features of sexual modernization such as liberalizing law reform or the contraceptive pill, it also sees the history of sexuality as a succession of movements towards a more progressive future. *Capital Affairs* sets out to challenge the idea that the post-war years marked the final demise of Victorian social morality and the dawning of a more enlightened era.

A number of factors inspired me to undertake a history of this sort. In part, I am continuing to explore key interpretative issues suggested by but left undeveloped in my earlier work, especially the question of how sexuality has become a privileged place to grasp the workings of modern power.[22] Confronted by London's immensely complex system of social organization, I have transformed the story of regulation from a history of official politics contained in my first book to show how sexual change was the contested outcome of encounters between a very wide spectrum of forces that competed for authority in the city's cultural and political spaces. The very fact that sexuality was and is a dispersed and decentred field, focused on bodies, identities and desires but also on government policies and systems of representation, has meant breaking out of the discrete and compartmentalized way that post-war English history has been traditionally told.[23]

My interdisciplinary ambitions reflect the challenges posed by a recent generation of cultural historians; they are entirely familiar to scholars researching early modern societies and the long nineteenth century, but they are still relatively unusual for those of us working on the years after 1945. This period has been dominated by the tight grip of political and economic narratives and by a type of social history that has understood social change as separate from culture transformations. Cultural historians have emphasized the need to bring together themes that political and social historians have conventionally kept distinct, to explore new ways of thinking about the connections between government and society, high and low culture, and public and private life. I have followed many of their leads, tempering their approach with an emphasis on the deep empirical and archival contexts favoured by social historians. Three issues which are central to the project for cultural history have informed my book: questions of social being and sexual identity, the cultural and representational character of urban life, and the resources of narrative.

Capital Affairs adopts a middle ground position between sexual and cultural power understood discursively and structurally and a more humanistic understanding of history propelled by egocentric actors and directed social movements. Recognizing that men and women are not at the centre of things (even though post-war men of power and influence profoundly believed they were) does not mean abandoning interest in them. As Judith Walkowitz has stressed, the historian's task still remains to explain cultural expressions in terms of their 'historically situated authorial consciousness'.[24] This means analysing the resources available to individuals to represent themselves and make sense of their world, rather than assuming that this process is natural or transparent. In post-war London the languages on offer for dramatizing the sexual self were multidimensional, and they involved fluid exchanges of meaning across social and cultural boundaries.

Take, for example, the issue that obsessed the Wolfenden committee and became such a vexed question for sexual politics later on: how did homosexuals recognize themselves and each other? Men like Peter Wildeblood, who gave evidence to the inquiry as a speaking homosexual subject, drew on social medicine and psychiatry as well confessional declarations familiar from autobiographical writing to announce their identity and distinguish their respectable condition from the degraded perverts and effeminate queans who populated the West End. Wildeblood was not fully in control of this process of bearing witness; his efforts to represent himself were governed by the languages available to make sense of his life, though they also involved active political choices about how best to speak publicly about his sexuality. In short, Peter Wildeblood and others like him in 1950s London were not free sexual agents but neither were they wholly trapped by circumstance; they made their own history in the face of events they could not fully control. Historians need to distinguish these public declarations of identity from the more intimate aspects of sexual and affective life. Sexual selfhood was shifting rather than fixed, and it was profoundly influenced by place as well as by society.

Cultural geographers and urbanists have reminded historians that the organization and representation of cities cannot be seen simply as background for 'real' social processes. Gyan Prakash has argued that cities are a distinctly 'spatial form of social life and power relations, not just a site of society and politics'.[25] Historians of modern London have recently shown themselves extremely receptive to this emphasis, and I have drawn on their insights to explore how London's social geography stimulated transgression and eroticized spectatorship in the years after 1945.[26]

The porousness of London's sexual cultures was encouraged by the city's extremely compressed urban layout and by its relatively haphazard ad hoc development, especially in the inner boroughs. In the 1930s the Danish architect Steen Eiler Rasmussen had famously celebrated the capital's piecemeal evolution because it offered a more humane design for urban living than the centralized Continental cities that were identified with the ambitions of the dictators.[27] Other urbanists profoundly disagreed with Rasmussen's panegyric to London's incoherence, especially the planners with their grand designs for the streamlined movement of people and goods and their moralized vision of organic urban communities. Despite their best efforts to reshape the environment, London in the 1950s remained, as it remains today, a recognizably nineteenth-century city in much of its infrastructure and social design.

Erotic encounters, scandalous incidents and many other forms of sexual activity that feature in the book were stimulated by central London's distinctive architectural and spatial layout. In the 1950s the grand commercial premises that fronted the West End's major shopping thoroughfares and the theatre district of Leicester Square backed onto Soho's narrow streets and alleys. The Palace of Westminster, the imposing government offices lining Whitehall, and Pall Mall's clubland were also only a short distance from bohemian Soho. This dramatically polarized geography had major consequences for public life. Politicians and policymakers whose ostensible brief was the regulation of social morality were in a constant dialogue with the sexual worlds on their doorstep, not just as problems demanding official solutions but also as erotic entertainment which provided them with the frisson of excitement. Dangerous sexualities pressed hard on government, especially when public figures brought London's *demi-monde* into the heart of the state through their personal liaisons.[28] Sometimes ordinary police officers working on their West End beats acted as intermediaries, delivering erotically charged accounts of capital city vice to a Whitehall bureaucracy eager to hear about their exploits. At other moments the connections were much more direct, when prominent politicians were exposed *in flagrante*, compromised by their associations with queer London or by their affairs with young women who defined themselves variously as prostitutes, mistresses and call-girls. These relationships generated social and sexual meanings that were enormously fluid, and they were played out in the social spaces of everyday metropolitan life.

Examining the city close up, from the standpoint of pedestrian spectators at street level, as Michel de Certeau put it, as well as from the panoramic vantage point of bureaucrats and administrators, I describe how the design of streets, buildings and urban interiors encouraged particular forms of sexual identity and personal intimacy.[29] Soho's pre-eminence as a place of social and sexual encounter was made possible by the narrow courts and alleys that enabled urban cruising, spectating and loitering of all kinds. The material fabric of the built environment, some of which was Georgian in its aesthetics and scale, also encouraged a distinctive type of romantic mythology in the 1950s, when sexually flamboyant characters from the past were seen to ghost the present. This enthusiastic reinvention of cosmopolitan Soho throughout the twentieth century (a phenomenon that was replicated across many European and North American cities with similar bohemian districts) disrupts the idea that London's development can be seen as a succession of distinctive economic phases or cultural epochs each succeeding the other (capitalist, modern, postmodern, global and so on). Soho's urban landscape was and still is porous and multilayered; it encourages the resourceful recycling of urban styles, bodies and personalities from earlier periods. The enthusiastic revival of the Edwardian suit and the urban pose of the man-about-town by local Teddy Boys, along with the take-up of theatrical styles of feminine glamour by young women who worked in the sex industry, were just some of the ways that images from the Victorian and Edwardian city were reinvented during the 1950s and 1960s.

It follows from all of this that I understand London not only as a complex material and social entity but also as a series of imaginary and contested landscapes that were produced by a wide variety of iconographic resources, especially photography, fiction, film and fashion. Jay Winter has criticized historians who emphasize the impact of this type of urban imagery, because in his view it reduces city culture to a regime of representations, at the expense of documenting the way it was actually lived.[30] My response is to insist that London as it was visualized and imagined during the post-war years cannot be divorced from all the other urban activities that shaped the city as a place of sexual danger and possibility.

Along with cultural geography, the resources of narrative history feature prominently in the book because so much of its sexual subject-matter is produced through the varied genres of story telling. Narratives of transgression and autobiographies told as true-life confessions were circulated by leading characters in many of the post-war scandals and then reworked with the help of the media. I have stayed close to their plot lines in order to convey the dramatic emotional impact involved in their unravelling and to show how many of the strongest disagreements about sex and culture were played out as disputes about the meaning and significance of key events. My commitment to presenting sexuality as the product of competing cultural and political forces has meant canvassing sexual stories from the widest spectrum of London society. It has involved questioning the confident voices of the intellectual and government elites by bringing their pronouncements about sex into a dynamic relationship with men and women positioned outside the world of the Establishment. Clashes between liberal-minded experts and homosexual men, or between high-ranking Tory politicians and ambitious young women, provide some of the richest studies of these sexual encounters in action.

Take as an example the role of the professionals and their claims to sexual authority. Kinsey's discovery of sexual London was driven by his enduring commitment to expert knowledge, a form of masculine competence that was deeply embedded in the city's public culture. London's pivotal role in the life of professional society was long-standing; since the eighteenth century urban surveys and official maps had generated social information about the city as part of the apparatus of civic government. 'Liberal governmentality', as Patrick Joyce has called it, played a major role in disciplining bodies and uncovering sexual secrets via technologies designed to make the city healthy, hygienic and morally secure.[31]

Capital Affairs continues the story of sexual experts and professionals into the post-war period in their role as doyens of the welfare state, championing policies of enlightened moral influence and increased surveillance in equal measure.[32] Doctors, lawyers, social workers and civil servants were instrumental in recasting ideas about private life, social responsibility, and normal as opposed to deviant conduct. In 1950s London, experts jostled for positions of power and influence with more overtly religious apologists for sexual morality, such as the leaders of the social purity movement, and frequently the professionals won out. Their ascendancy was particularly marked in the Whitehall committees and commissions which recommended major reforms to the laws on marriage and divorce, family welfare and sexual activity of all kinds.[33]

Noel Annan has defined the public professions as key players in the political consensus of the 1950s.[34] In my book John Wolfenden, the Yorkshire grammar school boy who went on to chair the hugely influential inquiry into homosexuality and prostitution, represents this tradition par excellence. However, major conflicts erupted in post-war London among the experts themselves, who displayed precious little consensus about the meaning of sex, let alone about appropriate forms of moral behaviour. Freudians clashed with behaviourists and sociologists about the biological and cultural significance of sexuality, and all of them took issue with the moral and religious prohibitions of the purity movement.

Struggles over sexual knowledge were also part of wider battles over masculine and feminine access to sexual information. Many historians have cast the 1950s as a hiatus period in English feminism, caught between the dynamic suffrage struggles of the early twentieth century and the renaissance of the women's liberation movement in the late 1960s. Feminism during the post-war period was partly circumscribed by a social democratic emphasis on equality and the 'foregrounding and integration of femininity in a masculine world'.[35] Yet the relative absence of large-scale campaigning did not mean that a feminist politics of sexuality was absent from the public agenda. Prostitution in particular continued to generate some of the most protracted disagreements between professional men and women, differences that reflected wider tensions about male sexual power and access to women's bodies that had remained unresolved for almost a century.

Sexual knowledge of a very different kind was on offer in the pages of the popular and middle-market press, as well as in the cinema and paperback fiction. Images of London loomed large in this coverage, where urban melodrama and the human interest story competed with more contemporary documentary features. Very often they drew on the world view of the elites and the experts, reworking Establishment obsessions to the demands of mass audiences. Elaborate stories of West End perversion and tales of sexual deviants in high places circulated information and entertainment to a culturally sophisticated reading public nationwide, following media patterns of production and consumption that had been established by the late Victorian popular press. Journalists were entirely familiar with the by-line that 'sex sells', but in the 1950s they were driven by a need to deliver ever more dramatic copy in the face of growing competition from the new medium of television. Sex plugged the demand for this type of sensational story.

During the post-war decades Fleet Street's editors were locked in a mutually reinforcing relationship with politicians and the Metropolitan Police, a triple alliance that provided all parties with effective self-promotion in their widely advertised battles against capital city vice. In the case of the Met this partnership affirmed a convenient and enduring idea of the morally upright London 'bobby', free from any hint of corruption, an image that was reinforced when officers themselves became influential media pundits. Chief Inspector Robert Fabian, alias 'Fabian of the Yard', led the field in this move from policing to publicity, reinventing himself on his retirement from the Met as a television policeman and the well-paid author of popular crime casebooks. Journalists for their part traded a tabloid discourse of sexual ethics, as Chris Waters has called it, a strategy dedicated to uncovering, naming and codifying sex for popular consumption that battled in the marketplace alongside expert opinion.[36] In the early 1960s the cosy tripartite relationship between the fourth estate, the political class and the police began to break down. Young single women, Caribbean newcomers and a new generation of homosexual men forced an entry into London's sexual scene, all hungry for lucrative publicity and much less mindful of Establishment rules and conventions.

These three urban personalities, who frequently collided in the West End's entertainment spaces, feature in the book as major players in London's fast-moving sexual culture. Socially mobile young women who appeared able to cross the city's social boundaries, and who drew on the resources of the sex industry as a form of empowerment, were centre stage in the changes. Public concern about sexually available women who were not prostitutes, but who sometimes exchanged sex for money and who sometimes gave it for free, was long-standing – part of a history of public anxiety about appropriate norms of female heterosexual behaviour that dated back to the nineteenth century. During the post-war period showgirls, models and nightclub hostesses made confident appearances in many contemporary scandals, regularly exploiting the influence of male patrons and the media to promote their interests. Christine Keeler, the leading female character in the Profumo affair, was celebrated as a new type of *femme fatale*. Drawing on the resources of consumer culture and pioneering an aggressive approach to chequebook journalism, her sexually charged performances aroused national and international interest.

Underpinning Keeler's erotic displays was the power of London's heavily commercialized sex industry. The West End's reputation as a city servicing the needs of almost every taste and sexual appetite was long established. Kinsey compared London to Havana, while other international tourists saw the city competing for their attention alongside sophisticated night-time haunts in Paris, Berlin and New York. Politicians and public moralists regularly feigned surprise when the extent and depth of the city's sex industry was exposed by raids on shady nightclubs or on queer bars and pubs, but the police were more realistic, exposing sex in

London as a highly lucrative and capital intensive industry that attracted large numbers of the paying public from across the world. Ambitious Soho entrepreneurs like Vivian Van Damm, manager of the Windmill Theatre, and Paul Raymond, owner of the Revuebar, catered to the demands of their affluent customers with glamorous sexual entertainment.

Commercial culture played an equally important role in promoting same sex relations between men. Kinsey saw only aggressive predators and abject punters on his sexual tour of London; in fact, the West End supported a densely textured homosexual culture that was sophisticated and urbane, as well as being heavily structured along class lines. Recent historians have shown that despite legal and social sanctions queer London was far from being the restricted and closeted world that supposedly predated the more openly gay scene of the 1960s.[37] What emerges in *Capital Affairs* is that these pubs, clubs and other meeting places were not distinct enclaves or subcultural milieus. Central London's commercial development pushed different types of sexual consumers into the same or adjacent spaces, rather than separating them off from each other by exclusive social zoning. During the 1950s a mixture of government policies, policing strategies and the tactics of the embryonic homosexual rights movement helped to define a more distinct and privatized version of homosexual identity.

As Kinsey was well aware, Soho was London's traditional centre for sexual sophistication of every kind; queer, straight and polymorphous. But during the 1950s Notting Hill, three miles further west, became a new site of experimentation. Notting Hill was London's 'wild west', as Stuart Hall has put it.[38] Its nineteenth-century squares and imposing middle-class villas had become decaying flats and rooming-houses where Caribbean immigrants now made their home. During the first stage of the migration cycle, young, single West Indian men were the subject of endless local fascination and anxiety. Exotic food, calypso music, drugs, and above all the sexual behaviour of the newcomers turned Notting Hill into an informal cultural laboratory and a major racialized conflict zone.

Jamaican and Trinidadian men possessed very different attitudes to women and family life compared with the indigenous local population, and their lifestyles generated possibilities and antagonisms that were distinct from Soho's bohemian atmosphere. In popular parlance Notting Hill was often referred to an extension of Soho, but the district produced a different version of cosmopolitanism, shifting the idea away from its European and Jewish associations and towards the Caribbean. Culturally as well as politically, the impact of West Indian newcomers was double-edged. Extending the idea of London as a multicultural city, they also encouraged a defensive, territorial sense of Englishness among many poor whites. In the miscegenist fantasies of urban everyday life that accompanied many of the post-war scandals, the idea of white women as victims of the sexual urges of Caribbean men erupted as a powerful negative image of interracial mixing.

These multiple intellectual agendas addressing sexuality and culture have shaped this history, but part of the book's origins also lies in my own autobiography. The themes I have chosen to explore echo the compulsions of many writers who have described their experiences of living through the post-war period, but my particular story brings to light other priorities as well that cut against received accounts and suggest a different way of interpreting the decades between the end of the war and the early 1960s.

The Queen's coronation in the spring of 1953, which is the London-centred event that introduces Chapter 1, has become a focal point for explorations in memory and personal testimony among the men and women who became the first post-war generation. I was a coronation child, born only days before the crowning of Elizabeth II. Along with thousands of other children at home and across the Commonwealth, I was given the regulation crown piece, silver spoon, mug and ribbon that singled us out as special and endowed us with a kind of talismanic significance. Annette Kuhn has argued that children were particularly associated with this coronation magic because they represented the extraordinary feelings of euphoria that accompanied the beginnings of the so-called Elizabethan era.[39] Among ordinary families like mine, the royal events of 1953 gave the popular aspirations invested in post-war children a particular inflection, linking them to monarchy and also to collective ideas about national renewal.

But the coronation was Janus-faced; it offered a supposedly dynamic vision for the country against a background of elaborate national and imperial tradition. It was this dynamic push and pull of the past and the future that I remember from my own childhood, where up-to-date ideas derived from television or from Americanized consumer culture jostled for my attention alongside images of Britain as a traditional and hierarchical society. The London comings and goings of royalty and social gossip about the leaders of aristocratic society were widely reported in Buxton, my home-town, which was physically and culturally close to Chatsworth, the imposing country seat of the Duke of Devonshire. Seven years after the coronation, the marriage of the Queen's younger sister, Princess Margaret, was the occasion for a day's school holiday and another bout of organized public celebrations.

In short, traditional emblems of prestige and authority were envisaged as socially potent rather than backward-looking in the 1950s. In our family this outlook (a belief that this 'was how things always had been and always would be', as David Cannadine has put it about his own childhood) co-existed uneasily with more obviously go-ahead ideas.[40] Competing versions of modernity loom large in the public histories covered in *Capital Affairs*, where conservative beliefs about a future rooted in the past confront progressive blueprints for social change. Both traditions were influential in shaping contemporary attitudes to sexuality because there was no consensus about how to disengage from the legacy of Victorian social morality.

By the 1960s there was a more disruptive and exotic side to my memories that echoes the themes explored in the book. My adolescent fantasies were heavily focused on London, now imagined as a cosmopolitan city that held out the promise of larger expectations and desires. The Sunday colour supplements were full of glamorous stories about the rise of swinging London, but I preferred a more down-market version of consumer culture which seemed to provide answers to a provincial adolescent's questions about sex and big city life. I read the tabloids and watched television specials that were full of suggestive features about 'sinful Soho' and 'permissive Paddington', coverage that mixed traditional exposés of vice and depravity with newer fantasies of liberated heterosexuality. My attention was also caught by the dramatic unravelling of the Profumo scandal, which prompted the boys in our school to exchange knowing whispers about the careers of prostitutes and ponces. All this was part of my informal sex education, supplementing the one rudimentary lesson in human reproductive biology that was on offer at our grammar school. Stories of this kind provided my first real glimpse of a world of sexual difference removed from family life.

London's cosmopolitan atmosphere also attracted my father. Down in the capital with his pals on their annual trip to the Cup Final for homosocial leisure, or in the West End for corporate business, he showed me the menu cards he kept as souvenirs of restaurant meals eaten in Soho's Chinatown. Savouring cultural exoticism abroad during wartime service in the Far East, he was now keen to try modest cultural sophistication at

home. Surreptitiously, I found out about the other places my father went
to on his London trips as well; in his briefcase were glossy programmes
commemorating his visits to the Windmill Theatre, with its world-famous
glamour reviews. Photos of blondes and brunettes, caught in decorative
poses with wholesome cheesecake smiles, advertised the girl-next-door
types who had been favourites with the Forces. The sexual appeal of the
West End's entertainment culture features prominently in the book, both
in the positive way it appealed to my father and also in its more negative associations where it signified urban impurity and cultural disorder.
These dual experiences of the cosmopolitan city have coexisted uneasily
together in London's commercial development.[41]

More personally and painfully, I was also aware of campaigns afoot at
Westminster to reform the law on homosexuality. By the mid-1960s I was
old enough to understand the significance of these debates; sitting with
my parents watching the TV news I blushed when the word 'homosexual'
was mentioned and realized it had some connection to me.[42] Suddenly,
abstract statistics about sex between men and distant press revelations
about London's subcultures became an intimate part of my own personal
drama at home. This was how sexual events in the capital began to impact
on the everyday life of ordinary families. A few years later, after homosexuality had been made just about legal, I followed in the footsteps of
earlier generations of provincials who had felt the sexual allure of the city.
Like a number of characters who appear in the book, London for me
was the place to be to experience the energy that was opening a new
phase of the gay male world.

I tell a slice of my own history not because it is unique; different parts
of this story have been rehearsed many times as part of the reminiscences
of the post-war generation. What is distinctive about my account is that,
perforce of personal circumstance, I map some of the social and sexual
contours of the period differently, and these differences influence the
history recounted in the book. I want to distinguish my own version of
the post-war years from other recent narratives not to insist that mine is
more accurate or comprehensive, but because the insights I deliver have
the potential to revise and complicate the histories that we already possess.

I do not present the 1950s as Peter Hennessy has recently evoked it, as
a 'golden time; a more innocent age before . . . illusion after illusion was
. . . painfully shattered'.[43] His nostalgic retrospective is coupled with more
negative images of the period as 'a right, tight, screwed down society',
waiting for the social and sexual 'ice-break' of the decade that followed.

It does not match my own childhood recollections, and more importantly it does not approximate to the cultural and social worlds explored here. Hennessy's history marks too sharp a break between the years of austerity and the colour, exuberance and fun that supposedly characterized permissiveness later on. In doing so he smuggles in negative and positive value judgements about both decades that are based on his progressive reading of the 1960s. Equally, I am not resurrecting post-war London via reassuring myths about community and kinship that shaped Roy Porter's memories of the capital, as a world of 'pea-soupers' and 'clanking trams', when working-class 'families stuck together' and 'everybody knew everybody'.[44] Porter's idea of the city conceals as much as it reveals; its cosy communitarianism does not allow space for different voices and for the disruptive social fantasies of transgressive sex and scandal that are the stuff of *Capital Affairs*.

My approach to post-war history shares most with Carolyn Steedman's account in *Landscape for a Good Woman* (1985). Steedman's writing differs from my own account of London in that hers is explicitly autobiographical, centred on a re-reading of her own awkward and unsettling personal past as a way of challenging contemporary histories of class, gender and social welfare. But the two books share common ambitions; both seek to disrupt dominant interpretations of the years after 1945 by bringing into focus lives and stories that sit awkwardly with many of the dominant post-war public narratives.[45] Tales of high society liaisons and of sexual lives lived on the margins, as distinct from the reassuring collectivities of class, welfare and social integration favoured by Hennessy and Porter, are what define my own book and Steedman's history in equal measure. *Capital Affairs* offers the historian a different lens through which to view a period that has become ossified by the repetition of familiar social myths.

Chapter 1 opens with the coronation; its staging recentred London in the national imagination and across the world. Coronation London was a city caught between the past and the future in ways that reflected wider uncertainties about Britain's imperial and international identity. Geographically, the coronation redirected public attention back towards the metropolitan central area, after the planning-inspired focus on suburban and 'greater London' in the 1940s. In fact and in social fantasy, the royal event intensified national concern about the moral state of the West End in streets and thoroughfares that lay adjacent to Establishment London. A cluster of public intellectuals produced social knowledge about sex in the city, refashioning overworld–underworld narratives that had been a familiar feature of Victorian urban encounters. Patrician characters, closely identified with the renaissance of fashionable society, also assumed a prominent role in this drama. Chapter 2 explores the impact of these elite personalities via the figure of the man-about-town and associated styles of upper-class femininity.

As London's distinctive rendering of the *flâneur*, the enthusiastic post-war reinvention of the man-about-town by younger, upper-class dandies testified to the continuing power of elite culture in a country that was now supposedly democratic and increasingly egalitarian. Being a man-about-town in 1950s London was quintessentially about masculine forms of privilege that gave access to the city's pleasures. Pall Mall's clubland, court and society functions in St James's and Mayfair, fashionable consumption in Jermyn Street, and all of the West End's varied night-time amusements were on offer to men-about-town. A number of leading society figures extended their itineraries into London's queer spaces, showing how the man-about-town displayed significant sexual fault lines that rendered his personality potentially dubious or problematic. Much further down the capital's social hierarchy, Teddy Boys empowered by nascent consumer culture fashioned their own styles of leisured gentlemanliness in inner city districts that were adjacent to the high society world of the West End.

Chapter 3 tracks the impact of these networks of sex and metropolitan society on the spectacular transgressive events that dominated London life during the 1950s and early 1960s. The highly publicized sexual murders by John Christie at Rillington Place, a dilapidated Victorian street in north Kensington, close to Notting Hill, are the chapter's focus for this collision of high and low cultural worlds. Shadowing coverage of the coronation, the Rillington Place murders concentrated public attention on one of inner London's 'twilight zones' as a place of blighted sexual relationships and racialized cultural difference. People and places at the centre of the Rillington Place episode provoked a deep-seated sense of uneasiness about contemporary sexuality and about the post-Victorian character of English society.

Chapter 4 moves the story away from narratives of urban decay and sex crime at street level and into the official glare of government and bureaucracy. The double-sided brief of the Wolfenden inquiry on homosexuality and prostitution was overwhelmingly metropolitan. A dedicated Whitehall committee of liberal-minded public figures tabled proposals to update the criminal law based on sexual information that was obsessively focused on a square-mile radius around Piccadilly Circus. Historians have cited the Wolfenden inquiry as a classic example of progressive policy-making, driven by reformers with a rationalist belief in the power of expert knowledge to redefine public and private life. This chapter's close-up view of the 'performance' of the state in action reveals a more dramatic and unstable picture, especially when the police and homosexual witnesses brought West End sex quite literally into the heart of government. Leading members of the political and intellectual elite embraced London's low society as a troubled component of their own fantasy life, as sexual practices that were officially defined as socially marginal became symbolically central to public culture.

Chapter 5 shifts the sexual action less than a mile from Whitehall's government complex into Soho, London's exotic foreign quarter and long-standing centre of the capital's sexual economy. Enclosed by the great rectangle of the West End's shopping and entertainment thoroughfares, Soho's provenance as the setting for cosmopolitan pleasures and dangers dated back to the eighteenth century. Successive Jewish and European immigrants, home-grown bohemians and dynamic entrepreneurs jostled for the attention of the English public, creating an exceptional cultural atmosphere that also pulled in tourists from across the world. In the 1950s an alliance of business leaders and ambitious media pundits reconstructed Soho's image as dangerous and sexually compelling for a new generation of discerning, affluent consumers. 'Continental' goods and services from selected parts of Western Europe were part of this commercial mix, while journalists and even local police chiefs now advertised Soho's reputation for vice and crime as an eccentric but invaluable part of the national culture.

Chapters 6 stays in Soho to explore how the area acted as a forcing ground for the rapidly changing performances of sexuality that were associated with permissive London. Resourceful theatre managers and night-club proprietors staged live sexual entertainment as a hugely profitable business and as sophisticated metropolitan leisure for well-heeled men. In the late 1950s erotic displays of female nudity were at the centre of a series of dramatic cultural contests fought out in Soho, as tasteful images of English feminine glamour were displaced by the international world of striptease. On-stage and off-stage, dancers and showgirls projected sexual personalities and bodily idioms that disrupted traditional dichotomies of vice and virtue with more assertive styles of femininity.

A close-up study of the Windmill Theatre and the Raymond Revuebar, two West End venues that were successively market leaders in erotic female nudity, poses the question: precisely what changed sexually in the 1960s?

Chapter 7 explores how the anxieties dominating post-war London life crescendoed in the Profumo affair. Profumo's plot drew on the resources of London's high and low cultures in equal measure. Driven by promiscuous Tory politicians, sophisticated showgirls and Caribbean interlopers, the scandal compromised public life at Westminster by revealing its links to the cultural and sexual worlds of Soho and Notting Hill. What marked out the Profumo case as a contemporary scandal, rather than just a dramatic re-run of Victorian *causes célèbres*, was the rapidly changing power balance between its major players. Young independent women and West Indian men-about-town produced their own influential scripts of sexuality, challenging the masculine authority of Establishment figures in the West End's entertainment spaces as well as in the national press. Intensive media coverage of events in the spring and summer of 1963 ensured that sexual London was advertised across the world as part of the wider problems of contemporary Britain. The scandal's legacy generated an atmosphere of moral confusion and social turbulence that reflected the dilemmas and possibilities associated with permissiveness. The Epilogue reveals that the story of London's capital affairs is by no means concluded, drawing out the long-term consequences for present-day society and culture.

Chapter 1   Majesty

Metropolis 1953

On 2 June 1953, the night of the coronation of Elizabeth II, London was *en fête*.[1] State ceremonial and popular spectacle throughout the day had given way to a 'glittering' evening scene of royal theatre that was baroque in its brilliance. At 9.45 pm a 'river of light' flooded across the city when the Queen herself, as the imagined source of the illumination, pressed a switch from the balcony of Buckingham Palace. Across the skyline of official London, public monuments from the Mall to St Paul's Cathedral rippled in floodlight, while a 'shimmer and iridescence' on the capital's horizon reflected firelight from a chain of beacons that were ablaze in the surrounding countryside (fig. 1).[2] An hour later 'Britain's biggest firework show' began with a massive salvo of aerial explosions, accompanied by cannon from the royal salute, a traditional *feu de joie*.[3] Thousands watched from the River Thames and from the city's bridges as ten tons of gold and silver rockets and Roman candles shot into the night. Gigantic Catherine wheels spun in circles over a hundred feet across, while colonnades of 'white . . . spray' ran along the length of the river's embankments. Maroons, with fanciful names like 'jade jets' and 'Martian comets', imitated cannon fire and then transformed themselves into clouds of golden moonshine, cascading 'silver . . . fragments' into the river below.[4] When the newly crowned Queen made her final appearance on the palace balcony just before midnight, a great pyrotechnic set piece celebrated the monarchy, as gigantic portraits of the royal family were picked out in fire.

The royal fireworks could be seen from the diverse public vantage points of central London, and as the press enthused with an upsurge of communitarian sentiment, they were enjoyed by Londoners from across

the social spectrum. The night-time spectacle was clearly visible from the
windows of Pall Mall's clubland, preserve of the masculine political elite,
and from gala balls organized by society hostesses in Mayfair and
Belgravia, but it was also seen from popular rendezvous in the entertainment settings of the West End, where an unending crocodile of revellers
snaked around Piccadilly Circus. Performers and audiences in theatreland,
close by in Leicester Square, joined in the night-time festivities, with stars
like Noël Coward appearing in special late-night cabaret. Meanwhile, in
working-class streets across London whole communities celebrated their
own popular version of monarchy throughout the evening and into the
night, with organized street parties and with endless music and dancing.[5]

The coronation was the most extended display of royal ceremonial
staged in Britain during the mid-twentieth century. There had been earlier
'rehearsals' for the event, notably the Queen's own wedding as Princess
Elizabeth in 1947 and the funeral of King George VI in 1952, but the
coronation was on an altogether different scale. It was seen by nearly a
quarter of the world's population. Inside Westminster Abbey a privileged
elite witnessed what was still essentially a medieval rite. They saw scep-
tres, swords of state and the relics of kings; they heard solemn promises,
invocations of saints and the swearing of historic oaths; they watched the
Queen anointed with holy oil and dressed in cloth of gold, acting out
the role of a resplendent, almost Byzantine hierophant.[6] Outside the abbey,
in London's major streets and public spaces, a much larger audience saw
the more familiar face of modern royalty, produced according to late nineteenth-century notions of official spectacle and tradition. Carriage processions of princes and rulers from around the world, Commonwealth
troops and massed bands accompanied the Queen on her procession to
and from the ceremony, framing monarchy as an imperial demonstration
of prestige (fig. 2).

In 1953 the new medium of television magnified the pageantry, orchestrating the coronation as a world event and inserting it into a developing network of international communications. The Queen was the first
monarch to be crowned, as protocol required, 'in the sight of all her
people'.[7] In Britain alone an audience of twenty-seven million, over half
the country, watched a two-and-a-half-hour broadcast of the ceremony.
A European link-up extended coverage to parts of Western Europe, and
within hours recordings of the BBC's television transmission were being
seen across the Atlantic on the Canadian and American networks.[8]
Monarchs and dictators of the past paraded their greatness on relatively

small stages; this was a qualitatively different production of spectacle in which time and space were hugely compressed. Elizabeth II was presented to an international audience who could participate in the coronation only slightly later than the guests in the abbey and the crowds outside.

As public spectacle, mass entertainment and world news the coronation was an overwhelmingly London-centred event. Modern ritual, as David Cannadine has reminded us, is a cultural form that requires a distinctive theatre to give its action significance and to make its symbolism meaningful.[9] The metropolitan focus of the coronation was more than simply a decorative regal background; London was recentred in the early 1950s through its close associations with monarchy, the attendant rituals of royalty and the court, and with the locations that provided the parade grounds for their displays. None of this was entirely new; since the 1870s, when the image of the Crown had been refashioned as 'splendid, public and popular', London was transformed as the setting for the 'improved performance of monarchy'.[10] Many of the official buildings and thoroughfares that provided the location for the events of 2 June (the frontage of Buckingham Palace, the Victoria Memorial, the Mall and Admiralty Arch) were the product of late nineteenth- and early twentieth-century civic improvements designed to provide a suitable *mise en scène* for royalty. But the powerful links between London and the monarchy were not just promoted by the infrastructure of the Victorian and Edwardian capital, they were also reinforced by more contemporary associations. During the early 1950s a wide variety of commentators sought to identify the Queen's accession with changes to London's geopolitical role, its public culture and its dominant structures of power and influence. These metropolitan perspectives were contradictory; they orchestrated competing understandings of what the city was, its position in the country and its relationship to the rest of world. Unpacking their significance is a necessary prelude to tracking some of the most important post-war changes to sex and morality because London provided so much of the social and imaginative infrastructure for these transformations.

At an overtly political level the coronation revived images of the capital's imperial role via the newly invented institution of the Commonwealth as the successor to the British Empire. Among political leaders, like Prime Minister Winston Churchill, and among large sections of the media still strongly committed to the imperial idea, especially the

Beaverbrook press, the hope was that the Commonwealth would re-establish London as the pre-eminent metropole and the hub of a revitalized international power bloc. Speaking on behalf of the white dominions, the Australian Prime Minister Robert Menzies, a committed Anglophile and 'the coming spokesman' of the Commonwealth, was the most vigorous apologist for the traditional political relationship linking London to cities in the imperial hinterland. In a confident rebuff to republican political institutions worldwide, Menzies insisted that all self-governing democracies owed their existence not just to the Westminster parliamentary system but to British constitutional monarchy as well.[11] Five days before the coronation ceremony Commonwealth ministers had toasted the Queen in Westminster Hall, scene of so many dramatic events in royal history. Assertively royalist, the *Daily Express* enthused that the members of fifty-two 'Empire Parliaments' had raised the roof of the ancient building with cheers of 'God Save the Queen', on behalf of the 600 million people who were subjects of the Crown.[12] The *Express* echoed Menzies, deliberately kaleidoscoping together coverage of the monarchy and the origins of parliamentary democracy with London's historic position as the foremost city of the empire.

Imperial sentiments of a different kind set the tone in much of the Commonwealth press during coronation year, when London's importance was reaffirmed as the setting for 'the British Empire's great day'.[13] What predominated in the Commonwealth media was the idea of a 'people's empire' which, as Wendy Webster has argued, emphasized the ideal of a multiracial community of supposedly equal nations, linked in partnership and shared international purpose.[14] 'From All Parts of the Globe They Come: London Takes on a Jamboree Air', announced Kingston's *Daily Gleaner* at the end of May, providing Jamaicans with a detailed description of the 'Coronation city' assembling 'the greatest show on earth'.[15] Caribbean readers were treated to day-by-day accounts of Commonwealth troops changing guard outside Buckingham Palace, the decorations in Oxford Street and the mounting atmosphere of excitement in the West End. In the antipodes the *Sydney Morning Herald*, keen to prioritize the Australian point of view, organized its stories through the eyes and ears of Prime Minister Menzies, conspicuous with his cine camera as he strolled among the crowds with his wife and daughters, admiring the decorations and chatting to Cockneys in the crowd.[16] Canadian reporters also encouraged close reader intimacy with the unfolding events in the capital: 'To have been in Westminster this morning was to have enjoyed one of the experiences of a lifetime', Toronto journalists enthused, as they invited their readers to 'slip into the Queen's golden coach' and look over 'the . . . route that Elizabeth . . . will follow'.[17] Only the *Times of India*, careful to preserve a degree of political detachment between the new Indian republic and London, remained lukewarm in its coronation coverage.[18]

Efforts by influential sections of the national and Commonwealth press and by committed imperialist politicians to recentre the British Empire around the double image of metropolis and monarchy were largely compensatory, in view of the actual diminished status of the Commonwealth and the Queen's role as its head. Elizabeth II's title was far less assertively imperial than that of her immediate predecessors; she was neither Empress of India nor ruler of 'the British Dominions beyond the Seas', but merely Head of the Commonwealth.[19] In that sense the coronation was a revivalist myth, the last great imperial display celebrating the continuity of Britain's great power status in an international situation that was increasingly dominated by the USA and the Soviet Union.[20] No amount of patriotic rhetoric could camouflage the fact that the Commonwealth represented a massive downscaling of imperial ambition.

However, not all commentators in 1953 sought to define London's international role in imperial terms. For the tourist industry, eager to relaunch the capital after the dislocations of world war and the economic restrictions imposed by rationing, London's appeal as a cosmopolitan city provided a much bigger draw, especially for foreigners. 'Why should a visitor come to Britain?' asked Fodor's *Woman's Guide to Europe* on behalf of their American readers in coronation year.[21] The answer was a panegyric to London's reputation for enlightened tolerance of 'every race and creed' and its celebrated atmosphere of cultural diversity. Cautioning visitors not to judge the city by American standards, Fodor's argued that London was the capital of 'one of the most civilised nations in the world – perhaps not the most progressive, nor the wealthiest, nor the most powerful', but a city that was 'easy to live in, that has given refuge to a score of nationalities, where the people live and let live'.[22]

Throughout the summer of 1953 this theme of social openness and metropolitan urbanity was embellished by the representatives of London's media and tourist industries. Was the English capital just like other big international centres, journalists asked? 'Not quite', because 'where else in the world could you see a man with a bowler hat and a briefcase' come out of the same house where moments before a 'colourfully-garbed

Negro with a saxophone under his arm' had gone in.[23] Evoking an implicit comparison with the racial segregation prevalent in many American cities, London was celebrated as a place of exotic encounters for international visitors. In an elite Mayfair nightclub, audiences could find the charismatic Caribbean cabaret artist Lesley Hutchinson entertaining Princess Margaret without any awkwardness or embarrassment.[24] While in Soho, dubbed the 'playpen of England', discerning visitors could experience a different form of sophistication that brought Europe into the heart of London. Soho was a place where 'fragments of Italy' were mixed with the 'warmth of France', where gourmets could demand the widest choice of foreign cuisine, and where men-about-town could savour glamorous night life.[25] Promoted by the leisure and entertainment industries and grounded in the city's stratified but exceptionally diverse consumer markets, cosmopolitanism in this sense implied a progressive internationalism, where London's indigenous traditions blended easily with the customs and cultures of Europe and the Commonwealth.

The celebration of cosmopolitan openness also had its negative underside, condensing suspicions of deracination, hybridity and displacement, especially in relation to new arrivals from the Caribbean, India and Pakistan. Evidence of these anxieties and their accompanying fears of miscegenation abounded in the early 1950s, not least among the leaders of the capital's tourist industry and in the market for housing, the most precious post-war commodity. Major West End hotels operated an obvious and explicit 'colour bar', discrimination that was paralleled for ordinary Londoners by adverts that announced with impunity 'no coloureds' in notices for rented flats and rooms.[26] Summing up his ten years spent in Britain, Trinidadian cricketer and broadcaster Learie Constantine believed that 'almost the entire population' expected 'the coloured man to live in an inferior area devoted to coloured people'.[27] Sociologists pioneering the academic study of race relations worried about this environmental segregation, speculating whether the growing concentration of migrants in run-down inner London districts such as Notting Hill and Brixton would lead eventually to American-style ghettos.[28] Far-right political groups, including the British National Party and Sir Oswald Mosley's Union Movement, campaigned around the negative vision of an urban dystopia that they argued would engulf British cities as a result of cosmopolitan mixing.[29]

Advocates and critics of London's imperial and cosmopolitan status positioned the capital either as the central point of an extensive colonial hinterland or as an entrepôt that was criss-crossed by an international traffic of people, cultures and commodities. London's role as the pre-eminent city of the United Kingdom of Great Britain and Northern Ireland involved different configurations of national culture and collective identity. Much of the Unionist imagery that surrounded the coronation, from the Queen's oath to maintain the United Kingdom and 'the Protestant Reformed Religion' to the traditional emblems of Scotland, Ireland and Wales woven into her dress designed by couturier Norman Hartnell, symbolized the various constitutional settlements that had shaped Britain as a political nation.[30] The popular conservative historian Arthur Bryant argued that London's acknowledged status as the capital of Great Britain was enhanced by the 'splendour and pageantry' of monarchy.[31]

Unionist perspectives like Bryant's did not go unchallenged in the run-up to the coronation, with some of the strongest criticisms coming from those parts of Britain with political traditions that rejected this centralizing, ethnocentric reading of national identity. Mass Observation, the research organization with a long-standing ethnographic interest in charting national attitudes and opinions and with experience of monitoring public reactions to the coronation of the Queen's father, George VI, in 1937, noted how there was a distinctive waning of enthusiasm for the royal event the further north its special team of observers went. People in Sheffield and York said they saw it as 'a London coronation', and there was plenty of evidence of downright hostility in Scotland.[32] Shopkeepers north of the border reported they could not sell 'Elizabeth II', partly because of nationalist objections that were focused on a dispute over the Queen's true title in Scotland.[33] Political activists, most notably those in the British Communist Party, sought to pull these regional dissatisfactions into their own class-based, republican agenda, claiming to give a voice to the millions of workers across all parts of the country who were 'carrying on the struggle for the things that really matter . . . higher wages . . . and peace'.[34] 'Long Live The People', proclaimed the *Daily Worker* on coronation day, and not the 'knights and barons, debutantes and their rich fathers' who herded into London.[35]

Perspectives of this sort, though minority views in 1953, suggested that the coronation represented a partial annulment of the 'provinces', an eclipse of the nation in its regional and ethnic diversity. In that sense the royal spectacle was in sharp contrast to the Festival of Britain staged only two years earlier, the only non-royal event held during the 1950s that was comparable in scale and ambition. Though the festival was also based in

London, with its specially built showcase site on the rejuvenated south
bank of the Thames, its cultural politics were self-consciously non–metropolitan. Conceived as a devolved rolling programme of exhibitions and
displays across Britain, the festival aimed to represent the country's
regional diversity, providing an inclusive 'autobiography' of the nation.[36]
With an agenda that was overtly educational and participatory, festival
events awarded a relatively minor role to the royal family. In marked contrast, the coronation enshrined the authority of the Crown, the importance of London as a metropolitan centre, and a conception of Britain as
a hierarchical society. As Tom Nairn has argued, one important effect of
this idea of 'regal' London was to reinstate a conservative version of state
power as traditionalist, centralized and immutable.[37]

Among some of the crowd camped out in the capital on the eve of
the coronation, royalist and nationalist sentiments were also tinged with
mild anti-Americanism. 'I'll say one thing,' remarked one middle-class
Londoner, who was showing his sister the decorations 'I think the
Americans . . . are just a little bit jealous as if they wished it were theirs.'[38]
A press cartoon entitled 'A Traveller's Dream of Home', showed 'Elmer',
a stereotypical post–war American tourist, dreaming that Manhattan had
been transformed into a royal city as New Yorkers celebrated the arrival
of 'Queen Elizabeth of the USA'.[39] Alistair Cooke, the assiduous transatlantic media correspondent whose letters from America had kept British
audiences in touch with their American cousins since the 1930s, told
readers at home about the mania for monarchy that was currently sweeping the USA. Cooke reported that New York's Rockefeller Plaza was now
wholly devoted to a near life-size, plaster-model display of 'Queen
Elizabeth's Coronation coach', accompanied by 'eight Windsor greys and
attendants fore and aft'.[40]

Many well-to-do Americans, especially committed Anglophiles visiting
London for the celebrations, were impressed by the way the coronation
seemed to be encouraging a social and cultural renaissance in the city.
'The transformation of London has to be seen to be believed . . . Britain
rediscovers herself', enthused Malcolm Muir, president and editor-in-chief
of *Newsweek* magazine, writing about the sea-change.[41] Keen to interpret
the significance of international events for readers at home, Muir confessed that most of his visits to the capital during the years after the war
had been depressing. Londoners' traditional self-confidence had vanished
amidst the difficulties of adjusting to the changed realities of a post–war
world, which involved a loss of their political and economic status on the

international stage. Now, low morale and drabness had given way to a 'rebirth' in the spirit of London. Muir's perception of the new atmosphere in the capital was supposedly informed by his talks with ordinary Londoners as he walked the streets, but it also reflected a semi-official idea, strongly promoted by romantic conservatives like Churchill, that the Queen's reign would usher in a new 'Elizabethan age' with London as its centre, mirroring the achievements of the first Queen Elizabeth.

Tudor mania, in the form of masques, pageants and commemorative decorations, abounded in the capital throughout the spring and summer in 1953. Bryant had already sounded an optimistic note about the idea of an Elizabethan revival at the time of the Queen's wedding, when he identified 'the reign of the first Elizabeth' as one of 'conscious national growth and vigour'.[42] In coronation year Robert Morley's *The Triumph of Oriana*, a collection of madrigals dedicated to Elizabeth I, was restaged at the Festival Hall, the newly opened concert venue on the South Bank. The Arts Council's musical pageant, *A Garland for the Queen* (with contributions from Vaughan Williams, Michael Tippett and Edmund Rubbra), also celebrated the new monarch with generalized references to Tudor England.[43] Benjamin Britten's specially composed coronation opera, *Gloriana*, an altogether darker account of the closing years of Elizabeth Tudor's reign, was given its gala performance in front of the Queen and an audience of British and foreign dignitaries at Covent Garden in June. An opera about failure and decay rather than rebirth and renewal, it was panned for not displaying the requisite upbeat elements of the new Elizabethanism.[44] Predictably, consumer culture was more positive, adding its own popular evocation of sixteenth-century England when Harrods, London's premier department store based in Knightsbridge, themed its coronation advertising around an exuberant celebration of the first Elizabethan age.[45]

More intellectual versions of Elizabethan nostalgia singled out the importance of this period in English history not only for its romantic associations, but also because it provided important lessons for the country's future. Journalist and long-standing liberal imperialist Sir Philip Gibbs set out the most developed version of these arguments in his book, *The New Elizabethans*, rushed out just before the coronation in 1952. 'We look back to the Elizabethan era . . . as our flowering time of genius, high adventure and national spirit,' Gibbs explained, 'and now there is a second Queen Elizabeth . . . many of us are inclined to take stock of ourselves and to compare our own character, conditions, manners and morals, and chances of a new blossoming, with those of our Elizabethan ancestors.'[46] Gibbs deliberately invoked 'Raleigh's vision of Empire', which he contrasted with the new shibboleths of 'self-determination and fanatical nationalism' that were undermining Britain's position across Africa and the Far East.[47] He projected a vision of the nation that was rooted in heroic individualism and masculine enterprise, so that British test pilots and scientists were celebrated because they demonstrated a revival of the Elizabethan spirit.[48] The Queen herself seemed to endorse a milder version of some of these ideas in her first Christmas radio broadcast when, with Churchill's political guidance, she spoke about the 'courageous spirit of adventure . . . given us by our forefathers' that would provide the country with 'the strength to venture beyond the safeties of the past'.[49]

Revivalist images of the country's future, and of London's central role in it, cut against the more obviously progressive accounts of national development evinced by many of the dominant figures in post-war consensus politics and by intellectuals and policymakers working in the expanding welfare state. These advocates of the post-war political and social contract emphasized the country's productive break with recent history, as represented by the Depression years of the 1930s or even the Victorian era, in order to argue that their policies were progressive. Romantics and conservatives, in contrast, drew enthusiastically on selective episodes from the past, insisting that such retrospectives had the power to shape the country's future. Their rhetoric emphasized the traditional conservative virtue of 'stability in an age of change', which in turn implied 'the continuity of Britain as a great power', but it also suggested a conservative reading of the national spirit that was driven by social forces and sentiments heavily rooted in history.[50]

Not all of the public discourse and social personalities associated with the coronation were backward-looking. Media technology that extended the coverage and the reliability of television was an obvious example of modernizing impulses that were closely associated with the royal event, and the British press displayed a marked fascination with this feat.[51] The conquest of Everest by Edmund Hillary and Tenzing Norgay, announced the day the Queen was crowned, with their ascent assisted by oxygen technology, was another instance of scientific research enhancing national prestige. The widely screened documentary film version of their ascent, *The Conquest of Everest* (1953), paid tribute to these efforts, with scenes showing the testing of oxygen equipment and efforts to overcome altitude sickness.[52] In a very different way, one of the most prominent figures now associated with the Windsor monarchy, the Queen's husband Prince Philip, was self-consciously go-ahead. A newcomer to court, he had alarmed some of its stuffier members with his enthusiasm for all things contemporary. Supported by his enterprising private secretary Mike Parker, Philip set about installing an intercom system and the first answering machines at Buckingham Palace.[53] He regularly piloted his own helicopter, and as a naval officer he took a keen interest in the design of the new royal yacht *Britannia*. Despite his conservative political views, his public impact was generally on the side of innovation.

In 1953 London itself was also portrayed in overtly progressive terms as a 'world city'. This urban idea differed from that of the imperial metropolis inasmuch as it explicitly defined London through the triple post-war obsessions of movement, money and culture. The capital was now the centre of an integrated communications system, a dynamic and expanding financial entrepôt (building on the City of London's long-established role as the international focus for banking, currency markets and trade), and a major cultural hub. New York's newly acquired status as the pre-eminent world city, measured against all of these criteria, was not lost on London's business community and its politicians as they talked up their capital's renaissance. Encouraged by the large-scale influx of foreign visitors, the chairman of the British Travel and Holidays Association predicted that coronation London would receive well over 200,000 American visitors alone and that many of them would travel by jet.[54] The appearance of the new Comet fleet of planes introduced by BOAC, Britain's long-distance commercial airline, the proposed expansion of Heathrow airport, and the recent opening of an air passenger terminal at Waterloo station added to the expectations of a new era in travel, when London would be linked to other major centres across the world in a streamlined system of communications.[55]

In the City, the Conservative government's relaxation of planning controls on business development was the cue for a commercially led building boom that began soon after the coronation. At the annual Lord Mayor's Banquet in 1953, Churchill laid the recent neglect of the financial square mile directly at the feet of 'socialist prejudice' and promised to 'rip down' the bomb-blackened ruins and create a 'new and full skyline' for the capital.[56] Deliberately pitching his arguments against the state-led policies of urban planning that had dominated the rebuilding of London in the aftermath of wartime destruction, Churchill placed his confidence in the ability of the private sector to redevelop the capital's central areas. In the City, financial journalists noted approvingly that 'business was moving eastwards again', back to its 'old haunts', encouraged by the reopening of London's commodity markets and by the Treasury's commitment to a reinvigorated sterling area.[57] The sound of mechanical hoists and concrete mixers on bomb sites across the City was a tangible sign that this major rebuilding programme was under way.[58] What materialized were the heavy brick and stone-clad office buildings that characterized the early 1950s property boom. Blocks such as Atlantic House on Holborn Viaduct and Millocrat House in Great Tower Street presented a conservative aesthetic with their imposing neo-Georgian facades, the embodiment of an architectural style that aimed to stabilize the image of the City of London as the centre of financial power.[59]

The expansion of business in the City was matched by a revival of elite forms of metropolitan culture, most notably in the West End, the traditional setting for ostentatious displays of wealth and glamorous spectacle. The reappearance of patrician social life organized around the idea of society, the ritualistic forms of upper-class solidarity in the capital, was in sharp contrast to the experiments in egalitarian social engineering pioneered by the Labour government during the late 1940s. Two weeks before the coronation, fashion photographer John French captured the mood of 'social glamour' in his picture from the Chelsea Flower Show at the start of the London season. It showed two extremely well-connected young people in an exchange of discreet mutual admiration. The immaculately groomed young woman in costume, hat and gloves was leading débutante Priscilla Greville, while the spruce young man in bowler hat and City suit was Vere Eliot, merchant banker and younger son of the 8th Earl of Saint Germans, who had been a page of honour at the coronation of George VI.[60] French shot his picture with characteristic brio and a subtle touch of irony, but the symbolism was intensely traditional: aristocratic personalities epitomizing the power of landed wealth and money moving to the rhythms of established social protocols.

Hostesses and socialites seized on the coronation as an opportunity to revive an extended version of the season that had not been seen in its full form since 1939. Along with French's coverage of the Chelsea Flower Show, society columnists claimed that Wimbledon tennis, racing at Royal Ascot, and the Henley Regatta had all been given an added éclat by the coronation. Monied foreign tourists and visiting dignitaries chorused their approval about the return of these elite forms of entertainment. American socialite Jackie Bouvier, covering royal events in her column for the *Times-Herald* newspaper, confided to audiences at home that she 'went dancing at the 400, a tiny private night club in Mayfair. Lined with . . . red velvet, it looked like the inside of a jewel box.'[61] Bouvier, who was about to extend her own social position through her engagement to Senator Jack Kennedy, was impressed by London society, which, as she noted enthusiastically, was patronized by the royal family and the aristocracy. Reviewing the flurry of the 1953 season, *Queen* magazine, the dedicated gazette for upper-class social sentiment, concluded that Londoners should feel well pleased that etiquette, manners and the capacity for civilized enjoyment remained intact among the country's top ten thousand, despite the ravages of the twentieth century.[62]

The optimistic coronation mood in the capital was not confined to the metropolitan elites; it was also present in many areas of popular culture. Here a softer, less hierarchical version of the city predominated, in which leisure and the entertainment industries took the lead. Throughout 1953 BBC Radio's Light Programme was full of live variety shows, broadcast direct from the heart of the West End, with upbeat coronation sketches and gags performed by comedians like Arthur Askey and Ted Ray. Television's first magazine-style programme, *London Town*, hosted by the new anchor-man of broadcasting, Richard Dimbleby, devoted a special edition to the coronation route.[63] Popular songs with commemorative lyrics augmented the festive mood. Noel Gay, whose musical *Me and My Girl* (1937) had captured national sentiment at the time of the previous coronation with his show-stopping tune 'The Lambeth Walk', now composed a special coronation ballad, 'In a Golden Coach'. Sung by a variety of top vocalists, it was the most widely played of many coronation melodies. Gay's cockneyfied lyrics associated the Queen with a revival in the spirit of London:

> In a golden coach
> There's a heart of gold
> Riding through old London town.
> With the sweetest Queen
> The world's ever seen
> Wearing her golden crown.
> As she drives in state
> Through the palace gate
> Her beauty the whole world will see.
> In a golden coach
> There's a heart of gold
> That belongs to you and me.[64]

The ballad's sentimental formulaic verses, sung in the style of an old-fashioned slow waltz, personalized Elizabeth II, associating her beauty and warm-heartedness with the traditions of 'old London town'. Gay's words claimed the new monarch for the people, evoking a long tradition of royal populism. The Queen paid lip-service to some of these sentiments when she self-consciously referred to herself as 'a Londoner' at a reception given in her honour by the London County Council (LCC) at County Hall.[65]

In popular discourse the idea of 'magic' was invoked repeatedly to describe the change that the coronation had brought about in the city. 'Mr Magic . . . Waves a Wand Over London', enthused the *Daily Mirror*, supposedly describing the experience of one spellbound provincial reader on a visit to the capital.[66] Part of this transformative effect, as the 'Golden Coach' ballad suggested, was promoted by the public persona of the Queen herself, projecting a unique blend of radiance, royal glamour, and even discreet sex appeal. Sceptics and even some ardent republicans who had approached coronation day with distaste and disapproval found themselves unwittingly drawn to these personal dimensions of the drama. A 21-year-old bank clerk, who had previously thought of Elizabeth II as supercilious and remote, wrote of 'a rising excitement in myself when the Queen came past in the State Coach'.[67]

The Queen's personal allure and her embodiment of youthful promise were in stark contrast to the personification of monarchy under her father. A dutiful constitutionalist, George VI lacked royal charisma; a pronounced stammer exaggerated his appearance of public diffidence, while in later years the King (by now prematurely aged) was seriously ill with heart disease and lung cancer. Though he was supported by his extrovert consort, Queen Elizabeth, with her flamboyant personal style, monarchy under George VI was strongly identified with the national struggles and privations of wartime and subsequently with post-war austerity. Elizabeth II, the first queen regnant for over fifty years, was poised, glamorous and regal; above all she was a woman. Churchill referred to the Queen as 'this gleaming figure', and comparisons with Hollywood were not lost on a politician who was himself a master of charismatic public presentation. 'Lovely, inspiring. All the film people in the world, if they had scoured the globe, could not have found anyone so suited to the part,' the premier confided to his doctor Lord Moran.[68] Enthusiastic courtiers and members of the royal family heralded the new reign as a 'phoenix time'; 'there was this gorgeous-looking, lovely young lady, and nothing to stop anything getting better and better,' Princess Margaret remembered.[69] For committed royalists and for many others who identified less strongly with the Windsor monarchy, the coronation seemed to promise a benign and more luminous period in the nation's history, traits that were personified in the Queen's own display of femininity.

In London the new royal era was engineered quite literally by the skilful use of props and scenery, especially with the official decorations designed by the architect Sir Hugh Casson (a wartime expert in airforce military camouflage) and overseen by the Ministry of Works. The general aesthetic effect was of height, light and scale pushing the city skywards, 'like a rainbow coming out of a dark cloud', according to the *Illustrated London News*.[70] The capital's official buildings were cleaned with new pressurized water sprays, while landmarks such as Eros, Sir Alfred Gilbert's aluminium statue in the centre of Piccadilly Circus, were taken away for repair.[71] Beyond the central areas of the West End and the City, all the London boroughs and many local working-class communities participated energetically in the coronation displays. Tenants in Lillie Walk, a condemned slum terrace in a poor part of Fulham, spent large sums of money not only on flags and traditional street decorations but also on makeshift floodlighting. Rows of bunting, white paper garlands and lines of miniature Union Jacks were strung across the narrow Fulham passageway, doors were embellished with gold and silver crowns, and pictures of the Queen and her family were pasted up in parlour windows.[72] One local woman, speaking on behalf of her street community, felt that the time and expense were 'worth it' because the young Queen's personal appeal made her feel very positive about the new reign. As she explained to Mass Observation on the eve of the celebrations: 'It's something . . . to remember. We've always liked her as Princess Elizabeth. . . . She seems so homely. Let's hope she'll be happy and we'll all have peace.'[73]

The street decorations and the official ceremony produced a powerful image of London that was *in colour*. One of the most significant visual effects of the coronation events, along with the countless printed souvenirs, newsreels and films that commemorated them, was the impact of heightened chromatic tones in silver, red and gold, and other vibrant colours. The obvious contrast was with the monochrome and sepia shots of London that predominated in press photography and in the cinema during the war and its aftermath. As Churchill hinted, there was a strong sense that much of the coronation imagery paralleled and sometimes imitated the lavish cinematic Technicolor used by Hollywood, as well as the widescreen visual format of Cinemascope.[74] The result was a dramatically heightened panoramic display of London and its leading characters.

Part of this coronation atmosphere was shaped by forces that were associated less with royalty than with the beginnings of a new era of mass consumerism for Londoners, albeit as yet only on a modest and embryonic scale. During the festivities shops and key consumer industries, backed by the power of advertising and marketing, worked hard to redefine London as a city of material abundance. In reality, rationing for foodstuffs and other goods remained in force well into the early 1950s, so that efforts to promote the capital as a centre of buoyant consumer culture were largely prefigurative.[75] Along the length of Oxford Street, the West End's principal shopping thoroughfare, Selfridge's and the other major department stores carried the traditional large-scale decorations that they had mounted for coronations and royal jubilees throughout the first half of the twentieth century. What was new, though, were the prominent displays of household consumer durables that were to become such a hallmark of mass affluence by the mid-1950s. The Electrolux showroom in Regent Street presented 'Loyal Greetings to Her Majesty', with fridges and washing machines topped with royal regalia and draped in national colours, while car dealers adopted similar patriotic window dressing.[76] Some of this economic populism was politically inflected; recently elected Tory ministers were keen to play up the contrast between a new Conservative society of freedom and plenty and 'the shortages, black markets, power cuts, [and] identity cards' they identified with the Labour government's previous regime of rationing.[77] Labour and Liberal critics for their part highlighted the 'enormous expense and trappings of the coronation' which sought to convince the public 'there is an affinity between the throne and the Tory party'.[78]

Taken together, the coronation celebrations circulated competing images of the capital that were a product of the widely different interest groups who claimed a stake in the event. The overall effect of these representations was to project London as a city centred by monarchy and by the political and cultural associations of the Crown. Partly by official design and partly as a result of popular sentiment, the capital's festive atmosphere was closely linked to royal tradition and to a conservative idea of English society.

Vice

Shadowing the exuberant coronation coverage as its negative underside, a wide range of commentators identified vice as a significant part of London's urban culture. During the late 1940s and early 1950s, as in earlier periods, this collective noun was used by politicians, the police and public moralists as an expansive referent for a litany of contemporary problems. Sex crimes and misdemeanours in public places, pornography in the West End, drug trafficking and pimping by young Caribbean men in Notting Hill, gang warfare in Soho, 'unmarried mothers' in 'twilight zones' of the city, a rising tide of juvenile delinquency epitomized by the esoteric working-class youth culture of London's Teddy Boys, this extensive list documented old and new urban pathologies and ranged across the spaces of central London and its adjacent areas.[79] Metropolitan police chiefs highlighted many of these problems in their annual reports, arguing that the long-term consequences of the war on the home front and the subsequent rapid pace of social change had led to a general 'lowering of standards of integrity' among otherwise law-abiding Londoners.[80] Social documentary photographers reinforced these perceptions in visual terms, producing atmospheric images of the capital's low-life haunts and their shady cast of characters (fig. 3). A dossier prepared by the International Criminal Police Commission pointed to feelings of moral dislocation across many other European cites, reporting rises in sex offences, drug use, and a general tendency towards self-centred 'materialism' in urban populations as far apart as Rome and Amsterdam.[81] In New York a similar set of urban problems focused the minds of city officials in an extensive discussion about social delinquency.[82]

In London, the coronation imposed a distinctive frisson onto this cluster of anxieties. Royal events, focusing intense public scrutiny of landmark or official London as the 'Mecca for all visitors' and the setting for national demonstrations of prestige, exaggerated the perceived impact of disturbances to moral values.[83] Compromising societal norms and established ethical systems, metropolitan vice was seen as a threat to the ritualistic display of social cohesion personified by monarchy in the capital city.[84] Public attention was focused on the dark sexual underside of the coronation in a series of escalating incidents that highlighted the West End as the setting for heavily organized public prostitution and sex between men. These cases, which were initially orchestrated by representatives of the tourist industry and influential foreign visitors and then rapidly taken up by the popular press in conjunction with the police and the Home Office, were the precursor to a wide-ranging national debate about transgressive displays of sex in the capital that ran throughout the 1950s. Alfred Kinsey's energetic fieldwork was part of this escalating anxiety and fascination with West End vice.

A few months before the coronation, in the autumn of 1952, Malcolm La Prade, an American vice-president of the travel company Thomas Cook, was visiting London on a business trip.[85] Accompanied by his wife, the couple were staying at the May Fair Hotel, off Piccadilly, and among La Prade's colleagues in the capital was James Maxwell, the General Manager of Cook's bureau at Piccadilly Circus. One evening in early October Maxwell entertained his American guests to dinner at the Dorchester Hotel on Park Lane, introducing them to his English colleagues in the travel business. The party went well and the group stayed until one in the morning, when Maxwell drove the couple back to their hotel. La Prade's wife went to bed, but La Prade himself was in no mood to turn in immediately. Not having visited London since the war, he asked Maxwell to show him a little of the city's night life.

Shop window lights and advertising signs had been turned on again in the West End that autumn for the first time since 1939; the two men took a leisurely stroll around Piccadilly Circus before turning towards Soho. La Prade was a cultivated New Yorker who had studied in Europe and was the broadcasting voice of 'The Man From Cook's' radio travelogues. A forward-looking American and clearly no prude, according to Maxwell he had an 'international outlook' and was one of the widest travelled men in the world.[86] La Prade was amazed to see the change that had come over the capital since his last visit; central London appeared utterly transformed. All along Piccadilly, which formed part of the official route for the coronation procession, 'street ladies' were spaced out every few yards on the pavement.[87] Shop doorways and even hotel foyers were thronged with prostitutes who made direct approaches to almost every man who passed by. On some street corners young policemen were seen casually chatting to the girls. Just up from the Park Lane Hotel something more unusual caught La Prade's attention. A group of 'obvious' homosexuals were busy propositioning two American tourists outside one of the large stores.[88] There was no attempt at concealment, and La Prade noticed how the men advertised themselves by their dress and 'effeminate mannerisms'.[89] It was the first time the American had seen such overt and seemingly uninhibited displays of homosexuality in the West End. Like Kinsey, La Prade identified public prostitution and sex between men as graphic evidence of London's contemporary erotic atmosphere.

La Prade viewed London as the well-informed and endlessly interested visitor, the most recent of generations of educated American men who had explored the city and its pleasures.[90] Maxwell, in contrast, saw himself as the embarrassed representative of domestic tourism facing an important foreign visitor. 'The state of affairs is not going to do you or me any good in our efforts to publicize Britain abroad,' he complained to the Chairman of the British Travel and Holidays Association, with his eye on the forthcoming celebrations, 'I shudder to think what conditions are going to be like during the Coronation next year.'[91]

Driven by the urgency of impending royal events, official responses to La Prade's and Maxwell's revelations were rapid. The Metropolitan Police Commissioner, Sir Harold Scott, ordered an internal inquiry, and the Home Secretary, Sir David Maxwell Fyfe, was prompted to deliver a special lecture on the dangers of public immorality from the church pulpit of St Martin-in-the-Fields in nearby Trafalgar Square. Stiffening the resolve of his audience, Maxwell Fyfe admitted that 'virtue' was not a popular word in London today, while its opposite 'vice' had increasingly acquired a 'carnal connotation'. In an urban environment dominated by 'speed, spacelessness and a spate of ever-changing problems', it was necessary to reinstate moral integrity into the hearts of the people of London.[92]

What concerned Maxwell Fyfe was not just the type of scandalous incident reported by La Prade but something more politically worrying from a Home Office standpoint; London's rapidly rising crime statistics. As the capital's police chief, Scott had already put the Met's case very forcibly in his recent annual reports; the 'transition from war to peace' had been accompanied by a serious increase in all indictable crimes, but the most striking rise had taken place in reported sexual offences, an area that he singled out for special mention.[93] Not only were rape and other sex crimes against women escalating, but also 'unnatural offences', especially male indecency.[94] A staggering rise of over 300 per cent since 1938 was not simply a 'reflection of greater activity by the police', Scott insisted.[95] Like his political masters at the Home Office, he argued that the West End had become the forcing house for unnatural sex of all kinds, where 'a general slackening of sexual morals' and a 'reckless pursuit of excitement', 'pleasure' and 'financial gain' were making the work of the police particularly difficult.[96]

Historians have argued over the reliability of this reported post-war rise in sex crime, as well as about its multiple causes, in a debate that has concentrated on homosexuality.[97] The idea of an official 'witch hunt' against homosexual men in London, orchestrated by senior political figures like Maxwell Fyfe and backed by increased surveillance from the Metropolitan Police, has been put forward by some commentators to explain the escalating crime figures. But an equally important feature of the numerical increase was the social impact of these statistics about sex, understood as part of a wider public culture of knowledge production and dissemination. Official statistics were part of a long-established strategy of information gathering which, as James Scott has argued, defined the 'legibility' of the modern state.[98] In the case of the rising incidence of sex crime, the impact of the figures was politically problematic; rather than legitimizing government policy, they raised more questions than they answered.

American criminologist Thorsten Sellin defined the problem succinctly at a lecture given at Cambridge University in 1951. Most people were innately distrustful of statistics, Sellin argued, yet a superstitious belief in the 'magical properties of numbers' made the community look with 'awe' on statistical tables.[99] The difficulty for criminologists was that their statistics represented only a small percentage of 'total criminality', the latter being in reality 'an unknown quantity'.[100] While some offences had a high degree of reportability, there were many others where the recorded sample was 'extremely small and sometimes . . . microscopic'. Sellin insisted that most sex offences were in this latter class, including homosexuality, criminal abortion and rape.

Sellin's hypothesis, which lay at the heart of post-war debates about the so-called 'dark figures' for crime, was taken up vigorously by Leon Radzinowicz at the newly created Department of Criminal Science in the Law Faculty at Cambridge. Examining data from over 3,000 cases of 'sexual transgressions', mainly in the capital, Radzinowicz believed that the nature of these offences, most of which took place in private, meant the level of concealment 'must be enormous', adding ominously that 'it must be doubted whether the amount of illegal sexual misconduct which is revealed can ever represent more than five per cent of the actual crime committed'.[101] As quantitative social scientists, Radzinowicz and Sellin insisted that the dark crime figures could not be ignored. As public commentators with their eyes on a wider audience, they also enshrined a distinctive social frisson into their seemingly dispassionate statistical argument about the number of concealed sex offences, suggesting an infinite mathematical regress to an almost unknowable core of criminality.

Official concern about the rates of sex crime in London was the precursor to a series of coordinated responses by central government which ran throughout the mid-1950s.[102] The most notable of these was the Home Office inquiry set up to investigate homosexual offences and prostitution. But information about the moral condition of the West End was not just the intellectual property of influential politicians and policymakers; the national media were also in competition with official sources for sexual news, with the police and reporters responding to each other's respective needs for political solutions and good editorial copy. Journalists regularly sought the ear of police commissioners and home secretaries, who were themselves under constant pressure from the press to deliver information about West End crime in order to satisfy the demands of national newspaper audiences.[103]

The Piccadilly Circus incident represented a clear case of the mutually reinforcing relationship that existed between the police and the media over access to sexual knowledge. Acting on a tip-off from the Met, the press got hold of La Prade's original disclosures that had been made to Scotland Yard and the Home Office. The *Sunday Graphic* launched an exposé of what it now billed as 'The Scandal of Piccadilly Circus', with reporters skilfully incorporating a version of the American visitor's nighttime excursions into their own newspaper copy.[104] The two accounts differed sharply in their style and cultural content; La Prade had expressed the detached interest of the man-about-town and the cultivated foreign visitor, but the *Graphic*'s journalists mixed the language of documentary reportage and popular melodrama, engaging the support of public morality campaigners to insist that the state of the West End was a national problem demanding immediate and long-term solutions.[105]

The *Graphic*'s coverage was the first in a sequence of carefully orchestrated press revelations pointing to direct links between the coronation and the escalation of 'commercialized vice' in London. One young crusading Catholic journalist, Duncan Webb, seized the initiative, extending the initial revelations by turning them into a quasi-official report about public morals that also functioned as voyeuristic sexual tourism. Running throughout April and May 1953 and scripted as a dossier that Webb insisted was intended for none other than the Home Secretary himself, 'Vice in London' took the nation's weekend reading public on a series of armchair tours of the capital.

Webb published his story in the *People*, one of the mass market Sunday papers that had enhanced its post-war reputation and its circulation figures by regularly printing 'hot' sexual stories.[106] He opened his series with a well-rehearsed theme that had been at the centre of his own recent pursuit of the Messina brothers, the Maltese and Italian gang of pimps and racketeers whose vice empire linked London's traffic in women to many Continental cities in an international network of crime. In the English capital, large-scale prostitution organized by foreign syndicates was flourishing in areas adjacent to the coronation route; with the event now only 'seven weeks away' gangs were planning an 'immense haul'.[107] Fresh from his own fact-finding tour of Europe, Webb showed how the coronation was actively encouraging 'the . . . dregs of Paris, Brussels, Sicily and Malta' to converge on London.[108] Pimps and ponces were turning parts of the West End into a 'sort of clearing house for foreign prostitutes'.[109] Far from encouraging a clean-up, Webb insisted that impending royal events were having a negative impact on public morality.[110]

Webb claimed narrative authority for his exposé by demonstrating his own intimate contacts with London's underworld.[111] Drawing on the well-established genres of urban exploration and cultural ethnography, he presented a detailed account of the prostitution trade and its associated forms of metropolitan low life 'from the bottom up'. Masquerading as a punter in the capital's long tradition of cultural slumming, Webb revealed how, in the public interest, he had allowed himself to be 'solicited by a French woman' in Soho and had then followed her to her 'gaff'. Moving his participant observation a few hundred yards south to the corner of Leicester Square, he hung around with 'extortionists, blackmailers' and 'homosexuals' and posed as a regular in the West End's 'speilers' or illicit gambling dens.[112] Following the contours of nineteenth-century urban topography that placed 'overworld' and 'underworld' side by side, Webb went on to sketch a map of London in which high and low society existed in the same or adjacent spaces. But his use of Victorian social imagery was augmented by more contemporary developments as well. The capital's 'vice underworld' had 'spread its tentacles' well beyond 'the normal haunts' of the West End, reaching out as far as 'dignified Kensington' and Chelsea, while Webb's catalogue of crime documented the appearance of new social types, especially a highly organized 'class of Chicago-like' gangsters who had 'dug themselves in' to London's central areas and built up a 'minor reign of terror'.[113]

Webb's exposé pushed together many of the distinctive public images of the capital that predominated in coronation year, revealing the underside to London's post-war renaissance and its much-vaunted urban sophistication. Combining representations of the socially bifurcated city with more up-to-date themes, his message was that expanded tourism and consumerism could mean an accelerating trade in commercial sex, as well as a revival of demand in more conventional markets. An open cosmopolitan society also permitted the influx of 'foreign undesirables', men and women from Europe and the Commonwealth whose business was vice. Turning to the opposite end of the social spectrum, Webb and his fellow journalists also placed elite society glamour under the spotlight; fashionable nightclubs and other rendezvous provided plentiful opportunities for 'young Lotharios' among the 'smart set' to prey on vulnerable women.[114]

Following well-established traditions of investigative journalism, Webb closed his Sunday series, like his colleagues on the *Graphic*, by casting himself as a crusading campaigner who drew on the authority of national opinion to demand that the government clean up the capital. Calling for the replacement of 'out of date laws' that allowed prostitutes to solicit openly on London's streets and 'a vicious circle . . . of blackmailers, thieves and gangsters' to profit from their operations, he insisted that a constant moral watch also needed to be kept on aristocratic men-about-town who were enmeshed in the city's underworld.[115] His 'hackles of patriotism' also forced him to admit that London's cosmopolitan atmosphere needed stronger protection from disreputable foreigners by an immediate tightening of the nationality laws.[116]

Despite his rallying cry, Webb's articles produced no sense of closure to the problems he raised; nor were they intended to do so. Exposé journalism of this kind projected a dynamic atmosphere of moral disturbance onto London's central areas, while giving readers a vicarious thrill of sexual excitement that appeared all the more transgressive because of the proximity of royal events.[117] Webb's revelations were part of a proliferation of competing genres of sexual knowledge produced during the early 1950s that took London's urban cultures as their central focus. These accounts of sex in the city were circulated by a wide variety of commentators who operated from very different social vantage points. Ranging from the leisured perambulations of the capital's men–about–town and other society figures, through the official surveillance of the police and numerous public intellectuals and commercial entrepreneurs, they also included the activities of men and women who moved within London's sexual subcultures at street level. All these figures had a major impact on the changing sexual politics of the capital during the post–war years, and their influence was felt well beyond the confines of the metropolitan area because London occupied a paradigmatic status in public discussions of national morality. Mapping this field of urban sexuality more closely involves profiling the personalities and tracking the movements of its principal protagonists.

Chapter 2   Society

Good Time Guides to London

When Douglas Sutherland, a young Fleet Street journalist and aspiring socialite, returned from army service to live in London after the war, he was immediately struck by the city's double consciousness. There was, he recollected, a tangible and 'immense war-weariness' among so many sections of the population that cast its shadow over life in the capital well into the 1950s.[1] A *bon viveur* who was well connected to the aristocracy and to influential members of the metropolitan gentry, Sutherland bemoaned the disappearance of anything approaching elite social life in its expansive pre-war forms. He saw the great town-houses of the rich 'with their armies of servants and lavish entertainment' shuttered and empty, or in the process of being converted into new post-war urban landmarks: the headquarters of oil companies and advertising agencies.[2] At a more personal level, the business of acquiring the necessities of life that were important for a gentleman to maintain an appropriate social style was a constant headache, given the limited clothing ration and Sutherland's own meagre standard demob kit which the army had issued him with. He remembered being grateful for clothing parcels sent by American friends, including two cast-off suits from the Broadway impresario Oscar Hammerstein. After discreet alterations by his Mayfair tailor, these outfits enabled him to pose for a while as 'one of the best dressed men-about-town'.[3] Finally, there was the headache of housing. Sutherland recalled that 'to find a furnished flat' for himself and his wife, who was a dancer with the Sadler's Wells Ballet, 'required complete dedication'.[4] Such was the pressure on accommodation that the couple were delighted when a property developer friend found them a small basement (overlooked by a request stop for the number 74 bus) at the unfashionable end of the Cromwell Road, near Earl's Court.

Yet as a young man in his twenties Sutherland was also optimistic about life in the capital; as he experienced it, the whole urban scene was changing as the city relaxed. Seen from the vantage point of youth and social opportunity, the picture was far from gloomy; there was a sense of continual restlessness in the air, a sort of shifting gear as a post-war generation started to get into its stride. For Sutherland, this atmosphere materialized in the appearance of urban personalities who were noted for their public styles of sociability. They included property tycoons, such as the multimillionaire developers Harold Samuel, Jack Cotton and Charles Clore, who were transforming the skyline of the City of London and the West End's social life with their corporate financial ventures and lavish parties.[5] Advertising executives, archetypal figures of the post-war consumer economy, also featured prominently in Sutherland's urban perspective, driving mergers and take-overs and setting the tone in the most exclusive restaurants. Sutherland was also aware that for the first time 'the voice of the public relations man was being heard in the land', with the result that it was now 'possible to have a ready-made glittering occasion to open almost anything from a night club to a fashion house'.[6]

Sutherland noted approvingly that there were feminine characters to match these masculine personalities, especially the figure of the society hostess who made a reappearance in the early 1950s. He acclaimed Lady Sonia Melchett, wife of the merchant banker Julian Mond, as 'London's party-giver par excellence', while Norah, Lady Docker, a former dancer at the Café de Paris, was also entertaining from her Mayfair home in flamboyant style.[7] If 'high Society' in the pre-war meaning of the term had gone forever, Sutherland was convinced that a new sort of 'Café Society was appearing in London'; an eclectic mixture of worldly politicians and international visitors, along with socialites, photographers, actors, models and fashion designers were beginning to stimulate London's cultural atmosphere after the years of austerity.[8] Many of these individuals congregated in fashionable pubs and clubs, which enterprising landlords had established as spaces for informal socializing and for relaxed displays of heterosocial and homosocial leisure.

After an initial desk job at the War Office administering the resettlement of foreign nationals, Sutherland reinvented himself as a Fleet Street gossip columnist on the *Evening Standard*. This was the point when his London life really began, he recollected.[9] The leisured pace of work and the need to fish for good stories left him ample time to explore the city and its pleasures. One of the hazards of 'marrying into the theatre', he

admitted ruefully, was that it was not 'conducive to a well–ordered domestic life'.[10] Sutherland confessed that he 'squandered disgracefully' the
leisure time of his late afternoons and evenings while his wife was appearing on the West End stage.[11]

Like Duncan Webb, Sutherland was particularly keen to show off his
knowledge of London's square mile of vice, but the contrast between the
perspectives of the two journalists was striking. Webb dealt in the language of the cultural ethnographer and the 'courageous' public morality
campaigner, while Sutherland expressed a mixture of delight and interested amusement in the capital's sexual scene that was more akin to
Malcolm La Prade's outlook.[12] In the West End 'when the lights went up
again in Piccadilly' after the lifting of the blackout, he too strolled among
the prostitutes who lined street after street, mingling with the 'youngest
and the prettiest' who were jostling for attention along the pavements of
Piccadilly and Bond Street.[13] Turning off the main thoroughfares in
Mayfair and St James's, it was quite easy to get a drink or place a bet
during the afternoon in one of the hundreds of illegal 'members only'
clubs that had sprung up during the war.

Sutherland's own favourite venues where he chose to while away his
'hours of idleness' were Frisco's in Mayfair's Shepherd's Market, run by a
'well preserved West Indian negro', and the Colony Room in Soho's
Dean Street, a self-styled bohemian venue presided over by its flamboyant Jewish hostess Muriel Belcher.[14] But for those who were less well
connected to the capital's sophisticated social networks, Sutherland recommended a number of informal guides to West End entertainment that
offered advice and information as part of de luxe tourism.[15] 'Welcome to
Clubland,' announced Harry Meadows, the manager and suave host of
Churchill's exclusive nightclub in New Bond Street, in his introduction
to *The 1953 Guide to London Clubs*. 'When the lights of London are low'
and the West End's cinemas and theatres emptied, Meadows recommended that visitors wend their way to the 'plush purlieus of Mayfair
when the revelry continues undiminished . . . until the early hours'.[16]
Meadows's golden rule was that everyone who had 'a reasonable standard
of education and culture' and who held 'his liquor like a gentleman' could
gain entry to clubland – provided he came equipped with the 'correct
introductions'.[17] Progressive publisher Francis Aldor, in his *The Good Time
Guide to London* (1951), proffered similar advice to visiting foreign businessmen and provincial tourists. Giving a suggestive twist to the international tourism pioneered by Fodor's travel guides, Aldor promised to 'put

in the visitor's hand a key which ensures that the right doors will open for him', while reminding the traveller of the rules he needed to remember if he didn't want his party cut short.[18]

Like Sutherland's itinerary and Kinsey's sexual explorations, Aldor's and Meadows's guides invariably started their conducted tour of the West End from Piccadilly Circus, the hub of London's night life and the imagined 'centre of the universe'.[19] With an eye on the influx of American businessmen after the war, Aldor described Piccadilly in terms more usually reserved for New York's Times Square as a crazy place, the home of 'playland', which kept 'brighter lights' and 'later hours than the rest of the town'.[20] This was the cue for a welter of detailed advice about where to find London's own version of live sexual entertainment, or what US visitors knew as burlesque theatre. Around Leicester Square, Aldor reported, you could usually find the newest 'leg-show' from Paris, the 'big spectaculars . . . packed with impassive nudes'.[21] But he also recommended that his readers pay a visit to a much smaller outfit with a 'more sophisticated presentation . . . tucked   away . . . behind   Piccadilly'.[22]   The   Windmill Theatre, on the corner of Archer Street, was a place that dealt in quintessentially English girls, where the management mixed glamorous nude displays with the fast-paced traditions of variety theatre. Visitors could spot the place quite easily by the queues of men stretching down towards Shaftesbury Avenue, and once inside, Aldor enthused, they were in for a treat.

Sutherland made it clear that personally he had no need of guidebooks or ciceroni; his boast was that he had discovered London's masculine pleasures at first hand by being 'out on the town'. His assumed right to experience the full range of the West End's amusements drew on the customary privileges of generations of upper-class men to stroll across the capital and encounter its cosmopolitan diversity. Being in the city positioned Sutherland not simply as an interested spectator but as a potential consumer of leisure and entertainment. In this respect he was careful to distinguish himself from ordinary businessmen and tourists. Sutherland advertised his own elevated credentials by announcing his membership of the metropolitan cognoscenti, defining himself as part of an informal group of sophisticated initiates who were closely connected to the capital's elite social networks.

Sutherland's participation in these elite milieus dictated a specialized urban itinerary. On Thursdays, a favourite stroll was from his War Office outpost in St James's Square, up through Piccadilly, to his weekly afternoon rendezvous on the top floor of Wheeler's Restaurant in Soho's Old Compton Street.[23] This was the location of the celebrated and extremely private drinking and dining venue, the Thursday Club. Over 'long meandering lunches' interspersed with 'speeches, pranks and jokes', an exclusive set of guests including 'politicians, artists, pressmen, noblemen, tycoons and royalty' met regularly to affirm the informal and sometimes eccentric rituals of patrician masculine solidarity.[24] Prominent club members ranged from Prince Philip, his cousin David Mountbatten, Marquess of Milford Haven, and Lord Glenavy (better known as the wit and raconteur Patrick Campbell) to the Conservative politician Iain Macleod and the editors of the *Daily Express*, *Punch* and *Tatler*. There were also stars from the film and theatre worlds, including the actors David Niven, James Robertson Justice and Peter Ustinov, as well as the American entertainer Larry Adler, together with a number of more unorthodox personalities. Kim Philby, the Foreign Office official later revealed as a Soviet spy, was an invited guest, as was the sexual sophisticate and society osteopath Stephen Ward, who ten years later became a key figure in the Profumo scandal.

The prevailing atmosphere of the Thursday Club was raffish and urbane; its unofficial master of ceremonies was a Jewish outsider, the society photographer Baron Nahum, son of an Italian shipping merchant. Nahum had already gained a reputation for revitalizing London's postwar social scene with impromptu Mayfair parties hosted from his house off Park Lane. As one guest enthused: 'Take all these people. Take them to Baron's in Brick Street. Give them food, wine and music. The resulting pattern is a swirl of crazy colour. Wisps of conversation – on Cyprus, on women's shoulders, on poetry. Nothing, of course, serious for more than a moment.'[25] Baron's parties were renowned for their individualism, informality and caprice. Gossip columnist William Hickey, journalistic pseudonym of the Labour politician and socialite Tom Driberg, believed that Baron helped to create an atmosphere of fun and social exuberance in a city that was otherwise dominated by rationing and the sheer struggle for existence during the immediate post-war years. Baron himself endorsed Hickey's impressions, insisting that the Thursday Club 'lifted us completely out of the veil of monotony and austerity in which we lived'.[26]

The Thursday Club was a 'men only affair' (reputedly the only female guest ever to be invited was the glamorous opera diva Maria Callas), and its emphatically homosocial culture worked to affirm exclusivity.[27]

Members had a penchant for wild practical jokes which, as Sutherland remembered, usually involved 'boisterous ragging', a form of public schoolboy humour often instigated by Prince Philip.[28] There was also a liberal supply of 'hard liquor' and good food served in Wheeler's second-floor private dining room.

The flamboyant behaviour of Thursday Club devotees was deliberately pitted against other styles of masculine conduct that dominated public life in the late 1940s and early 1950s, most notably the renewed emphasis on sobriety and seriousness projected by many members of the Labour government. The majority of club participants were intense individualists and many were committed social conservatives. Their code of manners, combining personal gratification with assumed rights of social leadership, contrasted sharply with the high-mindedness and reforming zeal championed by many left-leaning politicians and bureaucrats. Thursday Club members were suspicious of intellectual earnestness, and the slightest hint of highbrow pretentiousness or pomposity was met with derision. Whenever any member of their party tipped over into really serious conversation, the company would break out into a hearty, mocking chorus of 'Lloyd George Knew My Father'.[29] 'The truth is that we enjoyed going round with people who knew what was going on,' explained Mike Parker, Prince Philip's boisterous Australian private secretary.[30] One of the unwritten club rules was a propensity for 'lewdness'. There were 'no dancing girls', said one of the starchier members of the court who kept an eye on Prince Philip, but 'quite lewd talk. Quite lewd.'[31] Sexual conversation ranged from beautiful women to buggery. The Queen herself, as Princess Elizabeth, sensed something of the club's dubious reputation, laconically referring to its members as 'Philip's funny friends'.[32]

An important factor encouraging the fun-loving rituals of the Thursday Club was the contradictory experience of wartime. Most younger members of the club had seen active service either during the Second World War or in its immediate aftermath. Sutherland served in the invasion of Germany in a regiment of the Royal Army Corps, and he was subsequently an officer with Allied Liaison Branch in the British zone during the country's military occupation. Prince Philip and Mike Parker were Royal Navy officers on the destroyer flotilla that patrolled the notorious 'E-Boat Alley' from the Scottish base at Rosyth down to the Thames estuary.[33] Both men later saw action against the Japanese in the Pacific.[34] David Niven returned from Hollywood in 1939 to join the Rifle Brigade; he took part in the Normandy landings in 1944 and was a recruit to the

1 Coronation night in the floodlit Mall, 2 June 1953, photographer unknown. Popperfoto/Getty Images.

2   Coronation procession Admiralty Arch, 2 June 1953. Fox Photos.

3   Love in Southwark, 1949, photographer Bert Hardy/Stringer, Hulton Archive. Getty Images.

4   Princess Margaret with members of her party after her first visit to the Café de Paris, undated, photographer unknown, in Charles Graves, *Champagne and Chandeliers: The Story of the Café de Paris* (London: Odhams Press, 1958).

5   Lady Docker with dancer and band leader Victor Silvester, undated, 1950s, photographer unknown. Popperfoto/Getty Images.

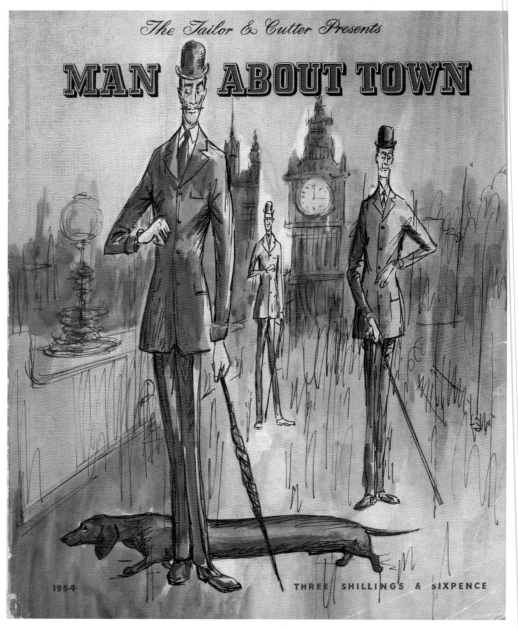

6   Front cover, *Man About Town*, 1954. Reproduced by permission of VinMag Archive Ltd.

7 'Back to Formality', *Vogue*, April 1950, p. 108, photographer Norman Parkinson. Courtesy of Norman Parkinson Archive.

8　Lord Edward Montagu arrives in New York, 29 September 1952, photographer unknown. TopFoto.

specialist Phantom Signals Unit, responsible for reporting enemy positions. On occasion, the wartime experience of all these young men was life-threatening, and they had witnessed the carnage and brutality of the conflict close up. As an observer at the execution of the Nazi high command at Nuremberg, Sutherland confessed that he had seen his 'fair share of the human detritus of war', which 'stayed with me in nightmarish clarity over the years'.[35] Niven rarely spoke publicly about his wartime career, but he was dismissive about journalists who glorified battle. As he put it tersely in his autobiography: 'Anyone who says a bullet sings past, hums past, flies, pings, or whines past has never heard one – they [sic] go crack.'[36]

The strenuous avoidance of seriousness, a constant search for light-hearted amusement, and the restless, individualist style of zany humour that motivated Thursday Club members were partly a reaction against the enforced discipline of military life and the wholesale collectivism of society during the 1940s. On returning to Civvy Street these young men were also keen to keep alive memories of their hedonistic wartime exploits. 'Of course we had fun' and there were 'always armfuls of girls', Parker admitted about his offshore leave with Prince Philip, which was the start of endless rumours about the Prince's sexual exploits.[37] Sutherland remembered that military life in Germany was made bearable by the 'prettiest of . . . young ladies', including society figures such as Fiona Smith, a member of the Guinness family, and Sonia Graham, who later became Lady Melchett.[38] The Thursday Club represented a post-war need to reassert masculine individualism on the part of the leaders of fashionable London life and a desire to preserve the pursuit of pleasure that had been a hallmark of their wartime careers.

With its secret society atmosphere and its rumours of excess, the Thursday Club also displayed continuities with the traditions of aristocratic libertinism that had been a marked feature of elite forms of masculinity during the eighteenth and nineteenth centuries. Young bloods, rakes and roaring boys with their private clubs, closed sites of assignation and stylized displays of disruptive behaviour had shaped the capital's social rituals and its gendered entertainment spaces over a long period. But Sutherland's personal style also drew on the resources of a different type of social personality, with an equally extensive pedigree, that exerted a major influence on cultural life in London during the 1950s; this was the figure of the man-about-town.

The man-about-town was London's highly distinctive version of the *flâneur*. This privileged male spectator, who encountered the city by 'botanizing on the asphalt', was initially associated with Parisian urban life, while the accompanying sociology of modernity elevated the *flâneur* to the status of a generic urban type.[39] London's own version of male world-liness displayed important links with the experience and analysis of *flânerie*, but the man–about–town also revealed significant differences from his Parisian counterpart that were shaped by the English capital's specific historical development.

Both the man–about–town and the *flâneur* were quintessentially leisured personae, with entertainment and sensory stimuli heavily privileged. Like the *flâneur*, Sutherland and his associates claimed imaginative rights to the whole of the city, rights that encompassed both high and low–life ver-sions of the capital's pleasures. In London, the ability of elite men to expe-rience diversity, as opposed to a confined localism, drew heavily on the urban genres of social investigation and metropolitan journalism, cultural resources that identified the city's capacity to stimulate its privileged inhabitants. Sutherland's sense of being at home in the metropolis, like generations of men before him, was frequently expressed in visual terms as a long 'fascinated gaze', a way of looking at the city that simultane-ously exercised rights of cultural ownership while preserving an appro-priate sense of distance and detachment.[40] But London's own version of urbane masculinity was bound up with the class and status hierarchies of metropolitan society. The post-war reappearance of the man–about–town, along with the prominence awarded to a number of associated upper-class female personalities, was closely linked to the renaissance of London's social elites and their styles of public display. These elite characters and their institutions need analysing in detail, not only on account of their intrinsic social importance but also because they exerted a powerful influ-ence on sexual behaviour in the capital and beyond during the 1950s and early 1960s.

Upper-Class Revivalism

Historical interpretations of English society in the years after 1945 have charted the relative decline and partial disintegration of the country's upper class.[41] The political and social power wielded by a network that included the monarchy, the extended royal family and senior functionar-ies of the court, the old aristocracy, the political class attached to the peerage, a good part of the gentry, and many of the very wealthy is understood to have substantially diminished during the immediate post-war period. Historians have explained this erosion of upper-class authority in terms of the sustained reorganization of the social hierarchies inherited from the nineteenth and early twentieth centuries. The combined democratizing effects of the Second World War, the Labour government's own programme of economic and social redistribution, along with the cultural impact of mass affluence in the 1950s, are among the reasons cited as to why this strata did not survive in its pre-war forms. Confronted with difficulties that threatened its public role, the upper class is seen to have retreated increasingly into the cultivated safe haven of private life.[42] Ross McKibbin, in an important reassessment of the changing role of the upper class, has extended this argument about decline not simply to its formal institutions but also to its more informal systems of solidarity, especially to the rituals of social honour that shaped the idea of metropolitan society. Inasmuch as part of the upper class defined itself, and was defined by others, not simply by accumulated wealth or political influence but also by its symbolic capacity for public display in the capital city, McKibbin has argued that the failure of these practices to survive in the post-war world was a serious symptom of the diminished power and prestige of elite society.[43]

There is plenty of contemporary evidence from the members of London society in the late 1940s and early 1950s to lend weight to McKibbin's thesis. Monarchy itself, the traditional focal point of social prestige, was not immune from some of these perceptions of decline. Seen from the perspective of the royal family, the compromised authority of the Crown after the formal ending of empire was a particularly unwelcome fact of life. It was an issue that the royal matriarch Queen Mary, the Queen's grandmother and a powerful representative of monarchy's pre-eminence in London throughout the first half of the twentieth century, felt compelled to comment on. Writing on the back of the envelope of a letter received from her son George VI after Indian independence, she noted: 'The first time Bertie wrote me a letter with the I for Emperor of India left out, very sad.'[44]

Figures less eminent than the dowager queen and former empress were equally emphatic about the diminished aura surrounding both the Crown and the aristocracy. Witnessing the marriage of Princess Elizabeth and Prince Philip in Westminster Abbey, Queen Mary's lifelong friend and lady-in-waiting, Mabell, Countess of Airlie, noted that despite the 'gaiety' and 'fairy tale' atmosphere of the wedding 'most of us were sadly shabby'.[45]

Post-war social conditions and rising prices had killed off many of the traditions that had added lustre to such events before 1939, especially the elaborate formal dress and civil uniforms worn by members of the court. Lady Airlie's conclusion was starkly pessimistic: 'The new setting for Monarchy is far less brilliant than that of my youth.'[46] Her perceptions were endorsed by many other female members of the upper class whose social life spanned the pre- and post-war years. When Margaret, Duchess of Argyll (who as Margaret Whigham had been 'deb of the year' in the season of 1930) returned to the 'white and gold State Ballroom' of Buckingham Palace for a reception in 1955, she too lamented that in comparison with the grand assemblies that characterized these events during the 1930s 'the splendour' had now 'vanished forever'.[47]

For some traditionalists even the 1953 coronation lacked the stamp of genuine prestige and authenticity. Observing the peerage massed in Westminster Abbey, James Lees-Milne's wry comment was that their robes and uniforms, with such 'depth of colour and glitter of gold', were now 'far too splendid' for most of their aristocratic wearers.[48] Lees-Milne was an architectural historian and ardent conservationist whose professional life during the late 1940s was taken up with his role as Historic Buildings Secretary to the National Trust. A high Tory who was unwavering in his opposition to Labour's post-war politics of social levelling, he saw the country's landed elite at close quarters, struggling on their estates under the government's regime of democratic taxation and death duties.[49] The freezing weather that gripped the country during the winter of 1947 was symptomatic of wider social and material privations confronting the English upper class, Lees-Milne argued. Acting as their champion, he complained that 'we live in the twentieth century' yet 'even the basic elements of civilization are denied to us'.[50] Acute fuel shortages, rationing and a general atmosphere of unremitting dreariness were inhibiting the activities and depressing the mood of the group who had once provided genuine social leadership. Lees-Milne agreed with Ian Anstruther, secretary to Lord Inverchapel, when he argued that 'to be a gentleman today . . . is a disadvantage' because 'for the first time in its history the upper classes are not wanted'.[51]

Part of Lees-Milne's sense of alienation had to do with the formation of competing axes of power and opposing political cultures that cut against elite institutions. The Labour government's period in office during the late 1940s brought into Westminster members of an alternative governing class, with increased representation from the trade union movement, municipal politics and the newer professions. Men like Herbert Morrison, with his power base in the London Labour Party and the LCC, and Harold Wilson (who though Oxford-educated was a product of provincial Nonconformism and the meritocratic wartime civil service) had little time for London's established social round. Lees-Milne dismissed the majority of Labour's new parliamentarians as 'upstarts, snobs and icon-oclasts', though he confessed to feeling threatened by Wilson's type, whom he christened one of the '*New Statesman* highbrows'.[52] A few Labour MPs, like Driberg and Nye Bevan, leader of the Labour left, were attracted to elite institutions, especially to the masculine privileges of the gentleman's club, but Sutherland remembered how many of these West End venues became 'fortresses' for 'die-hard Tories' after the war, concrete manifesta-tions of the 'escalation of class warfare'.[53] In 1948 Bevan himself was famously roughed up and kicked out of the intensely Tory White's Club in St James's by a loutish young aristocrat, John Fox-Strangeways, shortly after he made his inflammatory speech denouncing the Conservatives as 'lower than vermin'.[54]

After the war clubland resumed its function as a privileged site of elite political influence, with the gentleman's club continuing to endorse the rituals of masculine sociability removed from the company of women. When Churchill formed his first peacetime government in 1951, almost a third of his Cabinet were members of one London club, Brooks's, in Pall Mall.[55] But clubs like Brooks's were experiencing practical difficul-ties during the 1950s that reflected some of the wider problems facing the upper class. Repeated financial crises, an ageing membership and a growing reputation for 'stuffiness' were symptoms of a relative decline in this version of masculine culture.[56] Lees-Milne noted how the décor of Brooks's grew 'shabbier' and the atmosphere became 'singularly staid', while the rising young Conservative MP and junior minister Ian Harvey observed how even the Carlton Club, the bastion of high Toryism, never really recovered from the egalitarian social changes brought about by the war.[57]

In the heat generated by Labour's challenge to privilege, many mem-bers of the upper class felt displaced in post-war London. Harold Nicolson, whose personal networks included the court and the diplo-matic corps, Parliament, the old universities, the learned societies and the BBC, testified to feeling particularly disorientated during the late 1940s, despite the proximity of a range of familiar personal landmarks. Taking rooms in Albany Chambers, off Piccadilly, meant that he was close to his own favourite clubs, the Travellers in Pall Mall and the Beefsteak close to Leicester Square, as well as to the London Library and the National Portrait Gallery. In his 'privileged sanctuary', where the porters still wore tail-coats and top hats, Nicolson held court to a small circle of close friends on most weekday evenings, a gathering that he ironically referred to as his 'Grande Levée'.[58] Members of his circle included fellow Tory MP Bob Boothby, Giles St Aubin, then a master at Eton, and Sir Alan Lascelles, the Queen's private secretary. The conversation was always cultivated and urbane, but as Nicolson noted ruefully, this type of informal and essentially private entertaining was a far cry from the public displays of socializing that had characterized his London life during the inter-war years.[59]

In Nicolson's view one important reason for the diminishing influence of the upper class was that established men-of-the-world now had few opportunities to hand on the rules of social etiquette and savoir faire to a younger generation. As he put it in a BBC forum entitled Are Cliques Necessary?, broadcast in 1951, the declining role of society meant that young men of the post-war era were less and less able to meet with and learn from the great men of their age.[60] One of Nicolson's pet projects in the 1950s involved a defence of traditional patterns of civilized conduct. His Good Behaviour (1955), subtitled 'a study of certain types of civility', upheld the gentlemanly ideal as a flexible role model that retained its importance, even in so-called classless societies. Characteristically mixing personal predilections with intellectual argument, Nicolson justified his preference for 'polite people' as opposed to 'rude people', and the cultivated to the uncultivated, on the grounds that 'to love and desire the elegant or the eminent is surely a symptom of fastidiousness and taste'.[61] Whatever the ultimate effects of democracy, mass education and the welfare state, he doubted whether 'the citizens of London will ever slouch along their pavements like mumbling Muscovites'.[62] Yet the very fact that Nicolson had to make his arguments explicit, rather than naturally assuming their centrality, revealed a degree of defensiveness on the part of many apologists for patrician behaviour. His intervention was part of a wide-ranging debate about the relevance of elite forms of culture that reverberated throughout the 1950s. The much publicized controversy that erupted in 1956 over the essay by Nancy Mitford, Lord Redesdale's daughter, about 'U' (upper class) and 'non-U' (not upper class) linguistic usage, was another example of the tensions generated by patrician culture within English public life.[63]

If part of society's problems was the result of changing political and cultural circumstances, they were also in a very real sense practical and material. Fewer and fewer upper-class characters now had the resources to devote to elaborate and costly forms of entertaining. Conservative MP and socialite Sir Henry 'Chips' Channon observed that most members of society lacked the money and the confidence to take over its leadership after the war. Channon himself had ample resources for both. Married to the brewing heiress Lady Honor Guinness, eldest daughter of the Earl of Iveagh, in the late 1930s, the Channons had been well known for their grand social style, with 'a large London establishment' in Belgrave Square, a country house at Kelvedon Hall in the Essex countryside, and impeccable connections. In 1952 Channon's political colleague Maxwell Fyfe deplored the lack of social contact between ministers, MPs, and their wives, and Channon wondered, 'shall I begin entertaining again, politically? But they are all so damned dull, I cannot face it.'[64] It was not money that deterred him, but a perceived lack of lustre to contemporary London life; compared with the personalities of the 1930s the post-war world, as Channon saw it, was dominated by mediocrities.[65]

Channon's complaints about London's social round, like those voiced by the Duchess of Argyll and Lady Airlie, were partly generational; they evoked a characteristic nostalgia for a lost, inter-war idea of metropolitan society. This understanding of the 1920s and 1930s as marking the final, elaborate flowering of elite social mores was reinforced after 1945 by many patrician commentators, including novelist Evelyn Waugh, who famously identified the inter-war *jeunesse dorée* as the starting point for a wider narrative of upper-class decline and fall in his novel *Brideshead Revisited* (1945). But in fact inter-war London society was notable less for its traditionalism than for its social porousness and cultural fluidity. Predominantly associated 'with glamour, with success, and with wealth', society's membership became Anglo-American and plutocratic in character rather than being led solely by the English upper class, as selected international figures from the entertainment industries, notably film stars and sports personalities, joined its ranks.[66] The 1930s also saw a carefully cultivated and mutually reinforcing relationship established between patrician public figures and the mass media, an alliance that produced a regular diet of glamorous gossip and rumour principally designed for consumption by middle-market and popular newspaper audiences. Many of these elements remained central to the revived conception of society during the post-war years, though their meanings were often inflected in new ways.

McKibbin's argument about society's post-war demise, or decline, both overstates the case and ignores the way the elites transformed themselves and their spheres of influence in the years after 1945. The role of upper-class figures moving in London's public and entertainment settings continued to exert a powerful hold on post-war urban culture. Positions of social leadership were not only assumed by men–about–town; upper-class women were also heavily involved in the revival of society. Female members of the royal family, aristocratic hostesses and newer *arrivistes* played their part in the renaissance of elite social rituals in the varied entertainment spaces of the West End.

As the apex of the social hierarchy, monarchy was central to the revival of elite culture. After the war, George VI personally intervened to re-establish the Crown and the Court of St James's as focal points for the upper class. In doing so the King partly shifted the public display of monarchy away from its wartime role as a symbol of national unity. In 1946 the King claimed for Crown patronage the royal orders of the Garter, the Thistle and the Patrick, while the resumption of formal investiture ceremonies, taking place at Buckingham Palace and Windsor Castle with full pageantry, was a self-conscious attempt to reinforce the glamorous functions of monarchy.[67] George VI opened Parliament in full state in 1948, reviving a ceremony that was played out in the House of Lords where members of the royal family and the peerage were both the protagonists and the principal audience.[68] 'The State Opening . . . was magnificent,' Channon eulogized in his diary entry that October, 'one had forgotten such splendour existed. The Royal Gallery was gay and red with peers in their robes . . . and bejewelled peeresses.'[69] Evening parties at Buckingham Palace were also gradually resumed, though the elaborate and ostentatious evening courts that flourished before the war were finally abandoned.

Society papers confided that applications for these ceremonial displays were enormous, and optimistically hailed the spring and early summer of 1948 as the year that saw the season almost 'back to its pre-war proportions'.[70] Part of the reason for the enthusiasm was that court presentations were the launch pad for debutantes, involving the formal introduction of upper-class young women to the reigning monarch; a ritual that had been introduced by Queen Charlotte, consort of George III, in the late eighteenth century. When Buckingham Palace announced the revival of these presentation parties in 1947, 20,000 debutantes rushed to apply.[71] The 'eccentric tribal initiation ceremony', which the insider critic of upper-class social mores Jessica Mitford described in quasi-anthropological terms as a 'version of the puberty rite', marked a young woman's passage into society and onto the marriage market.[72] Presentations were not abolished until 1958. Another marker of the debutante's career, Queen Charlotte's Ball, held at Grosvenor House in Mayfair, was also reinstated. The ball fitted Mitford's description of an eccentric tribal initiation ceremony, culminating in a collective curtsey from the massed debutantes clad in long white ball gowns in front of a huge white birthday cake representing the defunct Queen Charlotte.[73] Other milestones in London's social calendar such the Royal Academy Private View at Burlington House, marking the official opening of the season, Ascot, and yachting at Cowes were also reinstated.[74] Such occasions were celebrated by society magazines like *Queen* and *Country Life*, which used them to mount a political defence of the 'cultured leisure class', with a corresponding attack on socialist versions of mass society and 'the herd instinct'.[75]

In the early 1950s one member of the royal family epitomized the dynamic revival of London society: the Queen's sister, Princess Margaret. For more than a decade, from the time of her sister's wedding to her own marriage in 1960, Princess Margaret was one of the most widely profiled women in the world.[76] Other post-war female icons with comparable international charisma were products of the Hollywood film industry, prominent among whom were the actresses Grace Kelly (herself partly 'turned royal' through her marriage to Prince Rainier of Monaco) and Elizabeth Taylor. But film stars were not serious rivals to an English princess in a period when royalty still counted over the movies. 'She is Britain's No. One item for public scrutiny,' announced an American paper under the headline 'The Blooming of Princess Margaret', and the report continued: 'People are more interested in her than in the House of Commons or the dollar crisis.'[77]

The majority of Princess Margaret's activities, in public as well as in private, took place under the auspices of society, and her début in the London season of 1948, aged eighteen, coincided with the revival of elite social life. The press and the newsreels often suggested that the Princess broke new ground for royalty with her outward-looking schedule and her choice of friends, yet in reality most of her social appearances followed precedents set by leading members of the royal family during the 1930s. The gregarious Duke and Duchess of Kent had mixed extensively in upper-class circles before the war, but Princess Margaret's eagerness to take the lead in setting standards of fashionable behaviour seemed more reminiscent of her uncle, the semi-exiled Duke of Windsor. As Prince of Wales and then as Edward VIII, he led the 'smart set' during the inter-war years, an involvement that culminated in his marriage to the twice-divorced American socialite Wallis Simpson after his spectacular abdication in 1936.[78]

In the late 1940s and early 1950s Princess Margaret's immersion in society contributed to a partial transformation of its rituals and meanings, both for some of its members and for a wider mass public who followed her comings-and-goings in the media. Not only did she represent a return to glamour and an implicit rejection of the politics of social levelling championed by the Labour government, she also embodied a strong sense of feminine individualism, 'high-spirited' youthfulness and a degree of public accessibility – characteristics that were all in marked contrast to the stiff royal protocol that had begun to envelope her sister.[79] As her first biographer and former governess Marion Crawford put it in 1953: 'Princess Margaret belongs to this age . . . she represents the spirit of youth in the nineteen-fifties . . . a young woman with a will of her own.'[80]

The Princess's immersion in the world of up-to-date consumption seemed to echo the restlessness of a generation of proto-teenagers. She changed her fashions and hairstyles regularly, she copied fads and gim-micks without embarrassment, and she was keen to learn about some of the nuances of popular culture. At the age of nineteen the Princess was first seen at a fashionable West End restaurant smoking in public through a long ivory cigarette holder that became her trade-mark.[81] Her decision to embrace Dior's extravagantly feminine New Look in 1948, in the face of considerable hostility from feminists in the Labour Party, reputedly set a trend for the fashion among many women.[82] Identifying the members of her social circle as 'the Princess Margaret set', the press quickly accen-tuated her up-to-date outlook through her supposedly democratic choice of friends. The vast majority of her close companions were in fact young men and women from leading aristocratic families, but some of her con-temporaries were from less traditional backgrounds.[83] The Princess's inter-est in two exuberant young Americans, the Brooklyn-born Jewish entertainer Danny Kaye (who reputedly addressed her as 'Honey') and Sharman 'Sass' Douglas, daughter of the US ambassador, exemplified this wider outlook.[84] As Crawford acknowledged with the apt use of a London theatre metaphor, acquaintances of this sort gave the Princess an introduction to the West End not from the isolated position of the royal box but from the stalls.[85]

Partly by dint of her personality but also by virtue of being the King's younger daughter and not heiress presumptive, Princess Margaret was more culturally mobile than her sister. Though her royal duties took her on official tours across the country and on European and colonial visits to the Netherlands and the Caribbean, her regular circuit quickly became the West End's social scene of fashionable nightclubs, restaurants and private parties. The 400 Club, at Leicester Square, was one of her favourite haunts; the Milroy Club, at the bottom of Park Lane, was another, and a table was reserved for her at the most famous nightspot of the period, the Café de Paris in Coventry Street, close to theatreland. Noël Coward, who had been an important master of ceremonies for society through-out the 1930s and was a confidant of the royal family, observed the Princess as guest of honour while he was playing in cabaret at the Café in 1951 and noted approvingly that 'the glittering audience' was 'headed by Princess Margaret . . . very glamorous'.[86] A photograph of the Princess on her first visit to the nightclub showed her keen to smile and pose for onlookers, a technique that she later perfected as a look of artful know-ingness in front of the camera (fig. 4).

All this enthusiasm for life displayed by a prominent member of the royal family was newsworthy; it also encouraged a moral debate about Princess Margaret's character among the more conservative members of society, especially those close to the court. Lees-Milne confided to a friend as early as 1949 that the Princess was 'high spirited to the verge of indis-cretion', while Channon gossiped that she already had a 'Marie Antoinette aroma about her'.[87] When the Princess's love affair with Peter Townsend, a middle-class RAF fighter pilot turned royal equerry, was disclosed shortly after the coronation, it revealed the Princess as a private person with a deep attachment to a man fifteen years her senior. A court offi-cial and a divorcé, Townsend was considered to be wholly unsuitable as a royal marriage partner. Princess Margaret's emotional commitment to Townsend undercut her image as a fashionable and superficial West End socialite.[88] The ensuing clash between love and duty, which culminated in the Princess renouncing her lover in 1955 on the advice of senior members of the government, the Anglican Church and her own family, generated a sustained attack on the moral hypocrisy of society and on the informal power and influence wielded by a network that critics now dubbed the Establishment.[89]

Princess Margaret's position as a female member of society during the 1950s was exceptional by virtue of her royal status, but beyond the royal circle upper-class women traditionally had played a very active role in elite social organization in their position as hostesses. In Victorian and Edwardian London, this impresarial tradition developed into a quintessentially political form of entertaining that was associated with wives of the leading Tory, Whig and Liberal families and was closely allied to the calendar of the season. Unlike the masculine world of clubland, the dinners, balls and receptions promoted by these female characters relied heavily on a 'mixed' idea of society, where women presided over an influential form of heterosocial culture that was also cemented through family relationships and friendship networks. The political hostess maintained her position well into the inter-war period, with aristocratic women such as Lady Londonderry promoting Londonderry House as a hub of Tory politics.[90] But the Londonderry's Greco-Italian-style mansion on Park Lane, replete with its famous grand staircase and an immense ballroom, never functioned in this way after the war (it was finally sold off and then demolished in 1962), nor was the Londonderrys' overtly political form of entertaining ever seriously revived.[91] None of the wives of the major Conservative political figures during the 1950s, Clementine Churchill, Clarissa Eden or Dorothy Macmillan, ever aspired to the role of political hostess in their own right.

The end of this public profile for upper-class women was influenced not only by the ongoing financial difficulties confronting their class but also by broader changes reshaping political culture after 1945. One of the unwritten rules of post-war mass democracy was that the display of political power as leisured wealth was not permitted. However, a different type of hostess emerged during the inter-war years. Women like Sybil Colefax, Laura Corrigan, Emerald Cunard and Maggie Greville were less concerned to exert direct political influence and much more interested in promoting an overtly glamorous tone within society.[92] It was no accident that some of the most successful and energetic hostesses of the 1930s were socially ambitious Americans: Lady Astor, Lady Cunard and Mrs Corrigan.[93] A number of these figures resumed social entertaining immediately after the war, albeit in a diminished form, but the deaths of Emerald Cunard and Laura Corrigan in 1948 and Sybil Colefax in 1950 seemed to mark the end of an era in metropolitan life, especially for the doyennes of the pre-war social order. Writing in his weekly column for the *Spectator*, Nicolson testified to the deep sense of bewilderment and disorientation that Lady Colefax's death aroused: 'the members of her circle . . . feel that they have suddenly been abandoned and dispersed'.[94]

Yet the inter-war social role pioneered by figures like Cunard and Colefax was sufficiently flexible to survive in a different form into the

1950s. Post-war versions of their feminine social style combined a traditional emphasis on glamour and celebrity status, advertised for consumption by mass audiences, with a stress on more personal forms of
entertaining that were cemented through cultural networks rather than
via political channels of influence.

'To those who . . . bemoan the fact that no young hostesses follow in
the tradition of Sybil Colefax and Emerald Cunard we now advocate Ann
[Fleming]', society photographer and designer Cecil Beaton wrote in his
diary in September 1953. Fleming's party to celebrate author and journalist Cyril Connelly's fiftieth birthday was small, Beaton noted, but the
group had 'unity and character'.[95] Here were people 'born in all different strata of life' enjoying the fruits of success in the company of others
they respected or had most in common with. Conversation was 'on target',
Beaton noted approvingly, no one wasted time in banalities. Guests
included Clarissa Eden, who was Churchill's niece, painters Francis Bacon
and Lucien Freud, poet Stephen Spender, Oxford don Maurice Bowra,
philosopher Freddy Ayer and writer Peter Quennell.[96]

Ann Fleming (née Charteris), who married the novelist Ian Fleming
as her third husband in 1952, epitomized the post-war revival of a style
of social entertaining that was still loosely allied to a conception of
society.[97] A bone fide member of the upper class with personal connections to many of the leading titled and gentry families, she carried exemplary cultural capital. Her paternal grandparents, Lord and Lady Elcho,
were members of the Souls, the late Victorian and Edwardian intellectual
coterie. Ann's first marriage to Lord O'Neill in 1932 was a conventional
alliance with landed wealth and City money, but during the 1930s she
was taken up by her grandmother, herself a prominent Edwardian hostess,
and by Emerald Cunard and Sybil Colefax, who introduced her to a
wider metropolitan circle. Ann O'Neill developed a flair for entertaining
during the war when, along with many of London's displaced socialites,
she used the Dorchester Hotel on Park Lane as an ad hoc social base.

Ann's marriage to the press baron Esmond Harmsworth, Viscount
Rothermere, in 1945 equipped her with the resources and the necessary
status to develop her persona as a grand hostess in the tradition established by her mentors. As Lady Rothermere her social life entered its
most spectacular and energetic phase. The Rothermere's London home,
Warwick House, on the edge of Green Park, became a beacon for gregarious royalty, leading politicians, theatrical and literary figures, and all
those who pressed for a revival of some version of society amidst the
privations of post-war austerity. Lady Rothermere's triumphalist general

election-night party in October 1951, celebrating the return of a Tory
government, was one of the most lavish social events of the early 1950s.[98]
But her formidable style was also more nuanced than the extravagant
public entertaining espoused by London hostesses during the inter-war
years. Guests were attracted not only by lavish hospitality, but also by her
deliberate effort to revive the art of conversation and intellectual discussion, which was always leavened by patrician notions of wit and bril-
liance. As Fleming's wife and now operating from the more modest
surroundings of her house in Victoria Square, Ann increasingly promoted
intimate forms of socializing at gatherings where politicians such as
Anthony Eden and the Labour leader Hugh Gaitskell mixed with painters,
writers and artists.[99] This was not exactly society as civilized private life,
because it was still glamorous and eminently well connected, but it did
mark a further subtle shift in elite social networks and in the meanings
invested in them by leading players.[100]

   Ann Fleming was unrepentant about the fact that her version of society
sprang from an aristocratic tradition that many dismissed as anachronistic.
Echoing the views of her confidant and relative Evelyn Waugh and other
high Tories, she announced that she believed only in an 'oligarchy, a ruling
class employing contented craftsmen, cooks, charcoal burners, ladies' maids
and laundry maids, all bobbing and curtseying'.[101] Assertions of this sort,
like Waugh's own reactionary posturing, threw down a defiant challenge
to common-sense ideas about post-war democracy. Yet Fleming also
spotted that mass culture held out distinctive opportunities for upper-class
characters who could demonstrate a degree of entrepreneurial flair.
During the 1950s she developed a new role, assiduously promoting the
idea of society in the popular media, advertising the comings and goings
of celebrities for the gossip pages of the press and latterly for television.
Sutherland remembered that as a young journalist he was summoned to
Warwick House and ordered to contribute to a social column that Lady
Rothermere was organizing for her husband's paper, the *Daily Mail*.[102]
The features were written by a group of in-house reporters, but as Ann
insisted, 'most of the news comes from me'.[103]

   This was by no means Fleming's only venture into the burgeoning field
of public relations; during the 1950s she turned herself into a minor
television personality, appearing on arts and current affairs programmes
with intellectual heavyweights like historian Hugh Trevor-Roper and
Randolph Churchill.[104] One of these early TV appearances actually took
the form of a society lunch party, with cartoonist Osbert Lancaster and

writers Angus Wilson and Antonia Fraser seen live on camera, chatting about books and literary culture between courses. Fleming's participation in the event earned her a stiff rebuke from Waugh: 'What honourable motive can you have for lunching on television?' he remonstrated.[105]

Ann Fleming was not just a formidable socializer; she also used society networks as the setting for her numerous love affairs that she pursued throughout her married life. She was a sexually active, confident woman who continued long-standing liaisons and started new relationships in her role as a hostess and socialite. Upper-class women had never been circumscribed by the same moral code that governed their middle-class counterparts, and Fleming took full advantage of this aristocratic tradition of feminine autonomy. Her emotional and sexual commitments to a variety of different lovers and to three husbands were played out in the spotlight of London's elite social round. Some of her encounters assumed the status of society myths. Her sister-in-law Virginia Charteris recalled that Ann conducted her thirteen-year-long affair with Ian Fleming from Warwick House, while still married to Harmsworth, on those evenings when her husband was away or still at his Fleet Street office. 'There was an atmosphere you could cut with a knife,' Charteris remembered.[106] Ann's relationship with Fleming, himself a notorious womaniser, was sexually experimental; they both enjoyed lovemaking as a ritual of erotic power, and their letters revealed a strong interest in sadomasochistic sex.[107] In the mid-1950s she took a new and more surprising lover, Hugh Gaitskell, who was himself a well-known socialite, attracted to metropolitan glamour as an antidote to the political culture of the Labour Party. Meeting publicly as dancing partners at the Café Royal in Piccadilly, they used the London home of Gaitskell's colleague, Tony Crosland, for their intimate encounters. Ann used to joke to friends that when she went to bed with Gaitskell she liked to imagine she was with the more debonair Crosland![108]

Ann Fleming's biography points to the continuing importance of upper-class women in promoting a sexually glamorous version of society well into the post-war period. But in 1950s London social personalities who were much less elevated than Fleming also competed for the attention of national audiences. One consummate female populist who epitomized a glamorous idea of metropolitan social life in the public imagination was Lady Docker. Norah Docker's career dramatized a twentieth-century version of a traditional feminine story: the provincial girl from a very modest background who married a millionaire. Born Norah

Turner, the daughter of a Birmingham motor engineer, she made her
London début as a West End dance hostess in 1924.[109] As one of the Café
de Paris's 'young ladies' she was required to accept invitations from all
unescorted men, and as she admitted such arrangements often involved a
discreet form of prostitution.[110] Yet Norah Docker's life, which was constantly recycled for public consumption in the press during the 1950s, was
the reverse of the story of the 'fallen' provincial girl. Her dancing partners, who included 'dukes, earls and knights', 'young millionaires' and 'old
millionaires', were escorts on her way to celebrity status.[111] Norah's first
elderly husband was Clement Callingham, chairman of Henekey's wine
importers. On his death, she promptly consolidated her alliance with
boardroom wealth by marrying 69-year-old Sir William Collins, chairman
of Cerebos Salt.[112] But it was as Lady Docker after her marriage in 1949
to Sir Bernard Docker, chairman of one of the largest British companies,
Birmingham Small Armaments, that her persona became much more
extravagant and self-promotional. 'I didn't intend to be a hostess,' Norah
Docker insisted in her autobiography, 'I became one by circumstantial
accident.'[113]

From their Mayfair mansion the Dockers launched themselves into a
'Front Page' lifestyle, a social whirl that was enthusiastically endorsed by
their 'close friends in Fleet Street'.[114] Coverage of the couple centred on
some very traditional trappings of luxury: Lady Docker's much-publicized
shopping trips to Bond Street and Knightsbridge, her collection of jew-
ellery, an ocean-going yacht, the *Shemara*, and a succession of ostentatious
social events where she mixed with Hollywood stars and British entertainers, like the dancer and band leader Victor Silvester (fig. 5). In an
effort to promote one of her husband's companies, the coach-builders
Hooper's, Lady Docker produced her spectacular *pièce de résistance*, a gold-
plated Daimler, which caused a sensation at the 1951 Motor Show and
stopped the traffic when she took the car into the West End.[115]

At the outset the Dockers' escapades were celebrated in the press as a
welcome antidote to rationing and austerity; by the mid-1950s they had
become synonymous with the promotion of a pseudo-gentry social style
and its close association with the media.[116] Observing the couple's antics,
many contemporary commentators believed that the Dockers' exaggerated efforts to revive a grand manner were proof that society in any meaningful sense had become redundant by the 1950s.[117] But Norah Docker's
principal audience was not society as such but a much broader mass
public, mainly composed of women. Tudor Jenkins, editor of the *Evening*

Standard's social column, believed that news of elite personalities continued to be of special interest to his female readers, who demanded to know 'when an heiress was getting engaged' or when a celebrity was giving a party.[118] For Jenkins, Lady Docker's enviably populist style spoke directly to the general public; she signed autographs for women celebrity hunters outside the Royal Enclosure at Ascot and invited groups of Yorkshire miners and their wives to champagne parties on her yacht.[119] The *Standard*'s women's column celebrated her as a 'fabulous star' in an 'all-too-utilitarian sky', stressing that she was a highly intelligent woman who deserved success because she used her femininity, rather than inherited wealth, to achieve her goals.[120] Kaleidoscoping images of social glamour with the spectacle of conspicuous consumption, Lady Docker personified the allure of elite society for mass audiences; the fact that her activities were seen as eminently newsworthy testified to the salience of real and imitative upper-class cultural rituals throughout the 1950s.

The social activities of Sutherland and Nicolson, Princess Margaret, Ann Fleming and Lady Docker all testified to the revival of London society during the early 1950s. Yet though this renaissance was the subject of endless media comment and was widely discussed by the members of society themselves, initially it stimulated little debate within intellectual or academic circles. Sociologists, in particular, with their much-vaunted claims to understanding contemporary social structures, seemed altogether uninterested, concentrating their energies instead on people and patterns of behaviour that highlighted the modernity of contemporary Britain, rather than focusing on the country's traditional elites. The impact of affluence, documented in endless discussions about the new working class and changing patterns of family and kinship organization, was a topic that regularly attracted the attention of British social scientists during the post-war period.[121] In comparison, the role of monarchy and gentry society was either cast as part of a conservative and backward-looking agenda, or more usually it was simply ignored altogether.

It was an American, Edward Shils, Professor of Social Thought at the University of Chicago, who first drew attention to the renewed importance of what he termed the 'aristocratic-gentry' formation. A transatlantic visitor to the UK during the 1950s, teaching at the London School of Economics, Shils identified with the LSE's 'moderate and conservative anti-socialist liberalism' represented by political philosophers like Frederick Hayek and Karl Popper.[122] He co-authored a provocative interpretation of the coronation with fellow sociologist Michael Young, in which he interpreted the ceremony as an act of 'national communion around the sacrality of kingship'. Shils and Young famously justified the continuing charisma of monarchy on account of its socially cohesive role that reaffirmed 'the centre' of society.[123]

Expanding these themes, Shils's famous essay on 'The Intellectuals', first published in the liberal and avowedly anti-Communist journal *Encounter* in 1955, made powerful claims about the revival of an elite and exclusive form of culture that drew its strength from the aristocracy and the gentry. For nearly a century these classes had been in retreat, Shils argued, but their cultural outlook had now regained 'moral ascendancy'.[124] Influenced by his American colleague Robert Park's sociological studies of capital cities and their hinterlands, as well as by T. S. Eliot's conservative reading of the cohesiveness of English national culture, Shils gave this patrician tradition a distinctive spatial axis, linking it to the 'supremacy of London society, and with it Oxford and Cambridge, over the provincial centres'.[125] An elite, mandarin culture 'of delicate but not deep voice', articulating 'subtlety without grandeur', it rested ultimately 'on the authority of the Crown and on the land'.[126] Shils characterized it as a way of life permeated by an ethic of refined consumption and gentlemanly pursuits that were remarkably unambitious: 'the connoisseurship of wine and food', 'acquaintance with the writings of Jane Austen', and a 'knowing indulgence for the worthies of the English past'.[127] Noel Annan, who as Provost of King's College, Cambridge, was part of these patrician networks, remarked that with the publication of his essay Shils gave the intellectuals a lecture: 'He told them they were self-satisfied, insular and genteel.'[128]

In fact, Shils's essay was programmatic in its sociological ambitions; it sought to stimulate debate about a perceived shift in post-war society rather than offer detailed proof that it had actually materialized.[129] It was the most prominent and closely argued of a whole series of critical commentaries that linked the re-emergence of elite culture to London's metropolitan dominance during the 1950s. Related contributions included the wide-ranging debate about the Establishment, stimulated by the historian and novelist Hugh Thomas and journalist Henry Fairlie, together with a series of provocative articles by journalist Malcolm Muggeridge and the young hereditary peer Lord Altrincham which challenged the overly patrician style of the Queen and members of her family.[130] Many of these dissenting voices came from within liberal intellectual or Establishment culture itself, but in the early 1960s the New Left also highlighted the negative impact of aristocratic influences (what Tom Nairn later called the 'glamour of backwardness') as a major obstacle to social and economic progress, in a series of arguments focusing on the 'peculiarities of the English'.[131]

What characterized all of these critiques was not just the prominence they awarded to the English upper class, but also the way they positioned elite culture as archaic and even atavistic. The resurgence of the court and presentation parties, society hostesses, London's clubland, the season and the turf, the old universities and the Foreign Office represented in Shils's phrase a massive 'narrowing' of national 'sensibility and imagination', when compared with the democratizing impulses at work during the Second World War.[132] Yet arguments of this kind remained partial on a number of counts. First, they ignored the way upper-class institutions and personalities were themselves partly transformed during the 1950s by many of the same forces that affected other social strata. By implicitly pitting the traditionalism of the elites against what was perceived as an urgent need for progressive social change, these critiques simplified the complex forms of modernization that characterized English society during the years after 1945, reducing them to a polarized choice between progress and backwardness. Shils and his contemporaries also tended to see upper-class rituals as wholly distinct and separate codes of behaviour, whereas in reality they were not isolated from the cultures of other social groups in a society that was heavily urbanized and manifestly porous.

The social elites were more than simply a residual presence in postwar London: they featured as active and frequently dynamic players in metropolitan culture. Masculine and feminine characters associated with the resurgence of elite social life brought together many of the contradictory features of traditionalism and innovation that characterized English society during the 1950s. In particular, the burgeoning impact of post-war affluence exerted a powerful influence on the experience of a younger generation of elite personalities. Douglas Sutherland's account of London life contrasted sharply with the experience of characters like Nicolson not only by virtue of age and social position, but also as a result of his participation in urban consumer culture. One important consequence of the impact of post-war affluence was that the resources of the man-about-town became more widely available and more broadly disseminated beyond the confines of the upper class. This commercially sponsored hybridization of patrician styles of masculinity had a significant impact on sex and social morality.

Men-About-Town

In his study of the fall of public man, Richard Sennett has argued that
the period after the Second World War witnessed the final decline of nineteenth-century conceptions of the public sphere.[133] Characterized by a
collapse of confidence in established rituals of civility, Sennett has charted
the way traditional forms of city life were challenged by the inexorable
rise of intimacy and privacy. Yet viewed in the context of the history of
twentieth-century London and many other metropolitan centres in
Western Europe and North America, Sennett's account ignores the rise
of alternative forms of sociability, especially those centred on the expansion of consumer culture.

From at least the mid-nineteenth century this commercial world was
distinct from the established public political sphere. Department stores,
restaurants, entertainment culture and all the other attractions of cosmopolitan life competed for the attention of city folk alongside parliamentary politics, political clubs and meetings, and the quality press. The
boundaries separating these domains were shifting and porous, while their
mutual tensions often reflected contradictions between the masculine
ethos of high politics and the perceived feminization of consumerism. But
in 1950s London personal consumption was one of the most dynamic
areas of activity for the man-about-town. The fast-expanding sectors of
fashion, design and publicity played an important role in the renaissance
and partial transformation of this urban personality. Equally important was
the way younger men from subaltern social groups drew on commercially sponsored forms of patrician symbolism and models of leisured, gentlemanly behaviour to fashion their own versions of cultural and sexual
identity. The urban poses adopted by homosexual men and London's
Teddy Boys represented distinctive negotiations of English dandyism.
These disruptive appropriations of style had significant consequences, as
deviant and dangerous masculinities became serious public issues in post-
war London.

In the spring of 1953 the *Tailor and Cutter*, trade paper of the British
tailoring industry, announced the launch of a new magazine for men, aptly
named *Man About Town*. Initially retailing for 3s. 6d., at a time when
leading newspapers like *The Times* sold for 4d., the title boasted art-
influenced photography, quality paper and a stylish design layout. The
magazine was unashamedly elitist; with a provocative opening editorial
Man About Town set itself against the trend towards cultural democracy

and mass society that it characterized as the dominant post-war ethos, 'where lump is a virtue and the mass is king'.[134] In-house journalists agreed with Harold Nicolson when they complained that 'humanity' was turning away from refined and civilized values; this was particularly galling for a new generation of younger men in London who were just becoming old enough to appreciate 'rich and fine living'.[135] The magazine aimed to reassert 'the higher aspects of elegant life' through its written copy and superior production values.[136]

Distancing itself from the political weeklies and monthlies, 'those solemn and high-minded journals' whose sole aim was the 'ultimate improvement of readers', *Man About Town* was an early attempt to create what later came to be known as a lifestyle magazine for men.[137] Its comercial ambition was to speak to men as a community of consumers, using a range of personal goods and services to promote selective ideas about masculinity. Placing a high value on connoisseurial taste because, as the magazine explained, 'there is no substitute for quality', the cover of the first issue advertised features on 'the what, when and how of men's clothes', 'eating out', 'men's sports', 'knowing about wine', the 'inside story of the theatre', 'mixing your drinks', and intriguingly, in what read like the trailer for a proto-agony column, the 'answers to all the problems of the Man About Town'.[138] Subsequent editions, which advertised the title as 'the magazine for the gay dog' before the term became associated with homosexuality, carried a more overtly sexual message. Targeting the unmarried, sexually active man, the magazine featured American-style pin-ups, intimate interviews with West End showgirls and quirky articles with a social message, such as a discussion piece on bachelordom versus-marriage, billed as 'A Man Wants To Be Alone'.[139]

The magazine's pitch to elite consumers strenuously avoided the aggressive commercial selling techniques of contemporary advertising and marketing. Journalists hailed their readers in cavalier fashion as the denizens of clubland or as the members of other privileged masculine coteries: 'If you are too damned idle to turn over the leaves and see for yourself,' it berated its audience in the language of the smoking room, 'then we are done with you, and there is an end of the matter. . . . We have your money.'[140] But *Man About Town* also sought to make a more serious point: the return to peacetime and the beginnings of the new 'Elizabethan age' held out exciting possibilities for younger men, especially in the sphere of personal consumption. The magazine claimed to speak up for a generation of affluent but neglected consumers, who had 'dwelt in draughty halls and itchy materials' for six long years of war and who were now eager to experience the fruits of their own prosperity.[141] If part of its brief was to counteract the negative effects of austerity, *Man About Town*'s long-term aim was to educate readers 'along channels of individuality' and away from the 'levelling machinery of contemporary sameness'.[142]

Predictably, the magazine's defining environment was fashionable metropolitan London. Visually, the capital city featured regularly on the front cover, as well as in fashion plates and photo shoots, where men-about-town were pictured against a backdrop of the West End's public landmarks, or in their clubs, or at their desks in City boardrooms (fig. 6).[143] Placing a high value on consumerism as urban mobility and echoing the itineraries supplied by de luxe tourist guides, the magazine invited its readers on a tour of the capital's central areas. Soho featured regularly on account of its foreign restaurants and nightclubs, where magazine journalists claimed their own privileged rights of access; nearby Savile Row and Sackville Street were included for their tailors of distinction and celebrated wine merchants, while looking further afield London airport was profiled for its new BOAC 'speedbird' jet routes to North America and Australia.[144]

Man About Town served as an etiquette manual for men with money and high levels of cultural capital who lived and worked in central London and aspired to a degree of social recognition through consumer culture. In circulation terms the magazine was a minority venture that went through various permutations during the 1950s and 1960s, as editors and advertisers searched for a de luxe, general interest publication to attract the male consumer.[145] In these respects *Man About Town* was not a prototype for mass market customers, who dominated so much of the debate about affluence during the 1950s, but for what Labour politician and consumption theorist Tony Crosland termed discriminating consumers. According to Crosland, this was the group who understood that 'high quality consumption', associated with an elevated social style, assumed increasing importance in an era when the 'mass-distribution economy' involved near-universal provision of basic goods and services.[146]

Journalists on the new magazine wholeheartedly agreed with Crosland's arguments about the importance of taste and discrimination, but they were equally careful to stress that their understanding of elite consumers was not limited to members of the upper class. In a pseudo 'symposium' on 'The Hangover', a survey of the best cures for the morning after from devotees of London's night life, the magazine took advice not just from the Marquess of Bristol's son but also from up-and-coming comedian Peter Sellers, star of *The Goon Show* on radio, from leading couturier Charles Creed, and from Freddy Mills, ex-boxing champion and now a successful restaurateur.[147] The message from this eclectic roll call of enterprising young aristocrats, entertainers and sports personalities was that post-war London was characterized by a marked degree of social mixing.

Prominently displayed biographies of the magazine's editorial team also highlighted the theme of class mobility. Cover designer Frank Bellamy had been a humble army sergeant during the war, who later worked on the provincial press before moving to London in 1949 to become a successful illustrator for Gibbs toothpaste and a habitué of the Swallow Club, a 'select little nightclub' just off Piccadilly.[148] Fashion illustrator Walter Wyles listed his hobbies as fast sports cars and sailing, while Franz Goodman, a publicist with the Royal Opera House Covent Garden and 'one of the few really talented photographers concentrating on male fashion', advertised himself as the 'poor man's Cecil Beaton'.[149] Most of these individuals were in their thirties or forties, many of them shared common experiences of wartime military service, and all of them had a professional and personal involvement in fashionable consumption.

Man About Town endorsed the aspirations of younger men, not themselves always from patrician backgrounds, who identified with sophisticated forms of metropolitan consumer culture. This commercial marketing of elite cultural values was one important way that the figure of the man-about-town was disseminated to wider audiences during the 1950s. Manufacturers and retailers selling cars, suits, food and wine, as well as sexual entertainment, regularly drew on images of upper-class masculinity to endorse the luxury values associated with high-quality goods and services in an increasingly crowded mass market.[150] The cult of James Bond, which spawned a vast array of commodities and images associated with the hero of Fleming's novels, represented one of the most successful attempts to synthesize the traditional personality of the English gentleman with up-to-date consumerism.[151]

This commercial version of the man-about-town was not simply a marketing ploy or a literary conceit; it shaped the actual careers of a number of younger men from elite backgrounds who were actively involved in the capital's consumer industries. One particular advertising agency, the London offices of the leading American company J. Walter Thompson (JWT), played an important role in cementing an alliance between patri-

cian values and commercial publicity. With prestige offices in Mayfair's
Berkeley Square, replete with 'impressively upholstered meeting rooms'
and antique furniture, JWT developed a reputation as a 'posh' agency.[152]
After 1950, when it became the top-ranked advertising business in Britain,
the company employed a deliberate policy of hiring younger men from
public school backgrounds as a way of supposedly raising the professional
status of advertising in London. The agency's reputation as a refuge for
'toffs' and 'gents' stuck, though not always positively; business journalists
John Pearson and Graham Turner disparagingly referred to JWT's recruits
as 'old Etonians with carnations rather than brains'.[153]

The careers of Robin Douglas–Home, employed at JWT as a copywriter, and Mark Birley, who worked in the agency's art department,
revealed how well-connected men-about-town were recruited into the
rapidly expanding world of advertising. Douglas–Home's family and social
pedigree were impressive; a nephew of the Earl of Home, then Tory leader
in the House of Lords, and a friend of the Queen's cousin, Edward, Duke
of Kent, he acquired a reputation as a 'debonair escort of beautiful
women'.[154] His close friendship with Princess Margaret, together with his
much publicized affair in 1957 with Princess Margaretha of Sweden,
grand-daughter of the Swedish king, confirmed his reputation as one of
London's most eligible bachelors.[155] Douglas–Home was also a regular in
London's exclusive nightclub scene, promoting himself as copywriter by
day and 'a Mayfair cocktail pianist by night', a reference to his regular
appearances as a jazz pianist at the Casanova Club in Mayfair's Grosvenor
Street.[156] Personally involved in the international worlds of fashion, photography and journalism, he was highly valued by his bosses at JWT for
his 'particular gift for being with it'.[157]

Birley's background was slightly less elevated than Douglas–Home's, but
he was equally well connected socially. Son of a respected society portrait artist, in the early 1950s he was in demand as an escort for upper-
class young women, a so-called 'deb's delight'.[158] Birley married Lady
Annabel Vane Tempest Stewart, daughter of the Marquess of Londonderry,
in the *déclassé* wedding of 1954.[159] Like Douglas–Home, he moved
between elite society and the de luxe consumer sector. After leaving JWT
to set up his own advertising business, he reinvented himself as an interior designer and an importer of luxury goods. In the early 1960s Birley
reappeared as a master of ceremonies for London's younger smart set,
opening Annabel's nightclub in Berkeley Square, which he promoted as
the sophisticated place to go for minor royals, international celebrities and
rich visiting businessmen.

Birley's and Douglas-Home's commercial ventures epitomized forms of upper-class entrepreneurship that were celebrated later as part of the success of 'swinging London'. Like the editor and designer Jocelyn Stevens, who relaunched *Queen* magazine in 1958 as an etiquette manual of fashionable consumption, and Alexander Plunket-Greene, the upper-class husband and business mentor of fashion designer Mary Quant, both Birley and Douglas-Home made much of the fact that that their position at the interstices of society and London's creative talent gave them access to new market trends developed by 'the pace-setters'.[160] Their activities also focused attention on the power of what Sutherland defined as the 'cult of personalities', which as he saw it dissolved traditional status hierarchies into a new cocktail of 'big business and show business'.[161]

The profiles of Douglas-Home and Birley showed how the post-war man-about-town was a hybrid rather than a unified figure, projecting competing understandings of elite masculine behaviour. In one important respect, however, these displays of social identity were heavily circumscribed: this was in the area of sexuality. The Thursday Club was a homosocial environment where any amount of lewd talk could go on, about buggery as well as brothel visiting, but the club's atmosphere and the public personas of the majority of its members were strenuously heterosexual. *Man About Town* sought to promote distinction and elegance in fashionable dress for its readers, though the magazine worked hard to avoid accusations of 'eccentricity', that cryptic code word for so many forms of deviant masculinity in the 1950s.[162] As journalists ruefully acknowledged in one prominent editorial, the most harmful criticism aimed at a gentleman of fashion was the accusation 'that to be interested in your appearance is to be effeminate'.[163] Advertising men, for all their enthusiasm about the world of up-to-date consumption, adopted a conventional ethic of restraint in dress and manners that characterized professional life in the 1950s. Their formal business suits in black and grey cloth epitomized the attire of business leaders which, as Ruth Rubenstein has argued, denoted self-control and focused energy directed at achieving organizational goals.[164]

Yet other groups of men who participated in metropolitan culture were much less restrained in their forms of embodied self-presentation, using dress, pose and social manner to advertise themselves as sexually different. These alternative appropriations of the figure of the man-about-town centred on the world of *haute couture* fashion, where they served as coded cultural expressions of homosexuality. One particular style became the focus for these social and sexual experiments in fashionable dress: the neo-Edwardian look for men.

In April 1950 the celebrated fashion photographer Norman Parkinson included a double-page spread in *Vogue* magazine entitled 'Back to Formality'.[165] One of Parkinson's photographs profiled three immaculately tailored young men caught in conversation on the pavement of Savile Row (fig. 7). Sporting starched white collars, burnished shoes, bowler hats and tightly furled umbrellas, these characters and their accompanying settings emphasized the patrician roots and military overtones of contemporary fashionable dress, grounding their sartorial style in the cultural authority of the capital city. *Vogue* pointed out that the gents in the photographs were not models, but bone fide members of the upper class with distinguished wartime service records. Peter Coats, now on the staff of Condé Nast publications, was former Comptroller to Field Marshall Earl Wavell in India, while William Ackroyd had been awarded the Military Cross for officer gallantry during the Allied invasion of Normandy.

Parkinson's images and *Vogue's* accompanying fashion copy had a specific aim: to promote a 'new, almost Edwardian formality in men's clothes . . . reminiscent of the pre-1914 period' that was in sharp contrast to the 'studied sloppiness' of fashion between the wars.[166] Major shifts in style for men were usually heralded by 'tiny points of details', *Vogue* confided, and recent events confirmed the significance of these small but important changes. The ubiquitous double-breasted, dark blue overcoat that had been *de rigueur* for almost twenty years was being cast aside in favour of the single-breasted black or grey worsted coat that was often 'collared in velvet'.[167] Loose-fitting suits worn with slouch hats, that were the trademark of Hollywood heroes like Humphrey Bogart during the 1940s and represented the democratic uniform of 'Mr Everyman', had given way to a renewed emphasis on the Englishness of English dress.

By celebrating the return of a national fashion that was championed by the country's social elites, *Vogue* threw down a challenge not only to Americanized mass culture but also to distinctively 'Continental' styles of dress that had made their mark in London during the 1940s. The magazine singled out for special criticism the sharply cut spiv look, associated with the capital's black-market racketeers and with the 'shady' masculinity of Italian and Maltese pimps and ponces.[168] The renaissance of the English gentleman heralded the revival of more positive role models. *Vogue* announced that bowlers were now seen again around Pall Mall and Bond Street, encouraged by the recent order issued by the guards regiments that ex-officers or officers wearing civilian clothes should adopt this dress code. At the same time, journalists drew attention to some of the more exaggerated features of the new men's fashion. Jackets were increasingly styled with narrow sleeves that were often cuffed, pockets were flapped, and fancy ticket pockets were frequently thrown in for good measure. Trousers were also being worn much narrower and would soon recall the stove-pipe cut of forty years ago, the magazine disclosed, while other echoes of the Edwardian period included the popularity of high-cut, patterned waistcoats in contrasting colours.

The revival of Edwardianism for men followed hard on the heels of the New Look in women's fashion, launched by Parisian couturier Christian Dior in 1947, which spread rapidly as an international style. Edwardianism complemented the New Look, with the latter's stress on flamboyant elegance and the return to an ultra-feminine profile promoted through cut, colour and a *belle époque* silhouette with its wasp waist and long billowing skirts. The social impact of these styles also paralleled each other; though both began life as high fashion, they were transformed by young men and women from subaltern groups, where their take-up promoted an anxious debate about consumerism, youth and sexuality.

Commercially, the launch of Edwardian styling in London was encouraged by the bespoke tailoring trade, with the aim of giving a much-needed fillip to the men's clothing industry, a sector that had remained stubbornly static after the war.[169] Fashion journalists who launched the campaign insisted on a 'trickle down' model of consumption that mirrored wider understandings of the status hierarchies at work within London society. Traditional tailoring, centred on the capital and catering to the needs of English gentlemen, was championed to set dress standards for all because, as fashion critics writing for the trade paper *Men's Wear* patiently explained to the industry in 1952, 'styles that start in the West End stay the test of time'.[170] Up-market tourist guides like Aldor's, keen to attract affluent visitors, amplified the point by suggesting that a number of well-known London thoroughfares now constituted a men's shopping district. Pinpointing three streets just off Piccadilly, Savile Row, Sackville Street and Jermyn Street, as the nucleus for this geography of masculine consumption, the British Travel and Holidays Association suggested it was here that discerning men-about-town could discover 'the best . . . tailors in the world'. Renowned tailors such as Henry Poole and Huntsman and Sons and shirt-makers Turnbull and Asser, all of whom were 'a byword for perfection in English quality', were the names to patronize.[171]

In drawing attention to the metropolitan origins of the new Edwardian style, Parkinson's iconic photographs suggested that the fashion also had a distinctive appeal among men from the social elites. Sociologist and broadcaster Tosco Fyvel endorsed Parkinson's visual point, noting that soon after the war debutantes' escorts and young men-about-town were seen in the West End wearing well-cut Edwardian suits with 'longer jackets, tighter trousers and curled bowler hats ... [and] their hair worn at exaggerated length'.[172] Other commentators were even more precise in identifying the source of the new look, noting its first appearance among fashion conscious young guards officers in the late 1940s.[173]

Fyvel believed that the dandies who paraded through the West End were making a cultural 'proclamation' as much as a fashion statement.[174] Understanding Edwardianism as a style 'revolt', with his interpretation influenced by the renewed ethnographic interest in social class as well as by the burgeoning sociology of consumption, Fyvel's conclusion was that the Edwardian fashion heralded a 'new era', marking a definite break with 'the war' and 'its uniformed heroes and general drabness'.[175] For many commentators including the journalists at *Vogue*, this revolt into style represented a reassertion of the inviolability of upper-class English masculinity against the double threat of Continental spivery, on the one hand, and the import of Americanized mass culture, on the other. As such, the new fashion encapsulated a paradox: it appeared to project an up-to-date style by appealing to the symbolic authority of social hierarchies that were grounded in the past. Couturier and man-about-town Hardy Amies, the Queen's dressmaker, summed up the contemporary hunger for glamour as a welcome reassertion of upper-class *savoir faire*, and in doing so he insisted that contemporary ideas about what was modern were heavily influenced by the weight of historical tradition. 'And what of the future ... of fashion itself?' Amies asked. 'It seems to me that the basic principles of our ways of life have not changed much. We still like to be ladies and gentlemen.'[176]

A style that projected a powerful sense of patrician values was also open to more disruptive, sexualized interpretations. In the early 1950s, versions of the Edwardian look appeared in a number of the West End's queer social spaces that were adjacent to the elite milieus of Mayfair and Piccadilly.[177] Worn by younger homosexual men as a way of signalling fashionability and sexual difference, this version of Edwardianism was in vogue among a smart set who patronized the discreet private members' clubs that had sprung up in the West End after the war catering to a moneyed, professional clientele. One queer club where the new fashion was visible was the Rockingham, which opened in Archer Street in 1951, where some members sported neo-Edwardian dress as part of a mannered evocation of the atmosphere of a gentleman's club or officer's mess, earning the venue the epithet of the 'poufs Athenaeum'.[178]

The sexual potential of the new fashion lay in its presentation of the male body. In contrast to the double-breasted suit that tended towards physical camouflage, the tight single-fitted jacket and narrow trousers advertised the male physique, especially torso, legs and thighs. The overall look of fitted physicality was elaborate and ornate; the more dedicated proponents of Edwardianism struck dandified poses by carrying canes and wearing light-coloured gloves, while their taste in fancy waistcoats, turned-back cuffs and velvet collars suggested ostentatious luxury.[179]

Fashion journalists advertised the sexual suggestiveness of the Edwardian look to a wider public, discreetly suggesting links between fashionable men-about-town and the capital's homosexual cultures. Berkeley West, self-appointed style critic writing for *Men's Wear*, worked tirelessly to create opportunities for flamboyance in men's dress, insisting that fashion innovation made good economic sense in the post-war climate because 'style consciousness' always increases 'when it has been necessary to offer out-of-the ordinary merchandise to tempt the . . . customer'.[180] Consistently inventive and resourceful, he used his own colourful personality, along with coverage of other society figures, to increase fashion awareness and to draw attention to the visibility of homosexuality in the capital.

West's report of a cocktail party held at the Ritz Hotel in Piccadilly during coronation season noted archly how 'certain Edwardianisms had been adopted' by many of the male guests.[181] He went on to introduce two figures who were known to be homosexual or bisexual within the closed circles of London society: journalist Godfrey Winn and theatre designer Oliver Messel. West's commentary on their clothes, along with accompanying photographs of Winn and Messel in fashionable dress, emphasized both men's exaggerated sense of style. Readers were told that 'Mr. Winn dislikes stiff collars' and that 'his tailor suggested gauntlet cuffs edged with braid to lend a formal note', while Messel was photographed posing informally in an unbuttoned jacket that revealed his legs and thighs.[182] A subsequent article about couturier Digby Morton, billed as 'A Peep into the Wardrobe of a Man Who Designs Women's Fashion', was more daring. Morton was pictured 'wearing clothes of an unusual flavour' that 'were cut to the shape of his figure', including a 'chocolate brown two-piece suit in . . . spun rayon cloth with cuffed sleeves and narrow trousers' and an exotic dinner jacket in 'midnight blue mohair fabric with black satin facings'.[183]

West's fashion journalism drew on a strategy that was later to become widespread as burgeoning subcultural communities reappropriated fashion to advertise solidarity among their members and to signal social differ-ence to a wider audience.[184] The 'meaning of style', as Dick Hebdige has put it, involved the subversion of dominant cultural codes by the deliberate manipulation of small but significant details.[185] In the 1950s, when clothes were meant to convey unambiguous social messages, these alternative readings of fashion conveyed a powerful sense of cultural disturbance.

The extent of the disruption could be gauged from the hostility that the Edwardian look provoked among society's gatekeepers. At the begin-ning of coronation year *Queen* pronounced the style 'tawdry'; when fashion went to extremes there was always the danger of 'ridicule and exploitation', the magazine intoned.[186] *Queen* hinted that those men who wore their 'trousers a little tighter' and their 'hat brim curled as though with a pair of tongs' were 'grotesque' and tasteless, because their appear-ance violated acceptable codes of masculinity.[187] *The Times* also felt the need to add its voice to the criticism when it covered a 'style presenta-tion' organized by the Men's Fashion Council in June. This 'little pageant' with its 'Edwardian flavour' went 'straight to the heart of the matter', jour-nalists insisted.[188] What was at issue was whether a man's clothes should conceal his identity, or whether they should make him conspicuous to the point of being commented on.

In the autumn of 1953 the full glare of hostile media attention was turned on the sexuality of the fashionable man-about-town. The arrest and subsequent trial of the young aristocrat Edward Montagu on charges of indecency, along with his friends Michael Pitt-Rivers and Peter Wildeblood, provoked a national debate about fashionable society and its links with London's queer cultures. Lord Montagu of Beaulieu was covered in the gossip columns as one of the country's most eligible bach-elors. With a country estate in Hampshire and a flat in Mayfair, he was profiled as a gentleman with a natural air of distinction who added bril-liance to the coronation season. Eton-and Oxford-educated, an officer in the Grenadier Guards, and a habitué of clubland, Montagu was an ener-getic member of London society.[189] As a contemporary man-about-town he declared a strong interest in fashionable dress and immaculate groom-ing (fig. 8). *Men's Wear* reported how this good-looking young aristocrat regularly demanded more 'daring' designs from his tailor.[190] Like Douglas-Home and Birley, Montagu was also an energetic entrepreneur, one of the first peers to recognize the commercial possibilities of opening his stately home to the paying public. In 1953 he was employed by a firm of publicity agents to organize press promotions for consumer products. Gregarious and affable with a wide social circle, friends commented how he was 'equally at home amongst all kinds of people'.[191] Wildeblood, a society columnist on the *Daily Mail*, testified to the very different types of guests who congregated at Lord Montagu's London home: 'Duchesses and model-girls, restaurateurs and politicians and musical comedy actresses and Guards officers and Americans wearing hand-painted ties.'[192] Wildeblood's description of the guest list evoked his friend's eclectic and individual lifestyle, but the coded references to guards' officers and fashionable Americans also hinted obliquely at Montagu's sexual tastes for those in the know.

In August 1953 the social column of *The Times* announced Lord Montagu's engagement to Anne Gage, a major's daughter from Bridgnorth.[193] Three months later a warrant was out for his arrest; along with the film director Kenneth Hume, Montagu was charged with 'serious offences' against two boy scouts on his Hampshire estate.[194] The subsequent trial at Winchester Assizes in November proved inconclusive, but Montagu was arrested again only two months later. Together with Pitt-Rivers and Wildeblood, he was now charged with indecency against two young RAF airmen. This time Montagu was found guilty and he was given a twelve-month prison sentence.

The Montagu-Wildeblood scandal has been seen by historians as a significant moment in the post-war history of homosexual law reform. Exposing dubious police tactics and culminating in a partisan show trial, the affair led indirectly to the setting up of the Home Office inquiry into homosexual offences and prostitution the following year.[195] The case was one of the *cause célèbre* exposés in which members of society and other prominent public figures were seriously compromised by their involvement in the capital's queer cultures. Other similar scandals included the prosecution of the actor Sir John Gielgud for soliciting in a notorious public toilet in Chelsea in October 1953, coverage of the sexual career of the British Foreign Office official and spy Guy Burgess after his defection to the Soviet Union two years earlier, and the exposure of Ian Harvey for sexual offences with a guardsman in Hyde Park in 1958.[196]

All these cases focused public attention on the questionable lifestyle of the man-about-town, which was probed in the courtroom and magnified by the national media as part of a wider interrogation of the sexual atmosphere of elite London society. At Montagu's trial, aggressive prosecution questioning of the defendants threw the spotlight on champagne parties and theatre visits that the young aristocrat had supposedly arranged for his friends and the two working-class airmen, with their suggestions of 'sinful glamour'.[197] In a case that turned on the transgressive nature of cross-class sexual liaisons, Montagu's world was pictured as a 'gilded den of vice', where immorality and the corruption of young working-class men apparently took place 'under the seductive influence of lavish hospitality'.[198] Even liberal commentators like the novelist J. B. Priestley argued that the affair revealed how 'the cultural life of London' was now 'largely dominated by homosexuals' who were members of 'a great secret society'.[199]

The Montagu scandal probed the darker side of the man-about-town, but the case also highlighted the porousness and malleability of this masculine personality. Ranging from the boisterous homosocial antics of members of the Thursday Club and the creative energies of well-connected men like Douglas-Home and Birley through to the take-up of Edwardian style by prominent aristocrats, these varied examples revealed how privileged men appropriated fashionable masculinity in 1950s London. The simultaneous appearance of the Teddy Boy, an overtly working-class urban stylist, showed that the cultural impact of the man-about-town was not confined to the social elites. Drawing on elements of the new Edwardian look for men, the Teds combined fashionable display and traditional proletarian flamboyance with aggressive rituals of territoriality to forge the first post-war youth culture.

As Paul Rock and Stanley Cohen have noted, the Teddy Boy emerged in London without much warning as a 'fully fledged deviant'.[200] Outbreaks of ritualized violence by young working-class men erupted across Europe in the 1950s, associated with what some sociologists called the 'welfare criminality' of embryonic post-war affluence. The *blouson noirs* or black windbreakers in France, the *Halbstarken* in Germany and the *skinknuttar* in Sweden were all identified with particular urban styles and special fashions.[201] In inner London, working-class youths combined the wearing of neo-Edwardian clothes with localized traditions of gang culture to assemble their own distinctive look. Fyvel was the first public commentator to make the point that Teddy Boys were not simply imitators of upper-class dress codes; they took Edwardianism out of the West End and turned it into a dandyism of their own in south London neighbourhoods around the Elephant and Castle, Southwark and Clapham, and further north in Islington and Tottenham.[202]

9　Teddy Boys at the Mecca Dance Hall, Tottenham, 29 May 1954, photographer Alex Dellow/Stringer, Hulton Archive. Getty Images.

10　'Social and Functional Analysis', Arthur Ling and D. K. Johnson, in J. H. Forshaw and Patrick Abercrombie, *County of London Plan* (London: Macmillan, 1943), Colour Plate 1. Reproduced by kind permission of the Corporation of London and London Metropolitan Archives.

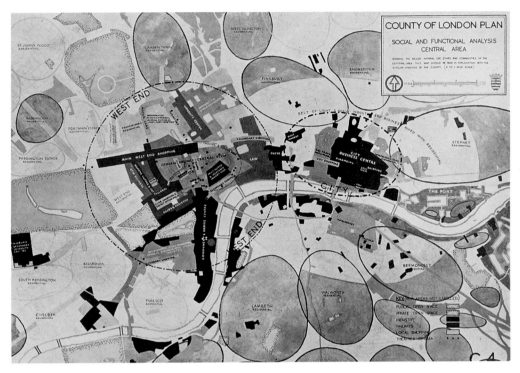

11   'Social and Functional Analysis of the Central Area', Arthur Ling, in J. H. Forshaw and Patrick
Abercrombie, *County of London Plan* (London: Macmillan, 1943), Plate VI, 2. Reproduced by kind
permission of the Corporation of London and London Metropolitan Archives.

12 'Eye level view of St Paul's Cathedral from the south side of Cannon Streeet (widened on north side) at corner of Friday Street', perspective by J. D. M. Harvey, no. 4a, Corporation of London, Court of Common Council, *Report to the Right Honourable the Lord Mayor etc. on the Preliminary Draft Proposals for Post War Reconstruction in the City of London* (London: Batsford, 1944), p. 17. Reproduced by kind permission of London Metropolitan Archives.

13   Neighbours chatting while police guard number 10 Rillington Place, 25 March 1953, photographer unknown. Popperfoto/Getty Images.

14   Family snapshot of John Christie, undated, in Criminal Cases: Christie, John Reginald Halliday (1949–1953), TNA PRO HO 291/228. The National Archives, reproduced by kind permission of the Metropolitan Police Authority.

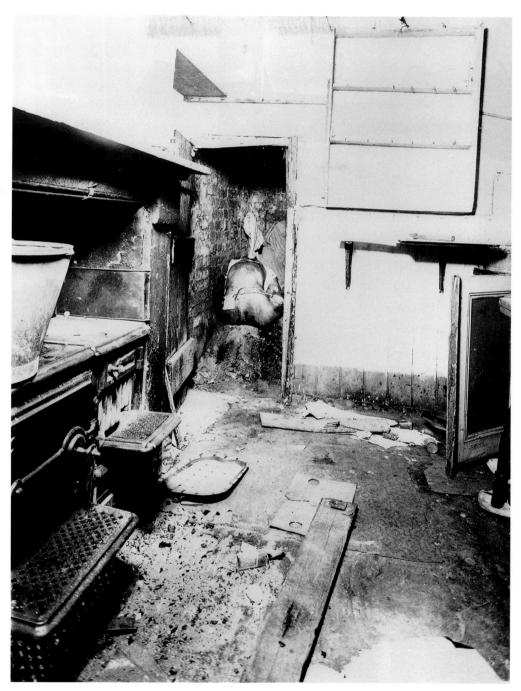

15   Kitchen of 10 Rillington Place showing the body of one of the murdered women, 1953, photographer Chief Inspector Percy Law, Photographic Department Scotland Yard, in Criminal Cases: Christie, John Reginald Halliday (1949–1953), TNA PRO HO 291/228. The National Archives, reproduced by kind permission of the Metropolitan Police Authority.

16   Front room of 10 Rillington Place showing the body of Mrs Ethel Christie, 1953, photographer Chief Inspector Percy Law, Photographic Department Scotland Yard, in Criminal Cases: Christie, John Reginald Halliday (1949–1953), TNA PRO HO 291/228. The National Archives, reproduced by kind permission of the Metropolitan Police Authority.

The Teddy Boy broke emphatically with established traditions of working-class culture which dictated that young men adopted the clothes, manners and forms of masculinity dictated by their fathers and elder brothers. In one of the numerous press exposés of the Teds, *Observer* journalist Hugh Latymer observed how 'in cafés, public houses or milk-bars which the Teddy Boys favour' the boys sat 'posed in groups, conscious of arranged hair [and] creased "drains" [trousers]'.[203] Hairstyles registered the contemporary influence of Hollywood movies, combining heavy sideboards and a high wave over the forehead, the so-called D.A., which was worn long at the back in a manner reminiscent of movie star Tony Curtis. The suit jacket came closest to the upper-class Edwardian look: fully draped with extra pockets and flaps, and topped with a velvet or moleskin collar for those who could afford it (fig. 9). Shirts were frequently worn with a black knotted string tie or 'Slim Jim', waistcoats were usually plain though particularly showy Teds sported patterned varieties, while trousers were tight fitting and tapered onto heavy shoes with round toecaps, or onto so-called 'brothel creepers' with thick crêpe soles. The full outfit cost over twenty pounds, five times the weekly wage of the young unskilled and semi-skilled workers who were regular recruits to the Teddy Boy gangs.[204]

At first the Teds were not recognized as a youth phenomenon at all. In the early 1950s the press and public moralists still identified young men who dressed 'in Edwardian' as spivs or cosh boys, 'old deviants in new clothes' who had appropriated some features of the revived patrician style.[205] But during the summer of 1953 a dramatic incident occurred in south London that crystallized the links between Edwardian fashion and contemporary expressions of working-class youth culture. On the evening of 2 July local youths and girls congregated around the bandstand on Clapham Common, listening to popular tunes from the hit parade.[206] As one of the group recollected later, most of the boys 'would not show interest in the girls'; they were 'there to see and be seen', to strike a pose and to show themselves off to each other.[207] Trouble erupted when a youth who was not himself in fashionable dress insulted one of the Edwardians as a 'flash cunt'.[208] After a chase and a scuffle between rival south London gangs, John Beckley, a 17-year-old bank clerk from Walworth, lay bleeding to death on the pavement near the Common from multiple knife wounds.

In the public anxieties that surfaced at the trial of six youths for Beckley's murder at the Old Bailey in the autumn of 1953, the press and the police began to make the first direct links between Edwardian dress and the social problems posed by young men from London's inner city areas. The *Evening Standard* was quick to demonize one of the local youths, Ronald Coleman, a 16-year-old shop assistant, as 'the leader of the Edwardians', a 'teenage gang of hooligans' whose trade-mark was 'their eccentric suits'.[209] Coleman himself drew attention to his distinctive sartorial style, putting on record in his police witness statement the fact that he dressed in 'a very dark grey suit, single breasted with three buttons . . . after the style of what is called Edwardian'.[210] At a key moment in his trial the prosecution demanded to know if the 'youths on the Common' wore 'tight trousers and strange-looking coats with a slit down the back?'[211] When one of the gang, Michael Davies, a 20-year-old labourer, was convicted of Beckley's murder in October, journalists pronounced that the Edwardian suit was 'mortally wounded' as a result of the delinquencies committed by south London's young dandies:

> The Clapham Common thug . . . took great pains to look like a dandy. Like most of his companions, nearly all his money went on flashy clothes, and just before the murder, he borrowed twelve pounds from his uncle to buy a suit. . . . This man was a born coward beneath his bravado and his 'gay dog' clothes.[212]

This naming of the Teds by the media and their direct links with working-class disreputableness forced an immediate *volte-face* on the part of upper-class men-about-town who had championed the Edwardian revival. One young ex-guards officer reportedly complained that after the Clapham murder 'absolutely the whole of one's wardrobe immediately becomes unwearable', while the Mayor of Harrogate insisted that there was now 'a very real connection between the action of individuals and the dress they wear, and this is no-where more marked . . . than in the so-called Edwardian style'.[213]

Searching for ways to explain the phenomenon of the Teds, some commentators believed that the new 'boy gangsters' were one of many unwholesome imports from the USA. Capitalizing on widespread anxieties about American forms of popular culture, local politicians and journalists now dubbed Clapham London's 'little Chicago': a place where city blight and urban dislocation had disturbed the indigenous structures of class and English neighbourliness. The behaviour of 'hardened thugs' and their 'molls' involved outbreaks of senseless violence, 'rowdyism' and 'hustling' which resembled the urban disorder prevalent in many US cities.[214] The editors of *Man About Town* agreed with this evils extrinsic argument; sounding a similar note of disapproval about 'enveloping American influences', journalists explained that the 'misnamed Teddy Boy is not Edwardian but Mid Western'.[215]

In contrast, sociologists like Fyvel insisted on a more complex reading of the Teds' expression of contemporary style that refused to blame extraneous cultural imports. Claiming close-up evidence as an ethnographer, Fyvel saw 'Teddyism' as a home-grown response to the contradictory social influences that were transforming life in the 'wasteland' of London's working-class neighbourhoods.[216] He believed that the Teds' affirmation of local territory in their violent gang culture was a defensive response to the erosion of traditional patterns of employment and community and to the break-up of racially homogeneous, white neighbourhoods by the arrival of Caribbean migrants. Fyvel went on to argue that the Teddy Boys' proletarian style drew on a wide range of resources: from the patrician influence of Edwardian fashion through to the 'plush cinemas, modernized dance halls', and 'late-night cafés with juke-boxes blaring' that were the landmarks of London's embryonic youth culture. The Teds' display of working-class authenticity combined these modern influences with ritualistic behaviour that was heavily rooted in the past.

Elite society was a significant factor shaping metropolitan culture during the 1950s. Its ongoing importance problematizes accounts of the post-war period that have highlighted the terminal decline of the English upper class and the dominance of mass political and cultural democracy. London's social elites were active in shaping the modernity of mid-twentieth-century urban experience, rather than simply appearing as regressive or reactionary forces. The renaissance of patrician characters and their institutions exerted a powerful influence on sexuality in the capital, encouraging the reappearance of the man-about-town and a number of associated female personalities in the entertainment and leisure spaces of the West End. Many of the men and women who took up these roles provided significant cultural leadership by virtue of their own influential status, while the machinery of publicity ensured that their social activities and intimate personal relationships were endowed with a continuing sense of national importance or notoriety. One consequence of the promotion of elite styles by the press was that fashionable upper-class types were cast as social and sexual mediators who crossed and recrossed the boundaries conventionally separating high and low culture.

The man-about-town reaffirmed a powerful vision of London as a man's city, but in the 1950s this urban identity was highly unstable, a testament to the fact that it was the product of competing social and sexual scripts. Networks of clubbable masculine solidarity were cross cut by more sexualized and potentially dangerous versions of homosociability that held up upper-class society to hostile moral scrutiny. Established forms of aristocratic display were reshaped by influences from metropolitan journalism, by the fashion industry and by the promotional cultures of advertising and marketing in ways that generated distinctive masculine styles. One important consequence of the impact of affluence was that some of the characteristics of the man-about-town were taken up and reworked by social groups placed well outside the parameters of the upper class. Young working-class men drew on commercially sponsored ideas about gentlemanly behaviour to produce their own homosocial rituals and fashionable poses in inner city areas that existed in close proximity to the de luxe entertainment spaces of the West End.

During the 1950s and early 1960s high-profile metropolitan scandals and other transgressive events intensified public debate about the porous connections between elite society and a variety of social and sexually marginal groups, in specific London environments as well as in more generic accounts as social fantasy. In part these collisions between overworld and underworld confirmed the continuing legacy of Victorian urban encounters, but they also generated more contemporary accounts of sex and culture that had long-term consequences. By bringing into public visibility areas of the city and social actors that were perceived to be troublesome or dangerous, these scandals acted as a powerful catalyst to wider processes of sexual and moral change. High society with its links to metropolitan low life was one recurrent feature of the episodes; an equally significant influence was the impact of planning and urban sociology, projecting their own powerful utopias and dystopias of order and disorder.

Chapter 3   Pathologies

Plans

Social historians have highlighted two major trends shaping the development of London's metropolitan area and its urban populations during the 1940s and 1950s.[1] The most significant force for change in the face of wartime enemy bombing by the German *Luftwaffe* and all of the attendant social dislocations was the partial implementation of a planning-inspired blueprint for the capital. Driven by Labour politicians, both at Westminster and across the river at the headquarters of the LCC in County Hall, working in close alliance with the enhanced power of the planning profession, this represented the most ambitious attempt to reorder London's physical and social environment since Christopher Wren's grand scheme for rebuilding the city after the Great Fire of 1666. Self-consciously progressivist, planning in its most expansive form identified London as a paradigmatic metropolis of the future. Insisting that the capital would need to serve multiple functions in the post-war years ahead, planners simultaneously envisaged London as a modern imperial metropole for the newly invented Commonwealth, a contemporary world city functioning as a hub for international communications, finance and culture, and a supra-urban conurbation with a hinterland dominating most of southern England.[2] All these visions for the city were in circulation at the time of the coronation. In policy terms three well-known advisory planning documents, emanating from the LCC, the City of London and Whitehall and forged during the war, set the terms of the discussion about London's future. The *County of London Plan* (1943), the *Report on Post-War Reconstruction in the City of London* (1944) and *The Greater London Plan* (1944) produced an influential body of planning doctrine that provided a broad consensus about the capital's development, both at the level of public debate and in parliamentary and local politics, which lasted into the early 1950s.

All of these plans began by confronting the serious problems posed by the bombing of much of the metropolitan core, especially in the City of London and the East End. From that centrifugal point they proposed major redevelopments in the inner and outer suburbs, as well as an environmental Green Belt and new satellite towns beyond. Comprehensively addressing London's physical and social geography, they envisaged population movements, planned coherent transport systems and instituted a modicum of industrial zoning. This story of planning, together with its subsequent reversals and failures, is extremely familiar and well rehearsed; not only does it dominate histories of mid-twentieth-century London, it has become part of a series of much broader master-narratives about the modernization of English society. Given that schemes for urban redevelopment were replicated across many areas of the country, planners and planning in London have been cast as key professional players in the implementation of the post-war social contract, founded on the principles of increased state intervention, extended citizenship rights and the power of expert knowledge.[3]

The systematic erosion of this planning consensus from the early 1950s has been seen as a consequence of the collapse of public confidence in the planned society. In London, as elsewhere, it involved the reassertion of a much more familiar facet of urban growth. Speculative development, especially in the capital's central areas, driven by an alliance of financiers, property developers and architects was the major force behind the rebuilding of the city for much of the 1950s and early 1960s.[4] Commercial expansion epitomized a new and aggressive phase of London's post-war transformation. In particular, the lifting of building controls by the Conservative government in November 1954 opened the way for a property boom that continued unabated until 1964, when Labour again instituted strict regulations on development throughout the greater London area.[5]

Property 'tycoons' as they were dubbed in the period, such as Clore, Cotton and Harry Hyams, along with their dedicated architect Richard Seifert, were the public face of this commercial transformation of post-war London. Their overwhelming legacy was the modern office block, with around twenty-four million square feet of new office space built in the City and the West End during the decade from 1954, an increase of

50 per cent on the figure for 1938.[6] Developers were not just commercial speculators on land and property values; they were also significant figures in the post-war renaissance of metropolitan society, despite their own often humble origins. Sutherland remembered how the 'new property millionaires' featured prominently in the social circles of the urban gentry. Charles Clore in particular was an energetic participant in the reinvented society networks of the 1950s, while the acquisitions, takeover bids and personal rivalries of the new 'landlords to London' were covered avidly in the gossip columns of the press.[7]

Historians have tended to assume that commercial developers consistently won out over the planning profession after the high moment of government intervention in the 1940s. The subsequent property boom, together with the later bursts of free-market entrepreneurialism associated first with the political project of the Thatcher governments in the 1980s and then with the power of global capital, all reinforced assumptions that private-sector development triumphed over coordinated planning in most of the central areas of the city.[8] Developers have also been credited with putting in place part of the material infrastructure for major post-war changes to personal and sexual life. Transformations associated with 'swinging' or permissive London, involving the reorganization of the sex industry and the fashion and youth markets, have been identified not just with new forms of consumer culture but also with changing portfolios of property ownership and retail use in the West End.[9]

These are important issues about the power of commerce to reshape cultural and sexual behaviour, but historical arguments that emphasize the dynamism of London's entrepreneurs underestimate how planners themselves generated their own distinctive moral vision for the city. Despite the fact that their grandiose policies for rebuilding the capital were checked from the mid-1950s onwards, the impact of planning was not felt at the level of the physical organization of the built environment alone. Planners offered a series of utopias which privileged a heightened ethical sense of how London would function in the future and projected images of the city that were often disproportionate to their enactment as actual schemes. The influence of the planning profession was felt not just at the level of policy, but also in terms of its particular understanding of how order was to be imposed on the physical and social confusion that they perceived to be contemporary London.[10] Visions of urban utopia and dystopia were not new, given the extensive municipal campaigns waged by environmentalists in the nineteenth and early twentieth centuries to reform and reshape the city. But the impact of the Second World War on the home front intensified the scope for a wide-ranging programme of urban intervention that had important consequences for the way moral and sexual problems were understood in the 1950s.

The *County of London Plan*, prepared by the architects and town planners John Forshaw and Patrick Abercrombie, together with the report for the City of London coordinated by the Corporation of London's engineer Francis Forty, dealt heavily in the business of image making and forms of representation. Cultural geographers have recently reminded historians that far from being transparent exercises in expert neutrality, acts of mapping are 'creative, sometimes anxious, moments' in the production of particular forms of spatial knowledge about the urban environment. Maps draw on a 'complex architecture of signs' through which the worlds they construct are selected and organized.[11] The maps, diagrams and photographs contained in Forshaw and Abercrombie's plans imposed a distinctive way of seeing London, whereby key urban functions were highlighted and other uses were deliberately occluded. Their immediate context was the political and intellectual debate about reconstruction on the home front which gathered pace during the final years of the war. William Beveridge's comprehensive review of the social security system, *Social Insurance and Allied Services*, launched in December 1942, was the precursor to a whole series of ambitious public policy statements on the future of the welfare state that also confronted the challenge of rebuilding Britain's war-damaged urban centres. Significantly, too, the launch of the *County of London Plan* on 9 July 1943 coincided with an intensified phase in the Allied bombing of Germany, making the plan part of the propaganda battle over the destruction and rebuilding of European cities that had been recognized as a key theatre of ideological conflict since the First World War.[12]

Professor of Town Planning at University College London, Abercrombie was the acknowledged doyen among English town planners in the 1940s, a profession that was itself a loose amalgam of different intellectual, aesthetic and public policy traditions rather than a unified field of expertise.[13] Beginning his career in private architectural practice, he combined this commercial role with a series of academic appointments and government commissions during the inter-war period.[14] Forshaw's career was more tightly defined as an architect; having held commercial and municipal posts throughout the 1930s, he was also an active member of the think-tank on metropolitan affairs, the London Society, and sat on a number of architectural associations and housing trusts.[15] Both men represented different facets of town planning, and Abercrombie in particular epitomized the confidence of a genteel, high-bourgeois outlook that played an important role in the formation of liberal and nascent social democratic politics during the first half of the twentieth century.[16]

Forshaw and Abercrombie opened the *County of London Plan* with a series of plates and illustrations, all of which worked to reinforce their argument that modern London's dramatic and sprawling growth had been largely unplanned and under-regulated. This familiar point had also been at the heart of the recommendations from the inter-war Unwin Committee and from the Barlow Commission on economic and industrial development in the capital, which reported in 1940.[17] Leading urbanists and town planners such as Patrick Geddes and Lewis Mumford had mounted similar intellectual arguments in public discussions about London's future throughout the first decades of the twentieth century.[18]

Abercrombie's preferred image for demonstrating the negative development of modern London was the visual metaphor of the city as an octopus, unfurling its tentacles ever outwards to strangle more and more of the independent settlements on the outskirts in its grasp. The use of this type of imagery to dramatize the effects of uncoordinated urban growth had featured regularly in commentaries on the capital for nearly 200 years.[19] During the early twentieth century the octopus image was used repeatedly by planners and preservationists to evoke the dynamic sense of disorder produced by uncontrolled urban development and to point to the need for an equally vigorous, planned response. Social Darwinist and town planner Patrick Geddes, in his *Cities in Evolution* (1915), described the 'octopus of London' as 'a vast irregular growth without previous parallel in the world of life', going on to visualize the city expanding from its 'daily pulsating centre' and 'spreading over . . . a great part of south-east England'.[20] In the *County of London Plan* a figured drawing of the capital's built-up areas provided a striking illustration of this process, with the bloated metropolitan centre inked in black and the suburban tentacles hatched as ever-extending feelers.[21]

These graphic reminders about the capital's development were accompanied in the plan by another more modern technique for visualizing metropolitan sprawl: aerial photographs portrayed endless vistas of haphazard and uncoordinated urban growth stretching away to the horizon.[22]

During the inter-war years this idea of viewing the city from above was drawn on extensively by novelists and poets, documentary photographers and politicians, as well as by planners, all of whom used aerial perspectives to augment their social and cultural arguments.[23] In the *County of London Plan* aerial photographs, taken by commercial pilots from shallow-angled viewpoints out of their plane windows, captured the endless, straggling ribbon development of London's suburbs. These images also encouraged a more optimistic argument when placed alongside the plans for reconstruction; they suggested a mappable disorder, in which planners held the key to enhanced future control.[24]

Forshaw and Abercrombie's account of urban disorder was immediately followed by their visualization of how London could be replanned. For their city of the future they drew on quite different iconography, producing an elaborate sequence of diagrams of the LCC area. Schematic coloured plates idealized and simplified London as a series of organic, naturally grouped communities (fig. 10). Drawing on a functionalist reading of the city by dominant use, circles delineated the 'social groupings and major . . . zones' within the LCC boundaries. The aim was to show how 'the present . . . use zoning and community structure' could be conveniently simplified and better ordered.[25] In a diagram of the central area the two largest circles represented the West End and the City, inside which were blocked the 'natural' sub-zones of government and empire, business, law, the university centre, the press, the produce and meat markets of Covent Garden and Smithfield, and the fashionable shopping streets, together with the surrounding residential communities (fig. 11). Acknowledging that central London was and would continue to be multi-functional, with its social and institutional features strongly interrelated, the planners' express aim was to demonstrate how a greater sense of civic order could be imposed on the pre-existing 'natural zoning' through stricter control of future development.[26] Here the planners parted company with the more radical calls for decentralization advocated by followers of the garden cities movement.[27] Forshaw and Abercrombie demonstrated a strong commitment to the renaissance of London's metropolitan core in the interests of national and imperial renewal.

Interpretations of the *County of London Plan* have overlooked the authors' obsession with the reconstruction of central London, emphasizing instead their policies for the decentralization and dispersal of population and industry from the worst congested areas of the inner city.[28] Yet this metropolitan-centredness set the tone in the document's important opening sections, it recurred in subsequent chapters ostensibly addressing questions of community and neighbourhood, and it was heavily present in the accompanying visual material. A similar concern dominated Forty's City of London report a year later. This focus on the capital's central area reveals how a concern with 'landmark' or official London, and with the urban pathologies that were understood to be located inside its perimeters or on its borders, coexisted in these plans alongside the emphasis on decentralization.

Forshaw and Abercrombie's sense of what they perceived to be the heart of the capital involved a partial but significant recasting of what constituted the metropolitan centre. Many of the state-sponsored schemes to transform central London in the early twentieth century had focused on the West End as the locus of monarchy and imperial spectacle, with an anxious eye on competitors in Wilhelmine Berlin or Habsburg Vienna.[29] The *County of London Plan* acknowledged much of this monarchical perspective, but it was also influenced by a more statist and bureaucratic understanding of official London as the seat of domestic and imperial government. Abercrombie and Forshaw focused their vision for London on the 'government and Commonwealth' district of Whitehall, running south from Trafalgar Square to the Houses of Parliament. The stated aim was to restore an appropriate urban aesthetic and a planning standard that had been lost in the chaos of inter-war development. Firmer controls of building heights and densities would promote a panorama suitable for the nation and for the empire's administrative centre.

Schemes for the beautification of the central area were aired in many inter-war planning projects, such as the collection of essays *London of the Future*, published by the London Society in 1921 and edited by the architect Aston Webb.[30] In the *County of London Plan* long perspective drawings of the nation's historic buildings at Parliament Square, in the newly named Westminster Precinct, envisaged the creation of an Italianate piazza and a spacious reservation for ceremonies of state, flanked by ornamental gardens, all safeguarded by architectural controls and efficient traffic zoning.[31] These sketches projected idealized, panoramic vistas in which only the great monuments and government buildings were included; the entire jumble of central London, with its traffic chaos, its rows and rows of speculative building and its inner city slums, had disappeared from view.

A similar version of civic monumentalism informed the vision for reconstruction in the heart of the City of London. Here Forty's detailed plans for building zoning, street improvements and freely circulating traffic were enhanced by six full-page, pastel-wash perspective drawings by the artist J. D. Harvey.[32] Centring on St Paul's Cathedral and the immediate neighbourhood, Harvey's views of the City, which were inserted into the Corporation of London's report, dealt in visionary streetscapes and river views.[33] For Harvey and for his political masters in the City, what was at issue was the way that successive waves of commercial development around the cathedral had massively restricted visual access to Wren's baroque dome, campaniles and portico. Extensive enemy bombing now made it possible to rethink this environment, and the Corporation concentrated on widening the western approach to St Paul's at Ludgate Hill and improving the southern perspective from the Thames and the vantage from Cannon Street to the east.[34]

Washed in half colour, Harvey's drawings embellished and enlivened these proposals for rebuilding the City. They presented a harmonized and sanitized panorama; the horizontal lines of all the surrounding buildings were regularized to echo the classicism of the cathedral, approaching thoroughfares were boldly curved, opening onto expansive vistas, Victorian railway bridges were discreetly removed, while traffic and pedestrians were sketched in as decorative additions (fig. 12).[35] The impression was of what the report approvingly termed 'a quiet formality', where chaos had been replaced by the modern ordering of people and spaces, overseen by the grandeur of St Paul's. So as to emphasize the proposed planning gains, these sketches were interposed with a very different set of images. Drawn from a 1934 photographic survey of the cathedral, they depicted the grimy reality of the area surrounding St Paul's, replete with snaking queues of vans and cars, advertising hoardings, soot-blackened buildings and disorderly pedestrians.[36]

David Matless has shown how the intellectual ambition contained in these planning programmes was driven by a powerful sense of where things appropriately belonged.[37] For Abercrombie in particular, this was a fundamental tenet of his philosophy, informing much of his early architectural work in private practice, as well as his inter-war surveys of the northern industrial areas and his interest in rural preservation.[38] In London, Abercrombie's sense of geographical appropriateness was focused on the division of functions within the urban environment. Throughout the *County of London Plan* this sense of appropriateness also involved identifying *misplaced environments*, or people and matter out of place. Such a process, involving a highly selective reading of dominant use, was strongly influenced by functionalist models of planning, especially those that predominated among urbanists in the USA. In their authors' note to the plan, Abercrombie and Forshaw singled out for special mention the

encouragement they had received from the team of the New York
Regional Survey, which reported regularly during the inter-war years and
led to the creation of a permanent City Plan Commission for New York,
with Thomas Adams as its head.[39] Adams's approach, which Forshaw had
encountered at first hand during his period in private architectural practice in New York during the 1930s, defined 'mis-planning' as the failure
to identify 'the ultimate social character and quality of development of
neighbourhoods and communities', a failure that was all too often the
result of reckless profiteering in land.[40] Informed by a socially integra-
tionist reading of the physical and human environment, Adams placed
strong emphasis on social zoning in order to avoid the type of urban dysfunction that currently bedevilled many American cities.

In the English town planning tradition, ideas about urban dysfunction
and social blight competed with home-grown agendas for transforming
the urban environment derived from London's own municipal traditions.
Policies of metropolitan improvement, originating in Victorian campaigns
for social reform and stressing the dynamic interrelationship between
moral and material conditions, remained an influential force in public discussions about the capital's central areas well into the post-war period.
Unsurprisingly, the state of the West End posed the most direct challenge
to London's planning luminaries as well as to a range of other public
agencies concerned with the management of the central area.

Planners were far from unique in staking out their claims to knowledge and authority over the West End. The Metropolitan Police, especially in the areas covered by C and B Divisions (administrative districts
covering the West End, Victoria and Chelsea), politicians at Westminster
and Paddington councils, together with local conservation groups and
purity campaigners, all had long-standing concerns about the social condition of an area that occupied such an important place in national life.
But there were significant differences between these traditional social
agencies and the initiatives championed by the planning profession.
Planners distinguished their own approach in terms of the scope of their
urban ambitions. Recognizing the limitations of local schemes, Forshaw
and Abercrombie insisted on a comprehensive reordering of the West End,
based on policies of approved social use.[41] They proposed that the capital's
central axis, running from Oxford Street southwards through Regent
Street and into Piccadilly Circus and Leicester Square, should become the
core of a redesignated 'shopping, business, restaurant and amusement' district.[42] Acknowledging that currently the West End was 'one of the worst

planned and architecturally designed areas of London' which in parts was now nothing more than 'a central slum', planners argued the West End needed detailed redevelopment in its own right.[43] Cinemas and theatres were to be rebuilt on prominent and spacious sites, sub-zoning would cater to the demands of specialized consumers, while inexpensive flats were needed for service-sector workers.[44]

Planners targeted their anxieties about the West End on the neighbourhood that Forshaw and Abercrombie coyly referred to as the capital's 'restaurant area'.[45] This was Soho, home of English bohemianism and political radicalism since the mid-nineteenth century, focal point for a diverse range of European and Jewish migrant and artisanal cultures, and the centre of London's thriving sex trade. Forshaw and Abercrombie grudgingly acknowledged that Soho had its 'own peculiar charm', but they also warned that the positive side of its exotic atmosphere 'might not maintain itself indefinitely'.[46] Here the planners' perception of moral and material deterioration went hand in hand; with a sidelong glance at the area's sexually dubious reputation, they noted that any proposed new development would have to compete with what they described as 'deteriorated mixed . . . use'.[47] Their answer was a stricter rationalization of commercial functions; the restaurant trade would henceforward define the district's cultural economy, with a hoped-for marginalization of its other irregular activities. In this respect the LCC planners were drawing on schemes for Soho's improvement that had long been advocated by local businesses. Forshaw and Abercrombie concurred, championing an approach to urban regeneration that privileged orderly commerce as the most effective form of counter-publicity to offset the area's disreputable reputation.

This quintessentially English synthesis of economic and civic functionalism with a moralized approach to human geography dominated Forshaw and Abercrombie's stance on all the other significant sub-districts in the West End: the 'professional and residential' streets of Fitzrovia, north of Oxford Street (in reality another socially mixed, 'bohemian' area), the 'University centre' in Bloomsbury to the east, and the river frontage along the South Bank, which had long been a focus for redevelopment plans that were partly realized on the rebuilt Festival of Britain site.[48] There were also major schemes to relieve London's traffic congestion, including futuristic road diagrams illustrating a proposed system of new arterial roads, underground expressways and flyovers designed to siphon off traffic in the West End, along with proposals for an inner ring encircling the central area.[49] Aerial sketches depicted a city dominated by an abstract idea of communication, purged of actual cars, buses and people.

Urban historians have counselled against too literal a reading of the planners' vision for central London, stressing how in reality their schemes were always necessarily much more pragmatic and ad hoc, both in intellectual conception and as they were implemented during the late 1940s, when political and financial constraints, powerful vested interests and the war-damaged state of the built environment limited their ambitions.[50] All of this was certainly the case; but assessing the full impact of these metropolitan plans involves tracing their complex afterlife in the 1950s, not simply as policy but in terms of an intellectual legacy that prioritized functionally ordered social systems, on the one hand, and dysfunctional urban pathologies, on the other. During the immediate post-war years, a whole range of official and professional bodies explicitly concerned with the management of the capital's social problems directed their attention to those individuals and environments written out of 1940s planning discourse. In part these initiatives marked a revival of public anxiety about long-standing urban dilemmas that were associated with London's central areas, but they also revealed how much post-war social policy continued to be shaped by the moral and ethical ideas about place and environment that were part of Forshaw and Abercrombie's outlook.

More than ten years after the LCC unveiled their scheme, the Institute of Psychiatry, a postgraduate research centre based at the Maudsley Hospital in south London, turned to highlight one of London's social problems. Their detailed study, *Suicide in London* (1955), was a contribution to the school of urban sociology that Emile Durkheim had inaugurated in the 1890s, but it also marked the beginnings of a post-war resurgence of a specifically English tradition of empirical research, with its close attention to social setting, backed by quantitative and qualitative methods.[51] Suicide represented the dark side of the city, and its perpetrators posed a dysfunctional challenge to the idea of a socially integrated metropolis that inspired Abercrombie and his team. Suicide also drew attention to those people and places that had been erased from the planned, functionalist vision for London. Peter Sainsbury, the research assistant on the institute's project and the report's principal author, believed that it was in London neighbourhoods with particularly high levels of social mobility and isolation, where community life tended to be unstable, 'without order or purpose', that men and women were most prone to suicide.[52]

Sainsbury's hypothesis was in no sense new; Durkheim had famously grounded his own classic study in an understanding of the moral and psychological dislocation produced by the anomie of city life.[53] What was significant about the Maudsley Hospital's project was the way that it mapped the capital; the report registered a characteristic shift in the geographical focus of much post-war social research away from the planners' grand schemes for the whole of the London area, seen as a macro-system of functionally integrated environments. Sainsbury chose instead to focus on a series of small-scale, dislocated districts in the inner city that he identified as the sites of many contemporary problems. Here the intellectual origins of his report were indebted neither to Durkheim nor to the tradition of American urban research based on social zoning. It was Chicago School sociologists Robert Park and Ezra Burgess, with their insistence on the complex interaction between dysfunctional and delinquent behaviour and the organization of particular neighbourhoods, who provided Sainsbury with a way of grasping the city's pressing social and moral problems.[54]

Drawing on evidence from the coroner's records for the inner boroughs of north London, Sainsbury examined the social and geographical make-up of those districts where suicide rates were high. Describing a northerly arc abutting the West End and the City, he drew attention to Finsbury and St Pancras, Holborn, Westminster and Marylebone, along with Paddington, Kensington and Chelsea further west, as the areas with the highest rates. In contrast, traditional working-class districts in the East End and east London, together with the residential outer suburbs, were below the average.[55] What, Sainsbury asked, was distinctive about these inner city environments? Following Park and Burgess's ethnographic studies of inter-war Chicago, Sainsbury believed that they represented London's own version of 'rooming districts' or 'zones of transition' so characteristic of American cities.[56] Squeezed between the established infrastructure of the metropolitan centre and more settled communities further east and north, areas of this sort were populated by individuals and groups caught in a web of transient and impersonal social relationships, or what the urban sociologist Ruth Glass termed 'twilight zones' containing a 'motley collection of people' ranging 'from the top to the bottom of the social scale'.[57]

Glossing this vision of alienated inner London more precisely, Sainsbury delivered a sociological snapshot of the rented rooms and bedsits in Kensington, Bayswater and parts of Bloomsbury, where the social consequences of loneliness and anonymity were major factors driving suicides. In Hampstead, with its high proportion of immigrants and a substantial foreign-born population, the problems were those of the 'newcomer', forced to adopt 'unaccustomed values', and of the 'lonely boarding house dweller'.[58] Sainsbury also noted that the social composition of these different districts was so varied that it was impossible to link suicide to the traditional determinants of class, poverty or overcrowding; instead, he returned again and again to focus on the atmosphere of impermanence and instability that marked these areas.

Sainsbury's ecological perspective, which associated modern social and psychological problems with liminal spaces in the inner city, was not an isolated occurrence.[59] During the 1950s a wide range of academics and policymakers focused repeatedly on these inner city areas, which became informal laboratories for research and debate about contemporary urban change. The work of the Social Research Unit of the Town Planning Department at University College London, coordinated by Glass and later renamed the Centre for Urban Studies, provided one important institutional base for projects ranging from studies of Caribbean immigrants in Notting Hill and Brixton to the analysis of inner city gentrification.[60] In 1954 sociologist Michael Young started his independently run Institute of Community Studies in Bethnal Green, with its ethnographic focus on working-class life. Pioneering in its cultural methodologies, the institute's early work confronted the break-up of traditional working-class communities in the inner East End.[61] Policy research on unmarried mothers and problem families undertaken by the Family Welfare Association (formerly the Charity Organization Society, the Victorian clearing house for information on the poor) and the National Council of Social Service took inner city boroughs like Paddington and Fulham as the focus for their social exploration.[62]

On first reading, projects of this kind contrasted sharply with the civic schemes of the planning profession, both in the nature of their analysis and in their tendency to view the metropolis not as a unified geographical entity but as a set of fragmented and extremely localized areas. Yet what linked them intellectually to the discourse of the planners was the way they posed sociological and ethical questions in the language of human geography, not in the abstract, but in relation to specific zones or quarters of the city. In this way post-war social researchers and urban policymakers carried an important legacy from the planning projects of the 1940s.

Anxieties about dysfunctional or problematic areas in the capital were not confined to the concerns of public intellectuals; they also shaped larger and more dramatic metropolitan events during the immediate post-war years. In the spring and summer of 1953 a series of grotesque and highly publicized sexual murders intensified concern about one such inner city district. Recounted by the police, by the sanitary inspector, by local prostitutes, and by the barristers in the courtroom, these serial killings gripped national audiences and metropolitan residents alike. They were one of many transgressive episodes running throughout the 1950s and early 1960s that generated a wide-ranging debate about pathological and wayward forms of sexuality and their links to contemporary urban life.

Murders

Two months before the coronation, in March 1953, four Jamaican families were living in the end house of an insignificant Victorian cul-de-sac in north Kensington.[63] Contemporary photographs showed Rillington Place as a shabby street lying close to the Metropolitan Railway line; its dilapidated late nineteenth-century houses, with their bay windows and soot-blackened brick, were dominated by the wall of a disused iron foundry (fig. 13). It was a street where the average wage was about eight pounds a week, where most of the families had to share a toilet, and where more often than not there was no bath. In the row of terraced houses there was at least one resident, 77-year-old widow Margaret Ploughman, who could not even write her own name.[64]

A poor and racially mixed part of west London, Rillington Place epitomized the type of inner city district that loomed large in contemporary debates about the capital's problem areas. In 1953 the street gained spectacular notoriety as the setting for the grotesque serial killing of six women by a local man, John Christie. Covered as major national and international news, the Rillington Place murders focused intense media attention on the 'small squalid' street that had become a 'chamber of horrors' and on the psychology of the 'monster' who had perpetrated the crimes.[65] At one level the murders were the contemporary dramatization of a very traditional poetics of the city as an encounter with poverty, debased sexual relationships, and death, and they drew heavily on a set of genres for understanding social life that had first been rehearsed in London more than a hundred years before. But this episode was not simply backward-looking; events and characters in the case, together with their representation as urban fantasy, also stimulated intense discussion about the modernity of sexual relationships and about the city that produced them.

The Rillington Place murders were not isolated events; they were part of a series of highly publicized metropolitan cases, variously involving homicide, sex, treason, espionage and political scandal that punctuated the immediate post-war period. Other sensational murder cases included the trial and execution of the faux London playboy Neville Heath in 1946 and the 'acid bath killer' George Haigh in 1949, as well as the *crime passionnel* of Ruth Ellis, the last woman in England to hang for shooting her lover in 1955.[66] Exposés of sexual scandal centred on the Montagu–Wildeblood trial for homosexual offences the previous year, as well as the Profumo affair in 1963, which compromised the Conservative government as a result of the sexual entanglement of the war minister, John Profumo, with call-girl Christine Keeler.[67] The Profumo affair also had a double plot that coupled sex and espionage; it therefore needs to be seen in relation to the other genre of public scandal dominating the post-war years: the high-profile cases of spying that involved sexually deviant characters, especially homosexual men, as security threats. The most prominent episodes in this latter category were the defections of the Foreign Office officials Burgess and Maclean to the Soviet Union in 1951, together with the fall-out from the Vassall spy scandal in 1962–3, involving the exposure and trial of the Admiralty clerk John Vassall for stealing military secrets for the KGB.[68]

All of these incidents highlighted particular problem zones in the inner city, and they were characterized by the mutual association of high and low cultures that were seen to be dangerously interrelated in London's central areas. Men-about-town and other society figures made regular appearances in the cases, personalities who were frequently shown to be compromised by their association with low-life or disreputable characters. Equally, the episodes pushed together competing beliefs about pathological forms of masculinity and sexually wayward femininity, set against the norms of marriage and family life. Many of them probed the psychology and motivations underpinning the nature of evil, treason, sex, and passion – forms of human behaviour that were seen to be stimulated by the capital's urban environments. A number of these scandals also brought into play anxieties about the capital's immigrant cultures, and especially about the way that cosmopolitan areas were being transformed under the impact of Caribbean migration.

This was by no means the first time that metropolitan scandals had functioned as conduits for wide-ranging social problems. Throughout the nineteenth century a succession of murder trials and sexual intrigues had allowed different groups to engage in struggles over meaningful stories about urban danger and moral truth.[69] It was no accident that so many of these cases culminated in courtroom dramas, for the modern courtroom stands as 'one of the great social spaces for the enactment of access to the secrets of sex'.[70] The scandals and homicides that erupted during the immediate post-war years were influenced by earlier events and drew heavily on their cultural and political resources. But they also orchestrated decidedly contemporary versions of public morality that functioned as major interpretative devices within English society.

Overwhelmingly, these post-war incidents dramatized quintessentially modern anxieties that eventually led to changes in social mood and in attitudes towards sexual mores and criminal conduct, as well as in some of the key markers defining national identity. Yet the cases were in no sense unproblematically forward-looking. The characters who dominated them were not the familiar range of liberal experts or progressive reformers that historians have identified as the main agents driving forward the moral and sexual changes of the 1950s and 1960s. Legislators and enlightened parliamentary or pressure-group campaigners featured very little in most of the cases, or if they did make an appearance their actions were usually subordinated to the demands of very different interest groups. What shaped these transgressive incidents were some very traditional elements within English public life: murder, treason and sexual scandal. By focusing in detail on the narrative of the Rillington Place murders and on the trial of the killer, John Christie, along with the attendant media coverage, I show how the case functioned as a grotesque site of moral disturbance, acting as a catalyst to a prolonged debate about the social and sexual characteristics of dangerous or vulnerable people, viewed in their urban settings. These concerns were taken up and magnified in many of the subsequent scandalous episodes during the 1950s and early 1960s.

Rillington Place was a liminal space in the extremely localized social geography of inner London. Only a short bus ride away from Marble Arch and the heart of the West End, the street was part of an area of traditional, white working-class poverty known as Notting Dale, but it was also close to the more racially mixed and culturally cosmopolitan, though equally dilapidated, district of Notting Hill. These neighbourhoods featured in Sainsbury's list of classic transition zones in his study of suicide, and they were listed as archetypal twilight areas by Glass.[71] The *County of London Plan* had argued that better public housing and the enhancement of amenities like parks and green spaces would significantly improve life in north Kensington, but in the early 1950s residents were not benefiting from any such urban renewal schemes.[72] There were few council house rebuilding projects in Notting Dale's back-to-back slum terraces, and there was no evidence of private-sector gentrification that, according to the local press, was now transforming 'workman's cottages' into 'bijou residences' in Campden Hill and Earl's Court, in the southern part of the Royal Borough of Kensington.[73]

Notting Dale, or 'the Dale' as it was invariably known locally, had an extensive pedigree as a London slum. In the nineteenth century noxious local industries, repeated outbreaks of cholera and typhoid, the presence of Irish navvies and a Gypsy settlement had all contributed to the area's negative reputation. In the 1890s journalists had christened it 'Avernus', after Lake Avernus, the mythological entrance to hell.[74] Notting Hill, immediately to the east and south, had a more socially genteel pedigree. It was developed in the 1860s as a proposed westwards extension of the fashionable squares and crescents situated along the residential Bayswater Road, on the north side of Hyde Park. But the proximity of 'the Dale' meant that the area was never fully established as a premier residential quarter. By the inter-war period, with the accelerated middle-class exodus to London's western commuter suburbs, Notting Hill's imposing villas had been converted into cheap flats and rooming houses. In the 1920s the area was known locally as 'little India', because many of the houses had been settled by Asian students studying for the Indian Civil Service examinations.[75] Along with Brixton in south London, Notting Hill became one of the first major sites for Caribbean settlement during the 1950s, as well as for smaller numbers of Cypriot and Maltese immigrants.[76]

In marked contrast to Notting Hill's cultural exoticism, Notting Dale retained its defensive, proletarian character, and during the 1950s groups of local residents increasingly projected this defensiveness as racially homogeneous and white. Public displays of aggressive and flamboyant working-class territorialism from local Teddy Boy gangs, along with the political presence of Sir Oswald Mosley and his Fascist Union Movement, made this part of west London a flashpoint for tensions between local men and women who were encouraged to see themselves as 'white Englanders' and newer residents from the Caribbean.[77] According to the local press, who played a major role in orchestrating the growing atmosphere of racial tension in the area, 'the Dale' was a place 'of toughs and wide-boys and street corner gangs', of layabouts, and 'sordid everyday petty crime'.[78] Championing the concerns of 'respectable' whites, the *Kensington News* and *West London Times* ran together traditional anxieties about the metropolitan poor with reports about the problems posed by Caribbean settlers. The paper hinted that schemes for social integration were futile; however much local people might 'polish, rub and scrub', the only real solution was to move out, into one of the homes being offered to the more fortunate Kensington tenants in the new satellite towns proposed by the *County of London Plan* and now being built in places like Harlow and Crawley.[79]

Public anxieties about areas like north Kensington highlighted long-standing connections between social and moral decline and the urban environment. Reporting sixty years earlier in the 1880s and 1890s, social scientist Charles Booth and his team of metropolitan researchers mapped poverty in Notting Dale via an intellectual framework that was derived from his vast sociological survey of life and labour in London's inner ring. Booth identified 'the Dale's' degraded migrant population as the root cause of the district's social and economic instability; he called it a 'temporary halting place', composed of the 'very dregs of . . . central London' moving westwards like a 'foul stream'. Booth viewed the pauperized, transitory inhabitants of north Kensington as a sub-category of his collective entity of the metropolitan poor: the residuum or 'submerged tenth'.[80] But by the 1950s local social workers and council officials argued that the area's complex problems could no longer be understood via class-based models of social deprivation essentially based on patterns of unemployment. The presence of the Caribbean population, and the emergence of new urban characters such as unmarried mothers and local Teddy Boys, meant that north Kensington rapidly became identified as one of the capital's inner city problem locations. Echoing Sainsbury's account of postwar dislocation, one local social worker, Pearl Jephcott, dubbed the district a 'troubled area' that was marked by massive official indifference and large-scale neglect.[81]

In microcosm, number 10 Rillington Place epitomized many of these social and environmental problems. Like most of the other houses in the street, it showed all the outward signs of landlord negligence, with peeling paint and rotting stucco. It was let out not as flats but, in the desperate conditions of post-war overcrowding, as rooms. Living conditions in the house condensed social antagonisms that were becoming increasingly prevalent in London's inner city areas, as Caribbean immigrants began to compete with the local working-class population for scarce material resources.

One of the focal points for this competition was the economic and racial tension that marked the lower end of the rented housing market. Abercrombie's policies had been designed to curb London's seemingly inexorable population growth by dispersal, but the planners failed to anticipate that central London would remain a magnet for workers employed in the expanding service sector.[82] Competition from Caribbean settlers, many of them young single men, intensified an already deepening housing crisis during the mid-1950s. Discrimination was rife in the private sector, and most accommodation in London was filtered by a 'whites only' housing policy that was sanctioned by local councils. West Indians were also regularly charged higher rents, a practice that Glass described as the 'foreigners' levy'.[83] As a result, housing was the most significant factor in the volatile crucible of post-war race relations that erupted only five years later as the Notting Hill riots.[84]

Number 10 Rillington Place had long been occupied by poor but respectable whites, who included a retired railwayman and a young van driver and his family. In 1950 the house was bought by a West Indian landlord, Charles Brown, who began letting the accommodation to his fellow Jamaicans.[85] Contemporary studies of property purchases made by enterprising Caribbeans like Brown, which were typically slums bought at inflated prices, revealed how the new class of landlords were driven both by a desire for economic and social status and by the need to secure some degree of personal control over a housing situation in which 'blacks were the least secure players in an increasingly insecure rental market'.[86] Employed as a commissionaire at a south Kensington hotel, Brown was also something of a Caribbean man-about-town, who used his new accommodation to hold shebeens, the boisterous impromptu parties hosted by young West Indian men.[87] By the following year seven Jamaican men and women were living on the upper floors of his house, through a process of rooming or subletting.

Tension was greatest in inner city areas when an incoming West Indian landlord like Brown acquired white sitting tenants like those living at 10 Rillington Place.[88] Predictably, disputes were not just about rents and repairs but also about social attitudes and lifestyles. Brown's gregarious-ness within the local Jamaican community meant that his house became a cultural conflict zone between West Indians and the indigenous north Kensington residents who were long-time tenants. Many of the young Jamaican men who Brown moved into his house played loud calypso music and brought with them women who were clearly not their wives.[89] Reactions from local whites veered between grudging tolerance and latterly outright hostility, when formal complaints mixed with racial abuse about their Caribbean neighbours were lodged with the local council.[90]

On 24 March 1953 the rooms on the ground floor of number 10 were empty, after the previous tenant had left hurriedly a few days earlier. John Christie and his wife Ethel, who had lived there for fifteen years, were poor but they presented a public face of respectability, and they were white. A quiet, reserved Yorkshire couple, they cut a distinctive pose in the decaying area. Judged in terms of income and access to housing, the Christies' status was extremely precarious. Repeated bouts of ill health and criminal convictions for petty theft and assault had confined John Christie to a variety of low-grade clerical jobs. Despite their downward mobility, the couple maintained a superior social tone in the street. Working-class neighbours were impressed by Christie's quiet genteel voice, by his neat appearance and his mock club tie, and by an assumed air of authority (fig. 14).[91] A local furniture dealer in nearby Portobello Road described him as 'a marvellous bloke, sort of parsonical [sic], full of scientific knowledge . . . a very good mind, very refined and nice to talk to'.[92] Ethel Christie was equally 'quiet and reserved' and she too cultivated a discreet aura of superiority, telling neighbours that she had a relative 'who was a singer with the BBC'.[93] Most of the locals, especially the Jamaican tenants, believed that the couple 'didn't like coloured people'.[94]

One of the new tenants in the house was a Jamaican labourer, Beresford Brown. Brown was something of a handyman, and he asked his landlord's permission to do up the back room of the empty ground floor as a kitchen.[95] When he went downstairs on that March afternoon in 1953, he found a scene of dereliction and squalor. Overlooking the overgrown back garden full of weeds, newspapers and rubbish, the room contained only a filthy mattress and an ancient cast-iron kitchen range. Brown looked round for a place to fix a wireless set. Tapping one of the walls, it sounded hollow and he pulled away the wallpaper to find a hole in the lath and plaster about two inches across. Peering in with his torch, he could just make out the 'bare back of a human being'.[96] In a state of shock he ran out of the house and telephoned the police.

Brown's account, which he later delivered in court, enacted a significant feat of cultural ventriloquism. Privileged by the law as an embryonic 'good coloured citizen', the Jamaican immigrant rehearsed his
evidence as an extraneous commentator on the scene of urban poverty
that he found in the rooms below his home. He was aware that he had
stumbled across a scene of multiple murder, and he evoked the atmosphere through a series of powerful images: images of the all-pervasive
odour of decomposition, of a scene of violent domestic disorder, and of
death, personified as unidentified female detritus. In his witness statements
that were later taken down as part of the murder investigation, Brown
rehearsed his story across a sensory borderline between smell and vision
and through a spatial narrative that dramatized his discoveries as a journey
from the external world into a small claustrophobic space or lair. Alain
Corbin has identified this type of tight spatial metaphor as a device used
predominantly by official agencies to delineate and distantiate the homes
of the urban poor.[97] More unusually in Brown's testimony this language
was drawn on by a post-colonial migrant to describe an interior that was
suffocating, derelict and suffused with death.

Scotland Yard decided to excavate the whole of 10 Rillington Place; it
was literally taken to pieces, floor by floor and wall by wall. Chief
Inspector Percy Law, from the Yard's photographic department, was immediately called in to record the scene, which resembled a charnel house.
Working with well-established visual codes of criminal photography, Law
produced images that were used as part of the forensic evidence to map
the *mise en scène* of the crime.[98] They depicted a sequence of six corpses
– all of them women – encased, quite literally, in the decayed Victorian
fabric of the building or buried in the garden. The removal of the first
body exposed a second, wrapped in a filthy blanket, lying on its back (fig.
15). Behind body number two there was a third body, propped upright
and neatly stacked behind the others. Law then turned his forensic attention to the main areas of the house, photographing another corpse laid
out under the floorboards in the front room (fig. 16).

Two days after the discovery of the bodies in the house, the police dug
up the back garden, where they found a collection of bones marking a
shallow grave of two more women. Forensic tests of their remains showed
that all the corpses were, with one exception, young women in their
twenties or early thirties who had died either a few months previously
or long before, sometime in the 1940s. On the basis of detailed post-
mortems, Dr Francis Camps, the police pathologist and an expert in

forensic medicine, confirmed suspicions already circulating in the press and in the local community that the murders were 'sex crimes'.[99] Three of the women had been subjected to sexual intercourse, immediately before being killed by a lethal dose of carbon monoxide. Police records identified them as prostitutes who had worked the streets, pubs and lodging houses of north Kensington and the nearby Edgware Road.[100] After examining the vaginas of the dead women for the 'number and condition of . . . spermatozoa', Camps initially suspected necrophilia, though he later rejected this hypothesis.[101] His provisional conclusion was that the women had been the victims of 'systematic' murder 'with a sexual basis', while the remains under the floorboards were identified as those of Ethel Christie, the wife of the previous tenant.[102]

Police photography and forensic science released powerful negative images of the killings that were in excess of their official representation as scientific and legal evidence.[103] In the Rillington Place case, as in so many modern serial murders, the fact that all the corpses were female immediately endowed the homicides with an erotic charge; images of transgressive urban horror were evoked by the association of the women's bodies with decay and putrefaction.[104] 'The grim house has given up another secret yesterday', announced the *Daily Mail* in one of many front-page headlines, as journalists disclosed how three of the murdered women, one of them pregnant and wearing only a 'pink silk slip', had been found 'boarded up in a ground-floor scullery'.[105] The press was quick to point out that 10 Rillington Place had already gained a reputation as a 'chamber of horrors'.[106] In 1949 the bodies of Mrs Beryl Evans and her baby daughter Geraldine had been found lying together in the washhouse. They had been strangled and Timothy Evans, the husband and father, had been hanged for the murder of his daughter. The hunt was now on for the missing man who had left the ground floor rooms so suddenly – John Reginald Halliday Christie.

The Christie case was the macabre sensation of coronation year. Ruth Fuerst, Muriel Eady, Ethel Christie, Kathleen Maloney, Rita Nelson, Ina Maclennan, Beryl and Geraldine Evans – the names and mug shots of these murdered women were circulated continually by the police and the press throughout the spring and early summer of 1953. In the popular and middle-market dailies and in London's evening papers, editors and reporters ran Christie's trial and subsequent execution as a macabre counterpoint to the spectacle of the coronation. The *Evening Standard* covered the Rillington Place story as a front-page leader more than a dozen times between March and June, in the teeth of fierce competition from royal news.[107] Media interest in the case was so intense that it eclipsed coverage of the death of Queen Mary in late March, pushing reports of her funeral preparations off the front pages.[108] In May, the *Daily Express* showed pictures of London jammed with spectators watching the coronation rehearsals, side by side with the grisly police exhumation of the bodies of Mrs Evans and her daughter from Kensington Cemetery.[109] There were also regular reports of 'blood-thirsty' coronation tourists and 'bands of morbid souvenir hunters' who arrived in 'garish holiday motor coaches', queuing to peer through the Christies' letter box to get a glimpse of the chamber of horrors.[110] The juxtaposition of the sublime and the monstrous was a long-established media device for producing sensational news copy, but in the immediate context of the coronation this double imaging suggested that the stories of majesty and murder were somehow related and that they existed in adjacent spaces of the capital city.

Starkly contrasting visions of high and low London were generated at John Christie's murder trial and in the powerful cultural imagery that circulated throughout the case. Paralleling Duncan Webb's revelations about the moral condition of the West End that had surfaced only seven weeks before, the media organization of Christie's story played a major role in centring events on the capital's divided social topography of underworlds and overworlds, thereby shaping the social anxieties unleashed by the killings. The highly wrought cultural rituals of the courtroom drama were cross-fertilized with equally elaborate codes of publicity, to produce an expansive commentary on post-war London society and its instabilities. As in earlier notorious homicides, London was imagined as lying at the epicentre of murderous crime. The case was an international scoop, with leading reporters arriving from as far afield as New York and Sydney to cover the case. Albert Pierrepoint, the nation's public executioner who had hanged many Nazi war criminals, noted perceptively how serial killings like Christie's were reported to a readership 'greedy for details of death and the dealers of death', a public that had become immune to horrific scenes of violence by media coverage of world war and the horrors of the concentration camps.[111]

Overwhelmingly, print journalism shaped not just the transmission of information about the Christie case but also its overall gestalt. All the scandals that punctuated the post-war period were reported at a time when the national press was under commercial pressure to forge more aggressive reporting methods, and coverage of the Rillington Place murders reflected this search for new approaches to news transmission. Steeply rising costs, an urgent need to secure advertising revenue, and an intense battle for circulation at the middle and lower ends of the market were accelerating demands that editors should search out different ways of reaching their readers. The growing impact of television was also pushing reporters to write copy that was, in the words of Hugh Cudlipp, editorial director of the *Daily Mirror* and the *Sunday Pictorial,* 'alarmingly provocative' and 'sizzling and topical on every issue'.[112]

Fleet Street's perception was that television had thrown down a challenge to print journalism to revamp its language of communication. 'Television animates the scene while the printed word "freezes" it,' observed the editor of the *Daily Express,* Arthur Christiansen.[113] Sounding a wake-up call to his colleagues, Christiansen revealed how the new medium had taught him to 'always think in pictures'.[114] Even journalists working at the quality end of the market were forced to confront the fact that television's impact aroused readership demands for a more dynamic alignment between words and images, with significant implications for the production of narrative stimulation and excitement. The plain truth is, reflected Colin Coote, editor of the *Daily Telegraph,* 'vast numbers of people like to be titillated', and 'when something is *seen* as well as *heard* there is less tendency to look for it in print'.[115]

Fleet Street responded to these challenges by capitalizing on its traditional reporting strengths. The advantages of the press were particularly apparent in a classic murder case like Christie's, as they were in most of the subsequent sexual and political scandals. With their fast-moving stories and localized settings these accounts demanded continuous and on-the-spot coverage of a kind still beyond the scope of television, but ideally suited to the hour-on-hour editions circulated by the popular dailies and the London evening papers.[116] Equally important was the ability of the press to mix genres in order to appeal to multiple readerships. Treatment of the Rillington Place murders, like Webb's exposés of West End vice, blended the traditions of documentary journalism with melodrama and detective fiction to circulate a powerful version of tabloid morality. Reporters drew on this eclectic mixture of styles to address a wide range of urban problems during the 1950s. Homosexuality, prostitution, gangland feuds, as well as homicide were all influenced by this type of media treatment. Directly rebutting attacks on their exaggerated tone, the newspaper industry used the Christie case to mount an aggressive defence of the human interest story. Self-consciously evoking the moral authority of crusading journalist W. T. Stead, whose coverage of child prostitution had set new standards of sensationalist news in the 'Maiden Tribute' scandal of the 1880s, editors claimed that reporting of this kind was best able to move the Christie case from darkness to light which justice demanded. Only the press angle, with its unique blend of heightened realism, could amplify the details of a story 'without parallel in British criminal history'.[117]

Media interest in the murders drew together many of the subjects dominating public debate about the condition of central London that surfaced at the time of the coronation: issues about traditional forms of power and cultural authority exercised by the social elites, about the dubious glamour of the West End and its cosmopolitan characters, and about the racial and sexual pathologies that were generated in neglected inner city areas. In the Christie case these themes were also framed by discussions of history and geography: in particular, by arguments about the way many of the inhabitants and spaces of contemporary London were shadowed by the legacy of a Victorian past.

Christie's high-profile prosecution, along with the courtroom dramas that concluded the other post-war London scandals, contrasted sharply with developments in the public cultures of many other European cities during the immediate post-war years, when a sequence of politically motivated show trials dominated civil society. These latter episodes were overdetermined initially by the Allies need to bring some degree of legal and moral closure to the Nazis' wartime atrocities and subsequently by the increasingly polarized international politics of the Cold War period.[118] Between October 1945 and November 1946 the International Military Tribunal at Nuremberg tried and convicted the main figures of the Nazi leadership, while American, British and French military courts prosecuted lesser figures in their respective occupied zones and the incoming governments of liberated France and the Netherlands began to punish collaborators. Trials of this kind were as much about pedagogy as justice. In Germany they were understood as an essential part of the process of denazification, while their widespread international coverage served to legitimate the Allied victory. A different type of juridical process dominated in Eastern Europe, where national Communist regimes subjected their citizens to successive waves of arrests, purges and political show trials.

Partly modelled on the Moscow trials of the 1930s, these post-war prosecutions enacted a crude form of morality drama. Extolling the virtues
of the Soviet dictator Stalin and castigating his enemies and their crimes,
they orchestrated 'judicial murder as public theatre'.[119] Their parallels in
the West were the espionage cases running throughout the 1950s, including the set-piece prosecutions in the USA that were generated in the
politically charged atmosphere of McCarthyism.[120]

A number of the trials and public scandals that occurred in London
were also influenced by Cold War politics. Burgess's and Maclean's activities were essentially those of Soviet agents, Vassall's career as a spy combined espionage and homosexual blackmail, while the Profumo affair
involved immensely complex claims and counter-claims about the operation of the British and Soviet security services. Yet in their form as well
as their content, most of these domestic cases differed from the public
prosecutions in Europe. The episodes at home framed social and ethical
problems largely as questions of individual character and motivation, not
as issues of collective guilt and atonement. In contrast to events on the
Continent, these intensely personalized stories of transgression rarely generated clear-cut answers to the moral dilemmas they raised. A more characteristic feature of their unfolding was the way that they worked to
complicate or destabilize traditional moral beliefs and values. This was certainly true in the Christie case.

Christie was tried for the murder of his wife at the Old Bailey, London's
principal show courts, over four days in the middle of June 1953. Coming
midway through the social calendar of the season, and taking place within
weeks of the coronation, Christie's courtroom appearances were framed
by the press as popular entertainment and as part of the rituals of elite
society.[121] This dual focus was immediately apparent from the diverse social
character of the audiences who were drawn to the trial. Outside the
entrance to the court's public gallery in Newgate Street, overnight queues
formed fourteen hours before the opening day. Many who flocked to the
court were ordinary interested members of the public, including a high
proportion of women from the London suburbs. Society journalists
writing in *Queen* dismissed the crowds as insignificant: those 'very ordinary women' and men 'in pork pie hats' who always hang around English
murder trials.[122] Along with this familiar group of spectators, the media
also drew attention to the fact that prominent members of the audience
at the Old Bailey were celebrities, precisely that section of a national and
international elite who were already in London for the coronation.[123]

The gossip column of the *Evening News* observed that getting into the court was proving more difficult than gaining access to the Royal Enclosure at Ascot, disclosing that reserved seats, just above the well of the courtroom, had been set aside for 'forty specially invited guests of the City'.[124] Eminent foreign tourists wrote in to the court pleading for special passes.[125] Closer to home, Cecil Beaton came every day; so did the dedicated socialite and gregarious hostess Lady Lowson, wife of a former Lord Mayor of London, as well as the actress Margaret Leighton. American dramatist Terrence Rattigan and Fryniwyd Tennyson Jesse, the famous crime writer, both covered the case. Journalists disclosed how 'fashionable women' strained forward in their seats when psychiatrists entered the witness box to testify about the state of Christie's mind.[126] When Lady Lowson was asked on the last day of the trial if she had found the revelations horrifying, she insisted that from her standpoint the case provided edifying entertainment: 'because the location, the motion and the interest of it all was so absorbing that it took away all the horrors'.[127]

The society atmosphere was heightened by the fact that Number One Court, scene of some of the most famous prosecutions in English criminal history, with its particular atmosphere of intimate theatre, was specially reopened for Christie's trial, having been restored after wartime bombing. The prosecutions of Heath, Ellis, Ward and Keeler involved equally elaborate stagings at the Old Bailey. The court's reputation reinforced the status of these cases as significant national and international events, part of the orchestrated theatre of the criminal law as public spectacle. Post-war restoration work on the courtroom preserved intact the intricate arrangements of juridical and social power and forms of urban spectatorship that had their origins in much earlier periods of London's history. The vast entrance hall with its Renaissance dome and marbled walls and floor, massive statuary and echoing central corridors encapsulated the power of the English judicial process (fig. 17).

According to legal custom Mr Justice Finnemore, the presiding judge, left the high-backed centre chair on his bench vacant, reserving it for the City of London's most prominent dignitary, the Lord Mayor.[128] To Finnemore's left, the seats of the City Lands Committee, held for members of the bar and their distinguished visitors, were raised to a higher level than the counsel benches and directly confronted the jury. The octagonal-shaped dock, topped with glass panels in black wooden frames and capable of holding up to twenty prisoners, dwarfed individual defendants. Above them all, removed from the court on a different floor, were the thirty seats of the public gallery. The whole chamber was backed by a Palladian arch, with the royal arms of Edward VII above and a symbolic sword of justice pointing upwards in the centre. The American playwright and Anglophile Robert Sherwood marvelled at the 'dignity and majesty' of English justice, all superbly calm and businesslike, he reported, with an air of distinguished ceremonial about it, which was quite different from the histrionics of a courtroom in New York or Chicago.[129]

In a post-war world that proclaimed an era of mass democracy and extended citizenship rights, Christie's trial, like many of the other transgressive events, dramatized a much more hierarchical view of social life. Leading members of society made significant appearances in many of these cases, either as active participants, or as energetic spectators, or via the authority awarded to selected forms of gentry or aristocratic symbolism.[130] In contrast to the progressive versions of cultural and moral change that were orchestrated by consensus politicians and policymakers, these scandalous incidents dealt in traditional, caste-like images of English society. Why was this the case?

Part of the reason was the significant revival of interest in society figures and their social rituals that was fuelled by the media. But in most of the cases public enthusiasm for upper-class characters was not purely celebratory; the focus on elite London society highlighted the moral deficiencies of the upper class as much as on their positive social influence. Many of the scandals also pointed to explicit and disturbing connections between prominent patrician characters and London's underworld, via their shared sexual tastes or politically motivated actions. The idea of metropolitan people and settings moving in close and disturbing proximity resurfaced periodically throughout most of the episodes, especially in relation to the portrayal of sophisticated men-about-town. Guy Burgess's public and private career gained notoriety not only on account of his role as a Soviet spy, but also because his life criss-crossed elite institutions, such as the Foreign Office, the BBC and the salons of literary London, on the one hand, and the homosexual clubs and pick-up joints in nearby Soho and Piccadilly, on the other.[131] Lord Montagu's status as a prominent aristocrat was compromised on account of his sexual assignations with men from the lower ranks of the armed forces. John Profumo, the ambitious Conservative minister *par excellence*, with a family history rooted in the Italian nobility and on friendly terms with members of the English royal family, epitomized another version of this story of social and sexual transgression, via his links with call-girls, Caribbean pimps, and racketeers in Soho and Notting Hill.

The Christie episode also highlighted the contiguity of the divergent spaces of high and low London. In that sense the case was distinctively different from other notorious serial murders that took place in the capital during the immediate post-war years. The multiple homicides committed by Heath and Haigh attracted national publicity on a scale comparable to the coverage of the Rillington Place case, but neither killer had any links with the capital's low-life cultures. Heath was personified as a playboy with 'sadistic fixations', who moved between central London hotels and the holiday resorts of the south coast, while Haigh was typed as a 'psychopathic personality' whose habitus was the fashionable gentility of south Kensington and the Home Counties.[132] Christie in contrast was overwhelmingly depicted as the product of inner city decay, but through a narrative logic and a set of visual images that juxtaposed his world against the environments of elite London society.

It was through the representations of John Christie's own character and the territorially based nature of his crimes that the courtroom audience and a wider reading public encountered London as a city of polarized social milieus that were mutually related. For much of his trial Christie was represented as the archetypal 'little man', entirely fixed by custom and locality to a few north Kensington streets. Christie himself embellished this persona in his own carefully crafted newspaper story released to the Sunday press: 'I am a quiet humble man who hates rows or trouble. . . . I come from a solid, respectable old-fashioned type of Yorkshire family. . . . I am the sort of chap you would never look twice at in a bus.'[133] Observing him *de haut en bas* in the courtroom, Tennyson Jesse noticed how insignificant the defendant actually appeared in the flesh. With a life that was almost wholly circumscribed by his neighbourhood, Christie's story was a narrative of 'dustbin lids', of 'human bones used to prop up a fence', of 'squalor and quarrels' and 'ignoble personal relations'.[134] She also noted that Christie's personality was a horrific example of the banality of evil: the case of a very ordinary man made extraordinary by 'lust, unnatural and uncontrolled'.[135]

With her trained eye for courtroom history, Tennyson Jesse believed that the murderer's character most closely resembled that of an earlier beleaguered 'little man', Dr Crippen. Crippen's trial for killing his wife

Cora in 1910 had positioned the murderer as a subaltern anti-hero, the representative of a form of lower-middle-class masculinity that was becoming increasingly squeezed by the rapidly changing social and gender relations of Edwardian London.[136] John Christie represented a mid-twentieth-century reworking of the story of subaltern man, who was a combined product of urban decline, the precariousness of lower-middle-class existence, and the sexual and racial tensions in post-war London. Camps, the police pathologist, noted that Christie's trial exemplified a particular category of murder, where the motive and the criminal seemed securely established but where the murderer's identity became 'the central problem of the case'.[137]

Time and again as the evidence unfolded, Christie was depicted *in situ* as the product of the degraded cultures that existed close by Rillington Place: the cafés, street corner pubs and rooming houses of north Kensington where he picked up women. It was here that the jury also encountered many of the murderer's victims, pathologized by the prosecution and the defence lawyers as prostitutes and street people. These were precisely the inner city characters who planners and sociologists highlighted in their debates about London's problem zones. They inhabited a world where poverty and moral blight existed side by side with traditional wealth, and where isolated men and women like Christie and his young female victims were identified as the products of profound urban dislocation.

Yet as Christie's story unfolded in court, it became clear that there was a counterweight to these revelations of inner city horror. Telegrams and anonymous letters sent to the Metropolitan Police from astrologers and amateur sleuths announced that the murderer had *doppelgängers* all over London and across the world.[138] His speed of movement and his seeming ability to mesmerize his female victims before killing them was also redolent of Svengali-like evil. Now, Christie was transformed into a figure of metropolitan modernity, a character who could juggle time and compress space through disguise and masquerade.[139]

The killer and a number of his victims were also seen to move outside the confines of Notting Hill and into more glamorous locations in the West End. At this point Christie's itinerary shifted into areas of elite London, social environments that must have been recognizable to many of the celebrity audience at the trial. The 'bluebeard of Notting Hill' appeared to take on the characteristics of a man-about-town, a sophisticate who was well acquainted with the capital's up-market sexual economy.[140] Helen Sunderland, a prostitute whose patch was in Piccadilly, recalled that Christie was well known to the girls who worked the de luxe areas around Bond Street and Park Lane.[141] Another police informant living in Upper Berkeley Street, Mayfair, who described herself as a 'model', with all of its ambiguous sexual status, came forward with similar information about the murderer; she believed he was one of a number of rich male clients whom she had entertained in her 'studio'.[142]

Christie's excursions around the West End had taken him to more genteel venues as well; he had been spotted stalking female members of the concert audience at the Royal Albert Hall in south Kensington and lady shoppers in St James's.[143] The social itineraries of the murdered women extended well beyond north Kensington's street corners and low-grade brothels or 'knocking shops' and into central London's nightclub scene. Rita Nelson had been spotted many times at the Benelux Club, near Piccadilly, and at the Welbeck Club in Baker Street.[144] During the trial the prosecution barrister and Attorney General, Sir Lionel Heald, worked strenuously to isolate Notting Dale for the jury, portraying its inhabitants as part of a 'strange country', or an exotic district that was distant both from the quotidian city and from the world of elite London.[145] Christie's appearances in and around the West End blurred that distinction, suggesting that the demarcations between upper-class society and the capital's dangerous or troublesome spaces and characters were porous and not clearly boundaried.

One important effect of this coverage was to bring together the city's high and low cultures in a series of powerfully resonating visual oppositions that were part of wider pictorial techniques for representing the capital during the immediate post-war years. The north Kensington world of Christie and his victims was depicted in monochrome as a world of chiaroscuro tones of half-light and shadow, where human endeavour was drained of warmth, colour and vibrancy. The press photographs released as iconic representations of the murders were invariably establishing shots of the bleak frontage of the Christies' terraced house and the derelict back garden. They showed a city caught in the grip of austerity, where life was dominated by the sheer struggle for existence. Familiar from the media coverage of many other war-torn European metropoles, such imagery figured prominently in Roberto Rossellini's film of contemporary Berlin, *Germania Anno Zero* (1948), and in Carol Reed's depiction of devastated Vienna in *The Third Man* (1949).[146] Visual and literary representations of derelict London also featured regularly in crime thriller films and in

detective fiction during the immediate post-war years, when the capital
was imaged as a city of grey shadows, bomb sites and treacherous moral
quicksand.[147]

Coverage of the Rillington Place murders evoked a pictorial contrast
between monochrome images of London and the Technicolor magic of
a city alive with purposeful and ceremonial movement in preparation for
the coronation. For one moment in early June 1953 these worlds of
majesty and murder actually collided. In her post-coronation drive
through west London, the Queen passed close by the street in north
Kensington that had come to resemble a charnel house. Gaudily festooned
with flags and patriotic ribbon, the local press noted how the Queen's
smile and royal aura momentarily dispelled the horror of the murders.[148]

Along with many of the other post-war exposés and public scandals,
the Christie case oscillated between depictions of the capital as the setting
for traditional displays of wealth and power, on the one hand, and extreme
social deprivation, on the other. Almost entirely absent from this coverage was any acknowledgement of the world of post-war reconstruction:
as evidenced in Forshaw and Abercrombie's vision of the replanned city
with its optimistic commitment to improving the urban environment, in
the political discourse of mass democracy with its extended access to citizenship and welfare rights, or in the sphere of consumer culture with
the implied democratization of social relationships. The meanings generated by the Rillington Place killings were anchored in traditional hierarchies of place and power. As part of this process experts and the police
as well as the press drew on representations of the Victorian city in order
to render the Christie case meaningful. These were accretive versions of
the nineteenth-century past that were sufficiently flexible to include
images and environments from the Edwardian period as well. Such uses
of history were not simply residual; 'Victorianism' was understood to be
an active presence in the development of contemporary social and sexual
relationships. How was this connection between past and present articu-
lated and what were its consequences?

Much of the material environment for the murders was quintessentially
nineteenth century, with corpses buried in the decrepit Victorian house
and the narrow streets and terraces providing the dominant setting for
the action. Many witnesses in the case were also presented as nineteenth-
century urban types. There were the workers and local residents of
Notting Dale's street scene: pawnbrokers, second-hand furniture dealers,
seamstresses, and street women whom Christie had met with or accosted.
There were also charity workers, city missionaries and other public moral-

ists with their legacy of philanthropic reform. Christie's own murderous travels through the city at times resembled a bizarre progress of the late Victorian swell, with his assumed right to move freely across the metropolis. These characters and urban environments were endowed with social significance partly as a result of their connectedness to a nineteenth-century past.

In the months before the coronation there were a number of other events, natural disasters and human dramas which, along with the Rillington Place murders, were vivid reminders of how the legacy of the nineteenth-century city continued to shadow present-day London. In December 1952 a dense fog settled over the capital. Combined with industrial pollution and the freezing weather, it recalled the great Victorian smogs of 1873 and 1880, both in terms of its spiralling death rates and on account of the eerie atmosphere that enveloped the capital.[149] Visibility dropped to near zero as public transport and airline flights were halted, while recorded mortality in the metropolitan area during the first three weeks of December 1952 was between 3,500 and 4,000 higher than in other years.[150] Emergency services were wholly unprepared for the scale of the disaster, and scientists and statisticians began comparing fatalities with the major epidemics that had blighted London in the nineteenth century.[151] One correspondent complained to *The Times* that despite major advances in modern science, the city continued to endure the serious handicap of dense fog and smog, environmental conditions that were a throwback to an earlier era.[152] Like the Rillington Place murders, discussion of the fog focused public attention on Victorian inner city areas with their decaying industrial infrastructure that generated heavy atmospheric pollution.[153] Presented as both a natural disaster and a social drama, the London fog brought significant aspects of Victorian London into renewed visibility.

The fog evoked the nineteenth-century urban past as an overwhelmingly negative presence in contemporary London life. In March 1953 the process of national reflection about the meaning of Victorianism took a different turn when Queen Mary died at Marlborough House, only days before Christie was arrested. Even before her death Queen Mary had become a legendary figure. The Dowager Queen's studied formality and her elaborate dress and deportment still embodied the manners and public style of nineteenth-century royalty. Implacably opposed to what she perceived to be the modern weakness of 'selfishness', her strict code of personal morality had stiffened national resolve during the 1936 abdication crisis.

Queen Mary's death precipitated an outpouring of national reflection about the Victorian age and about the social distance that the country had travelled since the end of the nineteenth century. Churchill's radio broadcast celebrating her long life was an extended romantic reverie on Victorianism and modernity, commemorating 'the passing of this last great link with . . . Victoria's reign'.[154] Listeners were reminded that when Queen Mary was born the railways were still comparatively new, while electric light and the internal combustion engine were unknown. Observing the elaborate public ceremonial of her funeral, as the cortège wound its way down the Mall to Westminster Hall for the lying-in-state, Queen Mary's biographer James Pope-Hennessy, a member of Nicolson's and Lees-Milne's intensely traditionalist social circle, mourned the event as a unique occasion in which 'an essential part of London life' was passing away.[155]

Each of these incidents dealt in a version of the city where a nineteenth-century inheritance was used to define the contemporary nature of events and people in the present, and where Victorianism featured as an active presence in the development of the new. There were multiple and competing ideas about England as a post-Victorian society in circulation during the years after 1945. The overtly progressive version, championed by public intellectuals and politicians intent on using the state to modernize what they saw as outmoded nineteenth-century social policies, invariably drew attention to the distance between the world of the Victorian past and the present. Forshaw and Abercrombie's plans for reconstruction, for example, defined the nineteenth-century city as an obstacle to modernization, while sexual and moral reformers regularly contrasted 'repressive' Victorian morality with more enlightened present-day attitudes.[156] The burgeoning heritage and conservation movements emerging in London during the 1960s emphasized a more sentimental idea of nineteenth-century culture, with Victorian buildings and artefacts endowed with authentic significance.[157]

Victorianism as it appeared in the Rillington Place murders conveyed a different understanding of the relationship between the nineteenth century and the present. Lawyers, journalists and even Christie himself repeatedly drew on Victorian urban narratives and characters in order to explain why post-war London appeared the way it did. What they emphasized were the social and cultural continuities across the two periods as well as the differences between them; Victorianism explained the present and brought it into greater relief. The condition of inner city areas, the

motivations of the murderer and his victims, together with broader questions of public and private morality, were all referred back to nineteenth-
century systems of conduct in order to understand the contemporary
character of English society.

Sex and 'Colour'

Nowhere was this movement between past and present more evident than
in the gender specific treatment of dangerous or wayward sexuality that
became one of the central moral issues in the case. Coverage of John
Christie's mental state, along with speculation about the lifestyles of his
female victims, was part of an ongoing debate about pathological or
deviant urban characters that erupted in most of the other murders and
scandals as well. Competing paradigms of criminal or deviant behaviour
jostled for public attention, and these explanations were then selectively
enlarged by the popular media.

Neville Heath's trial in 1946 had introduced centre stage, almost for
the first time in an English murder case, the concept of sexual sadism,
twinning it with more traditional legal interpretations of moral degener-
acy and debauchery.[158] Haigh's career was covered both as a study in
repressive psychology and paranoia and as a latter-day Gothic horror story,
positioning the killer as a rapacious vampire who disposed of his victims
in vats of acid.[159] Ruth Ellis, who shot her feckless lover David Blakely
outside a Hampstead pub, was memorialized both as the victim of diminished responsibility (a new legal category that was written into the
Homicide Act of 1957 partly as a result of the public outcry over Ellis's
hanging) and as a glamorous blonde guilty of a classic *crime passionnel* executed in cold blood.[160] The dissection of Guy Burgess's character and
accounts of the activities of Stephen Ward, the playboy at the centre of
the Profumo scandal, coupled scientific and popular explanations of
homosexuality with much more traditional accounts of male libertinism.
While all these varied explanations focused on murderous, dangerous or
troublesome personalities, they also showed how normal and pathological conditions were intimately linked.[161]

Writing about London's most infamous sexual monster, Jack the
Ripper, Judith Walkowitz has demonstrated how the Whitechapel murders
of the late 1880s drew on a 'transitional language' in order to represent
sex crime. The characterization of the Ripper as a monster, Walkowitz has

argued, with its roots in the cultural codes of nineteenth-century melodrama, coexisted with an emergent scientific discourse that eventually
transformed the figure of the sex beast into that of the medicalized sexual
deviant.[162] Sixty years later the Rillington Place murders pointed to the
ongoing instability of the concepts used to define deviant and transgressive male sexuality.

Overwhelmingly, Christie's pathology was located in his mind: 'Is
Christie Sane?' and 'Three Doctors Argue the Vital Question', announced
the daily and evening papers partway through the trial.[163] This interpretative framework was partly set by Christie's own plea of insanity; analysis of the murderer's mental state triggered a series of expansive intellectual
exchanges between the various experts co-opted onto the case about the
mental capacities of sex offenders and the nature of their disorders.[164]
Older but nonetheless influential notions of mania, sadism and hysteria,
essentially derived from late nineteenth- and early twentieth-century sexology and clinical psychiatry, competed for attention with the claims of
modern psychology and psychoanalysis.

Echoing debates that had surfaced at Heath's trial, William Wells, the
barrister and Labour MP, believed that psychiatric definitions of sadism,
pioneered by the criminologist Sir Norwood East in the inter-war period,
most closely fitted Christie's aberrant behaviour.[165] Brixton Prison, under
its Principal Medical Officer, Dr John Matheson, had a growing reputation for the psychiatric treatment of offenders, and Christie was taken
there for a variety of diagnostic tests. Prison reports suggested that he was
not insane but suffered from 'acute anxiety hysteria . . . mostly centred on
sexual fears'.[166] Matheson concluded that at all times the killer's actions
were 'purposive' and that he was thus fit to stand trial.

Christie's defence team argued the medical point, trying to prove insanity or mental illness, a legal defence against criminal responsibility established under the McNaughton rules in 1843. Carted across London again,
this time to the Middlesex Hospital for a further round of tests, Christie
convinced the resident consultant physician, Jack Hobson, that he was
'one of the most severe hysterics that I have met with on my psychiatric
practice' and that his condition should be regarded as a 'disease of the
mind'.[167] Desmond Curran, Senior Psychiatrist at St George's Hospital,
was eventually brought in to adjudicate on the competing claims about
the murderer's mental state. Curran had an established reputation for the
treatment of homosexuality, and his own report on Christie was a mixture
of behaviourist psychology and clinical judgement spiced with Freud-

ianism, a combination that reflected the pluralistic understanding of many categories of sex offenders during the 1950s. Christie showed all the signs of an overdeveloped ego and a highly abnormal character, and Curran typed him as an 'inadequate psychopath with hysterical features'. Drawing on psychoanalysis, he argued that the root cause of the murderer's condition lay in his repressive childhood and family background.[168] The dissection of Christie's mind and character brought together a wide range of experts, all of them keen to promote their own medical or psychiatric subdisciplines and to enhance their professional authority.

Expert opinion, with its strong endorsement of medical knowledge in speaking about sex, collided with the popular media throughout the case. The daily and Sunday papers produced their own distinctive rendering of the drama of popular science, focusing on the wonders of medical technology and modern forensic methods. The *Sunday Empire News* reported that Christie was taken 'in conditions of complete secrecy' to the Maudsley Hospital, where he was subjected to 'electro-encephalogram tests'. Placed on a couch with 'his head covered with a complicated "hairnet" of solid silver leads', white-coated assistants prepared to operate the hospital's 'brain machine'.[169] This type of psuedo-scientific reporting positioned Christie as a quintessentially modern anti-hero, disaggregating him from any connection with earlier criminal types.

In a remarkable twist to the endless dissection of his character, Christie turned the process self-reflexive, adopting a popular language of psychology to promote himself and his story. A number of the men and women at the centre of the post-war *cause célèbre* cases demonstrated a similar talent for self-publicity, encouraged by the pressure on editors for sensational stories and by growing readership demands for intimate sexual secrets. Stephen Ward drafted fragments of his autobiography that were clearly intended for publication, shortly before his dramatic suicide at the height of the Profumo affair, while Keeler traded regular instalments of her confessions as the scandal unfolded.[170]

Christie proved to be particularly adept at courting media attention, assiduously comparing his treatment to that of other serial killers and even to the coverage of Hollywood celebrities. After his initial hearing at the magistrates' court he reputedly boasted: 'See what they are saying about me – look at the space I'm getting. No film star ever had such a show.'[171] Christie was also flattered to hear how his effigy was on public view in the waxworks, occupying centre stage at Blackpool's chamber of horrors. Across the Atlantic thousands of New Yorkers flocked to a Long Island slide show that featured the life and 'deeds of the multiple murderer'.[172] Emboldened by the publicity, he sold his story to the *Sunday Pictorial* from the condemned cell in order to achieve maximum impact, in what appeared to be an early macabre form of chequebook journalism. Smuggled out to reporters, his serialized autobiography was released only days before he was due to hang, prompting a Home Office investigation and questions in Parliament about the murderer's audacity.[173]

Christie chose to frame his life as a Freudian narrative of guilt, shame and psychosexual damage. It dealt in scripts of the unconscious, narrating 'the strange dark dreams . . . which haunted me for so many years'.[174] There were primal scenes, seduction theories and unresolved Oedipal conflicts. Christie told how he saw his grandfather laid out after death and experienced feelings of sexual fascination and pleasure. His first sexual encounter, with a girl on the 'monkey run', or lover's lane, in his hometown of Halifax, was a humiliation; since then he had been unable to experience the sexual act properly.[175]

Christie in his self-analysis, the expert witnesses who examined him in prison, and most of the commentators on the case were agreed on one significant point: this was the negative impact of Victorian morality. 'My parents were Victorians of the old school,' Christie explained 'I always lived in dread of my father. He was stern, strict and proud.'[176] George Haigh, whose parents were members of the religious sect the Plymouth Brethren, also recounted his upbringing as a struggle between the normal desires of childhood and his father's patriarchal regime: 'From my earliest years my recollection is of my father saying . . . "Thou shalt not". Any form of sport or light entertainment was frowned upon and regarded as not edifying. There was only condemnation and prohibition.'[177] Both murderers portrayed themselves as victims of a repressive sexual culture that demanded unattainable moral standards. The result was psychosexual damage, guilt, and sexual murder.

Christie's modernity was defined by his distance from and links to a nineteenth-century past. His career was seen to be tied to a Victorian legacy inasmuch as family, class and background all pointed to the ongoing impact of nineteenth-century beliefs and attitudes. Yet simultaneously the murderer was understood to be post-Victorian on account of the ideas that were used to explain his character. In that sense he embodied a hybrid form of masculinity that was compromised by its allegiances to competing models of social conduct.

A different transitional language of sexuality was used to understand the character and motivations of the young murdered women. The most significant difference between the pathological treatment of Christie and that of his victims was the identification of their respective sites of cultural and sexual disturbance. While Christie's behaviour was firmly located in his aberrant psychology, in the case of the women it was their bodies, handed over to the mortuary and the coroner, that were scrutinized for signs of sex and then read back to the unstable social environments that had produced them.

Christie's victims were not gynaecologically mutilated, as victims often are in classic cases of sex crime, but the bodies of the murdered women were read for what Jane Caputi has called 'fetishized', 'absolute sex'.[178] From the police standpoint their corpses testified not only to the monstrous nature of Christie's acts, but also in a number of instances to their own wayward sexuality. With the exception of Christie's wife, the women's bodies were represented as potentially suffused with sex. Camps, the police pathologist, examined the stomach contents of the dead women for what he termed signs of their 'erratic life'.[179] Accompanied by all the visible evidence of decomposition as they were exhumed, the corpses evoked powerful negative images of the female body as putrid, confirming the strongest associations between sex and death.

Local evidence about the activities of these women presented a more complex account of their relationship to the city. The character and career of Christie's first victim, Ruth Fuerst, a young Austrian woman from a small town near Vienna, was a case in point. Fuerst had come to London in 1939 as a student nurse aged seventeen in search of the bright lights. Demanding better pay and less intrusive moral supervision, she switched to munitions work during the early part of the war, living in a single furnished room only a few minutes walk from Rillington Place. The reputation of wartime munitions workers like Fuerst for 'low moral standards' posed a considerable headache for government and voluntary bodies during the 1940s.[180] Fuerst told Christie, whom she met in a Ladbroke Grove snack bar around this time, that 'she used to go out with American soldiers and one of them was responsible for a baby she had previously'.[181] Attractive and feisty, Fuerst was well known to local rescue workers and welfare agencies. She was precisely the type of 'wayward girl' turned 'amateur prostitute' whose profile loomed large in the files of London's reclamation societies and purity groups. Edith Willis, a family friend who stood as Fuerst's 'guarantor' when she first arrived in London, described her as 'very difficult to manage' because she was so 'keen on the company of men' and liked to go out on the town as often as possible.[182] Mrs Willis decided Fuerst was in need of reform and placed her with the House of

Mercy in Highgate. But Ruth ran away and shortly afterwards she was working in West End hotels. Gravitating to Soho, where she had a child with a local restaurateur, she also spent time in a home for unmarried mothers before her fateful meeting with Christie.

Fuerst was young and culturally mobile; her character was not abject, as the police suggested was the case with many of the murdered women. Her short adult life involved a number of sexual affairs that were part of a wider search for metropolitan excitement and a degree of feminine independence. Fuerst's biography did not fit the traditional definitions of prostitution, and her sexual exploits demonstrated how young unattached women developed their own assertive sexual personalities in London's workplace and entertainment cultures during the war. Official reactions to Fuerst's career epitomized what Sonya Rose has described as a con- tinuous and frequently shifting public discourse about appropriate norms of female conduct.[183] Young women at the centre of the other scandals crystallized similar anxieties on account of their sexual and cultural mobil- ity. Ruth Ellis was a West End nightclub hostess who also had a bit part in a British film. Christine Keeler, who worked as a 'photographer's model' and a Soho showgirl before achieving public notoriety, developed a confident sexual persona that evaded her categorization as a traditional prostitute.

The three known prostitutes in the Christie case, Kathleen Maloney, Rita Nelson and Ina Maclennan, were framed by a comprehensive lan- guage of social pathology that twinned long-standing concerns about active female sexuality with more recent fears about delinquency and mis- cegenation (figs 18–20). Nelson and Maloney had convictions for prosti- tution, disorderly behaviour and petty theft dating back to the 1940s. Classified as 'uncontrollable', a succession of juvenile courts had placed care and protection orders on Maloney, and she had been sent to a Catholic mission.[184] The cellarman at a pub on the Edgware Road had watched her with punters in the streets around Marble Arch, while police witnesses confirmed that she was known to associate with 'Lascars', sea- faring men, Irish navvies and 'men of all nationalities'.[185] The press depicted Maclennan as another 'bright lights girl' and also reported on her taste in foreign men. Playing up a sense of the sexually exotic, the *Daily Mail* informed readers that her real name was 'Mrs. Klim Mauny Soe Hla', as she had once married a Burmese airman.[186] Nelson's record of petty crime was similar to that of the other two girls, and the police portrayed her as a modern prostitute, a woman driven not by economic hardship but by her desire for sexual thrills. As the local station sergeant in Notting Hill put it, she was essentially a deviant 'with a kink for men'.[187]

The police and expert witnesses established interpretative authority over the murdered women, but friends and neighbours produced their own counter-truths about Christie's victims. Their accounts suggested a greater three-dimensionality to the women's characters, undercutting official reports that saw their lives as part of a world of undifferentiated horror. Maloney, McLennan and Nelson were members of a dense friendship network of prostitutes and other women that was cemented on the streets and in the reformatories and prisons. Maureen Riggs, known in the area as 'Edgware Road Jacky', worked the West End pubs with Kay Maloney. The two girls 'knocked around together all the time', and Riggs testified that 'we never separated if we could help it'.[188] Along with Maloney, Riggs posed nude for Christie, and she was mindful to warn her friend about him. Mariana Papajotou-Jarman was a local Greek dressmaker separated from her husband who used to meet up with Rita Nelson, going 'up West' to the nightclubs around Piccadilly Circus.[189] Nelson herself was a glamorous and vivacious blonde, an aspect of her personality that came across even in Scotland Yard's grotesque mug shot.

The treatment of London and its inhabitants during the Christie case suggested a compromised version of modern urban life, in which images and characters from the past coexisted alongside present-day social relationships. But one feature of the murders was much more resoundingly contemporary; race, or to use the contemporary lexicon 'colour', ran through the episode like a leitmotiv. The intrusion of London's Caribbean population and their cultures into a story that was in other respects profoundly influenced by traditional ideas of Englishness disrupted the social understanding of events. The racialized element differentiated the Christie killings from most of the other sensational twentieth-century English murders, such as the Crippen homicide, the Haigh and Heath incidents, or the Ruth Ellis case. It also distinguished the Rillington Place affair from many subsequent serial killings: the moors murders in the 1960s, the 'Yorkshire Ripper' in the 1980s and the Gloucester homicides committed by Fred and Rosemary West a decade later.[190] In both the earlier and later murders the killers and their victims were circumscribed by extremely localized, racially homogeneous settings, with attention focused on subtle distinctions of social class, on marital discord, or on oppressively close-knit neighbourhoods. While this was partly true of the Christie case, the Caribbean presence in north Kensington suggested an environment that was less fixed by the traditional markers of class and community and where Englishness was itself a problematic category. In that sense, the Rillington Place murders anticipated elements in the Profumo affair, where the presence of West Indian characters and cultures in nearby Notting Hill added a new dimension to the meaning of English scandal.

The racialized aspect of the Christie case was influenced by north Kensington's rapidly changing social and ethnic character. By 1953, the year Caribbean migration into London began to rise sharply, the boroughs of Kensington and Paddington contained the second highest proportion of New Commonwealth migrants, after Lambeth.[191] By the early 1950s, too, an emergent sociology and anthropology of race relations were beginning to give a distinctive intellectual gloss to the impact of postcolonial migration on British cities. Much of this work continued the debate about twilight zones that already characterized the treatment of areas like north Kensington. What was distinctive about the race relations agenda, however, was the way it produced more overtly racialized definitions of the urban environment, where districts, streets and even houses were marked by the problem of colour.

Emergent race relations viewed immigrants from the Caribbean, India and Pakistan predominantly through the lens of cultural rather than physiological or genetic difference.[192] Official and intellectual discourses on race up to and through the 1960s overwhelmingly privileged social and anthropological rather than biological understandings of race, where the difficulties of cultural assimilation were defined through a perceived opposition between the national host community and the 'out group' of the immigrant. Drawing again on the resources of Chicago School sociology, the anthropologist Kenneth Little observed in his study of Cardiff's docklands in 1947 that it was in the 'rooming house quarters' where the great metropolitan centres had their 'racial colonies'. Removed from the networks of family and neighbourhood organization that characterized traditional working-class areas, these were districts where 'community' was especially difficult to define because of the 'peculiar mobility of the modern city'.[193] In the London-based appendix to his research, Little noted with concern that the area westwards from Bayswater, centring on north Kensington, also had the highest percentage of 'aversions' among whites to accepting coloured people, a testament to the district's defensive ethnic character.[194]

Anthony Richmond's research on colour prejudice in Liverpool, based on material collected between 1941 and 1951, built on the work of his mentor Little to give a similar definition to this port city and long-time centre for inward migration to Britain. Citing Robert Park's definition of prejudice as 'an instinctive and spontaneous disposition to maintain social distance', Richmond warned of a potentially dangerous 'similarity with the American situation' in terms of the 'definite tendency for the coloured population to congregate in a particular part of the city', a phenomenon that provoked feelings of resentment and hostility among the indigenous population.[195] Researchers at the Centre for Urban Studies challenged Richmond's conclusions, arguing that 'images of Notting Hill and Brixton as the "Harlems" of London' were 'still far from reality'.[196] In areas like north Kensington, as well as in Stepney and in the south end of Liverpool, immigrant difference was defined as a problem of environment and setting. Glass's study of Notting Hill produced in the aftermath of the 1958 riots acknowledged: 'The . . . buildings tell whether they are the ones in which the migrants are concentrated. If you look at the condition of the streets, and their surroundings, you see an important aspect of the so-called "colour problem."'[197] For Glass, as for many other proponents of race relations research, such perceptions involved a spatialization of race, and it was overwhelmingly in play in the Christie case.

Christie's defence team drew on this professional knowledge in order to bolster his plea of insanity, as a condition that was exacerbated by growing cultural tensions in the inner city. But medical experts and lawyers, along with Christie himself, also raided more popular languages of contemporary racism that were being forged in frontline areas like north Kensington. Christie's trial played out a highly charged version of the phenomenon that Bill Schwarz has termed the re-racialization of the national culture and its white urban populations.[198] The post-colonial encounter in north Kensington, as in other cities, produced a vocabulary of white Englishness that was different from both the older languages of popular domestic imperialism and the newer sociologies of race. As Schwarz has noted, two interrelated sentiments cohered around these rituals of everyday life: the fantasized figure of the white man as victim and, commensurably, a conception of white womanhood as prey to the rapacious and uncontrolled appetites of black men.[199]

Christie's defence was that his insanity had been brought on by persecution from his Jamaican neighbours, and his lawyers ran through the gamut of post-war 'colour prejudice' to demonstrate the 'terrible pressures' which he had been living under. The murderer and his dead wife were positioned as little people, striving to maintain respectability and social standards in a district facing an alien culture. When Christie's new landlord began letting out the upper floors of 10 Rillington Place to his fellow Jamaicans, Christie's stream of letters to Kensington Council drew on powerful cloacal imagery to make direct connections between the degraded conditions of his own environment and the presence of the Caribbean tenants.[200]

Colour for John Christie was an odour, a noise, a sex, a proximity, a persecution, indeed anything that was 'other', and he drew on a moralized environmental language, with its origins in nineteenth-century public health fears, to come to terms with his neighbours. Damp, overcrowding and filthy sanitation were not simply blamed on 'these coloured people', the West Indian 'newcomers' and their urban conditions became metonymically linked.[201] Many of these associations drew on ideas of cultural difference that had first been identified by Victorian social explorers investigating the condition of the urban working class. In the 1950s long-standing discourses about 'darkest England' and 'darkest Africa' were fused together in public discussion about the country's 'coloured quarters'.[202] In one expansive courtroom exchange, Christie's defence lawyer insinuated to one of the new Jamaican tenants living at Rillington Place that the reason his client continually sprinkled the hallway with disinfectant was not because he was deliberating trying to hide the smell of the corpses, but because of the filthy habits of coloured tenants like himself![203] Much was made in court of one of Ethel Christie's letters, written to her sister in Yorkshire, in which she complained: 'It is awful with these "people" here,' comparing London's negative cosmopolitanism to the traditional, northern values of homeliness and neighbourliness.[204] Grounded in the dispossessed streets of decaying urban areas, stories like that of John and Ethel Christie became a catalyst for the new forms of popular racism that characterized the 1960s.

This vision of whiteness, a belief about 'living in a white man's country', was built on miscegenation fantasies of extraordinary virulence. Christie had clearly wanted to talk about race during and after his killing spree. 'I know the Notting Hill district very well,' he confided to Ena Baldwin, a secretary whom he had chatted up in a Lyons' tea-shop, 'it has changed a lot lately, a lot of coloured people, foreigners there.' Christie embellished his account by highlighting the predatory sexuality of black

17   Restored interior of the grand hall of the Central Criminal Courts, known as the Old Bailey, 8 September 1952, photographer Central Press/Stringer. Getty Images.

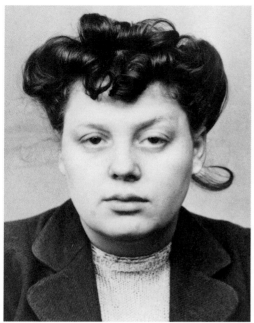

18 (*left*) Kathleen Maloney, undated, photographer unknown, in Criminal Cases: Christie, John Reginald Halliday (1949–1953), TNA PRO HO 291/228. The National Archives, reproduced by kind permission of the Metropolitan Police Authority.

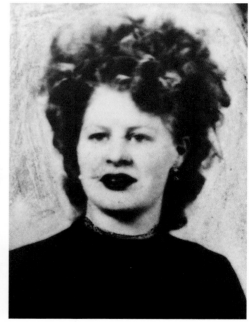

19 (*above*) Rita Nelson, undated, photographer unknown, in Criminal Cases: Christie, John Reginald Halliday (1949–1953), TNA PRO HO 291/228. The National Archives, reproduced by kind permission of the Metropolitan Police Authority.

20 (*left*) Hectorina (Ina) Maclennan, undated, photographer unknown, in Criminal Cases: Christie, John Reginald Halliday (1949–1953), TNA PRO HO 291/228. The National Archives, reproduced by kind permission of the Metropolitan Police Authority.

21 Remembrance Sunday in Whitehall showing the old Home Office, November 1957, photographer unknown, front cover, *Sphere*, 16 November 1957. © *Illustrated London News*/Mary Evans Picture Library.

22　John Wolfenden at work in his office, 3 February 1956, *Evening Standard* photographer/Stringer, Hulton Archive. Getty Images.

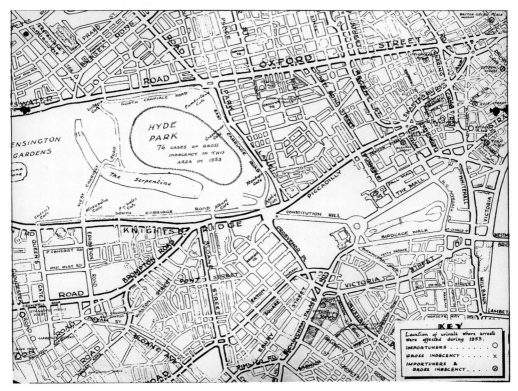

23 Location of urinals where arrests for importuning and gross indecency were made during 1953, Metropolitan Police map with hand-drawn key and annotations, in Memorandum by Sir John Nott-Bower, Commissioner of Police of the Metropolis, 22 November 1954, app. D, Committee on Homosexual Offences and Prostitution, Committee Papers (1954–1955), TNA PRO HO 345/7. The National Archives, reproduced by kind permission of the Metropolitan Police Authority.

24   Prostitutes in Macclesfield Street, Soho, 1 August 1953, photographer Fred Ramage/Stringer, Hulton Archive. Getty Images.

25   Girls from the Club de la Côte d'Azur, Carnival Parade Soho Fair, 14 July 1957, photographer unknown. Topham Picturepoint/TopFoto.

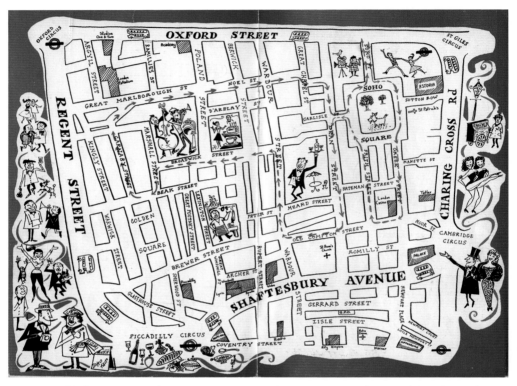

26   Map of Soho Fair carnival procession, 1958, in Soho Association, *Soho Annual* (London: Soho Association, 1958), pp. 49–50. Reproduced by kind permission of The Museum of Soho.

men. In doing so, he evoked the segregationalist politics of many of the southern states of the USA, highlighting the sexual dangers of interracial mixing: 'The blacks are hated in parts of America. . . . where there is a white family living, and if they have any young children, especially little girls, they have to watch the black boys. . . . Do the same to them as they do to Tom Cats.'[205] In court, Christie claimed he was 'terribly upset' when his landlord let the upstairs rooms to 'coloured people and to white girls'.[206] Local officials at Kensington Council added their own support-ive gloss to his story, insinuating that Christie's Jamaican landlord Beresford Brown was a brothel-keeper, citing as evidence the fact that his other property in Notting Hill 'was occupied by approximately a dozen coloured men and various white girls'.[207]

The Rillington Place murders and their associations with cosmopoli-tan London fuelled wider popular fears about the capital as a centre for interracial sex that surfaced in the run-up to the coronation. One father from Liverpool wrote to the police anxious to trace the whereabouts of his missing daughter, a girl with fair hair and blue eyes who, he confessed, was 'a sex maniac towards coloured people'. Her disappearance had led her father to think that she might have made 'her way to London with some black' and then fallen into Christie's hands.[208]

Sexual anxieties and fantasies about Notting Hill and Notting Dale were flashpoints for miscegenation fears that surfaced again and again during the 1950s and early 1960s. A catalyst to the 1958 riots, they were part of the defensive proletarianism of local Teddy Boy gangs, who enforced informal codes of social honour in local working-class commu-nities by policing white women when they crossed the sexual boundaries of 'the colour line' via their relationships with Caribbean men. During the Profumo affair interracial sex in the area became an issue for national politics, through disclosures about the sexual slumming of Keeler and Ward with Keeler's Caribbean boyfriends at local clubs and parties.

In the spring and summer of 1953 these miscegenation fears were given an international resonance as the Christie case unfolded. The Rillington Place murders occurred at the height of the Mau Mau raids in Kenya. The press was replete with stories about terrorist attacks on the farms of European settlers, with their inhabitants tortured, mutilated and then mas-sacred in an implied return to African savagery.[209] In March the first rein-forcement of British troops left London for Nairobi, and in April Jomo Kenyatta, leader of the Kenya African Union, was sentenced to seven years hard labour for his part in orchestrating the Mau Mau movement. Though almost all of the violence was directed at other African Kenyans, at home the obsession was with the threat to white women and children. Nuns and other female missionary workers were portrayed as under attack from forest gangs who, it was claimed, drank human blood and regularly engaged in shocking sexual orgies.[210] In London the colonial secretary, Oliver Lyttleton, stuck doggedly to the official line that Mau Mau was not a politically inspired, anti-colonial movement but was essentially an 'anti-European and anti-Christian' force that had committed the worst crimes 'you can imagine'.[211] The new Governor of Uganda, Sir Andrew Cohen, characterized the movement as wholly atavistic: 'a reversion to tribalism in a perverted and brutal form'.[212]

Coverage of Mau Mau involved a deep projection of home-grown fantasies about African culture and African masculinity, and its impact influenced domestic politics and culture. In the cinema these miscegenation fears were visible in a number of feature films of the 1950s, including *Simba* (1955), which showed African insurgents ransacking and burning the farms of white Kenyan settlers and butchering their occupants.[213] Fears about black nationalists slaughtering whites, with their subtext of interracial sexual violence, began to be transferred onto concerns about the growing presence of Caribbean settlers in London. Coverage of the disintegration of British colonialism and the situation in inner city areas like north Kensington produced fears about cultural and sexual disturbance that reshaped the boundaries between black and white. In microcosm, Christie's trial represented an early working through of these newly racialized urban fault lines

✳

John Christie was hanged for the murder of his wife at Pentonville Prison on 15 July 1953. Albert Pierrepoint, the executioner who dispatched so many notorious killers, remembered that blinking behind National Health spectacles as he approached the scaffold, Christie was 'no trouble'.[214] A crowd of about 200 people waited outside the gates, some pressing their ears up against the prison walls in the hope of hearing the trap-door slam open in the execution shed.[215] Despite this sense of narrative ending to the murder story, the Rillington Place affair offered no conclusion to the ethical and moral problems that it raised and to the city that had produced them.

It was not an isolated occurrence. Read in conjunction with the other metropolitan cases of scandal, treason and murder that punctuated London life during the post-war years, these episodes performed significant cultural work. They precipitated an atmosphere of crisis or turbulence that was brought about by infraction of the rules of morality, law or custom, and their development followed a characteristic pattern.[216] Beginning with a crime or scandal, they were enlarged by the press into events of national significance. What usually followed was an intense moral debate that typically remained unresolved at the close of each case. The overall effect of the various incidents was not so much a change in legislation or policy (though this sometimes followed indirectly) but a profound questioning of ethical and sexual values as a result of the activities of the main characters and the unravelling of their complicated plots.

The Byzantine way that these cases unfolded contrasted sharply with the more overtly progressive versions of post-war social and cultural change. Stories of dangerous or wayward sexuality, acted out in quasi-Victorian environments that juxtaposed metropolitan high society and its low underworlds, appeared on first reading to confirm a backward-looking agenda. Yet in almost every instance the impact of the episodes was to destabilize traditional moral certainties via characters and settings that drew heavily on the resources of the past. Many of these scandalous events highlighted the continuing force and adaptability of nineteenth-century cultural forms in a period that was increasingly characterized as post-Victorian, especially on issues of sex and morality.

The Rillington Place murders were one extreme manifestation of a much wider official preoccupation with dangerous or troublesome forms of sex in London that began with the build-up to the coronation and intensified throughout the 1950s. These metropolitan anxieties were centred on homosexuality and prostitution, becoming part of an expanding network of socio-technical surveillance that was energetically pursued by politicians and civil servants, as well as by a wide spectrum of intellectuals and experts. One important consequence of initiatives of this sort was that the Home Office, as the department of state responsible for the regulation of public morals, became a control centre for sexual management, driving forward proposals to regulate and reclassify normal and deviant conduct. But the plans were not driven by government alone; they were the outcome of confrontations between official discourse and London's varied sexual subcultures, encounters that exerted their own powerful influence on public policy and legislation. We now turn to these dual processes of control and sexual incitement, generated inside and outside the confines of Whitehall's bureaucracy.

Chapter 4   Governance

Whitehall

'I know that this is going to be a difficult and in many ways a distasteful operation; but in a queer sort of way I am rather looking forward to it.'[1] So wrote Jack Wolfenden with characteristic equanimity to his new committee secretary, W. Conwy Roberts, after his appointment to chair the new Home Office committee on sexual offences in August 1954. Wolfenden's brief was specific but double-sided: to consider the law and practice relating to 'homosexual offences' and 'offences . . . in connection with prostitution and solicitation for immoral purposes'.[2] Prostitution and homosexuality, two gendered forms of sexuality with extensive historical pedigrees, were yoked together in a departmental committee that was focused primarily on the operation of the criminal law.

Wolfenden's new committee was the Conservative government's response to the escalating anxieties about vice and public immorality in London. Ranging from the statistics of the Metropolitan Police and leading criminologists, through the sexual ethnographies of men-about-town and sensationalist news reporters, and crescendoing in the show trials of prominent public figures, all these various incidents identified homosexuality and prostitution as the focus of national disquiet. During the winter of 1953 Churchill's Cabinet debated both issues repeatedly, largely as a result of pressure from the Home Secretary, Maxwell Fyfe.[3] Competing for ministers' attention alongside urgent international business on the situation in the Suez Canal, the hydrogen bomb and the convertibility of sterling, such extended discussion by senior political figures was exceptional. It testified to the seriousness given to sexual offences in current government business and to the way these policy discussions sat uneasily with conventional ideas about the remit of national politics.

In the overwhelmingly masculine culture of Westminster and Whitehall, intervention on sexual matters was seen as a classic issue of conscience, not governed by formal party allegiances and best devolved to religious leaders and secular experts, or consigned to the extra-political sphere of private life. Rab Butler, one of the most significant reforming home secretaries of the post-war period, believed that morality was a minefield for politicians, while Harold Macmillan always felt it was best left to the 'archbishops'.[4] Churchill was particularly reluctant to encourage any fresh government intervention on either homosexuality or prostitution. From an older political generation, and carrying memories of the fiasco over the Contagious Diseases Acts, the last great attempt by the state to regulate prostitution, which ended in government defeat at the hands of a broad coalition of feminists and radical liberals, he held to a laissez-faire approach.[5] But the Home Secretary was insistent. Maxwell Fyfe was a traditional moralist, but he was also a modernizing Tory. A firm believer in law and order and a strong supporter of capital punishment, his lawyer's instincts made him acutely aware that the current system of criminal law regulation had broken down.[6] He was also concerned about what he referred to as 'a considerable body' of liberal opinion that regarded the existing law on homosexuality as 'out of harmony with modern knowledge and ideas', making it imperative that the government should be seen to act.[7] The Home Secretary initially proposed setting up the full apparatus of a royal commission, but Churchill and other Cabinet colleagues opposed the idea, with its connotations of a nationally prominent, semi-autonomous public body. A Home Office departmental committee, supposedly more amenable to control by ministers and civil servants and hopefully less politically visible, was the Cabinet's compromise solution.[8]

The significance of the Wolfenden committee, as it invariably became known, rested on more than the controversial nature of its subject-matter. The inquiry's historical importance has been durable because its proposals on homosexuality and prostitution formulated a new approach to the regulation of sexual and moral behaviour. The committee's best-selling report, published in 1957, laid out an ethic of privatized morality, marking a clear separation between the public domain of legal intervention on sexual matters and the sphere of individual consent, all of which had very different implications for men and women. As the report famously defined these general principles in the opening chapter:

> the function of the criminal law so far as it concerns the subject of
> this enquiry [is] . . . to preserve public order and decency, to protect

the citizen from what is offensive and injurious, and to provide suffi-
cient safeguards against exploitation and corruption of others. . . . It
is not, in our view, the function of the law to intervene in the
private lives of citizens, or to seek to enforce any particular pattern of
behaviour.[9]

This deep-seated moral pragmatism, which Wolfenden later defined as
the necessary disassociation of the 'morality of actions' from 'legality',
combined with the studious avoidance of any explicit religious framework for discussing sex, made the report a minor *succès de scandale*.[10] So
influential were the principles of public regulation and private consent
introduced by Wolfenden and his team that they profoundly influenced
the raft of so-called permissive legislation passed by successive
Conservative and Labour governments in the decade from the late 1950s.
A series of statutes reformed various aspects of sexual and cultural behaviour from obscenity, theatre censorship and pornography to divorce, abortion, incest, suicide and gambling.[11]

Subsequent commentators, often with a brief derived from gay and
feminist sexual politics that emerged out of the social movements of the
1960s, have revised their assessment of the Wolfenden committee's liberalism. They have concentrated on the report's extremely limited conception of reform, both in relation to homosexual men and more especially
in its approach to prostitution which, with its exclusive focus on the punishment of street women and a corresponding lack of interest in their
male clients, updated a contemporary version of the double standard on
female sexuality.[12] Despite these criticisms, there is widespread agreement
that the Wolfenden committee remains an important starting point for
any exploration of post-war morality, not because it was the cause of
everything that followed, but because, as Stuart Hall has noted, it initiated a process and identified a tendency that had a lasting impact.[13] The
role of national policy and legislation, backed by a cross-party alliance of
politicians and the authority of expert opinion, has been seen as pivotal
to the reformist moral project of the post-war years. In contrast to the
spate of scandals and transgressive episodes that punctuated the 1950s, historians have seen the Wolfenden committee as a modernizing intervention by national government, an important precursor to the liberal
reforms that continued until the end of the 1960s.

These are important issues that I intend to address as well, but there is
another line of inquiry surprisingly ignored by previous commentators:
the specific social and moral geography within which the committee's

deliberations were set. Though it was framed as a national project, Wolfenden's investigation was not about the condition of the country as a whole but about London. It was quintessentially a metropolitan account of sexual behaviour which was then transposed onto a much broader canvass in order to shape recommendations for future legislation. The inquiry's work was a dramatic example of localized policy making, where close observation of the central areas of the capital city influenced proposals for important changes to the criminal law and a wide-ranging debate about normal and deviant sexual conduct. Charting the impact of these micro-environments on national government and state bureaucracy shows how the committee's ideas about public and private morality were grounded in specific settings that were overwhelmingly located in London's West End.

The work of the committee was not just metropolitan-centred, it was also complexly dialectical. Onstage, in their policy discussions, and offstage in their informal conversations and sometimes also in their own personal life, committee members not only assembled a dossier of official information about sex in the city, they also produced more idiosyncratic forms of knowledge and emotive experience at the margins of their official work. Wolfenden's team, along with many of their witnesses, cemented a mutually reinforcing relationship between surveillance, sexual incitement and sexual secrets. Official discourse was caught in collision with individuals and social environments that were in some cases quite literally adjacent to the corridors of Whitehall. These were the homosexual men, street women, call-girls and pimps who had been conscientiously tracked by the police and eroticized by leading journalists. Often the encounters between the committee's public intellectuals and the world of West End sexuality were traumatic and intense. The men and women who sat on the Wolfenden inquiry were frequently drawn into imaginative engagements with the capital's *demi-monde*; despite their best efforts there was no clear separation between the official and the illicit elements of their work. This complex symbiosis, linking the world of Establishment London to its supposedly distant sexual 'other', showed how leading members of the political and intellectual elite dramatized cultural difference as their own antithesis.[14] The working out of these anxieties in the life of the inquiry revealed how transgressive sexuality became symbolically central to public culture during the immediate post-war years.

As the committee's secretary, Roberts believed that the 'meat' of the inquiry's work was to be found in the transcripts of the hearings, and the existence of these papers, documenting members' and witnesses' very full conversations, along with their confidential minutes and memoranda, presents the historian with a challenge and an opportunity.[15] The multilayered texture of this archive, crossing from the top of the government hierarchy through to London's criminal underworld, enables it to be presented stereophonically, as the product of multiple voices competing to define sexuality in the post-war period. Such a detailed record also makes it possible to read the material not simply as documentary evidence but as revealing the tensions and contradictions that marked official discourse. Significant questions about the investigative methods and the personal obsessions that shaped the committee's work, along with their gendered vocabularies for discussing sex and their competing ideas about sexual behaviour, can be brought into focus via an interpretation that highlights culture as an active ingredient in the making of policy.

The task of chairing the committee was Jack Wolfenden's first major government commission, and he was keen to prove his intellectual and administrative credentials in a post-war world where the state mattered more and more.[16] Wolfenden was forty-eight at the time of his appointment and intensely ambitious, the product of a lower-middle-class background rooted in Methodism which, as he later remarked with pride, was dedicated to 'social mobility' and getting on in the world.[17] His profile was typical of the very first generation of talented grammar school boys, born in the late Victorian and Edwardian period, who were moving into political and administrative positions of authority during the immediate post-war years, and in doing so were beginning to counter the hegemony of the public school network that dominated Whitehall.[18]

But Wolfenden worried that his new appointment might prove to be a poisoned chalice, attracting negative publicity that might 'rub off harmfully' and outweigh the potential gains to be had from a successful outcome.[19] He was also anxious about a personal matter that threatened to intrude into his professional life; his brilliant elder son Jeremy, dubbed by contemporaries as 'the cleverest boy in England' and about to become an Oxford undergraduate, was 'precociously and openly homosexual'.[20] There is no direct evidence documenting Jack Wolfenden's attitude towards Jeremy's sexuality, only rumour and traces of anxiety amidst an overwhelming public silence. Wolfenden supposedly confronted Jeremy about the potential damage that his son's behaviour might inflict on his own career, demanding as a minimum that Jeremy stay out of his way and 'wear rather less make-up' than usual if he accepted the Home Office job![21] His parental concern also emerged periodically in the committee's discussions; he worried about giving sex education to his children, arguing that 'the real problem for young people is the emotional problem', and warned against simply giving them 'the facts'.[22] Whether the chairman's family secret influenced his approach to public policy is difficult to establish. What is clear is that Wolfenden hesitated before taking on this government brief. He talked over the various official aspects of his appointment (though not his personal difficulties) a great deal with senior colleagues at Reading University, where he was the Vice-Chancellor, and especially with his mentor and patron, Lord Templewood, who as Sir Samuel Hoare had been Conservative Home Secretary during the 1930s. It was Templewood who persuaded Wolfenden where his 'duty lay'.[23]

The chairman's first encounter with his fellow committee men and women took place on the afternoon of 15 September in the old Home Office, halfway down Whitehall (fig. 21). They met in one of the main committee rooms, overlooking the inner courtyard of the great Victorian quadrangle of government buildings which had been designed in 'modern Italianate style' by Sir George Gilbert Scott in the 1870s. Framing the Home Office facade at the front of the building, Scott's imposing granite columns and elaborate friezes depicted the quarters of the globe, topped by a sculptured group of Britannia supported by a lion and a unicorn, symbolizing the imperial reach of the Victorian state.[24] A nineteenth-century legacy also lay heavy on the informal culture of the department. 'Club-like' would describe it best, reflected one insider, noting that the general feeling of calm and quiet, along with the overwhelmingly masculine ambience, most closely resembled the male preserve of a gentleman's club.[25] Post-war politicians were acutely aware that this Victorian environment, with its weight of tradition, seemed to epitomize the compromised status of government institutions during the post-war years, especially after the demise of empire. Macmillan reflected wearily that though Whitehall was still the 'centre and source of power' and the 'pivot of all political action', its dilapidated condition and antiquated atmosphere made it feel more like a 'mausoleum'.[26] Members of the Wolfenden inquiry conducted their business in an environment that contrasted sharply with their intellectual outlook; they produced quintessentially post-Victorian proposals for reforming sexual conduct in an official setting that epitomized the faded grandeur of the nineteenth-century state.

Institutionally, the Home Office was one of the great departments of government, occupying the politically charged ground between public order and personal liberty. Remaining partly aloof from the rest of Whitehall, it was and still is regarded as quicksand for ambitious politicians.[27] In the early 1950s the department had developed a reputation for secrecy and for the enforcement of strict administrative hierarchies, presided over by the powerful figure of the Permanent Secretary, Sir Frank Newsam. Identified by the press as one of Whitehall's 'Men of Power', Newsam was a classically trained generalist whom the *Daily Mail* heralded as a mandarin with a 'self-confident determination to have his own way'.[28] He also epitomized the confidence and urbanity of the cultured and sophisticated senior civil servant; a man-about-town and a 'womanizer' in his private life, he carried himself 'as one to whom the good things in life came naturally', acting with 'splendid bravura and getting away with it'.[29]

Newsam's forceful and decidedly uncollegiate leadership style meant that independent thinking was rarely encouraged among his subordinates.[30] After 1945 the Home Office, like the nation, experienced the conflicting desires for 'all change' and 'back to normal', observed one of the department's historians.[31] Newsam's management style was dedicated largely towards preserving the institutional status quo.[32] His laissez-faire instincts, coupled with an authoritarian streak, had contradictory implications for the Wolfenden inquiry. With the Permanent Secretary's tacit approval and in the absence of any internal departmental initiatives, the committee developed into an ad hoc centre for the coordination and development of sexual and moral policy. Wolfenden and his team embarked on a massive information gathering exercise, listening to witnesses and exchanging sexual knowledge that went far beyond their original brief to focus on the operation of the criminal law.

Newsam's support for this ambitious venture came at a price; he wanted speedy results that were framed as clear policy recommendations, especially on the pressing problem of prostitution in London. When the committee began to prevaricate with what Newsam believed were over-lengthy discussions, he applied repeated pressure.[33] His civil servant's bias in favour of professional opinion meant that he encouraged the inquiry to prioritize the evidence of particular types of expert witnesses, at the expense of campaigning organizations and activists who were perceived as a threat to the Home Office because they questioned professional hierarchies and implicitly challenged government control.

'Vice, sir? Room 101', Wolfenden remembered the doorkeeper quipping to each of the committee members in turn as they came in to take up their appointments that mid-September afternoon.[34] Introducing their work with an agenda-setting welcoming speech, the chairman's tone was a carefully crafted mixture of Yorkshire plain speaking (Wolfenden took pride in his northern origins) and mild pomposity, which he used as an effective tactic in the face of problematic witnesses or contentious issues over the next three years. Theirs was a 'distinguished gathering', but the task ahead was difficult and a 'heavy responsibility' lay on all of them.[35]

Wolfenden's letter of appointment gave his committee a superficial coherence in terms of its legal remit, but there were glaring anomalies about the way homosexuality and prostitution had been conflated.[36] While all sexual acts between men were illegal, the result of legislation introduced from the 1880s onwards that had expanded earlier laws prohibiting buggery, prostitution as such was not an offence. It was public soliciting that was punishable (along with brothel-keeping, living on the earnings of prostitution and procuration) under a variety of different statutes and various local by-laws concerned with public order and vagrancy.[37] Almost immediately they started their official business, Wolfenden and his committee began to regret that they had been forced to confront 'two quite different' sets of sexual problems that had been run together as part of the same government remit, largely as a result of political expediency.[38] It was almost certain that whatever they recommended would be opposed by a 'large section of the public', Wolfenden concluded. Colleagues should take courage and follow their consciences; he hoped to chair the business with as little formality as possible compatible with 'proper efficiency'.[39]

Along with these preliminaries, Wolfenden also got quick resolution on two much more contentious issues. First, the committee would meet 'in private' rather than holding public hearings, ensuring that members and witnesses could 'talk freely', away from the glare of sensational media coverage.[40] Second, they would begin their business by hearing from the experts, going 'straight to the top' by inviting government witnesses and other key professionals to present their evidence early. Under Newsam's paternalistic guidance, the Home Office had already tabled a list of the obvious suspects, ranging from representatives of the British Medical

Association, the police and the Bar Council through to the churches and the various learned societies.[41] Displaying his own Whiggish commitment to top-down ways of working and echoing the views of his superiors, secretary Roberts encouraged members to avoid what he dismissed as 'the lunatic fringe', with whom 'it would be quite pointless' to engage.[42] This was not simply a reference to the whacky individuals and oddballs who were already petitioning the committee; it was, as Helen Self has argued, an early attempt to tightly circumscribe the range of witnesses, with the aim of endorsing only those experts who had won the approval of the Home Office Establishment.[43]

Outside the department, political tactics of this sort were hotly contested, especially by a loose alliance of purity associations and women's groups who had long claimed a special place in the social policing of the capital. The skirmishes that broke out almost immediately between Wolfenden and his team of civil servants and politicians, on the one hand, and the organizations that Roberts dismissed as the 'lunatic fringe', on the other, were not just a result of the chairman's *in camera* decision; they also highlighted clear differences about gendered competence, access to sexual knowledge and attitudes towards the state.

Wolfenden's postbag was deluged with letters of complaint from vigilance societies, the Methodist churches, feminist organizations and opinionated members of the House of Lords. Arguing that the Royal Commission on Venereal Diseases (1913–16) and the work of the Street Offences Committee (1927–8) held open sessions, they insisted that closed hearings would weaken the new committee's public accountability and prevent the publication of valuable evidence for future use by campaigning organizations.[44] One London women's group, Teddington and the Hamptons Women Citizens' Association, went much further, protesting that 'secret enquiries' could lead to the setting up of a morals police, or *police des moeurs*. Common in many European countries, such a system guaranteed a regular supply of prostitutes for male clients in tolerated districts, but the association warned that it was wholly 'alien to [the] British tradition' of individual freedom and women's rights and hence 'abhorrent to the British people'.[45]

Protests of this kind revived the tactics and the language of the nineteenth- and early twentieth-century crusades against the sexual double standard; indeed, some of the figures who led the objections to Wolfenden's *in camera* ruling had cut their teeth in the campaigns over sexuality that emerged as part of the first wave of feminism in the years before the First World War. They carried with them the legacy of two competing strands of Victorian social reform: the anti-statist tradition of individual and personal rights and a much more coercive emphasis on the use of the criminal law to improve and educate public morals and to safe-guard women and children.[46]

Most of these activists suspected that Wolfenden's decision to go into closed session was a government stitch-up, deliberately designed to exclude them from decision-making. They were right! In the spring of 1954 a combined deputation from the feminist-led Association for Moral and Social Hygiene (AMSH) and the National Council of Women, rep-resenting twenty-six affiliated societies, confronted Home Office minis-ters with their own proposals to replace the existing solicitation laws with a new public order offence that was not weighted against women.[47] The deputation had been politely received by Sir Hugh Lucas-Tooth, Maxwell Fyfe's deputy, but campaigners came away from the meeting with the dis-tinct impression that their views were not part of Home Office think-ing. The coalition's efforts to get at least one of their members co-opted onto Wolfenden's new committee proved equally unsuccessful.[48] They responded with a full-blown campaign, culminating in a 'conference'-cum-protest rally held at Westminster's Caxton Hall. Here delegates warned Wolfenden against his decision to proceed in secret, and stressed that though the Metropolitan Police deserved support for their efforts to improve public order on London's streets, police activities should not threaten 'female liberty'.[49]

Jack Wolfenden's response to these political tactics was decisive. He issued a courteous standard letter to the protesters (though he was careful to massage the egos of their upper-class and aristocratic leaders with more hand-crafted replies), affirming his chairman's right to decide on the most effective methods to use in his own committee. In his opinion, the proper time for the expression of differing points of view was after the publica-tion of the inquiry's final report.[50] In private, Wolfenden was much more dismissive. 'The more I read this . . . tendentious bilge,' he fumed against the evidence from women's groups, 'the more ridiculous it seems to me to be.'[51] Drawing on his favourite public persona, that of the 'ordinary plain citizen' who was sturdily armed with the resources of common sense, he castigated Nonconformist church leaders as 'a nuisance' and fem-inists as partisan campaigners who were driven only by petty self-interest.[52] Claiming that he 'found the intensity of the women's organizations difficult to understand', both he and Roberts moved quickly to caricature them as 'stale' and out of date, obsessed with old-fashioned arguments about prostitution that had little relevance to the modern world.[53]

This early series of hostile exchanges was symptomatic of what was to come; they heralded the marginalization of purity and feminist campaigners from the operation of the inquiry, in ways that reflected the overall weakening of these traditions of sexual politics during the 1950s. Inside the Home Office their defeat was the result of Wolfenden's own deft political manoeuvring, supported by Newsam and Maxwell Fyfe, which was based on his express desire to steer his committee away from 'controversy', a position that he identified with the women's groups. The weakening of organized feminism after the Second World War, combined with the successful challenge posed by a post-war generation of state-orientated professionals to what they saw as the 'amateurish' and 'unscientific' character of the purity associations, also contributed to the overall decline of public morality crusading.[54] The Wolfenden inquiry privileged the expert witness over the moral campaigner with all the gendered consequences that this decision involved. The way lay open for the inquiry to hear witnesses in an atmosphere of confidentiality that was supposedly free from the intrusive noises of protest and dissension.

The fifteen committee members who had been selected by the Home Office, possibly in consultation with Churchill himself, epitomized a distinctive type of public intellectual long favoured by governments since the expansion of the modern state in the early nineteenth century.[55] Almost every member represented a specific branch of knowledge, but their professional outlook was invariably tempered by practical administrative or political experience and in many cases by both. Wolfenden's own public profile was characteristic; ostentatiously declaring himself to be 'scientifically illiterate', he was the product of an Oxford and Princeton University education in classics and classical philosophy.[56] Rejecting an academic career, Wolfenden achieved 'lightning promotion' as a public school headmaster, first at Uppingham and then at Shrewsbury School, before taking up the Vice-Chancellorship at Reading in 1950.[57]

Jack Wolfenden has received a lukewarm press from many of his contemporaries and from subsequent commentators. A prominent figure in post-war educational and cultural politics who was knighted in 1956 for his work chairing the committee, he has been criticized variously as a political opportunist, a 'self-satisfied social climber', and a faceless and impassive administrator who hid his personal feelings behind the studiedly impassive mask of his public persona.[58] A portrait photograph taken of him at his desk in 1956, bespectacled, pipe-smoking and balding, confidently leafing through his neatly arranged papers, seems to confirm this caricature (fig. 22). But critical assessments of Wolfenden have tended to oversimplify his character, portraying him as a monolithic study in masculine bureaucracy and neglecting the tensions that marked his own personality, especially the anxieties generated by his own meritocratic drive for success and his son's wayward sexuality. Equally, they have downplayed Wolfenden's enthusiastic support for homosexual law reform inside Whitehall and beyond. These commitments were underwritten by his astute political instincts, especially his 'well-honed skills' in dealing with sensitive administrative issues and his undoubted talents as an intellectual generalist, qualities that helped to frame an important part of the practical philosophy of post-war moral liberalism.[59]

Wolfenden's colleagues on the committee included an Anglican theologian and Oxford professor (Canon Vigo Demant), a minister of the Church of Scotland (Rev. R. V. F. Scott), a secular Jew who was also a barrister and a London local councillor (Victor Mishcon), three doctors (Desmond Curran, Lady Lily Stopford and Joseph Whitby), a scientist-cum-modernizing Conservative politician (Sir Hugh Linstead), a Fabian Labour MP and barrister who had intervened in Christie's trial (William Wells), a Conservative Catholic peer (the Marquess of Lothian) and three academics (Goronwy Rees, Principal of the University College of Wales, Demant and Wolfenden). There were twelve men and three women (Mary Cohen, Vice-President of the Scottish Association of Mixed Clubs and Girls Clubs, Kathleen Lovibond, a JP, and Stopford), a ratio that was considered progressive by the standards of post-war policy and administration.[60]

All these figures were marked by a strong commitment to public service, and with a single notable exception, the Scottish lawyer and church elder James Adair, they were mildly liberal on questions of morality and public affairs.[61] All of them viewed social problems from a collectivist and an individualist standpoint, a dual perspective which they agreed needed updating from its ameliorist, nineteenth-century origins in order to meet the demands of the twentieth-century 'Welfare Society'.[62] Intellectually, they were decidedly not polemicists or controversialists; the majority of committee members set great store by empirical methods of deductive proof and public policy reasoning, with the result that they tended to be critical of more abstract 'Continental' theorizing about sexual behaviour, and most especially about Freudian psychoanalysis and its derivatives.[63]

A number of these individuals, who were mostly strangers at the outset, became friends, allies and sometimes opponents, as they sat together for nearly three years sifting through a mass of evidence. Their chairman testified to the remarkable 'corporate spirit' that grew up between them, recollecting later that as they confronted material that was frequently 'distasteful and sometimes embarrassing' and encountered egocentric, boring or repetitive witnesses, none of them 'lost heart' or lost their temper.[64] They met in morning and afternoon sessions, twice a month for the first part of the committee's life, many of them travelling long distances from outside the capital to attend. Fifty-two professional and public bodies wrote memoranda or gave oral testimonies, along with thirty-eight submissions from individuals.[65] Half the sessions were devoted exclusively to listening to evidence. Many of the committee, most notably Wolfenden himself, underwent something of a 'conversion' on the issue of homosexuality, as they learned more about sexual behaviour that was radically different from their own. As the chairman put it without exaggeration, they 'had lived through a good deal together'.[66] The inquiry's three-year-long encounter with homosexuality and prostitution brought sex quite literally into the heart of government.

Mapping Sexual London

Wolfenden and his colleagues began to take stock of the enormity of their task during the autumn of 1954, but initially they confessed to feeling somewhat 'rudderless' because they were still 'feeling their way in unfamiliar fields'.[67] They were aware that 'the public interest' demanded something more from them than simply a 'bare statement of the law and proposals for changing it'; what was also needed was a résumé of ethical or philosophical principles that would justify any policy recommendations they made.[68] To this end Wolfenden proposed drawing up a 'glossary of terms' for use among themselves and in talking to witnesses, arguing that a shared intellectual vocabulary would hopefully avoid the pitfalls of 'ambiguity' resulting from the 'shifting connotations' of their 'tangled and complicated' matter.[69] Coupled with their search for a common language, the chairman highlighted a related issue: most of his team, albeit in their own 'slightly uninformed way', already felt that the condition of 'London and the immediate neighbourhood' would dominate their work.[70]

Over the life of the inquiry these two questions became inextricably linked; members' emphasis on investigating homosexuality and prostitution in the capital city became an integral part of their search for a shared conceptual framework. The committee's London-centred focus was driven by a number of different priorities. Overwhelmingly, it was influenced by the pressing problems posed by the rising statistics for reported sexual offences in the metropolitan area, as criminal and political facts and as social fantasy. It was also shaped by perceptions of London's exceptional but potentially paradigmatic status, a point that was stressed again and again by committee members and witnesses alike. 'Nowhere do you have the gathering of people in this way that you have in the West End of London,' was how the former Procurator Fiscal of Glasgow Adair put it, with his characteristic Presbyterian suspicion of the English capital. Underlining Adair's point, the Chief Constable of Glamorgan in his evidence insisted that unnatural vice and even street prostitution were problems created by the metropolis, troubling the provinces only marginally.[71] The metropolitan emphasis favoured by most committee members was more intellectually nuanced. Reacting against abstract sexual theorizing, they sought to prioritize the 'where', as well as the 'when' and 'how', of social explanation; in the best investigative traditions of the government's 'blue-book' inquiries, they held firm to the belief that in any discussion of sex, location mattered enormously. The capital, and more particularly the social environments of the West End, provided the *locus classicus* for the committee's extensive survey of sexual behaviour.

In the autumn of 1954 the inquiry called in London's magistrates along with the Metropolitan Police to produce the first detailed accounts of homosexuality. In drawing on these official witnesses, members believed that those in the front line of sentencing and law enforcement could provide the inquiry with precise local knowledge, enhancing the picture presented by abstract national statistics. The early written and oral evidence about homosexuality from Sir Lawrence Dunne, Chief Metropolitan Magistrate, and from Sir John Nott-Bower, Commissioner of the Metropolitan Police, was expansive. Both men took as their point of departure two of the legal categories that preoccupied the committee: male importuning and gross indecency between men. Both witnesses were against decriminalization, and they made their arguments in language that worked simultaneously to incite homosexuality and to condemn it.

'Laurie' Dunne was a paternalist and moral conservative who had risen steadily as a London barrister during the inter-war years, joining the magistracy in 1936. The inheritor of his father's sizeable fortune, he was also a gregarious man-about-town. Combining his official work on the bench with life as a dedicated *bon viveur*, Dunne was a popular member of the Garrick Club, the convivial meeting place for lawyers, writers and their publishers close to Leicester Square. His patrician boast was that when he walked through Covent Garden market to his court in Bow Street, the porters always greeted him with a friendly 'Good morning, Guv', while in police folklore he was celebrated for his fair-mindedness, a reputation that had reputedly won him the respect of London's criminal fraternity.[72]

During the 1940s Dunne inveighed against the depredations of the spiv and the black market, features of contemporary London life that he attributed to lax personal morality, weak parenting and a breakdown in national discipline.[73] He prefaced his memorandum to the Wolfenden committee with a robust defence of the law and in particular the bench in regulating homosexuality, arguing that only magistrates like himself were in a position to establish appropriate standards of punishment, because they were in touch with the 'day-to-day incidence of the various classes of crime'.[74] In 1952 Bow Street and Marlborough magistrates, who covered central London's police districts, heard nearly half of all prosecutions for homosexual offences in the capital.[75] Dunne vigorously opposed any attempt to dilute the efficacy of the criminal law, especially the efforts of liberal-minded laymen on the Appeals Committee of the London Sessions, who regularly quashed sentences for importuning and gross indecency. Equally, he argued against the use of medical treatment as an alternative to sentencing on the grounds that social therapies would diminish the remedial power of punishment.[76]

Dunne combined his defence of the judiciary with a dramatic and emotionally charged discourse on London's homosexual cultures, drawing on the long tradition of juridical sermonizing from the bench dating back to the eighteenth century. Highlighting the dangers of luxury and idleness that stimulated unnatural sex of all kinds, he quoted the famous lines from the dissenting eighteenth-century hymnodist, Isaac Watts: 'Satan finds some mischief yet for idle hands to do.'[77] Believing that the 'animal appetites' once stimulated were voracious and progressive, Dunne's reading of human nature was ultimately pessimistic. He conjured up an image of the rake's progress, familiar from earlier studies of metropolitan vice and perversion, with homosexual men spiralling downwards from adult contacts to the inevitable corruption of young boys. 'To countenance homosexual practices in private is playing with fire,' Dunne insisted; 'a homosexual sated with . . . adults, without hindrance, will be far more likely to tempt a jaded appetite with youth.'[78] The Chief Magistrate added darkly that though 'homosexual practices between females were unknown to the law', he believed that lesbianism was undoubtedly growing in clubs and other licensed premises where these women congregated.[79]

Side-stepping the question of whether homosexual offences were on the increase, 'it is impossible to produce any reliable figures . . . few things remain static in this world', Dunne claimed that he relied on his own eyes and ears for information.[80] Drawing on his own court records, he took the committee on their first of many armchair tours of queer London, recasting some of his own West End itineraries as a man-about-town. Dunne covered the capital's landmarks and major thoroughfares, but he also included the public lavatories and urinals that catered to 'the desires of perverts'.[81] He described the notorious sites at Victoria Station, Piccadilly Circus underground station, Leicester Square, and the urinals at Brydges Place, off the Strand, Rose Street, close by St Martin's Lane in theatreland, and Babmaes Street, adjacent to the haunt of fashionable men-about-town in Jermyn Street.

Dunne also supplied an answer to a question that was preoccupying the inquiry: how do homosexuals recognize each other? Committee members learned about the 'aphrodisiac appeal' of the old, tight walking-out dress supplied for soldiers in the guards and the Household Cavalry, which was now being abandoned in favour of supposedly less provocative kit in khaki serge.[82] Serving soldiers by day, at night these men reappeared as professional importuners who pandered 'to perverts for purely mercenary reasons' in the royal parks as well as in the West End.[83] They were the 'dare devils' whom Kinsey encountered on his night-time tour of Soho. The committee heard about the 'nests' of homosexuals in Mayfair and Paddington that had grown up during the war, and about the public houses where 'these pests' descended 'like locusts', driving out the respectable clientele.[84] Dunne also narrated more sentimental vignettes of the wasted lives of male prostitutes and of the countless waiters, kitchen hands and domestic workers who arrived homeless in London and who drifted into the trade in vice.[85] Understanding sexual behaviour as more or less fixed, he distinguished between different homosexual types according to social class, sexual motives and moral character. In his experience, all 'homosexuals' were not only unashamed of their conduct, they adopted a superior stance, actually looking down 'on those not similarly addicted as intellectual inferiors'.[86]

For an inquiry keen to endorse the authority of expert evidence, Dunne's melodramatic testimony about homosexuality came as a disappointment. The Chief Magistrate wilfully elided moral and professional judgements; he had little sense of scientific neutrality and his insistence on the absolute primacy of the criminal law, with his side-swipe at other experts as soft or ineffectual, challenged committee members' belief in intellectual pluralism. Nott-Bower's disclosures as Metropolitan Police Commissioner were more technical and precise, though they were also politically motivated by his campaign to bolster public confidence in the force in the face of repeated criticism. Nott-Bower had succeeded Sir Harold Scott soon after the coronation. In contrast to Scott's civil service outlook, Nott-Bower was a professional policeman who had spent over twenty years with the Indian force before his appointment as a chief constable at Scotland Yard during the 1930s. An Establishment figure, seen by Churchill's government as a 'safe' Tory appointment, he immediately cast himself as the stout defender of the London bobby in the face of a spate of accusations about police corruption.[87] But Nott-Bower's failure to halt the capital's rising crime rate on his watch provoked a fresh round of anxieties about lawlessness and public indiscipline. His widely publicized offensive against homosexual men running throughout 1953–4 was the commissioner's attempt to demonstrate that in one area at least the Met were winning the battle against crime.

Nott-Bower proffered a classification and a geography of homosexual acts, both in his memorandum to the committee and in his verbal evidence. Mentally bracing himself on behalf of the whole of his team, Jack Wolfenden wanted to know how trials for sodomy, the most serious crime, came before the courts: 'Take the sodomy case straight off and let us know the worst,' the chairman insisted grimly.[88] But Nott-Bower was keener to raise the lesser offences of importuning and gross indecency

because they took up so much police time and on account of the fla-
grant breaches of public morality that they involved. Importuners came
from 'all walks of society', but there was a marked clustering among men
in 'quasi domestic occupations' such as the catering and hotel trades.[89]
Providing the committee with a full list of the most notorious West End
rendezvous, Nott-Bower explained that 'gross indecency' was usually
committed in public lavatories or in 'public house lavatories without an
attendant' and normally between 'two men masturbating each other'.[90]

Warming to his evidence, Nott-Bower went on to sketch the architectural space of the urinals and to outline the sexual possibilities of the
lavatories in front of the committee. 'Perverts' were adept at cutting holes
'about 2 inches square' in the partition separating the WCs, which functioned as a means of social communication (so that men could pass notes
to one another) and as a form of sexual contact. When one local authority placed zinc sheets on both sides of the partition to prevent further
indecent acts, more holes appeared and more offences occurred! Nott-
Bower concluded his written report with an appendix that showed the
central London police divisions running from Kensington, Knightsbridge,
Bayswater and Hyde Park, in the west, through Victoria, Mayfair and
Piccadilly and across to Soho and the Strand, in the east.[91] The map was
annotated with a hand-drawn key of colour-coded circles and crosses in
red, showing the urinals where arrests for gross indecency and importuning had been made in 1953 (fig. 23).

Nott-Bower's map and his accompanying statistics exemplified the
techniques of surveillance associated with the exercise of modern state
power.[92] The commissioner's account of transgressive West End sex drew
on the work of local beat constables as well as their senior divisional com-
manders inside the Metropolitan Police, who generated sexual knowledge
as part of the informal rituals of policing. Matt Houlbrook has argued
that these 'ways and means' tactics, aimed at identifying and containing
public displays of homosexuality, were well established by the early twentieth century and were inherited and developed by successive generations
of officers.[93] What was more unusual, in terms of Nott-Bower's appearance in front of the committee, was the way that this internal police
know-how was shared with a wider community of experts and civil servants in Whitehall. The commissioner's evidence brought the Wolfenden
inquiry into close contact with the capital's homosexual cultures, highlighting the way same sex relations between men were part and parcel

of the urban culture of central London. Nott-Bower's circulation of this police information made homosexuality knowable in ways that began to shift the committee's focus away from abstract criminal statistics and towards more visceral and concrete modes of sexual understanding.

Despite Nott-Bower's detailed evidence, his top-down approach quickly prompted criticism from members of the inquiry. Hugh Linstead, who knew the government machine from the inside, warned that senior figures tended to regurgitate their own departmental policies.[94] Paper experience, generated from inside the sheltered confines of Whitehall or from Scotland Yard, was not the same as first-hand testimonies heard from West End station sergeants or from experienced warders working in Wandsworth Prison. Secretary Roberts took up· Linstead's campaign for the committee to hear from a much wider cross-section of official witnesses in the autumn of 1954. 'You will by now have read the . . . memoranda from the Commissioner of Police,' Roberts wrote to Wolfenden about Nott-Bower's evidence, 'and a dull bit of reading it is, too! I gather he has been a little reticent for fear of shocking the ladies . . . but . . . when we see them we shall want dirt and all.'[95]

Roberts's man-to-man injunction to 'talk dirty' served a double purpose.[96] His ostensible aim was to encourage much lower-level police officers to come forward, in the interests of providing detailed information about conditions at street level. But it was also an invitation to the men on the inquiry to discuss homosexuality in the vernacular, a move that had significant effects on the gendered balance of power and knowledge inside the committee. Initial disclosures from the Metropolitan Police provoked an extensive debate about sex among the men which continued throughout the life of the committee. As their work gathered momentum, homosexuality increasingly dominated the intellectual outlook and the narrative compulsions of most of the male members of Wolfenden's team, with a corresponding downgrading of prostitution.

The use of plain-clothes officers to police West End lavatories and urinals and secure convictions for importuning and gross indecency had been an established part of Metropolitan Police practice since at least the 1920s. It was highly controversial, provoking periodic criticisms from the Home Office, from magistrates, and at times from senior police officers themselves. Two government inquiries had confronted the issue as part of a wider debate about public morality and police powers during the interwar years. The Street Offences Committee acknowledged that the use of policemen in plain clothes was an 'unpleasant necessity', deployed in order to detect acts of gross indecency between men, but their report published in 1928 cautioned against the widespread use of such tactics. Noting how plain-clothes officers could easily turn into *agents provocateurs*, the committee recommended that the police should always act 'in couples', with regular changes made to their beats and routines.[97]

These arguments were reinforced by the *Report of the Royal Commission on Police Powers and Procedure* (1929), which emphasized that the primary duty of the police was to *prevent* crime. Commissioners insisted that this was always best served by using police in uniform, arguing that conduct by plain-clothes officers that encouraged the commission of an offence was utterly reprehensible.[98] An internal directive issued in 1936 refined the Met's position: while plain-clothes officers were never to be recruited in prostitution cases, chief superintendents could authorize their use if complaints were received about 'annoyance by *male* persons'.[99] Officers working in this way were to be carefully chosen for their steady character, and as an aid to observation they were to be supplied with special diaries, in addition to their usual police pocket books, where they could record the type of detailed evidence needed to secure convictions in court.[100] In homosexual cases, police officers were also taught to look out for incriminating items such as jars of lubricant, rags, and linen likely to contain traces of semen.[101]

Official concern about police tactics of this kind was recurrent throughout the 1930s and 1940s. The case of Frank Champain, a schoolmaster, First World War hero and former Oxford cricket blue, sentenced to three months' hard labour for importuning in the urinals around the Strand in 1927, whose conviction was quashed on appeal, brought to a head public anxieties about plain-clothes methods of entrapment. Reginald Handford, the police constable from E Division whose evidence convicted Champain, was subjected to severe cross-examination in front of the Street Offences Committee by the lawyer Sir Joseph Priestley. Priestley put it to Handford that the police officer's third appearance in plain clothes in the stall of the Strand urinal at York Place might very well have led Champain to conclude that 'you were going to a urinal for an improper purpose also?'[102] In what senior officers acknowledged was another very 'unsavoury file' involving the prosecution of Frederick Allen, a trunk maker, for gross indecency in 1933, W. H. Oulton, the Tower Bridge magistrate, cautioned the police about their aggressive tactics, insisting that plain-clothes methods not only threatened the reputation of

the force but also potentially compromised the masculinity of the officers involved. In his summing up, Oulton stated categorically that a police
officer should not 'invite and endure' an insult 'to his manhood' of such
a 'gross character' because his 'own self esteem must suffer', in addition
to that of 'the dignity of the Force'.[103]

Controversial prosecutions during the Second World War for offences
at West End lavatories generated similar anxieties about the character and
motives of plain-clothes policemen. The case of George Bronson, a
pattern cutter caught for persistently importuning in urinals at Leicester
Square and Piccadilly Circus, who was convicted by Dunne at Bow Street
Magistrates Court in 1943, provoked explicit accusations from the defence
lawyer that one of the plain-clothes policemen involved actually invited
sexual overtures from Bronson.[104] Objections voiced in all these cases
drew attention to the fact that plain-clothes officers were exposed to
greater temptations than men in uniform, and that their masculinity was
in danger of becoming temporarily undermined as they masqueraded as
homosexual punters. Immediately before the Wolfenden committee was
scheduled to hear from the police in the autumn of 1954, the Director
of Public Prosecutions sent a cautionary note to the chairman, reaffirming his view that the Met's system of entrapment was 'most unfortunate'.
Police who kept watch in public lavatories and then went into the witness
box telling 'identical stories' about 'grunts emerging from the defendant
coupled with glances and smiles' exposed themselves not just to ridicule
and to accusations of falsifying evidence, but also to much more serious
slurs on their character.[105]

Nott-Bower set the scene for the appearance of his own carefully
selected plain-clothes officers in the memo he sent to the committee in
November 1954. He judged his words carefully because Metropolitan
Police numbers dedicated to this type of work had been increased by
over 50 per cent during the immediate post-war years, and the inquiry
had already discussed whether increased surveillance was driving up the
number of recorded offences for importuning and gross indecency.[106]
Nott-Bower was at pains to stress that securing convictions for importuning involved lengthy periods of police observation that usually took
place inside the urinals. Patrols consisted of two men who were always
specially authorized by a senior officer at Scotland Yard. Because of the
unpleasant nature of the work such duties were, he insisted, 'most unpopular', and police officers were not normally employed in this way for
more than four weeks at a time.[107]

When Nott-Bower appeared in person a fortnight later, he suggested to Wolfenden that the committee might like a 'little more detail' from his colleague, Commander Robertson from A Department at Scotland Yard. Jack Wolfenden accepted this invitation from the police to move his investigation towards a more endogenous and intimate account of sex between men. The opening dialogue between the chairman and the two senior police officers was significant not only for its account of police methods of entrapment, but also for what it revealed about the institutional structures of sexual disclosure that shaped the committee's work:

> *Sir John Nott-Bower:* Mr. Robertson could describe the methods used by police officers employed in plain clothes. . . .

> *Wolfenden:* We should like to hear that. I can well believe, as your memorandum says, that this is an unpleasant job and very unpopular.

> *Sir John Nott-Bower:* Very unpleasant and very unpopular. I would suggest that Mr. Robertson describes that, and then perhaps if you would like to hear full details of one case. . . .

> *Wolfenden:* Mr. Robertson, could you tell us how this unpleasant job is done?

> *Mr. Robertson:* Yes. . . . I will take the lavatories first. They go down there – and may I say that these men who are employed on this have a sense of knowing the suspects, and they may follow them in, they may go down and see them in these lavatories, but once they do know that they are on a pervert of this sort, that he is there for the purpose of importuning, they watch him very carefully.[108]

Exchanges of this kind highlighted how the inquiry's education about homosexuality was orchestrated through specific bureaucratic mechanisms designed to produce official knowledge. Both Wolfenden and the police witnesses were committed to a highly structured speech-exchange system: questions were intended to stimulate answers, which then prompted further questions by committee members, with the aim of compiling a dossier of evidence. These protocols had been developed initially in the work of the nineteenth-century royal commissions and government inquiries, with their ambitious commitment to deductive empirical proof and public policy reasoning.[109] Nott-Bower's and Robertson's sexual disclosures also adhered to a procedural logic followed by all those who gave evidence; witnesses moved from general discussion points, taken first, to more particular information based on their own specific fields of professional competence. This approach to knowledge generation encouraged members and witnesses alike to see their contributions as part of an overall sequence that moved towards possible policy recommendations. The physical lay-out of Home Office committee room 101 was designed to promote the exchange of information in a quasi-juridical atmosphere that was redolent of a courtroom or a tribunal hearing. Witnesses remembered how committee members were seated in an expanded semicircle, distanced from themselves by a large amount of floor space. Jean Graham Hall, a member of the deputation from the Society of Labour Lawyers who gave evidence in 1955, recalled that the committee 'sat in chairs far away' and seemed like a 'bench of magistrates. It was all very formal.'[110]

7 December 1954 was a strenuous day for the committee. PC Butcher and PC Darlington made their appearance immediately after Nott-Bower had testified about homosexuality. They spoke to the map of the West End that the commissioner had circulated previously, but from their own position as plain-clothes beat officers. Butcher worked C Division, while Darlington operated from B Division, running from Victoria westwards to Chelsea and South Kensington. For their plain-clothes work they wore Harris tweed sports jackets, a style of smart casual dress that was marketed by popular menswear chain stores like Burton's and Hepworth's in the mid-1950s.[111] Butcher and Darlington confirmed that they worked on plain-clothes duty in pairs for a month at a time, eight hours a day, developing their own surveillance routines.[112]

Both men spoke about the distinctiveness of their respective patches; each district had its own particular customs and characters. Mapping a wide variety of social and sexual types, Butcher understood his area to have different subdivisions. The Soho and Piccadilly side of C Division was the location of the 'criminal type of homosexual'. These professional prostitutes were in his opinion 'the lowest form of animal life . . . in the West End'.[113] With their make-up, 'plucked eyebrows', painted fingernails and 'mincing gait', Butcher presented them as atavistic throwbacks; absolutely lazy and with low intelligence, they were despised by the rest of London's criminal community.[114] Homosexual culture at the Mayfair end of Butcher's beat was very different; it was most visible around midday, when men working at nearby offices in Berkeley Square came out during their lunch hour. Advertising agencies and estate agents were concentrated in this part of the West End, and Butcher explained knowingly that 'there are certain business organisations' in which 'these men are inclined to be found' where 'the communal office consists entirely of male staff'.[115] The Mayfair type stalked back and forth between three urinals that had become famous throughout the world: Providence Court, close to Oxford Street, Three Kings Yard, by the showrooms of the Standard Motor Company at the back of Grosvenor Square, and the urinal attached to the pub close by in George Yard.

Butcher proceeded to move members of the inquiry from the outside to conditions inside the urinals via his evidence. In promoting this cognitive shift he was encouraging them to see the urinals as liminal spaces; neither fully public nor fully private, they provided the setting both for homosexual sex and for the physical ablutions performed by normal men.[116] Butcher also contrasted their potentially illicit atmosphere (it is 'dim in there', he told the committee) with the bustling, daytime world of the surrounding streets. Some of Soho's urinals were still lit by gas, and he suspected that their Victorian setting and decrepit ambience attracted men looking for anonymous sex. Butcher also noted other erotic stimulants; as places of urination and defecation, their odour, the 'staleness' as he put it, excited many men. They would rarely visit the large, brightly lit public toilets that were serviced by attendants, such as those at Leicester Square and Green Park, nor would they go near conveniences that had been 'scrubbed clean . . . with dettol'. But as soon as the 'cleanliness' had gone they would return, working themselves up into a frenzy like the proverbial 'bitch' on heat. Butcher continued the animal comparison when he insisted: 'once they have the scent there is no holding them, they are oblivious to everything else'.[117]

Committee members and witnesses alike speculated about the reasons for these transgressive patterns of homosexual desire. Citing cases drawn from his own Harley Street practice, Dr Curran explained that 'uriniferous odours have an aphrodisiac effect on some'.[118] W. Lindsey Neustatter, a psychologist based at the Royal Northern Hospital in Holloway, ascribed such 'obsessional-compulsive' acts to the inordinate and irresistible sexual urge displayed by so many homosexuals, which was itself an expression of more general psychopathic tendencies.[119] Treating men for venereal disease at St Mary's Hospital Paddington, Dr F. J. Jefferiss was convinced that sex in public conveniences was part of the illicit atmosphere of excitement that attracted so many homosexuals; cloaked in secrecy, it became all the more appealing to the adventurous.[120] Butcher agreed with Jefferiss; he believed his Mayfair men did it 'for the love of the thing', and that their pleasure was enhanced by the thrill of the chase.[121]

Butcher and Darlington were keenly aware of the reciprocal dialogue that took place between themselves and the men under their surveillance; police lore emphasized that it was the officers who understood this connection who made the best policemen. The two young constables recognized how both sides were locked in a double structure of recognition, as Darlington put it: 'It is the same faces that you see. They see you and we see them, and they get to know us.'[122] Both men also pointed to the habitual rituals of offenders, and they went on to describe how many West End rendezvous had become sexual meeting points not just for Londoners but for a community of homosexual men that was drawn from across the world.[123]

Butcher had been on his West End beat for eight years, since being demobbed at the end of the war, and he had a particularly detailed knowledge of the international character of queer London. He revealed how the capital's much-vaunted status as a world city was being reinvented after 1945 as a centre of unorthodox sexual tourism. Along with authorized travel literature publicizing the usual landmark sights, homosexual men traded their own subcultural information; informal guides to the whereabouts of 'cottages' and other pick-up points were exchanged as far afield as Russia, Hong Kong and South Africa. A masseur with a visiting Russian ballet troupe, whom Butcher arrested in Mayfair, confided that he found his way around the West End's urinals with the aid of a map that had been drawn for him back at home.[124] Butcher also told the story of an American naval chaplain who docked one morning at Southampton on the *Queen Mary* and then travelled up to London, where he made nine separate visits to the urinals at Piccadilly Circus, before leaving on the night train for Glasgow.[125]

Listening to Butcher's evidence the committee had already acquired more intimate knowledge of London's homosexual culture than Nott-Bower had provided. Then the chairman turned to PC Darlington: 'we have kept "B" Division just sitting and listening for far too long,' Wolfenden interjected. 'Is there anything you would like to tell us . . . ?' This was the cue for Darlington to rehearse his own account of public sex in the West End:

> In B Division, Chelsea, which I am more conversant with, we get it in the evenings. We get very very little, if any, during the lunch hour.

We very seldom keep observation outside the urinal. We are two a month detailed off to do this and we decide to actually go to certain urinals, and we go there, and we take it in turn to go in. One goes in and the other stays outside. We never speak to each other, we have a certain look, a code where we can give certain signs. You go in and you sort of look as if you are going to urinate. We make it our business that we just stand there as if we are urinating and look about us to see what we can see. These people come in and one out of every 50 urinates, you get occasionally one that does, but it is one in 50, the man on B never does. They stand there and there are three or four or more and you are all standing there, and it is deathly quiet. There is no sound of anybody urinating at all. Somebody is in there for some other purpose. You see these men, they start to look about them and give each other the glad eye. They nod their head, they sometimes speak and reach out and touch one another, and practically everyone you see will be masturbating himself. In B Division they do it quite openly. They are in there for two or three minutes and some of them are cunning. Some of them go in for three or four minutes and will not do a thing, they just stand there, and you cannot tell what they are doing, but the majority of them do it quite openly. They masturbate themselves, that is the main thing. You see somebody comes up and starts to do the same thing and through that we get gross indecency. Then we change round and the other one comes in. We do two or three minutes and then we go out because you cannot stay in too long. . . . They go to these different urinals, but it is pretty well all the same on B, all in the evening, they all do practically the same thing, and it is with a view I think either to getting together, some of them, in these urinals and committing gross indecency, to masturbate with each other, or picking up a friend to take back to their flat or their home to indulge in what we call the finer arts – what they are I do not know.[126]

Darlington's expansive account of the methods of observation and entrapment used against homosexual men affirmed the privileged role of the police in producing what Les Moran has defined as an officially sanctioned version of 'the male genital body and its genital relations with other male bodies in law'.[127] The policeman recreated an elaborate choreography of same sex relations between men in time and space that sought to explain the various subcultural codes of communication to the committee. Darlington revealed how he and his colleague rehearsed these performances in the urinals as part of the somatic techniques of policing: approaching the stall, taking up a sexual position, signalling, foreplay, masturbation, and so on.[128] But his testimony also highlighted the dangers attendant on this kind of work that had shadowed official debate about plain-clothes tactics since the 1920s. Darlington made the committee fully aware of just how intimate he was with the men under his surveillance, via his assumed identity as a would-be homosexual in search of anonymous sex and through his evocative, sensory account of the atmosphere inside the urinal. His interjection, 'you cannot stay in too long', tacitly acknowledged the potential threat that plain-clothes work posed to the officially sanctioned version of his masculinity as a police officer. Towards the end of the account, Darlington drew back from this close-up position, returning to third person pronouns and a panoramic point of view in order to re-establish an appropriate distance between himself as a policeman and the sexual world he revealed to the inquiry.

For the most part, committee members did not enter into a detailed dialogue with these police officers, nor did they attempt to gloss the graphic testimonies that Butcher and Darlington had provided.[129] Some historians have suggested that such explicit accounts of non-reproductive, public sex delivered in a government setting involved a clear 'breaking of . . . taboos'.[130] Modes of informal communication used between low-ranking police officers and delivered in the vernacular suddenly became elevated to the status of official evidence, to be heard by prominent public figures. Yet other witnesses who testified in front of the inquiry noted how committee members developed their own collective strategy for listening dispassionately to these detailed testimonies about anonymous sex. Patrick Trevor-Roper, a consultant ophthalmic surgeon at Westminster Hospital and one of the homosexual men invited to give evidence in the summer of 1955, recollected how the atmosphere inside room 101 was 'so glacial, almost wooden . . . that sex didn't appear to arise'.[131] Wolfenden himself was particularly 'dry', Trevor-Roper remembered, giving 'no sign' either of interest or disapproval. Jean Graham Hall, a trainee barrister accustomed to the courtroom, ascribed such responses not to embarrassment but to the quasi-legal atmosphere that framed most of the committee's discussions. She remembered that sex was dealt with as if Wolfenden and his team were listening to offences at a 'Quarter Sessions, all very properly done. It was a code of manners, you see, which is understood, especially in legal circles.'[132] What Graham Hall experienced was an atmosphere of clinical detachment that committee

members had created in order to preserve an appropriate distance
between themselves and the graphic police accounts of public sex
between men.

After the visit by these police witnesses Roberts speculated again to
Wolfenden that 'the ladies' may have been shocked at their 'gruesome
details'.[133] His repeated affirmation of a homosocial language for discussing sex was part of the informal way that the men restricted women's
access to official conversation and debate. Despite their wide experience
in public life, Mary Cohen, Kathleen Lovibond and Lily Stopford regularly spoke less at meetings, especially in discussions about homosexuality when they mostly refrained from comment. On the infrequent
occasions when they did voice opinions, they often appeared hesitant or
apologetic.[134] Trevor-Roper recollected that when he gave evidence the
women 'were silent totally', though they seemed generally supportive,
giving off 'body language and smiles, to encourage us along'.[135] The corol-
lary to this growing gender divide in discussing homosexuality was
that prostitution was increasingly relegated to secondary status, despite
protests from the women about the unbalanced way that matters were
proceeding.[136]

When committee members turned to confront street offences, the
questions that obsessed them about homosexuality were not the issues.
Detailed official knowledge about London's public cultures of prostitution was readily available in ways that information about homosexuality
was not. While criminologists and social scientists worried that convictions for buggery and gross indecency represented only the tip of a submerged iceberg (the 'dark figures' for crime), prostitution presented the
reverse problem.[137] Prostitution was an all too obvious part of the capital's
street life; photographers regularly recorded the lines of women waiting
for customers strung out on the West End's pavements (fig. 24). It was
this palpable visibility that had pushed Churchill's government to set up
the committee. Research and debate about the aetiology of the prostitute, her male client, and the sexual economy that sustained their commercial relationship was well established, the product of more than a
century of sexual politics that was deeply embedded in metropolitan traditions of social investigation. Vigilance societies and feminist pressure
groups, the police and social workers, sociologists and the medical profession, environmental campaigners and municipalists, all staked out
competing claims to knowledge which they pressed forward onto the
committee.[138]

Overwhelmingly, Wolfenden and the majority of his team responded by compressing prostitution into a debate about public order, prompted by the perceived visibility of sexually disorderly women soliciting on the streets of central London. Homosexuality demanded a sustained process of reflection and philosophical inquiry, an intellectual journey as Wolfenden put it, whereas prostitution was increasingly understood as 'an issue of practicalities' designed to 'ameliorate a situation which could not be radically altered'.[139] The chairman outlined his proposed policy for street offences at an important meeting convened as an informal 'exchange of views' in October 1955. Wolfenden wanted to achieve a working consensus on prostitution by sounding out his team prior to drafting the report. With a watchful eye on his political masters at the Home Office, he insisted that the central practical question undoubtedly was: 'how are we to alter the appearance of the West End streets?'[140]

From a lawyer's perspective Victor Mishcon agreed. He believed that the whole problem of prostitution was 'comparatively simple', centring as it did on the offensiveness of prostitutes '"on parade"'.[141] Mishcon bolstered his point about public annoyance with a widely held argument about the changing economics of the sex trade. 'Everyone knew,' he insisted, 'that in these prosperous days other work was available and there was no financial need for women to go on the streets; those who did simply liked a lazy but financially rewarding life.'[142] Vera Williams, a probation officer in Cardiff, also believed that prostitution was 'definitely better off the streets', arguing that this should be the focal point of discussion, 'without going into the moral side of it'.[143] Drawing on his political skills as a consensus builder, Wolfenden insisted that the choices facing the inquiry over prostitution were essentially pragmatic; they were about matters 'of degree' and the 'balance of disadvantage'.[144] He acknowledged that if central London's streets were cleared many prostitutes 'would retire into flats and use street corner advertisements, and some would resort to a call-girl system', but 'such arrangements' were already part of the West End's sex trade.[145]

Committee members were confirmed and challenged in their public order approach to prostitution by evidence from the most famous witness to appear in front of the inquiry. Alfred Kinsey's West End experiences were fresh in his mind when he arrived at a specially convened Saturday morning meeting of the committee, arranged by the doctors not at the Home Office but in the more informal atmosphere of Drayton Gardens, South Kensington.[146] Kinsey's graphic account of public sex in Soho strengthened many committee members in their view that clearing the capital's public spaces was a necessary precondition to effective long-term action against street offences.

However, Kinsey took a different position about regulation, aiming to shift members away from their obsession with the criminal law and towards an extended social analysis of sex. Generalizing about what he had seen on London's streets, he concluded that public soliciting on this scale was a symptom of English sexual repression; such a demand for commercial sex could never occur in a society that was genuinely open and tolerant.[147] Kinsey's overall argument was that prostitution and homosexuality could only be understood as part of the infinitely malleable patterns of human sexual variation, which highlighted the power of culture and the environment to shape sexual behaviour in a wide variety of ways.

Kinsey made these points forcefully in his discussion points about male homosexuality, which were already well known to medical men like Desmond Curran. Summarising his famous heterosexual–homosexual rating scale, he took the committee through the various permutations, from 0 (exclusively heterosexual with no homosexual tendencies) through to category 6 (exclusively homosexual). Kinsey's model was cited approvingly in the inquiry's published report as evidence that 'homosexuals cannot reasonably be regarded as . . . separate from the rest of mankind'.[148] Penalizing homosexual experiences simply forced everyone to 'declare themselves as exclusively one way or the other', Kinsey argued.[149] He was equally doubtful about the effectiveness of the law to regulate prostitution. As he put it in response to questions by Roberts: 'I think that the current value of the law has been grossly exaggerated. So far as sexual behaviour is concerned, the social acceptance, or non-acceptance . . . of a phenomenon is . . . much more important.'[150] Draconian legislation prohibiting public prostitution in many of the American states simply channelled sex in different directions, stimulating a massive growth in premarital intercourse. The current fashion for 'heavy petting' among American teenagers was an entirely logical response from a post-war generation caught between conflicting messages about sexual morality.[151]

Committee members were highly selective in their use of Kinsey's evidence. The doctors in particular drew on his relativist approach to homosexuality to argue that sexual orientation could be modified by effective treatment, despite the fact that Kinsey himself was sceptical about the possibilities.[152] The women for their part took up Kinsey's arguments about the futility of legal sanctions against prostitution that were not framed by a broader social analysis of sex. For most members of the inquiry, though, these extra-legal considerations did not undermine their stress on the importance of restricting the public visibility of prostitution and public sex of all kinds. Kinsey championed an expansive American idea of social science to provide hard and soft data that would help 'soften the rules' of 'sexual restraint' determined by the law.[153] In contrast, committee members favoured a version of English pragmatism that was governed by public policy demands and by utilitarian notions of jurisprudence.

The committee was not alone in working to redefine prostitution as a public order offence in the 1950s. The dominant planning ethos championed by Abercrombie and Forshaw in the County of London Plan, and finessed in countless local initiatives across the metropolitan boroughs, understood public morality primarily via an environmental logic, with prostitutes and other social offenders seen as an affront to a revitalized idea of community and neighbourhood.[154] Police and social workers in north Kensington took this view of the three prostitutes who were Christie's murder victims, defining them as part of the detritus of inner city blight. Delegates from Paddington Borough Council were enthusiastically received by the Wolfenden committee when local officials explained how they adopted a practical approach to street offences, successfully pressing the Ministry of Works to fence off the northern boundary of Hyde Park to prevent soliciting and improving street lamps in red-light districts.[155]

Academics and policy researchers also argued strongly for workable responses to public prostitution that decoupled legal sanctions from questions of public morality. Psychoanalyst Edward Glover, who gave evidence on behalf of the Institute for the Study and Treatment of Delinquency, insisted that the sort of 'moralistic fulmination' against prostitutes so frequently displayed by the magistrate's bench simply aggravated the situation and was a positive encouragement to recidivism.[156] Glover emphasized that it was preferable to contain what he termed the prostitute's 'sexual backwardness' within the rubric of enlightened public indecency legislation.[157] Within jurisprudence there were related moves to abandon moral absolutes in favour of policies based on social expediency. Thomas James, barrister and London University law lecturer, argued that current attitudes towards prostitution had been formulated during a period of moral certainties; in civilized democracies the time had now come for prostitutes to be classed as public nuisances.[158] Here in embryo was the nub of the debate about the law's disaggregation from the enforcement of morals that was to find fuller expression in arguments put forward by the legal philosopher H. L. A. Hart in his exchanges with the law lord, Lord Devlin, in the late 1950s and early 1960s.[159]

Wolfenden for his part was assiduous in championing an analysis of prostitution that could be converted into workable legislation. As he put it approvingly in response to the Paddington Council's delegation: 'apart from questions of morality, which we have all I think rather deliberately kept out . . . apart altogether from that, as an issue of public order and decency I take it that would be your approach, primarily?'[160] The chairman was fully aware that his public order strategy would antagonize feminist campaigners who had pressured the committee from the outset to adopt a principled stance on social morality. Leading activists from the AMSH repeated their arguments in extensive evidence delivered to the inquiry. 'Legislation', they insisted, could not 'be divorced from the whole system of individual and national morality upheld by law and practised by a people'.[161] Feminist purity groups argued that sexual encounters between prostitutes and their clients should not be treated in isolation; they needed to be considered alongside all the other heterosocial environments that sustained the various markets for commercial sex: the pubs, cafés, hotel lounges, dance halls and nightclubs that were 'the working ground of many prostitutes . . . in London'.[162] Women's groups argued that these leisure and entertainment venues continued to be experienced as antisocial by most women, because so much popular culture fed 'the disastrous idea that there should be a different moral standard for the two sexes', implicitly condoning a man's 'lack of control over his body and its passions'.[163]

Despite his best efforts to marginalize purity feminists, Wolfenden began to feel their heat inside the Home Office, because the women on his team were raising their own collective doubts about the committee's approach to prostitution. Mary Cohen provided much of the focus for dissent because she represented an important link to national women's organizations via her prominent role in the Glasgow branch of the National Council of Women and the National Vigilance Association of Scotland. Acknowledging that 'the streets were the ultimate degradation' for women, Cohen was increasingly troubled by the restrictive notions of public space and public order that were beginning to dominate the inquiry's work.[164] Nervous about confronting the chairman face to face, she wrote to Wolfenden, worried by 'the proposed formula about prostitution', feeling that it did not 'attempt to do what I was told we were trying to do'.[165] Drawing on her personal experience with the girls' clubs movement and the Girl Guides, Cohen believed that the inquiry was not getting to grips with what she termed 'the beginning' of prostitution, nor were members confronting all the places beyond the street where women and girls were sexually exploited by men.[166] Mary Cohen was generally an obedient member of Wolfenden's team; slightly in awe of the chairman, she could usually be relied on to toe the majority line. On this occasion she issued Wolfenden with a rebuke for pushing his formula for the public control of prostitution too far and too fast.

Cohen's outburst was symptomatic of a deepening gendered split inside the committee over the politics of prostitution. For many of the men, the proposed formula for containing public soliciting was an appropriate response to a problem that had no real solution. Under growing pressure from the Home Secretary and Newsam to deliver policy recommendations fast, Wolfenden summed up his draft recommendations: 'Simply, we want to clear the streets of London . . . so that ordinary decent citizens can use them without being offended. This, we recognize, is not to abolish prostitution – but that is not, frankly, our concern.'[167] Along with this ameliorist stance, members continued to argue that street offences did not involve the 'matters of principle' that were raised by homosexuality, while informally many of the men still regularly discussed prostitutes in the language of sexual innuendo and suggestive fantasy.[168] Curran, Whitby and even the arch-moralist Adair seemed relaxed about the potential growth in the privatized sex trade that would result from restricting public soliciting. When Lily Stopford suggested that the names of men found in massage parlours should be made public, Curran confronted her with wry amusement, demanding to know 'what was the strong objection to brothels'.[169] William Wells adopted the studied nonchalance of the man-about-town when he mocked evidence given by Miss Long, a social worker with the Central After-Care Association. All the reclamation and rescue work in the world, Wells insisted, could not detract from the fact that it was always more stimulating for a young man to saunter down Piccadilly and Bond Street with its street girls than to 'walk down a little street in his home town where he sees nobody but the policeman'.[170]

Feminist protests did not seriously challenge Wolfenden's public order strategy for prostitution. This was partly because of the inquiry's prevailing masculinist ethos, but it was also due to the fact that the women on the committee were not wholly opposed to the policies of regulation that shaped members' overall common sense. Cohen, Lovibond and Stopford demanded stiffer penalties for those living on the earnings of prostitution, on account of a new class of 'middlemen' such as flat-farmers, taxi-drivers and hotel porters, and part of their proposals were successfully incorporated into the Street Offences Act.[171] Where the women parted company with their male colleagues was in pressing for greater control of the expanding sphere of privatized commercial sex, which for them was a necessary adjunct to clearing the streets.

Huntleys and Palmers

For much of its life the Wolfenden committee's knowledge about sex in London was supplied by official witnesses. Despite their overwhelming belief in the authority of experts, Wolfenden and his team always insisted that they wanted to go beyond government disclosures and professional evidence. Hugh Linstead's initial warning to his colleagues about the limitations of a Whiggish approach to the problem was bound up with a related issue that he referred to coyly as the 'Huntley and Palmer' question.[172] This was the very English euphemism, originally coined by Wolfenden from the name of the local biscuit factory in his adopted town of Reading, to refer to homosexuals and prostitutes themselves. Was the inquiry going to take on board what these men and women were thinking and saying, Linstead asked. 'What were their complaints against the police? What were their grudges against society?' He proposed that 'some of us' should talk to homosexual men 'off the record' about what really happened 'under the surface of the law and its administration'.[173] Mary Cohen was equally concerned that committee members should get to meet some of the prostitutes who worked the West End's streets. As a leading member of the National Vigilance Association of Scotland with extensive contacts among working-class and 'delinquent' girls, she suggested that the Home Office should hand pick one or two 'regulars' from the summons lists at Bow Street Magistrates Court and ask them to come and speak informally to the committee.[174] There was even the offer of evidence from 'an ordinary member of the public' who claimed he was a regular client of West End prostitutes.[175]

In seeking to move closer to street level, committee members were situating their work in the extensive traditions of metropolitan social exploration and urban ethnography which dated back to the mid-nineteenth century. Progressive members of the inquiry like Linstead and Goronwy Rees also genuinely believed that men and women who were the objects of official scrutiny should be represented as part of the committee's dossier of sexual evidence. This latter argument was potentially explosive as it implicitly challenged the inquiry's commitment to the power of expert knowledge.

Wolfenden was already encouraging a carefully selected group of homosexual men to put their case to the committee. In January and again in June 1955 he reported that he had been approached by a number of homosexuals, 'rather distinguished blokes' in their own lines, whom he mysteriously referred to as his 'Cambridge-Harley-Street party'.[176] Clearly impressed with the social cachet of his potential witnesses and careful to preserve confidentiality, Wolfenden disclosed that these men were anxious to discuss their problems and that he had agreed to see them as part of what he rather grandly termed his 'personal education'.[177] In an exchange with Roberts, the chairman and secretary agreed that all of them seemed 'decent sorts of chaps' with 'no axe to grind', precisely the sort of 'genuine inverts' whom the committee were looking for.[178] Prominent among Wolfenden's potential witnesses were Trevor-Roper, who had recently been elected a fellow of the Royal College of Surgeons, and Angus Wilson, who had left the staff of the British Museum Reading Room to pursue a full-time writing career. Wolfenden was keen to proceed via these elite personal contacts; at all costs he wanted to avoid adverse publicity by being forced to advertise for homosexual witnesses in the press. 'The more I think about it, the more frightened I am about a public advertisement,' he told Roberts.[179]

The setting up of the Wolfenden inquiry had aroused high expectations among a wide variety of pressure groups and activists, including homosexual men who were appalled by the show trials and negative press exposés that dominated their lives in the early 1950s. Trevor-Roper was one of many who remembered how the 'dark shadow' cast by the law over his personal life made him feel that a 'mark had got to be made'.[180] A founder member of the Homosexual Law Reform Society, he was sounded out about giving evidence via his Oxbridge connections and contacts in London's clubland. Initially, Trevor-Roper spoke to Goronwy Rees, a Fellow of All Souls College, Oxford. Rees complained that few members of Wolfenden's team had ever encountered a homosexual 'in a social way', though this was somewhat disingenuous given his own personal contacts. He suggested that Trevor-Roper should meet Wolfenden and other interested parties as a prelude to giving evidence.[181]

The ensuing dinner at Wolfenden's club, the United Oxford and Cambridge in Pall Mall, revealed how the social networks of upper-class masculine culture influenced the development of the inquiry at critical stages. Gentlemanly etiquette, grounded in a common Oxbridge educational background and a shared clubbable language for discussing sex among men, enabled Wolfenden and his potential witnesses to broach the subject of homosexuality after a protracted initial period of embarrassment. The dinner party consisted of Wolfenden, the barrister Wells, Trevor-Roper and Wilson. Trevor-Roper recollected that the evening started as an 'awkward affair'; even after port and brandy conversation was still desultory, pirouetting around the social niceties of the recent Test match. He remembered thinking, 'Christ, we can't finish off with nothing being said.'[182] Finally, it was Wolfenden who broke the ice, Trevor-Roper recollected, by raising the subject of a recent homosexual trial. ' "Terrible case, you know, where those three City directors were buggered by the . . . young soldiers".' Wolfenden began.[183] With that opening gambit the group began to talk more seriously. Trevor-Roper remembered: 'Finally Wolfenden said, "Right", and he agreed to have us meet the committee.'[184]

Making contact with West End prostitutes involved the use of quite different intermediaries; female social workers provided committee members with their link to the women who serviced the capital's sex industry. Jean Graham Hall had studied at the London School of Economics before training as a social worker and a probation officer in Gosport and Croydon in the late 1940s, where she dealt mainly with delinquent girls on remand.[185] In 1951 she began her bar pupillage, combining legal briefs with polytechnic lecturing, joining the Labour Party and the Society of Labour Lawyers, and becoming the society's secretary in 1954. As a woman who was outside the Oxbridge legal Establishment, progress in the law was extremely difficult. She was 'active on prostitution', she remembered, for two reasons: on account of her feminist politics and because it provided her with an entrée into current debates about criminal law reform.[186]

Gerald Gardiner, the Labour Lawyers' chairman and subsequently a Labour Lord Chancellor, originally floated the idea of bringing West End prostitutes forward as witnesses, but it was Graham Hall who did the out-reach work. Using sampling techniques derived from her own experience in market research (she had already undertaken commercially sponsored work on the consumption of aspirins), she tried to talk to 'every fifth girl on the Mayfair beat'. In the early 1950s Graham Hall was often out two nights a week, interviewing prostitutes and their 'maids' at Gunter's, the fashionable tea-shop in Curzon Street. Later she moved on to explore the much rougher red-light district around King's Cross, but her favourite patch was Mayfair, where the girls were 'very intelligent and very talka-tive'.[187] Encouraged by Graham Hall's embryonic fieldwork, the Labour Lawyers contacted the Home Office in the spring of 1955, suggesting that they bring along 'a few practising prostitutes' when they came to give evidence later in the year.[188] Some committee members objected to the idea of what they termed 'sponsored' women, and Roberts and Wolfenden continued with their ribald jokes and innuendoes, but all were agreed that it was probably their only opportunity 'to hear the views of prosti-tutes at first hand'.[189]

The decision to call homosexual men and street women as witnesses marked a radical departure in terms of the official culture of a govern-ment inquiry. Never before had a departmental committee or a royal commission agreed to hear testimonies from men and women whose sex-uality was defined as outside the law. Nineteenth-century inquiries into the operation of the Contagious Diseases Acts, along with later investi-gations into venereal disease and street soliciting, had not taken evidence from prostitutes. Commissioners and committee members operated with a system of class and gendered representation, where middle-class femi-nists competed with medical and military men to speak on behalf of the women themselves.[190] Before the 1950s no government agencies had ever canvassed the views of homosexual men directly. The Wolfenden com-mittee's decision to extend their terms of reference marked an imagina-tive leap, testifying to their expanded liberalism. However, in the spring of 1955 neither Jack Wolfenden's hand-picked homosexuals nor Jean Graham Hall's carefully selected Mayfair girls were the first to appear in front of the inquiry. It was Peter Wildeblood who presented himself as the committee's first homosexual witness, in May 1955.

At the time of his interview Wildeblood had gained a degree of sexual notoriety. Only just out of prison, he had spent the previous year in Wormwood Scrubs, after his conviction for indecency along with Lord Montagu and Michael Pitt-Rivers. The scandal was personally traumatic for all three men, but Wildeblood turned the case to political advantage, drawing on his experiences to criticize police tactics and to campaign for criminal law reform. He believed that his publicly declared identity as a homosexual provided him with a *carte d'entrée* to the committee.

From a professional middle-class background with a public school education, Wildeblood interrupted his studies at Oxford to join the RAF in 1941.[191] Completing his degree after the war, he moved to London as a reporter for the *Daily Mail*, and it was during this period that he began to think of himself 'as a homosexual', as he put it in his autobiography.[192] Via Fleet Street contacts and his interest in the theatre he also began to move in fashionable London society. At his trial the press described him as a 'tall slim man' wearing 'a well-cut single-breasted suit', a reference to his smart neo-Edwardian style and to the sexual ambiguity that surrounded him as a well-dressed man-about-town.[193] After a brief liaison with Trevor-Roper, he started an affair with a foreign prince, who impressed Wildeblood with his cosmopolitan outlook and his knowledge of almost everyone in London's *demi-monde*, from 'Cabinet ministers to the proprietress of a Mayfair brothel'.[194] He also picked up Eddie McNally one night at Piccadilly Circus, the young working-class RAF corporal whose evidence was used later to convict him in court.[195] Moving in these eclectic circles, Wildeblood came to realize that the homosexual world did not obey conventional social distinctions.[196] His supposed predilection for cross-class liaisons, with their perceived threat of social levelling, became a major issue at his trial.[197]

Peter Wildeblood's critique of the rigidities of the English class system went hand in hand with his enthusiasm for London's sexual bohemia, though he remained publicly cautious about declaring his commitment to 'the homosexual world'.[198] Professionally and socially ambitious, he distanced himself from the West End's queer culture in order to mark out his respectability. Wildeblood was well connected via his friendships with Montagu and with the theatre critic Kenneth Tynan, and he was rapidly promoted to the *Daily Mail*'s most important news desk. Moving through the paper's gossip column and the court and social pages, where he was assigned coverage of the coronation, he became the *Mail*'s diplomatic correspondent in 1953, a post that gave him regular access to diplomatic briefings. Promotion also enabled him to buy a Georgian house in Canonbury, an area of Islington in north London that was on the verge of gentrification. Wildeblood's burgeoning professional career combined with his influential contacts enabled him to enlarge his social influence. Homosexual culture was part of these networks, despite what he termed the 'saloon bar' mentality that prevailed in Fleet Street, where 'every sexual excess was tolerated, provided it was "normal"'.[199] Professional pressures of this kind forced him to live out a classic double life, adopting what he termed a 'deceitful' role during 'working hours' and a more honest existence when he was 'free'.[200]

Wolfenden admitted that he was 'not looking forward very much to our interview with Mr. Wildeblood'.[201] Despite his enthusiasm for bringing forward selected homosexual men, the chairman was irritated by this witness's tactics of self-promotion, especially when he discovered that Wildeblood had proposed himself to the committee rather than waiting to be invited.[202] Rees acted as Wildeblood's sponsor, endorsing his 'very interesting' written statement and asking for the paper to be circulated among members in advance of his interview. Wolfenden agreed, but he remained critical of Wildeblood's motives, predicting that his appearance at the Home Office, straight out of prison, would inevitably involve the sort of special pleading they were all keen to avoid.

Jack Wolfenden's own copy of Wildeblood's memorandum, preserved in the National Archives, contains heavily pencilled marginalia that provide insights into the chairman's reactions to his first homosexual witness. More often than not, Wolfenden's energetic annotations were hostile; his queries, exclamation marks and critical asides inserted at key points in the text revealed his scepticism about parts of Wildeblood's testimony.[203] 'You broke the law,' was his terse, pencilled response to Wildeblood's assertion that 'the imprisonment of men like myself is logically indefensible and morally wicked'.[204] 'Do you believe everything anybody in prison tells you?' was his equally unsympathetic rejoinder to Wildeblood's account of systematic blackmail.[205] But Wolfenden's social conscience was pricked by Wildeblood's argument that professional men from his background were excluded from the benefits and obligations of citizenship because of their sexuality. As he put it in one scribbled aside, expressed as an exasperated question to himself and perhaps with his own son Jeremy in mind, 'what to do with them?'[206]

Wildeblood's eight-page statement mixed generic social and psychological observations 'on the question of homosexuality' together with a casebook of his personal experiences that aimed to dispel commonly held 'misconceptions and prejudices'.[207] He cited evidence of blackmail cases, of police assaults on men caught cottaging, and allegations about his own mistreatment at the hands of the Metropolitan Police. The committee read how Wildeblood's phone had been tapped and his house raided without a warrant and how he was pressured by the police to register a guilty plea on the understanding 'that, if I did so, I should not be sent to prison'.[208] Wildeblood's time in Wormwood Scrubs had convinced him not just that medical treatment for homosexual men was inadequate, but that there could be no 'effective "cure" for his condition'.[209]

Peter Wildeblood's evidence formed part of a broader public story about his life, trial and imprisonment that was published later the same year in his book, *Against the Law*. His initial decision to declare his sexuality as an integral part of his personality had been taken at his trial.[210] 'It was easy for me to speak for the homosexuals,' he explained, 'because my admission that I was one of them had received the most widespread publicity; I had nothing further to lose.'[211] He used similar arguments in his written statement to the inquiry, though here he justified his commitment to sexual openness on the grounds of truth and moral integrity rather than political expediency; a life lived in secret crippled the personality, while freedom brought 'decency and dignity' to a homosexual's sense of himself.[212]

Wildeblood's testimony in front of the Wolfenden committee has produced markedly divergent responses from historians. Celebrated as an early 'coming out narrative', with its brave and forceful argument about the importance of sexual honesty in the face of the law and public prejudice, his account has been seen as a milestone in the 'march of homosexual emancipation'.[213] Equally, Wildeblood's heavily publicized campaign of self-promotion, claiming the right to speak on behalf of a wide community of homosexual men, has been criticized as exclusive and exclusionary, foregrounding the role of privileged sexual actors like himself while marginalizing the outlook of many men whose experiences were altogether different.[214] Both interpretations assume that Wildeblood was authorially in control of his story, but this was only partly true. His testimony set out to achieve distinctive goals, but it was shaped by the specific languages available to him to advance his political aims. These linguistic resources were generated both by the structures of the Wolfenden inquiry itself and by the conditions facing homosexual men in post-war London, and they set the parameters for Wildeblood's dramatic coming out story.

Wildeblood's dialogue with committee members was heavily influenced by the specific mechanisms of knowledge disclosure that governed the investigation. Once inside the Whitehall committee room his exchanges followed the familiar, quasi-juridical pattern of interrogation and response. The difference in Wildeblood's case was that, unlike the approach taken with official witnesses, committee members prioritized the personal dimensions of his testimony as a form of autobiographical narration that was understood to be constitutive of his identity as a homosexual man. Wildeblood for the most part was complicit in this arrangement.

Wolfenden opened the interview with his usual routine preamble about speaking frankly and 'off the record' that he used to break the ice with all witnesses. He hoped, as he put it to Wildeblood, 'that you will feel free to be as frank as you want to be, at the same time, obviously, preserving your right to stop when you want to stop'.[215] In Wildeblood's case openness indicated the committee's eagerness to hear him speak as a homosexual. Throughout the question and answer session, members actively encouraged him to frame his responses in this way. With 'regard to yourself' and 'from your own knowledge' were standard questions put to Wildeblood.[216] 'Have you ever come across people who at one time had relations with adults and at other times with boys?' Dr Whitby prompted him slightly later, in response to medical discussion about the connection between homosexuality and paedophilia.[217]

In his replies Wildeblood was not averse to using personal testimony to enhance his arguments. 'I know at Wormwood Scrubs there were two warders who had some kind of sexual relations,' he answered in response to questions from Canon Demant and Whitby about the homosocial culture of prison life.[218] 'Of course, one does get frightfully touchy in prison,' he continued.[219] His most personal disclosures were in response to questions about the nature of sexual and emotional relations between men. When Wolfenden raised the issue of promiscuity and blackmail, Wildeblood replied by drawing on his own heavily publicized relationship with Eddie McNally: 'My own experience, I think, shows that if I had simply picked up this airman and taken him for a night or something, and it was simply physical contact, I should not have gone to prison. It was the trust that I placed in him that was used as corroborative evidence.'[220]

Wildeblood's strategic command of the first person to discuss homosexuality and the committee's eagerness to hear about it were part of a

much wider tactical use of confessional declarations in post-war Europe
and the USA. Their most dramatic take-up was in the military and political arenas, where the Allies placed great emphasis on the need to obtain
confessions from Nazi war criminals and collaborators. Show trials staged
by the new Communist regimes were also organized around heavily publicized declarations of guilt from political subversives.[221] In the USA the
McCarthyite campaigns used ritualized forms of personal interrogation,
followed by swift condemnation of the guilty. Mike Hepworth and Bryan
Turner have noted how this Cold War context stimulated renewed sociological interest in confessional forms, especially in relation to the impact
of totalitarian propaganda and brainwashing.[222] Peter Wildeblood's testimony was shaped by therapeutic and autobiographical versions of the
confessional, rather than by these blatantly coercive techniques. Citing
medicine and sexology as well as a humanist language of personal rights,
his declaration of homosexuality was caught within the dual structures of
surveillance and liberal tolerance that characterized the operation of the
post-war welfare state.

Wildeblood's evidence was dedicated to tackling the big issue that had
obsessed the committee during their first nine months: how homosexuality was to be understood and how homosexual types were to be classified. This was the question he had insisted on clarifying at his trial when,
in response to aggressive cross-examination, he called for an agreed vocabulary to discuss homosexuality.[223] In providing answers he drew fluently
on many of the concepts that committee members had laboured over
in their early interviews with medics and psychologists.[224] Wildeblood
divided the homosexual population into three distinct groups. First, there
were glandular homosexuals, who through physiological or psychological
maladjustment 'regard themselves as women and behave accordingly'.[225]
Individuals of this sort were not morally responsible for their physical and
mental make-up, Wildeblood argued. This was essentially the idea of
homosexuals as an intersex, outlined by Havelock Ellis and elaborated by
inter-war sexology. Looking to the nascent science of endocrinology to
account for this anomaly in hormonal terms, Ellis increasingly believed
that homosexuality was a 'congenital abnormality', and Wildeblood followed Ellis's lead for at least part of his evidence.[226]

Second, Wildeblood insisted, there were pederasts, 'in whom the sexual
impulse is directed towards young boys'.[227] This was an entirely separate
condition, and in response to repeated questioning from the committee,
he insisted that 'there is a very strong distinction between men who are

attracted towards . . . boys and adult homosexuals'.[228] Finally, he listed 'homosexuals within the strict meaning of the word; that is to say, being attracted to men like themselves'.[229] This was by far the largest group; it was more or less equally distributed among the various social strata, but its members were extremely cautious and discreet.

Wildeblood's rationale for drawing these distinctions was partly an act of political calculation; in his evidence, as in his book, he denounced the negative manifestations of homosexuality, or pseudo-homosexuality, in the first and second categories, in order to affirm the innate dignity and respectability of the third group, where he placed himself. His differentiations were not only demarcations of type and moral judgement; Wildeblood consigned each of these groups to a distinctive environment or setting within the spectrum of London's sexual cultures.

Drawing on his experience in Wormwood Scrubs, Wildeblood insisted that the majority of congenital homosexuals were found in prison. They were by and large effeminate types: 'prostitutes and blackmailers' living 'on the fridges of crime', who were really 'women to all intents and purposes', though they happened 'to have a male body'.[230] Wildeblood insisted that they formed only a 'very, very small proportion of homosexuals altogether', but the hothouse conditions of prison life fostered their outrageous antics.[231] Using make-up and calling each other by women's names, they were also seen congregating outside West End restaurants and in many notorious pubs.[232] Wildeblood was quick to dissociate himself from London's queer subcultures; as he put it primly in response to hostile questioning by Adair, 'I rather tend to avoid people like that.'[233] His criticism of effeminate queans also involved an attack on metropolitan popular culture. The notoriety this group enjoyed was not helped by the 'tolerant amusement' given to such men in the capital's entertainment venues, he pontificated. Part of the problem was the 'frankly homosexual' musical comedies, all-male shows with camp antics and lavish staging that were such a big hit in theatreland.[234] Billed as family entertainment, they flooded the market with female impersonators, while in local East End pubs men appeared regularly *en travesti* without a word of complaint from the regulars.

Wildeblood's use of these sexual and spatial demarcations was not new; they had been developed by early twentieth-century campaigners like George Ives, Edward Carpenter and John Addington Symonds to delimit respectable from unrespectable homosexuality in the interests of forging an embryonic discourse of sexual rights.[235] Wildeblood's own intense criticism of the abject pervert and the outrageous quean also seemed to function as a form of displaced personal anxiety. London's queer commercial and entertainment spaces that he denounced so vigorously in front of the committee were a part of his own sexual lifestyle during the 1950s. After his release from prison he set up an afternoon drinking club in Soho's Berwick Street, while in parts of his autobiography and in his later fictional writing he celebrated the West End as a cosmopolitan playground, where gangsters, West Indian pimps, prostitutes and homosexual men all happily rubbed shoulders together.[236] But in his official testimony he marked out a rigid distinction between his own approved sense of himself and the marginal people and places of queer London. Wildeblood's ostensible aim was to gain social acceptance for respectable men, but in doing so he distinguished between 'good' and 'bad' elements in his own character, splitting his personality into ethically differentiated parts.

When it came to his respectable self Wildeblood's explanations were characteristically heterodox, reflecting the competing languages available to him to discuss homosexuality. In his written statement to the committee, as in many of the arguments made during his trial, Wildeblood drew on a definition of himself as an invert, whose condition was not of his own choosing.[237] At other moments, especially when he was not forced onto the defensive, Wildeblood's understanding of his sexuality was more fluid and malleable. Echoing Kinsey's findings, he noted how difficult it was in reality to draw a clear line between homosexuals and normal men. Many individuals had had homosexual experiences without ever becoming exclusively homosexual, yet such desires were usually never wholly eradicated.[238] In his autobiography Wildeblood also read homosexuality in Freudian terms as a psychosexual condition, writing about 'repressed homosexuals' in the language of contemporary psychoanalysis.[239]

Spatial demarcations figured equally prominently in Wildeblood's understanding of his own respectable identity. While queans were confined to the incarcerated world of the prison and to London's low entertainment venues, homosexual men of his type occupied an abstract and interior psychological space. Implicitly, he presented this mental universe as more significant than the degraded environments of the capital's sexual subcultures. Wildeblood's eagerness to distinguish his own expansive psychological sense of his personality from the socially limited identities that he awarded to unrespectable homosexual men, where difference was tied negatively to place, formed a key part of his political case for law reform.[240]

Speaking on behalf of the majority of 'people like me', Wildeblood argued that the mental well-being of respectable homosexuals was dependent on the degree of sexual tolerance available to them.[241] The disclosure of his own sexuality had been forced on him by prosecution, but 'now that I do not have any need to conceal', he assured the committee, 'I am certainly very much happier'.[242] Wildeblood's version of this early 'coming out' narrative characteristically made sexual openness central to his sense of personal validation. He argued for the collective benefits that would accrue if greater tolerance were given to men like himself, linking their increased self-worth to a growing sense of social responsibility. This was an argument that also featured prominently in sociologist Michael Schofield's pioneering investigation into homosexual culture published in 1952: social intolerance and legal stigma tended to produce unhappy and anti-social people.[243] At the close of the interview Wolfenden offered the usual opportunity to 'add anything to what you have told us', and it was at this point that Wildeblood underlined his point that psychosexual freedom and social citizenship were one and the same thing. 'I do not know,' he began, 'if I have stressed enough the point that the principal reason why I feel that the law is wrong is that it makes life extremely difficult, almost impossible, for a very large number of men . . . who in all other respects are perfectly good citizens.' Warming to his theme, he went on:

> There is no doubt about it, once you fall foul of the law in one respect it is very difficult to behave as a proper citizen in other respects as well. It is a tremendous strain for anybody and of course . . . it is unjust because it falls on the people who would be leading completely continent lives.[244]

With these powerful observations about homosexuality and the rights and duties of full citizenship, Wildeblood rested his case.

Many members of the inquiry including the chairman experienced the personal exchanges with Wildeblood as unsettling. Subsequently, Wolfenden spoke with feeling about the genuine transformation that he and his colleagues had experienced in relation to homosexuality, understanding their change of heart in humanist terms as progress towards greater sexual knowledge and enlightenment.[245] Wildeblood's testimony made a deliberate appeal to what Wolfenden called 'the creation of a public conscience', and the impact of his evidence had a significant impact on the inquiry's ideas about criminal law reform.[246] Wildeblood's distinction between respectable and disreputable homosexual conduct, which was at once spatial and psychological, strengthened the committee's case for decoupling public from private sexual morality.[247] His effort to prioritize the respectable homosexual, freed from the constraints of the criminal law but governed by discretion and a commitment to good citizenship, found favour with committee members because it coincided with their own views about public order, on the one hand, and private ethics, on the other.

Wildeblood's evidence differed in tone and content from the testimonies of the other two homosexual witnesses who appeared in front of the inquiry in July 1955. Carl Winter, Director of the Fitzwilliam Museum at Cambridge (who substituted for Angus Wilson) and Trevor-Roper both came at Wolfenden's express invitation. They represented a patrician social and sexual outlook that was relaxed and urbane and which cut against Wildeblood's emotional account of his personal life. Trevor-Roper recalled how he and Winter lunched at the Athenaeum before strolling down Whitehall to the Home Office. Once inside the committee room they were treated by their interlocutors as 'cultural equals'.[248] Appearing under the confidential aliases of 'Mr. White' (Winter) and 'the Doctor' (Trevor-Roper), both men emphasized that they led fulfilling lives in spite of widespread discrimination.[249] Implicitly criticizing Wildeblood's confessional narrative, they believed that an obsessive focus on the 'personal aspect' of homosexuality was 'tiresome', involving what they termed a 'disproportionate emphasis on its more morbid aspects'.[250] From a Northumberland gentry background, Trevor-Roper joked about some of his earliest sexual encounters, telling the story of how 'as a homosexual boy' he had seduced his family's gardener against the older man's will 'and against his better judgement'.[251] Winter for his part talked openly about the 'disastrous failure' of his own marriage, which he claimed he had resolved with his wife 'on a friendly basis'.[252]

Winter and Trevor-Roper presented a confident account of their social lifestyles which rested on secure ideas about class and status. Winter told the lawyer Victor Mishcon that homosexuals 'did not move in circles or classes' or follow 'ordinary social prejudices and distinctions', yet he personified a privileged world in which men like himself moved 'in an accepted pattern through society', visiting each other's houses, travelling abroad, making visits to art exhibitions and to the ballet, and generally having 'a satisfactory life'.[253] Winter's outlook endorsed the kind of cross-class homosexual idyll that concluded E. M. Forster's novel *Maurice* (1971) where, as Winter put it, a 'peer may be attached to a farm labourer or an able seaman to a university professor'.[254] Both Winter and Trevor-Roper argued strongly for criminal law reform in the private sphere because of the 'personal unhappiness, the risks, the blackmail, and the suicides', yet neither of them believed that a 'change in the law' would 'affect the vast majority of homosexuals', the '95 per cent' who already lived 'perfectly ordered lives'.[255]

Despite their class and cultural differences from Wildeblood, Winter and Trevor-Roper were equally strategic about the version of homosexuality they wanted the committee to hear about. They too exercised careful editorial control over disclosures about the kind of 'homosexual society' which they moved in. London's burgeoning commercial scene was absent from their evidence, and they dismissed cruising and cottaging for public sex as 'anti-social behaviour'.[256] Historians who have criticized the restrictive character of these testimonies and their exclusive and exclusionary consequences for public policy have failed to take account of two important aspects of the exchanges between the three witnesses and the committee.[257] There was a necessary element of political calculation involved in homosexual men putting their case to Whitehall's official culture that made choices about their evidence an inevitable part of the process of bearing witness. Subsequent recollections by Trevor-Roper revealed that he was fully aware of the approach he was pursuing. 'We spoke pretty carefully,' he recalled, recounting how both he and Winter tried to agree on a strategy in advance of the meeting.[258] He was also aware of the bureaucratic and procedural mechanisms that prescribed what could be discussed by witnesses and committee members alike. When Trevor-Roper commented, 'we were only given occasion to speak in a certain way . . . certain issues were not really allowed to come up,' it was these structural and linguistic constraints which he was referring to.[259]

The testimonies delivered by the three homosexual men marked an important enlargement of the inquiry's dossier of sexual evidence, but efforts to encourage prostitutes to come forward proved much more problematic. The difficulties that surfaced over recruiting street women were symptomatic of the growing imbalance between the two aspects of the committee's brief, as homosexuality assumed an ever larger part of members' time and intellectual attention. Gerald Gardiner championed two of Graham Hall's Mayfair protégés as possible witnesses, explaining that the women he had in mind had a 'considerable sense of vocation'. They were of 'perfectly good character', both visited a doctor regularly, and with 200 convictions for soliciting they had a fund of experience to draw on.[260] The Society of Labour Lawyers worked hard to give these women convenient appointment times. The Mayfair girls were slotted into the committee's business at 11.00 am, rather than at the usual 10.00 am start, not just because as Roberts explained they were 'notoriously late risers' but also because it would give them a chance to get clear of Bow Street Magistrates Court, if it was 'their turn' to be fined.[261] Wolfenden looked forward to the encounter: 'It looks as if we shall have a lively time . . . on Friday morning,' he confided. Off the record, both Wolfenden and Roberts were interested in the potential entertainment value of the meeting, not least because it would 'be interesting to see how some of our colleagues react'.[262]

But the girls did not turn up. Graham Hall, who knew them personally, was resigned if critical after the event. 'I knew the girls wouldn't come,' she recollected 'they wouldn't make the commitment. Gardiner was very disappointed. . . . But this girl Dorothy said, "I might as well tell you, I won't be there." '[263] Wolfenden complained that 'first-hand experience' from prostitutes 'was denied to us', and that as a result the writing of those sections of the report covering street offences 'was all done by hearsay', hampered by the absence of direct testimony.[264] After this unsuccessful attempt, committee members abandoned their efforts to recruit street women. Homosexuality rather than prostitution increasingly dominated the inquiry's sexual outlook and their moral philosophy. In a significant exchange at the close of his evidence, Gardiner was asked to assess the specific problems associated with the two aspects of the committee's remit. He insisted that from a social as well as a legal standpoint homosexuality was relatively easy to address, while prostitution was 'very much more difficult'.[265] Wolfenden disagreed, concluding that 'where questions of principle' were involved, homosexuality presented the more challenging issue.[266] Meeting this challenge, philosophically and in terms of public policy, preoccupied the inquiry during its final stages. It was ironic that a government inquiry which began life overwhelmingly concerned with prostitution should have ended its business by becoming much more engrossed with sexual relations between men.

Intimate Disclosures

There was one further final twist to the committee's encounter with London's sexual subcultures that complicated their agenda for moral reform. This was an embarrassing story of homosexual scandal that erupted dramatically into their official business, forcing an awkward confrontation between the Home Office and the capital's *demi-monde*. Centring on the misdemeanours of one of Wolfenden's own team, this episode, like most of the other scandals which dominated the post-war years, highlighted the complex links between high and low society that were perceived to be promiscuously interrelated in the social spaces of Whitehall and the West End.

In the spring of 1956 Wolfenden's team had arrived at the drafting stage of their report, but the writing was not going smoothly. A majority on the committee had reached general agreement on plans to partly decriminalize homosexual offences, but Adair categorically refused to agree to any change in the law and Wolfenden was spending time and effort trying to include him in the consensus. There were also ongoing noises of dissent on prostitution led by Mary Cohen. Along with these policy differences, the personal dynamics of the committee were showing signs of strain. Dr Curran was particularly critical of the chairman's whole approach to writing the report. In a lengthy memorandum challenging Wolfenden's leadership style, he complained that members were losing sight of the big picture, marginalizing 'general issues' in favour of the minutiae of endless 'textual criticism'.[267] Wolfenden himself was under increasing pressure from the Home Office to produce the long-awaited report. Lunching at his club in the middle of March, he was buttonholed by Newsam about an expected delivery date and hastily committed himself to a September deadline – a decision that he instantly regretted.[268] Juggling his work as committee chairman alongside his duties as university vice-chancellor, he confessed to feeling altogether 'end-of-Termish'.[269] He decided to have a proper Easter holiday, taking his family to the seaside on the Gower peninsula in west Wales. Putting up at the King Arthur Hotel in Reynoldston, he hoped he would be temporarily out of reach of Home Office memos.

Wolfenden's holiday mood was shattered when he opened his newspaper on 29 March. An item on the London page of the *Daily Telegraph* announced that the anonymous author of a series of dramatic stories recently published in the *People* was none other than a member of his committee, Goronwy Rees.[270] 'Principals of universities seldom write serial articles in the sensational Press. More seldom do they write them anonymously,' the *Telegraph* intoned, voicing strong moral disapproval. Marking out traditional distinctions between quality journalism and cheap news, the paper insisted that the type of writing identified with Rees was 'not at all the scholarly analysis one would expect from a Principal'.[271] Indeed it was not. Rees's five articles were a heady mixture of gossip, intrigue and sex laced with stories of international espionage. They centred on the career of a man whom the *People* announced was now the 'greatest traitor' in the country.[272] This was none other than the Foreign Office official turned Soviet agent Guy Burgess, who had vanished from London, only to resurface in Moscow in February 1956 along with his fellow spy, Donald Maclean. Jack Wolfenden was profoundly shocked.

'Guy Burgess Stripped Bare . . . His Closest Friend Speaks at Last', ran the banner headline of Rees's opening article for the *People*, which had been heavily trailed the previous Sunday.[273] What followed were a series intimate confessions in which their anonymous author claimed to speak out frankly and openly about his fondness for Burgess, 'this strange and in many ways terrible man' whose 'Jekyll and Hyde career was a masterpiece of duplicity'.[274] Billed by the paper's editors as a national crusade designed to expose Burgess's treacherous defection to the Soviet Union, the articles highlighted the relationship between the two men, which Rees disclosed was one of the closest intimacy. Rees described how they had known each other for twenty-four years and how they were 'constantly in each other's homes', sharing their 'anxieties and joys'.[275]

Rees's tortured involvement with Burgess coupled with his excursion into sensationalist journalism astounded friends and colleagues and severely compromised his profile as a public intellectual. The year before his appointment to the Wolfenden committee, Rees had returned to his home-town of Aberystwyth to become the Principal of University College.[276] The son of a local Methodist minister, his career epitomized the values of social mobility through educational success, paralleling in some respects Wolfenden's own meritocratic rise from the ranks of the provincial lower middle class into university administration and public service. After an education at New College, Oxford, and then a Fellowship at All Souls in the early 1930s, Rees had become a leader-writer on the *Manchester Guardian* and assistant literary editor at the *Spectator*.[277]

Rees first met Burgess in the summer of 1934 at Oxford where, according to Rees, Burgess attempted to seduce him, though he desisted.[278]

Subsequently, Burgess tried to recruit his friend for Soviet intelligence work, and there was always speculation surrounding Rees's own possible role as a spy or even a double agent.[279] Contemporaries who encountered Rees at Oxford, such as the young academic Noel Annan, believed Rees's own sexuality was 'staunchly heterosexual', but others noted his ongoing flirtation with homosexuality.[280] Isaiah Berlin, who was with Rees at All Souls, noted how Rees moved regularly 'in homosexual circles', while Maurice Bowra, the Warden of Wadham College, described him disparagingly as 'a normally sexed pansy'.[281] Rees later attempted to analyse the appeal of these Oxbridge homosexual milieus, believing that they shaped 'an entire generation of . . . Englishmen of the governing class', by encouraging 'an attitude of mind and heart which took it for granted that the deepest emotional satisfactions were only to be found in a masculine society'.[282] His close friendship with Burgess was part of this sexual culture, even though subsequently Rees saw the relationship in purely negative terms, complaining that the shadow of Burgess haunted him for the rest of his life.[283]

Rees's newspaper revelations about his one-time friend drew on the varied reporting styles that defined press coverage of homosexuality throughout the 1950s. Mixing the confessional genre, the exposé and the moral homily together with more contemporary psychological readings of abnormality, they testified to the continuing dominance of print journalism in disseminating popular sexual knowledge. Like Webb's 'vice in London' disclosures and the media treatment of the Rillington Place murders three years earlier, Rees's coverage linked transgressive male sexuality to the social spaces of the West End. The *People*'s series also strengthened the connections between the Establishment world of Whitehall, London's 'secret society' of homosexuality, and Cold War espionage.[284] 'Men like Burgess' were only able to escape detection, readers were told, because they had friends in high places who practised 'the same terrible vices'.[285] Rees claimed neutrality on the question of the 'legal and moral guilt of homosexuals', but his articles associated Burgess's 'treachery' with his addiction to unnatural sex.[286] Evidence about the prevalence of homosexuality in London and its infiltration into the highest levels of government provided Rees and his press sponsors with the opportunity to launch yet another round of disclosures about the links between the capital's overworlds and underworlds.

It was generally assumed that journalists at the *People* had exaggerated Rees's original account of his relationship with Burgess, embellishing his

language and exaggerating the plot so that it conformed to prevailing
readership expectations. In fact the reverse was true; Rees's own manuscript was more salacious than the articles that appeared in print.[287] His
draft contained long passages dealing explicitly with homosexual promiscuity which his editors strategically omitted from the final copy. The published version was graphic enough; it dramatized the story of Burgess's
life as a sequence of drunken episodes, addiction to drugs, dissolute physical habits and continuous sexual encounters, as Rees tracked his friend
across the public and private spaces of the West End. Harold Nicolson
described Burgess as a 'filthy drunk' in his commentary on the spy's defection in 1951, and Rees now amplified Nicolson's account of Burgess's dissolute character.[288] His aim was to accentuate Burgess's high- and low-life
networks of sexual transgression and the urban dystopia that lay at the
centre of this amoral world.

According to Rees, the 'frantic disorder' of Burgess's Mayfair flat provided an appropriate setting for his 'unnatural love affairs', as well as for
the notorious parties that brought together 'men of high repute' with a
bizarre gallery of rogues 'who looked as though they had been picked
up off the streets'.[289] Readers also encountered sinister Frenchmen and
Communist spies who mixed freely with distinguished scholars and
working-class toughs recruited from the East End.[290] At one of these
bizarre gatherings, the high-ranking guests looked on while Burgess
orchestrated a drunken brawl between two young thugs, as they smashed
wine bottles over each other's heads for entertainment. Rees went on to
claim that Burgess's thirst for sexual adventure had even compromised the
inner sanctum of the Foreign Office itself. Taken by Burgess into the
Victorian splendour of the Foreign Secretary's suite, Rees was amazed to
find that Burgess kept his personal copy of Kinsey's *Sexual Behavior in the
Human Male* in Ernest Bevin's safe![291]

Centring on Whitehall and the West End, Rees's articles moved outwards to highlight the importance of the Oxbridge–metropolitan axis
in Burgess's career. Rees traced him back to his flamboyant inter-war
life as a Cambridge student, then to his disclosure that he was a
Comintern agent, and finally to his involvement in Cold War politics
in Moscow and Washington. There were also the first hints of a 'third
man' who was central to Burgess's operations. This was the figure of
'Mr X', one of the diplomat's 'boon sex companions', who was
rumoured to hold a high position in English public life.[292] Two of Rees's
articles were accompanied by illustrations drawn by Burgess during his

time at the Foreign Office, which supposedly revealed the extent of the spy's depravity. Cartoons and compulsive doodlings showed double-headed monsters and transsexual figures, which a consultant psychologist interpreted as 'nightmare fantasies' of Burgess's 'monstrous life' and 'his own secret soul'.[293]

Rees's disclosures generated immediate and long-term consequences for the Wolfenden inquiry and for the political and intellectual culture that Rees deliberately sought to expose. The impact of the scandal on the committee was swift and dramatic. Wolfenden was so alarmed about Rees's revelations that he took action immediately. Writing to Newsam from his holiday hotel in Wales, the chairman's main concern was Rees's public declaration that he had been Burgess's 'closest friend'.[294] Wolfenden was acutely conscious of the way Rees's sensational revelations had the potential to damage the inquiry, by bringing the carefully crafted proposals on homosexual law reform into awkward proximity with Burgess's dubious sexual world. The chairman believed Rees's actions meant that the committee was now improperly close to the promiscuity and anonymous sex they had encountered through the evidence of many of their witnesses. 'It is pretty tricky,' he went on to Newsam, 'that one of the members of the Committee should now be revealed as having this particular connection with a notorious homosexual.'[295] Wolfenden could already hear cries of foul from the press and public opinion if it became known that a report recommending homosexual law reform had been signed by a reprobate like Rees. As he put it: 'It would be regrettably easy for the "Telegraph" – or anybody else – to say, "What would you expect, with this man as a member of the Committee?"' The affair was made even more problematic because Wolfenden did not expect Rees to resign voluntarily from the inquiry.[296]

The Home Office responded quickly, resorting to discreet and well-tried methods to marginalize Rees. Newsam enveloped the case in Whitehall's culture of secrecy that was used to silence awkward individuals and block the disclosure of information.[297] He dealt with Rees in private, confronting him about the allegation that he was the author of the anonymous articles, and on extracting a confession quietly removed him from the Committee. Rees was given an assurance that the reasons for his departure would not be made public, on account of the difficulties that this would cause with his employers at the University College of Wales.[298] But either Newsam's tactics proved ineffective or he wanted Rees exposed. A group of academics at Aberystwyth had already got wind of the affair, and they used Rees's media disclosures to press for his dismissal as Principal.[299] After a series of bitter exchanges, Rees was forced to resign his post. He was also effectively ostracized from London's social networks. When he attempted to relaunch himself in the capital's literary and artistic circles, he was quickly made aware that he was no longer 'salonfaehig', as he put it.[300] Rees never held any form of academic or public office again.

The hostility that Rees's actions provoked, not only from Wolfenden and the Home Office but also from close friends, revealed how the episode touched a raw nerve among prominent intellectuals and members of the upper class. For many the issue was their perception of Rees's extreme disloyalty in exposing Burgess, further complicating an already difficult political situation. It was this personal aspect of the affair that 'sickened' Nicolson, with his unswerving adherence to caste-like modes of class cohesion.[301] Michael Berry, later Lord Hartwell, the editor-in-chief of the Daily Telegraph, described Rees as 'someone who could not be counted on to be loyal . . . that was automatically a crime'.[302] Maurice Bowra wrote a poisonous letter to Rees about his treachery in exposing Burgess, suggesting that the college grounds at Aberystwyth should now be sown with 'Judas trees'.[303]

Rees's account of Burgess's life marked out explicit lines of connection between the official world of the Foreign Office and the low-life milieus of queer London. His articles kaleidoscoped together the public sphere of high politics with private vice, and they hinted that these connections were endemic among leading figures in Westminster and Whitehall. Burgess's personality had the capacity to evoke these transgressive connections, not just for Rees but for many men from his generation and background. When Bowra, in a characteristically vigorous phrase, remarked that Burgess 'had shit in his finger nails and cock-cheese behind the ears', it was precisely these disturbing associations that he invoked.[304] Writing from inside the Oxbridge circle that Rees sought to expose, Annan believed that Rees's actions detonated an explosion in the 'blast walls of the Establishment', while for author and journalist Rebecca West the whole affair spread a spiralling climate of fear and mistrust throughout London society during the 1950s.[305] Rees for his part admitted that his articles had breached the 'complicated moral code' through which the upper class was bound together.[306] The significance of the scandal lay in the way it exposed the informal codes of social honour held by the capital's political and intellectual elite.

The anxieties unleashed by Rees's revelations were not an isolated occurrence. In September 1955, shortly before the affair broke, political columnist Henry Fairlie launched a prominent attack in the *Spectator* on the concealed power of the Establishment that had shielded Burgess and Maclean.[307] Fairlie's understanding of Establishment influence, like Shils's analysis of the resurgence of aristocratic–gentry networks published in *Encounter* the previous April, covered not just the workings of official power but also the whole matrix of elite social relationships where 'the right people' moved effortlessly through a world that was self-enclosed and self-reproducing. At its heart, Fairlie insisted, was the Foreign Office, a bastion of 'masculine English society'.[308] With its finger-pointing at the Tory government and its accusation that oligarchic privilege remained a significant presence in the nation's public culture, his article provoked immediate controversy. Individuals who were themselves members of the 'governing class' rushed to rubbish Fairlie's assertions in a series of heated exchanges in the letters pages of the *Spectator*. They included John Sparrow, Warden of All Souls, David Astor, editor of the *Observer*, and Hugh Trevor-Roper, Patrick's elder brother, who was about to become Regius Professor of Modern History at Oxford.[309]

In October 1955 a very different type of incident turned further critical light on the social forces exposed by Fairlie and Shils. Princess Margaret issued a statement from Clarence House finally breaking off the relationship with her divorced lover, Group Captain Peter Townsend, 'mindful', as she put it, 'of the Church's teachings that Christian marriage is indissoluble and conscious of my duty to the Commonwealth'.[310] Her communiqué provoked criticism not just about the wisdom of her involvement with Townsend, but also about the courtiers, Anglican clerics and Tory grandees who were thought to have exerted a malign influence on her decision to put duty above personal happiness. Twelve prominent young writers and artists, including Humphrey Lyttleton, Wolf Mankowitz, Lindsay Anderson and Kenneth Tynan, wrote to the *Daily Express*, exasperated at the underhand work of Establishment figures who, they claimed, had pushed Princess Margaret into her unfortunate course of action. In particular, the authors identified 'reactionary' individuals close to the royal family and the Conservative government who had brought pressure to bear on the Princess.[311]

Rees's exposé surfaced as a disruptive sub-plot to the Wolfenden inquiry's official business. Part of an accelerating critique of upper-class and Establishment power, his articles refocused public anxieties about the

West End and its hinterland as the site of promiscuous associations between elite and low-life cultures. The revelations not only compromised the committee's work, they were also an awkward reminder of the problems associated with the inquiry's much vaunted moral philosophy: namely, the difficulties inherent in separating public from private behaviour. Like many of the other transgressive episodes of the post-war period, the incident showed how sexual scandal and its urban locatedness had the power to compromise the committee's modernizing strategy for reform. In the mid-1950s this remained largely concealed behind Home Office bureaucracy, but the issues raised by the Rees scandal continued to reverberate, erupting dramatically in the sexual revelations surrounding the Profumo affair six years later.

＊

When Jack Wolfenden walked over from the Home Office to the House of Commons on the evening of 2 September 1957, clutching bundles of his newly printed report, he confessed to being totally unaware that he was carrying political dynamite.[312] In fact, the Wolfenden report was an immediate sell-out; within a matter of hours few copies of the 5,000 first run of the 155-page blue book, priced at five shillings, remained on the shelves of the Stationery Office in Kingsway. Three days later counter staff were reporting 'very brisk' sales of the second printing and also anticipating a high demand from abroad.[313] Unofficial, erotically packaged extracts from the report marketed to an American readership confirmed its popular selling power worldwide. Almost overnight, Wolfenden himself became a minor celebrity, instantly recognizable in the press and over the airwaves.[314]

The report's reception intensified the spotlight on London in the ongoing national debate about sex and morality. All the issues that dominated the inquiry's work, both in their official discussions and in their unofficial encounters with sex in the city, were now dissected in the full glare of political and media scrutiny. The publication of the report was the catalyst for an increase in sexual knowledge, especially about the identities and lifestyles of queer men and street women and about the urban environments associated with them.[315] The committee overwhelmingly endorsed the authority of modern sexual experts, whose claim to professional status was at the expense of feminist and purity campaigners, but the flurry of press and radio coverage that accompanied the report also highlighted the critical role played by the popular media in disseminating sexual information.

The committee's radical proposal that private sexual acts between men should be partly decriminalized produced a flurry of debate but no immediate legislation. It took a decade and a further phase of parliamentary and pressure-group politics for this controversial recommendation to reach the statute book. In contrast, the rapid passing of the Street Offences Act in 1959 encouraged a partial reorganization of commercial sex in the West End, broadly in line with Wolfenden's strategy of reducing the public visibility of prostitution. The more overt forms of street soliciting decreased dramatically, if temporarily, as the girls went 'on the phone' or relied increasingly on syndicated networks of massage parlours and call-girl networks that were usually controlled by pimps and other male entrepreneurs.[316] Arrests for public soliciting declined by 90 per cent in the three months after the introduction of the Act, creating a national myth that the Wolfenden committee had, single-handedly, cleared the capital's streets overnight.[317]

Social and sexual historians have identified the report's double-sided strategy for homosexuality and prostitution as its key feature, laying the foundations for the liberalizing moral agenda promoted by successive home secretaries over the following decade. While this was undoubtedly the most significant policy outcome, tracking the committee's working methods close up points to a more complex picture of sexual governance, as well as to some important unintended consequences. The inquiry's announcement of a new ethic of regulation, carefully separating the sexual public from the sexual private, owed its intellectual origins to English utilitarianism, but in practical terms it was the dramatic encounters with London's sexual subcultures that determined their philosophy. Graphic evidence from low-ranking police officers and first-hand testimonies from homosexual men were just as important as abstract debates in formulating policy. The committee's recommendations were put together by men and women who were driven by competing gender-specific obsessions about sex and urban culture that intruded into the workings of government bureaucracy. State policy was the product of these social fantasies just as much as it was determined by rational evidence. The scandal that disrupted the inquiry in its later stages showed how the committee's modernizing project for sexuality was undercut by some very traditional sexual themes and personalities that obstinately refused to go away amidst all the enthusiasm for reform.

Wolfenden and his team refrained from peering too closely into their newly designated sphere of privatized, consenting behaviour, but other players with vested interests in the West End's sexual culture were much less reticent.[318] Now that prostitution was supposedly cleared off the streets, entrepreneurs, journalists and contemporary men–about–town all eagerly anticipated the expansion of a discrete but more erotically sophis-ticated sexual world, based on the 'natural laws' of supply and demand and removed from moral surveillance. This was overwhelmingly the sphere of the capital's heavily commercialized sex industry that was centred on the compressed entertainment spaces of central London. The policies of the Wolfenden committee were part of wider shifts in the capital's sexual economy taking place in the late 1950s and early 1960s under the impact of increased affluence and altered patterns of consumer demand. It is to these changes, conventionally associated with the idea of permissive London, that we now turn.

Chapter 5 Cosmopolitanism

Carnival

In the summer of 1955 Soho was the venue for a cultural experiment that ran as an annual event in central London until the early 1960s. A week-long Soho Fair was variously billed by the national and local media as a fête of 'uninhibited gaiety', a 'fiesta' of 'high carnival', with 'singing and dancing in the squares' and processions through the streets, an arts festival, and a major draw for visitors at the height of the tourist season.[1] Soho was 'on parade', announced the *Evening Standard*, coverage that was embellished in the local press around the themes of exoticism and hedonistic excess.[2] 'Cosmopolitania Goes Gay', enthused journalists from the *Westminster and Pimlico News*, expanding on a well-worked idea that Soho was in reality another country, a bohemian oasis located only a few hundred yards from Piccadilly Circus. The 'multi-racial and multi-lingual inhabitants of Soho' would soon declare themselves a 'foreign republic', announced members of the area's literary cognoscenti, somewhat tongue-in-cheek. In a post-war world that was massively riven by discord, this carnival in 'Little Europe' was hailed as an expression of 'the great feeling of communality which was present among the many nationalities existing together so amicably within its boundaries'.[3] Soho's unique atmosphere seemed to transcend the national and ethnic differences that cast such a shadow over contemporary politics and culture.

Centring on Soho Square, in the north-east corner of the district, and fanning out across a network of narrow adjoining streets, the fair was promoted by the Soho Association, a recently formed alliance of commercial and cultural interest groups. Events in July 1955 mixed together the traditions of the English carnival with a wide variety of hybrid and mimetic forms of European culture, especially those from the Mediterranean. Home-grown customs and ceremonies were deliberately placed alongside an eclectic rendering of foreign sights, sounds and smells in a format for the fair that was to become its hallmark over the next six years.

Modern fairs, the anthropologist Frank Manning has argued, tend towards culture's subjunctive mood; with an emotional range expressing cultural possibility and desire, they belong less to the transgressive universe of total social reversal that characterized traditional carnivals and much more to the sphere of leisure as performance and spectacle.[4] Soho's fairs drew on the area's reputation for cultural and ethnic diversity to create an idiosyncratic mood of celebration that could be marketed to local and national audiences via the media and entertainment industries.

Opening with the waiter's race, a sporting competition between Soho's foreign restaurant staff, the fair's community-minded business leaders invoked the customs and ceremonies of France and Italy to explain that such events were regular occurrences 'in most continental countries'. Organizers were praised for keeping up what the festival programmers referred to as 'this good old tradition' in 'London's Quartier Latin'.[5] Part of the open-air religious service that followed, attended by the Mayor of Westminster and other local dignitaries in weather reminiscent of 'summertime in Provence', was conducted by the Anglican Rector of Soho in a mixture of English, German, Spanish, Italian and Greek, reflecting Soho's polyglot cultures.[6] All week long, performances of classical music, dance and folk arts ran alongside events with a more contemporary feel when the emphasis was mainly on youth. There were exhibitions from local students at St Martin's School of Art, in nearby Charing Cross Road, as well as jazz from the young musician George Melly and from Cy Laurie and his band. Fresh from their recent success at the fashionable nightclub Mac's Rehearsal Rooms, nearby in Great Windmill Street, these two performers were a particular draw with a younger crowd.

Broadcasters on the BBC's Light Programme worked hard to convey the fair's atmosphere of social diversity for national radio audiences. Over the airwaves Soho was described not as inalienably foreign but as part of the eclecticism of English popular culture. The area's special character was advertised to the country as an easy-going metropolitan style that appealed to a wide variety of Londoners.[7] Events from the carnival were broadcast live as part of a special edition of the quiz and interview programme *Have a Go*, hosted by the homely Yorkshire comedian Wilfred Pickles, while radio stars Jean Metcalf and Franklin Engelman mingled among Soho's crowds with 'roving microphones' for an edition of the famous *Two-Way Family Favourites* record request show. Radio journalists and performers, with their respect for quirky eccentricity, found it relatively easy to accommodate Soho into their established genres of light entertainment.

The highlight of the carnival, on the opening Sunday, was the big parade of decorated floats winding through Soho's streets. Recorded by Pathé News, the company with local offices in Wardour Street, a focal point for the film industry, the event was shown on newsreels across the country throughout the summer of 1955. Screened as a light-hearted coda for cinema audiences, it relieved more serious items of domestic and international news, such as the national dock strike and Britain's deteriorating relations with Egypt over the Suez Canal. 'All the world lives in Soho, even including some English,' enthused Pathé's reporter, in a further effort to explain the area's character to national audiences.[8] Newsreel clips of the parade showed floats advertising prominent West End businesses followed by decorated displays from London's costermongers and Soho's foreign restaurants.

Centre stage in Pathé's record of the carnival procession was an eclectic tableau of femininity that proved a particular favourite with the crowd. Cameras pictured young women, dressed in traditional Italian and French peasants' costumes, moving gracefully through the streets and representing Soho's foreign communities. There was also a float carrying waitresses from the restaurants in Soho's newly established Chinatown, around Gerrard Street. Clad in long silk dresses and standing in a painted pavilion, they bowed decorously to onlookers as their procession passed by.

But it was a more up-to-date carnival sequence that captured most attention on that summer Sunday afternoon, especially among the men in the audience. The appearance of young women clad only in swimsuits and bikinis, jiving and swinging their hips and breasts in pseudo-provocative poses and blowing kisses to the crowd, drew the loudest applause by far. Pathé's coverage showed that these young women were less ethnically diverse than other participants in the fair; it was only European girls, and then mainly fair-skinned blondes and brunettes, who danced their way through Soho's public spaces. Journalists were quick to point out that the performers were all 'local girls' who worked in the area; there were models who sat regularly for the local Visual Arts Club, based in Soho Square, as well as dancers and showgirls from Soho's famous Windmill Theatre, sited only a few hundred yards away.[9]

Fully aware of the provocative sexuality of the girls' displays, the fair's organizing committee opted for a more traditional choice when it came to selecting Soho's carnival queen. Resplendent with sash, cloak and coronet in the style of an English beauty pageant, the election of 'Miss Soho' represented a conscious attempt to stabilize Soho's image around a more conventional icon of feminine glamour. The Soho Association announced that over twenty girls, including art school students, models, secretaries, typists and shop assistants, had entered the beauty competition.[10] The winner was a 19-year-old receptionist from a local fashion firm, the type of girl whom 'a chap could take home to mother'.[11] She 'was not too . . . exotic', the association explained, neither a 'continental' 'nor a Latin', but 'half Irish and half English'.[12]

Over the eight years of the fair's life, Soho's carnival girls projected a distinctive erotic style that was assertive, mobile and visually charged, and their performances confirmed a link between sex and Soho's cosmopolitan cultures (fig. 25). These young women were not part of Soho's traditional sex trade of street prostitution and brothel houses that so concerned the Wolfenden committee. They projected female sexuality as suggestive bodily idioms and erotic displays that were staged in the area's theatres and nightclubs.

Social historians and historians of sexuality have highlighted the impact of aggressive forms of commercial culture in the story of permissiveness. They have identified post-war economic growth and the expansion of demand as significant factors driving forward changes in sexual attitudes and behaviour.[13] In particular, pleasure-seeking images of women circulated by consumer goods and services and the mass media have been seen as key sexual icons of the 1960s.[14] The dancers and showgirls who acted out their displays at the Soho Fair were part of these shifts in feminine self-expression and associated bodily symbolism, but their activities were also grounded in a much more specific history. They were part of Soho's heavily gendered networks of entertainment and erotic nightlife that had marked out the district as exceptional for more than a century.

During the 1950s, as in earlier periods, Soho emerged as one of the forcing grounds for changing rituals and performances of commercially organized sexual entertainment, and displays of the female body were an important part of this package. Analyzing Soho's contribution to London's sexual economy, and charting the area's wider impact on English culture, demands a more detailed excursion into London's social geography than has driven our account so far. Moving beyond the official maps of Whitehall's policymakers and Kinsey's ethnography of Soho, this chapter maps the shifting contours of an area that was central to the outlook of a wide variety of metropolitan personalities. Understanding the specific changes that occurred in Soho after the Second World War and the privileged place they occupied in national life involves documenting the district's distinctive version of cultural trespass over a much longer period, showing how this local history continued to influence developments well into the post-war years.

Bohemians

In the 1950s the habitués of Soho never tired of pointing out that the area's reputation for cultural difference, together with its relationship to the wider world of the West End, was embedded in its extremely localized public spaces, its complex history and its unique customs and characters. The young writer and journalist Daniel Farson, who arrived in London fresh from Cambridge University in 1951 to work first in advertising and then as a photographer on *Picture Post*, the progressive photojournalism magazine, embellished this idea of the district. An enthusiastic and extremely well-connected Sohoite on account of his Oxbridge networks and his links to the metropolitan elite, Farson insisted that the area was as much a 'state of mind' as it was a boundaried physical environment.[15] He evoked Soho as the only area in London where the rules did not apply, remembering it as 'an island' in the country's grey 'post-war malaise', as 'lively as Isherwood's Berlin', the 'Rive Gauche' in Paris, and New York's 'Greenwich Village in its heyday'.[16]

Farson was later to become one of Soho's principal historians, fixing the district's story via its bohemian associations in ways that had a long-term impact on London's sexual and cultural atmosphere.[17] His arguments about Soho's imaginative possibilities were not new; they drew on observations first made half a century earlier by journalist and essayist Arthur Ransome in his extremely influential topography of London's artistic and cultural avant-garde, *Bohemia in London*, published in 1907.

Part literary essay, part sophisticated tourist guide, Ransome's study was advertised to an educated reading public at home and in the USA who were motivated by the pleasures of cultivated urban exploration.[18] Ranging across Chelsea and Hampstead as well as Soho, he evoked comparisons between these indigenous bohemian spaces of the English capital and the Latin Quarter of Paris. Characteristically, Ransome presented a picaresque, cleaned-up account of Soho that omitted the area's more problematic *fin de siècle* decadents like Oscar Wilde. He was keen to show that for 'a few grand years' in the late nineteenth century London rivalled Paris in its reputation for 'extravagant conversation' and bohemian life.[19]

Setting out an important premise for locating and experiencing London's cultural quarters which Farson and many other post-war commentators followed to the letter, Ransome stressed that districts like Soho were as much 'a tint in the spectacles' as they were a concrete physical setting.[20] 'Where is the Quartier?' Ransome asked rhetorically. 'It is difficult to give an answer. . . . It is impossible to draw a map.'[21] Actual maps, Ransome went on, ignored the way that London was experienced in the mind, as part of the 'strange, tense, joyful and despairing, hopeful and sordid life that is lived . . . by young artists and writers'.[22]

Throughout its modern history Soho was always envisaged as both a real and an imagined space, where complex economic and social relationships intersected with the equally rich resources of urban fantasy. Writing about Greenwich Village, a similar twentieth-century laboratory of metropolitan modernity, Christine Stansell has argued that such areas were usually understood by their devotees to be socially and geographically permeable rather than fixed, because the notion of fluid boundaries served the varied agendas of different interest communities.[23] Like Greenwich Village, Soho was projected as part of the geographies of the imagination and as an intensely compressed but mutable social environment. These interrelated factors positioned the district as a major site for cultural and sexual experimentation throughout the twentieth century.

In terms of physical mapping, local histories, social surveys and tourist guides published in the 1950s conventionally took Soho to designate the square mile of closely packed streets that roughly followed parts of the late seventeenth-century parish boundaries of St Anne's, in the east, and St James's, further to the west. Originally sited north of the royal court of St James's, successive Tudor and Stuart monarchs had sought to protect this area as an open space and as a hunting ground for the Crown, in the face of the perennial depredations of disease, social disorder and population increase. Soho's initial street lay-out and many of its early building projects were pioneered by enterprising aristocratic landlords and merchants, who took advantage of a statute of 1667 encouraging urban development in the face of massive pressure on the capital's economy and its housing stock as a result of London's Great Fire the previous year.[24]

Despite many later changes, a considerable proportion of Soho's late seventeenth- and early eighteenth-century infrastructure survived into the twentieth century. One of the district's major public spaces that exemplified this pre-Victorian lay-out was Soho Square, the site of the fairs in the 1950s. Planned by the Restoration surveyor and map-maker Gregory King in the 1680s as a fashionable Italianate piazza surrounded by town-houses for the gentry, the square's aristocratic history and architectural legacy continued to influence ideas about Soho well into the post-war period.

For local historian Margaret Goldsmith, writing in the late 1940s, Soho Square's noble facades possessed a 'romantic air', despite the fact that most of the buildings were now occupied by publishing houses and the offices of leading film companies.[25] Goldsmith's word painting evoked the celebrated 'romance of Soho', a literary and historical trope already well established by the late nineteenth century which was drawn on by successive generations of essayists who sought to identify the area with picturesque interpretations of the eighteenth-century past. The most developed account in this genre was local historian Edwin Beresford Chancellor's *The Romance of Soho*, published by Country Life in 1931. Writing in a heightened literary-cum-antiquarian style, he contrasted the splendours of Soho's bygone era, when 'Princes, (and once a king) . . . politicians, authors and artists' jostled 'one another', with everything that had scarred London in the twentieth century.[26] For Chancellor, Soho's romantic appeal was the result of its dramatic contrasts between past and present and of the way the 'phantoms of . . . notable men and women who once congregated here' continued to ghost the district.[27]

The search for 'romantic Soho' intensified after the upheavals of the Second World War, in part as a reaction to the modernist planning programme enshrined in the *County of London Plan*, which had looked forward to the functional rebuilding of much of this part of the West End. Journalist Stanley Jackson's urbane tourist handbook, *An Indiscreet Guide to Soho* (1946), aimed at the post-war man-about-town, celebrated the raffish and colourful Georgian legacy of Soho Square. For Jackson this environment was identified with the sounds of 'Venetian gamblers' rattling the 'dice-box far into the night', with 'Hogarth sketching his drabs', and with the ghost of the romantic writer and essayist Thomas De Quincey slouching 'into that house on the corner' looking for opium.[28] A more populist blend of sentiment and nostalgia informed Simon Dews's fictionalized travelogue *Soho* (1952). It was told as the story of a young provincial couple on their first visit to London who rejected the contemporary agenda of the Festival of Britain in favour of Soho's enchanted heritage.[29]

Contemporary tourist guides aimed at discerning visitors to the capital regularly stressed that Soho was a charming backwater, an oasis amidst the bustle of 1950s London. Accounts of this sort marginalized Soho's later Victorian development in the interest of preserving the area's picturesque appeal. The eighteenth-century romance of Soho also fed into the enthusiasm for all things Georgian that was driven by the burgeoning post-war conservation movement. Yet in reality the area's reputation as a unique quarter of London was shaped as much by nineteenth- and early twentieth-century changes to the capital's built environment as by its earlier inheritance. Major Victorian and Edwardian clearance and improvement schemes that defined the modern character of London's central area also indirectly influenced Soho. Four major thoroughfares, which were either constructed or substantially remodelled during the hundred-year period after 1820, came to form Soho's material and symbolic outer limits. Oxford Street to the north, Coventry Street to the south, Charing Cross Road to the east, and Regent Street to the west functioned as Soho's boundary lines, enclosing the area in a 'great rectangle', or what was more precisely a skewed parallelogram (fig. 26).[30] Soho's relationship to its surrounding urban arteries was one of difference but also of complex association. These peripheral routes formed a significant part of the story of modern Soho, because by contrast and comparison they worked to define the area's cultural exceptionalism.

Oxford Street was one of the great medieval roads that ran westwards out of London. Improved as a turnpike in the eighteenth century, it was also cleansed of its unsavoury reputation as the site for public executions at Tyburn Tree, the massive triangular-shaped wooden gallows that stood on the north-eastern edge of Hyde Park until the 1780s. During the 1820s Oxford Street emerged as an important shopping location, with its appeal to a varied female clientele. By the late nineteenth and early twentieth century the street was consolidated both as a major traffic artery and as one of the capital's most dynamic and heavily capitalized commercial environments.[31] The opening of the new underground route on the Central Line in 1900 enabled lady shoppers and their families to move below as well as above ground between Tottenham Court Road and Marble Arch, at either end of Oxford Street, and then out to the middle-class residential districts of west London. In his famous diagrammatic map commissioned for London Underground in 1933, draughtsman Harry Beck, working with modernist designer and planner Frank Pick, imagined this movement through space and time as massively streamlined and compressed, with tube travel conceived as a defining feature of metro-

politan modernity.[32] Piccadilly Circus, the underground station at Soho's
south-western corner, rebuilt in 1928 to a plan by Pick and the architect
Charles Holden, was designed to embody the new public culture of transportation, with batteries of automatic ticket machines surrounded by a
circular arcade of subterranean shops and flanked by wall panels in luxurious Travertine marble.[33]

Yet many of Pick's contemporaries pictured Oxford Street rather differently. A 'nondescript street', choked with traffic and thronged with
crowds, was how Forshaw and Abercrombie saw the thoroughfare in the
County of London Plan.[34] For these doyens of modern English planning
the street epitomized all that was wrong with London's commercially
driven central area. Defining shopping as chaotic and implicitly feminine,
in ways that revealed the prejudices of their own masculine high-minded
outlook, Forshaw and Abercrombie believed that West End consumerism
needed to be more strictly rationalized and regulated through tighter
control of the urban environment.[35]

In contrast to the masculine pessimism of leading urbanists, Virginia
Woolf's self-consciously feminine panegyric to the excitement of Oxford
Street, published in *Good Housekeeping* in 1932, evoked a similar atmosphere of urban chaos, but pointed to very different conclusions. Admitting
that it was not 'London's most distinguished thoroughfare', Woolf
famously endorsed the street as a 'forcing house of sensation', a monu-
ment to modern metropolitan culture that was 'built to pass' but not to
last. Assuming the persona of a middle-class woman with 'only fifteen
pounds a year to dress on', Woolf came to Oxford Street to 'linger and
loiter and look, if I can, as well-dressed as my neighbours'.[36]

Woolf's was the most literary of many positive endorsements of the
commercial possibilities of the West End which were voiced by women
from across the social spectrum during the inter-war period. Her themes
of feminine consumerism and the excitement of shopping were taken up
in a more formulaic way by the writers of post-war travel guides, intent
on relaunching London's tourist industry with a distinctive appeal to
women. In a world that was now hailed by advertisers and marketers as
an era of mass consumption, Oxford Street was celebrated as a national
institution: the great popular centre for shopping. According to the 1953
edition of the *London A to Z* guide, it was beloved of every woman in
Britain and a particular 'Mecca of suburban housewives at sale time'.[37]
Still scarred by bomb-damaged sites and with none of the chic of nearby
Bond Street, it was marketed by property developers as prime retail space.
Commercial rents in Oxford Street topped more than forty pounds per

square foot by the mid-1950s, partly due to the presence of many of the
best-known flagship department stores: Peter Robinson, John Lewis,
Marshall & Snelgrove, as well as the great Edwardian emporium, Selfridge's.[38]

The environmental and cultural contrasts between Oxford Street and
Soho were dramatic. Soho possessed very few of Oxford Street's modern
distinguishing features; with its lay-out of narrow streets, squares, courts
and connecting alleys, much of the district was still essentially pedestrian.
Old Compton Street, which dog-legged into Brewer Street at its western
end, was the closest that the area came to a major east–west arterial route.
It was cross-cut by the north–south intersections of Greek Street, Frith
Street, Dean Street and Wardour Street connecting Oxford Street to
Shaftesbury Avenue in the south. Unlike Oxford's Street's linear lay-out,
many of Soho's smaller streets and lanes were mildly circuitous, reflecting the original complex patterns of aristocratic land ownership. Most of
them contained retail premises and artisanal outlets that were small scale
and often family run, in contrast to the large department stores and chain
stores that dominated Oxford Street. Though it was accessible by taxi, car
and van, Soho was not crossed by any of the capital's main bus routes,
with the exception of the traffic along Shaftesbury Avenue, nor was it
defined by the presence of any underground stations, except at its outer
edges.[39] This sense of Soho as culturally amenable to the pedestrian
rhetorics of strolling, spectating and loitering was seen as a significant asset
for widely different groups of users (fig. 27).

Coventry Street, on Soho's southern fridge, extended Piccadilly eastwards and fed into the theatreland and cinema district of Leicester Square.
Since the late nineteenth century this had been the 'centre of the entertainment and night life of London', while more recently Leicester Square
had acquired the headquarters of a number of major corporations.[40] By
the 1950s many of the area's imposing Victorian theatres had been converted into cinemas, reinforcing its contemporary associations with
transatlantic popular culture. Pre-eminent among the buildings on
Coventry Street was Fanum House, the offices of the Automobile
Association. Rebuilt during the inter-war years with an imposing
Palladian facade that was illuminated at night, it was designed to project
an image of permanence and modern administrative efficiency.[41] Soho
possessed none of these modern corporate buildings; its architectural style
was domestic, small scale and haphazard, rising at most to four or five
storeys and comprising an uneven mixture of Georgian facades and
Victorian commercial premises. Soho's cultural goods tended to be self-
consciously marketed to highly specialized consumers, or to members of

the cultural cognoscenti, rather than to the mass market purchasers and suburban customers who set the tone in Oxford Street and to some extent in Leicester Square.

Eastwards, Soho's boundary line was drawn by Charing Cross Road, with its eclectic mixture of official buildings, theatres, residential mansion blocks and retailing.[42] Originally laid out by the Metropolitan Board of Works in the 1880s, this major boulevard had been designed to ease the traffic flow north of the new Charing Cross Road Station.[43] In the 1950s Charing Cross Road was dominated at its southern end by some of the landmark sites of nineteenth- and early twentieth-century municipal and official London: Westminster City Hall, the National Portrait Gallery with its corner facade in Florentine Renaissance style, and in the centre of the road, opening out onto St Martin's Place, the grey granite memorial to nurse Edith Cavell, the First World War heroine and patriot.[44] Further north, the thoroughfare was fronted by shops and offices, including W. H. Smith and local booksellers such as Collet's and Zwemmer's music publishers, which were grouped near the entrance to Denmark Street, London's 'tin pan alley' and home to various theatrical agencies.[45] Leading up to Cambridge Circus, which abutted Soho's south-eastern corner, landmark buildings included the offices of the Ministry of Works, the four-storeyed 'cathedral-like' structure of Foyle's bookshop, the modernist bloc that housed St Martin's School of Art, and the Sandringham Buildings, Victorian tenements that were originally built for local artisans.[46] Cambridge Circus itself was dominated by the Palace Theatre, 'an exuberant expression of Victorian commercial enterprise', with its grand terracotta frontage housing a venue that had variously staged grand opera, displays of female nude tableaux, and latterly musicals and reviews.[47]

In comparison, most of Soho's built environment was largely untouched by this type of nineteenth-century urban redevelopment. The area contained no government buildings and very few official landmarks, and those that it possessed, like the statue of Charles II in Soho Square, commemorated Soho's pre-Victorian past. Soho's vaudeville shows and nightclubs were internationally renowned, but they were intimate and small scale. They were generally owned or supervised by individual entrepreneurs and impresarios, who often had a strong economic or cultural stake in the area, rather than by the managers of London's corporate entertainment culture.

Regent Street, on Soho's western edge, skirted the district in a north–south arc running from Oxford Circus down to Piccadilly. Originally laid out by John Nash in the early nineteenth century as a fashionable parade ground connecting the new royal green space of Regent's Park at its northern end, to the Prince Regent's palace at Carlton House in the south, the rebuilding of the street in the 1920s in ferro-concrete and marble substituted the original Regency proportions for neo-classical grandeur. Erica Rappaport has shown how the disputed plans for the redesigned thoroughfare condensed competing imperial visions of the West End. Architect Norman Shaw envisaged the rebuilding project in a heavy baroque style, with masculinist connotations of official metropolitan prestige, a style that also found favour with the street's freeholders, the Crown Estate. Regent Street's shopkeepers, who opposed Shaw's original plan, advocated an alternative blueprint involving uninterrupted expanses of plate glass showcasing domestic and empire goods, with a hoped-for appeal to female consumers and international tourists. It was this feminine and more visually spectacular plan for modern commerce that won out in the final building scheme.[48] Post-war shopping guides continued to promote Regent Street as the display cabinet for domestic and Commonwealth merchandise, where 'household name after household name follow each other for a mile'.[49] During the coronation season the street's patriotic window displays advertised a mass of consumer goods swathed in the Union Jack and festooned with red, white and blue ribbon.[50]

Soho possessed none of Regent Street's aspirations to national or imperial prestige, and the area's links to empire were most commonly seen as negative ones. In the late nineteenth century social investigators revealed how Soho's problems of poverty, prostitution, immigrant culture and political subversion were located at the very heart of the imperial metropolis. Public moralists and journalists continued a version of this theme in the crescendo of anxieties about the condition of London as the capital of the Commonwealth in 1953. As Duncan Webb's articles made plain, it was the proximity of Soho's dubious social and sexual spaces to the coronation route, and by implication to the world of official or landmark London, which served as an important catalyst for the expansive national debate about contemporary morality.

Viewed collectively, all of Soho's major boundary streets signalled the resumption of forms of metropolitan life – mass leisure, shopping, transportation, tourism and business culture – that were generally not found inside the district. These major thoroughfares characteristically privileged styles of feminine consumerism, mass heterosocial nightlife and the masculine cultures of corporate business that were either marginalized in Soho or differently inflected within its extremely localized spaces. The surrounding streets were the product of large-scale redevelopment, and they carried many of the hallmarks of urban modernity described by sociologist Georg Simmel in his classic early twentieth-century essay about the impact of metropolitan culture on mental life: speed of movement, massive capitalization of the commercial and technological infrastructure, and the chaotic excitement of city life.[51]

Soho's material separation from these features of modern urbanism influenced its reputation as a world set apart from mainstream life in the English capital. In particular, the district's notoriety as a site of urban danger, sexual transgression and exotic cultural fantasy was orchestrated by a series of overlapping genres of metropolitan exploration, social exposé and atmospheric cultural tourism dating back to the late nineteenth century. The influence of these traditions extended well into the post-war period. Characters like Farson and his contemporaries drew extensively on Soho's cultural and sexual past in order to define their own sense of the urban present. The ongoing significance of this history for the 1950s means that its impact needs to be unpacked in detail.

Late nineteenth-century social explorers pictured Soho as a dark and foreign labyrinth, a babel of foreign tongues and a flesh market. Reporting in the 1890s, Booth described Soho's gradations of poverty in ways that were familiar from his broader sociological account of the West End. 'Sin and vice' ran riot in the neighbourhood of St James's, bordering on Mayfair in the west, Booth noted, where material deprivation and immorality coexisted cheek by jowl with 'the houses of the rich'.[52] This was the familiar depiction of the capital as a city of social and spatial extremes that Booth repeated countless times in his study of London's life and labour. His inquiry also highlighted Soho's 'strange outlandish population' that distinguished the district from other parishes in the West End. East of St James's in St Anne's, Booth drew attention to the particular commingling of 'the criminal and outcast', the 'utterly vicious and the hopelessly drunken', the 'harlot and those who facilitate and live upon her trade', along with 'every kind and description of foreigner, including a rapidly increasing colony of Jews'.[53]

Life and Labour of the People in London (1889–1903) catalogued Soho's mix of European nationalities and cultures, noting instances where five languages were spoken in one house. Writing in a more popular vein, journalist George Sims, a devotee of metropolitan slumming who saw himself as part of the capital's 'Bohemian fraternity' of editors and pressmen, also celebrated Soho's 'clash of unfamiliar accents' and the 'busy crowd of men and women of alien types and un–English bearing' in his two-volume edited collection, *Living London* (1903).[54] As a rule, Sims noted that different national and religious communities tended to group together in particular streets, a tendency that was supported by local churches and synagogues, such as the French Protestant Church in Soho Square, St Alban's Place Synagogue in the Haymarket at Soho's southern end, and the Swiss Chapel in Endell Street to the east. Booth depicted the atmosphere in these neighbourhoods as 'completely cosmopolitan' yet at the same time 'curiously insular'.[55] This sense of Soho's extensive geopolitical reach, coupled with the experience of ghetto-like enclosure and claustrophobia, was recorded by many *fin de siècle* commentators. Growing up in the area's Jewish neighbourhood in Berwick Street before 1914, Chaim Lewis remembered Soho nostalgically as an urban village, a 'self-contained community' locked inside a 'narrow circumference of streets'. He also emphasized that 'Jewish immigrant life added its own . . . tumult to the noisy round of the great metropolis'.[56]

Underpinning these observations was the demographic fact that Soho had been a haven for successive groups of foreign migrants over a 200-year period. The district was home successively to Huguenot artisans, French and German political emigrés, including Karl Marx and his family, Swiss and Russian refugees, Italian economic migrants, Irish labourers, and from the 1890s Eastern European Jews fleeing the pogroms of imperial Russia. By the end of the nineteenth century around 13,000 people lived in Soho. Some local surveys claimed that up to 60 per cent of the area's population was foreign-born, a figure that mirrored broader trends in London's increasingly multiracial demography.[57] The resulting atmosphere produced another long-standing version of the romance of Soho, this time organized around the exoticism of the district's foreign sights, sounds and smells.

Novelist John Galsworthy, chronicler of the fortunes of London's Victorian and Edwardian upper middle class, evoked the disorienting yet appealing character of early twentieth-century Soho for a middlebrow reading public in his second volume of *The Forsyte Saga*, *In Chancery* (1920). The quintessentially bourgeois Soames Forsyte, about to marry the daughter of one of Soho's French restaurateurs, encountered the district as 'untidy, full of Greeks, Ishmaelites, cats, Italians, tomatoes, restaurants, organs, coloured stuffs, queer names, people looking out of upper windows'. Confirming the prevalent view of Soho's exceptional status, Galsworthy concluded that it dwelt 'remote from the British Body Politic'.[58] Romantic novelist and essayist Alec Waugh evoked similar themes, using more stylized literary language familiar from his travel writing about the Far East and the Caribbean, in an essay written for the *Wonderful London* collection and published in the late 1920s:

> Soho . . . suggests mystery and squalor and romance . . . the obscure destinies of harshly savoured lives. It has a swarthy duskiness, an Oriental flavour; a cringing savagery. . . . there is a quality peculiarly un-English in the life that seethes and shudders about this dozen acres or so of streets.[59]

This quasi-orientalist theme was also taken up by journalist H.V. Morton in his account of Soho's Berwick Street market as the 'Baghdad-in-the-West', with its Jewish stallholders and fast-talking pavement salespeople, or schleppers.[60] Drawing on cultural imagery that was widely circulated in the press and in popular fiction, both Waugh's and Morton's stories of Soho were part of an expanding genre of inter-war writing on London that was produced as atmospheric tourist literature and literary travel guides.[61]

Yet though journalists and social reformers defined Soho as a world apart, an exotic slum at the heart of the British Empire, they were also aware of the dynamic connections between the district and the West End's expanding pleasure zone that existed on its borders. Sustained by the skills of foreign artisans, who were often employed as outworkers in the luxury trades, Soho's dressmakers, upholsterers, food manufacturers and scenery painters variously serviced the court society of St James's, the shopping thoroughfares of Oxford Street and Regent Street, and the West End's theatres. The proximity of this prestigious foreground meant that Soho was regularly depicted as central London's 'backstage', the provider of goods and labour for the highly stratified and voracious forms of consumption generated by shops and customers in nearby elite locations. Lewis noted how Jewish retailers and manufacturers in the 'honeycomb of narrow streets' south of Oxford Street had a dual role during the inter-war years; they serviced the great department stores of the West End and also provided for the needs of 'lower income shoppers'.[62] During the 1940s Jackson made a similar point about the exotic fruit and vegetables on sale in Old Compton Street's greengrocers, where local Soho residents regularly rubbed shoulders with 'famous hostesses', 'stockbrokers' and 'newspaper lords'.[63]

A sophisticated and adventurous shopper like Woolf demonstrated both her social dexterity and her cultural capital by moving easily between these segmented spaces of West End consumption. Woolf not only celebrated Oxford Street's democratic allure, she also delighted in the more specialist sales outlets of Berwick Street's market, as she famously haggled over the price of silk stockings with Jewish schleppers.[64] Making forays into the West End from the gentility of her home in Bloomsbury's Tavistock Square to the north-east, Woolf portrayed Soho as an alluring space of cultural encounter for middle-class women during the inter-war years. Morton's portrait of the same local market profiled less elevated but equally demanding female consumers. His comic vignette of Berwick Street introduced 'Miss Jones', the archetypal City typist, who came to Soho in search of cut-price goods because she insisted on dressing 'like a duchess on seventy shillings a week'.[65] Negotiating the sales pitch of Jewish stallholders, 'the ripe young Rebeccas' and 'their smart younger brothers', Morton described Miss Jones as one of dozens of women who found their way into Soho's shops and markets because they possessed 'chinchilla minds' though only 'coney incomes'.[66]

Sex played a major role in the development of Soho's consumer economy almost from the area's inception. In the years before 1914 Soho and its environs were a focal point for the capital's expanding homosexual culture, organized around cross-class liaisons, a thriving trade in male prostitution, and the appropriation of some of the area's public spaces for sexual encounters between men. Piccadilly Circus, described by the young sexual radical George Ives as a 'great centre for inverts', had an established reputation as a site for male prostitution and sexual pick-ups by the 1880s, at a time when the West End was consolidated as the capital's centre for commercialized leisure and entertainment.[67] Grand hotels, theatres and music halls, especially the notorious gallery promenades at the Alhambra and the Empire theatres at Leicester Square, provided opportunities for cruising and sexual adventures.[68]

Soho was also written into the fictional erotic geography of central London, featuring prominently in the pornographic novel *Sins of the Cities of the Plain*, published privately from offices in Leicester Square in 1881. Opening with the gentleman narrator's story of his encounter with John Saul of Lisle Street, an eponymous 'Mary-Ann', or male prostitute, whom he met on the square, the novel identified Soho's streets and alleys as part of a picaresque world of slumming and eroticized transgression that included the varied pleasures of flagellation, sodomy and sexual orgies.[69] A more aestheticized image of homosexual Soho appeared in Oscar Wilde's account of the decadent metropolis in *The Picture of Dorian Gray* (1891), where the district featured as the setting for Dorian's sexual rendezvous in a 'little Italian restaurant' in Rupert Street.[70] More prosaically,

Soho's sexual spaces were regularly cited in police reports and courtroom evidence, especially during the Cleveland Street scandal of 1889–90, an affair that exposed Post Office telegraph boys and their aristocratic clients in a West End brothel network north of Oxford Street. John Saul featured again in the case; identifying himself as a 'professional sodomite' he was interviewed by the police at 150 Old Compton Street, where he lived with 'female prostitutes, men with women's names, theatre people and blackmailers'.[71]

The expansion of the West End's mass markets for leisure during the inter-war period, with their appeal to a more democratized idea of the metropolitan consumer, also influenced the development of homosexual Soho. The first ostensibly homosexual guide to London, with the coded, punning title *For Your Convenience: A Learned Dialogue Instructive to all Londoners and London Visitors*, was published by George Routledge in 1937. It was written by Thomas Burke, a long-time Soho habitué and a novelist who specialized in exotic and low-life themes. With its endpaper map of London's 'cottages', which anticipated Nott-Bower's police survey of homosexual London circulated at the Wolfenden committee, *For Your Convenience* was an esoteric product of widening market trends and readerships. Cast as the supposed record of a conversation between Mr Mumble, 'doyen of the Thélème Club', and a young commercial traveller with a secondary school education, Soho was identified as part of an eclectic tourist itinerary advertising venues for public sex between men. Burke's guide ran from Ludgate Circus westwards through Trafalgar Square and across to Piccadilly Circus and Green Park.[72] 'For Soho', it advised, 'you need only go a few steps down Macclesfield Street', indicating the whereabouts of the notorious Dansey Place urinal, nicknamed Clerkson's Cottage, or 'for another rendezvous', Burke suggested knowingly, 'you may go up Berwick Street, turn into Broad Street, where you will find full service.'[73] All of Burke's sexualized spaces, in Soho as elsewhere, were open to double meanings whereby homosexual sex (the 'full service') was advertised as an open secret to the initiated.

Beyond the world of these clandestine encounters, Soho's inter-war cafés, restaurants, pubs and clubs contained almost every type of homosexual customer. The first floor of the famous Lyons' Corner House in Coventry Street became a male rendezvous in the late evenings and at weekends. Renamed the Lilypond in subcultural argot, this sexual space was carved out of one of the flagship restaurants of the Lyons' chain of eating houses that first opened in the capital in 1909. Men meeting men shared the place with other Lyons' customers, including suburban female shoppers, West End shopworkers and a Jewish clientele.[74] With its exterior facade in Carrara marble, a resident band and chandeliers, the Corner House created the illusion of metropolitan grandeur and de luxe consumption for customers on moderate budgets. The Lyons' management rigorously policed any overt forms of homosexual contact, but the Lilypond was an important social rendezvous through to the 1950s, attracting men from different social classes and becoming what one of its resident waiters described as 'the absolute Mecca of the gay scene'.[75]

Barred from many West End pubs and clubs, the outrageously effeminate young quean Quentin Crisp, arriving in London in the late 1920s, felt more secure at the Black Cat café in Old Compton Street. 'The clientele is very "mixed",' *The Lure of London* (1929) warned unsuspecting tourists about the venue, and Crisp and his friends spent their days in the café 'buying each other cups of tea, combing each other's hair and trying on each other's lipstick'.[76] Crisp's choice of Soho location was in part a deliberate attempt to identify with the world of bohemian squalor, as the café was also a hang-out for 'other outcasts of various kinds', including male and female prostitutes and struggling writers, artists and musicians.[77] More discreet, middle-class meeting places, servicing customers whom Crisp sardonically referred to as '"them" who acted refined and spoke nice', and 'whose people had pots of money', were forged at intimate restaurants such as Gennaro's in New Compton Street, 'famous for its beautiful waiters', and the Isola Bella in Frith Street, catering to an elite clientele.[78]

Prostitution in Soho was reputedly as old as the area itself. As early as the 1770s the notorious White House, or Hooper's Hotel, on the site of the old Spanish Embassy at Soho Square, operated as a high-class brothel that was described as 'notorious in the annals of Fashion'.[79] Equipped with a discreet side entrance leading to rooms decorated in exotic styles and furnished with ornate, inlaid mirrors, the hotel catered to royal and aristocratic clients, such as George, Prince of Wales, and the Duke of Queensberry.[80] A century later Booth's team exposed a very different picture of organized vice in Soho, linking prostitution to all the other manifestations of metropolitan poverty: crimes of violence, petty theft and above all pimping.[81] On Shaftesbury Avenue, Booth's investigators observed how prostitutes walked on one side of the road, shadowed by their ponces on the other.[82] Prostitutes and their bullies ' "are of all nations . . . French, English, Belgian and German in particular"', confided one local policeman, reinforcing the district's status as an international sexual entrepôt. Booth's study also drew attention to the reputation of French street women, who were 'the cleanest and the healthiest' and often the best paid. Many of Soho's leisure and entertainment spaces doubled as houses of assignation, especially the burgeoning clubs and 'massages establishments' that were, according to Booth, simply 'brothels with another name'.[83] Local police argued that aggressive prosecutions against brothel-keepers only shifted prostitution elsewhere, while action taken against known houses pushed women and their ponces into more concealed sites of commercial sex. Soho's brothels changed month by month, and women who operated independently of male control simply 'flitted from room to room'.[84]

Extensive prostitution in Soho's streets and commercial spaces preoccupied Westminster Council's Watch Committee throughout the inter-war years, when they conducted regular prosecutions against disorderly houses. Brothels run by Italian pimps operated from the Dieppe Restaurant and the Bohemian Café, both in Old Compton Street, while flats and businesses in Gerrard Street and Lisle Street to the south, along with premises in Archer Street and Greek Street, were regularly cited in prosecutions brought at Marlborough Street Magistrates Court.[85] On some occasions these local incidents became major national news, as Soho became the flashpoint for multiple forms of metropolitan vice and organized crime.

The 1928 Goddard case, involving systematic and extensive police bribery planned by the enterprising Sergeant Goddard from Vine Street police station, off Piccadilly, exposed brothel premises at the Comfortable Restaurant in Greek Street and sexual networks run by restaurateurs and nightclub proprietors that were supported by other corrupt policemen.[86] Some West End officers later acknowledged that police bribery by prostitutes was almost institutionalized in 1930s Soho, especially in Lisle Street, revealing a sexual economy that was later confirmed by the Wolfenden committee. Policeman Harry Daley, who joined Vine Street station in 1935 and dined regularly in Soho's restaurants with his elite literary patrons and lovers Joe Ackerley and E. M. Forster, remembered that the local prostitution trade had its own strict if corrupt rules: 'Each whore paid a regular lump sum . . . which entitled her to be arrested in proper rotation. . . . they formed small queues waiting to pay their dues.'[87]

Recollections by Soho residents and service workers pointed to the relative tolerance of street women within local neighbourhoods. Jewish Sohoites growing up in Frith Street and Manette Street during the inter-war years remembered that our '*cheder* [school] was in an area surrounded by prostitutes. . . . we boys became very friendly with them. There was one very nice person we called her "Gifty" because she always gave us sweets and little presents,'[88] Italian restaurateur Elena Salvoni, who started work at the Café Bleu in Old Compton Street during the Second World War, recalled how prostitutes and their 'maids', 'beautifully dressed with their sheer black silk stockings and high-heeled shoes', often lunched discreetly at the café, where 'we always treated them with equal respect'.[89] But the war also introduced new lines of social division into the West End's prostitution trade. Jackson's guide to Soho's pleasures informed discerning male tourists that the girls on the 'Sackville Street "beat"', west of Piccadilly Circus, were usually well dressed and had a '"Berkeley Square manner" and expensive flats of their own'.[90] In contrast, Jackson warned that Soho was fast becoming the place for new types of downmarket young amateurs from the East End, women whom he referred to as 'Cockney pompadours' wearing snoods or headscarves, chewing gum and talking a 'blend of Brooklyn and Billingsgate'.[91]

Many of Soho's markets for commercial sex overlapped with or lay adjacent to the area's bohemian culture. Ransome had taken issue with French romantic novelist Henri Murger's classic assertion that 'Bohemia neither exists nor can exist anywhere but Paris', placing Soho at the centre of his account of unconventional London. In doing so he established a pedigree for the district that remained significant throughout the twentieth century, as it was reworked by apologists as different as Woolf and Farson.[92] The artistic and social influences that shaped this bohemian idea varied considerably in terms of their shifting personnel, varied locations, and the different ways that bohemian society was advertised among the cognoscenti as well as to a wider public. What linked them was the way that Soho was regularly defined as a playground for sophisticated consumers of food and drink, cultural goods and exotic nightlife.

In the years before 1914 Soho's cafés and restaurants were part of an avant-garde network that also included artists and writers meeting in the West End and in Fitzrovia, as well as in Bloomsbury. The Domino Room of the Café Royal, on Soho's western edge in Regent Street, was celebrated as London's answer to Murger's original bohemian space, the Parisian Café Momus. Serving 'coffee . . . in glasses [and] . . . pale cloudy absinthes', it was decorated in French style with large gilt mirrors and sawdust-strewn floors.[93] Its clientele included the artists Aubrey Beardsley, Walter Sickert and Rex Whistler, together with writers and critics George Bernard Shaw and Max Beerbohm. In the 1920s the café's social circle expanded to include Bloomsbury artists Roger Fry and Duncan Grant, as well as Augustus John and writer and artist David Garnett, who opened his antiquarian bookshop in Gerrard Street in 1923.[94]

Fitzrovia, the location of the West End's furniture and furnishing trades, was viewed by many members of London's cultural and literary avant-garde as coterminous with Soho, at least until the 1940s.[95] Bohemian districts, as Ransome pointed out, did not follow conventional geographical demarcations; they were spaces that criss-crossed established local boundaries.[96] Fitzrovia was separated from Soho by Oxford Street, and it was subject to a different metropolitan police jurisdiction and governed by separate licensing hours. Both Soho and Fitzrovia provided a range of cheap amenities such as restaurants, studios and living accommodation close to the heart of the West End, together with an ambience that mixed local artisanal and immigrant cultures with the comings and goings of London's social elites.[97] From 1905, Sickert's Fitzroy Street group of artists deliberately cultivated seedy proletarian themes drawn from the inner city as the subject-matter for their paintings and the basis for their artistic personas. Fitzroy Square was also the early adult home of upper-middle-class Bloomsbury members Virginia and Adrian Stephen, while Fry opened his Omega Workshops on the square in 1913, a project funded by Shaw to produce post-impressionist art, furniture and pottery.

Fitzrovia's restaurants, in nearby Charlotte Street and Percy Street, ranged from cheap cafés, including the Jewish salt-beef dining rooms, to the celebrated Eiffel Tower. Run by its Viennese proprietor Rudolph Stulik, the Tower restaurant had been discovered by Augustus John and the socialite Nancy Cunard. Self-styled vorticists Ezra Pound and Wyndham Lewis celebrated the launch of their magazine *Blast* there in 1914, and in the 1920s regular guests included Cecil Beaton, American actress Tallulah Bankhead, and the chronicler and critic of upper-class social mores, Anthony Powell.[98]

The decline of elite venues like the Tower and the Café Royal from the late 1920s was the result of a shift in London's avant-garde. The onset of the Depression, along with the appearance of a new generation of artists and writers keen to distance themselves from the aloof style of the Bloomsbury circle and from patrician literary figures such as T. S. Eliot and society patrons like Cunard, prompted the search for different types of West End locations.[99] The emergence of the pub as a focal point for bohemia marked a new departure in Fitzrovia's and Soho's development.

Pre-eminent among these pub venues was the Fitzroy Tavern on the corner of Charlotte Street and Windmill Street. Skilfully promoted in the 1930s by its Jewish landlords, the Kleinfeld and Allchild families, as the 'Rendezvous of the World', these assiduous publicans consolidated the Fitzroy's reputation as London's premier bohemian location.[100] Advertised in Hickey's *Daily Express* gossip column as Fizrovia's 'central shrine' and the 'Clapham Junction of the world', the pub mixed artists like Augustus John and Jacob Epstein, composers Constant Lambert and Peter Warlock, and politicians such as Hugh Gaitskell.[101] By the 1940s it was also attracting a wide-ranging homosexual clientele, including professional men in search of sexual excitement, queans and rough trade, together with female prostitutes. 'Drinks at a gay pub called the "Fitzroy" which is really the gayest pub I know,' the actor Kenneth Williams confided in his diary after the war. 'Charming. Full of sailors and queans with prying eyes . . . all searching for some new sensation.'[102] Other pubs where homosexual men mingled with a bohemian clientele, with the capital's criminal class, and with more regular West End drinkers included the Wheatsheaf, the Marquis of Granby and the Bricklayer's Arms, which were all to be found just north of Oxford Street in Rathbone Place, Percy Street and Gresse Street respectively.[103]

Pubs of this kind were representative of a new social style that Dylan Thomas described as the valorization of 'sordidness'. He explained the idea to novelist and dandy Julian Maclaren-Ross when both men were working as scriptwriters for Strand Films in Soho's Golden Square in 1943: 'Why don't you try to look more sordid? Sordidiness, boy, that's the thing.'[104] Thomas understood that a dishevelled appearance, coupled with heavy public drinking, could be used as a valuable trade-mark, distinguishing his persona from the perceived effeteness of literary London and from the gentlemanly manners that ruled in West End publishing. Thomas's behaviour was resourced not just by Fitzrovia's pub culture but also by the down-market cafés and illegal bottle parties that flourished in the area during the late 1930s and through the war years.

Overwhelmingly, this was a masculine representation of bohemia, dealing in appropriate pleasures and satisfactions. Women who moved on comparable terms with men were more unusual, reflecting their unequal access to the culture of the bar-room and to flamboyant displays of social eccentricity. Women artists, models and latter-day salon hostesses were part of the bohemian scenes of Fitzrovia and Soho. Most prominent among them was the artist Nina Hamnett, who had been part of the Café Royal circle and the Fitzroy group and had modelled for Modigliani and Henri Gaudier-Brzeska. A tall striking figure with 'bluntly cropped hair and a personality and a mouth to match', Hamnett was a significant painter in her own right, who had a number of successful shows in major West End galleries during the inter-war years. Along with the Allchilds, Hamnett promoted the Fitzroy Tavern as a bohemian centre, where she served as Fitzrovia's unofficial cicerone and local publicist. As she acknowledged, the Tavern 'became a meeting place' but 'not only did one meet people . . . one did a lot of business there also'.[105]

In Soho proper, Birmingham-born and Jewish Muriel Belcher operated as a self-styled hostess for privileged patrons of bohemian society. In the mid-1930s she opened the Sphinx nightclub with Dolly Mayers in Gerrard Street, followed by the Music Box in Leicester Place in 1937, which was a society and theatrical haunt.[106] Belcher was best remembered as the hostess of the Colony Room, or 'Muriel's' as it was known to regulars, the drinking club she started immediately after the war. In this small, bamboo-clad first floor bar in Dean Street, Belcher presided 'like a monarch' in a 'tightly knit kingdom' over customers who included the doyens of London's progressive arts and media scene, especially Francis Bacon and John Minton, Farson and Melly.[107] Outrageously witty and physically handsome, she promoted the 'atmosphere of a constant party', liberally fuelled by drink. Perched on a stool at the club's entrance, Belcher crafted an autocratic public posture, mixing a form of 1930s 'high camp' with a more streetwise argot of calculated rudeness that entertained her 'family' of regulars and excluded unwelcome punters.[108] Belcher's talent as a club owner lay in mixing her customers, so that though Colony members included homosexuals, artists and men–about–town, her club was never typed.[109] Novelist and Sohoite Colin MacInnes, who was one of her regulars during the 1950s, celebrated Belcher in a provocative essay on the pleasures of the West End drinking club published in *Encounter*, where she appeared as 'the platinum-tough girl with the heart of gold', 'sharp, hard, ruthless, and aggressive' but also 'generous, forgiving, considerate, and rather shy'.[110]

One final grouping complemented Soho's social mosaic in the first part of the twentieth century: the younger members of London's social elite. The heterosocial leisure and entertainment spaces patronized by society that began to expand before the First World War included venues in Soho or on its peripheries. The growth of the public restaurant was the initial innovation, as dining out became an expression of fashionable sociability among the metropolitan upper and middle classes. Burke remembered how in the 1890s 'those little places' in Old Compton Street came into fashion, providing 'new food, more varied menus, "different" surroundings, a vivacious atmosphere, and deft service'.[111] In Galsworthy's novel

Soames Forsyte admired Soho's fictional Restaurant Bretagne, where he encountered couples 'seated at little round green tables with . . . pots of fresh flowers on them and Brittany-ware plates'.[112]

During the 1920s Soho's nightclubs promoted an up-to-date social ambience for metropolitan society. Paramount among them was the Café de Paris, an 'oval, two-tiered basement' in Coventry Street, which was launched in 1924 for 'the aristocracy, millionaire industrialists, American play boys, Conservative M.P.'s [and] daring debutantes'.[113] It occupied a liminal space between the glamour of Leicester Square's theatreland and the visible street prostitution in nearby Gerrard Street and Lisle Street. Harry Foster, son of a theatrical agent, and Martin Poulsen, the Danish head waiter from the Embassy Club, mixed the atmosphere of a restaurant and cabaret, capitalizing on the current vogue for 'midnight follies'.[114] It quickly acquired the patronage of London's pre-eminent man-about-town, the Prince of Wales, who often visited the club accompanied by film stars, entertainers and his mistresses, Freda Dudley Ward and later Thelma, Lady Furness.[115] The club's famous 'dance hostesses', who discreetly mingled with royalty and West End celebrities, provided partners for unescorted men in return for a basic pay of two pounds a week, plus expensive gifts and tips.[116] A prominent Café de Paris hostess, Norah Docker, remembered how on one occasion she was handed a cheque for £200 by Sir Ernest Tate, chairman of the sugar company Tate & Lyle, as payment for 'services'.[117]

The Gargoyle Club, opened in 1925 by the society organizer David Tennant in an alley off Dean Street, cultivated a more self-consciously cultural and artistic atmosphere. 'A bohemian and bourgeois rendezvous', its members were drawn from London's literary and political class. Pictures by Matisse hung on the walls, and the club boasted a membership list that included Rebecca West, Noël Coward, William Beveridge and Maynard Keynes, together with the usual leavening of socialites.[118] 'Free and easy manners rule' at the Gargoyle, noted journalist Stephen Graham, a reference to the club's predilection for outrageous public school behaviour and its relaxed attitude to homosexuality.[119] Like Belcher at the Colony Room, Tennant's recipe for success lay in his ability to juxtapose different clientele in ways that suggested originality. His aim, according to one long-standing member, was to cultivate a reputation for whimsy and caprice, where self-professed bohemians would 'not be ill at ease' and yet 'not perfectly at ease'.[120]

In contrast, the 43 Club, an underground basement in Gerrard Street, epitomized a more illicit version of Soho's pleasure economy. It was started in 1922 by Mrs Kate Meyrick, the so-called queen of London's nightclubs, who presided as the venue's informal hostess for patrons ranging from young aristocrats, celebrity stage stars, exotic foreign invitees, gangsters and working dance hostesses. 'Ma Meyrick's' club, which was raided repeatedly during the 1920s, brought together many of the contemporary themes of West End nightlife: upper-class rituals of heterosociability, modern dancing, drugs, same sex encounters and discreet prostitution.

The 43 Club featured in Evelyn Waugh's *Brideshead Revisited* (1944) as part of Captain Charles Ryder's reminiscences celebrating the aristocratic metropolitan style of the inter-war years. Appearing in Waugh's novel as the 'Old Hundredth', run by 'a stout woman, in evening dress', the club was the quintessential night-time venue for the 'bright young things' of the 1920s.[121] Waugh's fictional account reinforced the 43's inter-war image as an experimental space where young bloods, 'fairies', grafting dance hostesses and corrupt policemen coexisted in exquisite tension. The society columns of the middle-market press ensured that the reputation of Soho's clubs was advertised beyond the elite circle of the West End's social scene to a much wider readership. Venues like the 43 cemented Soho's reputation not just as a traditional place of moral danger, but also as a semi-acceptable safety valve for all the irregular transactions that had come to define modern metropolitan life.

Soho's development in the first half of the twentieth century was exceptional and diverse. No one group of social actors dominated the area, nor were people and places wholly separate from one another. Modern Soho was not a series of distinctive subcultural milieus existing in isolation, as some historians have suggested.[122] Cosmopolitanism was the term used repeatedly to encompass the varied cultures that were kaleidoscoped together in the district. This was not the Kantian philosophical understanding of the concept, implying a sense of critical distance and universalist social detachment. As Judith Walkowitz has convincingly argued, cosmopolitanism had much more specific historical meanings in early twentieth-century public discourse, conveying a sense of modern metropolitan life that possessed strong 'positive and negative valences'.[123] The idea was strongly identified with 'transnational forms of commercialized culture and with transnational migrants', especially with Soho's

European and Jewish residents and service-sector workers. Cosmopolitanism also encompassed Soho's markets for sex, where transgressive behaviour was promoted by established and experimental forms of the entertainment industry. Cosmopolitan bodies and spaces came to mark Soho as a site of both pleasure and danger, behaviour that was encouraged in foreign restaurants and cafés, dance halls and variety theatres, pubs and clubs. Most of these settings were marked by the dual meanings of cosmopolitanism; they conveyed the optimistic possibilities of the modern city, produced through consumerism and the leisure industries, and a negative, deracinated idea of urban impurity, rootlessness and disorder.

During the 1950s cosmopolitanism in Soho underwent a series of subtle but significant shifts as an alliance of business leaders and cultural intellectuals worked to reshape the area's reputation. The Soho fairs were part of this process of rebranding, when the district was advertised both as an exciting part of contemporary popular culture and a sophisticated component of elite metropolitan leisure. A wide variety of urban experiences and commodities were included in the package, ranging from exposés of London's underworld and coverage of Soho's local food cultures to fashionable tourism. Sex was a key part of these commercial campaigns. Soho's cultural redefinition had significant consequences for the sex industry, as prostitution and homosexuality as well as erotic entertainment and nightlife were restructured on more contemporary, consumer-led lines.

Publicity, Crime and Consumerism

Soho's post-war cultural reconstruction began with publicity. Film makers, television directors, novelists and journalists, along with influential local entrepreneurs, produced explanations about the area's exceptional status that were advertised to national and international audiences. Soho was already understood to be a special place by the late nineteenth century, but it was during the 1950s that it was systematically marketed in this way. The district's double character as dangerous and compelling, combined with its reputation for sexual frisson, was incorporated into a set of generic media treatments that promoted Soho as an eccentric but acceptable part of English national culture.

The earliest and arguably the most enduring of these post-war campaigns fed off Soho's notoriety as the centre of London's criminal underworld. The social and sexual dislocations of the war and the problems of reconstruction focused public attention on Soho as the home of spivs, violent black–market racketeers, pimps, prostitutes and feuding rival gangland bosses. One of the most effective publicists for these criminal networks was the retired police chief, Robert Fabian. Fabian began his career with the Metropolitan Police at Vine Street in the early 1920s, rising through the ranks to become Superintendent.[124] Retiring in the late 1940s, he reinvented himself as 'Fabian of Scotland Yard, England's greatest detective'.[125] Fabian became an apologist for Soho, first as a reporter for the Kemsley newspaper group and then as an influential media personality, and his memoirs were turned into a successful Saturday night BBC television series, *Fabian of the Yard* (1954–56), which was exported to the USA. Inspector Fabian appeared in person at the end of each episode as the straight-talking detective, echoing a style of audience address that had been pioneered by the actor Jack Warner in *The Blue Lamp* (1950) and in the early television series *Dixon of Dock Green*.[126]

Fabian's published two-volume crime casebook was billed as 'an intimate record of night life in London'.[127] Situated in the ethnographic present of the early 1950s, it drew together events and stories that covered the whole of his thirty-year career. Introducing himself as the policeman who had 'tried cocaine', Fabian confessed that he had spent hours watching the clubs and brothels on the 'wickedest pavements of England'.[128] Covering every conceivable urban pathology, his *London After Dark* (1954) returned again and again to Soho as 'The Square Mile of Vice'.[129] Soho was 'that mixed up backyard' of clubs and drug dens filled with deviants and thieves, 'prostitutes and coloured boys'.[130] Echoing Ransome's earlier observations about Soho as an imaginary space, Fabian insisted that from a policeman's point of view the district was not just 'an area you could mark out', it was also an 'atmosphere that pervades part of the West End'.[131] Liberally illustrated with black-and-white photographs, Fabian's books portrayed Soho as a monochrome world of shadowy alleys that were dimly lit by lamplight and peopled by characters who congregated in London's 'criminal clearing house'.[132] In his television series this stylized imagery flashed past in shots of police car chases across the capital, with the detective in hot pursuit of some of London's most notorious villains.

Fabian felt free to suggest to his readers that Soho's vices were potentially intriguing and alluring rather than wholly corrupt, because his memoirs sought to explore the criminal mind *in situ*. This approach reflected the turn to more 'criminal-centred' styles of narration that were evident in criminology and in popular culture during the immediate postwar years.[133] Fabian also justified his remarks about Soho's appeal on

account of its exceptional location; part of the area's charisma derived
from its close proximity to the glamour of official London and to the
comings and goings of elite society. The police chief's stories about his
encounters with wide boys and 'whores' were told in the same breath as
his recollections of the Queen's and Princess Margaret's visits to West End
theatres and nightclubs.[134] The point was, as Fabian never tired of pointing out, that both types of activity took place in the same compressed
space of 'roughly one square mile'.[135]

Fabian was one of a number of writers who claimed a privileged position for their stories about Soho's underworld on account of their own
personal involvement and their close-up techniques of observation. Duncan
Webb's investigative journalism was legendary both for its assiduousness and
for its highly unorthodox reporting style. 'Crime news can be obtained
from a number of sources,' Webb noted in 1955; 'an extremely important
method by which I obtain some of my facts about the underworld . . . is
from members of the underworld themselves.'[136] His crime and vice
exposés always began at 'ground level' and more often than not in Soho.[137]

Webb tracked almost every manifestation of Soho's 'vice racket' for the
popular Sundays and daily papers during the 1950s. Like Fabian, he also
published his memoirs, which were marketed as a bestselling volume of
London's *cause célèbre* crime stories.[138] Webb's Soho assignments for 1955
alone included dope peddling among 'jazz crazy negroes' and white boys,
call-girl rackets, and serialized coverage of the 'gangland feud' between
two of the 'little Caesars' of Soho's underworld, Jack Spot and Albert
Dimes.[139] Along with Fabian, Webb was one of the first post-war crime
writers to sense that readers 'wanted to enjoy as well as condemn the
activities perpetrated in London's square mile of sin'.[140]

Webb's ability to market stories about Soho's netherworld as spicy
entertainment was a hallmark of his journalism, which mixed a hard-
boiled reporting style with the romantic and sentimentalized treatment of
London's more appealing villains. His ghosted autobiography of another
Soho gangland boss, locally born Billy Hill, confirmed how criminal
culture was now consumed as national publicity.[141] A month after the first
fair, a brawl and serious stabbing on the pavement outside the Continental
Fruit Stores, in Frith Street, was the cue for a new outbreak of gangland
warfare between Hill and Spot.[142] Spot's subsequent trial, with its extensive press coverage, rehearsed many of the familiar themes of sleazy Soho,
with its spielers, protection rackets, petty brutality and pimping. At the
launch party for Webb's book, held at the fashionable Gennaro's in

November 1955 and covered by William Hickey, leading underworld figures, journalists and Scotland Yard detectives rubbed shoulders with prominent socialites like Lady Docker.[143]

Webb and Fabian twinned the pleasures and perils of Soho's contemporary vice rackets with more traditional overworld–underworld images of the bifurcated Victorian city that had dominated coverage of inner London during Christie's murder trial. Post-war film directors and popular novelists enlarged these cultural and visual resources to make Soho meaningful for national and international audiences. Crime movies became a successful staple of British commercial studio production during the late 1940s, adapting features from the well-established genre of the American gangster film, as well as from home-grown melodramas and thrillers. As early as 1946 London tourist guides were noting ironically how 'death strikes suddenly and often' on contemporary film sets supposedly located in Soho, where everyone in Frith Street 'packs a gun or razor, or usually both'.[144] With their exaggerated half-tone lighting and asymmetrical framing, these movies drew on the visual repertoire of *film noir* in order represent the metropolis as what Charlotte Brunsdon has termed a 'doubled London', in which official images of the capital were played off against landscapes of crime and immorality.[145]

The British film *Noose* (1948), directed by Edmond Greville, was based on a popular inter-war West End stage play by Richard Llewellyn. The original film script, *Murder in Soho*, was decisively rejected by the British Board of Film Censors in 1937, on account of its close-up treatment of London's criminals.[146] By the late 1940s public demand for cinema treatment of low-life characters and themes meant that the censors now felt able to approve the film with only minor changes. Billed as a 'black market' story set almost exclusively in Soho, *Noose* was shot against a studio backdrop of nineteenth-century streetscapes and dimly lit interiors.[147] Soho was pictured as the cosmopolitan home of French prostitutes, Spanish showgirls and Caribbean valets, all of whom worked at the Blue Moon Club in the pay of the Italian gangster 'Sugiani' (played convincingly by the Maltese-born actor Joseph Calleia). Modelled on the Sicilian vice racketeer Eugene Messina, one of the infamous Messina brothers who dominated West End prostitution from the 1930s and who were finally exposed by Webb, Sugiani's schizophrenic character personified the dual spaces of Soho. In his sumptuous club he was a lover of fine things and an informal host to the members of elite society, while backstage he was depicted as a cheap modern punk: the 'nastiest thug in Europe'.[148]

The Hollywood film *Night and the City* (1950), produced in Britain by Twentieth Century Fox and directed by Jules Dassin, revisited the high and low spaces of Soho and its surrounding area. Recurrent panoramic shots of Trafalgar Square and Big Ben, depicting the public, monumental world of the capital, were mapped onto the back alleys, glistening wet flights of stairs and sordid interiors where much of the film's action was set.[149] Dismissed by film critic Dilys Powell for its lack of urban verisimilitude, *Night and the City* dealt largely in iconic images of London for American and international cinema audiences, with its cheerful Cockney stereotypes and easily recognizable establishing shots of the city's landmarks.[150] It focused attention on Soho as a world of dubious foreign club owners, pay-offs and underworld hierarchies. The film dealt in contrasted national stereotypes of criminality, playing off the untrustworthy American anti-hero, club tout Harry Fabian (Richard Widmark), against the skilled, 'honest graft' of the English criminal fraternity.[151]

The spiv cycle of films ended in the early 1950s, but representations of Soho as the backstage setting for the gritty realities of crime and immorality continued in post-war fiction. Cheap paperbacks with steamy covers and blurbs comparing West End vice to organized racketeering in New York and Chicago depicted Soho as a heavily commercialized and often violent sexual entrepôt.[152] Josh Wingrave's *A Room in Soho* (1953) traced the sexual career of its middle-class, provincial anti-heroine, who established herself in the area as a high-class prostitute and a successful club owner for moneyed tourists and rich businessmen.[153] Displacing austerity images of London with coverage of de luxe consumption promoted by a shady society elite, the novel advertised female sexuality as an assertive and commercially manipulative feature of this West End world.[154] Anticipating the Wolfenden inquiry's investigation into the changing character of prostitution, Wingrave's book stressed that the capital's up-market sex trade was flourishing in private flats, discreet call-girl rackets and West End nightclubs. Marty Ladwick's novel *Soho Street Girl* (1954), which was prosecuted for obscenity at the Old Bailey, was more explicitly pornographic, revealing English women caught in a sadistic Soho vice ring led by Italian and Cypriot pimps.[155] Ladwick packaged Soho as a space of violent, miscegenist fantasies, in which the area's highly charged sexual atmosphere was generated by its claustrophobic environments and its menacing brothels and low-life dives.

All these varied treatments advertised Soho as an exotic cultural and sexual elsewhere, using the modern media and the entertainment industry to promote the area to a wide cross-section of audiences and poten-

tial consumers. An equally effective style of informal publicity, highlighting different though sometimes overlapping themes, was produced by
Soho's influential bohemians. Historians of the area have awarded a privileged role to this group, not least because many self-styled Sohoites subsequently became important local chroniclers, fixing Soho's story
retrospectively via their own obsessions.

Farson's influential interventions in the 1980s and early 1990s worked
to define Soho's post-war character as one of the last settings for 'true
bohemia', arguments that were endorsed by his collaborators George
Melly and Soho personality and man–about–town Jeffrey Bernard.[156] Most
of this coverage affirmed Soho's uniqueness and its separation from mainstream life in the West End. Much of it, too, celebrated the area's reputation for sexual unorthodoxy among young educated men, especially its
attractions for émigrés to London released from suburban or provincial
constraints. Sometimes this was merely a celebration of 'girls, booze' and
'nutcases', as Bernard evoked it, but for Farson and Bacon being bohemian
also involved regular visits to Soho's queer pubs and clubs, which Bacon
referred to as his 'sexual gymnasium of the city'.[157]

With their extensive access to the media, Soho's bohemians heavily
influenced the area's character throughout the 1950s and beyond. As early
as 1951, London travel literature began to reflect their impact, when
Francis Aldor's unconventional guide included references to Soho's 'social
clubs', especially the Colony Room. Mainstream tourist itineraries now
also contained obligatory paragraphs on Soho as 'the foreign speaking
island' where 'the shops are as fascinating as the inhabitants'.[158] Coverage
of bohemian Soho featured in Sam Lambert's guide for independently
minded visitors, *London Night and Day* (1958), which promised to reveal
the nonconformism that lay beneath the surface of the capital. For
Lambert, bohemianism in Soho now meant an eclectic mixture of
European cultures and social types, a place where 'a Briton in a boiler
suit reading [the] *Daily Mirror*, a Spaniard in a leather jacket and beret, a
Frenchman and eight Italians' gathered 'talking twenty to the dozen . . .
with Luigi di Rossi at the cash till'.[159] Farson pulled these images together
in his role as a television presenter in the early 1960s, fronting the live
arts programme *This Week*, which he used as a vehicle to promote Soho's
contemporary personalities and aficionados.[160]

But Soho's bohemian character was changing in the 1950s under the
impact of the new music-based cultures with their emphasis on youth.
Among the most prominent of the new arrivals were jazz and blues musicians and their audiences, many of whom made guest appearances at the

Soho fairs. Ronnie Scott and John Dankworth opened their jazz venue, Club 11, in 1948 with 'bare lightbulbs', 'tatty settees' and 'dope'; skiffle and blues clubs started up slightly later.[161] The related phenomenon of the coffee bars, such as the Moka in Frith Street, the first with an espresso machine which opened in 1953, also acted as a focus for contemporary youth styles. Beatniks favoured the House of Sam Widges, on the corner of Berwick Street and D'Arblay Street in west Soho, while the plusher surroundings of the Partisan café, in nearby Carlisle Street, catered to the post-1956 generation of New Left intellectuals who partly overlapped with the beat world.[162]

Above all, it was Colin MacInnes who linked Soho's new youth cultures to wider audiences in his novel *Absolute Beginners* (1959). MacInnes was a one-time Soho resident who used the Colony Room as a public lounge for his journalism and his literary career and local clubs for sexual liaisons with Caribbean men.[163] His novel featured contemporary Soho alongside a portrait of his other favourite inner city location, Notting Hill, as seen through the cynical eyes and ears of a hip teenage narrator. Soho was evoked as 'the most authentic' of 'all London quarters', a place where 'vice of every kink', including 'speakeasies and spielers, and friends who carve each other up', was mixed with 'dear old Italians and sweet Viennese'.[164] Soho provided MacInnes with a literary opportunity to showcase the area's 'un-silent teenage revolution', where 'disc shops', 'shirt stores and bra-stores', 'hair salons' and 'cosmetic shops' sold 'all the exclusive teenage drag' to 'pale rinsed-out sophisticates'.[165]

MacInnes's emphasis on the power of consumer culture reflected wider debates about the impact of the teenager in the affluent society that were documented by social researchers such as Mark Abrams.[166] Three years after the publication of *Absolute Beginners* MacInnes rounded on Soho's 'commercialization' in the recently launched weekly *New Society*. He rehearsed a critique that was later to become widespread among successive generations of Sohoites, intent on marking out their own cultural authenticity from the supposedly inauthentic invasion of the market. 'Now Soho is dead, except commercially,' MacInnes complained; 'Soho, at one time, owed its reputation to its people: now, the area bestows a bogus reputation on almost anything.'[167]

This riposte to the perceived onset of consumer-led gentrification was reinforced by Frank Norman, one of the self-proclaimed members of Soho's criminal class, who also went public with his critique of modern Soho in 1958. 'One time I used to lay around Soho nearly all of the time,' Norman confessed. 'These days I keep as far away as possible from it.'[168]

An auto-didact, a reformed borstal boy and a leading cockney apologist for old Soho, Norman had a strong investment in preserving the area's traditional underworld story. His account gave centre stage to the 'bums, tealeaves, villains and tearaways' and the 'brasses' standing on street corners, who were now being 'pushed out by the tradespeople' and the craze for espresso bars.[169]

A jobbing journalist after his release from prison in 1955, Peter Wildeblood also acted as a Soho publicist. Opening his own drinking club in Berwick Street, Wildeblood showcased the area's low-life cultures as Soho's 'crooked mile' in his fictionalized autobiography *A Way of Life* (1956) and in his two novels of London life, *The Main Chance* (1957) and *West End People* (1958). Wildeblood's portrait of Soho was even more sentimental than MacInnes's, depicting the area as a refuge for golden-hearted prostitutes, muddle-headed gangsters, cockneyfied skifflers, evangelists and debutantes.[170] This Soho image was subsequently popularized in the successful musical *The Crooked Mile*, Wildeblood's collaboration with composer Peter Grenwell, which opened at the Cambridge Theatre on Soho's eastern border in 1959, starring Elizabeth Welch and Millicent Martin.[171] Other West End productions that publicized similar Soho themes included Norman's own hit *Fings Ain't Wot They Used T'Be*, which ran for two years from 1960, and Wolf Mankowitz's musical *Espresso Bongo* (1959), which was turned into a film staring Laurence Harvey and the young Cliff Richard.

Promotional work of this kind was not just the preserve of bohemian self-publicists, it was also part of a campaign closer to the ground that was put together by local business leaders, intent on relaunching Soho as the venue for sophisticated consumption. In the long term this initiative had a significant impact on Soho's economy. At the outset, however, there were sharp disagreements among entrepreneurs, journalists and community activists about the way forward, differences that reflected competing views about how to deal with Soho's shady reputation.

Speaking on behalf of Establishment London as well as the tourist industry after the success of the first Soho Fair in 1955, the illustrated magazine *Sphere* was unequivocal about the future; the explicit aim of such events was to rid the district of the 'unsavoury associations . . . attached to it'.[172] *The Times* agreed wholeheartedly, welcoming the summer carnival as an exercise in counter-publicity; journalists insisted that in future 'the name of Soho should cease to be linked in the public mind to all that denotes the underworld'.[173] Local community leaders understood Soho's problems rather differently. 'Soho is not exactly a shining example of virtue and modern righteousness,' admitted Father Tony Reid, assistant priest at St Anne's church, at the opening ceremony for the second fair, but he went on to emphasize how the new wave of activity energizing local businesses and voluntary groups was 'not interested in whitewashing people'. Reflecting the contemporary stance of progressive Anglicanism and committed social work, Reid insisted that Soho's hoped-for revival presented a chance to uncover new forms of community activism.[174] In contrast, Soho's bohemians rejected this appeal to social responsibility in favour of their own heavily gendered commitment to romantic individualism. Farson, who was himself indirectly involved in the fairs, spoke for many of his contemporaries when he insisted that in the dash for respectability Soho needed to retain its reputation for sexual and cultural nonconformity, as a place where bad behaviour was cherished and where 'nobody gave a damn'.[175]

Predictably, it was Soho's entrepreneurs who synthesized these different perspectives into a commercial blueprint for the area's renewal. The growing dominance of commercial interests distinguished these post-war efforts to rebrand the district from initiatives that had been launched periodically from the late nineteenth century onwards. Underpinning the change in style was a partial shift in Soho's hierarchies of social leadership away from traditional gentry patronage and towards to the dominance of family-based businesses, many of which were established in the third generation by the post-war period.[176] Soho's fairs were designed not to encourage traditional values of social solidarity but to stimulate market-oriented forms of communitarianism.

The earliest ideas were sketched out by Gaston Berlemont, the locally born proprietor of the York Minister pub, in Dean Street, and the first chairman of the Soho Association. Delighted with the 'boom week' of the 1955 carnival, he insisted that the fair had encouraged many Londoners to take their first real look at the area. Careful to stress that it was 'solid English folk' who streamed into this part of W1, Berlemont noted that visitors were pleasantly surprised to find that Soho's reputation 'was not all that it had been said to be'.[177] An astute businessman and a host to one of Soho's long-established bohemian pubs, he enthused about the district's reputation for excitement and exuberance over respectability: 'we are respectable of course. But we are colourful too.'[178] Berlemont spoke as a sanctioned representative of Gallic *joie de vivre*; it made economic sense to let his customers believe he was a recent French immigrant, even though his family had been Soho residents since before the First World War. He described the carnival as a unique combination of native hedonism, from 'these English' who had finally let their hair down, and the cherished traditions of Soho's foreign populations.[179]

In embryo, Berlemont was attempting to define a new type of Soho consumer; his aim was to enlarge demand by repositioning the meanings of and the markets for cosmopolitanism. Berlemont's ideas were not lost on watchful outside observers. An article originally published in the mainstream women's magazine *Good Housekeeping* noted astutely that many Sohoites admitted privately that the area's 'oh-so-wicked reputation' meant 'cash in the till', because 'the human animal . . . likes places with a spicy reputation'.[180] A genuine clean up, the article warned, would spell the end of 'many a *cordon bleu* restaurant and delightful nightclub'.[181] Berlemont's influential boosterism, designed to whet the appetites of selected groups of English consumers with a taste for foreign goods and services, was pivotal to Soho's commercial renaissance during the late 1950s.

Ideas of this sort aspired to transform Soho into a commodified space of specialized tourism, building on cultural policies that had first been aired by the restaurant trade in the years before the First World War, and later by Abercrombie and Forshaw in their ambitious plans for social zoning in the West End. An early post-war revival of these schemes was encouraged by the creation of the Soho Restaurant Association in 1952, founded with the explicit aim of marketing the district to the restaurant 'exile returning to London for the first time since before the war'.[182] The launch of the Soho Association three years later also traded on the area's established reputation as a centre for the catering trades and for customers who demanded specialist dining and food shopping. Prominent representatives of local businesses, like the Italian family firm of Jaeggi's, the catering equipment manufacturers based in Dean Street, appeared on the fair's organizing committee, alongside journalists and members of Soho's film industry. The Soho Association's list of influential patrons also included corporate figureheads from Britain's leisure and entertainment sectors, including the holiday camp proprietor Billy Butlin and 'Mr Piccadilly', Italian-born Charles Forte, owner of the West End's Café Monico and the national chain of Milk Bar restaurants.[183] This alliance of business interests aimed to promote Soho as a 'world in microcosm', a commercial district that according to the association combined 'the best of food and wine and entertainment' with 'craftsmanship and friendly trading'.[184]

Two elements formed the centrepiece of this activity: a renewed emphasis on Soho's environmental distinctiveness and an updated version of the district's cosmopolitan ambience that promoted sex and food in equal measure. Soho's markets for sexual entertainment and erotic nightlife, together with its local specialist food shops and restaurants, were reorganized as shifts in the local economy reflected broader changes in the tastes and habits of influential consumers.

For local businesses, promoting Soho as a concentrated site for commodities and styles of consumption made effective sense because it involved positioning goods and services in a compressed and clearly identifiable central area. Emphasis on the importance of 'grouped location' to market goods and services was a well-established maxim held by property developers and retailers in 1950s London.[185] Location also exercised an important influence on contemporary ideas about the power of 'below the line' advertising, promotional campaigns that relied heavily on the strategic placement of shops, elaborate window displays and local sales initiatives. The highly successful, Lithuanian-born Jewish émigré Sir Montague Burton, whose flagship menswear store occupied a prime corner site on the junction of Oxford Street and Tottenham Court Road in Soho's north-eastern corner, was one of the main proponents of this commercial philosophy. Burton never tired of pointing out that a well-dressed shop window in a premier location was a more effective form of sales promotion than any amount of full-blown advertising.[186]

Soho's traders echoed Burton in their emphasis on the importance of commercial location, and they were backed up by Westminster Council. Tourist guides now clearly marked the whereabouts of all of Soho's amenities on their maps and walking itineraries. In 1957 the Soho Association persuaded councillors to install enlarged street maps of Soho at Piccadilly Circus, in the interests of a hoped-for expansion of West End tourism.[187] At carnival time that year twelve 'Welcome to Soho' banners were strung across the main streets, marking out the area's boundaries in a clearly visible way.[188] Atmospheric coverage of Soho's venues and events put together by strategically placed bohemian 'ciceroni' like Farson, or evoked through cinema newsreels and the press, provided consumers with information about the district's commercial culture. Whether the focus was on the famous stallholders in Berwick Street, shopping in Old Compton Street, or afternoon drinking at one of Soho's members' only clubs, journalists supplied would-be visitors with local knowledge and market know-how.[189]

Commercial campaigns of this sort were underpinned by a distinctive approach to preserving Soho's infrastructure that cut against the policies of demolition and rebuilding championed by many contemporary planners and architects. In 1954 the *Architect and Building News* showcased ambitious plans for the wholesale redevelopment of Soho's central area. Spearheaded by an architectural consortium appropriately named the Glass Age Development Committee, a company that was sponsored by the glass manufacturers Pilkington Brothers, the scheme advocated West End 'clearance' on a grand scale. The committee's ambition was to replace most of Soho's existing streets and buildings with six high-rise glass towers, each housing 1,500 residents, air-conditioned shopping and office precincts, glassed-in arcades, topped by canals and water gardens, underground car parks and 'spacious open-air entertainment areas'.[190] The project was one of many contemporary schemes outlined by London's property developers that envisaged the rebuilding of large swathes of the capital in concrete, glass and steel.

In Soho these plans were confined to the architect's drawing board; unlike other parts of the capital Soho was not targeted for slum clearance, nor was it seriously considered for commercial redevelopment. Economic factors, coupled with local political pressures, guaranteed a much smaller scale approach to Soho's urban renewal throughout the 1950s. Depressed local property values and rents, compared with other West End areas, together with burgeoning residents and conservation groups in adjacent districts like Mayfair and the strong presence of community-minded businessmen as local Westminster councillors and aldermen, ensured that Soho's transformation remained piecemeal and relatively ad hoc, characterized by what David Harvey has called local entrepreneurialism, as opposed to state-led corporatism.[191]

An early site for these local improvements was Soho Square itself. Much of the square was torn up in 1939 for use as an underground air raid shelter. An engineer's report produced for Westminster Council in 1950 revealed a picture of wartime neglect and dereliction.[192] The coronation provided the initial impetus for restoration; flower beds were replanted, the mock Tudor folly in the centre of the piazza was restored, and the seventeenth-century statue of Charles II was taken away for renovation and cleaning.[193] Schemes of this type were an important part of Soho's post-war renewal, augmenting the role of local businesses by enhancing the surrounding infrastructure. Restoration schemes also encouraged efforts to promote Soho as a picturesque visitor's quarter, with renovated eighteenth-century buildings and public spaces making the area more attractive for tourists who were drawn to the historic 'romance of Soho'.

These varied improvements aimed to relaunch Soho as a space for specialist consumption, but what sorts of commodities were on offer in its shops and markets, and what types of customers did local retailers hope to attract into its streets? Soho's business community was energized by the rapid growth of consumer demand that characterized the expansion of the national economy during the mid-1950s. The coronation had been a significant splash of commercial colour in a London landscape still dominated by austerity; Soho's fairs emphatically proclaimed the end of post-war scarcity and anticipated the arrival of a culture of material abundance centred on domestic markets and on a more integrated relationship between producers and consumers. Soho's food shops, coffee bars, restaurants, nightclubs and music venues were showcased to a wide cross-section of metropolitan visitors, but the area's version of affluence differed from the dominant forms of consumerism that historians have associated with the 1950s. It was not driven by corporate retailing, nor was it greatly influenced by American selling techniques or by the spending power of suburban mass consumers.[194]

In Soho the keyword was specialization: specialization of goods, services and markets. In an era of perceived mass consumption, many advertisers concurred with leading sociologists and cultural critics, arguing that English society was experiencing a rapid erasure of social differences based on the traditional hierarchies of class and status.[195] Yet as Tony Crosland pointed out in his astute reading of the impact of affluence on the class structure, the advent of near-universal provision for a wide variety of commodities did not mean that differences based on the cultural meaning of goods and services had been erased. Consumption, he insisted, was still as much about markedly different 'styles of life' and visible signs of status distinction as it was about income levels and access to public and private-sector markets.[196] A sophisticated metropolitan himself, Crosland was quick to spot new lines of division that were re-emerging inside the culture of mass affluence.[197] In 1950s London Soho was one of the laboratories for these experiments in consumer behaviour.

Soho's sex industry was an important part of these changing consumption patterns. Local queer venues were in a constant state of flux during the immediate post-war years, subject to the varied pressures of local policing, changing urban fashions, and widely different practices of homosexuality. 'Meeting places of the underground changed all the time,' explained the main character in Rodney Garland's fictionalized account of the homosexual West End, *The Heart in Exile*, published in 1953.[198] Despite the emphasis on diversity, many of Soho's clubs and pubs were increasingly stratified by divisions that reflected wider transformations in social class, purchasing power, and latterly the growth of an identifiable youth market.

Soho was the preferred site for the newer private members' clubs that mushroomed after the war, catering to professional men like Wildeblood and Patrick Trevor-Roper. Largely queer-run and enforcing a strict door policy as well as high membership fees, they advertised themselves as private clubs in order to evade police surveillance, exclude rough trade and deter the straight public. Paramount among these venues was the Rockingham, opened by Toby Roe. Aping the gentlemen's clubs of Pall Mall, the Rockingham was derided by outsiders as the 'elephant's grave-yard', with its 'piss elegant' striped Regency wallpaper, wood panelling, white grand piano and a quiet reading room.[199] Membership was available only to those with a personal introduction, and Roe deliberately insisted on a collar and tie dress code which encouraged some patrons to pose in fashionable neo-Edwardian dress. Devotees liked the Rockingham because it offered a leisure space that was 'plush and quiet and a bit . . . classy', but critics attacked the place for its 'phoniness' and its closet queans who would only be seen in the sanctity of the club.[200]

Less formal if more fashionable than the Rockingham was the reopened A&B club, sited in Rupert Street from 1952. One of the managers explained that its target market was the 'nine to five type person', or the 'suit and tie brigade'. Again, the A&B worked strenuously to exclude 'roughs and hustlers' by 'keeping an eye on the door' and by giving rent boys the 'cold shoulder'.[201] Fictionalized in Garland's novel as the Aldebaran, the clientele were described by the book's narrator, Oxford-educated Dr Anthony Page, as 'well dressed and not tatty', men who regularly 'talked about theatres and places abroad'.[202] Other similar club venues included the Spartan in Tachbrook Street and the Festival in Brydges Place. Michael Schofield explained that clubs of this kind catered to 'well-adjusted' men who were 'capable of holding responsible high salaried positions in all walks of life'; the 'lawyers, accountants, businessmen and stockbrokers' for whom 'homosexuality is but one phase' of their personality.[203] They epitomized the post-war culture of sexual discretion strategically advocated by Wildeblood in his evidence to the Wolfenden committee and by early members of the Homosexual Law Reform Society, such as the campaigner Anthony Grey.[204]

One result of this growth in affluent homosexual leisure was that the meeting places for 'rough trade' and more outrageous queans were increasingly squeezed. The closure of the Fitzroy Tavern in 1956 marked a watershed. Charrington Brewery gave the Allchild family notice to quit after a long-running police prosecution against the pub for infringement of the licensing regulations and for keeping a disorderly house. Along with the charge of prostitution, the police made much of the Fitzroy's popularity with 'perverts', especially the types who 'rouged their cheeks and behaved in an effeminate manner' seeking 'to seduce members of the Forces'.[205] Despite its closure, queans and rough trade still congregated after midnight at Soho's snack bars and makeshift coffee stalls like the Bar-B-Q in Frith Street, the Little Hut in Dean Street, and Bill's Snack Bar, erected on a piece of derelict land in Bouchin Street.[206]

Highly visible Soho rendezvous of this sort were subject to regular official surveillance in the 1950s, as the police and public morality campaigners sought to differentiate informally tolerated spaces like the private clubs from venues they defined as wholly unacceptable. In 1954 the Public Morality Council were briefed about a Scottish working-class youth, Tony Hegan, a 'weak character' who arrived in London after doing his National Service in the RAF. Thrown out by his landlady, Hegan 'got into very bad company' and began frequenting Soho's 'sordid all-night cafés', especially the Bar-B-Q and the Little Hut. 'So-called males' who were Hegan's intimates called themselves by girls' names, and 'openly discussed the fact that they were . . . prostitutes'.[207] The council defined them as members of the city's new underclass: 'male and female prostitutes . . . tramps, army deserters, young soldiers on leave . . . and teddy boys too lazy to work', a list that reflected the concerns of urbanists like Ruth Glass and Peter Sainsbury, with their anxieties about the capital's 'twilight zones'.[208]

By the mid-1950s Soho's emerging youth cult of coffee bars, what one habitué referred to as the 'new cafe society', was adding a further layer to the area's networks of homosexual sociability.[209] The famous 2i's coffee bar on Old Compton Street was celebrated as the birthplace of home-grown, English rock 'n' roll, but it also attracted some younger queer men in search of the excitement on offer in the teenage music scene.[210] Alternatively, there was the Mousehole, just off Piccadilly Circus in Swallow Street, which was decorated like a Cornish fishing village with nets and glass balls hanging from the walls and ceiling, while the Matelot, in Panton Street on Soho's southern fringe, cultivated a Frenchified ambience, with its Cocteauesque wall cartoons showing sailors in striped sweaters caught in 'compromising positions'.[211] Both bars provided opportunities for younger men with less money and less interest in status to talk and flirt in an atmosphere that was not fuelled by alcohol. Despite recurrent police raids, these venues were also less 'closety' or 'furtive' by the late 1950s. As one young patron of the Matelot remembered: 'furtiveness . . . I didn't want anything to do with that . . . .'Cos I was scampering around town.'[212]

Along with sex, Soho's overwhelming obsession in the mid-1950s was with food. This was not surprising; the area had a well-established gastronomic reputation, and food remained the largest single item of household expenditure across all social groups, while most major foodstuffs were nationally rationed by government well into the 1950s. Ina Zweiniger-Bargielowska has demonstrated how rationing and its aftermath exerted a major cultural influence on English society that went well beyond government policy and party politics.[213] In Soho the release from scarcity produced sharply contrasted sets of meanings around food consumption that were shaped by social status, gender and ethnic traditions.

These trends were very much in evidence at Soho's fairs. At the time of the second fair author and television personality Peter Noble invited visitors to follow him on a 'gastronomic Cook's tour' of Soho, strolling along Old Compton Street with occasional forays into Greek Street, Frith Street and Dean Street.[214] Focusing on the cultural imagery of food rather than on the sensory pleasures of eating, Noble's address was emphatically masculinist in tone. But it was much more plural and eclectic than the injunctions to be found in traditional tourist handbooks, like Baedeker's and Fodor's guides, where metropolitan food consumption invariably followed a prescribed hierarchy dominated by de luxe hotels and restaurants serving an international version of *haute cuisine*.[215] Noble spoke to the established man-about-town, but he also reached out to a newer generation of gastronomes, those recently enfranchised, middle-class customers who worked in consumer industries like advertising and who were being targeted by fashionable magazines for younger men such as *Man About Town*.

Noble's journalism placed much less emphasis on the traditional emblematic status of food connoting leisured wealth and refined luxury and much more on the pleasures of individual self-discovery, as he encouraged his readers to explore Soho's hidden gems for themselves. 'What a thrill it is to discover an unknown restaurant and make it your own favourite haunt,' he enthused, 'to find a really fabulous claret in a tiny out-of-the-way French restaurant.'[216] Noble went on to hint that it was only a short and easy step from the enjoyment of a good dinner to a fuller celebration of Soho's masculine pleasures in London's 'Latin Quarter'. His local observations were given extensive coverage in Fodor's *The Men's Guide to Europe* (1955), aimed at moneyed American visitors to London, with 'an accent on good times'.[217] Pronouncing that 'England has put austerity behind', Fodor's 'Gastronomic Grand Tour' included a section on 'Cosmopolitan Cuisine' which previewed many well-known restaurants in Soho and Fitzrovia.[218] Tourist literature of this kind also made a pitch for fashionable male consumers by profiling the tastes of colourful local personalities like John Taylor, editor of *Man About Town*, and Milanese-born Attilio Bossi, whose family owned the Café Bleu.[219]

Images of discerning customers were the marketing hook used by Soho's publicists in their efforts to promote the area's shops and services. Addressed as independently minded characters who moved confidently across the social spaces of the West End, Soho's hoped-for patrons were distinguished by their taste, style and personal flair. Pursuing a parallel address to women, local journalists celebrated Soho shopping as an 'education and an entertainment'.[220] They announced a complementary feminine appeal to the idea of sophisticated cultural appreciation and individualizing connoisseurship, promoting a range of goods and services, including gown shops, lingerie and accessories, but again most especially food. There were different types of women shoppers in Soho during the 1950s. Salvoni was one of many West Enders who always called in at Frith Street's Italian grocers and delicatessens on her way to work nearby, following a tradition established by her mother in the 1920s.[221] Secretaries, theatre workers and shop assistants from Shaftesbury Avenue, Leicester Square and Regent Street were also regulars at Soho's many delicatessens and sandwich bars, where they could be seen grabbing lunch or coffee.[222] In public commentaries, however, it was leisured middle-class English women who were assumed to be the area's main customers.

Exotic foodstuffs, the hoped-for ingredients of the discerning housewife's kitchen and dinner table, loomed large in Soho's publicity campaigns. This positive emphasis on the importance of food shopping for women was influenced by a major shift in household labour during the 1940s as a result of the rapid disappearance of domestic servants. Along the street stalls in Berwick Street and Rupert Street, middle-class women were now being encouraged to explore Soho's 'mouth-watering profusion' of different foods *for themselves*. Their future shopping list was expected to include green and red peppers, purple aubergines and cele-

riac, avocado pears and Chinese lychees, along with other fruits and vegetables 'with names you'll only come across in a dictionary'.[223] Some of
these foodstuffs were genuinely on offer locally, but other items were
purely aspirational. In a post-war world where even bananas were still in
short supply, part of the aim was to present a tempting food cornucopia
for the future.

The address to discerning female shoppers built on Soho's appeal to
women that Woolf had foregrounded in the 1930s, as an encounter
between genteel English femininity and exotic goods and people. After
the war, one particularly dynamic entrepreneur epitomized the close associations between Soho and the outlook of a progressive feminine elite.
This was Elizabeth David, the most influential contemporary English
writer on the food and atmosphere of the Mediterranean.

David was from a conservative gentry family with aristocratic connections, but she was also inspired by what Keith Williams has identified as
the new mood of 'else awareness', a consciousness of cultural difference
that influenced many younger members of the upper class during the
1930s.[224] Like other English men and women from similar backgrounds,
David's pre-war travels took her to France, Germany and Italy, but she
also spent time farther afield in Egypt and India, where she worked for
the Ministry of Information during the war. Returning to London in the
late 1940s, and now married to a former cavalry officer in the Indian
Army, the Davids set up home in a restored Georgian house in Halsey
Street, Chelsea. Elizabeth David's first book of culinary writing, *A Book
of Mediterranean Food* (1950), published by Soho editor and bohemian John
Lehmann, aspired to reform Anglo-Saxon appetites by carefully guiding
readers through the preparation of regional dishes from France, Italy, Spain
and Greece, using good but not extravagant ingredients.

David's culinary aesthetic was highly critical of established notions of
haute cuisine, especially the traditions that dominated in many of London's
grand restaurants and hotels, which were influenced by anglicized versions of 'elegant' French food, the debased legacy of culinary writer and
chef Georges Escoffier.[225] But David's recipes also registered a wider social
shift; her books were the most prominent of a number of contemporary
household manuals written for what novelist Olivia Manning identified
as 'the New Poor': women who would have had housekeepers and servants before the war but who now had to do their own shopping and
cooking.[226] David's books aspired to be much more than household
manuals; they were a potent 'bundle of spells' in words and images that
she herself later described as 'a love letter to the Mediterranean'.[227]

Elizabeth David's meticulous research into the regional culinary traditions of Italy owed almost as much to her frequent visits to Soho for
essential ingredients and cultural stimulation as it did to the extended
research tour of Italy that she undertook in the early 1950s. *Italian Food*
(1954) was littered with knowing references to wines, herbs, and foodstuffs that were to be found in Soho: dried red peppers from Gomez
Ortega and olive oil from Del Monico's, both in Old Compton Street,
Cremona's famed *mostarda di frutta* from a variety of local outlets, good
copper pans from Jaeggi's and from Ferrari's of Wardour Street.[228]
Encouraging readers to follow her example, David explained how she
made regular expeditions to Soho's shops and markets, scouring the area
in her search for sophisticated simplicity.[229] Debutante Fiona MacCarthy
remembered that in the mid-1950s her own mother was 'already under
the influence of Elizabeth David', noting how David's cookery books
were 'beginning to encourage a new exoticism in the kitchens of the
King's Road'.[230]

French Country Cooking (1951) and *A Book of Mediterranean Food* were
illustrated with richly textured drawings by the neo-romantic artist John
Minton, a member of the Colony Room circle. Minton's eye-catching
dust jackets and atmospheric sketches dealt in images of France and Italy
that were a recurrent feature of Soho's renaissance during the 1950s. One
sketch pictured a matelot and peasant girl standing by a table piled high
with local produce, in a town set on the shore of the Mediterranean (fig.
28).[231] Tourist literature designed for Soho's fairs released similar representations of Continental culture. Quirky, decorative line drawings of
Soho's French and Italian waiters accompanied emblematic images of
'pane e vino' and beret-clad Frenchmen, evoking a European atmosphere
that could be experienced in the heart of the West End.[232]

David's vision, like the policies of Soho's progressive commercial sponsors, was driven by a rejection of many of the forms of indigenous English
culture that had dominated national life during and immediately after the
war. Orchestrating an idea of civilized renewal and challenging the puritan
legacy of sensory denial, she confronted the 'make-do-and-mend' ethos
of the austerity years. Foreignness in Soho was evoked as the tangible
excitement of cultural difference, an experience that was designed to
appeal to expanding groups of predominantly middle-class consumers.

In microcosm, Soho was an important focal point for a cultural project
that later assumed a much more significant role in the lifestyle of the
progressive middle class. A vision of civilized living, focused on European

food along with other emblems of contemporary taste such as Scandinavian design, French couture and more enlightened attitudes to sex, loomed large in cultural policies championed by social democrat politicians such as Roy Jenkins and Tony Crosland.[233] Post-war Soho epitomized England's partial entente with carefully selected parts of Western and Southern Europe, a rapprochement that was also encouraged by wider cultural and political developments in the 1950s, such as the growth of foreign holidays, the creation of the various European trade federations and after 1957 the establishment of the European Economic Community.[234]

These changing domestic and international conditions encouraged Soho's entrepreneurs in their efforts to rebrand the area's foreign character. Cosmopolitanism was redefined as 'continentalism', as carefully selected European motifs were used to promote Soho's positive reputation for cultural diversity and to offset the area's traditional connotations of sleaze and sexual danger. Soho's attempted rehabilitation was also encouraged by its shifting demographics. By the 1950s the local population totalled fewer than 3,000 (reflecting a general decline in most of the inner London boroughs), and Soho's French, Italian, Jewish and German residents no longer constituted significant communities.[235] 'Foreignness' in Soho was now largely carried by the presence of prominent businesses, by service workers who were not themselves local residents, and overwhelmingly by the area's cultural industries.[236] Soho was in the process of being transformed from a genuinely alien quarter of London to one where its exotic character was heavily reliant on the influence of intermediaries and media-generated images. Under the impact of these changing demographic and social conditions, Soho could be presented as picturesque and essentially consumer-led. The district's foreign character now appeared more acceptable because it was largely European; its Continental atmosphere contained none of the connotations of extreme cultural difference that characterized official and popular perceptions of Caribbean areas such as north Kensington and Brixton.

✳

Soho's fairs and the people who organized them represented an expansion of business culture that had its origins in earlier experiments in West End tourism and publicity. Under the enhanced economic conditions of the mid-1950s, local entrepreneurs and community sponsors proposed an enabling profile for the area. According to their philosophy, the regenerative effects of modern commerce had the potential to harness and transform Soho's older negative reputation as the centre of vice and social trespass into an up-to-date and varied consumer economy that was responsive to contemporary market trends. What were the consequences of this growing ascendancy of commerce and consumer culture? Did the various entrepreneurial efforts to reposition Soho prove successful? Modern promotional blueprints for the future rarely achieved the influence on consumers that their advocates originally intended. In Soho the impact of these commercial plans was not the diversified, Continental atmosphere that was initially promised. It would take much longer, and another set of cultural initiatives in the 1980s and 1990s, for policies of this kind to be successful.[237]

Paradoxically, the most important effect of the renewed commercial ethos was that it stimulated specialization rather than diversification. What emerged in Soho was a reorganized sex industry structured along more contemporary lines. The erotic performances of the girls who appeared at Soho's first fair were a precursor of things to come. Over the next decade displays of female nudity, along with a wide variety of other forms of erotic nightlife, were a defining feature of the area's commercial renaissance. Driven by energetic entrepreneurs and marketed to an expanding audience of male consumers, these performances of female sexuality were the most significant feature of Soho's modernization. Soho's privileged place in an ongoing national debate about sex and public morality ensured that their impact was felt well beyond their actual location in central London. Commercially sponsored female nudity was associated with the West End's changing sexual atmosphere, one of the consequences of the permissive society.

Chapter 6   Erotica

Striptease

On a rainy Friday evening in the autumn of 1961 a young policeman turned into Walker's Court, off Soho's Brewer Street, and walked towards a strip club, advertised from the street with a neon sign as the Raymond Revuebar.[1] A late seventeenth-century alley that was 'busy by day, even busier and more garish by night', Walker's Court epitomized the compressed nature of Soho's consumer economy in the early 1960s, when cafés, hardware stores and wine merchants coexisted alongside a thriving commercial sex trade.[2] Dressed in plain clothes and acting under the alias of James Edwards, a draughtsman from Fulham, Sergeant Derek Caiels was posing as a punter for sex. He joined a sizeable queue of men outside the strip club, including European and American tourists and London businessmen, as well as English provincials down for a night on the town. Caiels showed his newly acquired membership card at reception, paid 15s. 6d. for a ticket, climbed the stairs to the club's lounge bar and ordered a beer.

Judged by the standards of many Soho clubs the Revuebar was expensively furnished, with subdued lighting, lounge chairs and television. Hosting a restaurant and a fully equipped theatre, there was also a casino where members and their guests could play roulette and *chemin de fer*. The atmosphere was comfortable, luxurious even, and the promoters promised 'a first rate review in Continental surroundings'; sex was advertised as part of the ambience and the bar and stairs were liberally decorated with photos of nudes.[3] Sergeant Caiels opened his programme, replete with more nudes shot in soft focus, to see that what was on offer was a 'striptease spectacular', with a cast of 'American, Continental and English artists'.[4] Images and text revealed an international cornucopia of erotica, featuring personal appearances from the 'fabulous French Star Marina L'Amour' and 'Luigia [*sic*] Canova, from Rome'.[5] The unclothed, erotically mobile female body held out the promise of multiple pleasures: Continental sophistication, glamorous sensuality and the thrill of sexual arousal, framed by a masculine culture of sociability.

Caiels noticed that there was already a buzz of expectation in the crowded bar, where members and their guests mingled with the club's hostesses. Approached by one of the women, Caiels ordered her a champagne cocktail before moving across to the theatre for the show. He joined a table with two other men in a cabaret-style auditorium and stayed for the whole of the two-hour-long revue. Following police instructions and with an eye on a possible prosecution, Caiels took down a detailed record of the performance in his notebook. This is what he saw.

The band struck up for the opening number, which was an upbeat, fast-moving, high-kicking dance routine featuring 'the fabulous Raymond girls'.[6] Feathered and sequined, their costumes trimmed with silver lamé, the showgirls performed well-drilled steps in marching time to a version of Rodgers and Hammerstein's exuberant celebration of femininity, 'I Enjoy Being a Girl'. The only difference from the original version, as Caiels observed prosaically, was that half of Raymond's troupe revealed 'their naked breasts through flimsy nylon jackets'.[7]

What followed were a series of double acts featuring male as well as female nudity that projected sex as visceral and as complementary heterosexuality. Some of these routines were studiedly serious; at other moments the mixture of music and performance style set a lightly satiric tone. The first act was a free-form dance of simulated sexual arousal, involving a couple miming to the lyrics of American Stan Freberg's record, 'John and Marsha'. Caiels described the choreography in detail, how Marsha fondled John's buttocks and started to pull at her partner's braces, taking off his trousers and shirt. Then the pair embraced and the woman stepped back and took off her panties; her partner sighed deeply, Caiels noted, 'indicating pleasure', and as the music ended John led Marsha knowingly by the hand behind a screen.[8] In an abrupt scene change the same couple promptly reappeared, wearing only grey top hats and underwear, for a strip spoof performance of the waltz from the musical *Sweethearts* made famous in the 1930s by Hollywood stars Nelson Eddy and Jeanette MacDonald. Dancing and stripping in 3/4 time, their act revolved around comic foreplay with a bouquet of flowers that was used to conceal and reveal the couple's sexual anatomy.

After an interval pause for more drinks and socializing at the bar, there was another scene of erotic parody, this time on the up-to-date theme of psychosexual disturbance. The act was set in a psychiatric ward where the 'patient', a 'coloured man', lay on a single bed, tossing and writhing about to atmospheric blues-style music. A 'nurse' appeared from behind a bead curtain whom Caiels described as a 'coloured girl' wearing high-heeled shoes and a brassiere, with black pants, suspender belt and stockings showing under a transparent nylon skirt. Seeing her, the 'patient' got up from his bed and danced around making what Caiels recorded in his notebook as 'gestures of desire'.[9]

The programme announced the finale as a traditional striptease spectacular. Featuring an American artist who received star billing, her performance was a professional display of glamorous female nudity. Appearing in full-length evening dress, fur stole and long gloves, the showgirl stripped as she danced, until she was wearing only 'panties and brassiere', which she eventually removed to reveal what Caiels noted was 'a floral posy worn over her pubic parts'.[10] The act was meant to simulate an auto-erotic climax; it ended when she collapsed in mock sexual exhaustion, removing the posy to show her 'pubic hairs'.[11] By now it was well after midnight and the audience was invited to go on to the famous One O'Clock Spectaculars showing at the Celebrite Club in Bond Street, but Caiels was not tempted and he ordered a final nightcap before leaving the club and heading for home.

Sergeant Caiels was one of many plain-clothes officers who were used by the Metropolitan Police to monitor London's thriving sex trade. The graphic testimonies that PCs Butcher and Darlington had delivered to the Wolfenden committee highlighted the use of young policemen out of uniform to entrap homosexual men for importuning and gross indecency. But monitoring sex between men was not the only focus for plain-clothes police activity. From the 1930s onwards, prosecutions for prostitution and other forms of disorderly conduct in notorious West End pubs and the enforcement of regulations governing displays of public nudity in venues like the Revuebar were started by undercover police operations. Posing as sexual customers, officers gathered evidence via well-established rituals of disguise and masquerade.[12]

The Met supplied Caiels with the necessary resources to work as a punter, enabling him to treat his hostess to expensive drinks and to order a meal in the club's restaurant. His sexual impersonation, like Butcher's and Darlington's operations in the West End's public urinals, produced an

unstable testimony that shifted between detailed but detached observation and a much more personally engaged account of the sexual displays
he saw. Caiels's references to the 'posy' worn over one of the stripper's
'private parts' and to the sighs from John and Marsha 'indicating pleasure'
were his way of describing the *mise en scène* dispassionately using his own
improvised descriptors. Other sections of the report were much more
graphic; his account of how the 'coloured man' in the psychiatrist's sketch
ripped off his partner's skirt and 'ran his hands up and down her back,
buttocks and thighs' hinted at the policeman's own potential involvement
in this piece of erotic theatre.[13]

The Revuebar was successfully targeted several times by plain-clothes
officers during the late 1950s and early 1960s, but the police complained
that the club was only the tip of the iceberg. According to Caiels's commanding officer, the West End was full of 'indecent striptease shows',
where performers showed 'passionate lust' and no imagination was necessary to understand how 'their desires are directed'.[14] Striptease expanded
rapidly in London during this period and its epicentre was Soho.
'Stripclubs are now part of London's new social landscape,' explained the
Spectator in amused tones during the summer of 1960, revealing how every
night over a thousand young women were 'peeling off' in central London,
in front of a combined audience of 250,000.[15] Sunday journalists exposing 'Naughtiness in the Afternoon' confided that 'moving nudes', once an
attraction exclusive to Paris and to 'some rather sleazy establishments east
of Suez', could now be seen in the West End any lunchtime.[16] Across the
Atlantic, American observers suggested that London's craze for strip was
evidence of the demise of English puritanism, revealing to intrigued New
York readers how 'the strip tease club is conquering Soho' in this 'once
staid and buttoned up city'.[17] London's strip phenomenon was advertised
as far afield as Australia, and its reputation even reached raunchy Hamburg,
where Soho's erotic performances were promoted alongside the city's own
extensive market for sex strung out along the notorious Reeperbahn.[18]

At home, positions divided as striptease quickly became identified with
a growing liberalization of London's sexual atmosphere. Journalists identified strip's spectacular rise, with an estimated annual turnover of two
million pounds, as part of the huge growth in national leisure.[19] Post-war
sexology sought to provide an intellectual explanation for the appeal of
striptease that was rooted in its own empirical traditions of research into
sexual difference. Kinsey's findings claimed to uncover the pervasiveness
of male voyeurism; there are 'probably very few heterosexual males who

would not take advantage of the opportunity to observe a nude female', he announced in *Sexual Behavior in the Human Female* (1953).[20] Following Kinsey's lead, other sexologists probed the psychosexual dynamics of male audiences and the personalities of 'exhibiting females' who stripped.[21] In the cinema, film director Michael Powell turned the voyeur into a major issue for public debate in his film *Peeping Tom*, released in 1960.[22] Public moralists and feminists linked to the purity movement responded with their own political challenge to striptease; the increase in female nudity not only exploited women's bodies, it was an all too visible symptom of creeping materialism and social instability.[23] Striptease was a potent and heavily contested symbol of London's rapidly changing sexual culture; it stood alongside pornography, male homosexuality and the contraceptive pill as one of the icons of permissiveness. Promoted by the glamour artists and showgirls who appeared at Soho's first fair, strip was the most visible sign of the heavily commercialized sex industry that was consolidated in the area from the late 1950s onwards, as business leaders sought to reorganize the local economy.

Striptease is a productive point of departure from which to unpack important strands in the cultural meanings and forms of production and consumption associated with the sexual changes to London's post-war commercial culture. A performance that was principally though not exclusively centred on the female body, the striptease phenomenon highlighted the gendered dynamics of a market sector that was seen by its advocates and opponents to mark an emphatic break with earlier traditions of erotic entertainment. But striptease was not new; it was the product of long-standing genres of static and kinetic female nudity which had their origins in the expansion of the West End as the nation's premier entertainment centre. By situating striptease within this longer history of eroticized displays of the female body, my aim is to problematize the idea that the 1960s marked a radical break with established forms of sexuality and moral authority. Changes associated with the permissive moment were heavily influenced by much earlier traditions of sexual performance and female spectacle.

Over more than a quarter of a century two of Soho's performance venues were successively market leaders in publicly staged female nudity. From the 1930s to the 1950s the Windmill Theatre, situated on Soho's southern fringe at the corner of Archer Street and Great Windmill Street, enjoyed the status of a celebrated sexual institution, with its shows dedicated to glamorous but carefully contained static nude tableaux. The Windmill's displacement in the late 1950s by the more explicit striptease acts witnessed by Sergeant Caiels at the Raymond Revuebar was symptomatic of wider transformations in the style and cultural connotations of erotic entertainment. These changes reorganized official regimes of moral surveillance, and they highlighted different priorities within the entertainment industry as well as among male audiences. They also registered important shifts in the geopolitical associations of sexuality, as representations of feminine glamour, defined as part of a tightly circumscribed notion of Englishness, were displaced by the commercial vision of an international world of sex symbolized by the nude female body.

A National Institution

A 'legend in our own lifetime', 'as central a national emblem as Eros . . . itself', was how two generations of Jewish theatre managers from the Van Damm family billed their performances staged at the Windmill Theatre.[24] Even the Lord Chamberlain, acting as the state's theatre censor, famously described the Windmill as a 'national safety valve', evoking a hydraulic model of male sexuality to endorse the theatre as an institution guaranteeing collective sexual release.[25] Today, more than half a century later, the theatre retains its national significance, boasting one of the most extensively preserved archives and a recent full-length feature film starring Judi Dench and Bob Hoskins.[26] From the 1930s to the early 1960s the Windmill's 'Revudeville' shows, programmed from midday until half past ten at night, ran for nearly 60,000 performances and were seen by an estimated audience of more than ten million.[27] These statistics were regularly cited as evidence of the theatre's expansive social influence, for the 'mill', as it was invariably known, came to symbolize many of the permissible forms of popular eroticism within English social life.

Five stories high, with elaborate cornices, turrets and twin cupolas advertising the theatre's visual presence in the West End, the Windmill's location was important in terms of Soho's complex social geography (fig. 29). The theatre was surrounded by shops and businesses that were closely identified with the area's cosmopolitan atmosphere, including Italian restaurants and tailors, theatrical suppliers, boxing promoters and Continental grocers.[28] But the 'mill' also faced south; it was visible from the broad thoroughfare of Shaftesbury Avenue marking the beginning of the theatre and cinema district of Leicester Square. Accessible to tourists and suburban visitors who were not always au fait with Soho proper, the

Windmill occupied a transitional space: a point where traditions of cultural bohemianism and sexual trespass met the wider world of West End
mass entertainment and organized leisure.

The acts staged by the famous Windmill girls had their origins in a
hybrid amalgam of Anglo-American and European performance traditions
of dance and the sexual display of the female body dating back as far as
the eighteenth century. These were organized around a conception of
either static nudity, on the one hand, or representations of the erotically
mobile female body, on the other. Shaped by different conceptions of
taste, cultural value, and moral and aesthetic judgement, this distinction
was consolidated as a key principle of modern, commercially organized
sexual entertainment.

London's own particular vogue for nude female displays reputedly originated in the late eighteenth century. These beginnings were still cited by
local guides and histories published in the post-war period, confirming
the West End's provenance as a centre of sexual sophistication.[29] In 1779
Emy Lyon (later Lady Emma Hamilton, Nelson's mistress) posed in white
silk robes as the goddess Vestina for Dr James Graham in the quack
doctor's Temple of Health, off the Strand. Lyon's flowing drapery and rich
rose-coloured girdle revealed and concealed her body, which was reflected
in artfully arranged gilt mirrors.[30] Her nude routine was one of many
forms of eroticized entertainment in Georgian London that blurred distinctions between popular culture and polite taste. The Temple of Festivity,
promoted by the Venetian émigré, former opera singer, and friend of
Casanova, Teresa Cornelys, at Carlisle House in Soho Square in the 1760s
and 1770s, was a fashionable venue for balls and masquerades involving
'indecency and mocking of solemn feelings and principles'.[31] Male and
female displays of sexual excess, cultural transgression and sometimes
gender inversion were regular features of Cornelys's entertainments.
Elaborately costumed and masked semi-nudity gave ladies the opportunity to become sexually anonymous 'dominoes' and to flirt with fantasies
of lasciviousness, while guards officers in flesh-coloured silk and 'aprons
of fig leaves' burlesqued plebeian types such as chimney sweeps and 'saucy
dolls'.[32] These styles of male and female impersonation also echoed the
erotic performances and private theatricals staged by fashionable
sodomites in the 'molly houses' of Georgian London.[33]

By the mid-nineteenth century, displays of living pictures, *tableaux
vivants*, or *poses plastiques* had become incorporated into the newly capitalized leisure industry, appearing as standard items in the music hall and

popular theatre as well as in the circus.[34] The static semi-nude, or more usually pseudo-nude, female body was created with the aid of flesh-coloured tights and atmospheric lighting, with the model's breasts sometimes encrusted in Plaster of Paris to 'suggest nature'. These displays frequently raided more elevated genres of visual and literary culture, billing the tableaux as part of a classical *mise en scène* supposedly derived from history painting or from mythological and orientalist subject-matter. Emphasis on frozen poses was critical, enabling theatre proprietors and their managers to remain within the limits set by the indecency laws and the metropolitan licensing regulations. Immobile postures also associated the female body with nudity rather than nakedness, suggesting a boundaried, quasi-artistic aesthetic rather than the uncontrolled desires of pornography.[35] Nonetheless, living pictures were notable for their sexual suggestiveness, for the passivity of their forms of female display, and for their highly ambiguous use of the traditions of classical nudity. In the 1880s and 1890s the whole issue of nude displays in London's theatres erupted as a major concern for metropolitan politics. Organized challenges from the purity and feminist movements forced a public debate about the leisure industries and about the culture of prostitution that was exposed in many West End theatres.[36]

Displays of the female body in erotic motion developed via a different theatrical tradition. It was English burlesque, a cross between satirical revue, operetta, ballet and pageant, that dealt emphatically in female bodies that moved.[37] John Hollingshead, a self-proclaimed 'licensed dealer in legs', opened his Gaiety Theatre on the Strand in 1868.[38] At first the chorus girls wore tights and ballet dresses, which were later substituted for close-fitting short skirts. The celebrated dancer and actress Lydia Thompson pioneered this formula as a transatlantic export when her troupe of 'British blondes' arrived in New York in the late 1860s, championing the burlesque tradition in the theatres of the eastern United States.[39]

Burlesque and variety theatre were popular cultural forms that helped define the staging of erotic entertainment well into the twentieth century. Later versions included the well-drilled routines from New York's Broadway showgirls that featured in Florenz Ziegfeld's *Follies* before and after the First World War, John Tiller's high-kicking chorus girls and C. B. Cochrane's 'young ladies', both appearing in the West End, as well as the elaborately contrived cinematic fantasies of femininity contained in the dance sequences of Busby Berkeley's Hollywood musicals.[40] Written into their various performance styles were many of the gendered contradictions that characterized the new cosmopolitan entertainment industries in European and North American cities, especially the tension between what Susan Glenn has termed women produced as assertively spectacular and as passive spectacle.[41]

The management of the Windmill Theatre drew on these traditions of erotic entertainment in their theatrical staging and visual display of the female body. But the Windmill's particular brand of nudity was primarily influenced by the specific economic and cultural conditions of the Depression. In 1931 Mrs Laura Henderson, the widow of a wealthy Calcutta jute merchant, bought what was then the Palais de Luxe cinema in Great Windmill Street. In West End theatre circles a dominant image of Mrs Henderson was of a self-confessed ingénue in the entertainment world, a 70-year-old 'white haired, bright eyed little woman in mink' and broderie anglaise who had reputedly been shocked when her husband took her to a leg show at the Gaiety.[42] In reality, Mrs Henderson was an astute commercial investor; she was also the patroness of many metropolitan charities and was extremely well connected to the leaders of inter-war London society, part of an elite female circle that included Queen Victoria's grand-daughters and Lady Bertha Dawkins, Lady-in-Waiting to Queen Mary.[43] Laura Henderson's aim in launching the Windmill as a continuous variety theatre was boldly philanthropic: to 'help these brave out-of-work artists' whose employment prospects had deteriorated as a result of the coming of the 'talkies'.[44] Writing to the Labour paper, the *Daily Herald*, Mrs Henderson explained that her new pet project would contribute to national economic recovery because she would hire only British theatre workers.[45]

This idea of a native workforce was amplified by her manager, Vivian Van Damm, who turned it into a cultural and sexual vision that extended well beyond the theatre's employment policy. Van Damm's aim as manager of the Windmill between 1938 and 1955 was to promote a version of erotic entertainment that was influenced not just by his astute reading of national sexual taste and the demands of the theatre censor, but also by an ethnocentric commitment to a highly stylized version of English femininity.

Van Damm, the son of a Jewish Bishopsgate solicitor of Dutch descent, had a varied early career selling modern consumer goods, including work as an estate agent and a de luxe car salesman.[46] In the 1920s his go-ahead style quickly attracted the notice of entertainment managers working in Wardour Street's expanding film industry. Van Damm was also well connected to Jewish commercial life in the capital via his wife Natalie, who was a niece of the catering and restaurant millionaire Joe Lyons. Van Damm's decision to introduce living tableaux into the Windmill's variety

acts in the late 1930s was driven by financial expediency, for Mrs
Henderson's experiments in home-grown vaudeville theatre ran up losses
totalling £60,000 between 1932 and 1940.[47] His venture into stage nudity
was also driven by an astute sense of the changing dynamics of the West
End's entertainment market. As he explained in his autobiography:

> I determined to introduce living tableaux on the London stage. My
> idea was that perfectly proportioned young women should be presented
> in artistic poses, representing a frieze entablature or a famous classical
> painting. Standing perfectly still, they would of course form part of the
> glamorous stage *décor*. This was a revolutionary idea in British show-
> business.[48]

Van Damm's public image as a theatrical innovator was much exaggerated, given London's well-established traditions of *tableaux vivants*, nude
shows and even clandestine striptease that had sprung up in the West End
during the inter-war years.[49] What was distinctive about his management
style was his idea of a standardized blueprint of feminine glamour that
could be integrated into continuous variety theatre and offered as popular
entertainment.

Judith Walkowitz has argued that under Henderson's and Van Damm's
dual control the Windmill's decorous nudes came to embody the inter-
war suburban values of middlebrow culture, transposed to a metropolitan
setting.[50] Tasteful, acceptable, even cosy in their style of visual display, the
showgirls epitomized the feminine qualities of unpretentious ordinariness
for a paying public. The social and sexual impact of the Second World
War on the home front established the Windmill's position, both as a
financial success and as an icon of national popular culture. 'The war years
. . . were vintage years, the beginning of the Windmill legend,' remembered Van Damm's daughter Sheila, who began work in the theatre's publicity office in the late 1930s.[51] The management engineered a close
cultural fit between the glamorous performances of the Windmill girls,
the expectations of wartime military audiences, and the wider demands
of government propaganda.

British servicemen, American GIs, Polish airmen and countless other
Allied military personnel on leave in the capital queued daily to see the
theatre's showgirls, who were promoted as part of London's defiant
message to the Nazi enemy. Important organs of home front morale such
as *Picture Post* regularly advertised the fact that the 'mill' always remained
open for business, despite the constant threat of bombing from the

Luftwaffe, and the slogan 'we never closed' became the theatre's most valuable promotional one-liner.[52] A direct hit by a flying rocket attack in 1944 on the Regent Palace Hotel, across from the theatre, happened just as one of the Windmill girls was revealed in a graceful, Spanish-style nude pose. It went down in theatre mythology as the only time that the 'mill's' nudes moved; through an avalanche of dust the plucky showgirl thumbed her nose at the enemy, to a tremendous audience ovation.[53] On VE Day in May 1945 the Windmill became one of the West End's focal points for crowds of celebrating servicemen and their girlfriends. Across the Atlantic, Hollywood set on record its admiration for the embattled Windmill, now rechristened the Music Box, in the Columbia film *Tonight and Every Night* (1945), starring Rita Hayworth and directed by Victor Saville. Ever cheerful Cockney girls and boys of the theatre's company were depicted as bravely 'carrying on' during the nightly horrors of the Blitz, embellishing the contemporary propaganda theme of 'Britain can take it'.[54]

Wartime conditions shaped the Windmill girls' distinctive sexual style in ways that persisted well into the 1950s; here Van Damm's idea of feminine 'sex appeal' was of paramount importance. Promiscuity and even sexual waywardness in young women continued to receive strong disapproval from government and moral agencies during the war, but feminist historians have shown how images of sexually glamorous young women were prioritized as a national asset.[55] At the height of the first phase of the Blitz, in the autumn of 1940, the front cover of *London Life* magazine pictured one of the smiling Windmill girls complete with tin helmet sitting on the roof of the theatre, knitting for victory (fig. 30).[56] Introduced as 'Pat', she epitomized the sexual persona made famous by the Windmill troupe, with her photographer's smile, plucked eyebrows, sculptured eye mascara, stockings and suspenders. This was not the aloof ideal of contemporary *Vogue* models or society beauties; like the Edwardian Gaiety Girls of an earlier generation, Pat promised good fun and sexual friendship. The accompanying copy emphasized her approachable, girl-next-door credentials, qualities that were also to the fore in the marketing of Forces' sweethearts like Vera Lynn and Anne Shelton. This type of femininity was heavily tailored to the demands of the military audience on leave in London or serving at the front; promotional copy in the Windmill's programmes spoke to 'you boys out East', providing 'pin ups' of star artists 'for your tents' and 'your messes'.[57] Souvenir material was mailed across the world, enhancing the 'mill's' reputation and enlarging the market for acceptable, mass-produced images of semi-nude women.

Inside the theatre audiences and performers testified to an atmosphere of 'peculiar intimacy'. Seating fewer than 400, the much sought-after front rows were so close to the stage that audiences were able to 'look upwards', giving a close-up view of the intimate body parts of the artists.[58] In the 1950s most performances still began with the regular 'Windmill steeple-chase', as patrons leapfrogged forward in an effort to bag the front seats.[59] The theatre's famous glass stage floor, which had been copied from a Parisian nightclub, not only produced the illusion of depth and scale, it also reflected images of the scantily clad showgirls from below.[60]

The Windmill's traditional theatre lay-out in miniature, with its proscenium arch, high stage, scenery and lighting effects, was all designed to promote voyeuristic spectacle *at a distance*. Binoculars and other artificial aids to vision were confiscated by the management, while complex lighting tended to emphasize the chimerical and distantiated quality of the nudes.[61] Sheila Van Damm recalled that the footlights were a 'no-man's land which the audience could only cross in imagination'.[62] Unlike the erotic atmosphere in a strip club, there was 'no mingling' between patrons and performers. Only Van Damm, or VD as he was known in-house, awarded himself the fringe benefit of sexual access to the girls backstage, visiting the women's dressing rooms for casual liaisons and affairs. In the auditorium a different atmosphere prevailed. 'Revudeville' was like a 'picture in a frame', to be gazed at and admired 'but not entered into'.[63] The management operated a system of audience surveillance to deal with customers who became 'too involved' in the performances; 'over-excited' patrons caught masturbating would be 'whisked bodily from the stalls' and deposited outside on the pavement.[64]

On stage, the erotic highpoint of the Windmill's shows was the static nude poses framed by continuous variety theatre. During the 1950s production themes included dramatic scenes from English history, such as the execution of Anne Boleyn, and endless routines derived from Hollywood musicals, with their opportunities for glamorous female spectacle, together with more contemporary material derived from television. 'Top Hat', which ran in February and March 1953, presented the showgirls as Fred Astaire lookalikes, tap dancing up and down an illuminated staircase in white tie and tails, with their breasts revealed through transparent gauze 'shirts'.[65] 'Parlour Game' was a spoof on the popular early TV show *What's My Line?*, with the act providing an opportunity for the troupe to pose as models and belly dancers for the Eamonn Andrews-style quiz compere, who was expected to guess their occupations.[66] For London's coronation season in May and June, 'Revudeville' opened with the colourful and patriotic 'On Parade'. Saluting their sovereign commander, dancers and showgirls masqueraded as guards officers in tight-fitting, red and white cut-away uniforms, designed to expose maximum cleavage.[67] Five years later, soon after the Soviet Union launched the space race with the Sputnik satellite, the Windmill girls replied with 'Out of This World'. Marshalled on the launch pad as three phallic rockets, they appeared in space helmets, scantily but futuristically dressed for orbit.[68] The production content varied but the erotic performance structure remained the same: a rolling programme of variety routines, showcasing solo artists as well as dancers and showgirls, which culminated in the frozen, fully nude tableaux.

Robert Allen has demonstrated how the tension between diachronic and synchronic versions of sexual entertainment was a marked feature of much twentieth-century burlesque theatre.[69] But the choices facing Van Damm over motionless nudes as opposed to kinetic displays of eroticism were not governed primarily by issues of artistic style or genre; they were heavily influenced by the demands of the theatre censor, who exerted a significant influence on the way all English theatres organized their shows.

The Lord Chamberlain's Office was a masculine redoubt of cultural conservatism; technically part of the Royal Household rather than attached to any government department, it was staffed by elderly officials from elite army backgrounds.[70] A Crown commission that was not directly answerable to government, the department was responsible for royal ceremonial, the management of honours, and liaison with the diplomatic corps. The Lord Chamberlain's Office had only a tenuous relationship to the institutions of twentieth-century political democracy; its patrician regime of sexual surveillance made a department like the Home Office seem progressive and forward-looking. The Lord Chamberlain had absolute power to refuse a stage play's licence under the terms of the 1843 Theatres Act, legislation that was not revoked until theatre censorship was abolished in 1968 as part of the liberal reforms of the post-war period.[71]

The Lord Chamberlain's authority over stage entertainment contrasted sharply with the more overtly repressive forms of control that governed nightclubs and private members' clubs like the Revuebar. In club venues the Metropolitan Police and the LCC held control, armed with statutory powers to close establishments for infringing the licensing regulations, or for keeping disorderly houses that encouraged prostitution or male importuning. In public theatres like the Windmill, the Lord Chamberlain's Office focused on the minutiae of sexual inspection and cultural supervision, involving detailed scrutiny of the play-scripts and the visual erotic content of 'Revudeville' performances.

In his famous dictum made in 1940, Lord Clarendon, then Lord Chamberlain, restated the terms for permissible stage nudity, insisting that displays needed to be motionless and also carefully separated out from other acts by a pause or break in the narrative action.[72] This official stance was reaffirmed throughout the immediate post-war years, when it received strong moral backing from the LCC, who were concerned about the spread of striptease in private clubs and unlicensed premises. The Lord Chamberlain's strictures bore down on the 'mill', as Van Damm pushed at the permissible limits of eroticism and sexual suggestiveness and was frequently pushed back by the censor, whose own resolve was stiffened by repeated lobbying from well-organized purity groups, especially the Public Morality Council.[73]

'Much more care should be taken not to uncover during the actual dance, technically speaking, there should be a complete break between the dance and the nude pose following. . . . I saw certain "things" [in the dance] which I ought not to have seen,' wrote the aptly named Mr Titman, one of the Lord Chamberlain's officials, after his visit to the theatre in 1947.[74] Following these official inspections, dance routines, dresses and straps were adjusted, and suggestive gags and ways of walking were edited out, as scripts were subjected to the famous 'blue pencil' of stage censorship. Surveillance was ongoing and cyclical, with both sides fully cognizant of the rules of the game. In the short term the Windmill's acts were tidied up, but the offending material was usually reinstated in subsequent shows after a suitable time lapse. These rituals were rendered even more bizarre because the Lord Chamberlain's elderly team of inspectors were clearly motivated by their own erotic agenda when they visited the theatre. Salacious and prurient asides about the girls' breasts and legs punctuated their written reports, along with ribald jokes and other suggestive innuendoes.[75]

One long-running Windmill act proved particularly contentious; this was the famous 'fan dance', in which the showgirl moved through a choreographed ten-minute routine, revealing glimpses of her unclothed body (above but not below the waist) beneath the diaphanous covering of swirling ostrich feathers held by the supporting dancers or 'covers' (fig. 31). The denouement centred on the principal fan dancer, exposed with both fans above her head or with the fans removed, caught in a decora-

tive pose as the house lights dimmed. The fan dance sequence encapsulated the erotic rituals of concealment and revelation that were a central
part of all Windmill performances. Fully aware that both the audience
and the censor were on the look-out for an accidental exposure of full
female nudity, efforts to produce the theatrical illusion of 'concealing all
and revealing all' depended on split-second timing and endless rehearsals
in front of the theatre mirrors.[76]

This well-tried display went through numerous variations, and the act
was even recorded for BBC television after the war. In one version the
fan dancers, costumed in elegant but flimsy gauze ball gowns, were cast
in a high society setting, with elaborately stylized choreography that was
reminiscent of a Busby Berkeley musical.[77] Another act presented the girls
in more elevated classical poses; dressed in revealing Greco-Roman togas,
their routine ended with the fan nude gracefully displayed on an architectural plinth.[78] By 1954 audiences were being treated to a more up-to-
date display in the sketch 'It Pays to Advertise', a light-hearted spoof on
consumer society. Lady marketers working with the ubiquitous female
consumer acted out a story of shopping and sales talk, with the finale
presenting the fan dancer framed by a mock TV set.[79]

The Windmill's combination of mobile as well as static sexual displays
has encouraged some theatre historians to view their acts simply as a precursor to the type of full kinetic nudity staged by striptease.[80] But this
reading ignores the way that Van Damm's presentation of the female body
was fully integrated into the wider traditions of variety theatre. Acts such
as the fan dance, or the 'dance of the seven veils' that was a version of
the same theme, were erotic highpoints in an overall performance
sequence that was shaped by the traditions of popular entertainment.

Throughout his career Van Damm demanded what he termed 'light
relief' between his nudes, and it was at these points that the chorus, along
with singers, acrobats, magicians, jugglers, and above all comedians, took
to the stage.[81] The 'mill' was famous as a forcing ground for up-and-
coming young comics, many of whom later rose to the status of national
stars. Performers and commentators alike have tended to downplay the
significance of comedy at the Windmill, seeing it as wholly subordinate
to the show's main erotic action. Yet the comedians' warm-up acts, one-
liners, and patter lyrics to orchestral accompaniment that punctuated
'Revudeville' not only enhanced a sense of erotic anticipation, they also
contributed to an atmosphere of partial arousal or contained licence, with

their regular double entendres, crude lavatory jokes and sly innuendoes. Comedians and singers also introduced a different ensemble of sensory stimuli into the productions; their acts were heavily reliant on verbal communication with the audience, cutting against the emphasis on visual spectatorship enshrined in the fan dance and in the appearance of the tableaux nudes.[82]

During the post-war years there was a distinct shift of emphasis in the preferred genres of comedy at the Windmill. Traditional music hall monologists and sketch comedians, such as Gus Chevalier and John Tilley, were replaced by zanier, faster-paced performers. Fresh from military service or from entertaining troops at the front and looking for their first break in the West End, comedians of the calibre of Jimmy Edwards, Harry Secombe, Michael Bentine, Tony Hancock, and Morecombe and Wise all played at the 'mill'. Edwards, who was an RAF veteran of the D-Day landings, appeared at the theatre with his famous mad professor act, replete with spats, cycle clips and a huge handlebar moustache, as he attempted to play a trombone full of water. Welsh comedian Harry Secombe, who entertained Montgomery's army during the invasion of Italy, was famous at the Windmill for his shaving routine, involving a soldier performing his ablutions with a 'bucket of ice-cold water and a blunt blade'.[83] Blowing raspberries to the audience, Secombe's stage entrance was to the tune 'Wild About Harry', while he exited crooning the 'Sweethearts Waltz' covered in shaving foam.[84] Bentine was part of the double act Sherwood and Forrest, a duo who appeared in 'tall and narrow black top hats and ancient frock coats, reciting an imaginary Russian fairy story' and finishing with 'a frantic rendering of "Black Eyes" in boogie tempo'.[85]

These forms of zany humour, which had been developed under wartime conditions of emotional and psychological stress, cut against the Windmill's established traditions of music hall and variety comedy, both in their content and delivery. They also represented a democratic version of the elite clowning and buffoonery that was on display at venues like the Thursday Club. Bentine recalled that his own act was 'more like a cabaret' than a straight comedy turn.[86] Working with Secombe and fellow Windmill comic Peter Sellers, as well as with Spike Milligan, Bentine went on to perfect these techniques in the *Goon Show* during the 1950s, the hugely successful radio comic quartet that specialized in an eclectic mixture of absurd impersonations and dressing up, madcap satire, verbal gibberish, manic sound effects and other forms of inspired lunacy, all delivered at break neck speed.[87]

The Windmill's combination of nudes and variety entertainment was not unique in the London theatre. During the immediate post-war period, stage star Phyllis Dixey promoted her own very successful non-stop glamour revues from the Whitehall Theatre, just south of Trafalgar Square, while nude acts also began to be included in variety shows staged by many provincial houses as a hoped-for boost to declining audiences.[88] However, the long-term pre-eminence of the Windmill was a direct result of Van Damm's success in advertising his theatre as an authentic component of the national culture. Despite the frequently contentious dialogue with officialdom, the 'mill' was granted favoured status with the censor, as well as with the public, because its sexual displays of the female body were presented as consensual rather than sexually and culturally transgressive. As one of the Lord Chamberlain's team put it approvingly in 1951: 'It is true that with these young and pretty girls, together with the artistic lighting, the Windmill theatre can do what other managements dare not attempt.'[89]

After the war Van Damm worked closely with his assistant producer Anne Mitelle to retain his winning combination of youth, beauty and ordinariness as the Windmill girls' recipe for success. 'They are fresh perky lasses full of fun,' he always insisted. 'Attracted to stage life, they hear from other girls that conditions are better . . . than anywhere else.'[90] Principal singers or dancers were rarely engaged from outside the theatre's own company; most of the stars were graduates from the chorus, creating a pool of local talent who worked together in what Van Damm stressed was a 'well-paid, harmonious team'.[91] The theatre's reputation as a 'mill' or factory was not only driven by the elaborately scheduled production routines, with their quasi-Fordist arrangement of two companies, six-week performance runs and six shows per day; it was also carried by an elaborate system of sexual grooming that was designed to mould the girls on their arrival.

Van Damm's experience of more than twenty years of 'presenting British girlhood' convinced him that the 'average . . . girl is a perfect fool about her appearance'.[92] Distrusting 'an ultra-modernistic' style, he emphasized traditional feminine qualities, 'chiefly personality, figure, talent and beauty', for the chorus as well as for the showgirls who appeared nude.[93] Creating an appropriate sexual aesthetic involved the regular application of a permanent wave as well as stage make-up, dieting, exercise and costuming. Over a thirty-year period the Windmill girls presented a relatively standardized look that was only a mildly exaggerated

version of the image of feminine beauty circulating in mass market magazines for women and in consumer-led advertising. Like other entrepreneurs of leading brands, Van Damm's resistance to changing his successful
format was based on an unshakeable belief that his own preferences held
the key to understanding the sexual tastes of his customers. In particular,
he drew on the resources of Jewish entrepreneurial culture to promote
the Windmill girls as an acceptably English sexual style.

Like a number of Jewish film directors in pre-war Hollywood who
forged powerful cinematic images of American culture, Van Damm was
adept at advertising theatrical feminine glamour as a product for national
consumption. Part of this promotional success was influenced by his skill
as a cultural intermediary which was the result of his own outsider status
in relation to English society. Publicly, Van Damm was reticent about his
Jewishness, though he maintained strong Jewish business connections, but
like many similar entrepreneurs he crystallized elements of a national type
or style by heightening or sharpening the cultural associations of his
product. In this he was not alone. Montague Burton circulated an image
of English gentlemanliness for the men's clothing market during the same
period, while two generations of the Jewish Allchild family encouraged
an English idea of bohemia in the bar of the Fitzroy Tavern.[94] In the
1960s Brian Epstein's phenomenal success as the manager of the Beatles
and other English pop groups partly rested on his ability to promote a
heavily anglicized version of teenage masculinity for national and international youth audiences. (Epstein was a sexual as well as a cultural outsider by virtue of his closet homosexuality and his Jewish background.)[95]
Van Damm's achievement was that he reorganized key aspects of English
femininity into an acceptable and publicly recognizable sexual typology.

The eroticism of the Windmill girls rarely included any hint of foreignness. Fair skin tones, enhanced by stage make-up and lighting, privileged an emphatically Caucasian look, while press coverage introduced
the girls as 'pretty blondes' or brunettes. In-house publicity profiled
'Brunette Beryl Caitlin from Canvey Island' or 'pretty fair-haired' Pauline
Colegate, who 'lived with her parents in their comfortable little house in
Beckenham'.[96] One journalist noted approvingly that after all the 'rarefied
atmosphere of experimental plays and Continental films' experience had
taught Van Damm that West End audiences liked their erotic entertainment 'in English'.[97] Rather than adopting glamorous stage pseudonyms,
the performers generally retained their own names, while much was made
of their local or regional origins, their social ordinariness and their

approachability. Emphasis was on an open and transparent style, free from any troubling associations with reproductive sexuality, which was reinforced by the girls' physical presentation as statuesque, acrobatically mobile or purely decorative.

These management and performance techniques were underwritten by a vigorous heterosexual culture that was reinforced front and backstage in the theatre. Daniel Farson believed that Van Damm personally policed the Windmill's sexual boundaries for any hint of 'abnormality'.[98] In the 1950s this involved excising the growing number of homosexual jokes and gags about effeminacy that infiltrated 'Revudeville' scripts, appearing as comic innuendoes and knowing asides about 'Ralph the outdoor boy who loved to camp' and 'that boy from Sadler's Wells who always wore my frocks'.[99] When the young aspiring theatre critic Kenneth Tynan auditioned for the Windmill, he was rejected by Van Damm with the riposte: 'You're much too queer for our audience.'[100]

Van Damm's sexual gatekeeping was designed to protect the Windmill's erotic atmosphere and its target audience from the experimental sexual styles that were circulating in Soho on his theatre's doorstep: sex between men, the allure of bohemian sophistication, and Continental culture. The organizers of the Soho fairs advertised the 'mill' as a cosmopolitan 'Soho institution', while journalists reported how the Windmill girls would rush out from the stage door to grab a coffee or a liver pâté sandwich at nearby Continental cafés, such as the Frankfurter Bar, the Restaurant Mignon or the Buffeteria.[101] But the Windmill's style and ambience defined the theatre as an emphatically English presence within Soho's heterogeneous social spaces.

This self-conscious cultural insularity was reinforced by public perceptions of the Windmill's audience. The management were deliberately vague about their customer base, preferring to keep patrons in the background of a well-run publicity machine that was dedicated to showcasing their glamorous product. This encouraged endless speculation about the overwhelmingly male audience. One dominant image conjured up a quintessentially English version of sexual seediness. Customers were frequently described as the 'dirty mack brigade', or what Jimmy Edwards jokingly called an audience 'made up entirely of lascivious incipient perverts, and warped old men'.[102] Other commentators dismissed the patrons as the banal and degraded sexual consumers of mass society: a 'queue of expressionless men' who were motivated only by 'the promise of seeing naked girls in static poses'.[103] More positive samplings of the audience suggested a different national type: the idea of 'Mr Everyman', a masculine identity that was shaped by post-war mass democracy. *Picture Post*, one of the vehicles for this democratic style, described customers in terms of the personality traits of heterosexual ordinariness that focused on a perennial and entirely natural quest for the opposite sex: 'He, the average *he*, is generally not a Londoner; he may be a businessman from the provinces, an adolescent visiting town, a soldier on leave. . . . His demands are – to see Girls, and to see as much of them as possible.'[104]

The Windmill's interventionist management style and Van Damm's paternalist outlook pointed to the imposition of a restrictive regime on his female workforce, yet in terms of pay, prospects and working conditions, the 'mill' offered positive opportunities for young women who joined the company. At the outbreak of the war showgirls' pay was five pounds ten shillings a week, at a time when average wages for women in secretarial and office work were a good deal lower; salaries remained similarly competitive throughout the 1950s.[105] *Show News* acknowledged that though few girls made fortunes by posing nude, 'a fairly good livelihood is pretty well assured'.[106]

Many of the Windmill troupe testified to the bonds of companionship and female camaraderie that they forged among themselves. As one member of the company put it in an interview for the Sunday press: 'There is a nice crowd to work with. Full of fun and always ready to stand by each other.'[107] Standing by one another might mean helping a girl give a collective rebuff to unwelcome 'stage door Johnnies', but it could also involve supporting and encouraging the girls who posed nude. The potential stigma attached to appearing in the erotic tableaux was partly dispelled by the fact that showgirls were not isolated from the rest of the troupe but formed part of the overall 'Revudeville' team, while the Van Damms' continual public emphasis on respectability added to the theatre's moral guarantees.[108] As management successor to her father after 1955, Sheila Van Damm reiterated the theatre's commitment to the moral welfare of the girls, stressing that the theatre was 'run like a family with the same sort of rules of conduct and discipline'. Boyfriends were never allowed backstage, and the publicity machine stressed that girls were discouraged from 'going to late parties or visiting pubs in the vicinity of Piccadilly Circus'.[109]

Testimonies from the Windmill girls themselves revealed work routines organized around demanding rehearsal and performance schedules and conventional home lives, interspersed with glimpses of more glamorous metropolitan life that sometimes bordered on the fringes of elite society. Desiree, known in the company as 'Dizzie', started out as a photographic model and worked at the Windmill before being directed into munitions war work. She was later poached by Dixey for her Whitehall troupe. Dizzie's off-stage life included 'parties, and night clubs and the occasional late supper'. Her wartime boyfriends included a brigadier-general in the US Army, but she remembered that after a show 'more often than not, [it was] home on the District line to Mum in Kew'.[110]

More remotely, a place at the Windmill held out the prospect of star status, or at least moving up into serious West End drama or the cinema. Actresses such as Jean Kent and Anna Neagle, both with international careers, began work at the Windmill, and their names were enshrined on the theatre's 'honours board'.[111] Following the traditions of the Edwardian theatre, a more conventional route to social advancement was via a good marriage, and a number of showgirls married diplomats, company directors, and celebrities.[112] In 1960 the marriage of Tommy Steele, the first home-grown rock 'n' roll star, to ex-Windmill girl Ann Donoghue at St Patrick's church in Soho Square was the show business wedding of the year.[113]

For nearly two decades the Windmill was at the centre of a working consensus that defined the boundaries of permissible erotic entertainment in London's West End. The 'mill' came to exert a cultural influence that extended well beyond its actual presence in Archer Street. Endorsed by official agencies and opinion formers, the theatre's success as a national institution lay in its version of English erotica. By the late 1950s this carefully constructed consensus was rapidly breaking down. Striptease was one of the most visible signs of the change to London's entertainment industry. The performances staged at the Raymond Revuebar were not only more aggressive than the Windmill's stylized routines in their deliberate flouting of the limits of censorship, they were also organized differently in terms of both their presentation of the eroticized female body and the geopolitical connotations of their performances.

Swinging London?

From the moment it opened in April 1958 the Raymond Revuebar provoked controversy; dividing public opinion, the club stimulated a wide-ranging debate about sex and consumerism in London. Enterprising man-about-town Christopher Booker, a founding editor of the successful satire magazine *Private Eye*, who also scripted the irreverent BBC television late-night review, *That Was The Week That Was*, identified the club as part of a 'post-Suez' atmosphere in the late 1950s, a period he characterized as one of productive social instability, orchestrated by buoyant consumer demand.[114] Equally, the club's commercial style sharpened a growing critique of the sexual impact of post-war affluence. For opponents of the consumer society the Revuebar was a potent symbol of Harold Macmillan's 'casino economy' that had prospered under the Tory government. Striptease was cast as part of the unregulated world of the 'windfall state', a laissez-faire and increasingly Americanized cultural economy that had spawned so many vices: cheap pornography, drinking clubs, Mayfair 'gambling shindigs', and the 'rootless *rentiers* of London's property boom'.[115] Clubs like the Revuebar, driven by free-market principles of morality and economics, were compared to the 'Make-a-Buck and Shut-Your-Face' syndicates dominating sleazy sexual entertainment in cities like New York and Chicago.[116]

In Soho, leading members of the local bohemian coterie such as Farson attacked the Revuebar's owner, Paul Raymond, on account of his club's negative impact on 'authentic' artisans and traders.[117] Political commentator Bernard Levin took these arguments further; he believed that Raymond's aggressive commercialism led directly to the amorality exposed by the Profumo scandal.[118] In the 1970s the Revuebar was one of the targets of the contemporary women's movement, campaigning about the exploitative effects of the capital's sex industry.[119] The club rapidly assumed national notoriety, in excess of its specific location in Soho.

Paul Raymond encouraged this view of his enterprise, casting himself as a harbinger of the permissive society. 'When social historians tackle post-war Britain,' he wrote later, 'they will probably fasten on the Revuebar's arrival . . . as the start of the stampede into sensuality.'[120] For fifty years, from the late 1950s until his death in 2008, Raymond was identified with changes not only to Soho but also to the country's overall sexual outlook. 'A prophet of a new liberated sexuality', the 'original salesman of sex' and a 'profoundly British phenomenon' were just some of the obituaries on his career produced by supporters and opponents alike.[121] Raymond's own claims to pre-eminence, like Vivian Van Damm's earlier assertions, were part of his own carefully crafted publicity machine. Both men developed expansive commercial styles, with an ability to define sex as part of a broader remit of national and international culture.

Raymond was part of a group of provincial entrepreneurs from relatively obscure backgrounds who substantially reorganized London's cultural infrastructure during the 1960s. Statistical surveys of the capital's labour market revealed the rapid growth of service-sector employment at the expense of heavy industry and manufacturing throughout the 1950s, confirming a trend that began during the inter-war years. Concentrated in the West End and the City of London, this expanding sector included not just civil servants and white collar workers in the major corporations, it also covered the capital's retailing, fashion and entertainment industries.[122] Jonathon Green has argued that photographers, designers, advertisers and magazine journalists, as well as entertainers like Raymond, gained a 'new cachet' as part of the dynamic changes to the consumer industries.[123] Successful businessmen and women were part of a network of 'brokerage, persuasion, savantry and shows' that played an important role in repositioning the capital as contemporary, progressive and go-ahead.

At the beginning of his career Raymond possessed few economic or cultural assets. His contemporaries were other provincial new arrivals, such as his friend, the Irish-born nightclub owner and female impersonator Danny Carroll (Danny La Rue), and Glaswegian fashion designer John Stephen, who opened his first Carnaby Street boutique in west Soho in 1955.[124] Raymond was born Geoffrey Quinn into an Irish Catholic family from Liverpool in 1927. The son of a haulage contractor who left school at fifteen after a Jesuit education at one of the city's genteel Catholic grammar schools, he worked briefly as a Bevan Boy during the war, and later joined the RAF where he spent two years as a bandsman and as a self-confessed part-time spiv, selling nylons and petrol coupons.[125] His first business venture was the Raymond Shirt Company, a front for black-market goods.[126] Undeterred when the outfit folded, he moved quickly back into entertainment, launching himself as a stage clairvoyant on the pier at Clacton-on-Sea in 1947 and changing his name to Paul Raymond. When the act broke up Raymond promptly switched to the northern variety circuit.[127]

Raymond was willing to take economic and cultural risks, and he was able to spot market opportunities at a critical juncture in the fortunes of the entertainment industry. He was involved not in the embryonic youth or teenage market that was central to so many business success stories during this period, but with glamorous forms of adult entertainment.[128] In the early 1950s he began organizing his own touring revues, billing comedians and variety artists, including Hylda Baker and the young mixed race singer from Cardiff, Shirley Bassey. Faced with falling bookings, the manager of one provincial theatre told Raymond that his acts could continue only if the chorus girls appeared nude. Defying the Lord Chamberlain, he took on two 'strippers', offering them an extra ten shillings a week.[129] Raymond regularly told the story that his 'brainwave' to 'organize shows with naked girls' came to him on his honeymoon in 1952, when he decided to go into partnership with his wife Jean, who was herself a showgirl-cum-choreographer.[130] Paul and Jean Raymond circumvented the licensing regulations proscribing static nudity by introducing nearly nude elements as well as what the censor derided as 'sadistic exhibitions' into their touring stage plays with suggestive titles such as *The Brothel, The Vice Racket* and *Les Nues de Paris*.[131] Their decision to spice up the acts in this way was a calculated response both to shifts in the production and consumption of leisure and to changes in the representation of female sexuality.

All genres of live entertainment were affected by the growth of privatized leisure during the 1950s. The impact of what Labour MP Leo Abse called 'our increasingly home-centred society', a style of consumer affluence epitomized by the growth of television, resulted in the rapid decline of London's music halls and variety theatres, as well as affecting many elite West End venues.[132] Rising overheads compounded the difficulties, and in 1960 *The Stage* bemoaned the near 'funereal atmosphere' that prevailed in many leading theatres.[133] Two years earlier critic Richard Findlater had reviewed the 'shrinking world of art and commerce' that was London's theatreland, where audiences numbered 'only a nightly average of 250,000, compared to the two-and-a-half million at the cinema or the twelve million who are probably at home watching the telly'.[134] Findlater's reading of the impact of television identified the arrival of new forms of light entertainment screened on the commercial networks. Successful imported American comedy series such as *I Love Lucy*, or Granada's own northern soap opera *Coronation Street*, attracted audiences by foregrounding domestic situations which focused on the rituals of ordinary life; in doing so they challenged the vaudeville and music hall traditions of British popular theatre.[135]

Coupled with these changes, the late 1950s witnessed a partial shift in sexualized representations of the female body in the visual media and in the performing and decorative arts. Nudity, or semi-nudity, was increasingly integrated into a wider range of artistic and cultural genres, rather than being separated out as a specialized erotic or aesthetic category.[136] Cinema audiences in particular were treated to a new brand of heightened sexual imagery in the visceral portrayal of heterosexual relationships. Hollywood films such as Fred Zinnemann's *From Here to Eternity* (1953) famously shot Burt Lancaster and Deborah Kerr in a suggestive coital embrace, with the couple lying semi-nude on the sand.[137] Many national cinemas also dealt in new scripts of female sexuality, part of experimental film genres like the French new wave and the Italian challenge to neo-realism mounted by Federico Fellini. Brigitte Bardot, who began her career as a 'dancing model' in the Paris fashion industry, performed her own version of a strip routine in *And God Created Woman* (1956), a film that confirmed her status as a European 'sex goddess'.[138] Bardot's strip was followed by Nadia Gray's routine, part of an erotic party dance included in Fellini's celebration of Roman sensuality, *La Dolce Vita* (1960).[139] At home and much further down-market, Rank studios launched Diana Dors as an English response to Marilyn Monroe, with what Tynan described as her 'robust and open-hearted physical allure'.[140] Surveying English character in the mid-1950s, social anthropologist Geoffrey Gorer concluded that these cinematic treatments of sex were loosening the bonds of traditional morality among a significant section of the population.[141]

Erotic coverage of the female body in film and popular culture posed a challenge to the static nudity on display at the Windmill, which began to lose much of its allure. By the late 1950s the 'mill' was struggling to retain its position as the capital's leader in the market for glamour, as the theatre's management felt the competition from strip clubs over audiences, stage staff and even the employment of the showgirls themselves. This competitive situation was particularly intense in Soho's compressed social spaces, where the Revuebar was sited less than a hundred yards away from the Windmill. Sheila Van Damm launched a broadside against Raymond's 'low' cultural credentials, attacking him as an entrepreneur from a 'Soho alley', but even she was forced to admit that 'Revudeville' had become too respectable.[142] Fan dances and static nudes 'were now old hat, as too many of our faithful, regular patrons found the entertainment in the strip clubs more to their liking'.[143]

Raymond's aim in opening his Revuebar was to create a different erotic atmosphere that capitalized on contemporary shifts in sexual and cultural consumerism. The Windmill's democratic style had been forged under the conditions of a collective wartime emergency; the Revuebar in contrast evoked a world of contemporary metropolitan leisure. Overwhelmingly, the club's cornucopia of nudes that moved announced the arrival of post-war affluence in ways that built on the goods and services now on offer in Soho. Acknowledging the revival of the man–about–town, Raymond promoted stratified rather than mass consumption. There were calculated attempts to ape the style of a gentleman's club, with the Revuebar's wine committee and its house rules supposedly governing membership applications which were designed to comply with the LCC's licensing regulations governing access to private venues.[144]

Queen magazine, relaunched under its dynamic new owner Jocelyn Stevens as a manual of de luxe urban style, endorsed the Revuebar as part of Soho's piquant appeal for a younger generation of the metropolitan gentry. Nude shows were now a must for sophisticated urbanites intent on experiencing the area's authentic sights and sounds, the magazine insisted.[145] Strip clubs were there to be savoured not condemned, along with Soho's 'colourful natives', drinking clubs and jazz venues, and the 'cast-off and the kinky'.[146] Raymond also worked hard to associate the Revuebar with Soho's burgeoning post-war reputation as an exotic entrepôt among the progressive middle class. His club's advertising invited audiences to sample the new fashion for Italian trattorias, Angus Steakhouses and Chinese restaurants. Raymond's theatre programmes also carried regular features on Soho's stylish bespoke tailoring trade, specializing in sharp Italian and American-style suits, as well as the ubiquitous adverts for local 'Continental' bookstores, outlets for the trade in pornography.[147]

Some Soho entrepreneurs threw their weight behind Raymond, but others were more critical of his business tactics. 'It's nice to keep up tradition,' argued Tom Farrelly, manager of Mooney's Irish pub in the Charing Cross Road. 'But there is some tradition that is better forgotten,' he went on with pointed reference to the Revuebar; 'I would like Soho cleaned up a lot.'[148] Planners and architects also took issue with Raymond's commercial ethos from an environmental standpoint, in ways that paralleled Abercrombie's critique of Soho's blighted condition twenty years earlier. In the eyes of these professionals, strip clubs were evidence of urban decay: 'Narrow courts, crowded streets . . . there is much . . . in need of improvement,' insisted the *Municipal Journal*, the mouthpiece of local authority planning, in a feature article on Soho's dilapidated state, published in 1963.[149] Photographs of Walker's Court, with the Revuebar's neon sign in full view, served to make the case for the area's wholesale replanning 'in line with more modern needs'.[150] A programme of demolition and street clearance needed to be twinned with a campaign to dismantle the worst excesses of an Americanized sex industry, explained *The Times* the same year.[151]

The difficulty was that the Revuebar's commercial ethos was tailored to modern needs – those of a paying public. The siting and lay-out of the club testified to the way the glamour market was changing. Striptease at Raymond's was staged not in a traditional theatre but in a so-called members' club. Van Damm had been reliant on Mrs Henderson's patronage to establish himself in theatreland; Raymond also needed sponsorship to secure a Soho club venue, taking over a restaurant lease for his Archer Street premises on favourable terms from the Isow family, the influential group of Jewish impresarios.[152] His 'instinct for seizing opportunities' was backed by his willingness to shoulder a high degree of personal financial risk; he borrowed no money to open the club, selling his house and car to finance the new venture.[153]

Ironically, Raymond's business profited from the package of government measures designed to reorganize the West End's night life by redefining the boundaries between public and private morality. The club was an indirect beneficiary of the Wolfenden committee's recommendations on prostitution enacted in the Street Offences Act, which effectively restructured London's sex trade. Raymond claimed later that he had 'unhappy memories' of Wolfenden's policies, but the Revuebar was an astute commercial and cultural response to the capital's new regime of sexual regulation.[154]

Inside the club, customers consumed sex in cabaret-style surroundings; the front-of-house lay-out with its comfortable sofas, television, gaming tables and piano bar created a contemporary style of leisured sophistication. In the 240-seat auditorium patrons sat grouped at small tables rather than in fixed seating, where they were serviced by restaurant and bar staff as they watched the nude displays.[155] There were none of the elaborate physical barriers and management controls designed to separate performers from the audience. Regular 'Amateur Strip' contests 'open to all girls over 16' encouraged audience participation in choosing competition winners (fig. 32).[156] Raymond's showgirls worked from a raised apron stage that extended well forward into the club's auditorium, and patrons confirmed that they were often 'seated so close to the stage that we were practically on it'.[157] One club regular who kept a 'sex diary' for much of his adult life noted it was in this 'glitzy atmosphere' that he had his first 'clear view of the female pudenda', as a parade of nattily dressed showgirls passed close by him.[158]

Live sexual entertainment at the club was not just brash and arresting, it was far more exclusively centred on the sexualized female body than performances at the Windmill. Working closely with his wife, who billed herself as 'the World's premier expert' on glamour, Raymond quickly dispensed with the variety acts that were an integral part of Van Damm's conception of review theatre.[159] Comedians were abandoned in the interests of promoting a sexy atmosphere focused on erotic female display and audience arousal. Comedy at the Revuebar took a different format, centred on sexual parody, quirky humour and light-hearted 'foreplay'. Club audiences rarely heard blue jokes from stand-up or gag comedians as they did at the 'mill', nor was there any attempt to draw on the genres of low sexual comedy that characterized other forms of popular culture during the 1960s, such as the *Carry On* films, with their blend of scatological humour and exuberant farce.

Revuebar performances were organized as a running sequence of strip routines, billed as cabaret-style entertainment. In February 1962, after the opening high-kicking song and dance 'Overture' by the full company and orchestra, audiences watched a solo from 'Miss Strip-Tease' followed by the 'Artists and Models' sketch, showcasing dancers posed as erotic 'colours' to be manipulated on the artist's 'palette'.[160] Three more solo strips followed, with the first half of the show rounded off by yet another version of the ever-popular song and dance routine from *Top Hat*. After the interval the full company returned for 'A Stripper We Would Be', an erotic parody of contemporary mass society, with nurses, schoolgirls, charladies and socialites all supposedly driven by the urge to go nude. 'Roarin' 20's', which came next, was set in a speakeasy, with Chicago-style gangsters and their 'molls', while the strip number 'Witchcraft' was redolent with mildly sinister suggestions of erotic voodoo. The full company reassembled for the 'International Roundabout' finale, which was another display of glitzy spectacle.

Raymond's version of striptease dispensed with the elaborate illusion of concealment and revelation that characterized the Windmill's performances. Strip routines followed a sequence that invariably climaxed with the full 'flash', and as the police noted in many scenes showgirls removed 'their "G" string or fig leaf . . . showing their pubic hair'.[161] By emphatically rejecting the traditional formula of static tableaux in favour of kinetic nudity, showgirls were able to stage more overtly sexualized displays of eroticism. This was what the police in C Division referred to as 'passionate lust' that left little to the imagination.[162]

The Revuebar's management style along with the acts themselves posed a direct challenge to the rules governing stage censorship. 'This is a Club in name only,' observed the Met's Superintendent Strath, who was respon-

sible for West End clubs, after the first raid on the Revuebar for suspected
infringement of the licensing regulations in May 1958. 'In my opinion,'
Strath went on, 'there are no bona fide members . . . and the Management
provide a façade of legality . . . for private gain.'[163] Strath's views were
endorsed by his commanding officers, who confirmed that Raymond was
in effect running an 'unlicensed theatre', using the 'false premise' of a club
in order to circumvent regulation by the Lord Chamberlain, whose remit
did not extend to private establishments.[164] Police surveillance revealed a
massive 'doorstep membership' policy that in effect granted admission to
almost any casual passer-by. It proved extremely lucrative; by the end of
April 1958 Raymond had accepted over 8,000 membership applications
which netted him receipts totalling over £4,000.[165] 'Very good going for
a Club which has been opened for eleven days,' the police commented
dryly.[166]

Striptease at the Revuebar not only marked an escalation of the battle
over the regulation of nude displays, it shifted the terrain of official confrontation away from the Lord Chamberlain and into the orbit of the
Metropolitan Police and the LCC. Theatre historians and historians of
censorship have seen the displacement of a discreet, patrician system of
supervision by more direct clashes between the police, the licensing
authorities and sexual entrepreneurs like Raymond as a defining feature
of the moral conflicts of the 1960s.[167] But the official campaigns used
against Soho's strip clubs were far from new; they replicated long-established patterns of surveillance dating back to the inter-war years. During
the 1930s the police had regularly used plain-clothes officers in undercover operations against dubious clubs they suspected were infringing the
public morality laws or the licensing regulations, following up their observations with lightning raids and prosecutions.[168] Raymond's response also
echoed the strategy of an earlier generation of club proprietors; he constantly played cat-and-mouse with the police and almost certainly
'bought' periods of 'quiet' by bribing officers with illegal pay-offs.[169] Far
from being a specific product of permissiveness, these activities were
rooted in the customary traditions of West End policing and in the deft
tactical responses of Soho's nightclub owners.

Championing free-market principles, Raymond's management style displaced Van Damm's corporatism, though like his predecessor he took a
close interest in his showgirls (fig. 33). Showgirls at the Revuebar were
usually given only short-term contracts, and they were often forced into
multi-task employment, marking a return to working routines that were

common among West End chorus girls during the inter-war years. Hungarian-born Eva Kovac, who 'stripped to a "G" string', had done nude photography before answering an advert in the pin-up magazine *Reveille* and booking an audition at the Revuebar.[170] Many artists juggled a rapid succession of nightly appearances at different Soho clubs and were subject to fines imposed for lateness.[171] Patrick Marnham, a young journalist who worked for *Private Eye* magazine during the 1960s, remembered leaning out of his office window in Greek Street 'watching Maltese ponces, Jamaican gamblers and English strippers who formed the local working population'. He recalled how the new breed of showgirls were easily identifiable, hurrying from one performance to the next with their 'little vanity cases'.[172]

Raymond's employment policies inevitably influenced the expectations of his workforce. The Windmill troupe stressed the benefits of female solidarity; performers at the Revuebar displayed a more instrumental and individualistic approach to a career in Soho's glamour industry. 'René Lastair', who started out at the Windmill, justified her move to Raymond's in terms of better pay and an unabashed attitude to appearing nude: 'This pays better than ordinary chorus work. And it doesn't worry me . . .'[173] The Windmill girls were always encouraged to present integrated and authentic biographies on and off stage, but Lastair carefully differentiated her sexual persona as a striptease artist from the rest of her personality. As she put it emphatically: 'What you do on the stage has nothing to do with your private life.'[174] Many girls who worked at the Revuebar emphasized the sheer 'hard graft' involved in stripping, including the need to simulate sexual pleasure for their audiences. 'If I've got anywhere in this game,' observed 'Jan', who began work as a secretary, 'it's because I try to give the audience the feeling "I'm enjoying this."'[175] Some showgirls championed the libertarian sexual politics of the 1960s, campaigning for the abolition of stage censorship.[176] Organizing themselves into the British Association of Striptease Artists, they targeted the Greater London Council, successor to the LCC, demanding the reform of outdated licensing regulations. As Rhoda Rogers, the chair of the association, argued in 1965: 'It's high time that the council changed its ways. All these laws are old-fashioned. . . . Striptease is . . . a respectable business.'[177]

The most notable change in the Revuebar's performances lay in the way they handled the geopolitics of erotic display. Whereas Van Damm worked hard to advertise an exclusively English version of femininity, Raymond promoted his artists as sexually and culturally cosmopolitan.[178]

Castigating the English as a 'nation of hypocrites probably . . . the worst in the world', he marketed his club as a deliberate assault on the sexual culture which in his view had held sway in London for too long, under the combined forces of the Windmill and the theatre censor.[179] Raymond's idea of cosmopolitanism drew on Soho's established pleasure economy, but like members of the Soho Association he repackaged the area's traditional associations with foreign bodies and spaces.

Showgirls at the Revuebar represented a wide range of international sexual types, and while some artists were genuinely foreign, others posed as exotic imports via assumed stage names and personalities. Photographs included in club programmes in the early 1960s showed Raymond working to promote an international world of sex via performers' visual styles and bodily idioms. There was 'Ingrid' from Germany; crouching forward, her body posture carried mild suggestions of masochistic sex, while her costume of black suspenders, high heels and 'G' string set off against blond skin tones was mildly fetishistic (fig. 34, top right).[180] Unlike the nudes at the 'mill' who invariably posed with wholesome 'cheesecake' smiles, this showgirl looked out to the viewer with an overtly sexualized stare. French 'Gisele Paris' traded on the more familiar theme of Gallic sexual naughtiness; narcissistically pleasuring her semi-naked body, she appeared in a tightly laced satin basque. With pouting lips, wide-eyed stare and legs spread apart, her act suggested a nubile and available sexuality, echoing the type of contemporary pose struck by Bardot (fig. 34, bottom right). There was also 'Anna Sandor' from Hungary, naked except for a guitar and Gypsy-style pantaloons and stiletto heels, fondling her 'instrument' in suggestive sexual foreplay (fig. 34, centre).

Like many other entrepreneurs in 1950s Soho, Raymond drew on sexual and cultural styles associated with Continental Europe to promote a glamorous ambience. Continentalism was also used by Raymond and his management team to suggest heightened or specialized forms of eroticism. American producer Sam Wanamaker wrote approvingly that the influx of 'foreign talent' meant that performers now had that 'extra something' frequently lacking in English girls.[181] Sergeant Caiels noted that the club introduced 'coloured dancers' as well, performers who represented sex as instinctual and freed from cultural restraint. The Public Morality Council mounted a strong protest about the inclusion of 'a coloured stripper . . . quite repulsive', and also objected to 'a girl from Latin America'.[182] Despite this opposition, the club's policy was to highlight a greater diversity of body types, skin tones and physiognomies than had been the norm at the 'mill'.

The showgirls' strip routines and the forms of auditory culture used to support their acts distanced the Revuebar's erotic displays from the Windmill's ideal of English femininity. In addition to the well-drilled chorus line of bodies moving in collective motion that Raymond continued to use for the opening and closing numbers in his shows, many of the Revuebar's solo dancers choreographed their own free-form striptease displays, drawing on the international traditions of modern expressive dance. Some club performers acquired a basic dance training, as well as a knowledge of the drills of classical ballet, by attending the Conti Italian Stage School based in Great Windmill Street.[183] Audiences heard a mixture of mainly transatlantic musical sounds as the accompaniment to their acts. Played either by a live band or on tapes or records, jazz and blues music was used to provide suitable rhythms and create an appropriate sexual mood.

The showgirls' bodily idioms suggested an unstable range of erotic meanings that pointed to the contradictory sexual associations of striptease. Bodies with full breasts pushed forward, legs wide apart, and hands caressing the genital area projected sexual stereotypes for male consumption. When performers were paired with male dancers they acted out a version of liberated heterosexuality, with its 'complementary' styles of instinctual male arousal and female display. The 'John and Marsha' routine witnessed by Caiels centred on the couple's synchronized strip as a celebration of the joys of mutual sex, a performance that anticipated many popular sex manuals in the 1960s. Other strip acts presented more autonomous and culturally mobile representations of the female body, with autoerotic movements suggesting expressive and potentially assertive forms of sexuality. This was especially the case in the solo numbers, where the showgirls were given space to individualize their routines. Performers also parodied the erotic itself; their bodies and faces displaying exaggerated sexual movements and elaborately staged expressions of desire.[184] Quirky humour regularly undercut a commitment to full sexual seriousness in striptease.

Raymond's decision to include nude male dancers in his shows shifted his club's profile in a different direction, tacitly recognizing Soho's importance as a rendezvous for homosexual men. On the opening Sunday night, the Revuebar advertised a 'Fabulous All Male Revue – Call Us Mister'.[185] This was a version of the lightly disguised homosexual musicals that had so concerned Peter Wildeblood in his evidence to the Wolfenden committee and which outraged public moralists with a mixture of vaudeville, drag acts and low sexual comedy. Even Danny La Rue, who appeared briefly in one of these reviews, thought the antics of the all-male chorus line were 'outrageous', adding tongue-in-cheek that they were 'far too camp for me'.[186] The police confirmed that Sunday nights at the Revuebar had a 'distinct flavour of homosexuality'.[187] Plain-clothes officers encountered a chorus and dancers 'of very effeminate appearances' performing 'extremely suggestive' cross-dressing routines, crude pantomime turns (including a well-tried 'ugly sisters' parody from *Cinderella*), and a variety of 'smutty talk'.[188]

Raymond always insisted that his target audience for these special shows was not Soho's homosexual customers but an adventurous heterosexual clientele, women as well as men who demanded sexual variety as part of sophisticated metropolitan nightlife.[189] Revuebar publicity billed the shows as 'unbelievable . . . a must for both Ladies and Gentlemen every Sunday'.[190] Women, accompanied by husbands, boyfriends and sexual partners, certainly formed a minority audience at the club, apparently confirming a contemporary trend identified by Kinsey, who noted that women were regular and enthusiastic visitors to American burlesque shows.[191] They included women like Janet Pickering and Muriel Ambrose from Weybridge, taken to the Revuebar on a West End night out by Mrs Ambrose's husband George, who had seen an advert for striptease in their local Surrey paper.[192] Raymond responded to this heterosocial demand by offering reduced joint subscriptions for husband and wife members, a policy that he claimed was intended to attract more women.[193]

The police told a different story about the all-male shows, noting that overwhelmingly they attracted an audience of men who were sexually interested in other men. Young plain-clothes officers were propositioned by members of the audience while on Sunday night duty, highlighting again the problems inherent in police disguise.[194] The Revuebar's workforce also included a complement of homosexual men. Eighteen-year-old Roy Skinner from Streatham gave up his apprenticeship as a carpenter to work the spotlight at the club. His mother hinted anxiously that the attraction of the Revuebar was more than financial: 'In April he started staying out at nights. . . . he told me he was sharing a flat at 30s a week with a male friend.'[195] Later in his career Raymond rejected homosexuality, and homosexual shows, as unnaturally 'kinky', reasserting a vigorous commitment to heterosexuality that characterized the outlook of many libertarian apologists for sex.[196] But in the early years the Revuebar was committed to a varied style of erotic entertainment that reflected Soho's reputation for sexual diversity.

Raymond's sales pitch aimed to differentiate his patrons from the seedy sexual punters who formed the perceived audience for so much of the local sex industry, and his marketing strategy was part of the overall rebranding of Soho in the late 1950s. He explained his approach to the new style women's magazine *Nova*, which was busy promoting the idea of liberated heterosexuality: 'We're not aiming to attract the dirty little men in raincoats but international businessmen and their wives who want a good sexy night out. And why not? They're perfectly entitled to it.'[197] Like Van Damm, Raymond believed he owed his success to the fact that he 'understood his punters', enabling him to tailor his acts to customer demand.[198] Soon he was boasting about his appeal among London's social elites, emphasizing how 'MP's . . . millionaires . . . knights . . . and . . . peers of the realm' were now regular visitors, while strategically placed advertising in the provincial press and the practice of issuing temporary membership cards to overseas travellers pointed to tourists as another target audience.[199] *The New London Spy* (1966), a contemporary adult tourist guide to the pleasures of London, endorsed the Revuebar's de luxe image, billing the club as 'the most imaginative strip club in town', noting that 'the bars are comfortable, the restaurant expensive and the hostesses a little too persistent'.[200]

Like Van Damm, Raymond was deliberately vague about his customer profile, but the Revuebar's pricing structure pointed to a clear-sighted marketing strategy. In addition to targeting affluent consumers, the cut-price opening membership fee of 15s. 6d. showed how Raymond was aiming for the same type of audience who were regulars at the Windmill. The Revuebar maintained a considerable overlap with Soho's established markets for sex; what linked male audiences at the Revuebar with those at the 'mill' was their willingness to pay for sexual entertainment.

When the police raided the club in the spring of 1958, they encountered many of the 'ordinary punters' who were also customers at the 'mill'. Standing in the bar, drinking light ale, were a group who had 'come down' from Stockport for the FA Cup Final, men 'with their pals' who had booked tickets for the club along with their soccer seats, via a local tour company.[201] Jovial, rumbustious and with personalities made more expansive by drink, these provincial visitors demanded erotic entertainment as a part of their weekend on the town, to be savoured along with all the

other forms of homosocial leisure, such as spectator sport and the obligatory West End pub crawl. They demanded sex on a limited budget, as
part of time spent away from their wives and families, rather than as part
of the de luxe itineraries of the man-about-town. Mainstream customers
of this kind were the characters whom one Soho prostitute particularly
detested: 'The ones just up for the cup,' she remarked, 'they've got £3 to
spend and want the most out of it. . . . They've come to London on a
cheap trip, for a cheap day and a cheap bash.'[202]

But the police also noted different types of patrons when they raided
the club. There were genteel visitors from the Home Counties, sipping
their gin and tonics, as well as foreign tourists and military men from the
Royal Navy and the RAF, in town for business or for a few days sight-
seeing as part of their leave.[203] Harry Pitz, from Antwerp, and his friend
Faes Adolph, from Zurich, were 'just strolling around the West End' when
they caught sight the club's neon light and were immediately given membership cards.[204] And there was at least one 'coloured man' from Barbados,
drinking brandy and water and puffing his cigar.[205] What distinguished
these men from the Windmill's audiences were their social and sexual
expectations. They carried little sense of the furtiveness or seediness that
shadowed the 'mill's' patrons. Revuebar customers demanded sexual
glamour not so much as contained licence or clandestine arousal but as
an explicit part of contemporary masculine leisure.

Paul Raymond's commercial ambition to cater to the demands of a
new type of consumer was more developed by the time he expanded his
business ventures into pornography during the mid-1960s. Promoted on
the back of the financial success of the Revuebar, the launch of his
glamour magazine *King* in 1964, which appeared alongside other contemporary titles such as *Penthouse* and *Mayfair*, heralded a new genre of
pornography that campaigned around the libertarian ethos of sexual
freedom.[206] Retailing for 7s. 6d., printed largely in colour on glossy paper
with high-quality production values, *King* projected the idea of an erotic
universe dominated by affluent, internationally mobile, young adult men.
Making the familiar publisher's identification with his readers, whom he
envisaged as part of a shared sexual community, Raymond ran regular
soft-focus nude spreads of up-and-coming film stars like Ursula Andress
alongside articles on foreign travel, Grand Prix racing, wine connoisseurship and stylish restaurants. A suggested weekend itinerary in Copenhagen,
one of the early Shangri-Las of Raymond's 'permissive revolution', rang

the changes of this consumerist vision of masculinity: 'Lively girls, livelier nights, lush food, they're the high life ingredients of Copenhagen that add up to a KING-size weekend jaunt. . . . Europe is our playground . . . and we have already won thousands of friends there.'[207] This shift in the geopolitical associations of sex, away from the robust Englishness of the Windmill girls to the idea of the sexual good life as an international long weekend, stimulated by a full assortment of consumer appetites, was a defining feature of Raymond's cultural outlook during the 1960s.

✳

The Windmill Theatre finally closed its doors in 1964; faced with mounting debts and declining audiences for 'Revudeville', the Van Damm family were forced to sell off their theatre to a cinema chain. The Revuebar, in contrast, went from strength to strength. Building up an extensive local property holding, Raymond became the self-proclaimed 'Duke of Soho' and the recognized face of commercial sex in London.[208] Never tempted to float his company, he used his own personal wealth to expand and diversify his business interests beyond striptease and pornography.[209] Raymond bought Ronnie Scott's jazz club in Frith Street, the fashionable L'Escargot restaurant in Greek Street and a chain of theatres. An enthusiastic supporter of Thatcherism, by 1992 he had ousted the Duke of Westminster as Britain's richest man, with an estimated fortune of £1.5 billion.[210] Economic success went hand in hand with the cultivation of a distinctive public persona as Raymond became a contemporary man-about-town. Divorced from his wife, he was frequently pictured in nightclubs and discotheques accompanied by famous models and fashionable 'dolly birds'.[211]

Raymond's expansive business interests had major consequences for Soho's development. As the area's premier landlord he was upfront about promoting Soho as a sexual marketplace organized around his own goods and services. Raymond's supervision of rents and leaseholds enabled him to keep an eye on the activities of newcomers and bar unwelcome competitors. His controlling stake in Soho also meant that he could experiment with a version of the cluster economy, with entrepreneurs and consumers grouped in one convenient location. But unlike Soho's later gentrifiers Raymond's vision remained sex-centred, and despite his public denials he continued to draw on the seedy underside of the West End's sexual economy.

27 Street scene in Greek Street, Soho, 1949, photographer Bert Hardy, Hulton Archive. Getty Images.

28 Frontispiece illustration by John Minton, in Elizabeth David, *A Book of Mediterranean Food* (London: John Lehmann, 1950).

29   Windmill Theatre during VE celebrations May 1945, photographer unknown, in Vivian Van Damm, *Tonight and Every Night* (London: Stanley Paul, 1952).

30   Windmill girl 'Pat', front cover, *London Life*, 19 October 1940, photographer unknown.

31   Fan dance, Windmill Theatre, undated, photographer unknown, in Vivian Van
Damm, *Tonight and Every Night* (London: Stanley Paul, 1952).

32   Amateur striptease at the Raymond Revuebar, 21 May 1958, photographer John Pratt/Stringer, Hulton Archive. Getty Images.

33   Paul Raymond and the Revuebar showgirls, 1 January 1960, photographer unknown.
Popperfoto/Getty Images.

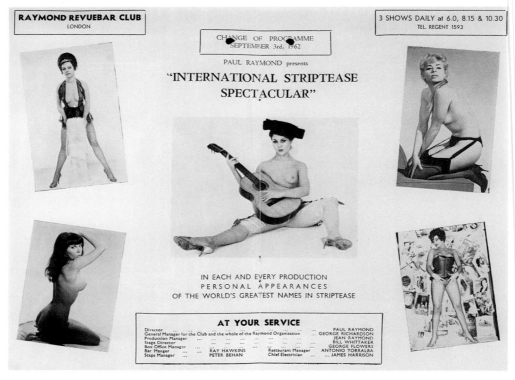

34   Pin-ups, *Paul Raymond's Raymond Revue Bar*, programme, 1962, in Raymond Revue Bar: Suspected Disorderly House (1961–1963), TNA PRO MEPO 2/10168. The National Archives, reproduced by kind permission of the Metropolitan Police Authority.

The rise to prominence of the Revuebar and the associated story of the Windmill's demise epitomized many features of the commercial story of permissiveness as it has been told since the 1960s. Tracing developments in one particular market sector over a longer timescale makes it possible to establish a better assessment of what precisely changed during the period. Certainly, the story of live sexual entertainment focused on erotic displays of the female body was as significant for sexual politics as some of the more familiar themes that have dominated post-war social history, such as the struggles over homosexuality and pornography.

The policing of commercially organized female nudity was not marked by a simple move towards the liberalization of official attitudes, at least not until the late 1960s with the abolition of theatre censorship. What occurred was an uneven and contested shift from patrician modes of supervision, based on supposedly consensual notions of taste and sexual etiquette, towards more direct intervention by the police and the local authorities. These conflicts were not just fought out as battles between public moralists and progressives over the sexual content of nude displays; they were also crucially about the cultural meanings associated with static and kinetic nudity, about the changing relationship between performers and audiences, and about shifting patterns of business organization. Corporate paternalism and traditional public spectacle gave way to more free-market principles and to a more intimate, privatized conception of masculine leisure. The theatrical staging of feminine glamour, anchored by a tightly circumscribed version of Englishness, was displaced by the international world of striptease centred on sexualized images of women from Continental Europe and the USA. Entrepreneurs like the Van Damm family and Raymond acted as influential cultural intermediaries, interpreting and shaping the sexual demands of their audiences in accordance with the social expectations of mass democracy, on the one hand, and stratified, individualized consumption, on the other. The Windmill Theatre and the Revuebar performed significant cultural work by maintaining the reputation of the West End in English sexual mythology. The impact of these iconic venues was felt not just through their actual presence in Soho, but also in terms of the wider resonances they carried in public debate and in the collective imagination about sex and the national culture.

In the summer of 1960 the activities of Soho's showgirls were projected onto a very large canvas indeed. Two young dancers appeared together on the stage of Murray's Club in Beak Street, one of Soho's more prestigious night-time entertainment venues. Eighteen-year-old

Christine Keeler was topless, dressed only in a shiny *cache-sexe* and an exotic assortment of feathers and sequins. Mandy Rice-Davies was costumed as an Indian squaw, with a feathered headband, short leather skirt, beads and ankle bracelets. Neither girl actually performed a striptease routine, but their visual style involving erotically clothed semi-nudity and a knowing contract between dancer and audience borrowed heavily from Soho's traditions of sexual entertainment. Offstage as well as onstage, Keeler and Rice-Davies acted out a series of powerful sexual performances that had the widest political reverberations. The major scandal that erupted as the Profumo affair kaleidoscoped together London's rapidly changing sexual cultures, highlighting transgressive sex as a major source of national anxiety.

Chapter 7   Scandal

The Profumo Affair

'It does not stop in Fleet Street. It goes to Westminster. It crosses the Channel, even the Atlantic and back again, swelling all the time.'[1] These were the comments of Lord Denning, senior law lord and Master of the Rolls, in his judicial review of the Profumo scandal, commissioned by Harold Macmillan and published in the autumn of 1963. The significance of the affair was extensive in the sense identified by Denning as 'a sensation which captured the attention of the world'.[2] The international dimensions of the scandal, linking government ministers to Soviet spy networks via a web of Cold War and society intrigue in London and abroad, ensured that it circulated as world news. In the arena of domestic politics Profumo's significance was equally compelling; it severely compromised an already weakened Conservative government, contributing indirectly to Macmillan's resignation as Prime Minister in the autumn of 1963 and to the Conservative Party's defeat in the general election the following year.

The Profumo case reproduced a number of the same anxieties that dominated the other post-war scandals, but its links to national politics along with its international resonances meant that the affair became much bigger. The consequences of the episode continue to shape public debate and popular memory almost half a century later, via an endless circulation of books, a feature film, and a continuous outpouring of memoirs and confessions from many of its key players.[3] It has also acquired the generic status of the 'standard' or classic twentieth-century scandal within English political culture, the median against which other subsequent liaisons and sexual transgressions have been measured.[4]

The Profumo affair was also expansive in terms of the social and sexual themes that it pushed together. The scandal had an immediate impact on the masculine world of high politics and on elite London society. It refocused the searchlight of publicity onto the problematic status of the man-about-town in the capital city and his connections with the metropolitan *demi-monde*. But Profumo's significance extended well beyond the usual purveyors of and settings for scandalous activity. Women and men from subaltern and marginal backgrounds who were empowered by consumerism, sexual knowledge and ethnic difference jostled for attention with members of the political and social elite in the public spaces and entertainment settings of the West End, as well as in cultural locations further afield. The scandal's denouement brought Westminster politics, Soho's traditional spaces of sexual encounter, and Notting Hill's racially exotic settings into an uneasy, triangulated relationship.

Historians who have written about the Profumo episode from the vantage point of high politics have underplayed the scandal's sexual dimensions, subordinating these intrigues to the Soviet spy story, which has been seen as potentially significant for British foreign policy in a Cold War context.[5] Espionage and rumours of espionage were crucial ingredients in the narrative to be sure, motivating a number of the leading players and creating an atmosphere of dangerous excitement. For the security services the spy angle was clearly paramount, but for the Home Office and the Metropolitan Police, for large sections of the national press, and for many Tory grandees the sexual and moral elements were judged to be equally critical. My account privileges the libidinous aspects of the scandal not just because they have been underestimated but also on account of the way they were read as symptomatic of the problems and possibilities of permissiveness.

Like most of the other scandalous events that dominated the post-war period, Profumo was London-centred, but in ways that reverberated well beyond the usual remit of these episodes. Both the Burgess and Maclean case and the Vassall spy incident focused public attention on the sexual misdemeanours and treasonable activities of Whitehall mandarins who were compromised by their alleged associations with low-life, West End characters. The Montagu–Wildeblood case highlighted the dubious activities of fashionable men-about-town. What elevated Profumo over and above these intrigues was the way the activities of the sexual actors and the environments at the heart of the affair became identified with symptoms of deep-seated moral problems. Once again historians have tended

to neglect the episode's metropolitan significance, seeing London simply
as background for the unfolding of events, with the result that the issues
of urban society and culture have been subsumed into the scandal's overarching political remit.[6] While not underestimating the impact of the affair
on national politics, I argue that at almost every stage the case was shaped
by the city's social relationships and environments.

Attention to the scandal's urban locatedness returns us to the larger
question that has underpinned this history: the links between metropolitan culture and wider processes of social and moral change. Sex and security were its main organizing principles, but these issues were run together
with other anxieties: the fallibility of upper-class political leadership, the
dark underside of the post-war consumer economy, Caribbean migrants,
media power, and an accelerating debate over the 'decline of Britain'. All
these dilemmas were superimposed onto the affair and were viewed
through a powerful metropolitan lens. As the case unfolded, scandal
became a highly marketable commodity with a high selling price, as it
had been in many earlier sensational sex cases, but it also became the currency for trading ideas and information about a wide range of contemporary moral problems.

This chapter explores the Profumo scandal's complex negotiation of
the themes of sexual and cultural modernity by situating them within the
history of post-war London that the book has charted. I do this in a
number of interrelated ways. I describe the main elements of the case,
introducing the principal actors and showing how their socially situated
biographies and personal relationships generated a dynamic and unresolved atmosphere of cultural and geographical disturbance in the capital
during the early 1960s. A careful and detailed reconstruction of the
Profumo story, which stays close to the development of the action and
its key locations, is important in order to demonstrate how the episode
refracted a number of expansive sexual themes via its intricate plot.
Mapping the interconnections between events, characters and their social
settings is particularly important not only because the case was manifestly
complex in terms of its genesis and denouement, but also on account of
the fact that so many of the key incidents are the subject of continuing
dispute. The scandal generated a bewildering variety of sensational story
lines and sub-plots that were told as gossip and innuendo or as deliberate deception, both at the time and in subsequent re-readings of the case.[7]
These uncertainties about the character of events were not simply problems relating to the reliability of witnesses in an evidential sense, impor-

tant though this was, nor can they be accredited to the generic features of scandal per se. They were the product of mounting disagreements within English society about morality, politics and culture. London's problematic geography loomed large at each stage in these debates; far from featuring simply as background, the metropolis was an essential component of the evidence itself.

This significance of Profumo's deep urban context is highlighted in the final part of the chapter, which describes how the scandal's sexual and political narratives were hotly contested. Different characters and social groups struggled to establish competing truths and fictions about the Profumo affair that were characterized by varying degrees of coherence. What was significant about almost of all of them was the way they returned again and again to the same cultural hinterland of metropolitan London. This recurrent focus on key locations and their cast of characters provides important clues to the complex versions of modernity that were carried by the case. John Profumo's political downfall as Minister of War and a member of the Conservative government and Stephen Ward's dramatic trial and suicide provided a degree of narrative closure to the affair, but many of the long-term questions remained unresolved.

Two Men-of-the-World

The Profumo scandal erupted into public consciousness in the spring of 1963, but its roots lay further back, in the activities of the men and women whose lives were part of elite London society during the 1950s. 'The story must start with Stephen Ward,' Lord Denning insisted at the opening of his report.[8] This was true in a literal sense; Ward's conduct and his social relationships set in train a series of incidents that eventually cost him his life and John Profumo his public reputation, and dramatically altered the careers of Christine Keeler and many of the lesser players in the affair. Equally importantly, Ward's personality served as a conduit for some of the most pressing moral anxieties about post-war metropolitan culture, especially the social and sexual uneasiness that surrounded the man-about-town. Ward's biography needs unpacking in detail, along with the activities of the other principal characters, notably Profumo and Keeler, because the contested readings of his personality featured as a major issue throughout the case.

Stephen Ward was the wayward product of a genteel, provincial English upbringing. Born in 1912, the son of an Anglican clergyman, Ward refused a settled middle-class career at home, preferring instead an itinerant and cosmopolitan existence. He explored the inter-war cultural and sexual scenes of Paris and Hamburg, acting as an informal guide at the famous Montparnasse brothel, Le Sphinx, and becoming a devotee of the red-light district of Hamburg's Reeperbahn, before travelling to the USA, where he qualified as an osteopath at Kirksville College, Missouri, in 1938.[9] On returning to Britain after wartime army service in India as a captain in the Royal Army Medical Corps, Ward discovered that osteopathy remained professionally dubious at home. He admitted that 'osteopaths weren't doctors. They weren't quite respectable.'[10] With their technique of directly manipulating the bodies of patients by feel and touch and their emphasis on holistic healing, they were regularly castigated as quacks, partly because osteopathy represented an alternative 'ethics of the flesh' to the scientific principles of controlled physiological intervention emphasized by conventional medicine.

Perceptions of Stephen Ward's close and potentially unhealthy proximity to his patients' bodies, as well as to the bodies of the young women who were part of his sexual circle, were eventually used to pathologize him as the Profumo scandal accelerated and Ward became its principal victim. But during the late 1940s and early 1950s the partial uncertainty that clouded Ward's professional status after his return to London contributed to his near-obsessive desire to be accepted socially. Stephen Ward aspired to enter the world of the upper class. Among friends and acquaintances Ward sometimes posed as an anti-Establishment figure, but he also acknowledged that 'big names were necessary to his personality'.[11] His guiding principle was axiomatic, 'start where you intend to finish – at the top', though friends pointed out that his intense social ambition was offset by enormous charm and by his attractive if unconventional lifestyle.[12]

The key to Ward's growing professional success and his enlarged reputation lay with his 'healing hands'. Stephen Ward's hands put him in touch, quite literally, with London's social and political elites.[13] His efforts to position himself as part of this metropolitan world represented a discreet but calculated exercise in self-promotion. Ward deliberately set up his clinic on the west side of Cavendish Square, situated close to Harley Street with its eminent consultants and physicians, and his practice began to be patronized by a succession of international public figures after he successfully treated both the American ambassador, Averell Harriman, and Winston Churchill.[14] Ward confided to friends that each of Churchill's twelve treatments became something of a battle of wills. He resisted the statesman's notorious bullying and eventually developed a friendly relationship with him, gossiping about Stalin and other world leaders while his patient was seated on Ward's treatment table wearing 'only the top half of his pyjamas!'[15] Society figures liked the idea of being treated by Churchill's osteopath, and by the early 1950s Ward was averaging a salary of around £5,000 a year, a figure roughly the same as that of Cabinet ministers and senior civil servants.[16] In Stephen Ward's world of osteopathy patients came almost entirely through recommendation, and by the middle of the decade his patient list boasted a mixture of 'Hollywood, the House of Commons, the peerage, the Church, and the City'.[17]

As a result of these professional connections Ward also became something of a 'social cocktail shaker' by virtue of his varied, but invariably distinguished, clientele.[18] He was a personal friend and long-standing confidant of Viscount Astor, and he had been treating Astor for back problems since 1950. A dilettante and an ageing socialite, Bill Astor had been a Tory MP. He was immensely rich, with an inherited family fortune that included a two-million-pound asset base in Britain alone and an impressive property portfolio in Manhattan.[19] Largely through Astor's patronage Ward was able to expand his social circle, with introductions to private homes and clubs that would otherwise have been closed to him. Via Astor, Ward was brought close up to a range of prominent public figures as acquaintances and potentially as personal friends, rather than simply as rich patients demanding treatment.

Stephen Ward's hands were not just the source of his growing professional success; they also provided him with a different type of entrée into London society, for Ward was a talented amateur portrait artist. Helped by the well-known West End gallery owner and dealer, Hugh Leggatt, and reputedly encouraged by Churchill himself, in 1960 Ward mounted a show of his sketches of statesmen, politicians and international celebrities. Going through his patients' lists and calling in favours, Ward's sketches of the titled, rich and famous acquired a distinctive cachet.[20] His charm and an undoubted talent for capturing a flattering likeness established him in the role of a latter-day society artist. During the season of 1960 the *Illustrated London News* profiled his work, publishing a selection of drawings of Macmillan, Hugh Gaitskell, Douglas Fairbanks Jr and Sophia Loren.[21] Also included in the magazine was a selection of Ward's portraits of leading members of the royal family. His sketches of Prince Philip, Princess Margaret and many other close relatives of the Queen were a clear indication that he had received the highest patronage.

Ward's ascendant career drew extensively on the resources of the man-about-town and the renewed valorization of this urban character during the 1950s. Though not from an elite background himself, he was able to assume elements of this metropolitan personality in order to claim access to the capital's privileged networks of informal power and influence. Ward's advancement highlighted the relatively porous nature of post-war London society (provided visitors came equipped with appropriate intro-ductions), and the way that the social style of the man-about-town could be taken up and reworked by individuals who were not bona fide members of the upper class. At the same time Ward's career pointed to the Tory associations of many elite characters; their belief in economic and cultural freedoms found its appropriate niche in Conservative politics.

Ward was fascinated by London life in all its variety, and he moved within it on a number of different but interconnected levels. His geo-graphical mobility across the city displayed traditional assumptions about the rights of the man-about-town to participate equally in high and low culture. Like other personalities associated with society's post-war revival, Ward was an acolyte of Baron Nahum and an occasional habitué of the raffish Thursday Club, the exclusive homosocial venue dedicated to the *bon vivant* pursuit of social excess. Just as important was the way his biography displayed a number of significant sexual fault lines that ren-dered the masculinity of the man-about-town potentially dubious or problematic.

In the West End's social scene Ward was known for his circle of beau-tiful young women. Tall, slim and remarkably youthful for a man in early middle age, Ward appeared regularly with a succession of glamorous female partners at parties and nightclubs like Les Ambassadeurs in Park Lane.[22] Connoisseurs of Ward's taste claimed they could spot a 'Ward girl a mile off'.[23] Society types rarely appealed to him, as he disliked what he termed 'the debutante droop' (a disparaging reference to the physique and deportment of upper-class girls).[24] Stephen Ward was an unashamed pop-ulist when it came to women; natural rather than sophisticated, with their blood 'refreshingly red', Ward's protégés, whom he would regularly launch into London's social round as models of untutored elegance, were often from obscure backgrounds.[25] One of his favourite recreations was what he called 'girl spotting' along Oxford Street. With an eye for the femi-nine ambience of mass culture, he christened this major shopping

thoroughfare his 'street of beautiful girls'.[26] He was also a regular customer at London's new coffee bars, taking advantage of the opportunity
they provided to sit and chat with young people and cruise the urban
scene.[27] In one esoteric venue where Ward was a regular, the Brush and
Palette in Queensway, customers could sketch or simply look at whichever
girl was posing nude among the tables.[28]

The girls Ward 'discovered' were all broadly of the same physical type;
svelte, slim-hipped and waisted, they were early versions of a gamine
London look that was popularized in the 1960s by models like Jean
Shrimpton. They were also 'acceptably voiced' and socially presentable, for
Ward always tutored his girls in pronunciation and deportment.[29] His role
as a latter-day Pygmalion was a source of social satisfaction, for Ward took
intense personal pleasure in grooming his girls. As he put it: 'There is a
great thrill in taking a Bayswater "alley cat" and doing a "Professor
Higgins" on her.'[30]

Stephen Ward was a self-professed libertine; briefly but unsuccessfully
married in the late 1940s, he was an apologist for 'free and unfettered
enterprise in sexual conduct'.[31] He was a strong advocate of the type of
entrepreneurial philosophy advocated by Paul Raymond, championing the
idea that sexual freedom and greater consumer choice needed to go hand
in hand. Equally, Ward supported the individual's inalienable personal right
to sexual privacy, in ways that pushed at the limits of the Wolfenden committee's liberal credo. Ward was emphatic that 'what people do in their
private lives, so long as they are not exploiting sex for money and so long
as it is between consenting adults and no one is forced to do what is
genuinely distasteful to them, simply cannot be a crime'.[32] Here was
Wolfenden's strictly delimited understanding of private morality and
informed adult consent transformed into an updated version of male
libertarianism.

Other aspects of Ward's sexual career as a man-about-town were much
more traditional, following the night-time itineraries of earlier generations of middle- and upper-class men who sought the company of prostitutes. Labour MP and self-appointed parliamentary sleuth George Wigg,
who later tracked Ward's sexual exploits relentlessly, observed: 'This man
knew his way around London and around the joints.'[33] Ward's sexual
tourism not only sought out prostitutes for sex, it also provided him with
access to various forms of cultural slumming in clubs and brothels.

Ward was particularly well acquainted with Soho's varied forms of cosmopolitan culture. There is no evidence that he actually visited the
Raymond Revuebar, but he was a patron of many similar Soho clubs that

mixed opportunities for late-night drinking and socializing with live sexual entertainment. In the early 1960s Ward also sampled the more contemporary atmosphere of Soho's jazz and dance clubs, venues that had mushroomed as a result of the influx of post-war youth culture. 'Stephen didn't like to dance, but he liked to mix,' observed one of his girlfriends from that period, referring to Ward's enthusiasm for mingling with the social scene of the moment.[34] Further down-market, Ward used Soho as a cruising ground for some of his pick-ups, though he always insisted that pimping was abhorrent to him. Distancing himself from the area's traditional sexual types, such as the Messina brothers or the 'cheap little Soho razor boy', he insisted that to 'live on women' in this way was antithetical to his whole style.[35]

In the early 1960s Ward's sexual interests took him further afield than the routes followed by conventional men-about-town and Soho's bohemians. His growing enthusiasm for drugs, black prostitutes and other types of transgressive liaisons propelled him outside the West End altogether and into much rawer social territory. This aspect of Ward's biography refocused attention on the cultural and sexual world of north Kensington, though in ways that were markedly different from John Christie's encounters with street women a decade earlier. For Ward, the district provided access to a range of experimental lifestyles that centred on the perceived exoticism of Caribbean culture, as it was seen by inquisitive English tourists. Ward regularly drove his white Jaguar from his mews flat in Marylebone across to Paddington and Notting Hill, where he cruised around for black prostitutes and spent time 'messing about with Negroes, smoking hemp [and] going to "rave parties"'.[36]

In the highly charged atmosphere that surrounded race relations after the Notting Hill riots in 1958, cultural and sexual contact between Caribbean settlers and the indigenous white population became a renewed source of concern, both locally and nationally. According to one Gallup poll survey taken at the time of the riots, white respondents declared themselves to be overwhelmingly opposed to racial intermarriage.[37] In Kensington, the British National Party and Mosley's British Union of Fascists campaigned explicitly around miscegenation fears, focusing public anxiety on the perceived sexual threat of Caribbean men. The local presence of young West Indian pimps who controlled white women epitomized this uneasiness. Notting Hill's Colville district, especially the large dilapidated Victorian houses surrounding Powis Square, south of Westbourne Park Road, was a major red-light area in the late 1950s and early 1960s, as prostitutes shifted away from the West End in

search of more discrete territory after the introduction of the Street
Offences Act.[38] Notting Hill became a well-established offshoot of Soho's
vice networks, accessible to pimps, sex workers and their customers via
the short journey down Oxford Street and the Bayswater Road.

Ward was one of a number of society figures who claimed imaginative ownership of parts of Notting Hill, a space that allowed privileged
initiates like himself to savour low-life experiences and related cultural
facilities. Following a route established by elite social and literary figures,
including the actress Sarah Churchill, the statesman's daughter, and Colin
MacInnes, both of whom had sexual interests in Caribbean men, Ward
was a regular customer for many of north Kensington's illicit goods and
services provided by young West Indians. He delighted in spending time
in coffee bars and local shebeens hosted in private rooms and flats, which
became centres for hustlers and dealers and where Trinidadians and
Jamaicans provided ska and bluebeat music, food and gambling.[39] Ward's
favourite hang-out was the El Rio café in Westbourne Park Road, which,
according to its proprietor Frank Critchlow, was a meeting place for 'all
sorts of West Indians . . . who were rebellious and . . . smart . . . for whom
the factory was not their speed'.[40]

Christine Keeler testified to the way that Ward used her as an escort
on his voyeuristic night-time excursions into Notting Hill, watching the
prostitutes and their black pimps and soliciting women who could cater
to his own specialized sexual tastes.[41] Ward also acted as an intermediary
for other society figures who were equally fascinated by his racialized take
on slumming, including Astor and the portrait artist and fellow member
of the Thursday Club, Vasco de Lazzolo. Ward's promotion of the exoticism of Notting Hill added the first in a series of twists to the meaning
of cosmopolitanism that circulated during the Profumo scandal, shifting
the idea from its European and Jewish connotations in Soho to more
contemporary associations with the culture and characters of the
Caribbean.

Ward's itineraries brought him into contact with the business dealings
and sexual career of another habitué of Notting Hall and Soho: the
landlord-cum-property developer Peter Rachman. Rachman's public
notoriety began after his death in 1962, as the Profumo scandal threw a
negative spotlight on his sexual involvement with Keeler and Mandy
Rice-Davies. The term 'Rachmanism' was coined by the north
Paddington MP Ben Parkin as synonymous with the worst excesses of
exploitative landlordism and with the corrupt underside of Macmillan's

affluent society.[42] Public reaction to Rachman's posthumous exposure tended to exaggerate his actual influence, using his name to symbolize much wider social grievances. His involvement with Ward highlighted a number of the dubious economic and sexual transactions that shadowed the Profumo affair.[43]

An expatriate Polish Jew and a victim of Stalin's Siberian labour camps, Rachman began his London operations very modestly in the late 1940s working for a Jewish tailor in Wardour Street, dabbling in black-market goods, and operating as a scorer at Jack Solomon's Soho billiard hall.[44] Like Paul Raymond and other successful entrepreneurs, he started up his businesses with profits generated from his involvement in London's sex trade. Rachman was on familiar terms with local prostitutes who worked the Bayswater Road, and he specialized in finding accommodation for them. On the back of these small-scale ventures he cofounded a series of companies that bought up end-of-lease properties in Notting Hill and Shepherd's Bush.[45] These business dealings benefited enormously from the accelerating property boom of the late 1950s, which followed from the Conservative government's relaxation of Abercrombie's planning restrictions. Rachman also took advantage of provisions contained in the 1957 Rent Act enabling landlords to decontrol tenancies and increase rents.[46]

Pressures stoked by the liberalization of the capital's rented housing sector were exacerbated by racial tensions in areas like north Kensington. The Rillington Place murders had already exposed conflicts between black and white over access to accommodation. Rachman found West Indian migrants flats and rooms, but he demanded rents well above market rates; he also stood accused of using strong-arm tactics to enforce his rule and of deliberately putting West Indians into houses with white, rent-controlled neighbours in order to drive out the sitting tenants. One former Caribbean resident recollected that the choices facing newcomers in Notting Hill were stark: 'The nice houses we lived in, we had to leave early in the morning and they didn't let us back until seven or eight . . . [at] night. Or you lived in the Rachman places where there was [sic] eight of you sharing one cooker.'[47] Other locals remembered Rachman as a figure of flamboyant wealth, elegantly dressed with 'handmade shoes and silk ties', arriving in his Rolls-Royce with 'a posse of young women'.[48] With the profits from his slum rents Rachman diversified his property portfolio; he purchased a string of fashionable nightclubs, including the El Condor in Wardour Street, which later became a sophisticated venue for a new generation of upper-class partygoers.[49]

In the late 1950s Ward and Rachman were part of a male friendship network that was cemented by shared interests in West End night life and in pretty and available girls.[50] Unlike Ward, who was a committed bohemian, Rachman's sexual interests were much more prosaic. Revelling in the supposed access to society networks that his business deals and his connections with Ward had opened up, he boasted to friends about a debutante who cost him £1,000 for a single night.[51] Rachman was also part of a *nouveau riche* group of self-styled playboys, who included Dennis Hamilton, the ex-husband of Diana Dors. It was through Hamilton and Rachman that Ward acquired his famous two-way mirror which was installed at his Bryanston Mews flat, enabling specially invited guests to 'spy on the amorous goings-on in the bedroom'.[52]

Rachman's sexual exploits were always strenuously heterosexual, but public perceptions of Stephen Ward's dubious career hinted at more unusual relationships with women. Ward's female friendships, together with associated gossip and innuendo about his own 'feminine disposition', placed his character at the outer limits of sex and gender norms. Ward claimed that the key to his sexual success was his 'basic interest in women as people', for he insisted that he was one of the few men in London who 'could understand a woman's mind'.[53] Keeler always insisted that Ward was 'a feminist', with a strong belief in 'equal rights for women'.[54] Many of his friends and acquaintances, along with those who disliked him, probed Ward's empathy with the opposite sex rather differently, using it as a way of questioning his masculinity. There was general agreement that he had a distinctively feminine side to his personality. For some it was his tendency to compulsive talking, especially on the phone, and his pretentious accent that seemed unmasculine, while for others it was his white, hairless body that had a curiously androgynous appearance.[55] Ward himself was known to joke about what he called his 'ambidextrous look'.[56] As Gillian Swanson has noted, it was his feminized character, evidenced by his body and by his intimate connections with the young women who were his protégés, that tainted Ward with suggestions of sexual deviancy.[57]

Ward's activities intrigued many of his friends, but in the long run his much-vaunted sexual sophistication compromised his claims to gentlemanly status. Some of his girlfriends testified that his appetite for experimental forms of lovemaking bordered on the perverted, pushing conventional masculinity to its limits, and beyond. Fashion model Patricia Baines, who was briefly and disastrously Ward's wife in the late 1940s, was 'desperately unhappy with him'. Baines hinted that Ward's sexuality 'put him in conflict with himself most of the time', though she also confessed that he did have 'a lot of charm'.[58] Model Margaret Brown, who was Ward's girlfriend a decade later, described him as a 'philosophical spectator', referring to his voyeuristic tendencies as well as his desire to shock.[59] Rice-Davies, who had a brief affair with Ward in the early 1960s, was characteristically blunter, insisting that his 'skill in love-making was . . . due partly to his dislike of normal sexual relationships'.[60] She confirmed Ward's role as a voyeur, though fellow man-about-town Graham Sutherland disagreed. Sutherland believed that Ward was an exhibitionist, describing how he arrived on one occasion at the fashionable Star and Garter pub in Belgravia with his girlfriend literally in tow, 'attached to his wrist by a very fancy collar and leash'.[61] In the sexual climate of the 1950s women as well as men speculated whether repressed homosexuality was the root cause of Ward's contradictory sexual persona.[62]

Conjecture about Ward's personality drew on the whole gamut of opinions about homosexuality that were canvassed so thoroughly during the immediate post-war years. Ranging from congenital theories that highlighted his supposedly inverted gender identity, through popular aphorisms and beliefs, to full psychoanalytic readings of his arrested development, homosexuality was used by Stephen Ward's friends and enemies to probe his social as well as his sexual status. Some of this speculation was aired informally during the 1950s, but the Profumo scandal intensified the questioning, enlarging it into a full-blown interrogation of Ward's character.

Many of his acquaintances read the signs of perversion onto the surface of his body; Rice-Davies saw in his hypnotic, 'cold fishlike eyes' clear proof of the fact that he was 'a homosexual'.[63] Other commentators suggested that Ward's artistic temperament and his commitment to the invasive corporeality of osteopathy were the most telling symptoms of an innate homosexual condition.[64] Tory MP William Shepherd, who loathed Ward and was responsible for the early inquiries into his activities as a potential spy, was convinced that the evidence for his sexual deviancy lay in his voice, with its recognizably 'homosexual intonation', as well as in his insinuating manner which had all the hallmarks of an interloper and a 'phoney'.[65] Shepherd ran together perceived ambiguities about Ward's social background and rumours about his ability to masquerade in a variety of high and low milieus as evidence of his homosexual inclinations and his Soviet sympathies, in ways that paralleled the treatment of Guy Burgess and John Vassall. In contrast, journalist Warwick Charlton, who interviewed

Ward shortly before his death, drew on Freudian explanations to suggest that feminine narcissism and homosexuality were inextricably linked in Ward's complex character. Charlton observed how Ward 'looked into the pool of a girl's beauty and saw therein the reflection of all that he imagined himself to be. In some cases the identification was complete.'[66]

No one had evidence that Ward actually had sex with men, but his varied social networks and his movements across the West End suggested that he was familiar with London's homosexual cultures. Via his friendship with Toby Roe, proprietor of the Rockingham club, Ward was in touch with the discrete world of homosexual clubland, with its up-market ambience and a social ethos dedicated to preserving the sexual privacy of professional men. Ward's association with the Scottish artists Robert Colquhoun and Robert Macbryde brought him into contact with Soho's bohemians, with their contemporary cultural style and their commitment to the West End as a space for transgressive, cross-class sexual encounters.[67] Via Colquhoun and Macbryde, Ward moved in the same scene as leading Sohoites like Farson and Bacon. A very different milieu was opened up to him via his friendship with Bobbie Shaw, Bill Astor's stepbrother. Shaw introduced Ward to an exclusive world of upper-class homosexuality involving characters from the Foreign Office and the Catholic Church. This elite circle also included Burgess and Maclean as well as the art historian Sir Anthony Blunt, Surveyor of the Queen's Pictures, and the 'fourth man' of the Cambridge spy ring, which had been exposed by Goronwy Rees in his sensational press revelations.[68]

Overall, an aura of intense sexual ambiguity surrounded Ward well before the start of the Profumo scandal, which his friends found intriguing and others castigated as repulsive. Many women found his manner 'creepy' and insidious, including Valerie Profumo, John Profumo's wife, while Rebecca West bluntly dismissed Ward as degraded, cold and mechanistic.[69] Reacting against his particular version of libertarianism, both women believed he represented all that was distasteful about so-called experimental sex, with its artificial and dehumanizing character and its overwhelmingly masculine bias. West put it memorably: Ward was 'the incarnation of a chemist's window in the Charing Cross Road'.[70] Gossip and innuendo about his personality drew together many of the unresolved anxieties about abnormal male sexuality in the 1950s; effeminacy, lack of sexual control, miscegenation fears and homosexuality all shadowed Ward's character, cross-cutting and compromising his elite social connections.

Stephen Ward's social and professional success in the highest circles testified to the revival and partial transformation of elite society during the
1950s, and it was this world that provided an important setting for much
of the Profumo scandal. Recalling its prevailing atmosphere in the early
1960s, Yevgeny Ivanov, Naval Attaché at the Soviet Embassy, remembered
how impenetrable it seemed to an outsider, especially to a visiting Russian
official whose acknowledged undercover brief was espionage. Ivanov had
already been identified by the British security services at MI5 as a Soviet
intelligence officer operating under diplomatic cover. He had been
recruited to the 'military diplomatic academy' in Moscow in 1949, a
covert branch of Soviet intelligence that was used for training secret
service personnel.[71] With his good looks and 'immense charm', Ivanov
was an energetic socialite during his posting in London.[72] His family connections to the old Russian nobility and his specialized military training
gave him a degree of social polish that enabled him to move with relative ease among the interrelated worlds of the diplomatic corps and the
metropolitan elites. Yet initially, when he arrived in the capital in 1960,
Ivanov found that the process of making influential contacts was much
more difficult than in Moscow because, unlike the atmosphere at home
where the Soviet governing class was garrulous and where social hierarchies were relatively transparent, a 'veil of silence' enveloped London 'like
a dense fog'.[73] Observing society from the outside and driven by his own
political priorities, Ivanov noted that it was as if 'an unseen sound editor'
had cut all gossip and chatter 'down to the minimum'.[74] Ivanov's reading
of this muted atmosphere was perceptive; he believed he was confronting
the barriers that the upper class had erected around themselves in order
to preserve privilege, prestige and privacy.

The interrelated worlds of metropolitan society, clubland and Tory
high politics were crucial settings for the incubation of the Profumo
affair, as they had been in many earlier high-profile sex cases. This was
partly because the scandal centred on the sexual misdemeanours and
political intrigues of privileged characters, especially Profumo and Astor,
along with rumours about the involvement of even more elevated public
figures, such as Prince Philip.[75] Individuals who were presented as enjoying the protection of closed cultures of influence were systematically
exposed to the full glare of national media attention, as the scandal
moved outwards from this exclusive world to full exposure via mass
publicity.

Elite political and social milieus were revealed as a part of an over-world that was intimately connected to and dependent on the capital's underworld. Elite society was seen to be compromised by its association with low or dubious characters and environments, reproducing a version of the high and low oppositions that had been a feature of so many nine-teenth- and early twentieth-century scandals. But there was a further reason why the Profumo episode revolved around the activities of the upper class, which had more to do with public perceptions of their con-tinuing power and influence. In the early 1960s there was still a consen-sus within English political culture, and among almost all of the national media, that for good or ill this elite strata still mattered, in terms of the social and moral leadership that it was expected to provide for the wider society.

The informal but highly elaborate rituals of upper-class power and influence preoccupied political analysts in the early 1960s who were obsessed with Britain's failure to modernize. Anthony Sampson, an *Observer* journalist fresh from working in apartheid South Africa, revisited arguments that had been developed by Shils in his own influential polit-ical sociology of the nation, the *Anatomy of Britain* (1962). Sampson described the 'white tribes' of ruling-class Britain as a series of inter-locking circles in which the court, aristocracy and urban gentry, with their strong links to the City, the press and Tory politics, continued to play a dynamic rather than a residual role in a country whose social structures had the appearance of a 'living museum'.[76] Sampson believed that the nation's contemporary intoxication with its 'monarchic and aristocratic past' and 'with the term "Establishment"' was a major impediment to a full and frank discussion about the failure of the governing class to reform the structures of state power.[77] Like Shils, Sampson also acknowledged the continuing salience of ritualistic forms of upper-class display in London, which he evoked sardonically as an image of 'glittering drawing rooms where all the key people gather together'.[78] The Profumo scandal accelerated critical public debate about the role and function of the capital's social elites, as part of wider concerns about national decline and backwardness.

'"Birds of a feather, flock together," but the plumage is finer in some than in others,' observed Sir Colin Coote, who was an important facili-tator for the influential coteries brought together by the Profumo affair.[79] The editor of the *Daily Telegraph*, Coote was a friend of Macmillan's from Oxford University days and a golfing partner of Sir Roger Hollis,

Director-General of MI5. He was a central figure in the political network that linked the Foreign Office and the security services to leading Conservative politicians and Fleet Street editors. A great social mixer, it was Coote, a patient of Ward's, who first introduced Ivanov to the osteopath at a lunch he hosted at the Garrick Club in January 1961. Via his growing friendship with Coote and Ward, Ivanov was able to peer behind the veil that screened the upper class. Ivanov gained access to clubland; there were also invitations to evenings with Tory politicians spent at Ward's newly leased Wimpole Mews flat, introductions to Princess Margaret and her husband Lord Snowdon, and weekend visits to English country houses.[80] Through these extensive contacts Ivanov claimed that he began to relay his 'numerous reports about the sexual preferences' of his various hosts and their guests (reports covering homosexuality, drug abuse and other peccadilloes) to Soviet intelligence in Moscow.[81]

Many of the metropolitan locations that sowed the seeds of scandal centred on Coote's traditional milieus of high Toryism and on an extensive informal network that was at once social and personal. Members of Macmillan's government who intervened politically in the Profumo affair or who were embarrassed by it, such as Viscount Hailsham, Lord President of the Council, the Commonwealth Secretary, Duncan Sandys, and younger men like Christopher Soames, Minister of Agriculture, as well as John Profumo himself, all moved between Westminster, the clubland milieus of St James's (especially the Carlton, White's and Boodle's), Buckingham Palace receptions, guaranteed by their membership of the Privy Council, and diplomatic and embassy functions hosted in Belgravia and Mayfair. As influential political figures in the government with public school and Oxbridge connections to leading press editors, they were guaranteed access to Fleet Street, as well as to national radio and television. All these political and cultural settings were located in the compressed metropolitan spaces of London's central area, and they were quickly and easily accessible by chauffeur-driven car, taxi or even on foot.

It was still predominantly a homosocial milieu (there were no women members of Macmillan's cabinet, and only two junior women ministers, one of whom was Margaret Thatcher). A photograph of leading members of the government assembled at Chequers in the spring of 1963 illustrates the masculine homogeneity of this world (fig. 35). However, it was augmented by the complementary sphere of mixed, heterosocial sociability that was in turn reinforced by ties of marriage and close-knit kinship networks. Duncan Sandys was Christopher Soames's brother-in-law before his divorce, both men having married Churchill's daughters, while Macmillan was uncle to the Duke of Devonshire (who was himself Under-Secretary of State in Sandys's department) through his own marriage to Lady Dorothy, née Cavendish. Macmillan's son Maurice, who was also an MP, was brother-in-law to both David Ormsby-Gore, the British Ambassador in Washington, and Julian Amery, Minister of Aviation.[82] In addition to these shared political and family allegiances, in 1963 the extended circle of the Tory upper class continued to revolve around a formal conception of public manners, governed by appropriate styles of deportment, and also around the cohesive power of the Crown and the royal family as the apogee of social honour.[83]

In 1963 John Profumo, or Jack as he was regularly known, was a modest but rising star in Conservative politics: MP for Stratford-upon-Avon, Privy Councillor, Minister of War, and Fifth Baron of the late United Kingdom of Italy. Profumo's career and family background testified both to the relatively porous character of the upper class and also to its powerful assimilationist tendencies. Only second generation British, Profumo's great-grandfather had been a Sardinian nobleman who had served as Principal Private Secretary to Cavour during the Italian Risorgimento.[84] The Profumos settled in London in the 1870s and took out British citizenship in 1885. Founders of the insurance company, the Provident Life Association, their considerable financial wealth was extended by Profumo's father's own highly successful career as a barrister and King's Counsel. The family's Italian connections were significant because they gave Profumo a cosmopolitan outlook wider than many of his political contemporaries which shaped his sexual behaviour and influenced his role in the scandal.

Educated at Harrow and Brasenose College, Oxford, Jack Profumo was brought up in a 'silver spoon' atmosphere during the 1920s, when the family's links to the Italian aristocracy were embellished by their close associations with the English landed gentry.[85] Profumo's father bought a grand 'squirish mansion', Avon Carrow, deep in rural Warwickshire, and their estate and pedigree were listed in *Burke's Landed Gentry*.[86] Profumo's own membership of the inter-war *jeunesse dorée* was advertised by his reputation as 'part daredevil and part lounge lizard'.[87] His sybaritic social life revolved around fast cars and flying, polo, hunt balls, pictures in society magazines, and friendships with foreign royalty. But there were also suggestions that the Profumo family's Italian background set them apart from the English upper class in terms of style and social mores. With a manner that was 'always bubbling with good form' and a 'slightly vulgar taste for conspicuous consumption', the Profumos were too immaculately presented in comparison with many of their Warwickshire counterparts.[88] Jack Profumo's 'darkly suave' profile and his 'oiled hairline', with its Rudolph Valentino look, appeared distinctly un-English among a generation of young men for whom deviations from the rigid norms of dress and deportment were considered dubious.[89]

Jack Profumo entered Parliament in 1940, aged twenty-five, as the youngest MP at Westminster, where he formed important early political friendships among the anti-Chamberlainite Tory circle that included Leo Amery, Bob Boothby, Quintin Hogg and Macmillan.[90] One Conservative Party official working in Profumo's local constituency at the time testified to Profumo's enduring belief in caste superiority: 'He and his family always clearly believed in the ruling class. This never showed in a nasty way, but he believed in it.'[91] Beyond his commitment to patrician Conservatism, Profumo's early political and personal interests also extended to the women's vote. In a magazine interview from the late 1930s, the young aspiring politician listed 'Beauty' as one of his main leisure pursuits, while lady members of the East Fulham Conservative Association (where Profumo canvassed on behalf of his friend Bill Astor) commented with a sly double entendre: 'There had never been a chairman of the association who had taken so much interest in the women's branch as Mr Profumo.'[92] Even at this early stage in his political career Jack Profumo's reputation as a Lothario seemed well established.

Profumo's ascendancy through a public school and Oxford education, and then via distinguished wartime military service in North Africa and the subsequent Allied invasion of Italy, into the ranks of Churchill's government in the early 1950s testified to his personal ambition. It also highlighted the upper-class credentials that remained important for success in Conservative politics. After junior and middle-ranking ministerial portfolios held at transport, the Colonial Office and the Foreign Office, Profumo was made Secretary of State for War in July 1960. Never a member of the Cabinet and not a political heavyweight, Profumo was nonetheless a capable minister and an effective advocate of one-nation Conservatism.[93] An elaborate, formal photograph taken around this time pictured him dressed in unusual costume, posed against a background of official Whitehall grandeur (fig. 36). Wearing a version of formal British court dress that was rarely used after the war, with its brocade uniform, silk stockings, knee breeches, buckled shoes, sword and feathered cap, this public image illustrated Jack Profumo's commitment to highly tradition-alist emblems of social prestige.[94] Though he was popular with many on both sides of the House of Commons, some of his fellow MPs disliked the ambitious member for Stratford. With a swipe at Profumo's Italian connections, they nicknamed him 'the Head Waiter', regarding him as a 'jumped-up opportunist'.[95]

Jack Profumo was a much more conventional man–about-town than Stephen Ward. In his private life he was '*un homme moyen sensuel*' who enjoyed the metropolitan privileges and facilities of the West End's varied nightlife.[96] Unlike Ward, Profumo was not attracted to the experimental fringes of the capital's pleasure economy, nor to the transgressive world of interracial mixing represented by Notting Hill. Profumo had been an eligible bachelor throughout his twenties and thirties, and there were rumours about his romantic involvements with a number of prominent women, including the actress Glynis Johns and the widowed Princess Marina, Duchess of Kent, the elegant, Greek-born member of the royal family who was a regular society patron.[97]

In 1954 Profumo married the divorced actress Valerie Hobson. This was not quite a marriage between the politician and the showgirl of the sort that was regularly advertised by the management of the Windmill Theatre, but on Profumo's part at least it represented a traditional form of sexual attraction. According to his family, Profumo held to a late Victorian and Edwardian view of the theatre as 'risqué' and 'slightly forbidden fruit', and he had an enduring fascination for women in 'feathery kit and spangled appendages'.[98] Hobson started out in the West End chorus in the 1930s, supplementing her stage appearances with fashion modelling for *Vogue*. After a film career that included a brief but unsuccessful spell in Hollywood, she returned to English films and finally to the London stage, where she played the female lead in the hit musical of 1953, *The King and I*.[99]

For Hobson, Profumo represented 'fun' and a degree of sexual sophis-tication, as well as assured wealth, in a post-war world where for her, as for many other women, these assets were in short supply. As she reflected much later in a remarkably frank observation that was meant to apply both to her own relationship with her husband and to Profumo's promis-cuity, 'he's totally free sexually, and in love with sex'.[100] Jack Profumo's appeal for Hobson lay in his charismatic style, and she recalled that there was an 'instant, electric sexual attraction' between them.[101] Publicly, Hobson remade herself on marriage as a model Tory wife. Poised, coolly beautiful, dressed by the designers Worth and Victor Stiebel, and with an expressed commitment to charity work as well as the arts, her personality was a distinct asset to her husband in a post-war public culture that was increasingly interested in the celebrity status of politicians and their wives, as a result of intensified media coverage. The Profumos' elegant and imposing Nash town-house in Chester Terrace, overlooking Regent's Park, testified to the couple's status as members of London's fashionable upper class.[102]

Yet marriage and ministerial promotion did not inhibit Jack Profumo's appetite for traditional forms of metropolitan glamour, and like earlier generations of privileged men he enjoyed the company of attractive young women who were sexually available. Astor introduced Profumo to Ward in 1956, when Profumo noted with relish that the osteopath 'always had a lot of pretty girls about the place'.[103] Thereafter, the fun-loving minister went to occasional cocktail parties thrown by Ward and confessed to finding him 'hugely charismatic'.[104] Like Ward, Profumo mixed freely with hostesses and showgirls, and he met Keeler at Murray's Club in Soho, a nightclub that staged semi-nude reviews and provided an erotic ambience for men-about-town. According to the code of honour adhered to by the majority of Tory MPs, Profumo's activity did not constitute immoral behaviour as such, but Jack Profumo was more indiscreet than many of his colleagues, showing a wilful disregard for conventional wisdom which stressed that the sexual affairs of political figures should be concealed from public view. This was society's golden rule, and it shaped reactions to almost all the contemporary scandals implicating upper-class figures.

Profumo's personal life points to the continuation of traditional forms of elite masculine behaviour in which the established privileges of the metropolitan man-about-town meshed with Tory politics. During the immediate post-war years this type of conduct was subjected to much closer scrutiny. Martin Francis has documented the growing emphasis on an emotional economy of restraint within parliamentary culture in the late 1940s and 1950s. The code of masculinity increasingly sanctioned in politics, Francis has argued, placed renewed emphasis on seriousness, sobriety and self-possession for politicians of all parties, together with a strenuous avoidance of emotional excess.[105] With his wartime military record and his style of gentlemanly leadership, Profumo conformed to some of these demands, though even in the public realm his personality was rather too buoyant and self-assured. What really disrupted Profumo's persona was his predilection for London's *demi-monde*, evidenced not just by his penchant for call-girls and 'very pretty' but 'very common' women, but also by his commitment to the 'risqué undercurrent' within society itself.[106] Fellow MP Shepherd, who was also a patron of the West End's nightclub scene, explained that by the early 1960s, even within elite Tory circles, it was 'not really acceptable' for 'Secretaries of State' to behave in the way that Profumo conducted himself in his private life. After Jack became Minister of War, Shepherd insisted, 'everybody expected him to be more discreet, but he wasn't.'[107]

Profumo was a transitional figure in terms of his personal and political conduct; his character was strongly influenced by the code of manners of an older masculine elite that tacitly sanctioned sexual adventures and marital infidelities. Over nearly half a century, until his death in 2006, Profumo remained an implacably silent witness about his part in the scandal, so the evaluation of his motives inevitably remains imprecise. His own aristocratic background and his Italian connections, together with a manifest desire to assert patrician values, all probably influenced his adoption of a sexual style that rejected more humdrum and conventional forms of morality. Regularly indiscreet before the scandal engulfed him, Profumo saw himself as part of a charmed and untouchable circle at a time when his world was changing rapidly. As his wife later testified laconically, 'He thought he could get away with it – after all, most of his friends did.'[108] When Shepherd secretly warned Macmillan and the Tory Chief Whip, Martin Redmayne, in the autumn of 1962 about the half a dozen ministers who constituted a risk to the government 'in moral/political terms', he included the war minister on his list of culprits.[109]

Neither Westminster politics nor the West End's night life provided the setting for the first phase of the Profumo affair. It was Lord Astor's architecturally monumental and imposing country seat, Cliveden House, sited twenty miles west of London on the Thames in Buckinghamshire, that was a key location in the initial development of the scandal.[110] During the inter-war years Bill Astor's parents, the American partnership of Waldorf and Nancy Astor, turned Cliveden into one of the most notorious salons in modern political history, when the 'Cliveden set' became synonymous with the appeasement of Nazi Germany.[111] In the early 1960s the third Viscount Astor and his third wife, the ex-model Bronwen Pugh, wielded less direct political influence than his parents, but the couple continued some of the same traditions of elaborate entertaining. Despite the Victorian scale of Cliveden, the Astors' social circle (dubbed the 'new

Cliveden set' by the press) was more intimate than the vast assemblies organized under Nancy Astor's regime, reflecting the move to increasingly personalized forms of upper-class sociability that was a hallmark of post-war hostesses like Ann Fleming.[112]

Cliveden mixed a country house ambience with the atmosphere of a latter-day salon; a venue for visiting international statesmen, writers and artists, as well as the usual leavening of politicians, it was more relaxed than the formal social environments in town. Convivial informality was enhanced, with Lord Astor's connivance, by Stephen Ward's regular weekend presence on the estate. In 1956 Ward had acquired from Astor the tenancy of Spring Cottage, a mock Tudor riverside hideaway in Cliveden's grounds, and it was here that he brought his girlfriends and associates for small ad hoc rendezvous. The guests at the cottage were frequently allowed to mingle with the grander party assembled at the big house, and Ward had a special arrangement with Astor that his own friends could use Cliveden's open-air swimming pool.[113] This social compact encouraged discreet sexual mixing, away from prying eyes, between Astor's distinguished male guests and Ward's girls, and it played a significant part in the collision of social worlds that characterized the Profumo affair. Macmillan later noted ruefully that while the 'old Cliveden set was disastrous politically', the new version of this coterie was proving to be 'equally disastrous morally'.[114]

In July 1961 Lord and Lady Astor were hosting a weekend house party for their principal guest Ayub Khan, the President of Pakistan, who was en route to Washington for talks with President Kennedy. Lord Mountbatten, Prince Philip's uncle, was also present, as were the Jewish businessman and philanthropist and his wife, Isaac and Edith Wolfson, the Conservative politician Lord Dalkeith, and the Profumos. Stephen Ward had his own party that weekend at Spring Cottage, including Captain Ivanov and 19-year-old Christine Keeler, who was living with Ward. It was an appropriately hot night, and after dinner Profumo and Astor, two mature men-of-the-world, strolled down to the swimming pool, a grand walled structure that was being used by Ward and his guests. Keeler was swimming nude, and as Ward deliberately switched on the floodlights, Profumo encountered her like 'a Venus emerging from the sea', according to Ivanov, as she came out of the pool.[115]

After this exotic encounter Profumo and Keeler began an affair, though there is considerable dispute about its length and seriousness. What is equally disputed is whether Keeler also started a sexual relationship with

Ivanov at roughly the same time.[116] This love triangle, the source of endless speculation, was at the centre of the scandal's sexual and political intrigue. The security services got to know of Profumo's association with Stephen Ward, and in view of Ward's friendship with Ivanov, they informed Sir Norman Brook, the Cabinet Secretary, who in turn warned Profumo about the potential dangers of his acquaintance with Ward. Believing that this intervention by a senior civil servant implied that his relationship with Keeler had also been discovered, an assumption that was in fact untrue, Profumo took steps to end his affair with Keeler, probably sometime late in 1961.[117]

A Sophisticated Showgirl

Thus far the Profumo story had a familiar ring; amorous entanglements involving senior ministers of the Crown in extramarital affairs replicated the structure of many late Victorian sex cases.[118] Even the new and potentially damaging Cold War twist to the episode, linking sex and espionage, echoed revelations familiar from the other post-war spy scandals that compromised Whitehall figures. An intrigue that was played out within relatively closed Establishment circles might have ended quietly at this point, except for one important proviso: Christine Keeler, with Ward's encouragement, also moved in very different worlds.

Keeler was culturally and geographically mobile in ways that enabled her to cross and recross social and sexual boundaries, both inside the capital and beyond. Like Ward, her career pushed together environments and characters from elite society, West End night life and Notting Hill's Caribbean culture via a succession of affairs and liaisons. But unlike Ward, who was cast as a victim of these triangulated relationships, Keeler revealed how the resources of female sexuality, extended by the full use of the media, could be drawn on as a form of social empowerment in London's cultural and entertainment settings. As a result of her heavily advertised role in the Profumo episode, Keeler became by her own self-confident assertion 'one of the most notorious femmes fatales of the twentieth century'.[119] But the intense public interest that her story aroused was not simply due to effective publicity. Her persona became closely identified with contemporary changes to female sexuality that had also preoccupied the Wolfenden committee as well as entrepreneurs like

Paul Raymond. The status of sexually active young women and their relationship to contemporary urban culture erupted as one of the central
issues in the Profumo affair.

Keeler was twenty-one when the scandal broke. The daughter of
divorced working-class parents, she was brought up by her mother and a
man she called her stepfather in a converted railway carriage on the banks
of a tributary of the Thames at Wraysbury in Buckinghamshire. The affluence of the 1950s passed her family by; the Keelers' modest house on
wheels had 'no bathroom, hot water was an unheard-of luxury', and they
had no electricity until Keeler was twelve.[120] What dominated her early
memories was a sense of material and psychological impoverishment; she
felt herself to be part of a post-war world of social problems: problem
families, broken homes and 'latch-key' children.[121] Sexually precocious, she
was first made aware of men by her stepfather's threatening presence; after
a number of casual boyfriends and a particularly gruesome self-induced
abortion, she had a child by a black American GI.[122] Keeler stressed that
these early experiences were not part of a world of permissive and liberated sexuality, which was the way her life was depicted at the time of
the scandal. They were shaped by traditional double standards in which
young women were regular casualties of what she termed 'prudish . . .
class consciousness' and random exploitation by men.[123]

In 1957 Keeler left Wraysbury and headed for 'the bright lights of
London'.[124] Rehearsing a variant of the generic provincial's story about
the perennial lure of the capital, London became central to her own burgeoning sense of identity and self-worth. She reflected later how the city
at that time 'seemed like the end of the rainbow to me – a never-never
land where I could finally achieve happiness'.[125] In reality, Keeler's London
début was in a series of low-status, service-sector jobs that already placed
her on the fringes of the city's sexual economy. Most of these were in
Soho and adjacent parts of the West End. She worked as a salesgirl-
cum-model in a dress shop in Poland Street, close by Oxford Street, as a
waitress and cloakroom attendant at a Greek restaurant in Baker Street,
and she also did some pin-up shots in a bikini for a queer photographer.[126] The photos were a success and they gave her semi-naked body
its first public airing in the popular news and picture magazine, *Tit Bits*,
in 1958. The paper billed her as a girl with a glamorous career ahead of
her: 'Though she is only fifteen,' the accompanying caption ran, 'Christine
Keeler is pretty enough to be a professional model.'[127]

Keeler was strikingly and unusually beautiful. Lithe and loose-limbed, with high cheek bones, expressive eyes and a sensual mouth, her looks and sexual allure went well beyond the typical Ward product, and her admirers competed with their compliments (fig. 37). 'The most beautiful girl [I] had ever clapped eyes on,' was the way one MI5 officer, not known for overstatement, described her.[128] Ivanov portrayed her as an exotic temptress in the tradition of female spies like Mata Hari, recollecting that she was 'devilishly attractive', with eyes that 'shone with passion, sensuality and cunning'.[129] Profumo was more conventional in his sexual appraisal, remembering that 'she was a very pretty girl, and very sweet.'[130] In a case populated by different young women, all assiduously courting media attention, Keeler's physical presence marked her as special. In contrast to most of Ward's other protégés, she stood out in terms of her looks and the distinctive aura of sexuality that surrounded her.

The *Tit-Bits* photo-shoot gave Keeler public visibility, but her first real break came the following summer when she was offered a job as a showgirl at Percy Murray's cabaret. With a regular starting salary of over eight pounds a week, putting her almost on a par with the top Windmill girls, and an opportunity to gain a foothold in London's entertainment business, the club offered a chance to stop 'worrying about the rent or money for the gas meter'.[131] At Murray's, Keeler remembered, it was 'the first time I felt I belonged anywhere'.[132]

Keeler's new job enabled her to begin her movement from Soho's backstage to the front stage of the West End's pleasure economy. The club was a different type of sexual and erotic space than either the Windmill or the Raymond Revuebar, both of which were sited only a few hundred yards away. Upmarket, reputable and with a de luxe if somewhat old-fashioned atmosphere, Murray's did not initially cater for the Windmill's mainstream sexual customer, nor did it represent the go-ahead form of commercialism epitomized by Raymond. Dating back to the expansion of heterosocial nightlife in the West End after the First World War, Murray's dance hostesses had reputedly introduced the slow foxtrot to London, and the club had a well-established reputation within society circles for sophisticated entertainment. During the 1940s and early 1950s Percy Murray remodelled the club, and his perennial boast was that along with 35,000 ordinary members, royalty and the nobility graced his tables, including Princess Margaret and King Hussein of Jordan, who was a regular patron.[133] Initial membership cost a guinea and the entrance fee was a guinea a time, which were double Raymond's prices.[134]

Murray's girls performed from a raised stage, flanked by a double orchestra, with the audience arranged in cabaret style; facilities included a full service restaurant and the opportunity for customers to sit 'out front' buying overpriced champagne and fruit cup for the hostesses and show-girls.[135] The aim was to augment the facilities of a supper club with a cabaret style of erotic entertainment and, most importantly, a carefully cultivated sexual ambience. The showgirls' dance sequences and bodily idioms established a glamorous atmosphere, though Murray's acts were circumspect and somewhat recherché, consisting of 'not very original dance routines performed by not very talented dancers', when compared with Raymond's up-to-the-minute striptease acts.[136] Photographs taken at the club that were circulated repeatedly during the scandal showed Keeler theatrically dressed in her 'grand showgirl outfit', consisting of a sequinned cloak, high heels, elaborate headdress and bare breasts. Another exotic wardrobe revealed her in the beaded *cache-sexe* costume, with her body eccentrically festooned with artificial love birds.[137] The overall effect at Murray's was of a conventional style of burlesque entertainment. Keeler and Rice-Davies danced and gyrated on stage like many of the Revuebar's performers, but they also echoed the sexual style of the Windmill troupe when they appeared in static, semi-nude poses.

The club's sexual atmosphere was the subject of contested interpretations. The official management line was that 'Pops' Murray, as he liked his girls to call him, was a strict, old-fashioned Scottish moralist, that his club was run protectively by a team of 'matrons' or 'head girls', and that any hint of impropriety between staff and customers was deemed a sack-able offence.[138] Rice-Davies always insisted that Murray's had a genuinely stylish and convivial atmosphere that marked it out as different from its competitors: 'a friendly oasis in the hard, after-dark world' of Soho's 'nightclubs, strip-tease-joints and drinking dens'.[139] Along with the Windmill girls, some of Murray's showgirls used the club to launch them-selves into successful careers in the entertainment business.[140] But Keeler told a different story about the venue, pointing out that its house rules existed largely to protect the reputation of its male patrons, and that Murray in fact ran a 'visual brothel'.[141]

What this meant in practice was that many of the familiar elements of Soho's sexual economy, short of obvious prostitution on the premises, fea-tured at Murray's in a discreet form. Hostesses fraternized with wealthy patrons and grafted for tips and other favours. There was ample oppor-tunity for the girls to meet clients after hours, and some of them were paid for sex.[142] This sort of erotic atmosphere appealed to Jack Profumo. Shepherd once saw his colleague argue with another customer over the attentions of Mandy Rice-Davies and then start 'physical trouble' with Murray's staff when he felt he was being ignored.[143] By the time Keeler arrived at the club in the summer of 1959, Murray's was targeting an audience of businessmen, international tourists and affluent provincial visitors as well as more distinguished patrons.[144] Murray acknowledged that competition from dynamic entrepreneurs like Raymond was forcing him to redouble his efforts to maintain his club's niche in an increasingly crowded market.[145]

During the early 1960s Keeler extended her sexual range well beyond the activities of a traditional showgirl and into more sophisticated territory. With Ward as her mentor, she was introduced as an invited 'special guest' at sex parties arranged from private houses in Mayfair, where the emphasis was on discreet group orgies.[146] In elegant surroundings after dinner, couples stripped off and used Keeler as an aid to sexual stimulation. Events of this sort were not explicitly organized around money transactions; they were part of an exclusive circle in which Ward provided young women like Keeler as erotic diversions for 'liberated' upper-class couples.

Some of Keeler's adventures were much more strictly financial. She got to know 'a very hard woman' who introduced her to a club 'where they just rang you to go and be screwed for a nominal £25'.[147] This was the Twenty-One Club, 'a glorified knocking shop with overpriced drinks and rooms to rent upstairs'.[148] In a scandal that later turned on the precise definitions of a call-girl and a pimp, Keeler's activities blurred the traditional economic relationship between prostitute and client. As the affair unfolded, much was made of the contrast between her glamorous image and the hard-nosed or abject stance of professional prostitutes like Ronna Ricardo and Vickie Barrett, girls who were also part of Ward's circle.[149] Unlike them, Keeler moved deftly between brief affairs, casual sex and more obviously commercial relationships. Her carefully cultivated sexual ambiguity enabled her to successfully evade control by the police and moral welfare agencies for relatively long periods during the late 1950s and early 1960s.

In all these episodes Keeler maintained that she just did it for kicks. Her emphasis on contemporary notions of transient fun contrasted sharply with the 'graft' of the prostitute and the nascent professionalism of the new breed of privatized call-girl. 'I trusted everyone,' Keeler remembered much later, 'and assumed that they wanted the same things out of life that I did – mainly, to have fun.'[150] This view of life as continual amusement, with an emphasis on sexual pleasure divorced from marriage and emotional commitment and championed by young women from obscure backgrounds just as much as by influential upper-class men, was a defining feature of the Profumo affair as a contemporary scandal.

While Ward acted as Keeler's mentor for her burgeoning sexual career, he also introduced Mandy Rice-Davies into his sphere of influence, another young woman empowered by consumption and cultural mobility (fig. 38). A former Birmingham salesgirl who arrived in London in 1960 aged sixteen to appear as 'Miss Austin' at the Motor Show, she was Keeler's junior at Murray's and subsequently Rachman's girlfriend. Excited by Rachman's 'aura of power' and presenting herself as the foil to Keeler in terms of her sexual style, Rice-Davies was always astute and calculating about the economic advantages to be had from a career dedicated to fun and pleasure. From the outset she was far more confident and assured in her negotiations with the upper-class men whom Ward introduced her to. After Rachman's death she listed the multimillionaire property tycoon Charles Clore and Hollywood actor Douglas Fairbanks Jr among her companions. Rice-Davies always denied any involvement in professional prostitution, presenting herself as a traditional 'courtesan', eager to savour the 'sensuous pleasures' offered by 'rich, lustful men', but Keeler typed her as 'a true tart'.[151]

Keeler's constant desire for sexual experimentation propelled her beyond a string of society boyfriends and casual encounters and into a series of affairs with Caribbean lovers. Rice-Davies always thoroughly disapproved of Keeler's 'lust for black men', but she believed it was the 'hypnotic Dr. Ward . . . in search of new sexual experiences to satisfy a jaded appetite' who influenced her friend 'to move in coloured society'.[152] Keeler's interest in West Indian men, coupled with Ward's own fascination with exotic slumming, began to shift the scandal's centre of gravity towards the cosmopolitan spaces of Soho and Notting Hill, with their distinctive atmosphere of racial and cultural disturbance.

Jealousy and personal rivalry between two of Keeler's boyfriends, Jamaican Aloysius 'Lucky' Gordon and Antiguan Johnny Edgecombe, erupted violently at the All Nighters club in Wardour Street during the autumn of 1962. In a heated argument at the club about sexual possession of Keeler, Edgecombe pulled a knife to Gordon's face and the five-inch cut needed seventeen stitches. Pursued by the police for serious assault of Gordon, Edgecombe went into hiding with Keeler in west London. He proved to be a sexually possessive and an extremely violent lover, and Keeler left him in December.

The Soho nightclub setting for the Edgecombe–Gordon affray introduced a more up-to-date version of the West End's entertainment culture, which was different from the world of glamorous showgirls and leisured upper-class men epitomized by Murray's. Catering neither to society patrons nor to mainstream sexual tourists but to Soho's burgeoning youth culture, the All Nighters was a hybrid space where music provided the social gel for its varied audiences.[153] Located in a steamy cavernous basement and promoting rhythm and blues and modern soul music, the venue attracted a growing black clientele, partly drawn from the contingent of American GIs stationed in southern England, as well as a crowd of early Mods who were in the West End for all-night raves.[154]

Drugs, and especially the new craze for amphetamines, were an integral part of these night-time experiences. Ricardo, a young prostitute picked up by Ward, who later gave evidence that compromised him at his trial, remembered the All Nighters as the first port of call in extended weekend sessions spent in Soho, with groups of her friends moving from club to club in search of fresh kicks: ' "We'd start in the Club, on Fridays . . . take some pills, crash out during the day, go to another club on Saturday night, take some more pills, then go to a Sunday afternoon dancing session." '[155] Ricardo's weekend party circuit represented another version of young women's active participation in transgressive fun that was fuelled by social as well as chemical stimulants. Not surprisingly, audiences at the All Nighters were lively and excitable, with fights like the skirmish between Gordon and Edgecombe being 'almost an accepted part of the . . . entertainment'.[156]

As Caribbean migrants Gordon and Edgecombe were complexly connected to London's cosmopolitan cultures, despite the fact that the media overwhelmingly positioned them as disruptive outsiders. Representing alternative appropriations of the man-about-town, their profiles highlighted yet again the multiple resources of this social type and the way that young, unattached West Indian men claimed their own cultural rights to the city.[157] Gordon came to London in 1948, very soon after the first arrivals from the Caribbean docked on the *Empire Windrush*. Variously referred to as a jazz singer and a 'stage artist', he had a record of police convictions for fraud, assault and shop breaking.[158] Sharply dressed and with a confident street style, according to Keeler he was 'cool', persuasive and extremely violent (fig. 39).[159] Even more go-ahead than Gordon, Edgecombe arrived in Liverpool a year later as a merchant seaman, and he too served prison sentences for larceny, living on immoral earnings and possession of drugs.[160] On his release he moved to London 'where it was all happening' and reinvented himself as a self-styled playboy-cum-entrepreneur.[161] Like many of his Caribbean friends, Edgecombe regularly visited Hyde Park and the Bayswater Road in order to cruise the urban scene and meet all the 'nice chicks' in 'the summertime'.[162] He also started up his own shebeen, known as Johnny's Place, at Colville Terrace, Notting Hill, in a flat leased from Rachman.[163] Providing a variety of illicit cultural goods, Edgecombe boasted that his club catered to every taste: a front room playing 'sounds', a 'casino . . . occupied by pimps', a 'restaurant' serving 'Caribbean soul food', and 'an extra dish . . . dope'.[164] His supply of these services enabled him to act as a facilitator for Notting Hill's drugs and party scene that fascinated Ward and his society friends.

But Edgecombe did not remain confined to north Kensington for long; his influence rapidly spread to the West End. In his autobiography he explained that 'jazz and dope' eased his social mobility.[165] Acting as a part-time chauffeur to visiting musicians of the calibre of Count Basie and Dizzy Gillespie, when they played at Soho's Ronnie Scott's club, Edgecombe was a ready supplier of drugs and local know-how. He admitted that his GIs 'were the best dope customers you could get'.[166]

Edgecombe's and Gordon's social profiles loomed large in public debate about the negative presence of Caribbean men in London which coalesced around the figure of the pimp. The police, purity campaigners and race relations sociologists cast the pimp as work-shy and economically parasitic, driven by low cunning and street nous; aggressive and lacking masculine self-control, he epitomized the immigrant's intractable problems of non-acculturation.[167] Superintendent Fabian exposed 'men who live on the immoral earnings of prostitutes' as the 'lowest form of animal life on the criminal scale'. Echoing inter-war anxieties about the white slave trade and 'dope girls', Fabian drew public attention to Soho's nightclubs where coloured pimps snared girls into a vicious spiral of sex and drug peddling.[168]

Black pimps inflamed miscegenation fears on account of their sexual access to and control of white women. Operating at street level, Edgecombe offered a different explanation for his career as a hustler. Justifying his activities in the context of the racism confronting him as a young immigrant in London, he remembered: 'Prostitution was big busi-

ness; it offered a chance to some to live a far more comfortable and prosperous life. . . . there was no way I was going to slave for the railways, to
be paid a pittance in wages for the rest of my life.'[169] Edgecombe's move
into the city's illicit sexual economy was an active choice made by many
young, disenfranchised Caribbean men. His affairs with English women
like Keeler also highlighted the fact that relationships between white
women and their Caribbean boyfriends were often characterized by
complex ties of emotional and financial interdependence. The cultural
status of the English girl and the sexual control exercised by her partner
coexisted in uneasy tension.[170]

Keeler herself was ambivalent about her relationships with West Indian
men in ways that reflected wider racial and sexual anxieties. Strongly held
miscegenation fears (she was terrified that her 'mother should find out
that I had black men as lovers'), alarm about being seen as a cultural
hybrid outside the boundaries of white Englishness, as well as the threat
of sexual violence were the reasons why she left both Gordon and
Edgecombe.[171] In a statement made under police pressure at the height
of the scandal, Keeler confessed that she had been 'silly living with a
coloured man'.[172] However, like a number of young women with
Caribbean boyfriends in Notting Hill, Keeler enjoyed the entrée that her
lovers provided into an expanded world of the senses, influenced by music,
drugs and a flamboyant style of masculinity. As she put it about her relationship with Gordon: 'I thought this was the escape I wanted. . . . his
love was so persuasive and the marijuana made it all dream-like.'[173]

Together with the Rillington Place murders a decade earlier, racial difference and its urban locatedness was a continuous thread running
through the Profumo episode. Understood by the white protagonists as
simultaneously dangerous and compelling, the Caribbean influence distinguished the affair from many of the other metropolitan sex scandals of
the post-war years, which turned on more tightly boundaried definitions
of Englishness. As West Indian migrants, Gordon's and Edgecombe's
involvement with Keeler and Ward placed domestic sexual mores under
the spotlight. The movement of these characters between Notting Hill
and Soho also disrupted the topography of the socially bifurcated city,
central to so many earlier scandals, which was organized predominantly
around the class divisions separating the West End from the East End.
Gordon and Edgecombe introduced a different sensory atmosphere into
the experience of domestic scandal, with their links to contemporary subcultural nightlife and exoticized sexual danger.

Keeler's relationship with Johnny Edgecombe quite literally returned to haunt her. At lunchtime on 14 December 1962 she was visiting Mandy Rice-Davies at Ward's Marylebone flat, when they heard shots outside the door and window. It was Edgecombe, who had arrived in a mini-cab in hot pursuit of Keeler, armed with a loaded pistol. Refused entry to the flat, Edgecombe repeatedly fired his gun. Stung by jealousy and furious at having been dumped by Keeler, he was by his own confession: 'Sick to the stomach over her . . . and when she came to the window and would not listen and told me to go away. The sickness in the stomach overcame me and I started firing the gun.'[174]

This dramatic incident first began to push the affair beyond London's elite milieus and low-life settings and into a much wider public domain that was shaped by the national media. Even without the knowledge of Keeler's relationship with a senior government minister or her rumoured involvement with Ivanov, a shoot-out involving a London model and two Caribbean men was a front-page story. 'Six Shots Fired at Girls' West End Flat', announced the headline of the *Evening Standard* in its late final edition that day.[175] Keeler remembered that 'after Johnnie Edgecombe had played his version of the Gunfight at the OK Corral', she became aware that she was seriously newsworthy.[176]

Breaking News

The Profumo scandal began to break in the early months of 1963 via a classic device that so often encouraged the discovery of modern sexual and political secrets: an English trial at the Old Bailey, amplified by the press. John Christie's prosecution in the Central Criminal Court a decade earlier had been the catalyst for an extensive public debate about pathological forms of masculinity and their links to London's low urban cultures. Edgecombe's trial for Keeler's attempted murder and other related offences, scheduled for March 1963, threatened to expose the capital's interconnected social and sexual worlds and their cast of characters. It was the first of a number of spectacular courtroom dramas punctuating the scandal that climaxed with Ward's own prosecution.[177]

Profumo and Lord Astor feared that Keeler would divulge her sexual story when she was called to appear in the witness box at Edgecombe's trial, but by the time the prosecution started on 14 March 1963, she had disappeared.[178] One of the reasons she later gave for her vanishing act was the worry that she would be asked in court 'if I had had sex with a black man, which in the early 1960s was a great stigma'.[179] Keeler resurfaced a few days later in southern Spain, flanked by her newly acquired publicity manager, Paul Mann. A racing driver as well as a journalist, Mann was a bridge-playing friend of Ward's who was also part of the osteopath's Cliveden party set.[180] It was widely presumed that Keeler had been spirited away by interested parties who were keen to keep the lid on the affair and protect Profumo, but as Keeler remembered the plan backfired spectacularly, turning the spotlight ever more intensely on what Fleet Street was now calling the case of the missing model.[181]

An important feature of the unravelling of the scandal was Keeler's ability to cast herself as the active feminine subject of the story, rather than simply appearing as the passive object of media attention. Titillating coverage of the sexual adventures of glamorous dancers and showgirls was hardly new in the post-war period, featuring as a staple item in the gossip columns of the daily and Sunday papers. But before the pop star phenomenon of the 1960s, it was extremely rare for an inexperienced young woman with little social capital to promote herself as a significant media event in her own right. Jack Profumo underestimated Keeler's ability to draw on sophisticated forms of publicity, dismissing her as 'completely uneducated'. 'All she knew about,' he insisted, 'was make-up and her hair, and . . . gramophone records and a little about nightclubs. . . . I simply thought that she was a very beautiful little girl who seemed to like sexual intercourse.'[182] Like many other Establishment figures, Profumo failed to grasp Keeler's astute use of alternative forms of feminine know-how. Keeler and Rice-Davies were adept at media self-promotion in ways that was anathema to the war minister. Profumo resorted to his solicitors in a desperate attempt to invoke the force of legal injunction to silence press rumours when they began to engulf him, while these two young women exploited the productive power of publicity to the full.

Keeler was assiduous in seeking out the professional advice of journalists and photographers to keep herself in the public eye. By her own confession she knew nothing about chequebook journalism, but she had friends who did. Working alongside Mann was a freelance writer and one-time sexual accomplice of Keeler's, Nina Gadd, who persuaded Keeler that she had a sellable story.[183] Keeler remembered later that the money Gadd promised 'certainly appealed to me', but her immediate follow-up question was: 'how much would I get?'[184] In the early months of 1963 she was involved in protracted negotiations with the editors of most of the mass market dailies and Sundays over the rights to her 'confessions' and about the content of her story. In a market that increasingly traded in 'sizzling' news coverage and what Coote admitted was provocative titillation, Keeler's disclosures aroused a lot of interest.[185]

Keeler framed her original account as a familiar overworld–underworld narrative about her life with ministers of the Crown, spiced with details of exotic encounters with her Caribbean lovers. It was this version of events that she showed first to the *Sunday Pictorial*, who offered her £1,000 for publication rights. But convinced that she could get more, Keeler walked straight along Fleet Street to the offices of its 'heavy hitting competitor', the *News of the World*, where she asked the paper's senior crime reporter, Peter Earle, to better her first offer. Earle replied that he was not joining any auction, so she promptly returned to the *Pictorial*.[186]

The *Pictorial*'s arrangement was that only £200 of their fee was payable in advance; the remainder was due on publication, and it was dependent on Keeler's story reaching the newspaper's expectations. She was now encouraged to dredge her memory for items of 'special interest'.[187] Sensing the need for a more sensational spin on events, Keeler and her publicity machine began to alter her account substantially, giving it an 'extra lift' by including the spy interest angle and the disclosures about the three-way sexual relationship between herself, the war minister and Ivanov.[188] These narrative embellishments reached epic proportions in the final version of the article that she signed off, in early February 1963. It now included the dramatic assertion that Ward had asked her to get nuclear secrets about West Germany's military hardware from the British Minister of War.[189] As Lord Denning commented later: 'The newspaper reporters saw how greatly the "spy interest" heightened the story.'[190] Frenzied efforts by Ward and Lord Astor, possibly acting on Profumo's behalf, resulted in the paper dropping the article from publication. Despite this temporary press embargo, three consequences followed from the wildly circulating rumours about the West End model: Ivanov was hurriedly recalled to Moscow, MI5 began to probe Ward's possible role in the security breaches that had been alleged by Keeler, while Ward himself began to run his own counter-publicity machine, negotiating with the *News of the World* for the sale of his version of events.[191]

Scandals begin when gossip becomes public, Anna Clark has observed.[192] The enlargement of the Profumo affair in the early months of 1963 was not characterized by a straightforward movement from secrecy to disclosure; what occurred was the complex mutation of events under the combined influence of media incentives and broader political pressures. The elaborate codes of mass publicity that were finely tuned for the circulation of sexual rumour, together with the compressed networks of metropolitan society gossip and Tory political intrigue, served to incubate the case. Initially, media coverage of events worked by suggestion and inference rather than by full exposure, a strategy heavily influenced by the current libel laws that were stiffened in the early 1960s with the award of massive damages against the press in a series of well-publicized court cases.[193] Legal restrictions on Fleet Street's scandalous revelations meant that journalists were extremely cautious about committing themselves to damaging exposés about public figures, unless their evidence was watertight. Instead, they elected to work with the safer journalistic form of allusion, or what editors termed 'message by code'.[194]

Several times in the spring of 1963 the *Daily Express* ran coverage of John Profumo's political engagements in ways that insinuated there was trouble in his private life. On one occasion the paper profiled a visit Profumo made with his wife to his Stratford constituency. The couple were pictured singing at the piano in the local committee rooms, while the caption, heavy with innuendo, read: 'Drink to Me Only with Thine Eyes'.[195] At the time of Edgecombe's trial in March the *Express* went further. Its front page carried a large photo of Keeler, separated by only one column from a story by political correspondent Ian Aitken speculating that the Minister of War had offered his resignation, at some future unspecified time, on the grounds of the coming reorganization of the defence departments. The proximity of the two news items suggested that they were in some way linked, especially for those in the know.[196]

At the same time, countervailing media pressures were encouraging editors to search out scandal as a means of attacking Macmillan's government. In February, Brendan Mulholland and Reginald Foster, journalists working on the *Daily Mail* and *Daily Sketch*, had been given contempt of court prison sentences for refusing to reveal to the Vassall Tribunal their sources for disclosures about the spy.[197] Press hostility to this legal judgement pointed the finger at the government, accusing the Prime Minister of political interference and deliberate heavy-handedness. As a result, the Profumo affair was generated in an atmosphere of rapidly deteriorating relations between the Tory administration and the fourth estate. Macmillan always believed that the subsequent animosity directed against him and other senior Tories was deliberately orchestrated by 'an exultant Press, getting its own back for Vassall'.[198]

Media culture was one crucial incubator for the scandal; Tory political culture with its links to London society was the other. At Westminster, rumours about a senior minister, a model and a member of the Soviet diplomatic corps had been circulating for months, both as political gossip and as the subject of ribald jokes exchanged between MPs in the clubs. Man-about-town Robin Douglas-Home, the nephew of the Foreign Secretary, first hinted that the names of Profumo, Keeler and Ivanov might be linked when he released the information as a morsel of delicious gossip in *Queen* in July 1962.[199] On hearing the disclosures at a party to mark the opening of an exclusive gaming club, the Clermont, in Berkeley Square in November, Christopher Soames reputedly joked: 'So what? At least it's a girl. You too could have her for five pounds a go.'[200] Unlike Shepherd, who believed that rumours of this kind seriously undermined the government, Soames's standpoint was relaxed and urbane. He epitomized the patrician attitude of a number of high Tories who continued to believe they were untouchable. As long as politicians were not publicly indiscreet and their affairs were vigorously heterosexual, their secrets remained secure, protected by the informal code of honour that governed the behaviour of the political elite.

But in March 1963 further disclosures from an esoteric but well-placed source, the parliamentary newsletter *Westminster Confidential*, escalated the rumours among a closed circle of politicians, lobby correspondents and foreign embassy staff. Run by Andrew Roth, an expatriate American, the political broadsheet was no more than three or four pages of mimeographed foolscap, with a print run of less than two hundred.[201] Under the heading 'That Was the Government That Was!' (a deliberate play on the current hit BBC television satire programme *That Was The Week That Was*, or *TW3*), Roth hinted again about the allegations surrounding the Minister of War, including information about 'a letter, apparently signed "Jack", on the stationery of the Secretary of W-r'.[202] The impact of Roth's journalism and Douglas-Home's society intrigue lay in the way that both writers assembled their fragments of gossip into a tantalizing bricolage of suggestive half-truths for consumption by the cognoscenti. Not only were these articles a calculated provocation to Profumo and the government to refute them, they also proffered counterfactual information that could be disclosed and then withdrawn, with the safeguard that they remained just inside the libel laws.

Eventually, the rumours and innuendoes surrounding Profumo began to erupt into open public debate, encouraged by the political immunity enjoyed by MPs and by the eccentricities of the British parliamentary system. On the afternoon of 21 March Ben Parkin was speaking in a House of Commons committee on the state of the London sewerage system. Taking advantage of a rule that allowed members to digress from their subject without interruption, Parkin made a deliberate reference to the recent case of the missing model, accompanying his remarks with a suggestive allusion to the fact that 'a model can be quite easily obtained for a Minister of the Crown'.[203] Parkin did not elaborate, but by the end of his speech press editors were calling his desk to expand on the story. In the late-night debate that followed on the imprisonment of the two journalists at the centre of the Vassall affair, George Wigg challenged the Home Secretary to deny the rumours that were circulating about a member of the government, or appoint a select parliamentary committee to investigate them.[204]

Woken at his home in the middle of the night, Profumo was rushed across London to the House of Commons to prepare a response, where he was interviewed by the government's chief whip and other Tory grandees. Iain Macleod, Joint Chairman of the Conservative Party and a close associate of Profumo, later told a journalist colleague that he had been blunt: 'Look Jack, the basic question is, Did you fuck her?' Macleod reputedly asked his friend.[205] Profumo recalled much later that he had replied, 'Something like that, yes', but he regarded his adultery as 'a side issue' in comparison with the allegations about his role as a security risk, which he emphatically denied.[206] However, the situation was now so grave that his colleagues sensed it was necessary to face down the rumours publicly.

Flanked by Macmillan and other senior members of the Cabinet, Profumo made a personal statement to the House of Commons the following day, insisting in his famous phrase that there had been 'no impropriety whatsoever in my acquaintanceship with Miss Keeler'.[207] According to parliamentary tradition, this set-piece rebuttal could not be challenged, because the integrity of an MP had to be accepted absolutely. Immediately before and after his declaration, Profumo reinforced his denial of wrongdoing with a series of socially symbolic acts designed to bolster his claims as a man of honour. All his activities drew their strength from the power of ritualized display in the parliamentary arena of high politics and in the entertainment settings of London society.

The elaborate semiotics of gesture and performance were a marked feature of the unfolding of the scandal, highlighting the continued impor-

tance given to traditional forms of elite metropolitan spectacle as a vehicle
for conveying political information. On the evening before his House of
Commons statement, in a very public act of bravado, Profumo made a
deliberate appearance at a political dinner at the Savoy Hotel hosted by
the Other Club, the 'most exclusive political dining club in the world',
in the company of prominent Tories including Churchill and Julian
Amery.[208] Minutes before making his parliamentary speech the following
day, Profumo was photographed by the press with his wife on his arm
on the steps of the War Office, in a forceful show of conjugal solidarity.
Valerie Profumo, looking 'dignified, composed and serious', then proceeded to the Speaker's Gallery to witness her husband's House of
Commons speech.[209] Later the same afternoon the couple's social position gained further endorsement when the Profumos were very prominent guests of their staunch supporter, the Queen Mother, at a racing
party held at Sandown Park in Surrey. In the evening they surfaced yet
again, this time at Quaglinos, the famous society restaurant in St James's,
at a fund-raising dance given by the Hatch End Conservative Party.[210]
The messages telegraphed by their appearances were deliberately crafted;
they were designed to show that the Profumos continued to enjoy the
confidence of the country's political leadership and the support of royalty.
They were played out for the benefit of two very different audiences: the
numerically small but highly influential circle of London's political and
social elite and the national readership of the popular and middle-market
press.

Profumo's defence of his position did not halt the gossip and speculation. One immediate consequence was that Keeler and her manager capitalized on the heightened interest in events by releasing a barrage of press
coverage about her life. They returned to the *News of the World*, now
demanding a higher fee for her full story, and Peter Earle duly ghosted
one of the earliest versions of Keeler's autobiography. Pictured on the
paper's front page 'modelling a bikini', the 'beautiful model's' progress was
tracked from 'a small village to the playgrounds of the Western world'.[211]
Constrained from making disclosures that would potentially breach the
libel laws, Earle raided an extensive vocabulary of female sexuality in order
to court public attention, variously projecting Keeler as naive ingénue,
modern young woman, sexual victim and wanton seductress. 'Take a Girl
Like Christine' and 'The Two Worlds of Christine Keeler' were just some
of the headlines and copy that Keeler endorsed in March and April

1963.[212] Avoiding any suggestion of prostitution, Earle presented Keeler as 'restless', 'lively, intelligent and charming', falling 'in love and out of it again' at a moment's notice.[213]

At this point Rice-Davies also entered competitively into the publicity stakes with a more straightforward but equally sellable sexual profile. According to Fleet Street, Mandy knew even better than Keeler what would sell, and 'she fed her ghost writer so much hot material that the . . . libel lawyers wore out . . . their blue pencils' bowdlerizing her story.[214] 'Mandy Talked – And It's Dynamite', was Earle's headline about 'the perfect popsie' who one moment appeared like a 'trim schoolgirl' and the next as a 'million dollar sophisticate'.[215] Rice-Davies's lavishly illustrated autobiography, released by Confidential Publications, embellished these character traits. Opening her 'wicked, wicked story' as 'the sorry tale of a young girl, barely more than a child' who was 'baited with mink and diamonds', she went on to recount tongue-in-cheek the fascinating events in a young life that had become 'trapped in a web of complete moral depravity'.[216] Exposing the 'truth, at long last, about the snake-pit masquerading under the title High Society', she pointed the finger explicitly at Ward as a perverted 'carrier of scandal' and as 'an international go-between, with the power to negotiate on both sides of the Iron Curtain'.[217]

One consequence of the frenzied media speculation was that government agencies and the police now began to make further inquiries about Stephen Ward. The politically motivated harassment of Ward that dominated the affair in its later stages was driven by official anxieties about security, sex and publicity. These different elements coexisted in uneasy tension among the various institutions and official interest groups that staked a claim over the osteopath's career. Contemporary commentators and later historians have argued that this campaign pointed to clear evidence of a coordinated Establishment conspiracy designed to frame him as a scapegoat for the more influential figures who were ensnared in the affair.[218] But the various branches of government and bureaucracy were far from unified in their pursuit of Ward; they were driven by competing political and cultural preoccupations that pushed the case in different directions.

The overriding concern among the intelligence services was with Ward's position as a potential security threat, in the light of Keeler's allegations about his role in her attempts to gain nuclear secrets from

Profumo. MI5 remained relatively uninterested in Ward's sexual peccadilloes, which was the issue that preoccupied the Home Secretary, Henry
Brooke.[219] An unpopular replacement for his reforming predecessor Rab
Butler, as a result of Macmillan's Cabinet massacre in July 1962, Brooke
was a social conservative on the right of the Tory Party.[220] He was
emphatically opposed to Wolfenden's proposal to liberalize the law on
homosexual offences, and during his twenty-seven months in office he
introduced measures tightening the obscenity legislation and further crim-
inalizing the use of cannabis. Denouncing all manner of 'sleazy stuff',
Brooke was alarmed about the trend towards permissiveness, which he
defined as the feeling among a 'growing number of people' that they
should 'feel free to do anything they liked'. His response was that government 'should be slow to loosen up'.[221] Brooke was particularly alarmed
about Ward's connections with London's underworld and his deliberate
self-promotion in the national media. His instructions to the Metropolitan
Police, authorizing them to begin a relentless investigation of the
osteopath's sexual activities, were motivated by the need to silence Ward
politically and also by a strong personal animus against the type of metropolitan society that Ward and Profumo represented.[222]

Police tactics used against Ward generated aggressive methods of information gathering that pushed the criminal investigation to its legal limits
and beyond. The scandal marked an intensification of police activity
directed at individuals without previous criminal records. Aggressive pro-
cedures of search and entrapment that had been used previously against
West End nightclub owners and brothel-keepers were now turned on a
leading society figure. Acting without either reported complaints or specific suspicions, Scotland Yard mounted a proactive campaign against Ward,
assembling an extensive dossier that probed his character and morals.
Chief Inspector Samuel Herbert, the officer in charge of the case, excelled
in prosecutions against West End gamblers, pimps and blackmailers, and
according to one contemporary witness his methods were 'pretty
dubious'.[223] Cross-examined at Ward's trial, Herbert was forced to reveal
the enormous amount of public resources that had gone into prosecuting the osteopath for what were mostly minor offences. A sizeable team
of detectives and regular beat officers fished for evidence about Ward's
unusual sexual tastes and hunted for his reportedly extensive collection
of pornography. Keeler herself was interviewed twenty-four times; Ward's
phone was tapped regularly, and the police team interviewed well over a

hundred witnesses, including many of his patients.[224] Tactics of this kind marked an increase in the surveillance mechanisms of Whitehall's secret state under the combined pressures of sex and security.

At Westminster, the rapid escalation of the scandal was beginning to engulf parliamentary politics. In May, Harold Wilson, Labour's newly elected leader, made political capital out of the case by accusing the government of incompetence in handling the reports of espionage.[225] Macmillan eventually responded by asking the Lord Chancellor, Lord Dilhorne, to investigate the security aspects of the affair. On 3 June Profumo returned with his wife from a holiday in Venice. Two days later Downing Street released a letter from the war minister to Macmillan admitting that he had lied to the House of Commons about his relationship with Keeler in order to protect his wife and family. Profumo resigned, both as a minister and an MP; his political career was over.

Macmillan always maintained that Profumo eventually came clean about his role in the scandal because at heart he was a still a gentleman, though now a disgraced one. 'Over-burdened' by a 'guilty conscience', Macmillan insisted that his minister's tragic downfall vindicated the innate morality of the governing class.[226] But it was more likely to have been mounting political and personal pressures and the imminent threat of even more scandalous disclosures which finally convinced Profumo that his strategy of denial was no longer viable. Not only was he facing the prospect of another round of interrogation in front Dilhorne's inquiry, Keeler was threatening more media revelations in a series of taped interviews that she had given as the tantalizing trailer to the impending release of her memoirs. On the political front, detailed inquiries by George Wigg had prompted Wilson to table a further parliamentary question just before Profumo left for Venice, casting doubt on the minister's original statement made to the House.[227] All these factors undermined Profumo's efforts to tough it out.

After Profumo's resignation, the scandal reached epic proportions, with stories of men in masks, whipping parties, widespread metropolitan orgies, and the alleged involvement of presidents and members of the royal family.[228] The climax of the Profumo affair was relayed not just through the channels of rational public discourse, but also via a series of mounting sensations – of rumour, fear, voyeurism and confession – that were focused on the spaces of the capital city. As Bill Sewell has noted, 'high pitched . . . excitement' orchestrated in a compressed urban space by the resources of ritual can act as a very significant factor in transforming particular events into potentially wider movements of social and political change.[229] Heightened emotionality shaped the course of the Profumo affair, especially in its crisis weeks, when the interaction of many of the key players in London's central area produced a form of contagious excitement. A slump in the stock market compounded the mood of nervous apprehension; even the English weather was 'hot and thundery'.[230]

Advertising the set-piece parliamentary debate on the scandal on 17 June as 'one of the great dramas of . . . public life', the press reported that overnight queues along with the volume of traffic in Parliament Square had brought central London to a standstill.[231] Inside the Commons, with the public galleries jammed, a three-line party whip meant that MPs spilled over into the gangways and squatted at the bar of the house.[232] Front bench members of the Labour opposition, Tony Benn and Richard Crossman, confided in their diaries that political society in London talked of nothing but the Profumo scandal.[233] Evoking comparisons with another incident that had been driven by wild rumour and accusation, the anti-Catholic Popish Plot nearly 300 years before, Macmillan believed that a 'Titus Oates atmosphere' prevailed in the country, as 'more than half the Cabinet were being accused of perversion, homosexuality and the like'.[234] Christopher Booker, who played a minor role in the affair as an editor of *Private Eye*, was one of the first to note how the scandal shifted gear in the late spring and early summer of 1963, moving from accusations aimed at a single minister to an outbreak of collective suspicion levelled against all those in authority.[235] Throughout June, Booker recalled, 'anything was possible and only the worst was to be believed'.[236]

Metropolitan anxieties released by the Profumo affair were intensified by a series of anti-government and anti-Establishment demonstrations that erupted in London during the first half of the year. In March, Parliament Square was the setting for protests by the north of England's unemployed, resulting in angry scenes and an attempt to break into the Palace of Westminster.[237] The following month the Aldermaston March converged on London, an annual event that provided the focus for so much extra-parliamentary opposition during the late 1950s and early 1960s. Led by the Campaign for Nuclear Disarmament and involving the London Federation of Anarchists, marchers threaded their way along Regent Street shouting anti-government slogans, before moving on to Hyde Park Corner where they clashed with the police.[238] In July there was the disastrous state visit to Britain by the reactionary King Paul and Queen Frederika of Greece. The couple's London appearances resulted in further demonstrations, and for the first time in over a hundred years a reigning British monarch was openly booed on the streets of the capital city, as the Queen arrived with King Paul at the Aldwych Theatre.[239] Brooke waded in to denounce the 'handful of communists, anarchists, beatniks, and members of the Campaign for Nuclear Disarmament' who were destroying the country's reputation.[240] All of these very visible protests, mounted in the heart of the West End, contributed to the growing sense of anxiety within government circles. The elaborately staged royal wedding of Princess Alexandra, the Queen's cousin, to Angus Ogilvy at Westminster Abbey in April was the only official ceremony that temporarily lightened the national mood.[241]

Improvements to the technology of news communication in the early 1960s meant that Profumo's story and images of the city that had produced it were now circulated across the world. Unlike most earlier English scandals, which remained relatively contained until reporters and editors had liaised with foreign newsdesks, the new American satellite communications system, Telstar, launched the previous year, followed by Syncom in 1963, meant that images and editorial copy could be transmitted across the Atlantic at high speed.[242] Press treatment of the affair was extensive and continuous in the USA and throughout the Commonwealth, as well as in Europe. In each case coverage was refracted through the specific political and cultural preoccupations of national readerships.

In the American dailies and weeklies editors placed Profumo as a leader item throughout June, when coverage of the scandal conveniently displaced pressing domestic issues from the front pages, especially reports of renewed race rioting in the southern states.[243] *Newsweek* promoted the affair as world news that was driven by Cold War politics; a traditional English sex scandal had assumed international dimensions as 'a . . . World Parliament of prostitutes, whoremongers, sex deviates, orgy-prone highbinders, and libidinous Soviet agents'.[244] The prurient head of the American Federal Bureau of Investigation, J. Edgar Hoover, took a particular interest in the case, motivated by rumours about President Kennedy's sexual involvement.[245]

Across the Commonwealth the overriding concern was with the negative impact of the scandal on British moral and political leadership. The affair was seen by the Foreign Office and by sections of the international press as potentially destabilizing the Commonwealth ideal that had been crafted in the wake of decolonization and the demise of empire. Australian journalists informed their readers that the 'gentleman's code', which for so long had meant that the 'Mother of Parliaments' was held in the highest regard among the 'old Dominions', was now irrevocably 'shattered'.[246] The British High Commissioner, Sir William Oliver, telegraphed back anxiously to Whitehall about local reactions in the antipodes, noting that the Australian 'with a slight chip on his shoulder' was 'rather pleased to be able to "knock" the . . . decadence of the "la-di-da" Englishman'.[247] Oliver's concerns not only highlighted the deficiencies of English upper-class leadership, they also focused on the declining influence of Westminster politics across the white dominions. Reporting a similarly hostile mood in New Zealand, the High Commissioner there noted a growing tendency among local politicians to distance themselves from the British government in the wake of the scandal.[248] In Pakistan and India, President Khan's rumoured involvement in Ward's sexual circle, as a result of his appearance at the Cliveden swimming pool incident, threatened to erupt as a major international issue between the two countries.[249] In Jamaica, press attitudes appeared to be more relaxed, if relentlessly satiric, with the Kingston papers suggesting tongue-in-cheek that Edgecombe and Gordon should be included in the next honours list for their contribution to English public life![250]

At home Keeler and Rice-Davies continued to use intelligent self-promotion and publicity to subject the political elite to the most sustained attack since Stead's exposé of aristocratic decadence nearly seventy years earlier. 'I do not remember ever having been under such a sense of personal strain,' Macmillan confessed in his diary, 'even Suez was clean – about war and politics. This was all "dirt".'[251] Keeler turned herself into a lucrative multimedia event; immaculately groomed for her various public appearances and exhibiting a deft sense of timing, she assumed the role of a fashionable celebrity. The *News of the World* began to serialize another round of her confessions, and the *Daily Express* reported that she had been successfully screen-tested in a 'top-secret location' for a 'dramatic documentary' about her life.[252] Her personality was endlessly commodified: there was a suggestive record with the title 'Christine', a planned autobiography and rumours of a lucrative contract with a West End nightclub, as well as an invitation to appear in Las Vegas. On the strength of the ongoing publicity Keeler switched managers and turned herself into a limited company.[253]

At the end of June, Stephen Ward appeared at Marylebone Magistrates' Court and was committed for trial at the Old Bailey on charges including living on the earnings of prostitution, attempting to procure a girl under twenty-one to have intercourse with a third party, and inciting Keeler to do the same. Ward pleaded not guilty on all counts.[254] His trial a month later marked the opening tragic denouement of the affair. After six days of hostile questioning Ward took an overdose of barbiturates. As he lapsed into a coma in St Stephen's Hospital on the Fulham Road, the jury found him guilty on the two charges of living on immoral earnings. He died without regaining consciousness three days later, unaware of the verdict against him. Macmillan survived the scandal but was seriously weakened politically, resigning his premiership as a result of ill health in October 1963.[255] Lord Denning's report, published a month earlier, was a damage limitation exercise for the government, concluding that there had been no serious breaches of security and that most of the sexual rumours surrounding leading politicians and public figures were unfounded.[256] Keeler received a nine-month prison sentence for perjury and attempting to pervert the course of justice in the Edgecombe trial. Profumo retired to philanthropic work at Toynbee Hall, the settlement and community trust in the East End, and into the silence of private life.

The status of the Profumo affair as one of the major scandals of the twentieth century was guaranteed by its sensational plot. The international reach of its rumours, coupled with the destabilizing effect of its disclosures and the dramatic performances from its principal characters, guaranteed that the episode received extensive coverage both at home and in an international context. The content of the affair, which drew together so many of the most pressing post-war domestic issues about sex, gender and social conduct, ensured that its influence extended well beyond the governing elites and into the sphere of mass politics and popular culture. But the unfolding of events cannot be divorced from another aspect of the episode's impact surprisingly neglected by most commentators: the narrative dimensions of the scandal itself. Along with a rich deployment of other related genres, notably fantasy, heightened imagery and mounting sensation, the Profumo affair was relayed as a series of diverse and frequently contested stories of metropolitan life. These representations of urban culture were not superficial factors in the development of the case; they were intrinsic to the meanings that were disseminated into post-war society. The concluding section traces these contested interpretations of metropolitan culture, identifying the scandal as a critical episode in the politics of English modernity during the 1960s.

35 Conservative ministers at Chequers, April 1963, photographer unknown.

36   John Profumo in British court dress, undated, photographer Paul Popper/ Popperfoto. Getty Images.

37 (*facing page top*)   Christine Keeler, 1963, photographer unknown. Popperfoto/Getty Images.

38 (*facing page bottom*)   Mandy Rice-Davies leaves the Old Bailey after the first day of Stephen Ward's trial, 22 July 1963, photographer Ted West/Stringer, Hulton Archive. Getty Images.

Daily Mirror

3d. Monday, July 22, 1963 · No. 18,533

Mirror Exclusive:

The man who faces trial today

WARD IN TV FILM

By BARRY STANLEY

THIS exclusive picture of osteopath Stephen Ward is taken from a half-hour TV film he has made while on bail.

The film is of a typical day in the life of Stephen Ward—whose trial opens at the Old Bailey today.

Already, the film has been sold on the Continent. And it may also be sold to a British TV company as well.

Our picture was taken at 7.30 a.m. in impresario David Pelham's flat in Montagu-square, Marylebone.

Sketching

Ward, 51-year-old clergyman's son and friend of Christine Keeler, slips out of bed and stretches . . . the start of another day.

A walk through London streets . . . a drive in the country in his white Jaguar car . . . treating a patient . . . sketching a friend.

Just a typical day for the man who will sit in the dock of the Old Bailey's famous No. 1 court to face seven vice charges.

The judge will be Mr. Justice Marshall. Crown counsel is Mr. Mervyn Griffith-Jones. Ward's counsel, Mr. James Burge.

The trial is expected to last several days. And more than 100 journalists will pack the court . . . ready to send reports of the trial to all parts of the world.

Mirror exclusive picture by DAVID STEEN

Stephen Ward, in pale blue silk pyjama trousers, faces a new day in a friend's flat in Montagu-square, Marylebone. Behind his bed is a pink curtain hung in a gilt frame. TV cameras moved into the room at 7.30 in the morning.

RACHMAN'S WIDOW SPEAKS—See Back Page

40 (*above*) 'Stephen Ward, in pale blue silk pyjama trousers', photographer unknown, front page, *Daily Mirror*, 22 July 1963. Mirrorpix.

39 (*facing page*) Lucky Gordon arrives at the Old Bailey on the second day of his trial, 6 June 1963, photographer unknown, Hulton Archive. Getty Images.

41 'Britain Gets Wythe Itte, 1963', cartoon by Timothy Birdsall, *Private Eye*, 31 May 1963, pp. 80–1. Reproduced by kind permission of *Private Eye* magazine/Timothy Birdsall/Christopher Booker.

te, 1963

42 'Oh, To Be In London', photographer Derek Bayes, in Piri Halasz, 'Great Britain', *Time*, 15 April 1966. Courtesy of Derek Bayes/Aspect Picture Library Limited.

Britain Gets With It

'High Society is dragged in the dirt and people love it,' gloated the journalist 'Cassandra' in his *Daily Mirror* column, written as part of an attack on the Establishment at the height of the affair in June 1963.[257] The scandal precipitated a major crisis in the informal networks of upper-class power and political influence, pushing together many of the anxieties about elite behaviour that had erupted during the previous decade. The *Mirror's* specific framework for understanding the case was the paradigm of aristocratic corruption and sexual decadence, and in-house reporters pursued this theme relentlessly in a series of articles exposing the 'intimate closed shop' of Macmillan's administration.

Cassandra, the pseudonym of William Connor, had pioneered his own eclectic mixture of social gossip and anti-Establishment journalism since the mid-1930s. Politics and perversion were the hallmarks of his famous 'polished barrack room style', and he used this combination ruthlessly and to great effect in his revelations about the private life of many public figures.[258] The Profumo scandal provided Connor with a golden opportunity to renew his brand of *soi-disant* popular radicalism that was dedicated to the titillating exposure of privilege. He took his readers on a tour of the City of London, through the corridors of Whitehall, and into the 'fly blown world' of the 'philanderer, the homosexual and the alcoholic', characters whom he depicted as representative of England's governing class.[259] Recounting what he believed was a traditional morality tale and deliberately echoing the language of W. T. Stead's crusading journalism, he cast Stephen Ward as 'one of the most dedicated whoremasters in London', who had been abandoned by both the 'high and mighty of this land' and by the 'female sexual monsters' he had so skilfully worked to create.[260]

Journalist and political commentator Malcolm Muggeridge echoed Connor's assessment. A former editor of *Punch*, Muggeridge had been one of the most vocal critics of monarchy during the 1950s. Now writing for the *Sunday Mirror*, the new forward-looking, populist weekend paper dedicated to modernization, he launched a sustained attack on the lax personal morality of the country's political elite, which he associated with a litany of vices: 'lying, fornication, corrupt practices, and . . . the public school system of sodomy'.[261] Again, Muggeridge's critique of the Profumo scandal was essentially class based; he argued that from at least the late nineteenth century vice and promiscuity had been 'more evident in stately homes than in semi-detached villas'. The relentless washing of the 'dirty linen of Debrett' in public, so evidenced by John Profumo and his kind, would ultimately spell the 'slow, sure death of the upper classes'.[262] As journalists working for committed Labour papers dedicated to exposing the negative moral effects of a patrician Conservative government, both Connor and Muggeridge understood the scandal as a traditional story of high and low life. They aimed it at a popular readership who, they believed, were eager to hear that the morals of so-called society were far lower than those of the middle and working classes.[263]

Connor and Muggeridge were not alone in their assessment of the affair; a polarized understanding of the scandal, with its contours shaped by the structures of upper-class power and class privilege, on the one hand, and London's sexual *demi-monde*, on the other, exerted a very powerful influence on the interpretation of events. Divergent interest groups drew on this framework in order to mount widely different types of moral arguments. Populists and progressives tended to view the episode and its cast of characters as archaic and backward-looking, in order to sharpen their own democratic vision of the political and sexual future. In contrast, traditionalists drew on similar perspectives but with very different aims, seeking to stabilize and contain the affair by reaffirming the importance of patrician leadership, while apportioning blame to guilty individuals like Profumo and to the malign influence of outsiders like Ward and Keeler. Ultimately, neither group was able to contain the moral dilemmas raised by a case that reverberated well beyond the contours of a conventional sexual intrigue.

Prominent members of society were vocal in their condemnation of the scandal, believing that it marked a crisis in their own patrician values. Noël Coward, an *éminence grise* in London life and a stalwart apologist for privilege, believed that the whole episode threatened upper-class prestige because too many authority figures had been compromised by their association with low-life characters. As so often, Coward's defence of traditional forms of authority also involved an attack on those who challenged the established hierarchy. 'Those miserable little tarts', with 'no standards left but the *Evening Standard!*' he exploded about Keeler and Rice-Davies, in response to a desperate letter from Valerie Profumo written at the height of the affair.[264] In his view these two young women were at best gold-diggers and at worst the lowest class of prostitutes, and he was vitriolic about the incursion of 'those disgusting girls' making 'pigs of themselves' into the upper echelons of society.[265]

Coward's emotional outburst of misogyny and class hatred concealed a more significant point: Jack Profumo had broken society's golden rule that affairs should never be publicly advertised but kept discreet, according to the conventions governing upper-class sexual etiquette. When Coward exclaimed, 'Poor Jack Profumo – idiotic Jack Profumo', he was not only voicing sympathy for a friend, he was expressing a widely held belief that the war minister had behaved idiotically by risking the exposure of private affairs in public places.[266] Echoing responses to the indiscretions of Lord Montagu and Sir John Gielgud a decade earlier, the cardinal sin for Coward was not that Profumo had committed sexual misdemeanours, but that he had been indiscreet about them, and then had lied publicly in a frantic effort at concealment.

As the affair reverberated ever more widely, with increasing numbers of society figures rumoured to be implicated, Coward began to see the scandal in much more apocalyptic terms, as heralding 'the almost universal decay of values'.[267] 'Values' for Coward meant the social and moral leadership of the English upper class. Rumours of 'sex orgies, flagellation, homosexuality, adultery and procuring' were not what shocked him, for he had always taken an urbane view of society's peccadilloes.[268] What outraged him was the way the case was being 'so widely and vulgarly advertised' to a mass public via the media.[269] This large-scale escalation of the scandal worried Coward enormously because it meant that the searchlight of negative publicity was turned on a group that hitherto had successfully avoided most attempts to diminish their prestige. It was no accident that he evoked the abdication crisis of 1936 as a point of comparison with the Profumo affair, because of the way the earlier scandal had compromised not just the monarchy but in his view the behaviour of a significant part of society as well.[270]

Coward's overall analysis of the Profumo affair was that its impact was deep seated and long term. He was one of a number of prominent society figures who believed that the scandal marked a watershed in English life. Norah Docker, the consummate populist who made a career out of advertising a version of the beau monde for popular audiences, clearly had the affair in mind when she listed the factors that brought 'England and its elegant age to an end'. Immorality, drugs, Mary Quant, the Beatles and Profumo were the root causes of the sudden collapse of what she referred to as 'my world, which we had restored after the last World War'.[271] Docker's sense of *après moi le déluge* was echoed by Lord Denning, who claimed that the affair was shaping a new chronology of twentieth-century Britain. 'Before and after Christine' had become a shorthand way of referring to the immense social and sexual changes of the late 1950s and early 1960s, he argued.[272]

Coward and Docker were both vocal apologists for patrician values, as well as being politically committed Conservatives. Yet similar arguments were made in reverse by leading Labour politicians, keen to demonstrate that the affair epitomized everything that was retrograde about Macmillan's government and about the informal society networks that sustained it. Echoing Connor's view that the scandal was driven by louche aristocrats and a supporting cast of deviants and tarts, Labour leaders sensed that Profumo's sexual symbolism could be annexed to their party's broader political agenda of social modernization. Richard Crossman, spokesperson on higher education and science and a long-standing critic of Establishment incompetence, noted with wry amusement how the usually invisible ranks of the English upper class had suddenly come into view during the spring of 1963, rallying round John and Valerie Profumo and 'doing everything possible . . . to try and save them from their fate'.[273] In a pre-election year, Crossman was convinced that 'the lying' and 'collusion' would undermine Macmillan's government and 'so assist in creating the conditions for a Labour victory'.[274]

Tony Benn wholeheartedly agreed with Crossman. Assuming an air of moral authority as Labour's election strategist, Benn believed that the affair was 'like wrestling with a chimney sweep'.[275] The murky world of call-girls and fantastic rumours was, he admitted, 'terribly bad for politics', but it would ultimately unmask the 'decay of the old British Establishment'.[276] Benn also felt that the Profumo revelations would help his party sharpen up their own egalitarian commitments. Like Muggeridge, he was convinced that in the long run the case would be good for democracy, because it could be used by progressive politicians to define a forward-looking social agenda that reflected the national mood. 'Republicanism', he concluded, with a side-swipe at monarchy as well as the Tory government, was 'on the move'.[277] Along with many other commentators Benn had his own personal motives for glossing events in this way. Having successfully fought a protracted battle to renounce his inherited peerage and keep his seat in the House of Commons, he was especially keen to demonstrate his commitment to modern democratic values and his hostility to hereditary privilege.

Harold Wilson extended this attack on the moral decay of the Tory governing class in his speech that opened the set-piece parliamentary debate on the scandal in June. The crisis was one of the first major tests of his leadership after succeeding Gaitskell earlier in the year, and Wilson revealed his skills as an adroit tactician and a committed political ideologue in his handling of the affair. Though his main argument focused on security and he warned MPs that 'we are not here as a court of morals', he repeatedly censured the type of metropolitan society that John Profumo and his circle represented.[278] Wilson's critique was aided and abetted by Wigg, the 'unofficial keeper of morals' in the House of Commons, who had thrown down repeated challenges to the 'permissive societies of our times' in his outbursts about homosexuality during the Burgess and Maclean affair and in his attacks on lax standards in public life.[279]

Identifying Macmillan's administration with London's negative underside, Wilson revisited many of the real and imaginary anxieties about the city that had circulated throughout the 1950s, posing them as urgent questions for national politics. He opened his speech by going straight to the disclosures 'which have shocked the moral conscience of the nation', identifying 'a sordid underworld network' that lay at the heart of the affair.[280] Ward was cast as the go-between linking high-ranking Tory politicians with 'vice, dope, marijuana, blackmail and counter-blackmail . . . violence [and] petty crime'.[281] At every moment Wilson was careful to stress how the scandal's cast of characters and their settings were antithetical to the values of a modern meritocracy. Returning in his summing up to the 'sleazy sector of society in London', he turned the spotlight on Keeler herself and on the world of commercialized sex that she represented. He told the story of an 'opportunistic nightclub proprietor' in the West End who was rumoured to have offered Keeler a job with a salary of £5,000 a week. 'There is something utterly nauseating,' Wilson taunted Macmillan, 'about a system . . . which pays a harlot 25 times as much as it pays its Prime Minister, 250 times as much as it pays its Members of Parliament, and 500 times as much as it pays some of its ministers of religion.'[282]

Wilson's assault on the moral consequences of Macmillan's affluent society, what he termed the 'social philosophy . . . of materialism and the worship of the golden calf', was a well-judged political attack. Careful not to criticize mass affluence or the expanded forms of consumer culture that had developed as part of the long post-war boom, he focused on London's shady, unregulated commercial sector. From the late 1950s Labour had identified striptease, pornography and illegal gambling as the negative consequences of greed and rampant individualism, associating them with the 'I'm alright Jack' decade.[283] The Profumo scandal enlarged

these anxieties, linking them to concerns about the impact of the capital's
property boom and disclosures about Rachman's business dealings. Local
Labour MP Ben Parkin claimed to show how Rachman's West End world
of 'white jaguars' and call-girls in 'mink coats' was reliant on the unseen
'victims of the free-for-all in inflated rents' and on north Kensington's sex
trade.[284]

Labour's challenge to the parasitic world of London was part of the
party's wider ideological campaign to construct a positive future for
Britain around an alternative geographical axis, and it was to have far-
reaching implications for political discourse during the 1960s, especially
after the party's general election success in 1964.[285] A language of possibility and aspiration that was designed to speak in electoral terms to
the skilled working and lower-middle class, Wilson sought to define
the ethical and egalitarian nation in powerfully provincial terms.[286] The
Labour leader's own very deliberate cultivation of northern values and
simple tastes, together with his insistence that he was neither a gentleman in the traditional sense nor from the officer class epitomized by
Profumo and Macmillan, meant that his political attack on the negative
features of London society took on a distinctly personal tone.

Wilson's political language was anti-metropolitan in a double sense; he
opposed the idea of cosmopolitanism championed by the capital's
bohemians and entrepreneurs, just as he challenged the world of privilege epitomized by Tory men-about-town. The eclipse of these values was
to become a defining feature of Labour's cultural project in government
over the next decade. *Queen* magazine, the vehicle for conveying so much
of the exuberance and excitement about elite society throughout the
1950s, anticipated the coming change in the political climate in its profile
of the opposition leader in September 1963. 'Out goes the hedonist', the
'greedy businessman', 'the landlords . . . [and] their call girls', the magazine warned; in comes the 'technocrat with clear eyes and clinical
mood'.[287]

Wilson's provincial, Nonconformist rhetoric was linked to a progressive agenda for change, but purity groups also drew on elements of the
same moral language to reinforce a very different reading of the scandal.
Campaigners seized on the affair as an opportunity to revive a traditional
conception of public morality, exposing the guilty cast of metropolitan
characters who threatened the social fabric of the nation. Making direct
links between Profumo and the great sex scandals and moral crusades of
the 1880s and 1890s, the Association for Moral and Social Hygiene glossed

the Profumo episode as a metropolitan tale of debauched aristocrats, evil procurers and the corruption of innocent women, a scenario that the great feminist 'Josephine Butler would have easily recognized'.[288] Casting Ward as a perverted London genius, he was compared to the original white-slave traders, a man whose career involved the 'most wanton enticement of girls and young women to whom he took a fancy, into sexual promiscuity'.[289]

Explanations of this kind continued to draw heavily on nineteenth-century typologies and social imagery. Framing the case via a traditional storyline and a recognizable cast of characters, public moralists sought to delimit the scandal's sexual dynamics in ways that pointed to relatively clear-cut resolutions. Purity campaigners hoped to make political capital out of the affair by reviving a language of popular nationalism that appealed to the idea of a virtuous community standing above party politics and sectional interests. These arguments were also championed by a wide variety of politicians, church leaders and press editors in their attack on contemporary moral values. Following Wilson, they marked out a strategic distinction between a negative and corrupt segment of London society and the moral soundness of the country as a whole. Mervyn Stockwood, the maverick Bishop of Southwark who moved between the conservative and progressive wings of the Anglican Church, defended the 'moral outlook of Victorian England' in a speech to his own diocesan conference held at Westminster in June. Stockwood's call was for a campaign to cleanse the 'national stables', especially the evil practices festering in the capital's 'high places', and for the country to 'bring ourselves under the scrutiny of the living God'.[290] Evidence from purity associations based in the provinces and in suburbia indicated that some local activists warmed to these familiar messages denouncing the decadence of London society.[291]

Senior figures in the Conservative Party also sought to revive an organicist conception of the healthy, moral body politic in a series of keynote public speeches and media appearances made at the height of the scandal. 'Britain is fundamentally moral at heart,' Rab Butler reassured national audiences on ITV's *About Religion* programme. Butler invoked Edmund Burke's eighteenth-century ideal of the Tory nation, insisting that politicians needed to bring the 'beauties of private life' back into the public realm.[292] Lord Hailsham, a former chairman of the party, endorsed Butler's views in his address to London's Public Morality Council; personal morality was essential to the well-being of political society, and when it was allowed to decay 'no mere cleverness' could save 'the state from ruin'.[293] Hailsham's belief in the essential interdependence of the public and private spheres and in 'objective moral values' threw down a challenge to the creeping relativism of the liberal intelligentsia and the moral laxity that he believed characterized Macmillan's handling of the case.[294] His polemical interventions during the scandal were designed to salvage a conception of public virtue and Tory honour from the havoc wrought by Keeler and Profumo. As Hailsham exploded in a famous BBC television interview: 'A great party is not to be brought down because of a scandal by a woman of easy virtue and a proved liar.'[295]

Not everyone agreed. By his own later admission, Hailsham was publicly mocked for 'being a bit of a prude about sexual morality', while a cartoon by Cummings in the *Daily Express* savagely derided such pretensions to righteousness via a satiric side-swipe at the recent goings-on in the metropolis.[296] Carrying the caption 'Visitez-L'Angleterre: Le "Can-Can" Anglais', it pictured a shocked French family on holiday in London, staring with embarrassment at a scantily clad Britannia dressed as a model, who winked down saucily at them.[297] *New Society*, the progressive weekly aimed at younger middle-class professionals, took up a similar theme, relishing the opportunity to expose the country's bankrupt moral reputation that had been brought about by the recidivism of its patrician elite. Journalists suggested that strait-laced London and hedonistic Paris had swapped their established roles in the aftermath of the scandal.[298]

It was this cynical mood that Sir William Haley set out to confront in his famous *Times* editorial on the affair published on 11 June, under the headline 'IT *IS* A MORAL ISSUE'.[299] Haley had established a reputation for moral rectitude as Director-General of the BBC during the immediate post-war years. In 1960 he had intervened on the side of 'decency . . . taste, and . . . morals' in the High Court obscenity trial of D. H. Lawrence's novel, *Lady Chatterley's Lover*.[300] 'Everyone has been so busy assuring the public that the affair is not one of morals,' Haley now opined, 'that it is time to assert that it is. Morals have been discounted too long.' His lurid picture of national woes claimed to reveal 'widespread decadence beneath the glitter of a large segment of stiff lipped society', and he went on to expose a dense network of unsavoury links between 'professional politicians' and what he luridly termed the 'fleshpots'.[301] Haley's Churchillian rallying cry to cut these associations evoked the wartime spirit of Dunkirk, insisting that the 'British are always at their best when they are braced'.[302]

The attempt by *The Times* to reaffirm traditional moral values was the first litmus test of public opinion about the Profumo affair; it was not an unqualified success. Responses to Haley's editorial revealed significant divisions that were beginning to open up over the scandal. The paper's postbag brought decidedly mixed reactions; many correspondents were highly critical of what they saw as the editor's divisive, sectarian morality. 'Your leading article today is the voice of . . . Puritanism,' insisted one of the paper's furious correspondents. 'It is a thread in . . . history which intertwines like a black snake with the other, gayer, more forthcoming thread which it tries to strangle.'[303] Younger members of Haley's editorial team privately panned him as hypocritical and out of touch.[304] Soundings from John Profumo's own rural Warwickshire constituency suggested that many local Conservatives also rejected Haley's arguments, challenging conventional political common sense that an attack on metropolitan morals would play well in the shires and middle England. 'Mr. Profumo's constituents are not Victorian moralists,' announced the *Guardian* in a direct rebuff to *The Times*.[305] Patrician Tories, forced into a tight corner by the relentless attacks on elite society, particularly disliked Haley's aggressive tone. 'Sir William Haley . . . seems to be obsessed with sex,' announced Randolph Churchill, reviving nineteenth-century arguments about the danger of purity fanatics, while Macmillan believed that Haley's 'nauseating' attitude had proved a spectacular failure.[306]

Progressive politicians from both main parties countered the traditional morality championed by Haley and Hailsham by stressing the need to distinguish between public and private behaviour in reviewing Profumo's conduct. As a progressive Tory, Macleod refused to condemn his colleague. 'I was, and am, a friend of Jack and Valerie Profumo,' was his response to an aggressive question thrown to him at the Press Club in Washington; 'I think it is a personal tragedy that this should have happened.'[307] Drawing on the Wolfenden committee's pragmatic ethical code, Macleod sought to distinguish the political and public implications of the affair from its personal dimensions, in order to confront more orthodox public moralists.[308] From the opposition benches, too, there was growing unease about Labour aligning itself with the moral lobby. Crossman continued to attack Establishment decadence, but he believed that Parliament and society were now more tolerant about the private lives of politicians, a state of affairs that marked a genuine social advance.[309] Barbara Castle, one of Crossman's close collaborators, insisted that she would be the 'last person to want to hound a politician for a sexual affair, as I knew that this could cover half the Cabinet of any government'.[310]

Despite their differences most politicians and leading editors were agreed that the scandal had precipitated a moral crisis, but only in a limited sense: in the metropolitan values that defined patrician culture. This perspective has also shaped the analysis of later political historians. Ben Pimlott has argued that the scandal needs to be seen as a significant episode in the updating of social attitudes because its exposure of sex and deceit at the heart of the Establishment provoked an 'inquisition into the mores of the governing class'.[311] Yet the crisis in formal politics was only one important strand in the affair. As events began to unravel, many commentators were aware that upper-class decadence did not exhaust the ethical and sexual dilemmas raised by the case. Anxieties about transgressive sex, Caribbean migration and commercially organized female sexuality that had surfaced throughout the previous decade extended the scope of the scandal, dramatizing these themes as part of a comprehensive debate about the capital city and its protagonists.

Much of the frisson of the affair was generated by the London settings that were exposed in relationships of corrupt and unhealthy dependence. In all the flurry of argument about the meaning of permissive morality that punctuated the case, one issue was recurrent: a widely held belief that the city's rapidly changing social geography occupied a pivotal role in influencing moral behaviour. Permissiveness understood in this way did not refer to the conventional markers of sexual liberalization, such as progressive legislation, the enhanced power of experts and entrepreneurs, or to shifts in personal habits and beliefs, but to a dynamic realignment of people and places in the capital.

Once again, different groups of protagonists advanced competing arguments about the consequences of changes that were understood to be both social and environmental. Self-confessed 'non-conformist' and 'outsider' Gerald Sparrow was a barrister and for ten years a judge at the International Court in Bangkok who returned to London to specialize in 'topicality-plus journalism'. His book on Stephen Ward argued that the cultural and sexual world revealed by Profumo and his friends exposed deep cracks in the facade of the Establishment.[312] He was convinced that the affair bore little resemblance to traditional Victorian and Edwardian scandals because of its distinctive geography.[313] London as it appeared to Sparrow in 1963 was not the divided terrain of overworld and underworld, with high- and low-life characters commingling in dubious sexual locations; it was 'made up of a Bohemian fringe, writers, photographers and young women, often beautiful, who are sometimes described inaccurately as models and sometimes as call-girls'.[314] Sparrow concluded that the case was the product of a 'new type of London', a world that had been reshaped by post-war affluence, by the social consequences of the property boom, and by the reorganization of the city's sexual economy as a result of the Wolfenden committee's stance on prostitution.[315]

Macmillan returned to many of the same themes from a different standpoint, both as the crisis unfolded and in his subsequent reflections on the affair. Under constant attack from the opposition and the press, as well as from many in his own party, for being 'old incompetent' and 'worn out' by the scandal, he was deeply anguished about the whole episode and about its consequences for public life.[316] Confiding to his diary by filling page after page with running analysis of daily developments, Macmillan struggled to understand how and why Profumo had behaved so 'fallibly and indiscreetly'.[317] He, too, sensed that part of the answer lay in London's changing social environments; as he saw it Profumo and his associates moved in a 'a raffish . . . society where no one really knows anyone and everyone is "darling"'.[318] Expanding on this theme in a television interview, he explained that the scandal revealed a world 'that has never come into my life before', a world 'that is quite foreign to me and very unpleasant'.[319]

Macmillan's claims to ignorance about contemporary social mores was disingenuous on a number of counts. He had clearly been warned about his minister's activities well before the scandal broke, while intimate personal knowledge of adultery in his own marriage (a result of Dorothy Macmillan's long-standing affair with Tory MP Bob Boothby) made him painfully aware of the type of moral fallibility that he castigated in others. The 'Boothby factor' may have made Macmillan flinch from confronting Profumo directly about a liaison with a call-girl.[320] Yet like Sparrow, Macmillan was convinced that the metropolitan settings uncovered by the scandal were neither conventional society assignations nor the West End venues of established cosmopolitans and bohemians. The new social landscapes were characterized by their deliberate cultural ambiguity, without any clear separation between licit and illicit activities. In his Edwardian youth and inter-war manhood, he recalled, 'you could be absolutely sure that you could go to a restaurant with your wife and not see a man that you knew having lunch with a tart. It was all kept separate, but this does not seem to happen these days,' he complained.[321] Macmillan drew attention to the extremely porous character of society in the early 1960s, as people and places collided in what was for him an alarming fashion. Equally, he lamented the collapse of the traditional privileges of the man-about-town, with his protected rights of movement and spectatorship across the varied terrain of London's social life.

The contrast between the Profumo episode and more traditional scandals was immediately apparent in the spring of 1963, because the affair ran concurrently with the denouement of the long-running Argyll divorce case. The extremely public divorce of the Duke and Duchess of Argyll in the Edinburgh courts was the subject of extensive media coverage. The supposedly insatiable sexual appetites of Margaret, the Duchess, together with compromising pornographic photographs of her lovers and herself shown as evidence in court (including shots of the infamous 'headless man' revealing intimate body parts), pointed to what the judge referred to as the promiscuity of the 'moderns'.[322] Suspicions of a link between the Argylls and leading characters in the Profumo case were aroused via gossip about Duncan Sandys, one of the Duchess's lovers, who was also believed to be a member of Ward's intimate circle.[323] Denning asked to see the Argylls' divorce papers as part of his inquiry, and he devoted a section in his report to rumours about the 'man without a head'.[324]

Yet what was striking amidst all of the revelations and sexual speculation that surrounded the Argylls' separation was how traditional their social world appeared in comparison with the much more contemporary associations that linked Keeler, Ward and Profumo. The Duchess's husbands and lovers were a familiar string of Scottish landowners, Italian and German aristocrats, and rich American industrialists, while her sexual itineraries covered the well-established terrain of Mayfair, English and Scottish country houses, Paris and Monte Carlo. The Argyll case was much closer to the world of late Victorian and Edwardian scandals, which centred on the adventures and peccadilloes of prominent upper-class characters, than it was to the Profumo affair.

Overwhelmingly, it was the linked themes of perverse masculinity, racialized cultural difference and pleasure-seeking female sexuality that extended and undercut the conventional meanings of scandal in the Profumo affair. Stephen Ward's character was the focus for these multiple anxieties. 'Ward: Pimp or Rake?' asked the *Daily Mirror* midway through the osteopath's trial.[325] The paper's headline probed Ward's sexual activities via a well-established template of unruly or disorderly masculinity, but journalists quickly concluded that his complex personality could not be contained by these traditional characterizations. Ward's rumoured exploits encompassed an exhaustive catalogue of perversions that were listed by the prosecuting counsel and assiduously relayed to a national readership by the press. There were Ward's interests in sadomasochistic sex (the tales of whippings and canings revealed in court by prostitute Vickie Barrett), his promotion of group orgies, a long-standing use of drugs and pornography, a voyeuristic streak that was supposedly evidenced by his use of the infamous two-way mirror left in his flat by Rachman, along with all the signs of effeminacy and deviancy that were marked on his body or evidenced by his character.[326] These latter traits were given relentless exposure during his trial. One of the *Mirror's* many front-page stories pictured 'the suave healer', whose 'slender fingers' had soothed the 'pain of tormented patients', exercising in 'pale blue silk pyjama trousers' at a friend's flat.[327] The accompanying photograph exposed Ward's puny, unmasculine body in a bedroom setting decorated with pink curtains and revealing an unmade bed that resembled a feminine boudoir or a brothel rather than a gentleman's bedroom (fig. 40).

Ward's perversions were polymorphous; his sexual character seemed to evade the more specific categorizations that were used to define and regulate sexual deviancy. One important consequence of this ambiguity was that it produced a fluid and expansive discourse about sexual dissidence that partly undermined established understandings of pathology. Ward, like Keeler, 'disarmed sexual categories and classifications'.[328]

Reflecting on the forms of transgressive sex that were supposedly practised by Ward and his circle, campaigning journalist Ludovic Kennedy, who reported on his trial, noted wryly: 'No-one . . . was interested in, or indeed capable of, doing it or having it straight.'[329] Observing the courtroom audience and the crowds outside at close quarters, Kennedy also believed that public reactions to Ward's exploits were qualitatively different from responses to similar revelations a decade earlier. Developing this argument, *Queen* believed that what distinguished this scandal was the way its version of 'mass produced libido', promoted by the capital's sex industry and circulated by the media, had gained a level of acceptance that would have been unthinkable in the 1950s. 'Sexual permissiveness', or what the magazine referred to as a 'do it yourself morality', had been encouraged by men like Ward and by young women like Keeler who now conducted smart business 'behind advertising nameplates of bland directness', profiteering from the Street Offences Act.[330] Neither Kennedy nor the journalists at *Queen* cited hard evidence for this supposed change of mood, but their reports began to raise questions about the long-term impact of the scandal.

The role of London's Caribbean population extended the meanings of the scandal in a different direction. From the moment the press announced Edgecombe's shoot-out at Ward's flat, speculation mounted about the two young West Indians who had been Keeler's boyfriends. Like the immigrant presence in the Christie case a decade earlier, Edgecombe and Gordon focused anxieties about London's changing cosmopolitan atmosphere and its implications for English culture.

Richard Crossman was entirely comfortable with the case as a story of debauched aristocrats, but he was much more concerned with revelations about the 'social seediness' of 'Keeler and her Negro friends', which he believed was one of the biggest shocks to public morality this century.[331] From the opposite end of the political spectrum, Evelyn Waugh also fixed on the miscegenist aspects of the case. Dismissing much of the affair as a rerun of earlier sex scandals, he admitted to his confidante Ann Fleming that the links in the story between 'the Minister of War' and 'a nigger' were unusual and highly disturbing.[332] Kennedy took up the same theme in his courtroom observations, describing Keeler as nothing more than a 'bin for the world's refuse'.[333] This image of Keeler as the receptacle for international detritus was heavily influenced by her choice of Caribbean lovers. Kennedy was a humanist and a politically committed liberal on most aspects of post-war social policy, but he too was troubled about Keeler's relationships with Edgecombe and Gordon. A 'teenage girl who counted negroes among her lovers was a thing that lingered in the mind', he noted; 'to many people it would seem about as far in depravity as one could go'.[334]

Anxieties about the racialized forms of transgression epitomized by the Profumo, Keeler and Edgecombe triangle became a major focus for media attention as events pointed to disturbing connections between the Caribbean cultures of Notting Hill and the West End's social elites. Press articles highlighting the overworlds and underworlds criss-crossed by Keeler portrayed her as 'a girl who had the homes of the great open to her' but who also 'sought the company of the bizarre and often squalid' section of 'London's less respectable coloured population'.[335] Keeler's continual movement between the 'colourful' Kensington scene of hustlers and grafters and her 'wonderful . . . high society' functions exacerbated public concern.[336] Ward was depicted as fraternizing with Gordon and Keeler at shebeens in Notting Hill before going on to socialize with royalty and Tory politicians.[337] The relentless exposure of Rachman added further links between north Kensington and West End society, because the proceeds of his property dealings exploiting Caribbean tenants enabled him to pose as a man-about-town. From a very different standpoint Johnny Edgecombe reflected on his experience of being brought into the orbit of 'top government circles' via his associations with Keeler and Ward, ascribing his role to the 'weird period' of 1960s London.[338] Casting himself as the 'black pawn' who was 'check-mated by the all-powerful white Kings and Queens of society', he remembered feeling 'the tension' as he was drawn onto the capital's 'aristocratic social ladder'.[339] All these perceptions pointed to the way London's cosmopolitan cultures were being reshaped by post-colonial migration, which marked out new urban connections between Caribbean migrants, Westminster politics and the lifestyles of the governing class.

From a different cultural angle the scandal provoked an extensive debate among women about the politics of marriage and personal life. These discussions shifted the affair's focus away from a concern with upper-class manners and morals and into the sphere of popular culture and the nascent feminist politics of the 1960s. Women's organizations linked to the purity movement continued to view the case as a problem of uncontrolled male sexuality and as evidence of a sexual system that exploited all women, but prominent women journalists produced an alternative reading of events.[340] Encouraged by Fleet Street's reinvigorated appeal to women readers in the early 1960s, columnists like Nancy Spain and Anne Edwards argued that the scandal needed to be understood from the feminine point of view, in ways that recognized the reality of women's lives and gave readers insights into 'real events and people, the things that really happen'.[341] Speaking a language of feminine populism, these writers evoked sympathy for 'Mrs. Profumo' as a classic 'wronged wife', claiming her for a traditional philosophy of marriage and stalwart wifely duty.[342] Writing 'woman to woman' in the *Daily Express*, Edwards also admired Mrs Profumo's 'flawless' performance as a public figure who managed to conceal her 'private feelings' beneath a veneer of carefully applied make-up and studied English reserve.[343]

Equal-rights feminist Mary Stott opened up a more complex set of arguments when she analysed the scandal as a story of modern marital breakdown. In a provocative women's editorial for the *Guardian*, Stott insisted that while a wife might have some sympathy for a husband who 'fell in love with another woman', she would be nauseated 'by the idea of his consorting with a prostitute'.[344] Did men understand 'this revulsion', she went on, 'or did they simply close their mind to it?' Stott emphasized the importance of women sharing their contradictory experiences of men in a rapidly changing world.[345] Her view of the case as an emotional triangle between the virtuous wronged wife, a philandering husband and the 'call girl . . . debased by . . . cash' dealt in what she believed was the reality of marriage for many women, and her message to readers was grittily realistic. In the 'present turmoil' of 'moral standards', Stott insisted, 'lifelong, monogamous marriage is clearly the best bet for a woman, even if, like all the best bets, it doesn't come off every time'.[346]

Stott's arguments raised an issue that reverberated widely in feminist critiques of the sexual politics of permissiveness during the 1960s; sexual freedom regularly produced casualties, and more often than not the losers were women not men. Many 'happily married women' wrote in with letters of support, but other readers were 'shocked' by Stott's 'lack of generosity of spirit'. Refusing to impute blame, they insisted that the scandal needed to be seen as commentary on the failure of modern marriage that involved both partners equally, rather than distinguishing between an innocent and a guilty party, as Stott implied. What the case demanded was human sympathy and compassion.[347]

Stott sought to prise open the gendered contradictions in the post-war ideal of companionate marriage that she believed were concealed below the surface of the affair, but her position remained exceptional before the advent of the women's movement in the late 1960s. More characteristic was the controversy over young single women and their seemingly enthusiastic involvement in London's sex industry.

Keeler and Rice-Davies appeared to be visibly empowered by consumer mobility, while much of their activity neatly evaded traditional definitions of prostitution. 'I have never considered myself a call-girl or prostitute,' Keeler insisted repeatedly in her press revelations.[348] Rice-Davies was equally emphatic in her best-selling disclosures billed as *The Mandy Report* (1964). 'Neither of us ever hawked our bodies for sale,' she stressed. 'We moved in the kind of world where the normal code of morals has no place; where there is no dividing line between good and bad, only that between a gay time and boredom.'[349] Both women claimed exemption from conventional morality because of the elevated rank of their male patrons.

If these two young women were not prostitutes, what was their sexual status? The question dominated Ward's trial, given the charges levelled against him of living on immoral earnings, but the issue also reflected a growing questioning of conventional ideas about female sexuality. Keeler and Rice-Davies seemed to have gained distinct material and social advantages from London's sexual marketplace.

'No simple differentiation between whores and non-whores is possible today,' explained the *Sunday Mirror* to its working-class readers in June; 'call girls with elegant flats, models, and nuclear disarmers will hop into bed as readily as prostitutes.'[350] Journalist Marjorie Proops, whose frank agony column was championing premarital sex, homosexuality and divorce by the mid-1960s, argued the point when she insisted 'a girl can't help noticing these days' how 'the wages of sin are anything but deadly'. Instead, Proops went on provocatively, payment for sexual services provided the things that most girls would absolutely love to have: 'minks, holidays in Majorca, villas in Spain . . . diamonds and scent at £9 an ounce . . . and people referring to you as a beautiful, fabulous model'.[351] Other columnists hinted that London's 'sweet life set' were not just 'champagne circuit girls', the starlets and stage folk who moved between Mayfair, Knightsbridge and the beaches of St Tropez, but ordinary girls as well.[352]

Arguments of this kind pointed to the changing character of the capital's sex industry by hinting at the potential benefits available to young single women. Light-hearted coverage of London life in a new genre of consumer magazines such as *Nova* and *Honey* endorsed the sexual lifestyles of girls-about-town, as part of a world of jet travel, modern luxury and high jinks.[353] These fantasies of feminine autonomy were given added weight when Helen Gurley Brown's *Sex and the Single Girl* was published in Britain in July 1963. A guide to 'living single in superlative style', it exhorted young women to opt for sexual independence as well as independent careers.[354]

Taken together, the overall effect of these competing accounts of sex and contemporary urban life was to undermine existing moral sureties, opening up fresh debate and sexual conversation, rather than resolving ethical dilemmas. This was what Michael Ramsey, the Archbishop of Canterbury, wryly termed 'the immense pre-occupation with Venus' that had surfaced as part of the Profumo scandal's revelations. Ramsey went on to admit that a prevailing atmosphere of moral uncertainty was one of the most striking consequences of the case.[355] Rebecca West, an assiduous commentator on so many sex and espionage cases, believed that this scandal differed from earlier disclosures because 'the community did not know what to think or feel about the Ward–Profumo affair'.[356] West believed that the lack of moral consensus about the scandal meant that it had released more general feelings of social uneasiness; a scandal of this kind might easily happen again, she argued, because the issues that underpinned it remained unresolved.

West's hunch that the Profumo case crystallized a prevailing national mood of anxiety was confirmed by political opinion polling and by a good deal of the media reaction. The scandal initially produced a massive 20 per cent poll lead for Labour, but by the autumn of 1963 there was a dramatic recovery of Tory fortunes. Political pundits concluded that 'the succession of scandal upon scandal and disclosure upon disclosure were producing fickle political allegiances'.[357] Across Fleet Street there were far fewer crusading voices calling for a return to traditional values than there had been in the exposés of scandalous behaviour during the 1950s, despite Haley's strident intervention in *The Times*.

A prominent editorial in the *People* suggested that attitudes to sex were more complex and robust than was often thought: 'The British . . . may not condone immorality, but they are not so horrified or naïve about the scandal.'[358] The country's new 'barrage of frankness', explained the *Evening Standard*, was part of a deep-seated 'public questioning of long-established Victorian moral standards'.[359] The paper's valedictory for nineteenth-century morality quoted approvingly from arguments outlined by anthropologist Professor G. M. Carstairs in his BBC Reith lectures broadcast the previous year. Agreeing with Carstairs's much-quoted insight that conventional 'popular morality' was 'now a waste land, littered with the debris of broken convictions', the *Standard* explained that the mood of national introspection was not simply negative; it was part of the search for a new approach to personal life in which sexual relationships would be seen primarily as a 'source of pleasure' and individual satisfaction.[360] Social researchers mapping public reactions to the scandal highlighted a move away from moral absolutes. A survey of younger professionals in the Cambridge area revealed them to be relatively unconcerned about John Profumo's sexual escapades and his marital infidelity.[361]

Many commentators welcomed this moral questioning as evidence of a more tolerant and open society, but for others the same facts indicated a deep sense of national malaise that accelerated into a wider debate about the 'decline of Britain'. A *Time* magazine editorial entitled 'Great Britain: The Shock of Today' dissected the problems for American audiences at the beginning of 1963, noting that for 'all their heady new affluence', the British felt 'disturbed and insecure'; their troubled mood was 'indefinable but inescapable'.[362] *Time* pointed out that the atmosphere of 'deepening national *angst*' had some very tangible underpinnings: rising unemployment, low productivity, a balance of payments deficit, coupled with General de Gaulle's dramatic French veto of the latest British application to join the Common Market early in 1963 and the humiliating weaknesses in national security exposed by successive spy cases.[363] Economic journalist Michael Shanks had laid out similar arguments in his Penguin paperback, *The Stagnant Society*, published two years earlier. Shanks warned that 'psychological factors' were now major impediments to the country adopting a 'greater degree of dynamism and common purpose', especially what he termed the tendency to embrace a 'narcissistic ecstasy of conservatism'.[364] Echoing Shils's and Sampson's readings of national backwardness, Shanks concluded that the problems lay ultimately with the culture of the political and bureaucratic class; their extreme cultivation of refinement and exaggerated sensibility, bordering on decadence, seemed like an elegant admission of defeat to the outside world.[365]

Arguments about inadequacies in the collective national psyche brought about by weak patrician leadership were taken up by novelist and journalist Arthur Koestler in his dramatically titled collection, *Suicide of a Nation?* (1963), which was written under the immediate shadow of the Profumo affair. Countering mainstream political analysis which held that national difficulties stemmed from material and structural weaknesses, Koestler agreed with Shanks that 'psychological factors and cultural attitudes' were the root cause of current 'economic evils'.[366] Together with his fellow contributors, who included Muggeridge and Goronwy Rees, Koestler returned to the twin issues of upper-class decay and collective psychic maladjustment.[367] The social and sexual obsessions uncovered by the scandal suggested that the country was fast becoming an emotional 'sick-bay', where the 'comforts of stagnation' appeared to outweigh the urgent need for change among the vast majority of the population.[368]

Anxieties of this sort remained largely confined to the political class and to an educated public, but a different genre of social commentary translated them into a wider currency designed for national consumption. The satire boom of the early 1960s drew together the political and sexual themes at the heart of the Profumo affair. Journalists on the cult magazine *Private Eye* and on the enormously successful television series *TW3* put together a more accessible language of social critique that exposed the deficiencies of the patrician elite as targets of ribald humour and ridicule. The early 1960s cult of satire was not particularly visionary, as David Frost, one of its leaders, recollected; its success lay in the fact that it remained deliberately just one step ahead of what people were thinking and feeling but not yet saying.[369] Cast as a harbinger of the permissive sixties by both its devotees and its opponents, it was 'anti-pomposity, anti-sanctimony, anti-snob and – blatantly – anti-Conservative'.[370]

Throughout the spring of 1963, in the thick of the Profumo rumours, *Private Eye* had been running stories about the sexual proclivities of government ministers and 'pansies and poofs' in high places. In April the *Eye*'s 'Last Days of Macmillan' issue pictured the Prime Minister as a decadent Roman emperor, reclining on the imperial couch, surrounded by scantily clad nymphs–cum–models and whispering, effeminate Tory courtiers.[371] Just before Profumo's parliamentary confession, *TW3*'s scurrilous coverage of the scandal escalated the rumours when comedian Millicent Martin introduced a sketch in negligee and dark glasses which ran: 'I was on first-name terms with top politicians and we often had discussions which went on far into the night . . .'[372]

In May, cartoonist Timothy Birdsall's double-page spread, 'Britain Gets Wythe Itte, 1963', was featured in *Private Eye* (fig. 41). Birdsall's visual theme focused on an elaborate dystopia of contemporary London, and he sketched it as an imaginary event in Trafalgar Square, the capital's historic setting for celebrations of national greatness and political revolt.[373] Centre stage in his extravagant urban panorama was the Prime Minister, eagerly tracked by television journalists. Macmillan was dressed in his familiar guise as a pseudo-Edwardian gent, declaiming manically about the fruits of prosperity from a soapbox attached to Nelson's Column. He was accompanied by a grotesque chorus of law lords, chanting about some of the major themes of the permissive society: divorce, capital punishment and homosexuality. In the background London had been partly transformed into a modern Americanized cityscape: the National Gallery, the church of St Martin-in-the-Fields and other familiar public monuments were dwarfed by the headquarters of modern corporate industry. Two archetypal ad men flew overhead, proclaiming banal messages about modern consumerism.

The foreground of Birdsall's cartoon contained every conceivable manifestation of London's sex industry. Here was a tattooed and bare breasted 'duchesse' disporting her 'million pound Dugges!' and Nell Gwynne-like strippers distributing 'swete pornographie' to lecherous businessmen. In the opposite camp there was a crowd of purity campaigners with placards demanding 'Burn the Homos' and 'Shoot the Nancy Boys', only to be confronted by young liberated homosexuals dancing 'our fairye dance'. At the heart of the melee was the editor of the *News of the World*, clutching his paper with its ludicrous parody of the Profumo scandal's sexual obsessions.

Birdsall, who died of leukaemia aged only twenty-seven less than a month after his cartoon appeared, was the leading visual exponent of the satire boom. Part of the same Oxbridge-metropolitan circle that also included the founder members of *Private Eye* and *TW3*, his cartoon drew heavily on the visual and social resources of the great satirists of London life, especially Hogarth and Gillray. Following Hogarth, Birdsall's modern urban subjects were depicted as grotesque parodies that dissolved the distinctions between high and low culture. From Gillray he borrowed a visual language of mock heroics, together with an elaborately detailed graphic style of fine-line drawing and the characteristic speech balloons that served as vehicles for satiric wit.[374]

But the content of Birdsall's satire was resoundingly contemporary; brash sexual actors and aggressive self-publicists rubbed shoulders with the doyens of elite society. Birdsall's message about London life was not simply one about the uneasy juxtaposition of contemporary versus traditional values; monarchy and aristocracy, the metropolitan gentry, Tory politicians and the judiciary, were all equally go-getting. They competed for the attention of a paying public alongside media moguls, sex workers, pop idols, and public moralists, old and new. Birdsall's inventive use of pseudo-Shakespearian English reinforced his point that contemporary cultural forms were contained within ritualized patterns of speech and social etiquette. With his stripping duchesses and entrepreneurial royals, Birdsall suggested that the representatives of patrician culture were themselves agents of modernization, as Britain got 'Wythe Itte'.

✳

Birdsall's sketch of the capital as a scene of cultural chaos dramatized the specific obsessions of the satire boom and the wider social confusion that characterized much of the debate over the Profumo case in the spring and summer of 1963. In microcosm, it also encapsulated many of the wider preoccupations that dominated the affair. A story that drew on the resources of nineteenth-century imagery and which most of the political and social elite sought to contain within the familiar contours of a Victorian scandal confounded public expectations, with its dizzying and unstable mixture of traditional personalities and much more contemporary characters. Metropolitan London featured as a major part of the anxieties released by the affair because the environments that the case pushed together generated an extremely powerful atmosphere of moral disturbance. The scandal was not just London-centred; the West End, Soho and Notting Hill featured as significant social facts in a national debate about sex and morality that centred on parliamentary politics and was orchestrated by the full scrutiny of the media. The episode represented a crisis of place and location, bringing to a head public concerns and social fantasies about the metropolis that ultimately reshaped the character of public and private life. The sense of moral turmoil noted by so many commentators was not simply the result of a battle between conservatism and progressivism or between old and new England; it was also a product of the dynamic interaction of these settings in the capital city and of the characters who moved between them. The case promoted contemporary sexual subjects via traditional scripts of scandalous behaviour in a convoluted tale of cultural modernization. The Profumo episode was neither the beginning nor the end of this story of social change, but it did mark the intensification of a process that had deep-seated origins and long-term consequences.

Epilogue

One very familiar, upbeat ending to our history of the capital city is the idea of swinging London. When the young American journalist Piri Halasz published her famous article advertising London as a swinging metropolis, as the cover story for *Time* magazine in April 1966, she introduced a neologism that fixed the metropolis in the world's imagination for years to come. Writing heightened breathless copy, and drawing on the eyes and ears of the 'switched on' staff at *Time*'s London bureau, Halasz's article was a panegyric to London as the 'city of the decade', paralleling the cultural excitement of *fin de siècle* Vienna, the 'savage iconoclasm' of Weimar Berlin, and 'thrusting' New York in the 1940s.[1]

Halasz's image of London as the swinging capital of the sixties is worth revisiting to illustrate its appeal and to highlight my disagreements with its conclusions about modern city life. In history writing and in popular memory, the liberalization of sexuality associated with London's permissive era is one of the master narratives defining the post-war period. *Capital Affairs* has marked out a different version of English modernity, challenging accounts of urban culture that have placed sex centre stage in the progressive story of the 1960s.

Time's atmospheric, colour photo-essay took the form of an imagined storyboard 'scripting the action' for the different urban 'scenes' that now made the capital move with 'verve and élan'.[2] Introducing his new young author as a committed Anglophile, writing in the best traditions of social exploration, Halasz's New York editor boasted that her journalism had been written over four days of the most dedicated participant observation.[3] Halasz's enthusiasm for cultural ethnography along with her outsider status curiously mirrored Alfred Kinsey's take on London's West End a decade earlier, but her conclusions were very different.

Halasz introduced her readers to the swinging city with a map that pinpointed the hot spots of London's renaissance. Partying late on weeknights at Annabel's, the ultra-fashionable discotheque in Berkeley Square, and in the even plusher aristocratic environment of the Clermont Club's exclusive casino, she then reinvented herself and her surroundings. She spent Saturday immersed in London's new eroticized fashion culture, shopping with the 'guys' and 'dolly birds' in Soho's Carnaby Street and on Chelsea's King's Road. Chelsea was the place to sample 'bird' boutiques like Granny Takes a Trip as well as the 'kinkiest' shop selling 'gear' for men.[4] Later, sitting in Soho's 'unpretentious but ever so In' little restaurants and in the new coffee bars that were springing up across the West End, the young American listened to the doyens of London's scene, whom she dubbed the leaders of a 'bloodless revolution'.[5] The old 'Tory-Liberal Establishment' had given way to a 'swinging meritocracy' based on youthful talent. 'Youth is the word and the deed in London,' Halasz announced. 'The war is over – the Mods have won.'[6] Halasz's deliberate name-dropping of celebrities on her party list was meant to show off the capital's commitment to a new-found social pluralism. Working-class success stories from the fashion and film industries like Jean Shrimpton, Vidal Sassoon and Terence Stamp rubbed shoulders with Princess Margaret and her photographer husband, while leaders of the progressive urban gentry were pictured chatting to the sociologists and TV executives who promoted themselves as the intellectual patrons of Harold Wilson's technocratic Labour government.

Halasz reported later that her essay was ultimately 'about sex' and that it was meant to have a lightly satiric edge, a quality that was lost in the earnest debate that followed about the merits and demerits of swinging London.[7] Certainly, 'chatter about sex' as well as the 'cheery vulgarity' of the sex industry loomed large in her account of a city that had 'burst into bloom'.[8] Predictably, at the top of *Time*'s list of must-see erotic venues was the Raymond Revuebar. Halasz pronounced Raymond's a 'totally uninhibited' nightclub, citing it as evidence of a growing disrespect for conventional morality, along with the 'dirty' but essentially 'healthy' performances from London's radical theatre and from street fashion's playful culture of narcissism – what she called 'a flash of leg and varicolored vinyl' (fig. 42).[9] Where Kinsey had uncovered a world of sordid prostitution and perversion, Halasz celebrated sexual fun.

She was serious, though, about her overall conclusions; if Britain had 'lost an Empire', it had 'recovered a lightness of heart lost during the weighty centuries of world leadership'. The end of Victorian morality meant a loosening of the country's traditional inhibitions. London now led the field in the 'art of living' and in the 'special quality' that was the

hallmark of all 'great cities; civility in the broadest sense'.[10] Economic
capital was yielding to cultural capital; the 'heart of London' was moving
westwards away from the City and towards a new elite whose collective
centre was somewhere 'between Hyde Park' and the 'statue of Eros in
Piccadilly Circus'.[11]

Time's upbeat conclusions about London were in stark contrast to its
story of national decline that had been aired only three years earlier. It
was not the only magazine to discover that the English capital had reinvented itself. Earlier rave notices about London as a happening city had
already appeared in the European press, and Halasz built on this genre of
urban publicity to produce a culturally sophisticated and internationally
influential account that was long lasting.[12] After *Time*'s intervention the
whole debate about swinging London really began in earnest, she
recalled.[13] Initially celebrated and then denounced as the product of
superficial journalism, the term entered popular mythology as something
of a joke. Nonetheless, Halasz's essay continued to attract the attention of
historians eager to identify the capital's leading role in the sexual and cultural changes of the 1960s.[14] Her story points to a very well-documented
conclusion to the histories of metropolitan culture charted in *Capital
Affairs*. One seemingly compelling outcome to the cosmopolitan mixing
of urban styles, the spectacular performances and the increasing chatter
about sex, and the new wave of consumer culture was *Time*'s idea of an
unstoppable 'social revolution', orchestrated by individualism and 'liberated by affluence', that made London the pre-eminent city of the 1960s.[15]
Explanations of this kind not only attracted aficionados like Halasz, who
identified enthusiastically with the changes, but also cultural conservatives
and traditional public moralists who attacked the consequences of the
permissive society.

Capital Affairs has presented a counter-narrative to this 'grand climacteric' vision of the post-war years.[16] Though I recognize many similar elements and environments as catalysts of change, I have resisted celebrating
them as the swinging tale of the 1960s. Unlike Halasz, who synthesized
her different 'urban scenes' into a confident narrative about London as an
exemplary progressive city, I have mapped sex in the capital as a story of
difference, dissidence and power. My account has highlighted sexuality as
a contested terrain, shot through with the divisions that marked contemporary England, and I have stressed that social outcomes were often
far from optimistic or forward-looking.

Many of the sexual stories covered in the book were not simply 'libidinous' or 'cheerfully vulgar', which were Halasz's preferred terms to desc-

ribe sex in the sixties; they were transgressive, sordid and threatening.
There were losers as well as winners from London's post-war cultural
revival; men and women became sexual casualties just as much as they
shot to fame as celebrities. Post-war London has often been described as
a 'soft city', without the political extremes and violence that characterized many other European capitals during the same period.[17] But this idea
of hedonistic freedom should not blind us to the structures of sexual and
social power that continued amidst all the excitement about urban innovation and renewal.

Halasz's vision of 1960s London conjures up the image of a group of
liberated, 'switched on' people moving the country forward towards a progressive future. *Capital Affairs* has not mapped cultural change as the
outcome of one single, dominant interest group driven by clear-sighted
goals. Instead, I see Establishment culture and government policies being
constantly undermined by men and women positioned well outside elite
society and Whitehall's sphere of influence. Young and increasingly sexually independent women, Caribbean newcomers and homosexual men
were key players in this combustible mix. Tense encounters between the
different groups who made up the fast-moving terrain of high and low
society were staged across the entertainment settings of the West End and
in adjacent inner city areas. Advertised to national audiences by the
capital's finely tuned networks of publicity, these cultural conflicts stimulated new blueprints for sexual identity among the customers and workers
who populated Soho's fashionable nightclubs and Notting Hill's happening scene.

Events and characters in the book have challenged another central tenet
of permissiveness: the idea that experts and entrepreneurs, working in
conjunction with enlightened public opinion, were forward-looking
agents of change. To be sure, professionals and sexual salesmen have featured prominently in this history, but their activities were not governed
by an overarching commitment to liberalizing social morality. Specialist
knowledge about sex was part of an expanding system of urban governance that combined well-tried methods of policing with newer modes
of control. The know-how of sexual experts and commercial innovators
needs to be seen alongside the activities of a different but equally influential group, the metropolitan social elites.

London's society networks and their associated raffish cast of characters generated their own scripts of sexual modernity; men-about-town,

go-ahead princesses, feminine adventurers and contemporary rakes were some of the most prominent personalities here. Halasz and other commentators recognized the importance of these society figures, but they tended to subsume their activities into a generalized dynamic of progressive change. The reality was more complex.

The metropolitan gentry and their displays of urban spectacle undermined traditional moral and sexual certainties, but the changes they introduced were more nuanced than the idea of the social elites getting 'with it', as the notion of swinging London suggests. Acting in uneasy and often bizarre alliance with less privileged characters, and projecting urban styles that attracted men and women from outside the upper class, society leaders intervened in metropolitan life with the aid of cultural rituals deeply rooted in London's history. The scandals and other transgressive events that erupted throughout the post-war decades were dynamic, but their impact challenges interpretations of this period that stress the inexorable rise of progressive social egalitarianism. The patrician characters dominating these cases were not simply backward-looking apologists for an aristocratic world; they were cultural modernizers who drew on the resources of the past in their efforts to change the present. Historians need to know more about the continuing influence of the social elites and their contribution to the remaking of post-war society, in a period dominated by perceptions of upper-class decline.

Social dramas pushing together high and low culture were played out in the glamorous and shady entertainment spaces of the West End, in the homosocial world of Whitehall and in twilight zones of the inner city. Their collective impact transformed the geopolitical contours of English culture. Soho and Notting Hill became flashpoints for moral anxieties about the changing sexual meanings of cosmopolitanism and the cultural consequences of decolonization. Home-grown bohemianism, European migrant culture and the growing presence of the Caribbean in London acted as critical factors repositioning sex in the national imagination. Halasz and other urbanists were acutely aware of the capital's 'patchwork quilt of differently coloured neighbourhoods and localities', what Jonathan Raban called villages 'inside the city' that produced their own influential ideas about metropolitan living.[18] This book has built on their insights about place and location, seeing urban life as a distinctive space of culture and power, not just as the passive setting for social action. From the 1940s through to the early 1960s many of the most significant sexual and cul-

tural changes taking place in England were focused on London, but this
was not the result of some natural metropolitan dominance nor of capital
city chauvinism. It was the product of time and circumstance; events that
began during the war and continued in the peace that followed recentred London in political life as well as in the national culture.

'London is the prophet's graveyard,' metropolitan historian Jerry White
has observed; it has regularly shrugged off the efforts of utopians to
reimagine it and planners to reshape its future.[19] Despite White's warning
about the perils of prediction, we can trace a number of routes out from
the histories covered in *Capital Affairs*. Many of these have multiple and
untidy endings; some are finite while others are by no means concluded.

The maelstrom of 1950s sexual politics forged a new system of governance that was one of the most enduring legacies to come out of
Whitehall. The Wolfenden committee's moral philosophy, a mixture of
high-minded principles and bureaucratic pragmatism, set the parameters
for legal reforms supported by successive Conservative and Labour governments that dealt not just with prostitution and homosexuality but with
a much broader portfolio of sex and culture as well. Policymakers and
political activists operating well beyond the liberal moment of the 1960s
continued to feel the committee's influence, because its ethical system had
won the minds if not the hearts of many in Whitehall and Westminster.

With the evasive understatement that was his hallmark, Jack Wolfenden
always played down the significance of his moral project, suggesting that
only a couple of decades later he and his colleagues were typecast as a
bunch of 'Victorian fuddy-duddies', with society asking in puzzled amusement, 'what on earth was all the fuss about?'[20] As usual, Wolfenden's dis-
claimer was intended to mislead. His distinction between the sexual public
and the sexual private, with its important caveats about adult consent and
behaviour likely to cause 'public offence', became part of the common-
sense of the political and bureaucratic class. Government responses to
pornography and visual censorship, to public sex in commercial entertainment spaces, and legal debates about the legitimacy of same sex part-
nerships were all regularly referred back to the first principles established
by the inquiry, especially inside the Home Office. The export of
Wolfenden's moral philosophy to Commonwealth countries founded on
English law was a further testament to the committee's political reach.[21]

Ostensibly, the Wolfenden committee represented the ascendancy of
'liberal and progressive' elements 'within the structures of authority', but

their sexual strategy was shot through with contradictions.[22] Masculine assumptions about free choice and movement supposedly exercised by moral subjects in public and private life, along with the vexed question of where to set the boundaries of liberal tolerance, were two of the biggest headaches for policymakers. They remained unresolved precisely because they were hotly contested, not just as abstract principles but also in the much messier world of real social politics. In the decades after the report's publication the women's movement threw down a challenge to liberalism's gender blindness in campaigns against prostitution and related crimes of sexual violence against women. Gay and lesbian campaigners and later queer activists pushed at the limits of Wolfenden's philosophy on the age of homosexual consent and over the restrictive notions of sexual privacy enshrined in the report. Moral authoritarians partly associated with the Thatcher governments also reignited opposition to progressive sexual reform. Liberal morality remained unstable, contested and subject to ongoing political and social pressures.

During the 1950s the state gave official recognition to a new type of homosexual subject. At the time, anxieties were focused on homosexual *acts*, but the political and intellectual context of the post-war years rapidly turned a debate about sexual activities into a discussion about identities and personalities, or at least about the links between the two. Peter Wildeblood's passionate declaration of himself as 'a homosexual' was an intimation of things to come. The subsequent claims of rights-based homosexual politics, along with the more radical sexual agenda set by the new social movements in the 1960s, returned again and again to the issue that became known as the identity question. Were sexual categories socially fixed or innate? Did the individual and collective take-up of sexual identities involve the expression of rights and character traits hitherto suppressed or denied, or was their adoption more strategic and provisional? What were the overall aims of movements organized not just around sexual demands but around the intense politicization of privileged forms of sexual identity?

The 1967 Sexual Offences Act sanctioned a discreet, responsible and heavily privatized version of homosexual selfhood, at the expense of all those individuals who did not conform to this ideal type, either in their personal life or in their political and cultural demands. It was a further testament to the influence of the Wolfenden committee that later campaigners were forced to negotiate the boundaries separating this officially

approved identity from sexual behaviour that was deemed to be defec-
tive and hence outside the body politic.[23] Wolfenden's legal litmus test of
acceptable conduct in appropriate places was applied not just to homosexuality but to many other sexual activities as well.

Changing patterns of surveillance and policing were important factors
in the subsequent history of sexuality; equally important were the changes
to London as the pleasure capital of England. Soho's status as the city's
most influential cosmopolitan quarter was transformed many times after
Daniel Farson and his contemporaries enthusiastically staked out their
claims to cultural authenticity and Paul Raymond opened his Revuebar.
Subsequent versions of bohemian Soho were driven by businesses marketing a wide variety of goods and sexual services to successive generations of customers and fashionable cognoscenti. In the 1960s and 1970s
the runaway success of Carnaby Street's youth fashion, celebrated by
Halasz, coexisted with a new and aggressive phase of the local sex industry. Pornography and call-girl prostitution, as well as live erotic entertainment staged by Raymond's showgirls, were defining features of Soho's
sexual culture, and they were underwritten by a fresh alliance between
local entrepreneurs, the Metropolitan Police and Westminster Council.

Halasz suggested that happening London emerged spontaneously out
of a 'creative mix' generated by 'swinging people', but as Raymond and
Vivian Van Damm were well aware, what was equally necessary was the
cultivation of a profitable customer base. Soho's much vaunted economic
renaissance since the mid-1980s has been the result of careful policies of
urban renewal and the deliberate promotion of an appealing cosmopolitan ambience.[24] So, along with youth culture and heterosexual entertainment, Soho became the venue for London's first gay village, in line with
similar commercial experiments across the world. Successive waves of specialized retailing and a modernized restaurant and bar scene also opened
up the area to a new generation of young professionals intent on using
Soho as a leisure extension of their West End workplace culture. At the
time of writing, and in the teeth of a grim economic recession, some of
Soho's spaces are being reappropriated for down-market cultural tourism
fuelled by alcohol and catering to more mainstream consumers.

All these developments built on Soho's reputation for cultural and
ethnic diversity generated by more than a century of cosmopolitanism.
In contemporary Soho food, sex and night-time entertainment are regularly rebranded with all the razzmatazz of innovation, but their promotion relies on established rituals of consumerism that are embedded in

the area's compressed urban spaces. Successive generations of publicists reinvent Soho for each new group of habitués, but their urban guides are grounded in the district's historically sedimented cultures laid down by earlier bohemians. Contemporary characters who lay claim to local spaces raid earlier scripts of city living and sophisticated behaviour via information about the area's celebrated personalities. The resourceful recycling of the district's selective urban myths is an important part of Soho's claim to cultural authority. These processes of making and living history now form an important part of the psycho-geographies of city life. They are carried by the personal and affective values that consumers invest in Soho's streets, buildings and intimate social spaces. Yet despite the enthusiasm for urban diversity, the sex industry remains a major part of the local infrastructure. Coverage of Raymond's death in the spring of 2008 revealed just how significant Soho still is for collective fantasies about sex and the national culture ('taking sex out of the dark corners of British life', as one obituary put it) and for the West End's real economy.[25]

Beyond Soho, progressive versions of cosmopolitanism have become part of London's bid to rebrand itself as a successful world city for the twenty-first century. With a sidelong glance at urban problems experienced elsewhere, the English capital is now lauded as 'one of the most tolerant . . . of the world's multicultural societies'.[26] Partly civic boosterism but also a testament to undoubted gains made in social management and cultural planning, London's cosmopolitan renaissance has been used to counter the recent terrorist attacks and to challenge the prevailing pessimistic mood about the future of Western cities. Political rhetoric drawn on by successive London mayors Ken Livingstone and Boris Johnson has built on this upbeat commitment to cultural pluralism and social inclusiveness, and it has emerged centre stage in the capital's projected status as an Olympic city, in preparation for hosting the 2012 games.

This cosmopolitan ideal now shapes high-profile cultural policies, but its unwavering optimism needs qualifying in the light of the history charted here. Cosmopolitanism was always more contradictory than the progressive version celebrated by successive generations of politicians and cultural pundits. From its eruption into late Victorian and Edwardian London cosmopolitanism was double-edged, implying not just a progressive commitment to transnational commercial culture but also a powerful idea of urban impurity and disorder. Both experiences coexist in uneasy tension in London today, and both are clearly visible in Soho. The capital's central areas are marked by high levels of social deprivation and crime as well as by glamorous entertainment and fashionable consumption. Soho's young homeless from across the world, drug users and female sex workers, exploited as part of the new trafficking trade from Eastern Europe, are as much a part of the cityscape as are all the attributes of London's global metropolitan status. Much of the area's night-time economy is fuelled by alcohol, causing major problems of antisocial behaviour, noise and nuisance. Cosmopolitan pleasures continue to rely on dangerous and transgressive associations with their negative underside. Twenty-first-century London reveals how pleasure and danger are part of the ongoing tensions of city life that continue to generate their own powerful possibilities.

Beyond Soho, the scandals that punctuated English life in the post-war years left a powerful legacy. Scandals, homosexual show trials and sexual murders were not part of the story of liberal England celebrated by Halasz, but a macabre reworking of tales of urban danger and Victorian melodrama. In the fifty years since the Rillington Place murders, heavily sexualized serial killings and spectacular homicides have continued as an all too familiar feature of public culture. The sadistic moors murders of teenagers and children by Ian Brady and his accomplice Myra Hyndley in the mid-1960s, together with the killing spree unleashed on thirteen women by Peter Sutcliffe, the Yorkshire Ripper, a decade later were two of the most dramatic cases. Incest, rape and serial murders committed by Fred and Rosemary West in their Gloucester 'house of horrors' were equally shocking. All these incidents and others like them aroused massive national and international interest, acting as the catalyst for renewed expressions of public anxiety about contemporary moral problems.[27]

These later ritualized slayings were different from the transgressive and murderous events of the 1950s. Set in the north and the provinces rather than in London, they were not stories of overworld–underworld encounters and none of them involved aristocratic or elite society. Instead, they addressed the consequences of industrial decline, the growing anonymity of English provincial life, and the sexual impact of dysfunctional families.[28]

While sex crimes moved north, sex scandals that twinned immorality with high politics remained London-centred. Westminster and Whitehall continued to be shadowed by the fall and disgrace of nationally prominent public figures, leading to claims that English politics was now the only place where such things mattered. In the 1970s Liberal Party leader Jeremy Thorpe, who epitomized a latter-day version of the man-about-town with his immaculate suits and silk waistcoats, was severely compromised by his friendship with male model Norman Scott; their association led not just to allegations of homosexuality but also to Thorpe's trial for Scott's attempted murder at the Old Bailey in 1979.[29] At the high moment of Thatcherism a succession of Tory ministers and MPs were exposed for sexual improprieties: Cecil Parkinson for an adulterous affair with his former secretary, Harvey Proctor for gross indecency after lurid revelations about his private life, and Jeffrey Archer for his alleged relationship with a prostitute.[30] All these individuals were eventually forced to resign from office, partly as a result of sexual misdemeanours.

Cases of this sort reflected the continuing influence of nineteenth-century codes of conduct that demanded moral rectitude from men holding political office, not the liberal separation of public from private life favoured by Wolfenden's philosophy. The media frenzy that fuelled these exposés mixed traditional sexual prurience with a revived tabloid discourse of newspaper ethics for disclosing sexual secrets, a formula that was compelling and socially corrosive in equal measure. Subsequent indiscretions committed by members of the political class have been treated less harshly, leading to suggestions that society has now 'lessened or removed altogether the social penalties incurred by the sexually immoral individual'.[31] After the Profumo episode the sexual dynamics of scandal changed; wronged wives and lovers were much less acquiescent, boyfriends and rent boys demanded a public hearing, and following Christine Keeler young women became extremely skilled in the art of selling lucrative self-publicity. The traditional casualties of sex had become empowered by the breakdown of social conventions that hitherto had protected philandering men-about-town.

A number of these later political affairs featured individuals who were recognizably members of the English upper class, but the values of elite metropolitan society were rarely on trial in the way they had been during the Profumo episode. By the 1990s scandals centring on the indiscretions of the aristocracy and the urban gentry seemed antiquated and passé, especially in the context of New Labour's efforts to update national institutions and public culture. Then an event occurred that confounded the buzz of modernization: the death of the renegade daughter-in-law of the House of Windsor, Princess Diana.

The roller-coaster career of the Princess of Wales revealed how the rituals of royalty and the upper class that were deeply embedded in the culture of the capital city continued to influence social and sexual values. Diana's life and death may have upturned the traditional symbolism of the Crown so carefully preserved by Elizabeth II, but her career drew heavily on the aura and mystique of royalty, updated for new times and new audiences. The 'people's princess' was a refusnik royal, a young woman in flight from the waxworks world of tradition and ceremony, who was nonetheless aristocratic in birth and manner and monarchical in aspiration.

The sexual and emotional turmoil of Diana's life horrified her adopted family and delighted her admirers in equal measure. Her story of marital revolt showed how the sexual options open to women were now very different from half a century earlier. Unlike Princess Margaret, the rogue royal of the 1950s, Diana went public about her love affairs and her treatment by senior members of the court. Denouncing the *ménage à trois* offered to her by her husband and his long-time mistress, she struck out as a sexual free agent and as a socially responsible individual. Diana launched few ships, but she shook hands with Aids patients and she was a committed public campaigner for a variety of good causes. Mobilizing to the full her prestige as a princess, she became an increasingly cosmopolitan personality who used and was used by the international media. She died a mundane celebrity death in a Paris traffic tunnel with her Muslim multimillionaire boyfriend, Dodi Fayed, by her side.

Diana's funeral refocused international attention on the turbulent story of royal London. It was a spectacular event that formed an appropriate climax to a tale of emotional and sexual defiance, and it drew on the traditional resources of the capital city as the setting for monarchy while disrupting some of its rituals. Watched by an estimated audience of two-and-a-half billion people in the summer of 1997, like the Queen's coronation nearly half a century earlier the drama required appropriate metropolitan settings to frame the urbanism of power and to make its symbolism meaningful. Diana's horse-drawn cortège, mounted on a gun carriage, travelled from Kensington Palace to Westminster along metropolitan routes and thoroughfares that were an established part of the invented tradition of royalty. Important family mourners processed on foot behind the coffin on its way to Westminster Abbey, the traditional Anglican setting for state funerals. These customs and ceremonies were as significant as the much publicized breaks with tradition: the Queen forced to stand on the pavement outside Buckingham Palace as Diana's funeral car passed by, the Union Flag flying at half mast on the staff above, and most of all the popular outpouring of sadness infused with anger at the Princess's treatment by her adopted family, which undercut traditional English reserve.

Diana's death appeared to represent a major contradiction within English society. On the one hand, it compromised the monarchy and generated powerful expressions of populist sentiment. On the other, public responses and private grief about the people's princess remained contained within structures of feeling that focused obsessively on traditional forms of prestige and social authority.[32] Republicans and democrats hoping for a more radical resolution to events were left puzzled by such manifest peculiarities of the English. Yet these displays of metropolitan spectacle testified to the ongoing cultural work performed by monarchy and the social elites in shaping influential public images of sexual behaviour and affective life. Equally, they embodied the contradictory impulses of tradition and innovation that still lie at the heart of contemporary London as the centre of the collective national imagination. Time will tell if the Diana phenomenon represents a finale to this sort of influential patrician symbolism or a new departure. Time will also tell whether London continues as the capital of majesty as well as a city of cosmopolitan modernity in the twenty-first century.

Notes

INTRODUCTION

1 Wardell Pomeroy, *Dr. Kinsey and the Institute for Sex Research* (London: Thomas Nelson, 1972), 407, 421, 427; James Jones, *Alfred C. Kinsey: A Public/Private Life* (New York: W. W. Norton, 1997), 757. See also Jonathan Gathorne-Hardy, *Alfred C. Kinsey: Sex and the Measure of Things; A Biography* (London: Chatto & Windus, 1998), 420–33; Helen Self, *Prostitution, Women and Misuse of the Law: The Fallen Daughters of Eve* (London: Frank Cass, 2003), 220–1.

2 Pomeroy, *Dr. Kinsey*, 419.

3 Gathorne-Hardy, *Alfred C. Kinsey*, 422.

4 Pomeroy, *Dr. Kinsey*, 415.

5 Ibid.

6 Ibid., 418–19.

7 Alfred Kinsey, Journal of 1955 European Trip, Notes, 12 October 1955, Alfred C. Kinsey Collection, Box 1, series 1, B, Diaries, Folder 1, Bloomington, Indiana, The Kinsey Institute for Research in Sex, Gender, and Reproduction, pp. 13–14.

8 Gathorne-Hardy, *Alfred C. Kinsey*, 422.

9 Kinsey, Journal of 1955 European Trip, pp. 13–14.

10 Notes of a Meeting, 29 October 1955, Committee on Homosexual Offences and Prostitution, Committee Papers (1955–1956), TNA PRO HO 345/9, pp. 12–13.

11 Kinsey, Journal of 1955 European Trip, p. 15.

12 For this tradition of social and sexual encounter in London see Judith Walkowitz, *City of Dreadful Delight: Narratives of Sexual Danger in Late-Victorian London* (London: Virago, 1994), 16.

13 Arthur Marwick, *The Sixties: Cultural Revolution in Britain, France, Italy, and the United States c.1958–c.1974* (Oxford: Oxford University Press, 1998), 5–7. See also from different perspectives Jeffrey Weeks, *Sex, Politics and Society: The Regulation of Sexuality since 1800* (London: Longman, 1989), 249–72; Lesley Hall, *Sex, Gender and Social Change in Britain since 1880* (Basingstoke: Macmillan: 2000), 167–84.

14 See Eric Hobsbawm, *Age of Extremes: The Short Twentieth Century 1914–1991* (London: Abacus, 1995), 257–344; Tony Judt, *Postwar: A History of Europe since 1945* (London: Pimlico, 2007), 324–53, 390–421.

15 Christopher Booker, *The Neophiliacs: A Study of the Revolution in English Life in the Fifties and Sixties* (London: Collins, 1969), 35–50. See also Mark Donnelly, *Sixties Britain: Culture, Society, and Politics* (Harlow: Longman, 2005); Mark Jarvis, *Conservative Governments, Morality and Social Change in Affluent Britain 1957–64* (Manchester: Manchester University Press, 2005); Peter Hennessy, *Having It So Good: Britain in the Fifties* (London: Allen Lane, 2006); Nick Thomas, 'Will the Real 1950s Please Stand Up?', *Cultural and Social History* 5, no. 2 (June 2008): 227–35.

16 See Betty Friedan, *The Feminine Mystique* (London: Penguin, 1965); Beatrix Campbell, 'A Feminist Sexual Politics: Now You See It, Now You Don't', *Feminist Review*, no. 5 (1980): 1–18; Rosalind Brunt, ' "An Immense Verbosity": Permissive Sexual Advice in the 1970s', in Rosalind Brunt and Caroline Rowan, eds, *Feminism, Culture and Politics* (London: Lawrence & Wishart, 1982), 143–70; Michel Foucault, *The History of Sexuality Volume 1: An Introduction*, trans. Robert Hurley (New York: Pantheon, 1978).

17 See Edward Shils, 'The Intellectuals 1: Great Britain', *Encounter* 4, no. 4 (April 1955): 5–16; Hugh Thomas, ed., *The Establishment: A Symposium* (London: Anthony Blond, 1959); Anthony Sampson, *Anatomy of Britain* (London: Hodder & Stoughton, 1962).

18 'Authors' Note', in J. H. Forshaw and Patrick Abercrombie, *County of London Plan* (London: Macmillan, 1943), vi.

19 Peter Ackroyd, *London: The Biography* (London: Vintage, 2001), 584.

20 Seth Koven, *Slumming: Sexual and Social Politics in Victorian London* (Princeton, NJ: Princeton University Press, 2004), 1.

21 See especially H. Montgomery Hyde, *A Tangled Web: Sex Scandals in British Politics and Society* (London: Constable, 1986); Patrick Higgins, *Heterosexual Dictatorship: Male Homosexuality in Post-War Britain* (London: Fourth Estate, 1996), 179–320.

22 See my own reappraisal of Foucault's contribution to the history of sexuality in the 'Introduction' to *Dangerous Sexualities: Medico-Moral Politics in England since 1830*, 2nd edn (London: Routledge, 2000), xi–xxvi.

23 For commentary on the traditional perspectives of post-war British history see Becky Conekin, Frank Mort and Chris Waters, 'Introduction', in Becky Conekin, Frank Mort and Chris Waters, eds, *Moments of Modernity: Reconstructing Britain 1945–1964* (London: Rivers Oram, 1999), 1–21; James Vernon, 'The Mirage of Modernity', *Social History* 22, no. 2 (May 1997): 208–15.

24 Walkowitz, *City of Dreadful Delight*, 9; Gabrielle Spiegel, 'History, Historicism, and the Social Logic of the Text', *Speculum* 65, no. 1 (January 1990): 59–86.

25 Gyan Prakash, 'Introduction', in Gyan Prakash and Kevin Kruse, eds, *The Spaces of the Modern City: Imaginaries, Politics, and Everyday Life* (Princeton, NJ: Princeton University Press, 2008), 2.

26 See David Feldman and Gareth Stedman Jones, eds, *Metropolis – London: Histories and Representations since 1800* (London: Routledge, 1989); Walkowitz, *City of Dreadful Delight*; Raphael Samuel, *Theatres of Memory, Volume 1: Past and Present in Contemporary Culture* (London: Verso, 1994); Miles Ogborn, *Spaces of Modernity: London's Geographies, 1680–1780* (New York and London: Guilford, 1998); Frank Mort and Lynda Nead, 'Introduction: Sexual Geographies', *New Formations*, no. 37 (1999): 5–10; Lynda Nead, *Victorian Babylon: People, Streets and Images in Nineteenth-Century London* (London and New Haven: Yale University Press, 2000); Patrick Joyce, *The Rule of Freedom: Liberalism and the Modern City* (London: Verso, 2003).

27 Steen Eiler Rasmussen, *London: The Unique City* (London: Jonathan Cape, 1937). See similar arguments in Lewis Mumford, *The Culture of Cities* (New York: Harcourt Brace, 1938).

28 For cultural analysis of the reciprocal relationship between high and low social and aesthetic categories see Peter Stallybrass and Allon White, *The Politics and Poetics of Transgression* (London: Methuen, 1986).

29 Michel de Certeau, *The Practice of Everyday Life*, trans. Steven Rendall (Berkeley: University of California Press, 1988).

30 Jay Winter, 'Paris, London, Berlin, 1914–1919: Capital Cities at War', in Jay Winter and Jean-Louis Robert, eds, *Capital Cities at War:*

Paris, London, Berlin, 1914–1919 (Cambridge: Cambridge University Press, 1997), 5. See my response in Frank Mort and Miles Ogborn, 'Transforming Metropolitan London, 1750–1960', Journal of British Studies 43, no. 1 (January 2004): 10–11.

31 Joyce, Rule of Freedom. See also Mary Poovey, Making a Social Body: British Cultural Formation, 1830–1864 (Chicago: University of Chicago Press, 1995); Christopher Otter, 'Making Liberalism Durable: Vision and Civility in the Late Victorian City', Social History 27, no. 1 (January 2002): 1–15.

32 For very different accounts of professional society in the post-war period see Harold Perkin, The Rise of Professional Society: England since 1880 (London: Routledge, 1989); Noel Annan, Our Age: Portrait of a Generation (London: Weidenfeld & Nicolson, 1990); Nikolas Rose, Governing the Soul: The Shaping of the Private Self (London: Routledge, 1990); Stefan Collini, Absent Minds: Intellectuals in Britain (Oxford: Oxford University Press, 2006).

33 See especially Report of the Royal Commission on Marriage and Divorce, 1951–55, Cmnd. 9678 (London: HMSO, 1955); Home Office, Scottish Home Department, Report of the Committee on Homosexual Offences and Prostitution, Cmnd. 247 (London: HMSO, 1957); Home Office, Report of the Committee on Obscenity and Film Censorship, Cmnd. 7772 (London: HMSO, 1979).

34 Annan, Our Age, 208–9, 342–3.

35 Birmingham Feminist History Group, 'Feminism as Femininity in the Nineteen-Fifties?', Feminist Review, no. 3 (1979): 48. For related analysis of post-war feminism see Elizabeth Wilson, Only Halfway to Paradise: Women in Postwar Britain (London: Tavistock, 1980); Martin Pugh, Women and the Women's Movement in Britain, 1914–1959 (London: Macmillan, 1992), 284–311.

36 Chris Waters, 'Disorders of the Mind, Disorders of the Body Social: Peter Wildeblood and the Making of the Modern Homosexual', in Conekin et al., Moments of Modernity, 139. The lack of an effective history of the popular press remains a major obstacle for twentieth-century cultural histo-

rians. For commentaries see Hugh Cudlipp, At Your Peril: A Mid-Century View of the Exciting Changes of the Press in Britain, and a Press View of the Exciting Changes of Mid-Century (London: Weidenfeld & Nicolson, 1962); Peter Chippindale and Chris Horrie, Stick It Up Your Punter! The Rise and Fall of the Sun (London: Heinemann, 1990); Matthew Engel, Tickle the Public: One Hundred Years of the Popular Press (London: Gollancz, 1996); Adrian Bingham, Gender, Modernity, and the Popular Press in Inter-War Britain (Oxford: Clarendon Press, 2004).

37 See especially Matt Cook, London and the Culture of Homosexuality, 1885–1914 (Cambridge: Cambridge University Press, 2003); Matt Houlbrook, Queer London: Perils and Pleasures in the Sexual Metropolis, 1918–1957 (Chicago: University of Chicago Press, 2005).

38 Stuart Hall, conversation with the author, June 2000.

39 Annette Kuhn, Family Secrets: Acts of Memory and Imagination (London: Verso, 2002), 79. For different memories of the coronation see Denise Riley, 'Waiting', in Liz Heron, ed., Truth, Dare, or Promise: Girls Growing Up in the 1950s (London: Virago, 1985), 239; David Cannadine, Ornamentalism: How the British Saw their Empire (London: Allen Lane, 2001), 174–99.

40 Cannadine, Ornamentalism, 183–4.

41 See Judith Walkowitz, 'The "Vision of Salome": Cosmopolitanism and Erotic Dancing in Central London, 1908–1918', American Historical Review 102, no. 2 (2003): 340–1.

42 See my own personal exploration of the 1950s in 'Social and Symbolic Fathers and Sons in Postwar Britain', Journal of British Studies 38, no. 3 (July 1999): 353–84.

43 Hennessy, Having It So Good, xvii.

44 Roy Porter, London: A Social History (London: Hamish Hamilton, 1994), xiii–xiv. From a similar perspective see also David Kynaston, Austerity Britain 1945–51 (London: Bloomsbury, 2007), 509–10.

45 Carolyn Steedman, Landscape for a Good Woman: A Story of Two Lives (London: Virago, 1985), 5.

CHAPTER 1   MAJESTY

1   For accounts of the celebrations on corona-
tion night see 'River Mirrors London's Feu-
de-Joie', *Daily Telegraph and Morning Post*, 3
June 1953, 1; 'The Queen Turns on the
Lights', *Daily Express*, 3 June 1953, 1; 'Plans
for Night of Rejoicing', *The Times*, 1 June
1953, 1. More general accounts of the coro-
nation that have been drawn on here include
Randolph Churchill, *The Story of the
Coronation* (London: Derek Verschoyle, 1953);
Richard Dimbleby, *Elizabeth Our Queen*
(London: Hodder & Stoughton, 1953);
Kingsley Martin, *The Crown and the Est-
ablishment* (London: Hutchinson, 1962);
Robert Lacey, *Majesty: Elizabeth II and the
House of Windsor* (London: Hutchinson,
1977); Conrad Frost, *Coronation, June 2 1953*
(London: Arthur Barker, 1978); Philip
Ziegler, *Crown and People* (London: Collins,
1978); Edward Carpenter, *Archbishop Fisher:
His Life and Times* (Norwich: Canterbury
Press, 1991); Kenneth Harris, *The Queen*
(London: Weidenfeld & Nicolson, 1994); Ben
Pimlott, *The Queen: A Biography of Elizabeth
II* (London: HarperCollins, 1996).

2   'A Glittering Scene', *Manchester Guardian*, 3
June 1953, 1.

3   'River Mirrors London's Feu-de-Joie'.

4   'Plans for Night of Rejoicing'.

5   For these multiple celebrations see 'The
Flowers and the Food Will Add to London's
Gala Occasion', *Sunday Herald* (Sydney), 24
May 1953, 23; 'Our London Correspondent',
Manchester Guardian, 3 June 1953, 10;
'Piccadilly Dances As Lights Go On', *Daily
Telegraph and Morning Post*, 3 June 1953, 12;
Frost, *Coronation*, 84; 12 June 1953, in
Graham Payn and Sheridan Morley, eds, *The
Noël Coward Diaries* (London: Phoenix,
1998), 214; M-O A: TC Royalty, 69/9/A,
Street Parties, London, May and June 1953.

6   These aspects of the coronation ritual, with
their connotations of mystic spirituality and
a more primitive idea of sacrifice, inspired a
range of public intellectuals to elevate the
ceremony to the status of an act of national
communion between the deity, the monarch
and her people. See Geoffrey Fisher, *'I Here
Present Unto You': Six Addresses Interpreting the*
*Coronation of Her Majesty Queen Elizabeth II,
Given on Various Occasions by His Grace the
Archbishop of Canterbury* (London: S.P.C.K.,
1953), 15–29; Edward Shils and Michael
Young, 'The Meaning of the Coronation',
Sociological Review, n.s., 1, no. 2 (December
1953): 63–81; Norman Birnbaum, 'Monarchs
and Sociologists: A Reply to Professor Shils
and Mr. Young', *Sociological Review*, n.s., 3, no.
1 (1955): 5–23.

7   Harry Hopkins, *The New Look: A Social
History of the Forties and Fifties in Britain*
(London: Secker & Warburg, 1963), 295.

8   For televised coverage of the coronation see
British Broadcasting Corporation, *The Year
that Made the Day: How the BBC Planned
and Prepared the Coronation Day Broadcasts*
(London: British Broadcasting Corporation,
1953); Jonathan Dimbleby, *Richard Dimbleby:
A Biography* (London: Hodder & Stoughton,
1975), 229–38; Asa Briggs, *The History of
Broadcasting in the United Kingdom*, vol. 4,
Sound and Vision (Oxford: Oxford University
Press, 1995), 420–32.

9   David Cannadine, 'The Context, Performance and Meaning of Ritual: The British
Monarchy and the "Invention of Tradition",
c.1820–1977', in Eric Hobsbawm and
Terence Ranger, eds, *The Invention of Tradition*
(Cambridge: Cambridge University Press,
1983), 101–64.

10   Ibid., 120.

11   A. W. Martin, *Robert Menzies: A Life*, vol. 2,
1944–1978 (Carlton South, Vic.: Melbourne
University Press, 1999), 281; R. G. Menzies,
'Many Nations: One Crown', *Daily Telegraph
and Morning Post*, 1 June 1953, 6.

12   'Opinion – From the Ends of the Earth',
Daily Express, 28 May 1953, 4; 'The Queen
Welcomes Her Empire Ministers', *Daily
Telegraph and Morning Post*, 28 May 1953, 7.
See also Martin, *Robert Menzies*, 231.

13   'Preparing for the Grand Day', *Daily Gleaner*
(Kingston), 20 May 1953, 1.

14   Wendy Webster, *Englishness and Empire 1939–
1965* (Oxford: Oxford University Press,
2005), 93. Speaking to the Commonwealth
in 1953, the Queen stressed that the institution was a 'world-wide fellowship of nations
of a type never seen before': Tom Fleming,

ed., *Voices Out of the Air: The Royal Christmas Broadcasts 1932–1981* (London: Heinemann, 1981), 74.

15　'From All Parts of the Globe They Come', *Daily Gleaner*, 26 May 1953, 1; 'The Crowning of the Queen', *Daily Gleaner: Coronation Supplement*, 30 May 1953, 1.

16　'Thousands Admire Decorated London', *Sydney Morning Herald*, 26 May 1953, 3; Martin, *Robert Menzies*, 231.

17　'Coronation Route', *Toronto Daily Star*, 28 May 1953, 1. In the general media build-up to the coronation which took place across the Commonwealth, the Indian press were conspicuous for their studied lack of interest; see 'A Letter from London', *Times of India*, 30 May 1953, 6; 'Britain and the Coronation', *Times of India*, 14 June 1953, 8.

18　'Britain and the Coronation'.

19　Cannadine, 'Context, Performance and Meaning of Ritual', 157.

20　The coronation coincided with what some historians have described as a short-lived imbalance between the new superpowers; see David Adamson, *The Last Empire: Britain and the Commonwealth* (London: Tauris, 1989), 118; Pimlott, *Queen*, 203.

21　Joan Erskine, 'Great Britain', in Eugene Fodor, ed., *Woman's Guide to Europe*, Continental edn (New York: Fodor's Modern Guides, 1953), 185.

22　Ibid.

23　'Eve Perrick Joins the "They're Here" Theme', *Daily Express*, 23 May 1953, 3.

24　'Encore', *Evening Standard*, 11 December 1953, 5.

25　Louis Stanley, 'London By Night', *Queen*, 4 November 1953, 30.

26　See Catering Establishments (Colour Bar), 14 December 1953, *Parliamentary Debates (Hansard), House of Commons Official Report*, 5th ser., vol. 522, session 1953–4 (London: HMSO, 1954), cols 24–5; 'Colour in the Hotels', *Evening Standard*, 15 December 1953, 5.

27　Leary Constantine, *Colour Bar* (London: Stanley Paul, 1954), 67.

28　See Anthony Richmond, *Colour Prejudice in Britain: A Study of West Indian Workers in Liverpool, 1941–1951* (London: Routledge &

Kegan Paul, 1954), 18; Ruth Glass, *Newcomers: The West Indians in London* (London: Centre for Urban Studies and George Allen & Unwin, 1960), 41.

29　See Nicholas Mosley, *Beyond the Pale: Sir Oswald Mosley and Family 1933–1980* (London: Secker & Warburg, 1983), 302–8; Edward Pilkington, *Beyond the Mother Country: West Indians and the Notting Hill White Riots* (London: Tauris, 1988), 118.

30　Pimlott, *Queen*, 212. For the Unionist symbolism in the Queen's coronation dress see Frost, *Coronation*, 52–3.

31　Arthur Bryant, 'Our Notebook', *Illustrated London News*, 13 June 1953, 974. See also Bryant, 'Our Notebook', *Illustrated London News*, 30 May 1953, 854.

32　M–O A: TC Royalty, 69/5/M, Pre-Coronation Diaries, Sheffield, 21 April 1953, and M–O A: TC Royalty, 69/5/L, Interviews Regarding Coronation Souvenirs, May 1953. For commentary on the marginalization of the provinces see Ziegler, *Crown and People*, 104, 120.

33　M–O A: TC Royalty, 69/5/L, Interviews Regarding Coronation Souvenirs.

34　'The Real Britain', *Daily Worker*, 1 June 1953, 1.

35　'Harry Pollitt on the Coronation', *Daily Worker*, 2 June 1953, 3.

36　Becky Conekin, *'The Autobiography of a Nation': The 1951 Festival of Britain* (Manchester: Manchester University Press, 2003). See also Mary Banham and Bevis Hillier, eds, *A Tonic to the Nation: The Festival of Britain 1951* (London: Thames & Hudson, 1976).

37　Tom Nairn, *The Enchanted Glass: Britain and its Monarchy* (London: Radius, 1988), 287. Though post-coronation events involved royal visits to the other capital cities of the United Kingdom and a tour around England, these efforts to define the programme as inclusive did not undercut the essentially London-based nature of the celebrations.

38　M–O A: TC Royalty, 69/4/E, Coronation Decorations, Comments on Decorations in Central London, 25 May 1953.

39　'A Traveller's Dream of Home', *Daily Express*, 26 May 1953, 4.

40 Alistair Cooke, 'As America Sees It', *Manchester Guardian*, 2 June 1953, 4. See also Alistair Cooke, *America Observed: The Newspaper Years of Alistair Cooke Selected and Introduced by Ronald A. Wells* (London: Reinhardt, 1988); Nick Clarke, *Alistair Cooke: The Biography* (London: Weidenfeld & Nicolson, 1999).

41 Malcolm Muir, 'Britain Rediscovers Herself', *Daily Telegraph and Morning Post*, 4 June 1953, 6.

42 Arthur Bryant, 'Throne and People', *Sunday Times*, 16 November 1947, 4.

43 For the Elizabethan revival in music see Heather Wiebe, ' "Now and England": Britten's *Gloriana* and the "New Elizabethans" ', *Cambridge Opera Journal* 17, no. 2 (2005): 141–72. For the performance of *The Triumph of Oriana* see Frost, *Coronation*, 84.

44 Britten's *Gloriana*, unlike most of the other Tudor revivalism, did not receive favourable reviews, partly because the composer's treatment of the ageing Elizabeth I and her relationship with the young Earl of Essex was seen by critics as inappropriate for a celebratory national occasion. See Humphrey Carpenter, *Benjamin Britten: A Biography* (London: Faber & Faber, 1992), 314–28; Christopher Headington, *Peter Pears: A Biography* (London: Faber & Faber, 1992), 166; Wiebe, ' "Now and England" '.

45 Advert, *Illustrated London News*, 30 May 1953, 899.

46 Philip Gibbs, *The New Elizabethans* (London: Hutchinson, 1953), 13.

47 Ibid. See also Philip Gibbs, *Life's Adventure* (London: Angus and Robertson, 1957), 31.

48 For the position of science and technology in the Elizabethan revival see R. J. Unstead, *People in History* (London: Adam and Charles Black, 1955); Robert Bud, 'Penicillin and the New Elizabethans', *British Journal for the History of Science* 31 (1988): 329–31.

49 'Queen Elizabeth's First Christmas Broad-cast', *Illustrated London News*, 3 January 1953, 4.

50 Cannadine, 'Context, Performance and Meaning of Ritual', 153.

51 'Historic Event in Television', *The Times*, 3 June 1953, 17; British Broadcasting Corporation, *Year that Made the Day*.

52 Peter Hansen, 'Coronation Everest: The Empire and Commonwealth in the "Second Elizabethan Age" ', in Stuart Ward, ed., *British Culture and the End of Empire* (Manchester: Manchester University Press, 2001), 62.

53 Robert Lacey, *Royal: Her Majesty Queen Elizabeth II* (London: Little, Brown, 2002), 189.

54 Richard Greenough, 'Stop Press New York', *Queen*, 8 April 1953, 38.

55 'Opinion', *Evening Standard*, 23 May 1953, 4; 'Crowning Year for the Airlines', *Daily Express*, 22 May 1953, 6; E.V. Parrott, *A Pocket History and Guide to Heathrow Airport, London* (Rickmansworth: EP Publications, 1977).

56 'Pledge to London', *Evening Standard*, 10 November 1953, 4.

57 'The Heart of London', *Evening Standard*, 19 February 1953, 4.

58 'The Scarred City, 1953', *Evening Standard*, 19 February 1953, 6.

59 On these new post-war office blocks see Simon Bradley and Nikolaus Pevsner, *London 1: The City of London*, new edn (London: Penguin, 1997), 152.

60 'An Eye for a Pretty Flower', *Daily Express*, 21 May 1953, 3.

61 Jacqueline Bouvier, article for *Times-Herald*, quoted in Carl Sferrazza Anthony, *As We Remember Her: Jacqueline Kennedy Onassis in the Words of her Family and Friends* (New York: HarperCollins, 1997), 76.

62 Colin McIver, 'End of the Season', *Queen*, 12 August 1953, 18; Sacheverell Sitwell, 'This Year of Grace', *Queen*, 18 November 1953, 44.

63 M-O A: TC Royalty, 69/5/A, Coronation and the Press, London, 18 February 1953, 10 April 1953.

64 M-O A: TC Royalty, 69/5/A, Coronation and the Press, Donald Peers Programme, Sunday Afternoon Radio, 29 March 1953; Ziegler, *Crown and People*, 104.

65 'Reception for the Queen at County Hall', *Queen*, 15 July 1953, 8.

66 'Mr Magic . . . Waves a Wand Over London', *Daily Mirror*, 25 May 1953, 4; 'Nellie in Wonderland', *Daily Mirror*, 30 May 1953, 6.

67 Ziegler, *Crown and People*, 114.

68 24 February 1953, in Lord Moran, *Winston Churchill: The Struggle for Survival 1940–1965* (London: Constable, 1966), 403.

69 Princess Margaret, quoted in Pimlott, *Queen*, 193.

70 Arthur Bryant, 'Our Notebook', *Illustrated London News*, 14 March 1953, 388.

71 'Coronation Year Grooming', *Illustrated London News*, 24 January 1953, 137.

72 M-O A: TC Royalty, 69/9/C, General Observations and Overheards, Lillie Walk Fulham Coronation Decorations, 30 May 1953.

73 Ibid., p. 6.

74 Moran, *Winston Churchill*, 403.

75 In February the news that sweets were to come off the ration (for the first time since 1942) was a minor cause for celebration, especially among children. One firm in Clapham distributed 150 pounds of lollipops to children: BBC, 'On This Day 5 February, 1953, Sweet Rationing Ends in Britain', http://news.bbc.co.uk/onthisday/hi/dates/stories/february/5/newsid_2737000/2737731.stm (accessed 22 August 2006).

76 M-O A: TC Royalty, 69/4/A, Observation of Shops, Coronation Decorations and Posters, Regent Street, 19 May 1953.

77 Conservative Research Department, *Three Years' Work: Achievements of the Conservative Government*, quoted in Ina Zweiniger-Bargielowska, *Austerity in Britain: Rationing, Controls, and Consumption, 1939–1955* (Oxford: Oxford University Press, 2000), 234.

78 M-O A: TC Royalty, 69/8/F, Economic Effects of the Coronation, 1953. For parliamentary criticism see Mr. Grimmond, Coronation Celebrations (Cost), 27 November 1952; Mr. Emrys Hughes to Minister of Works, Coronation Expenditure (written answer), 2 December 1952, *Parliamentary Debates (Hansard), House of Commons Official Report*, 5th ser., vol. 508, session 1952–3 (London: HMSO, 1952), cols 71, 138.

79 Sex crimes and pornography are dealt with below. For immigrant drug trafficking and pimping see Robert Fabian, *London After Dark: An Intimate Record of Night Life in London, and a Selection of Crime Stories from the Case Book of Ex-Superintendent Robert Fabian* (London: Naldrett Press, 1954), 36–43.

For Soho's gangland see Duncan Webb, 'Soho – Albert Dimes Takes the Lid Off', *People*, 2 October 1955, 1. For unmarried mothers see Paddington Council of Social Service, Family Service Units for Problem Families, 16 January 1953, London Metropolitan Archives, ACC 1888/53, London Council of Social Service, LCSS Administration, Correspondence Files, 1950–60; Family Welfare Association, *Eighty-First Annual Report . . . October 1 1946–September 30 1949* (London: Family Welfare Association, undated), 7. For London's Teddy Boys see 'The Leader of the Edwardians', *Evening Standard*, 22 September 1953, 1; 'Outbreaks of Violence due to Moral Sickness', *Clapham Observer*, 9 October 1953, 7.

80 See Chief Superintendent Z Division (Croydon), Drunkenness, 5 June 1951, Drunkenness: Commissioner's Views as to the Cause of Present Trends of Increase (1951–1952), TNA PRO MEPO 2/8946. Sir Harold Scott, Commissioner of the Metropolitan Police between 1945 and 1953, isolated 'petty dishonesty' as a major problem for police work: Harold Scott, *Scotland Yard* (London: Andre Deutsch, 1954), 12. An international criminal police commission identified 'fatalism and existentialism' among the causes influencing the rise of sex crimes across Europe: International Criminal Police Commission, 21st General Assembly, Stockholm, 9–12 June 1952, General Report re. Increase of Sexual Crimes after the Second World War to be Submitted to the General Assembly (1952), TNA PRO MEPO 2/9000, p. 16.

81 International Criminal Police Commission, General Report re. Increase of Sexual Crimes, pp. 6–11, 16.

82 See George Chauncey, 'The Child Molester, the Delinquent, and the Urban Jungle: Notes towards an Analysis of the Homosexual Specter Haunting Postwar New York and Postwar Urban Studies', unpublished paper to the Urban Atlantic Seminar, New York University, November 2005.

83 Chief Superintendent C Division, Prostitutes, Homosexuals, Pornography and Rowdyism in the West End, 30 October 1952,

Vice at Piccadilly Circus and Surrounding Area (1952–1953), TNA PRO MEPO 2/9367.

84 For similar moral exposés during the run-up to the coronation of George VI see 'Bottle Parties: Court Proceedings Against 26 Clubs', *The Times*, 22 January 1937, 11; 'Raid on Barn Club', *The Times*, 30 January 1937, 9; 'Soho Club Struck Off the Register', *The Times*, 17 March 1937, 13.

85 A full account of this incident is preserved in TNA PRO MEPO 2/9367.

86 James Maxwell to Sir Alexander Maxwell, 6 October 1952, TNA PRO MEPO 2/9367. For La Prade see 'Malcolm La Prade, the Man from Cook's', *New York Times*, 13 July 1974, 26.

87 J. Maxwell to A. Maxwell.

88 Ibid.

89 Ibid.

90 For accounts of American visitors to London see Henry Steele Commager, *Britain Through American Eyes* (London: Bodley Head, 1974), and for American sociological tourism in Europe see Daniel Rodgers, *Atlantic Crossings: Social Politics in a Progressive Age* (Cambridge, MA, and London: Belknap Press of Harvard University Press, 1998), 160–4, 208.

91 J. Maxwell to A. Maxwell.

92 David Maxwell Fyfe, *Virtue, the State and the Family* (n.p.: Home Office Library collection, 1954), 9. See also his *Political Adventure: The Memoirs of the Earl of Kilmuir* (London: Weidenfeld & Nicolson, 1964), 6, 165, 198.

93 See Home Office, *Report of the Commissioner of Police for the Metropolis for the Year 1945*, Cmnd. 6871 (London: HMSO, 1946), 4. The wartime and post-war crime statistics were rather more uneven than some public commentaries suggested, a point that Scott acknowledged. There was a fairly steady increase in all indictable crimes in the Metropolitan Police district until 1941, then a fall in 1942–3, and after that a large increase, bringing the total to a record level of 128,954 offences in 1945. Figures slowly fell again until 1949–50, when there was a fall almost to 1941 levels. In 1951 the trend was reversed and there was a substantial rise,

followed by a moderate fall in 1952. The great majority of crimes were against property, but crimes against the person also increased, especially woundings and sexual offences. See Scott, *Scotland Yard*, 58–9. For commentary see Home Office, 'Crime: Return to an Address of The House of Lords dated 23 March, 1950', *Papers Relating to the Large Number of Crimes Accompanied by Violence Occurring in Large Cities*, Parliamentary Papers, House of Lords, Session 1950, no. 121; Mr. Ede, Home Secretary, Criminal Justice Bill, Second Reading, 27 November 1947, *Parliamentary Debates (Hansard) House of Commons Official Report*, 5th ser., vol. 444, session 1947–8 (London: HMSO, 1947), cols 2131–2.

94 Reported unnatural offences and attempts to commit those offences, including indecency between males, totalled 512 in 1951, 228.6 per cent higher than the figures for 1938; see Home Office, *Report of the Commissioner of Police for the Metropolis for the Year 1951*, Cmnd. 8634 (London: HMSO, 1952), 45; Home Office, *Report . . . 1945*, 4; Home Office, *Report . . . 1947*, Cmnd. 7406 (London: HMSO, 1948), 38. The increase in homosexual offences (including buggery, indecent assault and gross indecency) to 736 in 1951 was a rise of over 300 per cent; see Scott, *Scotland Yard*, 60.

95 Stressing that his force now confined their interventions to cases of 'open scandal' or to the 'corruption of boys and young men', Scott insisted that such incidents were no longer treated 'with the same repugnance as in the past': Scott, *Scotland Yard*, 61.

96 Ibid.

97 For commentary on the figures and their relationship to the supposed growing police offensive against homosexual men in the 1940s and early 1950s see Jeffrey Weeks, *Sex, Politics and Society: The Regulation of Sexuality since 1800* (London: Longman, 1989), 240; Matt Houlbrook, *Queer London: Perils and Pleasures in the Sexual Metropolis, 1918–1957* (Chicago: University of Chicago Press, 2005), 33–5.

98 James Scott, *Seeing Like a State: How Certain Schemes to Improve the Human Condition Have*

Failed (New Haven and London: Yale University Press, 1998), 1–2.

99 Thorsten Sellin, 'The Significance of Records of Crime', *Law Quarterly Review* 67 (1951): 489. Sellin's paper was initially delivered as a lecture to the Department of Criminal Science, University of Cambridge, in March 1951.

100 Ibid., 494. See also M. Grünhut, 'Statistics in Criminology', *Journal of the Royal Statistical Society*, series A (General) 114, no. 2 (1951): 149–50.

101 Leon Radzinowicz, *Sexual Offences: A Report of the Cambridge Department of Criminal Science* (London: Macmillan, 1957), xv. Radzinowicz's study of sexual offences began in 1950 and focused on fourteen police districts in England and Wales. The areas covered included both rural and suburban communities, but most of the data collected was from London and other cities. Two-thirds of cases involved indictable offences.

102 For the immediate response of the police and the Home Office see Superintendent C Division to Commander 1, 30 October 1952; Sir Harold Scott to Sir Alexander Maxwell, 13 November 1952; JHW, Copy of Minute on H.O. pps. 976501, 20 October 1952, TNA PRO MEPO 2/9367. For the Home Secretary's speech see Maxwell Fyfe, *Virtue*, 9. For Cabinet discussions see Item 12, 11th Conclusions, 24 February 1954, Cabinet Papers, 1 January to 22 June 1954, TNA PRO CAB 128/27, p. 98; Item 4, 20th Conclusions, 17 March 1954, TNA PRO CAB 128/27, p. 156; Item 5, 29th Conclusions, 15 April 1954, TNA PRO CAB 128/27, pp. 6–7.

103 See Charles Eade to Sir John Nott-Bower, 26 June 1956; Eade to Nott-Bower, 10 July 1956, 'Sunday Dispatch': Contentious Articles on Police Matters: Correspondence with Editor (1929–1961), TNA PRO MEPO 2/9604.

104 'The Scandal of Piccadilly Circus', *Sunday Graphic*, 5 October 1952, 2; 'The Nation Backs Our Campaign to Clean Up Piccadilly Circus', *Sunday Graphic*, 12 October 1952, 2.

105 The *Sunday Graphic* cited support from prominent churchmen and politicians for its campaign, including Archdeacon C. E. Lambert of St James's Church Piccadilly, and Alderman C. P. Russell, leader of Westminster City Council; see 'The Nation Backs Our Campaign'.

106 For the culture of the popular press in the 1950s see Hugh Cudlipp, *At Your Peril: A Mid-Century View of the Exciting Changes of the Press in Britain, and a Press View of the Exciting Changes of Mid-Century* (London: Weidenfeld & Nicolson, 1962), 47, 292; Kemsley Newspapers, *The Kemsley Manual of Journalism* (London: Cassell, 1950); Arthur Christiansen, *Headlines All My Life* (London: Heinemann, 1961), 286; Colin Coote, *Editorial: The Memoirs of Colin R. Coote* (London: Eyre & Spottiswoode, 1965), 248–9; Matthew Engel, *Tickle the Public: One Hundred Years of the Popular Press* (London: Gollancz, 1996), 145–242.

107 Duncan Webb, 'Vice in London', *People*, 12 April 1953, 1.

108 Ibid., see also Duncan Webb, *Deadline for Crime* (London: Frederick Muller, 1955), 78, and his *Crime Reporter* (London: Fleetway Colourbacks, 1963), 60–1.

109 Webb, 'Vice in London', *People*, 19 April 1953, 2.

110 Webb, 'Vice in London', 12 April 1953. See also Webb, *Deadline for Crime*, 78.

111 'Crime news can be obtained from a number of sources,' Webb confided; 'an extremely important method by which I obtain some of my facts . . . is from members of the underworld themselves': Webb, *Deadline for Crime*, 9, and his *Crime Reporter*, 3–5. Webb had been prosecuted in 1950 for alleged contempt of court as a result of his contact with Mrs Cynthia Hume, wife of the murderer Donald Hume, and the publication of Hume's story in the *People*; see 'I Never Dreamed It of the Man I Loved', *People*, 20 January 1950, 1. The Metropolitan Police commented that Webb was 'attempting to specialize in obtaining the exclusive life story of condemned murderers': Metropolitan Police, Criminal Investigation Department to Chief Superintendent, 21 January 1950, Activities of Thomas Duncan Webb, Press Crime Reporter (1946–1956), TNA PRO MEPO 3/3037.

112   Webb, *Deadline for Crime*, 88.
113   Duncan Webb, 'Vice in London: The Facts', *People*, 17 May 1953, 2. See also Webb, 'Thugs Who Thrive on 40s. Fines', *People*, 24 May 1953, 2.
114   See Penny Gillard, 'His Lordship Said: "We Are Alone"', *People*, 16 January 1955, 3.
115   Webb, 'Thugs'.
116   Webb, *Crime Reporter*, 61.
117   See Webb, *Deadline for Crime*, 9.

CHAPTER 2   SOCIETY

1   Douglas Sutherland, *Portrait of a Decade: London Life 1945–1955* (London: Harrap, 1988), 68.
2   Ibid., 72. Sutherland believed that the reason very few upper-class Londoners still entertained on any scale in their homes was because of the difficulty of getting enough drink to throw a decent party!
3   Ibid., 50. See also Christopher Breward, *Fashioning London: Clothing and the Modern Metropolis* (Oxford: Berg, 2004), 138.
4   Sutherland, *Portrait of a Decade*, 56.
5   Ibid., 210.
6   Ibid., 210–11.
7   Ibid., 72. For other accounts of the revival of the society hostess see 'Hostesses of 1953', *Evening Standard*, 10 November 1953, 10.
8   Sutherland, *Portrait of a Decade*, 77, 72.
9   Ibid., 81–93.
10   Ibid., 67.
11   Ibid.
12   Ibid., 118, 67–8.
13   Ibid., 9, 68.
14   Ibid., 69–71. For Frisco's see Maurice Richardson, 'The Bottle Party Belt', *Night and Day*, 1 July 1937, 23. For the Colony Room in the 1950s see Colin MacInnes, '"See You At Mabel's"', *Encounter* 8 (March 1957): 21–6.
15   Sutherland, *Portrait of a Decade*, 69.
16   Harry Meadows, 'Welcome to Clubland', in Anonymous, *The 1953 Guide to London Clubs* (London: Regency Press, 1953), 7.
17   Ibid., 8.
18   Francis Aldor, *The Good Time Guide to London* (London: Harrap, 1951), 8, 15. For travel guides see Ira Grushow, 'Guidebooks', in Jennifer Speake, ed., *Literature of Travel and Exploration: An Encyclopedia*, vol. 2 (New York and London: Fitzroy Dearborn, 2003), 519–23.
19   Aldor, *Good Time Guide*, 118. See also Francis Marshall, *The London Week-End Book* (London: Seeley Service, 1953), 219–23; Anonymous, *1953 Guide to London Clubs*, 7.
20   Aldor, *Good Time Guide*, 19.
21   Ibid., 82.
22   Ibid.
23   Sutherland, *Portrait of a Decade*, 66.
24   Eileen Parker, *Step Aside for Royalty* (Maidstone: Bachman & Turner, 1982), 80; Warwick Charlton and Gerald Sparrow, *Stephen Ward Speaks Conversations with Warwick Charlton: Judge Gerald Sparrow Sums Up the Profumo Affair* (London: Today Magazine, 1963), 57. For other accounts of the Thursday Club see Baron Nahum, *Baron by Baron* (London: Frederick Muller, 1957), 129–31; Tim Heald, *The Duke: A Portrait of Prince Philip* (London: Hodder & Stoughton, 1991), 105–7; Larry Adler with Philip Judge, *Me and My Big Mouth*, ed. William Hall (London: Blake, 1994), 125–30.
25   Charlton and Sparrow, *Stephen Ward Speaks*, 43.
26   Nahum, *Baron*, 130–1.
27   Adler, *Me and My Big Mouth*, 130.
28   Sutherland, *Portrait of a Decade*, 70.
29   Adler, *Me and My Big Mouth*, 126.
30   Heald, *Duke*, 106.
31   Anonymous source, ibid., 105.
32   Parker, *Step Aside for Royalty*, 80. See also Charlton and Sparrow, *Stephen Ward Speaks*, 58.
33   'Commander Michael Parker', *Daily Telegraph*, 1 January 2002, http://www.telegraph.co.uk/news/obituaries/1380107/Commander-Michael-Parker.html (accessed 7 January 2009).
34   'Commander Michael Parker', *Independent*, 4 January 2002, http://www.independent.co.uk/news/obituaries/commander-michael-parker-729636.html (accessed 7 January 2009).
35   Sutherland, *Portrait of a Decade*, 19, 21.
36   David Niven, *The Moon's A Balloon: Reminiscences* (London: Hodder & Stoughton, 1971), 252.

37 'Commander Michael Parker', *Daily Telegraph*.

38 Sutherland, *Portrait of a Decade*, 37.

39 The term 'botanizing on the asphalt' was Benjamin's; see Walter Benjamin, *Selected Writings, Volume 4: 1938–40*, ed. Howard Eiland and Michael Jennings, trans. Edmund Jephcott et al. (Cambridge, MA, and London: Belknap Press of Harvard University Press, 2003), 36. However, *flânerie* has become elevated into a more generic, sociological idea designed to capture the quintessential experience of high modernity in a range of European and North American cities.

40 Jane Flax, 'Postmodernism and Gender Relations in Feminist Theory', *Signs* 12, no. 4 (Summer 1987): 624. See also Judith Walkowitz, *City of Dreadful Delight: Narratives of Sexual Danger in Late-Victorian London* (London: Virago, 1992), 16.

41 See Samuel Beer, *British Politics in the Collectivist Age* (New York: Alfred Knopf, 1966), 215; Arthur Marwick, *British Society since 1945* (London: Allen Lane, 1982), 43–5; David Cannadine, *The Decline and Fall of the British Aristocracy* (New York: Anchor Books Doubleday, 1990), 637–96; F. M. L. Thompson, 'Presidential Address: English Landed Society in the Twentieth Century: IV, Prestige without Power?' in Royal Historical Society, ed., *Transactions of the Royal Historical Society*, 6th ser., 3 (London: Royal Historical Society, 1993), 1–23; Peter Mandler, *The Fall and Rise of the Stately Home* (New Haven and London: Yale University Press, 1997), 309–53; Ross McKibbin, *Classes and Cultures: England 1918–1951* (Oxford: Oxford University Press, 1998), 1–43; Fiona MacCarthy, *Last Curtsey: The End of the Debutantes* (London: Faber & Faber, 2006).

42 Noel Annan, *Our Age: Portrait of a Generation* (London: Weidenfeld & Nicolson, 1990), 13–14; Peter Mandler and Susan Pedersen, 'The British Intelligentsia after the Victorians', in Susan Pedersen and Peter Mandler, eds, *After the Victorians: Private Conscience and Public Duty in Modern Britain; Essays in Memory of John Clive* (London: Routledge, 1994), 1–28.

43 McKibbin, *Classes and Cultures*, 41–3.

44 Queen Mary to George VI, 18 August 1947, quoted in John Wheeler-Bennett, *King George VI: His Life and Reign* (London: Macmillan, 1965), 716.

45 Mabell, Countess of Airlie, *Thatched with Gold: The Memoirs of Mabell Countess of Airlie*, ed. Jennifer Ellis (London: Hutchinson, 1962), 229.

46 Ibid., 239.

47 Margaret, Duchess of Argyll, *Forget Not: The Autobiography of Margaret, Duchess of Argyll* (London: W. H. Allen, 1975), 140.

48 2 June 1953, in James Lees-Milne, *A Mingled Measure: Diaries 1953–1972* (London: John Murray, 1994), 29.

49 For Lees-Milne's observations on the privations of the country's landed elite in the late 1940s see his *Diaries, 1946–1949: Caves of Ice and Midway on the Waves* (London: John Murray, 1996).

50 29 January 1947, ibid., 109.

51 2 August 1947, ibid., 159.

52 2 December 1946, ibid., 90.

53 Sutherland, *Portrait of a Decade*, 64.

54 Ibid. For Bevan's speech and its repercussions see Michael Foot, *Aneurin Bevan: A Biography, Volume 2: 1945–1960* (London: Davis-Poynter, 1973), 237–44; Martin Francis, 'The Labour Party: Modernisation and the Politics of Restraint', in Becky Conekin, Frank Mort and Chris Waters, eds, *Moments of Modernity: Reconstructing Britain 1945–1964* (London: Rivers Oram, 1999), 152–70.

55 Piers Dixon, 'The Members', in Philip Ziegler and Desmond Seward, eds, *Brooks's: A Social History* (London: Constable, 1991), 185. Brooks's was originally a Liberal/Whig club, but between 1925 and 1940 the number of Liberal MPs fell from ninety-five to twenty-five, while the number of Conservative peers and MPs rose; see James Neidpath, 'Brooks's Between the Wars', in Ziegler and Seward, *Brooks's*, 89.

56 For details of Brooks's difficulties in the post-war period see Christopher Ward, 'Brooks's since the War', in Ziegler and Seward, *Brooks's*, 103–16.

57 James Lees-Milne, 'The Second World War', in Ziegler and Seward, *Brooks's*, 97, 93; Ian

Harvey, *To Fall Like Lucifer* (London: Sidgwick & Jackson, 1971), 58–9.

58 James Lees-Milne, *Harold Nicolson: A Biography, Volume 2: 1930–1968* (London: Chatto & Windus, London, 1981), 274.

59 Ibid., 263, 274.

60 15 November 1951, in Nigel Nicolson, ed., *Harold Nicolson: Diaries and Letters 1907–1964* (London: Weidenfeld & Nicolson, 2004), 378.

61 Harold Nicolson, *Good Behaviour: Being a Study of Certain Types of Civility* (London: Constable, 1955), 3, 282.

62 Ibid., 284.

63 The debate originated in an academic article by Professor Alan Ross of Birmingham University entitled 'Linguistic Class-Indicators in Present-Day English', published in the Finnish periodical *Neuphilogische Mitteilungen*. Ross's argument was that by the mid-1950s linguistic distinctions were the sole factors distinguishing the upper class, as the old divisions of education and wealth had now been eroded. Nancy Mitford developed Ross's thesis into a popular essay on 'U' and 'non-U' terminology, which was first published in *Encounter* and republished as 'The English Aristocracy', illustrated with cartoons by Osbert Lancaster, in Alan Ross et al., *Noblesse Oblige: An Enquiry into the Identifiable Characteristics of the English Aristocracy* (London: Hamish Hamilton, 1956), 39–64.

64 28 November 1952, in Robert Rhodes James, ed., '*Chips': The Diaries of Sir Henry Channon* (London: Weidenfeld & Nicolson, 1967), 470–1.

65 11 July 1948, ibid., 427.

66 McKibbin, *Classes and Cultures*, 31.

67 For the royal orders see Wheeler-Bennett, *King George VI*, 757; Harold Nicolson, *King George the Fifth: His Life and Reign* (London: Pan, 1967), 655.

68 'News of Court and Society', *Queen*, 27 November 1948, 8.

69 October 1948, in Rhodes James, '*Chips*', 430.

70 'News of Court and Society', *Queen*, 21 July 1948, 7.

71 MacCarthy, *Last Curtsey*, 12.

72 Ibid., 1, 7.

73 Ibid., 85.

74 See 'Queen Charlotte's Ball for Debutantes', *Queen*, 26 May 1948, 10; Louis Stanley, 'Henley', *Queen*, 23 June 1948, 13.

75 Percy Colson, 'Collecting Can be Fun', *Queen*, 9 June 1948, 24. See also 'The Presentation Parties', *Country Life*, 13 March 1953, 763.

76 For biographies and studies of Princess Margaret see Marion Crawford, *Princess Margaret* (London: George Newnes, 1953); Nigel Dempster, *H.R.H. Princess Margaret: A Life Unfulfilled* (London: Quartet, 1981); Christopher Warwick, *Princess Margaret* (London: Weidenfeld & Nicolson, 1983); Paul James, *Margaret: A Woman of Conflict* (London: Sidgwick & Jackson, 1990); Theo Aronson, *Princess Margaret: A Biography* (London: Michael O'Mara, 1997).

77 Quoted in Aronson, *Princess Margaret*, 105.

78 For the Duchess of Kent's participation in society see Stella King, *Princess Marina: Her Life and Times* (London: Cassell, 1969), 133–49; Sophia Watson, *Marina: The Story of a Princess* (London: Weidenfeld & Nicolson, 1994), 194–7. For Edward, Prince of Wales, later Edward VIII, see Edward, Duke of Windsor, *A King's Story: The Memoirs of H.R.H. the Duke of Windsor* (London: Prion, 1998), 191–2; Philip Ziegler, *King Edward VIII: The Official Biography* (London: Fontana, 1991), 166–7.

79 Crawford, *Princess Margaret*, 9. Not only was Princess Margaret presented in the media as the talented and precocious little sister, she was also seen to play 'the Mary to her sister's Martha': 'Little Sister', *New Statesman*, 30 April 1960, 616.

80 Crawford, *Princess Margaret*, 75, 44. See also Crawford's famous study of the two princesses, for which she was ostracized by the royal family for breaching protocol, *The Little Princesses* (London: Cassell, 1950).

81 See Aronson, *Princess Margaret*, 110; 'Bigots Attack the Princess', *Daily Mirror*, 21 May 1953, 2.

82 See Pearson Phillips, 'The New Look', in Michael Sissons and Philip French, eds, *Age of Austerity* (London: Hodder & Stoughton, 1963), 143, 146; Aronson, *Princess Margaret*, 106.

83　Two of the escorts Princess Margaret was rumoured to be romantically involved with in
the 1950s were 'Johnny', Earl of Dalkeith,
heir to a number of Scottish dukedoms and
three huge estates, and 'Sunny', Marquess of
Blandford, the Duke of Marlborough's heir.

84　For Princess Margaret's relationships with
Kaye and Douglas see Aronson, *Princess
Margaret*, 109, 111; Warwick, *Princess Margaret*,
49; Martin Gottfried, *Nobody's Fool: The Lives
of Danny Kaye* (New York and London:
Simon & Schuster, 1994), 158–9, 215–16.

85　Crawford, *Princess Margaret*, 17.

86　29 October 1951, in Graham Payn and
Sheridan Morley, eds, *The Noël Coward
Diaries* (London: Phoenix, 1998), 179.

87　21 June 1949, in Lees-Milne, *Diaries 1946–
1949*, 386; 18 June 1949, in Rhodes James,
'*Chips*', 439. Queen Mary dubbed the
Princess *espiègle*, not bad but adventurous:
Warwick, *Princess Margaret*, 37.

88　For the affair between Princess Margaret
and Peter Townsend see Warwick, *Princess
Margaret*, 57–65; Aronson, *Princess Margaret*,
125–34; Peter Townsend, *Time and Chance: An
Autobiography* (London: Collins, 1978), 187–
239. For public reaction to the relationship
see M-O A: TC Royalty, 69/11/B, Townsend
Affair, 1955.

89　Princess Margaret issued a statement from
Clarence House in the autumn of 1955
finally breaking off her relationship with
Townsend, 'mindful', as she put it, 'of the
Church's teaching that Christian marriage is
indissoluble, and conscious of my duty to the
Commonwealth': 'Statement by Princess',
The Times, 1 November 1955, 8. For the
controversy see Lindsay Anderson, letter to
the editor, *Spectator*, 18 November 1955,
650–1.

90　See Brian Masters, *Great Hostesses* (London:
Constable, 1982); Anne de Courcy, *Society's
Queen: The Life of Edith, Marchioness of Lon-
donderry* (London: Phoenix, 2004); H. Mont-
gomery Hyde, *The Londonderrys: A Family
Portrait* (London: Hamish Hamilton, 1979).

91　Sutherland, *Portrait of a Decade*, 159. For
details of Londonderry House see H.
Montgomery Hyde, *Londonderry House and
its Pictures* (London: Cresset Press, 1937).

92　For the role of these women see Masters,
Great Hostesses; Daphne Fielding, *Emerald and
Nancy: Lady Cunard and her Daughter* (Lon-
don: Eyre & Spottiswoode, 1968); Peter
Quennell, ed., *Genius in the Drawing-Room:
The Literary Salon in the Nineteenth and
Twentieth Centuries* (London: Weidenfeld &
Nicolson, 1980).

93　McKibbin, *Classes and Cultures*, 26.

94　Harold Nicolson, quoted in Masters, *Great
Hostesses*, 194–5.

95　September 1953, in Richard Buckle, ed., *Self
Portrait with Friends: The Selected Diaries of
Cecil Beaton* (New York: Times Books, 1979),
273. For other accounts of the evening and
Fleming's social role see Ann Fleming to
Patrick Leigh Fermor, 7 October 1953, in
Mark Amory, ed., *The Letters of Ann Fleming*
(London: Collins Harvill, 1985), 133; Andrew
Lycett, *Ian Fleming* (London: Weidenfeld &
Nicolson, 1995), 248–9.

96　September 1953, in Buckle, *Self Portrait*, 274;
Peter Quennell, *The Wanton Chase: An
Autobiography from 1939* (London: Collins,
1980), 105, 145.

97　Andrew Lycett, 'Fleming, Ann,' *Oxford Dictionary of National Biography* (Oxford: Oxford
University Press, 2004), http://www.ox-
forddnb.com/view/article/40227 (accessed 6
July 2007).

98　Lycett, *Ian Fleming*, 214.

99　See Lycett, 'Fleming, Ann'; Lycett, *Ian Fleming*, 296.

100　Mandler and Pedersen have argued that one
of the defining features of upper-class culture
in the post-war period was its stress on 'civility in private life', in the face of what was
perceived to be the spurious domesticity of
post-war popular culture. Such notions of
civilized living, they have insisted, were personally and intellectually distinct from more
politicized versions of sexual radicalism that
had attracted sections of the cultivated elite
in the 1920s: Mandler and Pedersen, 'British
Intelligentsia after the Victorians', 17. See also
Quennell, *Wanton Chase*, 162.

101　Quoted in Amory, *Letters of Ann Fleming*, 43.

102　Sutherland, *Portrait of a Decade*, 87.

103　Ann Rothermere to Hugo Charteris, March?
1950, in Amory, *Letters of Ann Fleming*, 86.

104 Ann Fleming to Evelyn Waugh, 15 December 1957, in Amory, *Letters of Ann Fleming*, 210–11.

105 Waugh to Fleming, 28 July 1959, in Mark Amory, ed., *The Letters of Evelyn Waugh* (London: Phoenix, 1995), 525. See also Fleming to Waugh, 24 July 1959, in Amory, *Letters of Ann Fleming*, 232.

106 Quoted in Lycett, *Ian Fleming*, 176.

107 Ibid., 179, 217.

108 Ibid., 296.

109 'Docker, Lady Norah', *Bygone Derbyshire*, http://www.bygonederbyshire.co.uk/articles/Docker,_Lady_Norah:_Artificial_Blond _in_search_of_stardom (accessed 22 October 2009).

110 Norah Docker, *Norah: The Autobiography of Lady Docker* (London: W. H. Allen, 1969), 26.

111 Ibid., 26. See also Arthur Marshall, 'Bantam-Weights', *New Statesman*, 24 October 1969, 582.

112 Docker, *Norah*, 62.

113 Ibid., 86.

114 Ibid. 86–7, 119.

115 Ibid., 107–17. See also Peter Lewis, *The Fifties: Portrait of an Age* (London: Herbert Press, 1989), 34–5.

116 The exposure of Sir Bernard Docker's financial affairs also revealed characteristic types of deception that began to be associated with the Tory Party, notably his efforts to evade currency restrictions and his undisclosed expense accounts.

117 Harry Hopkins, *The New Look: A Social History of the Forties and Fifties in Britain* (London: Secker & Warburg, 1963), 352. See also Tudor Jenkins, *The Londoner* (London: MacGibbon and Kee, 1962), 75; Sutherland, *Portrait of a Decade*, 72–4.

118 Jenkins, *Londoner*, 128–9.

119 Ibid., 75. For coverage of these incidents see Docker, *Norah*, 182–93, 143–5.

120 'Lady Docker', *Evening Standard*, 7 October 1953, 11.

121 Margaret Stacey highlighted the continuing importance of the upper class in her social survey of the Oxfordshire town of Banbury between 1948 and 1951. Stacey argued that 'it was impossible to ignore the existence of upper-class people,' and she concluded, 'in so far as this class sets the standards and aspirations of traditional social class attitudes . . . it is important out of all proportion to its size': quoted in Marwick, *British Society since 1945*, 44–5. For the more characteristic focus of post-war British sociology see Michael Young and Peter Willmott, *Family and Kinship in East London* (London: Routledge & Kegan Paul, 1957); Ferdynand Zweig, *The Worker in an Affluent Society: Family Life and Industry* (London: Heinemann, 1961); John Goldthorpe et al., *The Affluent Worker in the Class Structure* (London: Cambridge University Press, 1969); Richard Hoggart, *The Uses of Literacy: Aspects of Working-Class Life, with Special Reference to Publications and Entertainments* (London: Chatto & Windus), 1957.

122 See Shils's reflections on this period of his life at the LSE in *The Intellectuals and the Powers, and Other Essays* (Chicago: University of Chicago Press, 1972), ix. See also Edward Shils, *A Fragment of a Sociological Autobiography: The History of My Pursuit of a Few Ideas*, ed. Steven Grosby (Somerset, NJ: Transaction Publishers, 2006).

123 Shils, *Fragment*, 88. For Shils's interpretation of the coronation see Edward Shils and Michael Young, 'The Meaning of the Coronation', *Sociological Review*, n.s., 1, no. 2 (December 1953): 63–81.

124 Edward Shils, 'The Intellectuals 1: Great Britain', *Encounter* 4, no. 4 (April 1955): 10, 12.

125 Ibid., 11. For Shils's indebtedness to Park and Eliot see Shils, *Fragment*, 113–14.

126 Shils, 'Intellectuals', 16, 13.

127 Ibid., 16, 10–13.

128 Annan, *Our Age*, 247.

129 Ibid. See also Stefan Collini, *Absent Minds: Intellectuals in Britain* (Oxford: Oxford University Press, 2006), 140–50; Mike Savage, 'Cultural Formation in England, 1939–1960' (unpublished paper, 2006).

130 See Hugh Thomas, ed., *The Establishment: A Symposium* (London: Anthony Blond, 1959); Henry Fairlie, 'Political Commentary', *Spectator*, 23 September 1955, 379–80; Malcolm Muggeridge, 'Royal Soap Opera,' *New Statesman and Nation*, 22 October 1955, 499–500; Lord Altrincham, 'The Monarchy To-

day', *National and English Review* 149 (August 1957): 61–6. For commentary see Peter Hennessy, *The Great and the Good: An Inquiry into the British Establishment* (London: Policy Studies Institute, 1986); Ben Pimlott, *The Queen: A Biography of Elizabeth II* (London: HarperCollins, 1996), 276–88.

131   Tom Nairn, *The Enchanted Glass: Britain and its Monarchy* (London: Radius, 1988), 213. See also Edward Thompson, 'The Peculiarities of the English', in Ralph Miliband and John Saville, eds, *The Socialist Register 1965* (London: Merlin Press, 1965), 311–62; Perry Anderson, 'Components of the National Culture', in Alexander Cockburn and Robin Blackburn, eds, *Student Power: Problems, Diagnosis, Action* (Harmondsworth: Penguin, 1970), 214–84.

132   Shils, 'Intellectuals', 13, 16.

133   Richard Sennett, *The Fall of Public Man*, (London: Faber & Faber, 1993), 15–16.

134   'Hors D'Oeuvres', *Man About Town*, Spring 1953, 41.

135   Ibid.

136   Ibid.

137   Ibid.

138   'Buying a Suit', *Man About Town*, Spring 1953, 73, and see also the cover page, *Man About Town*, Spring 1955. The men's problems addressed in the first issue focused on hair loss; see Cormac Swan, 'Hair Today and Gone Tomorrow', *Man About Town*, Spring 1953, 141–5.

139   See 'Friends of Man', *Man About Town*, Autumn 1955, 39; 'The Profile of a Mill Girl', *Man About Town*, 1954, 57–60; 'A Man Wants To Be Alone', *Man About Town*, Spring 1956, 5.

140   'Hors D'Oeuvres'.

141   'The Shape of Things in 1953', *Man About Town*, Spring 1953, 43–4.

142   'Buying a Suit', 94.

143   'Quality Street – an Advertisement for Good Tailoring', and advert, *Man About Town*, 1954, 73, 89.

144   'Buying a Suit', 91; 'The Weigh In', *Man About Town*, Spring 1953, 165. See also British Travel and Holidays Association, *Shopping in London* (London: British Travel and Holidays Association, 1953), 31, 42.

145   *Man About Town* was restyled and renamed in the 1960s, on its acquisition by publishers Michael Heseltine and Clive Labovitch. *About Town*, later abbreviated to *Town*, ran until 1968 with an ambitious mixture of photography and journalism. Paralleling the newspaper colour supplements of the period, the title blended fashion, politics and arts coverage; see Frank Mort, *Cultures of Consumption: Masculinities and Social Space in Late Twentieth-Century Britain* (London: Routledge, 1996), 18–19.

146   C. A. R. Crosland, *The Future of Socialism* (London: Jonathan Cape, 1956), 282, 281. Crosland himself was a habitué of metropolitan social circles in the 1950s; see Susan Crosland, *Tony Crosland* (London: Jonathan Cape, 1982), 63–4. For the wider Labour revisionist debates over consumption see Lawrence Black, *The Political Culture of the Left in Britain, 1951–64: Old Labour, New Britain?* (Basingstoke: Palgrave Macmillan, 2003), 82–3, 124–54; Jeremy Nuttall, *Psychological Socialism: The Labour Party and Qualities of Mind and Character, 1931 to the Present* (Manchester: Manchester University Press, 2006), 11–12.

147   'A Symposium Concerning the Hangover', *Man About Town*, Spring 1953, 58–9.

148   'Some Men About Man About Town', *Man About Town*, Spring 1953, 171. For specific details of Frank Bellamy see 'Nancy Bellamy Interview', http://www.frankbellamy.com/binter.htm (accessed 8 May 2007).

149   'Nancy Bellamy Interview'. For similarly varied social profiles see 'Some Men About Town', *Man About Town*, 1954, 156; 'Some Men About Town', *Man About Town*, Spring 1955, 23.

150   For the use of the image of the gentleman in clothes retailing see Frank Mort and Peter Thompson, 'Retailing, Commercial Culture and Masculinity in 1950s Britain: The Case of Montague Burton, the "Tailor of Taste"', *History Workshop Journal*, no. 38 (Autumn 1994): 106–27.

151   See David Cannadine, 'James Bond and the Decline of England', *Encounter* 53, no. 3 (September 1979): 46–55; Jeremy Black, *The Politics of James Bond: From Fleming's Novels to*

the Big Screen (Westport, CT, and London: Praeger, 2001), 211–12; James Chapman, *Licence to Thrill: A Cultural History of the James Bond Films* (London: Tauris, 1999), 65–110.

152 Sean Nixon, 'Apostles of Americanization? J. Walter Thompson Company Ltd, Advertising and Anglo-American Relations 1945–67', *Contemporary British History* 22, no. 4 (2008): 480.

153 John Pearson and Graham Turner, *The Persuasion Industry* (London: Eyre & Spottiswoode, 1965), 112.

154 Leslie Frewin, 'Publisher's Preface', in Robin Douglas-Home, *The Faint Aroma of Performing Seals* (London: Leslie Frewin, 1969), 7.

155 For Douglas-Home's relationship with Princess Margaretha see 'Proposal to a Princess Rejected', *The Times*, 6 May 1957, 10; 'Mr. Douglas Home's Stockholm Visit', *The Times*, 6 March 1958, 10.

156 See 'The Princess & the Pianist', *Time*, 20 May 1957, http://www.time.com/time/magazine/article/0,9171,809494,00.html (accessed 22 January 2009); 'Mr. R. Douglas-Home', *The Times*, 16 October 1968, 12.

157 Quoted in Nixon, 'Apostles of Americanization?', 490.

158 Annabel Goldsmith, *Annabel: An Unconventional Life; The Memoirs of Lady Annabel Goldsmith* (London: Weidenfeld & Nicolson, 2004), 83. For commentary on the 'deb's delight' see MacCarthy, *Last Curtsey*, 60–84.

159 'Lady Annabel's Wedding', *Daily Dispatch*, quoted in Goldsmith, *Annabel*, facing page 83.

160 Nixon, 'Apostles of Americanization?', 490.

161 Sutherland, *Portrait of a Decade*, 109. Tudor Jenkins, Sutherland's boss on the *Evening Standard*, saw this as the consolidation of a reporting style started in the inter-war period that smudged the boundaries between social commentary and gossip: Jenkins, *Londoner*, 128. See also Christopher Booker, *The Neophiliacs: A Study of the Revolution in English Life in the Fifties and Sixties* (London: Collins, 1969), 24–7.

162 One of the magazine's articles on evening dress warned that 'too much experiment in style is liable to end up with you looking like one of the band': 'A Military Air', *Man About Town*, Spring 1953, 48. For discussion of masculine deviation in dress in the 1950s see Mort and Thompson, 'Retailing, Commercial Culture and Masculinity'.

163 'Hors D'Oeuvres', *Man About Town*, 1954, 42.

164 Ruth Rubinstein, *Dress Codes: Meanings and Messages in American Culture* (Boulder, CO: Westview Press, 1995), 57–8. See also Sutherland, *Portrait of a Decade*, 125; John Harvey, *Men in Black* (London: Reaktion, 1995).

165 Norman Parkinson, 'Back to Formality', *Vogue*, April 1950, 108–9.

166 Ibid., 109. For discussion of this renaissance of formal styling in dress see Breward, *Fashioning London*, 125–9; Edwina Ehrman, 'Broken Traditions', and Caroline Evans, 'Post-War Poses: 1955–75', in Christopher Breward, Edwina Ehrman, and Caroline Evans, eds, *The London Look: Fashion from Street to Catwalk* (New Haven and London: Yale University Press in association with the Museum of London, 2004), 97–116, 117–37; Christopher Breward, Becky Conekin and Caroline Cox, eds, *The Englishness of English Dress* (Oxford: Berg, 2002); Claire Wilcox, ed., *The Golden Age of Couture: Paris and London 1947–1957* (London: V&A Publications, 2007).

167 Parkinson, 'Back to Formality', 109.

168 Ibid.

169 'Coronation Trade has Begun', *Men's Wear*, 28 March 1953, 37. See also 'Talk of the Trade', *Men's Wear*, 17 January 1953, 28; 'Hat Promotion in Piccadilly', *Men's Wear*, 14 March 1953, 12. See also Hardy Amies, *Just So Far* (London: Collins, 1954), 203–46; Edwina Ehrman, 'The Spirit of English Style: Hardy Amies, Royal Dressmaker and International Businessman', in Breward et al., *Englishness of English Dress*, 133–45.

170 Berkeley West, 'Fancy Waistcoats Are Here to Stay', *Men's Wear*, 21 June 1952, 17.

171 British Travel and Holidays Association, *Shopping in London*, 31, 42; Aldor, *Good Time Guide*, 260.

172 T. R. Fyvel, *The Insecure Offenders: Rebellious Youth in the Welfare State* (London: Chatto & Windus, 1961), 48.

173 Chris Steele-Perkins and Richard Smith, *The Teds* (London: Travelling Light, 1979), unpag-

inated. See also Tony Parker, *The Plough Boy* (London: Hutchinson, 1965), 20; Nik Cohn, *Ball the Wall: Nik Cohn in the Age of Rock* (London: Picador, 1989), 266.

174 Fyvel, *Insecure Offenders*, 49.

175 Ibid.

176 Amies, *Just So Far*, 245. See also Fyvel, *Insecure Offenders*, 49.

177 Steele-Perkins and Smith have argued that the Edwardian style originated in 'homosexual circles': *Teds*. See also Shaun Cole, *'Don We Now Our Gay Apparel': Gay Men's Dress in the Twentieth Century* (Oxford: Berg, 2000), 22–4.

178 Michael James, bar-waiter at the club, 1993, Hall Carpenter Oral History Project, British Library Sound Archive, C456/122/02. See also Patrick Trevor-Roper, ibid., C456/089/ 01–02; John Lehmann, *In the Purely Pagan Sense* (London: GMP, 1985), 210–12; Cole, *'Don We Now Our Gay Apparel'*, 23.

179 Ehrman, 'Broken Traditions', 112.

180 Berkeley West, 'The Beginning of a New Style Era', *Men's Wear*, 31 January 1953, 12.

181 Berkeley West, 'Seen at the Ritz', *Men's Wear*, 11 April 1953, 19.

182 Ibid.

183 Berkeley West, 'A Peep into the Wardrobe of a Man Who Designs Women's Fashion', *Men's Wear*, 18 July 1953, 14–15.

184 For this cultural strategy in relation to working-class youth see Stuart Hall and Tony Jefferson, eds, *Resistance through Rituals: Youth Sub-Cultures in Post-War Britain* (London: Hutchinson, 1976); Geoff Mungham and Geoff Pearson, eds, *Working Class Youth Culture* (London: Routledge & Kegan Paul, 1976); Dick Hebdige, *Subculture: The Meaning of Style* (London: Methuen, 1979).

185 Hebdige, *Subculture*.

186 'The Glass of Fashion', *Queen*, 14 January 1953, 23.

187 Ibid.

188 'Tailored Elegance for Men: Capes and Pleats', *The Times*, 10 June 1953, 3.

189 'Montagu of Beaulieu, 3rd Baron', *Who's Who 1953* (London: Adam and Charles Black, 1953), 2064.

190 'Can the Trade Sell the Lounging Suit to Me', *Men's Wear*, 22 August 1953, 13.

191 Peter Wildeblood, *Against the Law* (Harmondsworth: Penguin, 1957), 41.

192 Ibid.

193 'Forthcoming Marriages', *The Times*, 6 August 1953, 8.

194 For coverage of the affair see 'Charge Against Lord Montagu', *The Times*, 17 October 1953, 3; 'Allegation Against Lord Montagu', *The Times*, 16 November 1953, 4; Wildeblood, *Against the Law*, 48–9.

195 For analysis of the social and sexual significance of the Montagu-Wildeblood scandal see Jeffrey Weeks, *Coming Out: Homosexual Politics in Britain from the Nineteenth Century to the Present*, 2nd edn (London: Quartet, 1990), 159–65; Stephen Jeffery-Poulter, *Peers, Queers and Commons: The Struggle for Gay Law Reform from 1950 to the Present* (London: Routledge, 1991), 16–17, 24–7; Patrick Higgins, *Heterosexual Dictatorship: Male Homosexuality in Post-War Britain* (London: Fourth Estate, 1996), 231–46; Chris Waters, 'Disorders of the Mind, Disorders of the Body Social: Peter Wildeblood and the Making of the Modern Homosexual', in Conekin et al., *Moments of Modernity*, 134–51.

196 For coverage of these scandals see Sheridan Morley, *John G: The Authorised Biography of John Gielgud* (London: Hodder & Stoughton, 2001), 231–63; Hugh David, *Heroes, Mavericks and Bounders: The English Gentleman from Lord Curzon to James Bond* (London: Michael Joseph, 1991), 224–43; Annan, *Our Age*, 235; Harvey, *To Fall Like Lucifer*, 101–26.

197 Wildeblood, *Against the Law*, 44. See also 'Peter Wildeblood', *The Independent*, 25 November 1999, 6. Walter Jones, the head of Hampshire Constabulary's CID who was instrumental in securing the convictions of Montagu and Wildeblood, also emphasized the metropolitan atmosphere of luxury in the case: Walter Jones, *My Own Case* (Maidstone: Angley Books, 1966), 116.

198 Wildeblood, *Against the Law*, 63. See also 'Scout Tells of Bathe with Montagu', *People*, 15 November 1953, 7.

199 'Outlaws We Should Bring within the Law', cutting preserved from *Reynold's News*, undated, in Papers of John Frederick Wolf-

enden, MS 5311, uncatalogued, Special Collections Service at the University of Reading.

200 Paul Rock and Stanley Cohen, 'The Teddy Boy', in Vernon Bogdanor and Robert Skidelsky, eds, *The Age of Affluence 1951–1964* (London: Macmillan, 1970), 289. For other studies see Tony Jefferson, 'Cultural Responses of the Teds: The Defence of Space', in Hall and Jefferson, *Resistance Through Rituals*, 81–6; Hebdige, *Subculture*, 50–1, 81–4, 123–4; Steele-Perkins and Smith, *Teds*. Rock and Cohen have argued that the term 'Teddy Boy' was not publicly aired in the press until March 1954; however, coverage of the Clapham Common murder the previous year was a key moment in the identification of the working-class Edwardian look.

201 For discussion of related forms of gang violence elsewhere in Europe see Fyvel, *Insecure Offenders*, 32–3; Tony Judt, *Postwar: A History of Europe since 1945* (London: Pimlico, 2007), 347–8.

202 Fyvel, *Insecure Offenders*, 51.

203 *Observer*, 19 June 1955, quoted in Fyvel, *Insecure Offenders*, 53.

204 The Teds involved in the Clapham Common incident included shop assistants, carpenters, labourers, street traders and the unemployed; see 'I Only Booted the Fellow', *Clapham Observer*, 10 July 1953, 1.

205 Rock and Cohen, 'Teddy Boy', 290–1.

206 The account is taken from Murder of John Beckley by Michael John Davies at Clapham Common (1953–1967), TNA PRO MEPO 2/9538; Parker, *Ploughboy*. Parker was one of the original members of the Clapham Common gang. See also Rupert Furneaux, *Michael John Davies*, crime documentaries no. 4 (London: Stevens, 1962).

207 Parker, *Ploughboy*, 20. Parker's account was based on a compilation of anonymous witness statements to the Clapham Common murder inquiry; see Keith Soothill, *Criminal Conversations: An Anthology of the Work of Tony Parker* (London: Routledge, 1999).

208 Statement of Ronald Coleman, 4 July 1953, TNA PRO MEPO 2/9538; Parker, *Ploughboy*, 21.

209 'The Leader of the Edwardians', *Evening Standard*, 22 September 1953, 1.

210 Statement of Coleman, TNA PRO MEPO 2/9538.

211 'No Case Against 4 Youths in Clapham Murder Trial', *Evening Standard*, 14 September 1953, 8.

212 *Daily Mirror*, 23 October 1953, quoted in Rock and Cohen, 'Teddy Boy', 291. Davies was later reprieved by the Home Secretary and was granted an early release from prison in 1960. For the negative associations of the Teddy Boy and neo-Edwardianism in official debates see Hooligans, Clapham Common (Precautions), written answers, 22 October 1953, *Parliamentary Debates (Hansard), House of Commons Official Report*, 5th ser., vol. 518, session 1952–3 (London: HMSO, 1953), col. 295; 'Outbreaks of Violence due to Moral Sickness,' *Clapham Observer*, 9 October 1953, 7; 'Home Secretary and Reports of Hooliganism', *Clapham Observer*, 30 October 1953, 1.

213 *Daily Mirror*, 17 November 1953, quoted in Rock and Cohen, 'Teddy Boy', 290–1.

214 'London's Little Chicago', *People*, 19 July 1953, 3; 'Things I Hear', *Clapham Observer*, 24 July 1953, 4.

215 'The State of the Nation', *Man About Town*, Winter 1954, 5–6.

216 Fyvel, *Insecure Offenders*, 14. See also Jefferson, 'Cultural Responses of the Teds', 81–2.

CHAPTER 3   PATHOLOGIES

1 The social and cultural histories which have been drawn on here include Ken Young and Patricia Garside, *Metropolitan London: Politics and Urban Change 1837–1981* (London: Edward Arnold, 1982), 229–87; Steve Humphries and John Taylor, *The Making of Modern London 1945–1985* (London: Sidgwick & Jackson, 1986), 80–107; Andrew Saint, ' "Spread the People": The LCC's Dispersal Policy 1889–1965', in Andrew Saint, ed., *Politics and the People of London: The London County Council 1889–1965* (London: Hambledon Press, 1986), 215–36; Roy Porter, *London: A Social History* (London: Hamish Hamilton, 1994), 349–63; Stephen Inwood, *A History of London* (London, Macmillan, 1998), 814–17;

Francis Sheppard, *London: A History* (Oxford: Oxford University Press, 1998), 341; Jerry White, *London in the Twentieth Century: A City and its People* (London: Penguin, 2002), 37–45; David Kynaston, *Austerity Britain 1945–51* (London: Bloomsbury, 2007), 143–70.

2 For these different visions of the planned city see J. H. Forshaw and Patrick Abercrombie, *County of London Plan* (London: Macmillan, 1943), 1–17; Corporation of London, Court of Common Council, *Report to the Right Honourable the Lord Mayor etc. on the Preliminary Draft Proposals for Post War Reconstruction in the City of London* (London: Batsford, 1944), 1–5; Patrick Abercrombie and South East Regional Planning, *Greater London Plan 1944 . . . A Report Prepared on Behalf of the Standing Conference on London Regional Planning at the Request of the Minister of Town and Country Planning* (London: HMSO, 1945); General Register Office, *Census 1951 England and Wales: Report on Greater London and Five Other Conurbations* (London: HMSO, 1956), xiii–xiv.

3 For the planners' role in the post-war social contract see John Cullingworth, *New Towns for Old: The Problem of Urban Renewal* (London: Fabian Society, 1962); Wilfred Burns, *New Towns for Old: The Technique for Urban Renewal* (London: Leonard Hill, 1963); Peter Mandler, 'New Towns for Old: The Fate of the Town Centre', in Becky Conekin, Frank Mort and Chris Waters, eds, *Moments of Modernity: Reconstructing Britain 1945–64* (London: Rivers Oram, 1999), 208–27.

4 For accounts of London's property developers see Oliver Marriott, *The Property Boom* (London: Hamish Hamilton, 1967), 80–99; Simon Jenkins, *Landlords to London: The Story of a Capital and its Growth* (London: Constable, 1975), 209–27.

5 The boom was stimulated by the erosion of nineteenth-century patterns of land tenure, especially the disappearance of many of the large aristocratic estates in the West End during the immediate post-war years, as a result of the doubling of rates of legacy duty in the Finance Act (1947); see Marriott, *Property Boom*, 80–9; Jenkins, *Landlords to London*, 209–27.

6 The motor behind this demand was the highly successful renaissance of the City of London in the international financial markets, together with the pull of the capital for national and multinational corporations and for the expanding bureaucracy of modern government. By 1962 there were 114 million square feet of offices in central London; see Inwood, *History of London*, 842. For accounts of London's post-war office boom see Peter Cowan, *The Office: A Facet of Urban Growth* (London: Heinemann, 1969); Alan Delgado, *The Enormous File: A Social History of the Office* (London: John Murray, 1979).

7 Douglas Sutherland, *Portrait of a Decade: London Life, 1945–1955* (London: Harrap, 1988), 210. During coronation year Charles Clore and his wife hosted a number of flamboyantly staged parties for members of the royal family, which were endowed with added excitement when it was disclosed that the millionaire was engaged in an intense property battle with Harold Samuel for the Savoy Hotel group. See 'Mr. Clore Spends an Evening Bidding – All in Aid of Charity', *Evening Standard*, 7 December 1953, 5; 'Samuel Buys Up Clore Shares', *Evening Standard*, 4 December 1953, 1. For commentary on this group of developers see Marriott, *Property Boom*, 48, 105, 118, 132–8, 140–2, 154.

8 For very differently nuanced accounts of London's post-war development which all nonetheless assume that commerce triumphed over planning see Peter Hall, *London 2001* (London: Unwin Hyman, 1989); Porter, *London*, 344–63; Frank Mort, *Cultures of Consumption: Masculinities and Social Space in Late Twentieth-Century Britain* (London: Routledge, 1996), 149–82; White, *London*, 46–87.

9 See Christopher Booker, *The Neophiliacs: A Study of the Revolution in English Life in the Fifties and Sixties* (London: Collins, 1969), 172, 188; Porter, *London*, 419–44; Christopher Breward, *Fashioning London: Clothing and the Modern Metropolis* (Oxford: Berg, 2004), 151–76.

10 For the subliminal geography of policy see J. B. Harley, 'Maps, Knowledge and Power', in

Denis Cosgrove and Stephen Daniels, eds, *The Iconography of Landscape: Essays on the Symbolic Representation, Design and Use of Past Environments* (Cambridge: Cambridge University Press, 1988), 289.

11 Denis Cosgrove, 'Introduction: Mapping Meaning', in Denis Cosgrove, ed., *Mappings* (London: Reaktion, 1999), 2–3.

12 For examples see 'Nazi Morale Shaken, Says Air Ministry', *Daily Mirror*, 3 July 1943, 5; '50-Year Plan to Rebuild London', *Evening News*, 9 July 1943, 1; 'London Plan Exhibition', *The Times*, 15 July 1943, 6. For discusion of images of the bombed and reconstructed city in twentieth-century wartime propaganda see Angus Calder, *The Myth of the Blitz* (London: Jonathan Cape, 1991).

13 For the disparate nature of the planning profession in the early twentieth century see Gordon Cherry, *The Evolution of British Town Planning: A History of Town Planning in the 20th Century and of the Royal Town Planning Institute, 1914–1974* (Leighton Buzzard: Leonard Hill Books, 1974); Gordon Cherry, *Town Planning in Britain since 1900: The Rise and Fall of the Planning Ideal* (Oxford: Blackwell, 1996).

14 See 'Abercrombie, Sir Patrick', *The Dictionary of National Biography 1951–1960* (London: Oxford University Press, 1971), 1–3. See also Gerald Dix, 'Patrick Abercrombie 1879–1957', in Gordon Cherry, ed., *Pioneers in British Planning* (London: Architectural Press, 1981), 103–30; David Matless, '"Appropriate Geography": Patrick Abercrombie and the Energy of the World', *Journal of Design History* 6, no. 3 (1993): 167–78; Pyrs Gruffudd, '"Uncivil Engineering": Nature, Nationalism and Hydro-Electrics in North Wales', in Denis Cosgrove and Geoff Petts, eds, *Water, Engineering and Landscape: Water Control and Landscape Transformation in the Modern Period* (London: Belhaven Press, 1990), 159–73.

15 'Forshaw, John Henry', *Who's Who 1945* (London: Adam and Charles Black, 1945), 945.

16 For other comparable figures in this tradition see Ben Pimlott, *Hugh Dalton* (London:

Jonathan Cape, 1985); Robert Skidelsky, *John Maynard Keynes: A Biography, Volume 2: The Economist as Saviour, 1920–1937* (London: Macmillan, 1992); José Harris, *William Beveridge: A Biography* (Oxford: Clarendon Press, 1997). For more general discussion of mid-twentieth-century liberal intellectual culture see Noel Annan, *Our Age: Portrait of a Generation* (London: Weidenfeld & Nicolson, 1990).

17 See Greater London Regional Planning Committee, *First Report of the Greater London Regional Planning Committee* (London: Knapp, Drewett, 1929); Greater London Regional Planning Committee, *Second Report of the Greater London Regional Planning Committee*, (London: Knapp, Drewett, 1933); *Report of the Royal Commission on the Distribution of the Industrial Population*, Cmnd. 6153 (London: HMSO, 1939).

18 See especially Patrick Geddes, *Cities in Evolution: An Introduction to the Town Planning Movement and to the Study of Civics* (London: Williams & Norgate, 1915), 25–30, 216–18; Lewis Mumford, *The Culture of Cities* (New York: Harcourt Brace, 1938), ch. 2.

19 Horace Walpole had used the word 'polypus' in 1776 to describe London's 'rows of houses that shoot out in every way'; quoted in Asa Briggs, *Victorian Cities* (Berkeley: University of California Press, 1993), 12. See also H. J. Dyos, 'The Growth of a Pre-Victorian Suburb: South London, 1580–1836', *Town Planning Review* 25, no. 1 (April 1954): 59–78.

20 Geddes, *Cities in Evolution*, 26–7. For similar discussion of the octopus image of London see Clough Williams-Ellis, *England and the Octopus* (London: Geoffrey Bles, 1928). For commentary see Matless, '"Appropriate Geography"'. Abercrombie distinguished this type of 'tentacular' city development in his regional study of Doncaster, written in the early 1920s; see Patrick Abercrombie and Thomas Johnson, *The Doncaster Regional Planning Scheme* (London: University Press of Liverpool, 1922). For analysis of Abercrombie's contributions to inter-war planning see Clough Williams-Ellis, 'A Genial Wizard: An Appreciation of Sir Patrick

Abercrombie', *The Listener*, 8 August 1957, 199–200; Dix, 'Patrick Abercrombie'.

21 Significantly, this was the image of London that was repeated in the popular version of the plan published by Penguin; see Edward Carter and Erno Goldfinger, *The County of London Plan Explained* (West Drayton: Penguin, 1945), 14–15.

22 Geddes suggested that in order to grasp what he christened the new 'conurbations', it was necessary to photograph them 'from an aeroplane journey', as well as to map them 'street by street': Geddes, *Cities in Evolution*, 34–5.

23 For literary perspectives 'from the air' see Valentine Cunningham, *British Writers of the Thirties* (Oxford: Oxford University Press, 1988), 186–206. For the aerial vision of the documentary film movement see Mary-Lou Jennings, ed., *Humphrey Jennings: Film-Maker, Painter, Poet* (London: British Film Institute in Association with Riverside Studios, 1982); Kevin Jackson, ed., *The Humphrey Jennings Film Reader* (Manchester: Carcanet, 1993). For military uses of aerial photography see Association of Royal Air Force Photographic Officers, *The History of Air Photography in the Royal Air Force* (England: Association of Royal Air Force Photographic Officers, 1987); Alf Pyner, *Air Cameras: RAF & USAAF, 1915–1945* (Burnham-on-Crouch: Alf Pyner, 1988).

24 See Matless, '"Appropriate Geography"', and his *Landscape and Englishness* (London: Reaktion, 1998), parts I and III.

25 Forshaw and Abercrombie, *County of London Plan*, 21.

26 Ibid., 22.

27 Mumford proposed a wholesale dispersal of 'the great offices of government that . . . crowd around Whitehall', in the long-term interests of urban renewal: Lewis Mumford, *The Plan of the London County, etc.*, Re-building Britain series, no. 12 (London: Faber & Faber, 1945), 31.

28 See Young and Garside, *Metropolitan London*, 229–87; Porter, *London*, 349–63; Inwood, *History of London*, 814–17; Sheppard, *London*, 341. For more nuanced arguments about the metropolitan-centredness of the *County of London Plan* see Bronwen Edwards, 'Shaping the Fashion City: Master Plans and Pipe Dreams in the Post-War West End of London', in Christopher Breward and David Gilbert, eds, *Fashion's World Cities* (Oxford: Berg, 2006), 159–73.

29 The idea of the English capital as the improved site for monarchical display and patrician symbolism was underpinned by a series of coordinated changes to the built environment of the West End beginning in the early 1900s. Architect Aston Webb's refronting of Buckingham Palace, together with his architectural layout of the Mall as a great processional way, which was framed by the newly erected Admiralty Arch (commemorating Edward VII) at the Trafalgar Square end and the Victoria Memorial to the south, created a parade ground for grandiose state ceremonial in which monarchy played the leading role. See David Cannadine, 'The Context, Performance and Meaning of Ritual: The British Monarchy and the "Invention of Tradition", c.1820–1977', in Eric Hobsbawm and Terence Ranger, eds, *The Invention of Tradition* (Cambridge: Cambridge University Press, 1983), 101–64; M. H. Port, *Imperial London: Civil Government Building in London 1850–1915* (New Haven and London: Yale University Press, 1995); Felix Driver and David Gilbert, 'Heart of Empire? Landscape, Space and Performance in Imperial London', *Environment and Planning D: Society and Space* 16 (1998): 11–28; Jonathan Schneer, *London 1900: The Imperial Metropolis* (New Haven and London: Yale University Press, 1999).

30 Aston Webb, ed., *London of the Future* (London: London Society, 1921). For analysis see Helena Beaufoy, '"Order Out of Chaos": The London Society and the Planning of London 1912–1920', *Planning Perspectives* 12 (1997): 135–64.

31 Forshaw and Abercrombie, *County of London Plan*, plate LII.

32 Harvey was a draughtsman whose watercolour renderings of London's historic buildings had been widely displayed and publicized since the 1920s. His illustrated books, especially those on eighteenth-century English domestic architecture, had contributed to the Georgian revival of the 1920s. See James Burford and John Harvey,

Some Lesser Known Architecture of London (London: Ernest Benn, 1925); Stanley Ramsey and John Harvey, Small Georgian Houses and their Details 1750–1820 (London: Architectural Press, 1972).

33 The Corporation advertised these only as suggested schemes, insisting that the St Paul's area was of such significance that the 'ultimate solution should be determined by means of a competition, open possibly to the whole Empire': Corporation of London, Report of the Preliminary Draft Proposals, 15.

34 The Corporation rejected as 'unpractical' plans put forward by the Royal Academy in 1942 for the total redevelopment of the St Paul's area, which would have involved the permanent clearance of many high-value sites. For the Royal Academy's own version of civic monumentalism see Royal Academy Planning Committee, London Replanned: The Royal Academy Planning Committee's Interim Report (London: Country Life, 1942).

35 Corporation of London, Report of the Preliminary Draft Proposals, drawing nos 3, 4a, 5.

36 Ibid., plate D.

37 See Matless, ' "Appropriate Geography" ', 167.

38 Patrick Abercrombie, 'The Preservation of Rural England', Town Planning Review 12, no. 1 (May 1926): 5–56; Patrick Abercrombie, Sydney Kelly and Thomas Johnson, Sheffield and District Regional Planning Scheme (London: Hodder & Stoughton, 1931).

39 Forshaw and Abercrombie, County of London Plan, v.

40 Thomas Adams, 'Foreword', in SERA, Regional Survey of New York, vol. 7, Neighborhood and Community Planning Comprising Three Monographs . . . (New York: n.p., 1929), 3. See also Thomas Adams, Outline of Town and City Planning: A Review of Past Efforts and Modern Aims (London: J & A Churchill, 1935).

41 Forshaw and Abercrombie, County of London Plan, 22.

42 Ibid., 23.

43 Ibid.

44 Ibid. For proposals on the central area by local authorities see City Engineer's and Surveyor's Office, City of Westminster, Town and Country Planning Act, 1947, Summary of London Development Plan with Particular Reference to Westminster City Engineer's and Surveyor's Office, 8 June 1947, in City of Westminster, Town Planning and Improvements Committee, Minutes 1954–5, Westminster City Archives, p. 500.

45 Forshaw and Abercrombie, County of London Plan, 24.

46 Ibid.

47 Ibid.

48 Ibid., plate VI.

49 Ibid., 48–78.

50 See especially Young and Garside, Metropolitan London, 229–34, 248–51; Inwood, History of London, 814–21.

51 See Jennifer Platt, Realities of Social Research: An Empirical Study of British Sociologists (London: Chatto & Windus, 1976); Philip Abrams and Paula Lewthwaite, eds, Development and Diversity: British Sociology, 1950–1980; Transactions of the Annual Conference of the British Sociological Association . . . 1980 (London: British Sociological Association, 1980).

52 Peter Sainsbury, Suicide in London: An Ecological Study (London: Chapman & Hall, 1955), 30.

53 Émile Durkheim, Le suicide: Étude de sociologie (Paris: Alcan, 1897).

54 See especially Robert Park and Ezra Burgess, The City (Chicago: University of Chicago Press, 1925); Harvey Zorbaugh, Gold Coast and the Slum: A Sociological Study of Chicago's Near North Side (Chicago: University of Chicago Press, 1929); Robert Faris and H. Warren Dunham, Mental Disorders in Urban Areas: An Ecological Study of Schizophrenia and Other Psychoses (Chicago: University of Chicago Press, 1939).

55 Sainsbury, Suicide in London, 33–7.

56 Ibid., 13.

57 Ruth Glass, 'Aspects of Change', in Centre for Urban Studies, eds, London: Aspects of Change (London: MacGibbon and Kee, 1964), xx–xxi. See also Ruth Glass, Newcomers: The West Indians in London (London: Centre for Urban Studies and George Allen & Unwin, 1960), 48–58.

58 Sainsbury, Suicide in London, 70.

59 Sainsbury acknowledged the pioneering work of the psychometric psychologist Cyril

Burt on the capital's rising juvenile delinquency rates which, Burt argued, were highest in the central districts of Finsbury, Holborn and Shoreditch, directly abutting onto areas of 'business, pleasure and residential comfort': Cyril Burt, *The Young Delinquent* (1944), quoted in Sainsbury, *Suicide in London*, 15.

60 See especially Glass, *Newcomers*; Centre for Urban Studies, *London: Aspects of Change*. Glass was Research Associate at the Centre. In 1949–50 the Department of Town Planning at University College undertook an early conservationist study of the Georgian squares of London: University College London, *University College Annual Report 1949–50* (London: University College London, n.d.), 39.

61 See Michael Young and Peter Willmott, *Family and Kinship in East London* (London: Routledge & Kegan Paul, 1957); Peter Townsend, *The Family Life of Old People: An Inquiry in East London* (London: Routledge & Kegan Paul, 1957); Peter Willmott and Michael Young, *Family and Class in a London Suburb* (London: Routledge & Kegan Paul, 1960). For analysis of the methods of the Institute of Community Studies see Jennifer Platt, *Social Research in Bethnal Green: An Evaluation of the Work of the Institute of Community Studies* (London: Macmillan, 1971).

62 See (among very many) Paddington Council of Social Service, Family Service Units for Problem Families, 16 January 1953, in London Metropolitan Archives, London Council of Social Service, LCSS Administration, Correspondence Files, 1950–60, ACC 1888/53; Family Welfare Association, *Eighty-First Annual Report . . . October 1 1946–September 30 1947* (London: Family Welfare Association, n.d.), 7.

63 The following account is based on Francis Camps, *Medical and Scientific Investigations in the Christie Case* (London: Medical Publications, 1953); Reginald Paget and Sidney Silverman, *Hanged – And Innocent?* (London: Gollancz, 1953); John Grigg and Ian Gilmour, *The Case of Timothy Evans: An Appeal to Reason* (London: Spectator, 1956);

F. Tennyson Jesse, ed., *Trials of Timothy John Evans and John Reginald Halliday Christie* (London: William Hodge, 1957); John Chance, *The Crimes at Rillington Place: A Novelist's Reconstruction* (London: Hodder & Stoughton, 1961); Ludovic Kennedy, *Ten Rillington Place* (London: Gollancz, 1961); John Eddowes, *The Two Killers of Rillington Place* (London: Little, Brown, 1994); Rupert Furneaux, *The Two Stranglers of Rillington Place* (London: Panther, 1994); Anonymous, *Rillington Place* (London: The Stationery Office, 1999).

64 Statement of Margaret Ploughman, 28 March 1953, Murders of Ethel Christie and other Women at 10 Rillington Place, London, by John Reginald Halliday Christie (1953–1965), TNA PRO MEPO 2/9535, part 1B.

65 See Grigg and Gilmour, *Case of Timothy Evans*, 4; Furneaux, *Two Stranglers of Rillington Place*, 7.

66 For coverage of Haigh and Heath see John Haigh, *The Trial of John George Haigh – The Acid Bath Murderer*, ed. Lord Dunboyne (London: William Hodge, 1953); Gerald Byrne, *Borstal Boy: The Uncensored Story of Neville Heath* (London: John Hill Productions, 1954); Conrad Phillips, *Murderer's Moon: Being Studies of Heath, Haigh, Christie & Chesney* (London: Arthur Barker, 1956); Paull Hill, *Portrait of a Sadist* (London: Neville Spearman, 1960). For the Ruth Ellis case see Robert Hancock, *Ruth Ellis* (London: Arthur Barker, 1963); Denise Farran, *The Trial of Ruth Ellis: A Descriptive Analysis* (Manchester: Sociology Department, University of Manchester, 1988); Laurence Marks, *Ruth Ellis: A Case of Diminished Responsibility?* (Harmondsworth: Penguin, 1990); Georgie Ellis, with Rod Taylor, *Ruth Ellis, My Mother: A Daughter's Memoir of the Last Woman To Be Hanged* (London: Smith Gryphon, 1995).

67 For the Montagu-Wildeblood episode see Peter Wildeblood, *Against the Law* (Harmondsworth: Penguin: 1957); Jeffrey Weeks, *Coming Out: Homosexual Politics in Britain from the Nineteenth Century to the Present*, 2nd edn (London: Quartet: 1990), 159–65; Patrick Higgins, *Heterosexual Dictatorship: Male Homosexuality in Postwar Britain* (London:

Fourth Estate, 1996), 231–46; Chris Waters, 'Disorders of the Mind, Disorders of the Body Social: Peter Wildeblood and the Making of the Modern Homosexual', in Becky Conekin, Frank Mort and Chris Waters, eds, *Moments of Modernity: Reconstructing Britain 1945–1964* (London: Rivers Oram, 1999), 134–51. For the Profumo scandal see Chapter 7.

68 On Burgess and Maclean see Cyril Connolly, *The Missing Diplomats* (London: Queen Anne Press, 1952); Tom Driberg, *Guy Burgess: A Portrait with Background* (London: Weidenfeld & Nicolson, 1956); S. J. Hamrick, *Deceiving the Deceivers: Kim Philby, Donald Maclean and Guy Burgess* (New Haven and London: Yale University Press, 2004). For the Vassall case see Home Office, *Report of the Tribunal Appointed to Inquire into the Vassall Case and Related Matters*, Cmnd. 2009 (London: HMSO, 1963); William Vassall, *Vassall: The Autobiography of a Spy* (London: Sidgwick & Jackson, 1975).

69 On the culture of the courtroom and its relationship to sexuality see Nancy Erber and George Robb, 'Introduction', in George Robb and Nancy Erber, eds, *Disorder in the Court: Trials and Sexual Conflict at the Turn of the Century* (Basingstoke: Macmillan, 1999), 1–11; Ruth Harris, *Murders and Madness: Medicine, Law and Society in the Fin de Siècle* (Oxford: Clarendon Press, 1989); Angus McLaren, *The Trials of Masculinity: Policing Sexual Boundaries, 1870–1930* (Chicago: University of Chicago Press, 1997).

70 Kali Israel, 'French Vices and English Liberties: Gender, Class and Narrative Competition in a Late Victorian Sexual Scandal', *Social History* 22, no. 1 (January 1997): 1.

71 Sainsbury, *Suicide in London*, 70; Glass, *Newcomers*, 49–58.

72 Forshaw and Abercrombie, *County of London Plan*, 65, 108, 156, 162, 176, 226.

73 'Kensington Chimes: Homes in Peril', *Kensington News and West London Times*, 6 January 1953, 6.

74 Barbara Denny, *Notting Hill & Holland Park Past: A Visual History* (London: Historical Publications, 1993), 86. See also F. H. W. Sheppard, general ed., *Survey of London*, vol. 37, *Northern Kensington* (London: Athlone Press, University of London, 1973), 346–51; Mary Cathcart Borer, *Two Villages: The Story of Chelsea and Kensington* (London: W. H. Allen, 1973).

75 Edward Pilkington, *Beyond the Mother Country: West Indians and the Notting Hill White Riots* (London: Tauris, 1988), 56. For contemporary and retrospective commentaries on the area see Pearl Jephcott, *A Troubled Area: Notes on Notting Hill* (London: Faber & Faber, 1964); Glass, *Newcomers*; Anthony Richardson, *Nick of Notting Hill: The Bearded Policeman; The Story of Police Constable J. Nixon F.166, of the Metropolitan Police* (London: Harrap & Co., 1965); Charlie Phillips and Mike Phillips, *Notting Hill in the Sixties* (London: Lawrence & Wishart, 1991).

76 For Caribbean immigration see Glass, *Newcomers*; Jephcott, *Troubled Area*; Sheila Patterson, *Dark Strangers: A Sociological Study of the Absorption of a Recent West Indian Migrant Group in Brixton, South London* (London: Tavistock, 1963); Trevor Lee, *Race and Residence: The Concentration and Dispersal of Immigrants in London* (Oxford: Clarendon Press, 1977); Nancy Foner, *Jamaica Farewell: Jamaican Migrants in London* (London: Routledge & Kegan Paul, 1979); Mike Phillips and Trevor Phillips, *Windrush: The Irresistible Rise of Multi-Racial Britain* (London: HarperCollins, 1998). In 1966 1.5 per cent of the population of Kensington and Chelsea was classified as Cypriot/Maltese; see Joe Doherty, 'The Distribution and Concentration of Immigrants in London', *Race Today*, no. 1 (December 1966): 228.

77 For coverage of Notting Dale's racialized atmosphere see 'Threat Letters to Girls Signed "Klu Klux Klan"', *Kensington News and West London Times*, 20 February 1953, 2; 'Blackshirts on the March Again', *Kensington News and West London Times*, 9 March 1956, 1; 'Milk Bottle Gang of Twenty-Five Boys Attacked Jamaican Social Worker', *Kensington News and West London Times*, 1 February 1957, 1. For official reaction see Immigrants from West Indies Settled in Notting Hill, London (1959), TNA PRO CO 1031/2541; Racial Disturbances Notting Hill Activities

of Extremist Organisations; Deputation of MPs to the Secretary of State (1959–1961), TNA PRO HO 325/9; Disturbances Involving Coloured Persons in London: Metropolitan Police Reports on Incidents (1960–1961), TNA PRO MEPO 2/9992.

78 'Kensington Times and the Changes They Ring', *Kensington News and West London Times*, 3 April 1953, 6.

79 'Leaving Kensington', *Kensington News and West London Times*, 3 June 1953, 6. See also 'This No-Man's Land is a Disgrace', *Kensington News and West London Times*, 20 July 1956, 1; 'Colonial Invasion', letters to the editor, *Kensington News and West London Times*, 6 July 1956, 7.

80 Charles Booth, *Life and Labour of the People in London, Third Series, Religious Influences 3: The City of London and the West End* (London: Macmillan, 1902), 152–3. For perceptions of the area which emphasized north Kensington's respectability see London School of Economics and Political Science, *The New Survey of London Life and Labour*, vol. 6, *Survey of Social Conditions (2) The Western Area (Text)* (London: P. S. King, 1934), 427–30.

81 Jephcott, *Troubled Area*.

82 See Donald Foley, *Controlling London's Growth: Planning the Great Wen, 1940–1960* (Berkeley and Los Angeles: University of California Press, 1963), 90–2; John Davis, 'Rents and Race in 1960s London: New Light on Rachmanism', *Twentieth Century British History* 12, no. 1 (2001): 73. The Milner Holland Committee on Housing in London reported that though the population of greater London fell by 2.7 per cent between 1951 and 1961, the number of separate households rose by 1.5 per cent: Ministry of Housing and Local Government, *Report of the Committee on Housing in Greater London*, Cmnd. 2605 (London: HMSO, 1965).

83 Glass, quoted in Davis, 'Rents and Race', 78. For further evidence of the housing crisis in north Kensington see Evidence of Franklin Stewart, 22 June 1953, Regina v John Reginald Halliday Christie, Transcript vol. 1, Criminal Cases: Christie, John Reginald Halliday: at Central Criminal Court on 25

June 1953 Convicted of Murder; Sentenced to Death; Executed 15 July 1953 (1949–1953), TNA PRO HO 291/228, p. 36; Phillips and Phillips, *Windrush*, 120–42.

84 For discussion of housing as a critical factor in English race relations during the 1950s and 1960s see James Wickenden, *Colour in Britain . . . Issued Under the Auspices of the Institute of Race Relations* (London: Oxford University Press, 1958); London Council of Social Service, West Indians in London: Report of a Conference at Caxton Hall 8 October 1958, in London Metropolitan Archives, London Council of Social Service and Related Agencies, Administration: Correspondence Files 1922–77, ACC 1888/110.

85 See Kennedy, *Ten Rillington Place*, 210.

86 Davis, 'Rents and Race', 78–9. See also Patterson, *Dark Strangers*, 180.

87 Evidence of Charles Brown, Christie Trial Transcript, vol. 1, TNA PRO HO 291/228, pp. 20–22; Tennyson Jesse, *Trials*, 138; Kennedy, *Ten Rillington Place*, 210.

88 Davis, 'Rents and Race', 78–9.

89 See Statement of Cyril Edwards, 24 March 1953, and Franklin James Stewart, 29 March 1953, TNA PRO MEPO 2/9535, part 1B.

90 For complaints by local residents to Kensington Council see Statement of Derek Kennedy, Sanitary Inspector, 26 March 1953, TNA PRO MEPO 2/9535, part 1A. For evidence of racist abuse see anonymous postcard to Mr Beresford [Brown], TNA PRO MEPO 2/9535, part 3B. For commentary see Furneaux, *Two Stranglers of Rillington Place*, 102–3.

91 For the Christies' background and precarious social position see Kennedy, *Ten Rillington Place*, 40, 49–50; Eddowes, *Two Killers of Rillington Place*, 4–5.

92 Quoted in Kennedy, *Ten Rillington Place*, 49–50.

93 Statement of Edward Smith, 25 March 1953, TNA PRO MEPO 2/9535, part 1A. See also Statement of Henry Waddington, 26 March 1953, TNA PRO MEPO 2/9535, part 1B.

94 Statement of Edwards; Statement of Stewart.

95 See Statement of Beresford Brown, 24 March 1953, TNA PRO MEPO 2/9535, part 1B.

96　Ibid.

97　Alain Corbin, *The Foul and the Fragrant: Odor and the French Social Imagination* (Leamington Spa: Berg, 1986), 151–3. See also Carolyn Steedman, *Dust* (Manchester: Manchester University Press, 2001), 117–18.

98　The original photographs are preserved in TNA PRO HO 291/228. For Law's testimony see Tennyson Jesse, *Trials*, 134–7. Sir Lionel Heald, the Attorney General, paid tribute to modern science in the detection of crimes like Christie's; see Sir Lionel Held, 'Foreword', in Camps, *Medical and Scientific Investigations*, xv. For historical discussion of police photography as official surveillance see John Tagg, *The Burden of Representation: Essays on Photographies and Histories* (Basingstoke: Macmillan Education, 1988), 66–102.

99　Camps, *Medical and Scientific Investigations*, 40.

100　The women identified by the police as prostitutes were Kathleen Maloney, Rita Nelson and Ina (Hectorina) Maclennan. See Statement of Maureen Riggs, 31 March 1953, and Statement of Dorothy Symers, 8 April 1953, TNA PRO MEPO 2/9535, part 1B; Statement of Lillian Maloney, 28 March 1953, TNA PRO MEPO 2/9535, part 1C.

101　Camps, *Medical and Scientific Investigations*, 43–4. For speculation about Christie as a necrophiliac see Tennyson Jesse, *Trials*, lxi.

102　Camps, *Medical and Scientific Investigations*, 40.

103　For the excesses of modern official and documentary photography see Allan Sekula, *Dismal Science Photo Works 1972–1996* (Normal, IL: University Galleries, Illinois State University, 1999), 122, and his *Photography Against the Grain: Essays and Photo Works 1973–1983* (Halifax, NS: Press of the Nova Scotia College of Art and Design, 1984).

104　For the negative erotic associations of the female body in the history of modern sex crime see Deborah Cameron and Elizabeth Frazer, *Lust to Kill: A Feminist Investigation of Sexual Murder* (Cambridge: Polity, 1987); Jane Caputi, *The Age of Sex Crime* (Bowling Green, OH: Bowling Green University Popular Press, 1987); Judith Walkowitz, *City of Dreadful Delight: Narratives of Sexual Danger in Late-Victorian London* (London: Virago, 1992), 191–228.

105　'Murder House Girl Named', *Daily Mail,* 25 March 1953, 1.

106　'Crowds Wait All Night Outside Rillington Place Charnel House', *Kensington News and West London Times*, 27 March 1953, 1.

107　See 'Christie: Bodies in Cupboard', *Evening Standard*, 22 April 1953, 1; 'Christie Pleads Insanity says QC', *Evening Standard*, 22 June 1953, 1; 'Is Christie Sane? Doctors Clash', *Evening Standard*, 24 June 1953, 1. During the period April to June 1953, months that were dominated by coverage of preparations for the coronation, the Rillington Place murders appeared twelve times as headline news in this London paper, second only to the royal event.

108　See 'Multi-Killer: Police Fear', *Daily Mail*, 27 March 1953, 1.

109　See 'London Jammed 14 Hours in Coronation Preview' and 'Mrs. Evans: Dawn Exhumation', *Daily Express*, 18 May 1953, 1.

110　'The Ghouls of Rillington Place', *People*, 23 August 1953, 1.

111　Albert Pierrepoint, *Executioner Pierrepoint* (London: Harrap, 1974), 169. Pierrepoint saw demand for the reporting of 'colourful murders' as heralding the permissive society. For related comments about the impact of the concentration camps on the English popular imagination see Ludovic Kennedy, *One Man's Meat* (London: Longmans, Green & Co., 1953), 24–5.

112　Hugh Cudlipp, *At Your Peril: A Mid-Century View of the Exciting Changes of the Press in Britain, and a Press View of the Exciting Changes of Mid-Century* (London: Weidenfeld & Nicolson, 1962), 47, 292.

113　Arthur Christiansen, *Headlines All My Life* (London: Heinemann, 1961), 286. Christiansen was editor of the Beaverbrook-owned *Daily Express* in the early 1950s.

114　Margaret Cowen, 'Christiansen – Ideas Man!' *Stage and Television Today*, 13 April 1960, 15.

115　Colin Coote, *Editorial: The Memoirs of Colin R. Coote* (London: Eyre & Spottiswoode, 1965), 248–9.

116　For the primacy of print journalism in news transmission throughout the 1950s and the ongoing importance of the 'human interest story' see Christiansen, *Headlines All My Life*; Cudlipp, *At Your Peril*.

117 'End of a Monster', *Daily Mail*, 26 June 1953, 1.

118 For the Nuremberg trials see Bradley Smith, *The Road to Nuremberg* (New York: Basic Books, 1981); Rebecca West, *A Train of Powder* (London: Virago, 1984); Larry May, *Aggression and Crimes Against Peace* (Cambridge: Cambridge University Press, 2008).

119 Tony Judt, *Postwar: A History of Europe since 1945* (London: Pimlico, 2007), 186–8.

120 The most prominent American trials were the controversial prosecutions of Alger Hiss in 1950 and the Jewish Communists Julius and Ethel Rosenberg a year later. See Morton Levitt and Michael Levitt, *A Tissue of Lies: Nixon vs Hiss* (New York: McGraw-Hill, 1979); Ronald Radosh, *The Rosenberg File: A Search for the Truth* (London: Weidenfeld & Nicolson, 1983).

121 On the celebrity nature of the trial see Tennyson Jesse, *Trials*, lvi; Furneaux, *Two Stranglers of Rillington Place*, 9; Eddowes, *Two Killers of Rillington Place,* 93.

122 'Comment', *Queen*, 6 May 1953, 36.

123 For evidence of the different social constituencies drawn to Christie's trial see Mrs E. Clark [Slough] to the Clerk of the Court, Central Criminal Court, 28 May 1953; Geoffrey London [Kenton, Middlesex] to the Keeper of the Old Bailey, 14 June 1953; Herbert Drake [Southgate] to the Keeper of the Old Bailey, 14 June 1953, John Christie: Applications for Press and Visitors Passes (Regina v John Christie) (April–June 1953), TNA PRO CRIM 8/22.

124 'The Christie Judge', *Evening News*, 22 June 1953, cutting preserved in TNA PRO CRIM 8/22.

125 See A. Klapras to Central Criminal Court, Old Bailey, 6 June 1953; Arthur Jacobs to Leslie Boyd, Deputy Clerk, Central Criminal Court, undated, TNA PRO CRIM 8/22.

126 'Christie's Mind', *Daily Express*, 25 June 1953, 1.

127 'Express Diary', *Daily Express*, 26 June 1953, 6. For details of Lady Lowson see Fiona MacCarthy, *Last Curtsey: The End of the Debutantes* (London: Faber & Faber, 2006), 44, 55.

128 See Kennedy, *Ten Rillington Place*, 140–1.

129 Robert Sherwood, 'If Christie Had Been Tried in New York', *Evening Standard*, 26 June 1953, 6.

130 The trial of Stephen Ward, part of the denouement of the Profumo affair, aroused much society interest; see Ludovic Kennedy, *The Trial of Stephen Ward* (New York: Simon & Schuster, 1965), 18. In the Montagu-Wildeblood case the links between homosexuality and the metropolitan gentry were played up by the prosecution; see Wildeblood, *Against the Law*, 14.

131 For depictions of Burgess's relationship to London's high and low cultures see 'Guy Burgess Stripped Bare!', *People*, 11 March 1956, 3.

132 Phillips, *Murderer's Moon*, 45–6. See also Neville Heath, *The Trial of Neville George Clevely Heath*, ed. MacDonald Critchley (London: William Hodge, 1951); Francis Selwyn, *Rotten to the Core? The Life and Death of Neville Heath* (London: Routledge, 1988); Richard Davenport-Hines, 'Heath, Neville George Clevely', *Oxford Dictionary of National Biography* (Oxford: Oxford University Press, 2004), http://www.oxforddnb.com/view/printable/58803/ (accessed 30 July 2007). For Haigh see Arthur La Bern, *Haigh: The Mind of a Murderer . . . Psychiatric Analysis by Nöel C. Browne* (London: W. H. Allen, 1973); Stewart Evans, 'Haigh, John George', *Oxford Dictionary of National Biography* (Oxford: Oxford University Press, 2004), http://www.oxforddnb.com/view/printable/58803 (accessed 30 July 2007).

133 John Christie, 'My Dream and My First Victim', *Sunday Pictorial*, 5 July 1953, 6.

134 Tennyson Jesse, *Trials*, i.

135 Ibid.

136 See Julie English Early, 'A New Man for a New Century: Dr. Crippen and the Principles of Masculinity', in Robb and Erber, eds, *Disorder in the Court*, 209–11.

137 Francis Camps, with Richard Barber, *The Investigation of Murder* (London: Michael Joseph, 1966), 51.

138 See for example Percy Bibby, Sydney, to New Scotland Yard, 26 June 1953; Maria Fuchs, Astrologer, Bremen, to Chief Det-

ective to the Assize Court, Old Bailey, 5 June 1953, TNA PRO MEPO 2/9535, part 3B.

139 For Christie as Svengali see Mrs L. Hay to Superintendent Peter Berridge, 26 March 1953, TNA PRO MEPO 2/9535, part 3A. For a reading of the Svengali myth in terms of urban modernity see Daniel Pick, *Svengali's Web: The Alien Enchanter in Modern Culture* (New Haven and London: Yale University Press, 2000).

140 'Arrest of the London "Landru"', newspaper cutting extracted from *Le Soir*, 4 April 1953, trans. P. C. Langford, in TNA PRO MEPO 2/9535, part 3A.

141 Helen Sunderland to Metropolitan Police, 31 March 1953, TNA PRO MEPO 2/9535, part 1B.

142 Interested Onlooker, unsigned and undated letter to Scotland Yard, TNA PRO MEPO 2/9535, part 3B.

143 Statement of Arthur Turner, 25 March 1953, TNA PRO MEPO 2/9535, part 1A.

144 Statement of Mariana Demetra Papajotou-Jarman, TNA PRO MEPO 2/9535, part 1B.

145 Sir Lionel Heald, closing speech for the prosecution, 24 June 1953, quoted in Tennyson Jesse, *Trials*, 253. Mr Christmas Humphreys made a similar point about north Kensington in the prosecution's summing up at the trial of Timothy Evans in 1950: ibid., 81.

146 For the cinematic treatment of European cities see Pierre Sorlin, *European Cinemas, European Societies 1930–1990* (London: Routledge, 1991). For the urban landscape of postwar Vienna see Brigitte Timmermann, *The Third Man's Vienna: Celebrating a Film Classic*, trans. Penny Black (Vienna: Shippen Rock, 2005).

147 These films included *They Made Me A Fugitive* (1947), directed by Alberto Cavalcanti, *Noose* (1948), directed by Edmond Greville, and *The Blue Lamp* (1950), directed by Basil Dearden. See Charlotte Brunsdon, 'Space and Place in the British Crime Film', in Steve Chibnall and Robert Murphy, eds, *British Crime Cinema* (London: Routledge, 1999), 148–59; Charlotte Brunsdon, *London in Cinema: The Cinematic City since 1945* (London: British Film Institute, 2007), 21–56.

148 'And the Queen Smiled' and 'Gay Rillington Place', *Kensington News and West London Times*, 5 June 1953, 5.

149 See Ministry of Health, *Mortality and Morbidity During the London Fog of December 1952: Reports on Public Heath and Medical Subjects No. 95* (London: HMSO, 1954); London County Council, *Report of the County Medical Officer of Health and School Medical Officer for the Year 1952* (London: London County Council, 1953), 159.

150 'Fog Delays Air Services', *The Times*, 6 December, 6; 'London Buses Stopped', *The Times*, 8 December 1952, 8. For mortality rates see Ministry of Health, *Mortality and Morbidity*, 1–2; London County Council, *Report of the County Medical Officer 1952*, 159.

151 'Death Rate in London Fog', *The Times*, 31 January 1953, 3.

152 Ernest Fisk, letter to the editor, *The Times*, 10 December 1952, 7. Scientists at the Ministry of Health noted that modern medicine had eliminated the nineteenth-century scourge of cholera along with most of the other contagious and infectious diseases, but scientists seemed helpless in the face of the effects of industrial pollution: Ministry of Health, *Mortality and Morbidity*, 3.

153 Though scientific research into the effects of pollution was rudimentary, many local medical officers noted that large numbers of fatalities occurred in areas that were close to the 'sources of excessive smoke'; see 'Information from Dr. E. Smithard, Medical Officer of Health, Lewisham', Ministry of Health, *Mortality and Morbidity*, 26.

154 'Mr. Churchill's Broadcast', *The Times*, 26 March 1953, 8. See also 'The Genius of Queen Mary', *Daily Mail*, 25 March 1953, 5.

155 James Pope-Hennessy, *Queen Mary 1867–1953* (London: George Allen & Unwin, 1959), 621. For coverage of Queen Mary's death and funeral see 'A Lifetime of Gracious Service', *The Times*, 25 March 1953, 5; 'Queen Mary's Body Borne to Westminster Hall', *The Times*, 30 March 1953, 6.

156 For this version of moral and sexual progressivism see C. A. R. Crosland, *The Future of Socialism* (London: Jonathan Cape, 1956),

521–4; Roy Jenkins, *The Labour Case* (Harmondsworth: Penguin, 1959), 135–46.

157 For analysis of heritage and conservationist versions of the Victorian past in the post-war period see Patrick Wright, *On Living in an Old Country: The National Past in Contemporary Britain* (London: Verso, 1985); Robert Hewison, *The Heritage Industry: Britain in a Climate of Decline* (London: Methuen, 1987); Raphael Samuel, *Theatres of Memory, Volume 1: Past and Present in Contemporary Culture* (London: Verso, 1994).

158 Davenport-Hines, 'Heath'; Phillips, *Murderer's Moon*, 45–6.

159 Evans, 'Haigh'.

160 Jane Dunn, 'Ellis, Ruth', *Oxford Dictionary of National Biography* (Oxford: Oxford University Press, 2004), http://oxforddnb.com/view/article/56716 (accessed 31 July 2007).

161 For the relationship between the normal and the abnormal in twentieth-century social and psychiatric discourse see Nikolas Rose, *Governing the Soul: The Shaping of the Private Self* (London: Routledge, 1990); Peter Miller and Nikolas Rose, eds, *The Power of Psychiatry* (Cambridge: Polity, 1986). For contemporary studies of the sexual criminal see British Medical Association, Joint Committee on Psychiatry and the Law, *The Criminal Law and Sexual Offenders: A Report of the Joint Committee on Psychiatry and the Law Appointed by the British Medical Association and the Magistrates Association* (London: British Medical Association, 1949); Cecil Binney, *Crime and Abnormality* (London: Oxford University Press, 1949).

162 Walkowitz, *City of Dreadful Delight*, 197–8.

163 'Is Christie Sane?'; 'Three Doctors Argue the Vital Question – Is Christie Sane?' *Daily Mail*, 25 June 1953, 1.

164 Christie's defence lawyers maintained that he was insane and hence irresponsible, while the prosecution successfully argued that though Christie was mentally and sexually inadequate he was fit to plead. See Report on John Reginald Halliday Christie by Desmond Curran, 4 June 1953 and Dr. J. C. M. Matheson, Principal Medical Officer Brixton Prison, On Christie, John Reginald

Halliday, 18 June 1953, Christie, John Reginald Halliday: At Central Criminal Court on 16 June 1953 Convicted of Murder, Sentenced to Death; Executed (1953), TNA PRO PCOM 9/1668.

165 See William Wells to David Maxwell Fyfe, 24 June 1953, TNA PRO MEPO 2/9535, part 3A; J. C. Matheson to Reginald Seaton, 13 June 1953, TNA PRO PCOM 9/1668. For Norwood East's influential work on criminology see W. Norwood East, *Medical Aspects of Crime* (London: J. & A. Churchill, 1936); W. Norwood East, *Society and the Criminal* (London: HMSO, 1949). For commentary see Chris Waters, 'Havelock Ellis, Sigmund Freud and the State: Discourses of Homosexual Identity in Interwar Britain', in Lucy Bland and Laura Doan, eds, *Sexology in Culture: Labelling Bodies and Desires* (Cambridge: Polity, 1998), 165–79.

166 Stephen Coates, Clinical Psychologist, Rorschach Report, Mr. Christie, 19 June 1953, TNA PRO PCOM 9/1668.

167 Jack Abbott Hobson, Consultant Physician, Department of Psychological Medicine, Middlesex Hospital, Report on Christie, TNA PRO PCOM 9/1668.

168 Dr. Desmond Curran, Report on John Reginald Halliday Christie, 4 June 1953, TNA PRO PCOM 9/1668.

169 'Doctors Give Christie Secret Brain Test', *Sunday Empire News*, 7 June 1953, cutting in TNA PRO PCOM 9/1668.

170 For Ward's autobiographical story see Warwick Charlton and Gerald Sparrow, *Stephen Ward Speaks: Conversations with Warwick Charlton; Judge Gerald Sparrow Sums Up the Profumo Affair* (London: Today Magazine, 1963). For Keeler see (among very many) Peter Earle, 'Take a Girl Like Christine', *News of the World*, 7 April 1963, 6.

171 Furneaux, *Two Stranglers of Rillington Place*, 125.

172 'Ghouls of Rillington Place'.

173 See W. Montgomery, on behalf of Central London News Service, to J. Christy [*sic*], 1 April 1953, TNA PRO PCOM 9/1668. Christie's relationship with the press was in direct contravention of Home Office rules stating that it was not in the public interest

for those awaiting trial for serious crimes to give interviews to the press. Questions were asked in Parliament about how 'a long article that was advertised as being the first of a series had been delivered to the press by Christie'. The answer was that 'the Home Office were almost certain that Christie had smuggled out his story via his solicitors': Extract of a Note Sent by Mr. Plaice to the Home Office, 2 July 1953, TNA PRO PCOM 9/1668, and see Condemned Prisoner (Communications) Mr. Marlowe to Sir H. Lucas-Tooth, 9 July 1953, Oral Answers, *Parliamentary Debates (Hansard) House of Commons Official Report*, 5th ser., vol. 517, session 1952–3 (London: HMSO, 1953), cols 1477–8.

174 'Girls Laughed at Me', *Sunday Pictorial*, 12 July 1953, 6.

175 'Christie's Own Story: My Second Victim . . . We Kissed and Cuddled', *Sunday Pictorial*, 12 July 1953, 6. See also 'Christie Writes his Story for the Sunday Pictorial', *Sunday Pictorial*, 28 June 1953, 1, 4–5.

176 'Christie's Own Story', 6. See also 'Girls Laughed at Me'. For other readings of Christie as a Victorian casualty see Matheson, On Christie; Kennedy, *Ten Rillington Place*, 22–8.

177 'Serial Killers Casefiles, John George Haigh', http://hosted.ray.easynet.co.uk/serial_killers/haigh.html (accessed 31 July 2007).

178 Caputi, *Age of Sex Crime*, 129.

179 Camps, *Medical and Scientific Investigations*, 39.

180 See Penny Summerfield, *Reconstructing Women's Wartime Lives: Discourse and Subjectivity in Oral Histories of the Second World War* (Manchester: Manchester University Press, 1998), 164.

181 Second Statement of Christie, 5 June 1953, quoted in Camps, *Medical and Scientific Investigations*, 200–1. See also Trial Transcript, vol. 1, TNA PRO HO 291/228, pp. 99–100; Kennedy, *Ten Rillington Place*, 43.

182 Statement of Edith Willis, 21 May 1953, TNA PRO MEPO 2/9535, part 1B. See also Statement of Mrs Emma Le Bas, 20 June 1953.

183 Sonya Rose, 'Sex, Citizenship, and the Nation in World War II Britain', *American Historical Review* 103, no. 4 (October 1998): 1148; Sonya Rose, 'Girls and GI's: Race, Sex and

Diplomacy in Second World War Britain', *International History Review* 19, no. 1 (1997): 146–60; Lesley Hall, *Sex, Gender and Social Change in Britain since 1880* (Basingstoke: Macmillan, 2000), 99–166.

184 Statement of Lillian Maloney, undated, TNA PRO MEPO 2/9535, part 1C. For the treatment of delinquency in young women see Pamela Cox, *Gender, Justice and Welfare: Bad Girls in Britain, 1900–1950* (Basingstoke: Palgrave Macmillan, 2003).

185 Statement of George Noakes, 30 March 1953, TNA PRO MEPO 2/9535, part 1B.

186 'Multi-Killer: Police Fear'.

187 Report of Sergeant J. Brown, 28 March 1953, TNA PRO MEPO 2/9535, part 3A.

188 Statement of Riggs.

189 Statement of Papajotou-Jarman.

190 For coverage of these other homicides and serial killings see Fred Harrison, *Brady and Hindley: Genesis of the Moors Murders* (Bath: Ashgrove, 1986); Nicole Ward Jouve, *'The Streetcleaner': The Yorkshire Ripper Case on Trial* (London: Boyars, 1986); Colin Wilson, *The Corpse Garden: The Crimes of Fred and Rose West* (London: True Crime Library, 1998).

191 The number of Caribbean migrants to Britain was small until 1953 and then increased rapidly, reaching a peak in 1956. In 1958 and during the first half of 1959 there was a sharp decline, but in the second half of that year numbers rose again; see Glass, *Newcomers*, 4. Kensington was one of the few inner metropolitan boroughs to show a population increase between 1951 and 1961. The 1961 Census revealed that 40,500 residents, 24 per cent of the borough's total population, were born outside the British Isles; see Jephcott, *Troubled Area*, 23.

192 See Chris Waters, '"Dark Strangers" in Our Midst: Discourses of Race and Nation in Britain, 1947–1964', *Journal of British Studies* 36, no. 2 (April 1997): 207–38.

193 Kenneth Little, *Negroes in Britain: A Study of Racial Relations in English Society* (London: Kegan Paul, Trench Trubner & Co., 1947), 2–3.

194 Ibid., app. 1, 280–1.

195 Anthony Richmond, *Colour Prejudice in Britain: A Study of West Indian Workers in Liverpool,*

1941–1951 (London: Routledge & Kegan Paul, 1954), 18. See also Michael Banton, *The Coloured Quarter: Negro Immigrants in an English City* (London: Jonathan Cape, 1955); Barbara Ballis Lal, 'The "Chicago School" of American Sociology, Symbolic Interactionism, and Race Relations Theory', in John Rex and David Mason, eds, *Theories of Race and Ethnic Relations* (Cambridge: Cambridge University Press, 1986), 280–98.

196 Glass, *Newcomers*, 41.

197 Ibid., 51.

198 Bill Schwarz, ' "The Only White Man in There": The Re-Racialization of England 1956–1968', *Race and Class* 38, no. 1 (1996): 65–78; Bill Schwarz, 'Reveries of Race: The Closing of the Imperial Moment', in Conekin et al., *Moments of Modernity*, 189–207.

199 For sexual relations between white women and black men as a source of social anxiety see Clifford Hill, *Black and White in Harmony: The Drama of West Indians in the Big City, from a London Minister's Notebook* (London: Hodder & Stoughton, 1958); Majbritt Morrison, *Jungle West 11* (London: Tandem Books, 1964); Pilkington, *Beyond the Mother Country*, 64–6; Marcus Collins, 'Pride and Prejudice: West Indian Men in Mid-Twentieth-Century Britain', *Journal of British Studies* 40, no. 3 (July 2001): 391–418.

200 See Statement of Kennedy, TNA PRO MEPO 2/9535, part 1A.

201 See Statement of Christie, 31 March 1953, TNA PRO MEPO 2/9535, part 1B; Tennyson Jesse, *Trials*, xxx–xxxi.

202 See Waters, ' "Dark Strangers" ', 227.

203 Derek Curtis Bennett to Franklin James Stewart, Trial Transcript, vol. 1, 22 June 1953, TNA PRO HO 291/228, p. 36.

204 Ethel Christie to Mrs Lily Bartle, 15 December 1952 [date altered by Christie], exhibit no. 4, TNA PRO HO 291/228.

205 Statement of Ena Baldwin, 27 March 1953, TNA PRO MEPO 2/9535, part 1B.

206 Evidence of Christie, Trial Transcript, vol. 1, 23 June 1953, p. 109.

207 Statement of Kennedy.

208 John McGowan to Metropolitan Police, 25 March 1953, TNA PRO MEPO 2/9535, part 3A.

209 See 'Women Fight Intruders – Courageous Action Succeeds', *The Times*, 6 January 1953, 6; 'Settler Killed by Mau Mau', *The Times*, 9 February 1953, 8. For official reactions to and accounts of the Mau Mau movement see Colonial Office, *Historical Survey of the Origins and Growth of Mau Mau*, Cmnd. 1030 (London: HMSO, 1960); Donald Barnett, *Mau Mau from Within: Autobiography and Analysis of Kenya's Peasant Revolt* (London: MacGibbon and Kee, 1966); Robert Buijenhuijs, *Essays on Mau Mau* (Leiden: African Studies Centre, 1982); Robert Edgerton, *Mau Mau: An African Crucible* (New York: Free Press, 1989); Wunyabari Maloba, *Mau Mau and Kenya: An Analysis of a Peasant Revolt* (Bloomington: Indiana University Press, 1993).

210 'Mau Mau Massacre of Loyal Kikuyu', *The Times*, 28 March 1953, 8. See also 'Nairobi Declared a Special Area', *The Times*, 25 April 1953, 5.

211 'Mr. Lyttleton's Return', *The Times*, 7 November 1952, 6. For the impact of Mau Mau on race relations in north Kensington see Richardson, *Nick of Notting Hill*, 144–5.

212 Andrew Cohen, *British Policy in Changing Africa* (London: Routledge & Kegan Paul, 1959), 55.

213 *Simba*, set in Kenya, was directed by Brian Desmond Hurst and produced by Rank; see Wendy Webster, ' "There'll Always Be an England": Representations of Colonial Wars and Immigration, 1948–1968', *Journal of British Studies* 40, no. 4 (October 2001): 565, 576; Richard Dyer, 'White', *Screen* 29, no. 4 (1988): 44–64.

214 Pierrepoint, *Executioner Pierrepoint*, 205.

215 '200 Crowd at Prison as Christie Dies', *The Star*, 15 July 1953, 1.

216 For this idea of social turbulence see Victor Turner, 'Social Dramas and Stories about Them', *Critical Inquiry* 7, no. 1 (1980): 159.

CHAPTER 4   GOVERNANCE

1 John Wolfenden to W. Conwy Roberts, 28 August 1954, Committee on Homosexual Offences and Prostitution, General Corr-

espondence (1954–1957), TNA PRO HO 345/2. Roberts was a career civil servant who in 1954 was listed in the *Imperial Calendar* as Principal of the International Division of the Home Office. In 1955 he became Principal in the Office's Criminal Division.

2 David Maxwell Fyfe and James Stuart, Warrant of Appointment, 24 August 1954, Committee on Homosexual Offences and Prostitution, Minutes of Meetings (1954–1957), TNA PRO HO 345/6. The committee's brief also included investigation of the treatment of persons convicted of homosexual offences by the courts.

3 For Cabinet discussions see Item 12, 11th Conclusions, 24 February 1954, Cabinet Papers, 1 January to 22 June 1954, TNA PRO CAB 128/27, p. 98; Item 4, 20th Conclusions, 17 March 1954, TNA PRO CAB 128/27, p. 156; Item 5, 29th Conclusions, 15 April 1954, TNA PRO CAB 128/27, pp. 6–7. See also Memorandum by the Secretary of State for the Home Department and Minister for Welsh Affairs, C. (54) 50, 17 February 1954, TNA PRO CAB 129/66.

4 Lord Butler, *The Art of the Possible: The Memoirs of Lord Butler* (London: Hamish Hamilton, 1971), 198; Macmillan quoted in Henry Fairlie, *The Life of Politics* (London: Methuen, 1968), 16. I am grateful to Peter Caterall for the Fairlie source. For contemporary debates about sex as a political conscience issue see C. A. R. Crosland, *The Future of Socialism* (London: Jonathan Cape, 1956), 521–4; Roy Jenkins, *The Labour Case* (Harmondsworth: Penguin, 1959), 135–46.

5 Churchill proposed simply doing nothing, or at most encouraging some back-bench MPs to introduce a bill designed to prevent the publication of detailed accounts of criminal proceedings for homosexual offences: Item 4, 17 March 1954, TNA PRO CAB 128/27, p. 156. See also Patrick Higgins, *Heterosexual Dictatorship: Male Homosexuality in Post-War Britain* (London: Fourth Estate, 1996), 6.

6 D. J. Dutton, 'Fyfe, David Patrick Maxwell, Earl of Kilmuir', *Oxford Dictionary of National Biography* (Oxford: Oxford University Press, 2004), http://www.oxforddnb.com/view/

article/33301 (accessed 3 November 2007). See also David Maxwell Fyfe, *Political Adventure: The Memoirs of the Earl of Kilmuir* (London: Weidenfeld & Nicolson, 1964).

7 See Item 4, 17 March 1954, TNA PRO CAB 128/27, p. 156.

8 Item 5, 15 April 1954, TNA PRO CAB 128/27, p. 7.

9 Home Office, Scottish Home Department, *Report of the Committee on Homosexual Offences and Prostitution*, Cmnd. 247 (London: HMSO, 1957), 9–10. The report was invariably known as the Wolfenden report. See also Wolfenden's later comments on his strategy of legal reform in 'Lord Wolfenden on Public Law and Private Morality', *The Listener*, 8 February 1979, 211.

10 The Wolfenden inquiry was underpinned by an updated version of classic Millian principles of legal utilitarianism, as well as by a tighter definition of the boundaries separating crime from immorality, traditionally an indistinct division within English jurisprudence. For Wolfenden's own debt to John Stuart Mill see his Law and Morality, typewritten draft of a speech, undated, Papers of John Frederick Wolfenden, MS 5311, uncatalogued, Special Collections Service, University of Reading. For commentaries see Stuart Hall, 'Reformism and the Legislation of Consent', in National Deviancy Conference, eds, *Permissiveness and Control: The Fate of the Sixties Legislation* (London: Macmillan, 1980), 1–43; H. Montgomery Hyde, *The Other Love: An Historical and Contemporary Survey of Homosexuality in Britain* (London: Mayflower, 1972), 255–97; Jeffrey Weeks, *Coming Out: Homosexual Politics from the Nineteenth Century to the Present*, 2nd edn (London: Quartet, 1990), 156–82; Helen Self, *Prostitution, Women and Misuse of the Law: The Fallen Daughters of Eve* (London: Frank Cass, 2003), 69–160.

11 The legislation covered two moments of Home Office reform. The first, associated with Rab Butler's period as Home Secretary, included the limitation of the death penalty in the Homicide Act, 1957, 5 & 6 Eliz. 2, c. 11; the Street Offences Act, 1959, 7 & 8 Eliz. 2, c. 57, dealing with prostitution; the Obs-

cene Publications Act, 1959, 7 & 8 Eliz. 2, c. 66; the Suicide Act, 1961, 9 & 10, Eliz. 2, c. 60; and various legislation affecting licensing, betting, and gaming. The second period, largely coincident with the tenure of Roy Jenkins, included the second Obscene Publications Act, 1964, c. 74; the Murder (Abolition of Death Penalty) Act, 1965, c. 71; the Sexual Offences Act, 1967, c. 60, addressing homosexuality; the Abortion Act, 1967, c. 87; the Theatres Act, 1968, c. 54, dealing with stage censorship; and the Divorce Reform Act, 1969, c. 55. For political commentary see Butler, *Art of the Possible*, 198–205; Roy Jenkins, *A Life at the Centre* (London: Macmillan, 1991), 199–213; James Callaghan, *Time and Chance* (London: Collins, 1987), 229–49.

12 See especially and from very different perspectives Lucy Bland, Trisha McCabe and Frank Mort, 'Sexuality and Reproduction: Three "Official" Instances', in Michèle Barrett, Philip Corrigan and Janet Wolff, eds, *Ideology and Cultural Production* (London: Croom Helm, 1979), 78–111; Stephen Jeffery-Poulter, *Peers, Queers and Commons: The Struggle for Gay Law Reform from 1950 to the Present* (London: Routledge, 1991); Leslie Moran, *Homosexual(ity) of Law* (London: Routledge, 1996); Higgins, *Heterosexual Dictatorship*; Self, *Prostitution*.

13 Hall, 'Reformism', 6.

14 For an influential reading of cultural transgression that I have drawn on here see Peter Stallybrass and Allon White, *The Politics and Poetics of Transgression* (London: Methuen, 1986), 128.

15 Roberts to Wolfenden, 22 September 1954, TNA PRO HO 345/2. The records of the Wolfenden committee are preserved at TNA PRO HO 345/1–20. Material relating to police tactics used to entrap homosexual men engaged in public sex was removed from the files before their release, though this was denied by the Home Office librarian in his conversation with me in 1999; see also Higgins, *Heterosexual Dictatorship*, 10.

16 Wolfenden was appointed director of pre-entry training in the Air Ministry in 1941, and in 1942 he chaired the Board of Education's Youth Advisory Council and became

a member of the charitable Carnegie United Kingdom Trust: John Wolfenden, *Turning Points: The Memoirs of Lord Wolfenden* (London: Bodley Head, 1976), 79–87, 97–101.

17 For Wolfenden's social ambition see Speech of Lord Wolfenden, 12 November 1975, *Parliamentary Debates (Hansard) House of Lords Official Report*, 5th ser., vol. 365, session 1974–5 (London: HMSO, 1976), col. 1845. For his early background see Wolfenden, *Turning Points*, ch. 1; Jeffrey Weeks, 'Wolfenden, John Frederick, Baron Wolfenden', *Oxford Dictionary of National Biography* (Oxford: Oxford University Press, 2004), http://www.oxforddnb.com/view/article/31852 (accessed 10 Aug 2007).

18 See Noel Annan, *Our Age: Portrait of a Generation* (London: Weidenfeld & Nicolson, 1990), 8, 215. Annan distinguished this first generation of grammar school boys from later cohorts in terms of their continuing conformity to upper-class codes of behaviour, while in the 1950s and 1960s the manners of the grammar school boy 'became ascendant and the public school boys found themselves at a disadvantage': ibid., 3.

19 Wolfenden, *Turning Points*, 133.

20 Sebastian Faulks, *The Fatal Englishman: Three Short Lives* (London: Hutchinson, 1996), 218. For the only letter in Wolfenden's papers discussing Jeremy, after his son's death, see Wolfenden to John Sparrow, Warden of All Souls College, Oxford, May 1976, Wolfenden Papers.

21 Faulks, *Fatal Englishman*, 241. Faulks's account is not substantiated.

22 Wolfenden to Association of Municipal Corporations, Notes of a Meeting, 31 January 1956, Committee on Homosexual Offences and Prostitution, Transcripts of Evidence Hearings (1956), TNA PRO HO 345/16, p. 6.

23 Wolfenden, *Turning Points*, 133. See also Wolfenden to Lord Templewood, 23 May 1954, quoted in Higgins, *Heterosexual Dictatorship*, 7.

24 See Ian Toplis, *The Foreign Office: An Architectural History* (London: Mansell, 1987), 186; Robert Pittam, Highlights (and some dark corners) of Home Office History:

Lecture by R. R. Pittam, May 1982 at Lunar House, unpublished, 1982, typescript in Home Office library, p. 9; Robert Pittam, 'The Home Office 1782–1982', in Home Office, *The Home Office 1782–1982: To Commemorate the Bicentenary of the Home Office* (London: Home Office, 1982), 10. In the early 1960s the *Architect's Journal* condemned these nineteenth-century government buildings as 'an inefficient office slum'; see 'Loving Modernisation or Expedient Desecration', *Architect's Journal* 136, no. 13 (26 September 1962): 733. The problems associated with the Victorian structure and lay-out of the government offices are well described by M. H. Port, *Imperial London: Civil Government Building in London 1850–1915* (New Haven and London: Yale University Press, 1995), 141, 146, and by David Brownlee, 'That "Regular Mongrel Affair": G. G. Scott's Design for the Government Offices', *Architectural History* 28 (1985): 159–82.

25 Pittam, 'Home Office', 10.

26 Harold Macmillan, *Tides of Fortune, 1945–1955* (London: Macmillan, 1969), 492; Harold Macmillan, *Riding the Storm, 1956–1959* (London: Macmillan, 1971), 1.

27 For the Home Office's role see Frank Newsam, *The Home Office* (London: George Allen & Unwin, 1954); Sir Alexander Maxwell, *The Work of the Home Office: A Talk to the Staff by Sir Alexander Maxwell* (London: Home Office, 1944); Maxwell Fyfe, *Political Adventure*, 198–219; Royal Institute of Public Administration, *The Home Office: Perspectives on Policy and Administration: Bicentenary Lectures 1982* (London: Royal Institute of Public Administration, 1983).

28 'The Boy from Barbados', *Daily Mail*, 13 February 1956, 4. See also Allen of Abbeydale, 'Newsam, Sir Frank Aubrey', *Oxford Dictionary of National Biography* (Oxford: Oxford University Press, 2004), http://www.oxforddnb.com/view/article/35219 (accessed 3 November 2007); Butler, *Art of the Possible*, 199.

29 Annan, *Our Age*, 125; Austin Strutt, 'Sir Frank Aubrey Newsam', in E. T. Williams and C. S. Nicolls, eds, *The Dictionary of National Biography, 1961–1970* (Oxford: Oxford University Press, 1981), 792; Pittam, Highlights.

30 Lord Allen of Abbeydale, 'Reflections of a Bureaucrat', in Royal Institute of Public Administration, *Home Office*, 32. See also Neil Cairncross, 'Where Have All the Old Characters Gone?' in Home Office, *Home Office*, 42, 48.

31 Pittam, 'Home Office', 15.

32 See Newsam, *Home Office*, 41–2, 65, 78, 135, 139. See also Allen of Abbeydale, 'Newsam'. Under Newsam's regime little attempt was made to expand the government's capacity to address a range of issues that loomed large on the political agenda of all post-war home secretaries, especially the vexed questions of capital punishment, rising crime rates and the treatment of offenders. Departmental funds allocated to research were extremely low, with only £12,000 spent between 1948 and 1957, and it was not until after Newsam's retirement that a Home Office research unit was established. See Leon Radzinowicz, *Adventures in Criminology*, (London: Routledge, 1999), 172; T. S. Lodge, 'The Founding of the Home Office Research Unit', in Roger Hood, ed., *Crime, Criminology and Public Policy: Essays in Honour of Sir Leon Radzinowicz* (London: Heinmann, 1974), 11–24.

33 See Newsam to Wolfenden, 22 August 1956, and Wolfenden to Newsam, 5 September 1956, TNA PRO HO 345/2; Roberts to Wolfenden, 28 August 1956, Committee on Homosexual Offences and Prostitution, Committee Notes and Correspondence (1956), TNA PRO HO 345/5.

34 Wolfenden, *Turning Points*, 134. See also Patrick Trevor-Roper, interview by the author, August 1999.

35 Minutes of the First Meeting, 15 September 1954, Committee on Homosexual Offences and Prostitution, Minutes of Meetings (1954–1957), TNA PRO HO 345/6, p. 1.

36 For the ensuing problems resulting from the conflation of homosexuality and prostitution see Self, *Prostitution*, 82.

37 See especially Metropolitan Police Act, 1839, 2 & 3 Vict., c. 47, Section 54 (11); City of London Police Act, 1839, 2 & 3 Vict., c. 94,

Section 35 (11); Town Police Clauses Act, 1847, 10 & 11 Vict., c. 89, Section 28; Vagrancy Act, 1824, 5 Geo. 4, c. 83. For a summary of existing legislation in the 1950s see Home Office, Scottish Department, *Report of the Committee on Homosexual Offences and Prostitution*, 82–5, 98–112.

38   Minutes of the Second Meeting, 14 and 15 October 1954, TNA PRO HO 345/6, para. 6.

39   Minutes of the First Meeting, TNA PRO HO 345/6, p. 1.

40   Roberts to Wolfenden, 30 September 1954, TNA PRO HO 345/2.

41   Revised List of Organizations to which Invitations to Submit Evidence Might be Addressed, undated, 1954, TNA PRO HO 345/2.

42   Roberts to Wolfenden, 27 August 1954, TNA PRO HO 345/2.

43   Self, *Prostitution*, 84–5. At their first meeting committee members also agreed to 'establish among ourselves one or two general principles to guide us through these complicated affairs': Wolfenden, *Turning Points*, 134–5.

44   See (among very many) Association for Moral and Social Hygiene to Wolfenden, 14 October 1954; National Council of Women of Great Britain to Wolfenden, 20 October 1954, British Vigilance Association and the National Committee for the Suppression of Traffic in Persons to Wolfenden, 2 November 1954, TNA PRO HO 345/2.

45   Teddington and the Hamptons Women Citizens' Association to Wolfenden, 26 October 1954, TNA PRO HO 345/2. See also Methodist Church, Department of Christian Citizenship, to Wolfenden, 29 October 1954, TNA PRO HO 345/2.

46   For the history of these two traditions within nineteenth- and early twentieth-century English feminism see Judith Walkowitz, 'Male Vice and Feminist Virtue: Feminism and the Politics of Prostitution in Nineteenth-Century Britain', *History Workshop Journal*, no. 13 (1982): 79–93; Susan Kingsley Kent, *Sex and Suffrage in Britain, 1860–1914* (Princeton, NJ: Princeton University Press, 1987); Lucy Bland, *Banishing the Beast: English Feminism and Sexual Morality 1885–1914* (London: Penguin, 1995); Frank Mort, *Dangerous Sexualities: Medico-Moral Politics in England since 1830*, 2nd edn (London: Routledge, 2000), 49–116.

47   Association for Moral and Social Hygiene, 'Draft Public Places Order Bill', *Shield*, April 1953, 40. For details of the deputation to the Home Office see 'Notes and Observations', *Shield*, December 1953, 3–4. Directed at both sexes equally, the draft bill removed references to 'common prostitutes' and also required evidence from those 'annoyed' before charges could be pressed by the police. Part of the proposals were a restatement of the Home Office, *Report of the Street Offences Committee*, Cmnd. 3231 (London: HMSO, 1928).

48   See International Bureau for the Suppression of Traffic in Persons, British Vigilance Association, and the National Committee for the Suppression of Traffic in Persons, *Second Annual Report . . . for the Year Ending 1954* (London: International Bureau for the Suppression of Traffic in Persons, 1954), 7.

49   'Notes and Observations', *Shield*, December 1954–January 1955, 1.

50   See Wolfenden to the Dowager Lady Nunburnholme, 19 November 1954, TNA PRO HO 345/2.

51   Wolfenden to Roberts, 22 November 1954, TNA PRO HO 345/2.

52   For Wolfenden's persona as the 'ordinary citizen' see Wolfenden to Roberts, 22 November 1954; for his views on the Nonconformist churches, especially the Methodists, see Wolfenden to Roberts, 1 November 1954, TNA PRO HO 345/2. For the exchanges over feminism see Roberts to Wolfenden, 26 October 1954, TNA PRO HO 345/2.

53   Notes of the General Discussion on 24 February 1956, TNA PRO HO 345/6, p. 3; Roberts to Wolfenden, 23 September 1954, TNA PRO HO 345/2.

54   See Self, *Prostitution*, 88; Martin Pugh, *Women and the Women's Movement in Britain, 1914–1959* (London: Macmillan, 1992), ch. 10.

55   The procedure for selecting committee members is not clearly documented in the Home Office archive. Higgins has argued

that Wolfenden himself helped to choose the members, but there is no evidence for this; see Higgins, *Heterosexual Dictatorship*, 9. For Churchill's own possible involvement see Item 5, 15 April 1954, TNA PRO CAB 128/27, p. 7.

56 For Wolfenden's confession of scientific illiteracy see Wolfenden to Mrs E. Abbott, Vice-President of the Association for Moral and Social Hygiene, 18 October 1955, TNA PRO HO 345/2.

57 See 'Editorial', *Savelian Wakefield Grammar School Magazine*, December 1933, 2, in Wolfenden Papers.

58 Self, *Prostitution*, 154; see also Higgins, *Heterosexual Dictatorship*, 7–9. For other commentaries on Wolfenden's character written at the time of the publication of his autobiography see J. E. Morpurgo, 'A Very Private Person', *Yorkshire Post*, 8 April 1976, 9; Philip Toynbee, 'The Invisible Man', *Observer*, 11 April 1976, 9; C. H. Rolph, 'Turn Again', *New Statesman*, 30 April 1976, 580. All these authors commented on Wolfenden's ruthless suppression of his private life.

59 Weeks, 'Wolfenden'.

60 Wolfenden reflected later that 'it was very important that the Committee should not be all male': Wolfenden, *Turning Points*, 133.

61 One of the committee, Kenneth Diplock, Recorder of Oxford, also had a reputation for being a 'safe pair of hands' on government inquiries; see Stephen Sedley and Godfray Le Quesne, 'Diplock, (William John) Kenneth, Baron Diplock', *Oxford Dictionary of National Biography* (Oxford: Oxford University Press, 2004), http://www.oxforddnb.com/view/article/31031 (accessed 10 Aug 2007).

62 John Wolfenden, *The Creation of a Public Conscience: The Twenty-First Shaftesbury Lecture* (London: Shaftesbury Society, 1961), 4–5.

63 The exception was Curran, who was a committed Freudian. See Curran to Roberts, 16 September 1954, TNA PRO HO 345/2. For more characteristic responses to Freud's theories see Roberts to Wolfenden, 20 December 1954, TNA PRO HO 345/2.

64 Wolfenden, *Turning Points*, 134.

65 Home Office, Scottish Department, *Report of the Committee on Homosexual Offences and Prostitution*, 152–5.

66 Wolfenden, *Turning Points*, 139.

67 Notes of a Meeting, 15 October 1954, Committee on Homosexual Offences and Prostitution, Transcripts of Evidence Hearings (1955), TNA PRO HO 345/12, p. 1.

68 Minutes of the Second Meeting, 14 and 15 October 1954, TNA PRO HO 345/6, para. 6.

69 Minutes of the First Meeting, 15 September 1954, TNA PRO HO 345/6, p. 2. See also Homosexuality and Homosexual Offences: General Considerations, undated, February 1956, Committee on Homosexual Offences and Prostitution, Committee Notes and Correspondence (1955–1957), TNA PRO HO 345/4, unpaginated.

70 Notes of a Meeting, 15 October 1954, TNA PRO HO 345/12, p. 3.

71 James Adair, ibid., p. 57; Mr. C. H. Watkins, Chief Constable of Glamorgan, Notes of a Meeting, 31 March 1955, Committee on Homosexual Offences and Prostitution, Transcripts of Evidence Hearings (1955), TNA PRO HO 345/13, p. 6.

72 'Dunne, Sir Laurence Rivers', in E. T. Williams and C. S. Nicholls, eds, *The Dictionary of National Biography 1961–1970* (Oxford: Oxford University Press, 1981), 316.

73 Richard Davenport-Hines, 'Dunne, Sir Laurence', *Oxford Dictionary of National Biography* (Oxford: Oxford University Press, 2004), http://www.oxforddnb.com/view/article/32936 (accessed 30 October 2008).

74 Memorandum Submitted by Sir Lawrence Dunne, Committee on Homosexual Offences and Prostitution, Committee Papers (1954–1955), TNA PRO HO 345/7, p. 3.

75 In 1952 Bow Street Magistrates Court heard 194 cases of homosexual offences, while Marlborough Street heard 56, out of an overall London total of 583; see Matt Houlbrook, *Queer London: Perils and Pleasures in the Sexual Metropolis, 1918–1957* (Chicago and London: University of Chicago Press, 2005), 273.

76 Memorandum Dunne, p. 3. For objections to Dunne's position see Claude Mullins, Mem-

orandum, TNA PRO HO 345/7, p. 1. Dunne opposed the provisions of Section 17 (2) of the Criminal Justice Act, 1948, 11 & 12 Geo. 6, c. 58, which proscribed imprisonment for male offenders under twenty-one, except as a last resort.

77 Memorandum Dunne, p. 10. The lines were misquoted from Isaac Watts's poem 'Against Idleness and Mischief', in his collection *The Divine and Moral Songs for the Use of Children* (1715).

78 Memorandum Dunne, p. 3.

79 Ibid., p. 4.

80 Ibid., p. 2.

81 Ibid., pp. 2–3.

82 Ibid., p. 2.

83 Ibid.

84 Ibid.

85 Ibid.

86 Ibid., p. 3.

87 David Ascoli, *The Queen's Peace: The Origins and Development of the Metropolitan Police, 1829–1979* (London: Hamish Hamilton, 1979), 269–71; Higgins, *Heterosexual Dictatorship*, 261.

88 Wolfenden to Sir John Nott-Bower, Notes of a Meeting, 7 December 1954, TNA PRO HO 345/12, p. 1.

89 Memorandum by Sir John Nott-Bower, Commissioner of Police for the Metropolis, 22 November 1954, TNA PRO HO 345/7, p. 11.

90 Ibid., pp. 10, 8.

91 Ibid, app. D.

92 For these forms of surveillance see James Scott, *Seeing Like a State: How Certain Schemes to Improve the Human Condition Have Failed* (New Haven and London: Yale University Press, 1998); Frank Mort, 'Mapping Sexual London: The Wolfenden Committee on Homosexual Offences and Prostitution 1954–57', *New Formations*, no. 37 (Spring 1999): 92–113; Patrick Joyce, *The Rule of Freedom: Liberalism and the Modern City* (Lon-don: Verso, 2003).

93 Houlbrook, *Queer London*, 23.

94 Hugh Linstead to Wolfenden, 28 September 1954, TNA PRO HO 345/2.

95 Roberts to Wolfenden, 24 November 1954, TNA PRO HO 345/2.

96 See Higgins, *Heterosexual Dictatorship*, 16.

97 Home Office, *Report of the Street Offences Committee*, 25.

98 Home Office, *Report of the Royal Commission on Police Powers and Procedure*, Cmnd. 3297 (London: HMSO, 1929), 40–1. For discussion see Moran, *Homosexual(ity) of Law*, 162–4.

99 Plain Clothes, Employment of Officers of Uniform Branch . . . , n.d. (1936?), Metropolitan Police, Employment of Uniformed Officers in Plain Clothes (1936–1960), TNA PRO MEPO 2/8311.

100 Ibid. The importance of these diaries and notebooks was stressed repeatedly in police training manuals published before and after the Second World War; see C. C. Moriarty, *Police Procedure and Administration*, 6th edn (London: Butterworth, 1955); Alan Garfitt, *The Book for Police*, vol. 1 (London: Caxton, 1958), 148.

101 Garfitt, *Book for Police*, 435–7.

102 Meeting held 5 January 1928, Street Offences Committee, Report of Sub-Committee . . . on the Cases of Major Graham Bell Murray and Mr. Francis Henry Bateman Champain with Appendices, n.d., Metropolitan Police, Francis Henry Bateman Champain – Importuning: Successful Appeal Against Conviction on Grounds of Drunkenness Causing Strange Behaviour (1927), TNA PRO MEPO 3/405, p. 20.

103 Inspector on Duty at Police Court (M Division), Magistrate's Remarks, 30 August 1933, Metropolitan Police, Use of Plain Clothes Officers in Detecting Indecency Offences in Urinals: Magisterial Comments About "Agents Provocateurs" (1933), TNA PRO MEPO 3/990. The Metropolitan Police were divided over the case; the District Commander defended the use of specially selected plain-clothes officers to 'stamp out this objectionable practice', but more senior figures were concerned that such methods tended 'to provoke the commission of offences': DAC No. 4, 19 September 1933, and ACA, 26 September 1933, TNA PRO MEPO 3/990, pp. 14, 16.

104 ACA, 15 October 1933; W. Bronson to F. C. Watkins, 25 September 1943, TNA PRO MEPO 3/990. In the aftermath of the war,

efforts were made by the DPP to clarify the distinction between 'the somewhat sinister term Agent Provocateur' and genuine efforts by the police to 'gain evidence originating from participation' in a range of sex crimes including gross indecency. The DPP insisted that if the offence was such that 'ordinary methods of outside observation' were ineffective, then an officer was justified 'in participating in the crime . . . to obtain the necessary evidence': Metropolitan Police: Agent Provocateur: Definition of the Term "Agent Provocateur", Memorandum on the Use of Agents Provocateur by the Director of Public Prosecutions (1945), TNA PRO HO 45/25622, p. 3. See also Deputation re Scotland Yard Action, 31 January 1945, TNA PRO HO 45/25622.

105 JB, 14 October 1954, Director of Public Prosecutions, Departmental Committee on Homosexual Offences and Prostitution (Wolfenden Committee): Memorandum by Director (1954–1956), TNA PRO DPP 6/66.

106 See Memorandum Submitted by the Home Office 2: Homosexual Offences, TNA PRO HO 345/7, p. 3; Moran, *Homosexual(ity) of Law*, 119.

107 Memorandum Nott-Bower, TNA PRO HO 345/7, p. 11.

108 Notes of a Meeting, 7 December 1954, TNA PRO HO 345/7, pp. 6–7.

109 For these official traditions of information gathering see Mary Poovey, *Making a Social Body: British Cultural Formation, 1830–1864* (Chicago: University of Chicago Press, 1995); Scott, *Seeing Like a State*; Joyce, *Rule of Freedom*.

110 Judge Jean Graham Hall, interview by the author, August 1999. See also Trevor-Roper, author's interview.

111 Evidence of PC Butcher, Notes of a Meeting, 7 December 1954, PRO HO 345/12, p. 3. On casual clothes for young adult men in the 1950s see Frank Mort and Peter Thompson, 'Retailing, Commercial Culture and Masculinity in 1950s Britain: The Case of Montague Burton the "Tailor of Taste"', *History Workshop Journal*, no. 38 (Autumn 1994): 106–27.

112 Evidence Butcher, pp. 1–2.

113 Ibid., p. 4.

114 Ibid., p. 3.

115 Ibid., p. 2. There were thirteen advertising agencies in the vicinity of Grosvenor and Berkeley squares in the mid-1950s; see *Coles Classified Directories: The West End Directory Guide 1954–55* (London: Fudge, 1955).

116 For the liminal space of the urinals see Matt Houlbrook, 'The Private World of Public Urinals: London, 1918–57', *London Journal* 25, no. 1 (2000): 53. For their longer-term history in homosexual London see Angus McLaren, *The Trials of Masculinity: Policing Sexual Boundaries, 1870–1930* (Chicago: University of Chicago Press, 1997), 194; Randolph Trumbach, 'London', in David Higgs, ed., *Queer Sites: Gay Urban Histories since 1600* (London: Routledge, 1999), 89–111.

117 Evidence Butcher, pp. 6, 3.

118 Desmond Curran and Denis Parr, 'Homosexuality: An Analysis of 100 Male Cases Seen in Private Practice', *British Medical Journal* 1 (6 April 1957): 800.

119 W. Lindsey Neustatter, 'Homosexuality: The Medical Aspect', *Practitioner* 172, no. 1030 (April 1954): 371.

120 Memorandum on Venereal Disease and the Homosexual submitted by Dr. F. J. G. Jefferiss, Committee on Homosexual Offences and Prostitution, Committee Papers (1955–1956), TNA PRO HO 345/9, p. 5. See also Evidence of Dr. Peter Scott on Behalf of the Institute of Psychiatry, Notes of a Meeting, 13 September 1955, Committee on Homosexual Offences and Prostitution, Transcripts of Evidence Hearings (1955), TNA PRO HO 345/14, p. 7.

121 Evidence Butcher, p. 3.

122 Evidence of PC Darlington, Notes of a Meeting, 7 December 1954, TNA PRO HO 345/12, p. 11.

123 Evidence Butcher, p. 12.

124 Ibid., p. 3.

125 Ibid., p. 5.

126 Evidence Darlington, pp. 9–10.

127 Moran, *Homosexual(ity) of Law*, 118.

128 For these gestures and rituals as forms of communicative action in the urinals see Laud Humphreys, *Tearoom Trade: A Study of Homosexual Encounters in Public Places*

(London: Duckworth, 1970), 59–80; Moran, *Homosexual(ity) of Law*, 149–53.

129   Roberts noted that committee members dispersed rather more hurriedly than usual after hearing the police accounts; see Roberts to Wolfenden, 31 December 1954, TNA PRO HO 345/2.

130   Higgins, *Heterosexual Dictatorship*, 16.

131   Trevor-Roper, author's interview; Patrick Trevor-Roper, 1990, Hall Carpenter Oral History Project, British Library Sound Archive, C456/089/01.

132   Graham Hall, author's interview.

133   Roberts to Wolfenden, 31 December 1954, TNA PRO HO 345/2.

134   See, for example, Mary Cohen to Roberts, 25 September 1955, Committee on Homosexual Offences and Prostitution, Correspondence with Secretary (1955–1957), TNA PRO HO 345/3.

135   Trevor-Roper, author's interview.

136   See Cohen to Wolfenden, 30 July 1956, TNA PRO HO 345/5; Note by Mrs. Lovibond, n.d. (September 1955), and Note by Lady Stopford, n.d. (September 1955), TNA PRO HO 345/4.

137   See Note by the Secretary, 10 October 1956, Committee on Homosexual Offences and Prostitution, Committee Papers (1956–1957), TNA PRO HO 345/10.

138   For their submissions to the committee on prostitution see (among very many) National Council of Women, Draft of Evidence for the Committee on Enquiry into Solicitation and Prostitution, Committee on Homosexual Offences and Prostitution, Committee Papers (1955), TNA PRO HO 345/8; British Medical Association, Homosexuality and Prostitution: A Memorandum of Evidence Prepared by a Special Committee of the Council of the British Medical Association, November 1955, TNA PRO HO 345/9; Memorandum upon Prostitution and Kindred Offences Prepared by the Paddington Moral Reform Union, 1955, TNA PRO HO 345/8; Evidence of the Association of Municipal Corporations, Notes of a Meeting, 31 January 1956, TNA PRO HO 345/16.

139   Summary Record of General Exchange of Views at the 14th Meeting, 5 October 1955, TNA PRO HO 345/6, pp. 1–2, 6.

140   Ibid., p. 7.

141   Ibid. See also Notes of a Meeting, 31 January 1956, TNA PRO HO 345/16, p. 4.

142   Summary 14th Meeting, TNA PRO HO 345/6, p. 10.

143   Vera Williams, Notes of a Meeting, 13 July 1955, Committee on Homosexual Offences and Prostitution, Transcripts of Evidence Hearings (1955), TNA PRO HO 345/13, p. 31.

144   Summary 14th Meeting, TNA PRO HO 345/6, p. 11.

145   Ibid.

146   Notes of a Meeting, 29 October 1955, TNA PRO HO 345/9.

147   Alfred Kinsey, Journal of 1955 European Trip, Notes, 12 October 1955, Alfred C. Kinsey Collection, Box 1, series 1, B, Diaries, Folder 1, Bloomington, Indiana, The Kinsey Institute for Research in Sex, Gender, and Reproduction, p. 15.

148   Home Office, Scottish Department, *Report of the Committee on Homosexual Offences and Prostitution*, 12. Committee members were keen to know whether individuals were fixed on Kinsey's scale, or if there was any movement. Kinsey's reply was cautious; while sexual orientation was determined by the age of sixteen for the majority of men, there was nonetheless some fluidity in the middle range of the spectrum, though this was usually towards the homosexual end. Dr Whitby asked Kinsey if his findings were compatible with the idea that society was primarily organized into two groups, heterosexual and homosexual. Kinsey framed a culturalist reply that was consistent with his rejection of the notion of a distinctive homosexual identity. Kinsey emphasized that 'social factors' made it 'more convenient' for a boy of this sort 'to associate with an exclusively homosexual group where he is accepted': Notes of a Meeting, 29 October 1955, TNA PRO HO 345/9, p. 5.

149   Notes of a Meeting, 29 October 1955, TNA PRO HO 345/9, p. 5.

150   Ibid., p. 13.

151 Ibid., p. 4.

152 The final report agreed that 'total reorientation from complete homosexuality to complete heterosexuality is very unlikely indeed', but it nonetheless affirmed that 'there is evidence that the homosexual who is of a Kinsey rating lower than 5 or 6 provides opportunity for treatment with a better prospect of success', Home Office, Scottish Department, *Report of the Committee on Homosexual Offences and Prostitution*, 66.

153 See James Jones, *Alfred C. Kinsey: A Public/Private Life* (New York: W. W. Norton, 1997), xi–xii.

154 See, for example, Steen Eiler Rasmussen, 'Neighbourhood Planning', *Town Planning Review* 27, no. 4 (January 1957): 207; Lewis Mumford, 'The Neighbourhood and the Neighbourhood Unity', *Town Planning Review* 30, no. 1 (April 1959): 99.

155 For Paddington Council's strategy on prostitution see Prostitution: Bayswater Road, Metropolitan Borough of Paddington, Report of the General Purposes, Legal and Parliamentary Committee, 9 November 1950, in Metropolitan Borough of Paddington, Minutes of Council 25th May 1950–26th April 1951, Westminster City Archives, p. 188. The council also improved street lighting in local red-light areas as a means of prevention; see Minutes of a Meeting of Paddington Borough Council, 24 July 1952, in Metropolitan Borough of Paddington, Minutes of Council 22nd May 1952–30th April 1953, p. 15.

156 Edward Glover, *The Psychopathology of Prostitution*, 2nd edn (London: Institute for the Study and Treatment of Delinquency, 1957), 5.

157 Ibid., 16.

158 Thomas James, *Prostitution and the Law* (London: William Heinemann, 1951), 50–1, 124.

159 For this debate see Patrick Devlin, *The Enforcement of Morals . . . Maccabaean Lecture in Jurisprudence of the British Academy, 1959* (London: Oxford University Press, 1959); H. L. A Hart, *Law, Liberty and Morality* (London: Oxford University Press, 1963). For

Wolfenden's own intervention see Wolfenden to Hon. Mr Justice Devlin, 17 March 1959, Wolfenden Papers.

160 Notes of a Meeting, 2 February 1955, TNA PRO HO 345/12, p. 30.

161 Association for Moral and Social Hygiene, Evidence Presented to the Departmental Committee, July 1955, TNA PRO HO 345/8, p. 4.

162 Ibid., p. 5. See also National Council of Women, Draft of Evidence, TNA PRO HO 345/8, pp. 1–3.

163 Association for Moral and Social Hygiene, Evidence, p. 4; Evidence of Elizabeth Abbott, both TNA PRO HO 345/8, p. 1.

164 Notes of Discussion at Meeting on 17 October 1956, Committee on Homosexual Offences and Prostitution, Committee Papers (1956–1957) TNA PRO HO 345/10, p. 3.

165 Cohen to Wolfenden, 30 July 1956, TNA PRO HO 345/5.

166 Ibid.

167 Draft Section on Prostitution, in Wolfenden's hand, undated, TNA PRO HO 345/5.

168 Summary 14th Meeting, TNA PRO HO 345/6, p. 7.

169 Notes of Discussion, 17 October 1956, TNA PRO HO 345/10, p. 3.

170 Notes of a Meeting, 17 November 1955, Committee on Homosexual Offences and Prostitution, Transcripts of Evidence Hearings (1955–1956), TNA PRO HO 345/15, p. 13.

171 'Reservation by Mrs. Cohen, Mrs. Lovibond and Lady Stopford', Home Office, Scottish Department, *Report of the Committee on Homosexual Offences and Prostitution*, 128, see also 95–6. The Street Offences Act increased prison sentences for those convicted of living on the earnings of prostitution and of exercising control over prostitutes to a maximum of seven years.

172 Hugh Linstead to Wolfenden, 28 September 1954, TNA PRO HO 345/2.

173 Ibid.

174 Roberts to Wolfenden, 30 September 1954, TNA PRO HO 345/2. Cohen was Vice-Chairman of the National Vigilance Association of Scotland; she had been

President of Glasgow and West Scotland Union of Girls' Clubs (1924–31) and Emergency Officer for Youth in Glasgow (1939–43). See 'Cohen, Mary Gwendolen', *Who's Who, 1960* (London: Adam and Charles Black, 1960), 604.

175 Roberts to Wolfenden, 15 December 1954, TNA PRO HO 345/2.

176 Wolfenden to Roberts, 21 January 1955, TNA PRO HO 345/2, and Wolfenden to Roberts, 29 June 1955, TNA PRO HO 345/2.

177 Roberts, Minutes [untitled], January 1955, TNA PRO HO 345/2.

178 See Roberts to Wolfenden, 15 December 1954, Wolfenden to Roberts, 11 May 1955, and Wolfenden to Roberts, 29 June 1955, TNA PRO HO 345/2.

179 Wolfenden to Roberts, 11 May 1955. The committee did eventually make a limited announcement in the press asking for homosexual men to give evidence; see Roberts to Wolfenden, 18 May 1955, TNA PRO HO 345/2.

180 Trevor-Roper, author's interview. See also Trevor-Roper, Hall Carpenter Oral History Project, C456/089/01; Dudley Cave, 1987, C456/063/01; Tony Garrett, 1990, C456/090/01–02.

181 Trevor-Roper, author's interview.

182 Ibid.

183 Ibid. It is unclear what case Wolfenden was referring to.

184 Ibid.

185 'Jean Graham Hall', in Rebecca Abrams, *Woman in a Man's World: Pioneering Career Women of the Twentieth Century* (London: Methuen, 1993), 94–110. See also 'News and Information, Chartered Institute of Arbitrators – South East Branch, Obituary Her Honour Jean Graham Hall', http://www.arbitrate.org.uk/nvmay05/notices_1.htm (accessed 18 January 2008).

186 Graham Hall, author's interview.

187 Ibid.

188 See Roberts to Wolfenden, 16 March 1955, TNA PRO HO 345/6.

189 Minutes of the Eighth Meeting, 30 and 31 March 1955, and see also Minutes of the Fifth Meeting, 4 and 5 January 1955, TNA PRO HO 345/6.

190 See Judith Walkowitz, *Prostitution and Victorian Society: Women, Class and the State* (Cambridge: Cambridge University Press, 1980), 113–47; Mort, *Dangerous Sexualities*, 51–77.

191 For studies of Wildeblood see Higgins, *Heterosexual Dictatorship*, 40–1, 247–8; Simon Edge, 'Peter Wildeblood: Hero Without Applause', *Soundings*, no. 3 (Summer 1996): 175–84; Chris Waters, 'Disorders of the Mind, Disorders of the Body Social: Peter Wildeblood and the Making of the Modern Homosexual', in Becky Conekin, Frank Mort and Chris Waters, eds, *Moments of Modernity: Reconstructing Britain 1945–1964* (London: Rivers Oram, 1999), 134–51. See also Wildeblood's obituaries: 'Peter Wildeblood', *Guardian*, 16 November 1999, 20; 'Peter Wildeblood – Obituary', *The Times*, 16 November 1999, 27; 'Peter Wildeblood', *Independent*, 25 November 1999, 6.

192 Peter Wildeblood, *Against the Law* (Harmondsworth: Penguin, 1957), 31.

193 'I Went for a Quiet Holiday', *Daily Sketch*, 19 March 1954, 3.

194 For Wildeblood's relationship with Trevor-Roper see author's interview. For his affair with the Indian prince see Wildeblood, *Against the Law*, 32.

195 Wildeblood, *Against the Law*, 42.

196 Ibid., 31.

197 See Higgins, *Heterosexual Dictatorship*, 244; Waters, 'Disorders of the Mind', 146.

198 Wildeblood, *Against the Law*, 31.

199 Ibid., 36.

200 Ibid., 37.

201 Wolfenden to Roberts, 23 May 1955, TNA PRO HO 345/2.

202 Trevor-Roper, author's interview.

203 Alongside a key paragraph in which Wildeblood provided evidence of a particularly brutal case of police entrapment of an elderly man in the urinals on the Old Brompton Road, Wolfenden wrote: 'Nothing in all of that questions that the man *was* guilty'; Statement Submitted by Mr. Peter Wildeblood, TNA PRO HO 345/8, p. 4, Wolfenden's emphasis.

204 Ibid.
205 Ibid., p. 5.
206 Ibid., p. 8.
207 Ibid., p. 1.
208 Ibid., pp. 5–6. For the police account of Wildeblood's prosecution see Walter Jones, *My Own Case* (Maidstone: Angley Books, 1966), 114–23.
209 Statement Wildeblood, TNA PRO HO 345/8, p. 7. See also Notes of a Meeting, 24 May 1955, TNA PRO HO 345/13, pp. 6–8.
210 Wildeblood, *Against the Law*, 67. For Wildeblood's act of declaration at his trial see 'I Went for a Quiet Holiday'.
211 Wildeblood, *Against the Law*, 174.
212 Statement Wildeblood, TNA PRO HO 345/8, p. 8.
213 Waters, 'Disorders of the Mind', 135. For positive endorsements of Wildeblood see Edge, 'Peter Wildeblood', 176; Weeks, *Coming Out*, 159–65; Poulter, *Peers, Queers, and Commons*, 16–17.
214 This is the argument made by Higgins, *Heterosexual Dictatorship*, 231–50. See also Houlbrook, *Queer London*, 244–63.
215 Notes of a Meeting, 24 May 1955, TNA PRO HO 345/13, p. 1.
216 Ibid.
217 Ibid., p. 2.
218 Ibid., p. 3.
219 Ibid., p. 9.
220 Ibid., p. 11.
221 See Tony Judt, *Postwar: A History of Europe since 1945* (London: Pimlico, 2007), 186–8.
222 Mike Hepworth and Bryan Turner, *Confession: Studies in Deviance and Religion* (London: Routledge & Kegan Paul, 1982). For emphasis on the confessional form in the post-war period see William Sargant, *Battle for the Mind: A Physiology of Conversion and Brain-Washing* (London: Heinemann, 1957); James Brown, *Techniques of Persuasion: From Propaganda to Brain-Washing* (Harmondsworth: Penguin, 1963).
223 'I Went for a Quiet Holiday'.
224 For the committee's interviews with medics and psychologists see (among very many) Evidence of Dr. Clifford Allen, Dr. Eustace Chesser and Dr. R. Sessions Hodge and Evidence of the Royal Medico-Psychological Society, Notes of a Meeting, 31 October 1955, and Evidence of the Institute of Psychiatry, Notes of a Meeting, 13 September 1955, TNA PRO HO 345/14.
225 Statement Wildeblood, TNA PRO HO 345/8, p. 1.
226 See Henry Havelock Ellis and John Addington Symonds, *Sexual Inversion*, vol. 1 (London: Wilson and Macmillan, 1897). For analysis of Ellis's influence on theories of homosexuality in inter-war and post-war Britain see Chris Waters, 'Havelock Ellis, Sigmund Freud and the State: Discourses of Homosexual Identity in Interwar Britain', in Lucy Bland and Laura Doan, eds, *Sexology in Culture: Labelling Bodies and Desires* (Cambridge: Polity, 1998), 165–79; Waters, 'Disorders of the Mind'.
227 Statement Wildeblood, TNA PRO HO 345/8, p. 1.
228 Notes of a Meeting, 24 May 1955, TNA HO 345/13, p. 1; Statement Wildeblood, TNA PRO HO 345/8, p. 1.
229 Statement Wildeblood, TNA PRO HO 345/8, p. 1.
230 Notes of a Meeting, 24 May 1955, TNA PRO HO 345/13, pp. 2–3.
231 Ibid., p. 3.
232 Ibid, p. 4.
233 Ibid.
234 Statement Wildeblood, TNA PRO HO 345/8, p. 1. For these musical reviews see Danny La Rue, with Howard Elson, *From Drags to Riches: My Autobiography* (London: Viking, 1987), 71; Roger Baker, *Drag: A History of Female Impersonation in the Performing Arts* (London: Cassell, 1994), 182. La Rue joined the company of the notorious *Soldiers in Skirts* review, but left because of what he called 'the decadent and degrading antics of certain members of the company offstage': La Rue, *Drags to Riches*, 75.
235 See George Ives, *The Continued Extension of the Criminal Law* (London: J. E. Francis, 1922); Edward Carpenter, *The Intermediate Sex: A Study of Some Transitional Types of Men and Women* (London: Allen & Unwin, 1908); John Addington Symonds, *A Problem in*

Modern Ethics: Being an Enquiry into the Phenomenon of Sexual Inversion, Addressed Especially to Medical Psychologists and Jurists (London: privately printed, 1896). For commentary see Matt Cook, '"A New City of Friends": London and Homosexuality in the 1890s', *History Workshop Journal*, no. 56 (2003): 33–58, and his *London and the Culture of Homosexuality, 1885–1914* (Cambridge: Cambridge University Press, 2003), 32–3, 138–50.

236 See Peter Wildeblood, *West End People* (London: Weidenfeld & Nicolson, 1958), and his novel *The Main Chance* (London: Weidenfeld & Nicolson, 1957).

237 Statement Wildeblood, TNA PRO HO 345/8, p. 1. See also Wildeblood, *Against the Law*, 8. For discussion of these competing discourses see Waters, 'Disorders of the Mind', 148–50; Mort, 'Mapping Sexual London', 108–11.

238 Wildeblood, *Against the Law*, 10.

239 Ibid., 27.

240 Recent oral histories of homosexual men have revealed how a psychological as distinct from a social reading of homosexuality was partly the product of class, education and culture. See Jeffrey Weeks and Kevin Porter, eds, *Between the Acts: Lives of Homosexual Men 1885–1967*, 2nd edn (London: Rivers Oram, 1998); Hall Carpenter Archives and Gay Men's Oral History Group, *Walking After Midnight: Gay Men's Life Stories* (London and New York: Routledge, 1989).

241 Statement Wildeblood, TNA PRO HO 345/8, p. 8.

242 Notes of a Meeting, 24 May 1955, TNA PRO HO 345/13, p. 23.

243 Gordon Westwood [pseud. Michael Schofield], *Society and the Homosexual* (London: Gollancz, 1952), 151–3.

244 Notes of a Meeting, 24 May 1955, TNA PRO HO 345/13, p. 29.

245 Wolfenden, draft review of Quentin Crisp's *The Naked Civil Servant*, undated, Wolfenden Papers.

246 For Wolfenden's idea of moral conscience see his *Creation of a Public Conscience*.

247 A similar argument is made by Matt Houlbrook and Chris Waters in their reading of Rodney Garland's 1953 novel, *The Heart in Exile*; see '*The Heart in Exile*: Detachment and Desire in 1950s London', *History Workshop Journal*, no. 62 (2006): 142–65.

248 Trevor-Roper, author's interview.

249 For discussion of Trevor-Roper's and Winter's evidence see Higgins, *Heterosexual Dictatorship*, 42–4; Houlbrook, *Queer London*, 254–63.

250 Notes of a Meeting, 28 July 1955, TNA PRO HO 345/14, pp. 10, 3.

251 Ibid., p. 10.

252 Ibid., p. 14. Winter married Theodora Barlow, daughter of the banker industrialist Sir Thomas Barlow, in 1936. They had three children and divorced in 1953.

253 Ibid., pp. 4, 6.

254 Ibid., p. 4.

255 Trevor-Roper, author's interview; Notes of a Meeting, 28 July 1955, TNA PRO HO 345/14, p. 19.

256 Notes of a Meeting, 28 July 1955, TNA PRO HO 345/14, p. 17.

257 See especially Higgins, *Heterosexual Dictatorship*, 40–1; Houlbrook, *Queer London*, 254–63.

258 Trevor-Roper, author's interview.

259 Ibid.

260 Notes of a Meeting, 28 July 1955, p. 13. For retrospective comments by Wolfenden on the problems of getting prostitutes to give evidence to the committee see his blurb in Anonymous, *Streetwalker* (London: Bodley Head, 1959), unpaginated.

261 Roberts to Wolfenden, 19 April 1955, TNA PRO HO 345/2.

262 Wolfenden to Roberts, 20 April 1955, TNA PRO HO 345/2.

263 Graham Hall, author's interview.

264 Wolfenden, *Turning Points*, 138.

265 Notes of a Meeting, 28 July 1955, TNA PRO HO 345/14, pp. 27–8.

266 Ibid.

267 Curran to Wolfenden, 21 June 1956, TNA PRO HO 345/2. For Wolfenden's response see Note by the Chairman, TNA PRO HO 345/10, p. 1.

268 Wolfenden to Roberts, 24 March 1956, TNA PRO HO 345/2. See also Newsam to Wolfenden, 22 August 1956, TNA PRO HO 345/2.

269 Wolfenden to Roberts, 24 March 1956, TNA PRO HO 345/2.

270 For Wolfenden's account of his initial reactions see Wolfenden to Newsam, 29 March 1956, TNA PRO HO 345/2.

271 'London Day By Day', *Daily Telegraph and Morning Post*, 29 March 1956, 6.

272 'Guy Burgess Stripped Bare!', *People*, 11 March 1956, 3.

273 Ibid.

274 Ibid.

275 Ibid.

276 'A Welshman with a brilliant academic record' was how the local press received the news of Rees's return to Wales; see 'Aberystwyth's New Head a Scholar, Writer and Soldier', *Western Mail and South Wales News*, 27 June 1953, 3; Edward Ellis, *The University College of Wales Aberystwyth, 1872–1972* (Cardiff: University of Wales Press, 1972), 294.

277 For Rees's autobiographies see Goronwy Rees, *A Bundle of Sensations: Sketches in Autobiography* (London: Chatto & Windus, 1960); *A Chapter of Accidents* (London: Chatto & Windus, 1972). For biographical studies and sketches see Jenny Rees, *Looking for Mr. Nobody: The Secret Life of Goronwy Rees* (London: Weidenfeld & Nicolson, 1994); Kenneth Morgan, 'Rees, (Morgan) Goronwy', *Oxford Dictionary of National Biography* (Oxford: Oxford University Press, 2004), http://www.oxforddnb.com/view/article/31594 (accessed 8 January 2008).

278 G. Rees, *Chapter of Accidents*, 110–11; J. Rees, *Looking for Mr. Nobody*. For another version of this story see A. L. Rowse, *All Souls in My Time* (London: Duckworth, 1993), 95.

279 For Rees's intelligence work see Morgan, 'Rees', and J. Rees, *Looking for Mr. Nobody*, 155. Rees's daughter claimed that her father was a member of MI6 during the late 1940s.

280 Annan, *Our Age*, 229.

281 Berlin and Bowra, quoted in J. Rees, *Looking for Mr. Nobody*, 54. See also Michael Ignatieff, *Isaiah Berlin: A Life* (London: Vintage, 2000), 194. Rees admitted that he had a homosexual or a homoerotic relationship with an East End professional boxer in the 1940s; see G. Rees, *Bundle of Sensations*, 74–82. Journalist Michael Burn, who was briefly Burgess's lover in the mid-1930s, recollected that though Rees 'was not homosexual, homosexuality appealed to his mind'; Michael Burn, interview by the author, June 1997. See also Michael Burn, *Turned Towards the Sun: An Autobiography* (Norwich: Michael Russell, 2003), 97.

282 G. Rees, *Chapter of Accidents*, 94. For further speculation about the significance of homosexuality in inter-war elite culture see Goronwy Rees, *Brief Encounters* (London: Chatto & Windus, 1974), 83–4; Annan, *Our Age*, 97–121.

283 G. Rees, *Chapter of Accidents*, 216. See also J. Rees, *Looking for Mr. Nobody*, 1, 4.

284 For the original Cold War press coverage of Burgess's and Maclean's disappearance see 'Yard Hunts 2 Britons', *Daily Express*, 7 June 1951, 1; 'Diplomats: Cable Puzzle', *Daily Express*, 8 June 1951, 1; 'Pontecorvo Case: Expert Called in to Search Burgess Wire', *Daily Express*, 9 June 1956, 1.

285 'Guy Burgess Stripped Bare!'.

286 Ibid.

287 According to Nat Rothman, the *People's* deputy editor, Rees was obsessive in scrutinizing the drafts of his articles, making weekly visits to the newspaper's Fleet Street offices to oversee their publication; J. Rees, *Looking for Mr. Nobody*, 188.

288 For Nicolson's assessment see 'Who Screened Burgess?' *Daily Express*, 14 June 1951, 1.

289 'He Kept his Sex Book in Ernest Bevin's Safe', *People*, 25 March 1951, 3; 'His Farewell Party Ended in a Bottle Fight', *People*, 1 April 1956, 3. For Rees's own later account of these incidents see his *Chapter of Accidents*, 128–34.

290 'He Kept Blackmail Letters in his Room', *People*, 18 March 1956, 3.

291 'He Kept his Sex Book in Ernest Bevin's Safe'.

292 He Kept Blackmail Letters'. The Third Man was later confirmed to be Kim Philby.

293 For the cartoons see 'Guy Burgess Stripped Bare!' and 'He Kept his Sex Book in Ernest Bevin's Safe'. For commentary on Burgess's drawings see Tom Driberg, *Guy Burgess: A Portrait with Background* (London: Weidenfeld & Nicolson, 1956), 80.

294 Wolfenden to Newsam, 29 March 1956, TNA PRO HO 345/2.
295 Ibid.
296 Ibid.
297 For the closed culture of modern British government see David Vincent, *The Culture of Secrecy: Britain, 1832–1998* (Oxford: Oxford University Press, 1998); Peter Hennessy, *The Secret State: Whitehall and the Cold War* (London: Allen Lane, 2002).
298 Newsam to Goronwy Rees, 18 April 1956, and see also Wolfenden to Newsam, 19 April 1956, TNA PRO HO 345/2.
299 For details of the affair see Ellis, *University College Wales*, 293–8. For Rees's own account see G. Rees, *Chapter of Accidents*, 253–70, and 'Goronwy Rees Tells Why He Resigned', *Cambrian News*, 10 September 1971, 1.
300 Quoted in Annan, *Our Age*, 228.
301 Quoted in J. Rees, *Looking for Mr. Nobody*, 189. Other friends were disturbed less by the content of Rees's articles and more by the fact that they had appeared 'in so vulgar and sensationalist a paper as the People': G. Rees, *Chapter of Accidents*, 267.
302 Quoted in J. Rees, *Looking for Mr. Nobody*, 185.
303 G. Rees, *Chapter of Accidents*, 267; Rowse, *All Souls*, 166; Annan, *Our Age*, 228.
304 Maurice Bowra, quoted in Annan, *Our Age*, 226. Michael Burn also noted that Guy Burgess cast a shadow over many people, including Rees and himself, because 'you didn't know where he was going to pop up next and what he was going to say. Perhaps he'd say that he'd slept with the King. You didn't know what he was going to say': Burn, author's interview.
305 Annan, *Our Age*, 228; Rebecca West, *The Meaning of Treason* (London: Virago, 1982), 283.
306 G. Rees, *Chapter of Accidents*, 266.
307 Henry Fairlie, 'Political Commentary', *Spectator*, 23 September 1955, 379–81.
308 Ibid., 381.
309 John Sparrow, letter to the editor, *Spectator*, 30 September 1955, 418; David Astor, letter to the editor, *Spectator*, 7 October 1955, 448; Hugh Trevor-Roper, letter to the editor, *Spectator*, 21 October 1955, 531.

310 'Statement by Princess', *The Times*, 1 November 1955, 8. For analysis of the affair see Christopher Warwick, *Princess Margaret* (London: Weidenfeld & Nicolson, 1983), 57–65; Theo Aronson, *Princess Margaret: A Biography* (London: Michael O'Mara, 1997), 125–34.
311 See Lindsay Anderson, letter to the editor, *Spectator*, 18 November 1955, 650–1.
312 Wolfenden, *Turning Points*, 140.
313 'Three-Year Chairman', *Daily Express*, 5 September 1957, 9. See also '5,000 Copies Sold within Hours', *Daily Telegraph and Morning Post*, 5 September 1957, 11; Wolfenden, *Turning Points*, 140–2; Self, *Prostitution*, 163.
314 For Wolfenden's media presence see 'Sir John Wolfenden on Vice Law Proposals', *The Times*, 5 September 1957, 10; 'Discussion by TV Panel', *Daily Telegraph and Morning Post*, 5 September 1957, 13; 'Hidden Vice Less Harmful', *Daily Mirror*, 10 September 1957, 1.
315 For the call to expand sexual knowledge see Home Office, Scottish Department, *Report of the Committee on Homosexual Offences and Prostitution*, 77–8, 116.
316 Jerry White, *London in the Twentieth Century: A City and its People* (London: Penguin, 2002), 323. See also Lesley Hall, *Sex, Gender and Social Change in Britain since 1880* (Basingstoke: Macmillan, 2000), 161. For contemporary accounts of the changes brought about by the Street Offences Act see John Gosling and Douglas Warner, *The Shame of a City: An Inquiry into the Vice of London* (London: W. H. Allen, 1960); Paul Bailey, *An English Madam: The Life and Work of Cynthia Payne* (London: Jonathan Cape, 1982), 76–85.
317 In the period between August and November 1959 prosecutions for street soliciting dropped from 4,318 to 464 in central London; see Rosemary Wilkinson, 'Cleaning Up the Streets', *Shield*, September 1960, 15.
318 See Wolfenden, *Turning Points*, 142.

CHAPTER 5   COSMOPOLITANISM

1 'Soho Fair', *Listener*, n.d. 1955, and Muriel Segal, 'Fiesta in Soho', unnamed publication, cuttings in Westminster City Archives, St

Anne Parish Soho, Prints and Cuttings, Box A13 to 1985; 'All the Fun of the Soho Fair', *The Times*, 11 July 1955, 7; John Platt, *London's Rock Routes* (London: Fourth Estate, 1985), 7–9.

2 'Soho on Parade', *Evening Standard*, 12 July 1955, 4.

3 'Soho Fair'. See also 'After the Fair a Republic', *Westminster and Pimlico News*, 20 July 1956, 2.

4 Frank Manning, *The Celebration of Society: Perspectives on Contemporary Cultural Performance* (Bowling Green, OH: Bowling Green State University Popular Press, 1983), 3–33. See also Victor Turner, *The Anthropology of Performance* (New York: PAJ Publications, 1986); Ray Browne and Michael Marsden, 'Introduction', in Michael Marsden and Ray Browne, eds, *The Culture of Celebrations* (Bowling Green, OH: Bowling Green State University Popular Press, 1994), 2.

5 Soho Association, Soho Fair: Daily Programmes, 10–15 July 1955, Westminster City Archives, St Anne Parish Soho, Parish Registers and Parish Records, Acc 2288/33.

6 'All the Fun of the Soho Fair'.

7 'The Soho Fair', *Radio Times*, 8 July 1955, 19. See also 'Soho Goes Even Gayer', *Westminster and Pimlico News*, 1 July 1955, 3.

8 British Pathé News, 'Soho Goes Gay', 1955, www.britishpathe.com/record.phpid=39489 (accessed 21 November 2009).

9 'All the Fun of the Soho Fair'.

10 'All Set for Soho's Fair', *Westminster and Pimlico News*, 3 July 1955, 1.

11 'A Week of Carnival in Soho', *Radio Times*, 8 July 1955, 5.

12 Ibid. See also 'All the Fun of the Soho Fair'.

13 See especially Stuart Hall, 'Reformism and the Legislation of Consent', in National Deviancy Conference, eds, *Permissiveness and Control: The Fate of the Sixties Legislation* (London: Macmillan 1980), 1–43; Jeffrey Weeks, *Sex, Politics and Society: The Regulation of Sexuality since 1800* (London: Longman, 1989), 249–72; Arthur Marwick, *The Sixties: Cultural Revolution in Britain, France, Italy, and the United States c.1958–c.1974* (Oxford: Oxford University Press, 1998).

14 Birmingham Feminist History Group, 'Feminism as Femininity in the Nineteen Fifties?' *Feminist Review*, no. 3 (1979): 48–65; Elizabeth Wilson, *Only Halfway to Paradise: Women in Postwar Britain 1945–64* (London: Tavistock, 1980), 81–111; Lesley Hall, *Sex, Gender and Social Change in Britain since 1880* (Basingstoke: Macmillan, 2000), 167–84; Gillian Swanson, *Drunk with the Glitter: Space, Consumption and Sexual Instability in Modern Urban Culture* (Abingdon: Routledge, 2007), 73–99, 147–76.

15 Daniel Farson, *Soho in the Fifties* (London: Michael Joseph, 1987), 3. Robert Hewison makes the same point about Soho's interrelated imaginative and social geographies in *Under Siege: Literary Life in London, 1939–1945* (London: Weidenfeld & Nicolson, 1977), 56–66.

16 Daniel Farson, *Never A Normal Man* (London: HarperCollins, 1997), 108. See also his *Soho in the Fifties*, 7.

17 See 'Obituaries: Dan Farson', *Guardian*, 29 November 1997, 19; 'Obituaries: Dan Farson', *The Times*, 29 November 1997, 25; 'Obituaries: Daniel Farson', *Independent*, 1 December 1997, 16.

18 See Arthur Ransome, *The Autobiography of Arthur Ransome*, ed. Rupert Hart-Davis (London: Jonathan Cape, 1976), 114.

19 Arthur Ransome, *Bohemia in London* (London: Chapman & Hall, 1907), 112.

20 Ransome, *Autobiography*, 115.

21 Ransome, *Bohemia in London*, 10.

22 Ibid., 3.

23 Christine Stansell, *American Moderns: Bohemian New York and the Creation of a New Century* (New York: Owl Books, 2000), 43.

24 An Act for Erecting a Judicature for Determination of Differences Touching Houses Burned or Demolished by Reason of the late Fire which Happened in London, 1667, 18 & 19 Car. 2, c.7.

25 Margaret Goldsmith, *Soho Square* (London: Sampson Low, Marston & Co., 1947), 2.

26 Edwin Beresford Chancellor, *The Romance of Soho: Being an Account of the District, its Past Distinguished Inhabitants, its Historic Houses, and its Place in the Social Annals of London* (London: Country Life, 1931), 9–10.

27 Ibid., 10.

28 Stanley Jackson, *An Indiscreet Guide to Soho* (London: Muse Arts, 1946), 22.

29 Simon Dews, *Soho* (London: Rich and Cowan, 1952), 15–17.

30 Jackson, *Indiscreet Guide to Soho*, 24.

31 For histories of Oxford Street see Gordon Mackenzie, *Marylebone: Great City North of Oxford Street* (London: Macmillan, 1972), 72–98; Erika Rappaport, *Shopping for Pleasure: Women in the Making of London's West End* (Princeton, NJ: Princeton University Press, 2000), 151, 154; David Brandon and Alan Brooke, *Marylebone and Tyburn Past* (London: Historical Publications, 2007), 95–107.

32 See Michael Saler, *The Avant-Garde in Interwar England: Medieval Modernism and the London Underground* (New York and Oxford: Oxford University Press, 1999), 27–8, 92–121.

33 See Christian Barman, *The Man Who Built London Transport: A Biography of Frank Pick* (Newton Abbot: David & Charles, 1979), 121–3.

34 J. H. Forshaw and Patrick Abercrombie, *County of London Plan* (London: Macmillan, 1943), 10.

35 Their stance echoed Mumford's denunciation of the rituals of 'conspicuous expenditure' in major European and North American cities, where he argued that the 'ruthless concentration of human interest on pecuniary standards and pecuniary results . . . become the goals of vulgar ambition': Lewis Mumford, *The Culture of Cities* (London: Secker & Warburg, 1940), 230. For commentary see Bronwen Edwards, 'Shaping the Fashion City: Master Plans and Pipe Dreams in the Post-War West End of London', in Christopher Breward and David Gilbert, eds, *Fashion's World Cities* (Oxford: Berg, 2006), 164. Feminist and cultural historians have highlighted the fraught relationship between the doyens of urban modernism and feminine perceptions of city life. See Beatriz Colomina, *Privacy and Publicity: Modern Architecture as Mass Media* (Cambridge, MA: MIT Press, 1994); Mark Wigley, *White Walls, Designer Dresses: The Fashioning of Modern Architecture* (Cambridge,

MA: MIT Press, 1995); Christopher Reed, ed., *Not at Home: The Suppression of Domesticity in Modern Art and Architecture* (London: Thames & Hudson, 1996).

36 Virginia Woolf, 'The London Scene II: Oxford Street Tide', *Good Housekeeping*, January 1932, in *Ragtime to Wartime: The Best of Good Housekeeping 1922–1939*, compiled by Brian Braithwaite, Nöelle Walsh and Glyn Davies (London: Ebury Press, 1986), 138–9. For new female consumers in inter-war London see Sally Alexander, 'Becoming a Woman in London in the 1920s and 1930s', in David Feldman and Gareth Stedman Jones, eds, *Metropolis – London: Histories and Representations since 1800* (London: Routledge, 1989), 245–71; Mica Nava, 'Modernity's Disavowal: Women, the City and the Department Store', in Mica Nava and Alan O'Shea, eds, *Modern Times: Reflections on a Century of English Modernity* (London: Routledge, 1995), 38–76; Janice Winship, 'Culture of Restraint: The British Chain Store 1920–39', in Peter Jackson et al., eds, *Commercial Cultures: Economies, Practices and Spaces* (Oxford: Berg, 2000), 15–34.

37 John Metcalfe, *London A to Z* (London: Andre Deutsch, 1953), 91.

38 Anonymous, *Red Guide to London*, 61st edn (London: Ward Lock, 1957), 156. See also Basil Bazley and Frank Lambert, *Show Me London* (Tunbridge Wells: Graphic Studios, 1947), 29; Anonymous, *London Pocket Guide* (London: Ernest Benn, 1962), 36.

39 For the absence of bus routes in Soho see Jackson, *Indiscreet Guide to Soho*, 24.

40 William Morris, *The Homeland Guide to London* (London: Homeland Association, 1947), 93. See also F. R. Banks, *The Penguin Guide to London* (Harmondsworth: Penguin, 1958), 186.

41 David Keir and Bryan Morgan, eds, *Golden Milestone: 50 Years of the AA* (London: Automobile Association, 1955), facing page 165; Hugh Barty-King, *The AA: A History of the First 75 Years of the Automobile Association 1905–1980* (Basingstoke: Automobile Association, 1980), 175; F. H. W. Sheppard, general ed., *Survey of London*, vol. 33, *The Parish of St Anne Soho* (London: Athlone Press, University of London, 1966), 297–312.

42 Metcalfe, *London A to Z*, 26.

43 See 'Shaftesbury Avenue and Charing Cross Road', British History Online, http://www.british-history.ac.uk/report.asp?compid=41110 (accessed 9 November 2006); Sheppard, *Survey of London, St Anne Soho*, 297–312.

44 Anonymous, *Red Guide to London*, 128.

45 *The Post Office London Directory for 1958: Street Directory* (London: Kelly's Directories, 1958), 172–3.

46 Sheppard, *Survey of London, St Anne Soho*, 297–312. For the 'cathedral-like atmosphere' in Foyle's see Jackson, *Indiscreet Guide to Soho*, 61.

47 Judith Walkowitz, 'The "Vision of Salome": Cosmopolitanism and Erotic Dancing in Central London, 1908–1918', *American Historical Review* 102, no. 2 (2003): 346. See also Raymond Mander and Joe Mitcheson, *The Theatres of London* (London: Rupert Hart-Davis, 1961), 122–5.

48 Erika Rappaport, 'Art, Commerce, or Empire? The Rebuilding of Regent Street, 1880–1927', *History Workshop Journal*, no. 53 (2002): 94–117; Rappaport, *Shopping for Pleasure*.

49 Metcalfe, *London A to Z*, 101; Anonymous, *Red Guide to London*, 142; Anonymous, *Wonderful London* (London: Associated Newspapers, 1961), 122.

50 M-O A: TC Royalty, 69/4/A, Observation of Shops, Coronation Decorations and Posters, Regent Street, 19 May 1953.

51 See especially Georg Simmel, 'The Metropolis and Mental Life', in Kurt Wolff, ed., *The Sociology of Georg Simmel* (New York: Free Press of Glencoe, 1964), 409–24. For related discussion of Simmel's work see David Frisby, *Fragments of Modernity: Theories of Modernity in the Work of Simmel, Kracauer and Benjamin* (Cambridge: Polity, 1985).

52 Charles Booth, *Life and Labour of the People of London, Third Series, Religious Influences 2: London North of the Thames; The Inner Ring* (London: Macmillan, 1902), 183–4.

53 Ibid., 185.

54 George Sims, *Living London*, vol. 1 (London: Cassell, n.d.), 4. See also Matt Cook, *London and the Culture of Homosexuality, 1885–1914* (Cambridge: Cambridge University Press, 2003), 23.

55 Booth, *Life and Labour, The Inner Ring*, 185.

56 Chaim Lewis, *A Soho Address* (London: Gollancz, 1965), 7. See also Gerry Black, *Living Up West: Jewish Life in London's West End* (London: London Museum of Jewish Life, 1994), 46–53.

57 By 1911 nearly 4 per cent of the County of London's population was foreign-born; see London School of Economics and Political Science, *The New Survey of London Life and Labour*, vol. 1, *Forty Years of Change* (London: P. S. King, 1930), 82; Jerry White, *London in the Twentieth Century: A City and its People*, (London: Penguin, 2002), 104–5. There is great disparity between the different estimates of Soho's foreign-born population at the end of the nineteenth century; compare Arthur Sherwell, *Life in West London: A Study and a Contrast* (London: Methuen, 1897), 58, where his estimate is 11.5 per cent, with the Survey of London where the foreign population estimate is 60 per cent in 1903, see Sheppard, *Survey of London, St Anne Soho*, 11.

58 John Galsworthy, *The Forsyte Saga, Book II: In Chancery* (Oxford: Oxford University Press, 1995), 372.

59 Alec Waugh, 'Round About Soho', in Arthur St John Adcock, ed., *Wonderful London*, vol. 1 (London: Fleetway House, n.d.), 129–30. For similar long-standing impressions of Soho as London's foreign quarter see Count Armfelt, 'Cosmopolitan London', in Sims, *Living London*, 241; Sherwell, *Life in West London*, 172.

60 'Miss Jones in Bagdad', in H. V. Morton, *The Spell of London* (New York: Brentano's, 1926), 92. See also Jackson, *Indiscreet Guide to Soho*, 43.

61 See for example H. V. Morton, *The Nights of London*, 3rd edn (London: Methuen, 1930); H. V. Morton, *Ghosts of London* (London: Methuen, 1939). For commentary on the tourist literature of the inter-war period see David Gilbert, 'London in All its Glory – Or How to Enjoy London: Guidebook Representations of Imperial London', *Journal of Historical Geography* 25, no. 3 (1999): 279–97.

62 Lewis, *Soho Address*, 83.

63 Jackson, *Indiscreet Guide to Soho*, 36.

64 Quoted in Judith Walkowitz, Schleppers and Shoppers (unpublished paper, 2003).

65 Morton, *Spell of London*, 92.

66 Ibid., p. 93. J. B. Priestley highlighted similar feminine aspirations in his London novel *Angel Pavement*. Miss Matfield, a middle-class and world-weary secretary, always felt her spirits lift as she walked 'down Old Compton Street' with its 'faint colouring of adventure': J. B. Priestley, *Angel Pavement* (London: Heinemann, 1931), 234.

67 15 June 1905, George Ives, *Diary*, quoted in Cook, *London*, 26. Cook dates the consolidation of Piccadilly Circus as a homosexual space to the 1880s, linking this development to the intensification of 'cosmopolitanism, entertainment and consumption' in the West End: ibid., 22.

68 For cruising at the Alhambra and the Empire theatres see Cook, *London*, 223.

69 Anonymous, *The Sins of the Cities of the Plain; or, the Recollections of a Mary-Ann*, vol. 1 (London privately printed, 1881), 7–9. For discussion see Morris Kaplan, *Sodom on the Thames: Sex, Love, and Scandal in Wilde Times* (Ithaca, NY: Cornell University Press, 2005); Cook, *London*, 18–22; H. Montgomery Hyde, *The Other Love: An Historical and Contemporary Survey of Homosexuality in Britain* (London: Heinemann, 1970), 121–3, 126. For analysis of Mary-Anns see Jeffrey Weeks, 'Inverts, Perverts and Mary-Annes: Male Prostitution and the Regulation of Homosexuality in England in the Nineteenth and Early Twentieth Centuries', in Jeffrey Weeks, *Against Nature: Essays on History, Sexuality and Identity* (London: Rivers Oram, 1991), 46–67.

70 Oscar Wilde, *The Picture of Dorian Gray* (London: Penguin, 1985), 87. See also Cook, *London*, 108–9.

71 Cook, *London*, 28. In his evidence to the police at the Cleveland Street trial, the 'real' John or Jack Saul described a world similar to the one depicted fictionally in *Sins of the Cities*. For Saul and the Cleveland Street Scandal see Morris Kaplan, ' "Did My Lord Gomorrah Smile?": Homosexuality, Class, and Prostitution in the Cleveland Street Affair', in Nancy Erber and George Robb, eds, *Disorder in the Court: Trials and Sexual Conflict at the Turn of the Century* (Basingstoke: Macmillan, 1999), 78–99; Colin Simpson, Lewis Chester and David Leitch, *The Cleveland Street Affair* (Boston, MA: Little, Brown, 1976), 48–64.

72 Paul Pry [Thomas Burke], *For Your Convenience: A Learned Dialogue, Instructive to all Londoners and London Visitors Overheard in the Thélème Club and Taken Down Verbatim by Paul Pry* (London: George Routledge and Sons, 1937), endpaper.

73 Ibid., 51–2. For discussion of the West End's homosexual urinals see Matt Houlbrook, 'The Private World of Public Urinals, London 1918–57', *London Journal* 25, no. 1 (2000): 52–70; Matt Houlbrook, 'For Whose Convenience? Gay Guides, Cognitive Maps and the Construction of Homosexual London, 1917–67', in Simon Gunn and Robert Morris, eds, *Identities in Space: Contested Terrains in the Western City since 1850* (Aldershot: Ashgate, 2001), 165–86.

74 For the diversity of Lyons' customers see Peter Bird, *The First Food Empire: A History of J. Lyons & Co.* (Chichester: Phillimore, 2000), 101.

75 John Alcock, 1985, Hall Carpenter Oral History Project, British Library Sound Archive, C456/003/01. Alcock was born in 1927 and came to London at the end of the war. He attended a waiters' school before working at the Lyons' Corner House. See also Emlyn Williams, *Emlyn: An Early Autobiography: 1927–1935* (London: Bodley Head, 1973), 116. For a different account of Lyons' in the same period see Lillian Harry, *Corner House Girls* (London: Orion, 2000).

76 Robert Hopkins, *The Lure of London* (London: Cecil Palmer, 1929), 184; Quentin Crisp, *The Naked Civil Servant* (London: Jonathan Cape, 1968), 28.

77 Jackson, *Indiscreet Guide to Soho*, 105. See also Houlbrook, *Queer London*, 88–9. Other cafés like Harry Raymond's in Berwick Street and pubs like the Golden Lion in Dean Street catered to a similarly eclectic mix of customers.

78 For Crisp's comments on middle-class venues see Crisp, *Naked Civil Servant*, 28. For Gennaro's see Peter Parker, *Ackerley: A Life of*

J. R. Ackerley (London: Constable, 1989), 112–13; Houlbrook, *Queer London*, 74.

79 Edward Rimbault, *Soho and its Associations, Historical, Literary and Artistic: Edited from the MSS. of E. F. Rimbault by George Clinch* (London: Dulau and Co., 1895), 29.

80 Judith Summers, *Soho: A History of London's Most Colourful Neighbourhood* (London: Bloomsbury, 1989), 107.

81 Talk with Police Constable A. Gunn about the Soho district generally, Charles Booth Online Archive, Search Survey Notebooks, London School of Economics and Political Science, Booth B355, http://booth.lse.ac.uk/notebooks/b355 (accessed 12 November 2006), p. 33.

82 Ibid., p. 35.

83 Ibid., p. 43.

84 Ibid., p. 37.

85 For the Dieppe Restaurant see 'Antonio Rabiani convicted of keeping a brothel . . . and recommended for deportation' and 'Guiseppi Valla convicted of assisting in the management', 'Report of Watch Committee', 5 October 1922, City of Westminster, *Minutes and Proceedings of the Mayor, Aldermen and Councillors, 1922* (London: Harrison and Sons, 1926), 455. For the Bohemian Café see 'George Mack Gould convicted of keeping a brothel', 'Report of Watch Committee', 13 May 1926, City of Westminster, *Minutes and Proceedings of the Mayor, Aldermen and Councillors, 1926* (London: Harrison and Sons, 1927), 314. For other premises in the area see 'Madame Jean, 40a Greek Street, convicted of keeping a brothel', 'Report of Watch Committee', 5 May 1927, City of Westminster, *Minutes and Proceedings of the Mayor, Aldermen and Councillors, 1927* (London: Harrison and Sons, 1928), 271.

86 See 'Police Bribery Charges', *The Times*, 19 December 1928, 7. For the Goddard case see Clive Emsley, 'Sergeant Goddard: The Story of a Rotten Apple, or a Diseased Orchard?' in Amy Gilman Srebnick and René Lévy, eds, *Crime and Culture: An Historical Perspective* (Aldershot: Ashgate, 2005), 85–104.

87 Harry Daley, *This Small Cloud: A Personal Memoir* (London: Weidenfeld & Nicolson, 1986), 149. Daley was transferred to C Division seven years after Sergeant Goddard's exposure; see Emsley, 'Sergeant Goddard', 95. In 1935 the Piccadilly flat mystery focused public attention on the murder of 'French Fifi' (Mrs Josephine Martin), who operated from Archer Street; see 'Piccadilly Flat Murder', *The Times*, 27 November 1935, 8. Throughout the 1940s and early 1950s the police pursuit of the Messina brothers' network of brothels and protection rackets across Soho and Mayfair was regular media news, see Summers, *Soho*, 211–21.

88 Anonymous source, quoted in Black, *Living Up West*, 52.

89 Elena Salvoni, with Sandy Fawkes, *Elena: A Life in Soho* (London: Quartet, 1990), 57.

90 Jackson, *Indiscreet Guide to Soho*, 65.

91 Ibid.

92 Henri Murger, *The Bohemians of the Latin Quarter*, trans. Ellen Marriage and John Selwyn (Philadelphia: University of Pennsylvania Press, 2004), xxiv.

93 Virginia Nicholson, *Among the Bohemians: Experiments in Living 1900–1939* (London: Viking, 2002), 269. For the Café Royal see Guy Deghy and Keith Waterhouse, *Café Royal: Ninety Years of Bohemia* (London: Hutchinson, 1955); Summers, *Soho*, 190.

94 Summers, *Soho*, 190; Denise Hooker, *Nina Hamnett: Queen of Bohemia* (London: Constable, 1986), 38–9.

95 Beresford Chancellor described the environs of Tottenham Court Road as 'London's Old Latin Quarter' in his history of the area; see Edwin Beresford Chancellor, *London's Old Latin Quarter, Being an Account of Tottenham Court Road and its Immediate Surroundings* (London: Jonathan Cape, 1930). See also Ruthven Todd, *Fitzrovia & the Road to York Minster, or, Down Dean St.* (London: Michael Parkin Gallery, 1973); Nick Bailey, *Fitzrovia* (London: Historical Publications in association with Camden History Society, 1981); Michael Bakewell, *Fitzrovia: London's Bohemia* (London: National Portrait Gallery, 1999); Mike Pentelow and Marsha Rowe, *Characters of Fitzrovia* (London: Chatto & Windus, 2001). For Fitzrovia's relationship to Soho see Hewison, *Under Siege*, 59–66; Hugh David, *The Fitzrovians: A Portrait of Bohemian Society*

1900–55 (London: Michael Joseph, 1988), 172;
Jonathan Fryer, *Soho in the Fifties and Sixties*
(London: National Portrait Gallery, 1998), 3.

96   Ransome, *Bohemia in London*, 10–11.

97   Bailey, *Fitzrovia*, 26–8; David, *Fitzrovians*, 172.

98   Nicolson, *Among the Bohemians*, 268. See also
David, *Fitzrovians*, 123; Bailey, *Fitzrovia,* 52;
Hooker, *Nina Hamnett*, 102.

99   For the specific social style of Fitzrovia's
writers in the later 1930s and 1940s including Dylan Thomas, see David, *Fitzrovians*,
150–6; Hewison, *Under Siege*, 29–30; Nicolson, *Among the Bohemians*, 271–3. For
Dylan Thomas see Constantine Fitzgibbon,
The Life of Dylan Thomas (London: J. M.
Dent, 1965).

100   Sally Fiber, *The Fitzroy: The Autobiography of
a London Tavern; Sally Fiber's Story of the
Fitzroy as Told to Clive Powell-Williams*
(Lewes: Temple House, 1995), 2. For other
accounts of the Fitzroy's bohemian character
see Bernard Levin, 'Tavern Where the Arts
and Politics Mingle', *Manchester Guardian*, 27
March 1956, 5; Nina Hamnett, *Is She a Lady?*
(London: Allan Wingate, 1955), 61; Leslie
Hunter, *The Road to Brighton Pier* (London,
Arthur Baker, 1959), 217; Hooker, *Nina
Hamnett*, 175–6.

101   'No Moaning at this Bar', *Daily Express*, 27
March 1940, 4. William Hickey was the pseu-
donym of Labour MP Tom Driberg. See also
Fiber, *Fitzroy*, xi.

102   20 June 1952, Russell Davies, ed., *The
Kenneth Williams Diaries* (London: Harper-
Collins, 1994), 77. For other references to the
Fitzroy as a homosexual pub see Gordon
Westwood [pseud. Michael Schofield], *Society
and the Homosexual* (London: Gollancz, 1952),
19; Peter Wildeblood, *Against the Law*
(Harmondsworth: Penguin, 1957), 40; Julius
Horwitz, *Can I Get There by Candlelight*
(London: Panther, 1971), 14–15, 17, where the
Fitzroy is referred to as the Dog and Duck;
John Lehmann, *In the Purely Pagan Sense*
(London: GMP, 1985), 210–12; Jeffrey Weeks
and Kevin Porter, eds, *Between the Acts: Lives
of Homosexual Men 1885–1967*, 2nd edn (Lon-
don: Rivers Oram, 1998), 174.

103   The Wheatsheaf, in Rathbone Place, was the
regular of Julian Maclaren-Ross and the
Tamil poet and critic Meary Tambimuttu.
The Bricklayer's Arms was around the
corner in Gresse Street. The Marquis of
Granby, on the corner of Rathbone Street
and Percy Street, had a violent reputation.
Most commentators agree that by the 1940s
these pubs had replaced the Fitzroy Tavern
as the centre of Fitzrovia's artistic and
literary scene; see Nicholson, *Among the Bohemians*, 271. Regular social movement across
Oxford Street was partly driven by the later
closing times of pubs in Soho; see Hewison,
Under Siege, 58.

104   Julian Maclaren-Ross, *Memoirs of the Forties*
(Harmondsworth: Penguin, 1984), 123. Publisher and writer Dan Davin, who was
himself a Fitzrovia regular, described Maclaren-Ross's itinerary during the 1940s:
'Midday in the pub till closing time, a late
lunch at the Scala restaurant in Charlotte
Street. . . . A stroll to look at the bookshops
in Charing Cross Road. Opening time
again at the Wheatsheaf till closing time. A
hurried dash to the Highlander which
closed half an hour later. Back to the Scala
for supper and coffee. At midnight the tube
home from Goodge Street': Dan Davin,
Closing Times (1975), quoted in 'The Lost
Club Journal', http://freepages.pavilion-
.net/tartarus/maclaren-ross.html (accessed 2
December 2006). See also Alan Ross,
'Introduction', in Maclaren-Ross, *Memoirs of
the Forties*, x.

105   Hamnett, *Is She a Lady?*, 61. For women's
relationships to nineteenth- and twentieth-
century bohemia see Elizabeth Wilson,
Bohemians: The Glamorous Outcasts (London:
Tauris, 2000), 85–117; Griselda Pollock,
*Avant-Garde Gambits, 1883–93: Gender and the
Colour of Art History* (London: Thames &
Hudson, 1993).

106   Houlbrook, *Queer London*, 83.

107   Summers, *Soho*, 192. For other accounts of
Belcher and the Colony Room see Farson,
Soho in the Fifties, 40–8; Fryer, *Soho in the
Fifties and Sixties*, 40–1.

108   For the atmosphere of the Colony see
Hooker, *Nina Hamnett,* 248–9; Frank Nor-
man, *Norman's London* (London: Secker &
Warburg, 1969), 186–90.

109 Dan Farson, 'Muriel Belcher – Queen of Clubs', in *Artists of the Colony Room Club: A Tribute to Muriel Belcher: November 11 – December 4 1982* (London: Michael Parkin Fine Art, 1982), unpaginated.

110 Colin MacInnes, ' "See you at Mabel's" ', *Encounter* 42 (March 1957): 25.

111 Thomas Burke, *London in my Time* (London: Rich & Cowan, 1934), 183.

112 Galsworthy, *In Chancery*, 40.

113 Charles Graves, *Champagne and Chandeliers: The Story of the Café de Paris* (London: Odhams Press, 1958), 9.

114 Ibid., 10, 29, 34, 166–7. See also Norah Docker, *Norah: The Autobiography of Lady Docker* (London: W. H. Allen, 1969), 26–8.

115 Graves, *Champagne and Chandeliers*, 16–17.

116 Ibid., 27–9.

117 Docker, *Norah*, 26, 28.

118 Stephen Graham, *Twice Round the London Clock and More London Nights* (London: Ernest Benn, 1933), 131–2.

119 Ibid., 135.

120 Ibid.

121 Evelyn Waugh, *Brideshead Revisited: The Sacred and Profane Memories of Captain Charles Ryder* (New York: Little, Brown, 1999), 113–14.

122 Historians of London homosexual cultures have tended to isolate Soho's different uses in this way; see Cook, *London*; Houlbrook, *Queer London*.

123 Walkowitz, ' "Vision of Salome" ', 338. The proliferating sociological literature on cosmopolitanism mostly neglects the changing historical usages of the concept; see Timothy Brennan, *At Home in the World: Cosmopolitanism Now* (Cambridge, MA: Harvard University Press, 1997); Pheng Cheah and Bruce Robbins, eds, *Cosmopolitics: Thinking and Feeling Beyond the Nation* (Minneapolis: University of Minnesota Press, 1998); Ulrich Beck, *World Risk Society* (Cambridge: Polity, 1999); Bruce Robbins, *Feeling Global: Internationalism in Distress* (New York: New York University Press, 1999); Jacques Derrida, *On Cosmopolitanism and Forgiveness* (London: Routledge, 2001). For more historically nuanced accounts see Amanda Anderson, *The Powers of Distance: Cosmopolitanism and the Culture of Detach-ment* (Princeton, NJ: Princeton University Press, 2001); Mica Nava, *Visceral Cosmopolitanism: Gender, Culture and the Normalisation of Difference* (Oxford: Berg, 2007).

124 Robert Fabian, *London After Dark: An Intimate Record of Night Life in London, and a Selection of Crime Stories from the Case Book of Ex-Superintendent Robert Fabian* (London: Naldrett Press, 1954), 3–4.

125 Claims about Fabian as 'England's greatest detective' were made at the opening of the BBC television series *Fabian of the Yard*; see 'Fabian of the Yard', http://www.tv-ark.org.uk/drama/drama_e-k.html (accessed 10 November 2006); Susan Sydney-Smith, 'Fabian of the Yard 1954–56', Screenonline, http://www.screenonline.org.uk/tv/id/1010 225 (accessed 10 November 2006).

126 Fabian also appeared on the *Wheel of Fortune*, an early television game show; see Marek Cohen, *Dope Girls: The Birth of the British Drug Underground* (London: Lawrence & Wishart, 1992), 161.

127 Robert Fabian, *Fabian of the Yard: An Intimate Record by Ex-Superintendent Robert Fabian* (London: Naldrett Press, 1950); Fabian, *London After Dark*.

128 Fabian, *London After Dark*, 41, 10.

129 Ibid., 10.

130 Ibid.

131 Ibid., 9.

132 Fabian, *Fabian of the Yard*, 17.

133 Andrew Clay, 'When the Gangs Came to Britain: The Postwar British Crime Film', *Journal of Popular British Cinema*, no. 1 (1998): 84.

134 Fabian, *London After Dark*, 27. For the Queen's night-time visits to the West End see Ben Pimlott, *The Queen: A Biography of Elizabeth II* (London: HarperCollins, 1996), 159.

135 Fabian, *London After Dark*, 9.

136 Duncan Webb, *Deadline for Crime* (London: Frederick Muller, 1955), 9. See also his *Crime Reporter* (London: Fleetway Colourbacks, 1963), 3–5.

137 Webb, *Deadline for Crime*, 83.

138 Ibid., and Webb, *Crime Reporter*.

139 Duncan Webb, 'Dope Trade Danger', *People*, 23 January 1955, 3; Duncan Webb, 'He is

London's Call Girl "King" ', *People*, 13 March 1955, 3; Albert Dimes, 'Soho: Albert Dimes Takes the Lid Off', *People*, 2 October 1955, 1.

140 Robert Murphy, *Smash and Grab: Gangsters in the London Underworld 1920–60* (London: Faber & Faber: 1993), 137.

141 William Hill, *Boss of Britain's Underworld* (London: Naldrett Press, 1955). Hill was born in Seven Dials, Holborn.

142 'Soho Fight Charge: Alleged Use of Knife', *The Times*, 20 September 1955, 4; 'Tinpot Tyrant Jack Spot was "Tried" by his own Mob', *People*, 25 September 1955, 5. The affray in Frith Street in August 1955 was between Jack Spot (Jack Comer) and Albert Dimes, one of Billy Hill's favoured hardmen. Duncan Webb led much of the subsequent press exposé of the feud; see Wensley Clarkson, *Hit 'Em Hard: Jack Spot, King of the Underworld* (London: HarperCollins, 2002).

143 See Murphy, *Smash and Grab*, 135–7. The launch party for Hill's book, *Boss of Britain's Underworld*, attracted considerable media attention. The *Daily Mail* reproduced the invitation sent to its reporter, and Hickey profiled the underworld celebrities present at the event for the *Daily Express*. A few months earlier the BBC News and Information Service had opened a special 'gang warfare file', in which Soho featured prominently. See Duncan Campbell, *The Underworld* (London: BBC Books, 1994), 53.

144 Jackson, *Indiscreet Guide to Soho*, 17.

145 Charlotte Brunsdon, 'Space and Place in the British Crime Film', in Steve Chibnall and Robert Murphy, eds, *British Crime Cinema* (London: Routledge, 1999), 155. See also Brunsdon's *London in Cinema: The Cinematic City since 1945* (London: British Film Institute, 2007), 100–4.

146 Strict censorship ensured that British crime film scripts of the 1930s such as *At the Blue Café*, *Soho Racket* and *Murder in Soho*, which featured prostitutes and drug addicts, were rejected by the British Board of Film Censors; see Robert Murphy, *Realism and Tinsel: Cinema and Society in Britain 1939–1948* (London: Routledge, 1989), 148; Robert Murphy, 'Riff-Raff: British Cinema and the Underworld', in Charles Barr, ed., *All Our Yesterdays: 90 Years of British Cinema* (London: British Film Institute, 1986), 300–1; James Robertson, 'The Censors and British Gangland, 1913–1990', in Chibnall and Murphy, *British Crime Cinema*, 19.

147 See 'Noose', *Monthly Film Bulletin*, 30 September 1948, 125.

148 *Noose*, directed by Edmond Greville (Great Britain: Edward Dryhurst Productions, 1948).

149 Brunsdon, 'Space and Place in the British Crime Film', 154. See also Murphy, *Realism and Tinsel*, 164.

150 Dilys Powell, 'Never-Never London', *Sunday Times*, 18 June 1950, 4. See also Steve Chibnall and Robert Murphy, 'Parole Overdue: Releasing the British Crime Film into the Critical Community', in Chibnall and Murphy, *British Crime Cinema*, 7.

151 'Night and the City', *Motion Picture Herald*, 27 May 1950, 313. See also Brunsdon, 'Space and Place in the British Crime Film', 153.

152 See Gaston Lamond, *Soho Lady* (Stone: Curzon Publishing, 1948), cover blurb. Other novels in this genre included Ben Sarto, *Soho Spivs* (London: Modern Fiction, 1949); Josh Wingrave, *A Room in Soho* (London: Gaywood Press, 1953); Josh Wingrave, *Back Streets of Soho* (London: Kaye Publications, 1953); Marty Ladwick, *Soho Street Girl* (London: Kaye Publications, 1954); David Bateson, *The Soho Jungle* (London: Robert Hale, 1957).

153 Wingrave, *Room in Soho*.

154 Ibid., 72.

155 See 'Twelve Men Must Read Four Books', *Daily Herald*, 21 September 1954, 5.

156 Farson, *Never a Normal Man*, 108. See also George Melly, 'Introduction', in Farson, *Soho in the Fifties*, xiii; Taki and Jeffrey Bernard, *High Life, Low Life* (London: Unwin, 1982); Fryer, *Soho in the Fifties and Sixties*, 4–6; Frank Norman and Jeffrey Bernard, *Soho Night and Day* (Secker & Warburg, 1966), 3.

157 Jeffrey Bernard, quoted in Farson, *Soho in the Fifties*, 83; Bacon, quoted in Farson, *Never a Normal Man*, 125. For portraits of Bacon, Farson and Minton see Fryer, *Soho in the Fifties and Sixties*.

158 Francis Aldor, *The Good Time Guide to London* (London: Harrap, 1951), 135–6; Harold Hutchinson, *Visitor's London* (London: London Transport Executive, 1954), 82.

159 Sam Lambert, ed., *London Night and Day: A Guide to Where the Other Books Don't Take You*, 6th edn (London: Architectural Press, 1958), 46. See also Ian Nairn, *Nairn's London* (Harmondsworth: Penguin, 1966).

160 Fryer, *Soho in the Fifties and Sixties*, 51.

161 Platt, *London's Rock Routes*, 5.

162 See Frank Mort, *Cultures of Consumption: Masculinities and Social Space in Late Twentieth-Century Britain* (London: Routledge, 1996), 155; Platt, *London's Rock Routes*, 3–5.

163 In 1956 MacInnes took a room above an art gallery at 20 D'Arblay Street in west Soho; see Tony Gould, *Inside Outsider: The Life and Times of Colin MacInnes* (London: Allison & Busby, 1993), 110.

164 Colin MacInnes, *Absolute Beginners* (Harmondsworth: Penguin, 1986), 69.

165 Ibid., 74.

166 Mark Abrams, *The Teenage Consumer* (London: Press Exchange, 1959).

167 Colin MacInnes, 'Out of the Way', *New Society*, 6 December 1962, 24.

168 'Soho '58', *Sunday Graphic*, 20 July 1958, reprinted in Norman, *Norman's London*, 16.

169 Norman, *Norman's London*, 18.

170 Peter Wildeblood, *West End People* (London: Weidenfeld & Nicolson, 1958), cover blurb.

171 'Peter Wildeblood', *Guardian*, 16 November 1999, 20.

172 'Carnival in Soho', *Sphere*, 16 September 1955, cutting in Westminster City Archives, St Anne Parish Soho, Prints and Cuttings, Box A13 to 1985.

173 'Pride in Soho', *The Times*, 2 March 1955, 10.

174 'After the Fair a Republic'.

175 Farson, *Never a Normal Man*, 109.

176 The aim of a grand bazaar and fête held in Soho Square under royal patronage in 1893 and opened by Lady Randolph Churchill was to raise funds for the local parish church of St Anne's. Half a century later a fair launched in Soho Square in 1939 in aid of the Soho Hospital for Women was again under aristocratic supervision. See 'Bazaar in Soho Square', *The Times*, 9 June 1893, 10; 'Gaiety in Soho', *The Times*, 5 July 1939, 13.

177 'London Gets a Fair View of Soho', *Evening News*, 16 July 1955, 3.

178 Ibid.

179 Ibid.

180 Charlotte and Denis Plimmer, 'How Wicked Is Soho?' and Kenneth Hurren, 'The Spirit of Soho', in Soho Association, *Soho Fair*, Official Programme (London: Soho Association, 1957), 26, 21–2.

181 Plimmer, 'How Wicked Is Soho?', 26.

182 'Soho Changes since 1939', *The Times*, 9 December 1952, 3.

183 'The Remarkable Charles Forte', in Soho Association, *Soho Fair* (1957), 68–9. For membership of the Soho Association see Soho Association, *Soho Annual* (London: Soho Association, 1958), 19.

184 Soho Association, 'Why We Have a Fair', in Soho Association, *Soho Fair*, Official Programme (London: Soho Association, 1956), 15.

185 For the idea of grouped location see Frank Mort and Peter Thompson, 'Retailing, Commercial Culture and Masculinity in 1950s Britain: The Case of Montague Burton the "Tailor of Taste"', *History Workshop Journal*, no. 38 (1994): 112–13.

186 Ibid., 113. See also Eric Sigsworth, *Montague Burton: The Tailor of Taste* (Manchester: Manchester University Press, 1990), 50–1; Katrina Honeyman, 'Montague Burton Ltd.: The Creators of Well-Dressed Men', in John Chartres and Katrina Honeyman, eds, *Leeds City Business 1893–1993: Essays Marking the Centenary of the Incorporation* (Leeds: Leeds University Press, 1993), 186–216.

187 Town Planning and Improvements Committee, Minutes, 3 March 1954, and City Engineer's Report to Town Planning and Improvements Committee, 19 January 1955, City of Westminster, Town Planning and Improvements Committee: Minutes 1954–1955, Westminster City Archives, pp. 36, 370.

188 See Proposed Soho Fair, 14th to 20th July 1957, Town Planning and Improvements Committee, Minutes, 8 May 1957, in City of Westminster, Town Planning and Imp-

rovements Committee: Minutes 1956–1957, Westminster City Archives, pp. 59–60.

189   See 'Around Soho in Pictures and Quotations', in Soho Association, *Soho Annual*, 22–3.

190   Glass Age Development Committee, 'The Soho Project – 3', *Official Architecture and Planning*, February 1955, 56. For further coverage of the Soho scheme see 'Glass Age Development of Soho', *Architect and Building News*, 28 October 1954, 529–30; 'A Glimpse of the Glass Age', *Sphere*, 17 December 1954, cutting in Westminster City Archives, St Anne Parish Soho, Prints and Cuttings, Box A13 to 1985.

191   For these traditions of localized improvement see David Harvey, *The Urban Experience* (Oxford: Blackwell, 1989), and for their impact on Soho see Mort, *Cultures of Consumption*, 151. Close to Soho, the Mayfair Association, a conservation and residents group, started in 1952, while Soho's own Soho Society was founded in 1972. Councillors for St Anne's Ward during the 1940s and 1950s included local traders and business people; see Members of the City Council, Westminster City Council, Handbook (1946), 9–19; Members of the City Council, Westminster City Council, Handbook (August 1950–July 1951), 6–16, both in Westminster City Archives.

192   City Engineer's Report to Town Planning and Improvements Committee special meeting, 9 March 1950, City of Westminster, Town Planning and Improvements Committee: Minutes 1950–1951, Westminster City Archives, p. 190.

193   'A New Lease of Life for Soho Square', *Sphere*, 3 October 1953, 25; 'Work Goes Ahead in Soho Square', *Sphere*, 13 February 1954, 236.

194   For the impact of post-war consumption on the international economy and on the social politics of nation states see Eric Hobsbawm, *Age of Extremes: The Short Twentieth Century, 1914–1991* (London: Abacus, 1995), 257–86; Victoria de Grazia, *Irresistible Empire: America's Advance through Twentieth-Century Europe* (Cambridge, MA: Belknap Press of Harvard University Press, 2005); Tony Judt, *Postwar: A*

History of Europe since 1945 (London: Pimlico, 2007), 324–59. For effects on the British economy see G. D. N. Worswick and P. H. Ady, eds, *The British Economy in the Nineteen-Fifties* (Oxford: Clarendon Press, 1962); Alec Cairncross, *The British Economy since 1945: Economic Policy and Performance 1945–1990* (Oxford: Blackwell, 1992).

195   For contemporary debates about the culture of mass affluence see J. B. Priestley and Jacquetta Hawkes, *Journey Down a Rainbow* (London: Heinemann-Cresset, 1955); Richard Hoggart, *The Uses of Literacy: Aspects of Working-Class Life, with Special Reference to Publications and Entertainments* (London: Chatto & Windus, 1957); Peter Willmott and Michael Young, *Family and Class in a London Suburb* (London: Routledge & Kegan Paul, 1960); John Goldthorpe et al., *The Affluent Worker in the Class Structure* (London: Cambridge University Press, 1969).

196   C. A. R. Crosland, *The Future of Socialism* (London: Jonathan Cape, 1956), 278. See also Crosland's *The Conservative Enemy: A Programme of Radical Reform for the 1960s* (London: Jonathan Cape, 1962). For an appraisal of Crosland's cultural programme see Philip Dodd, 'The Arts of Life: Crosland's Culture', in Dick Leonard, ed., *Crosland and New Labour* (Basingstoke: Macmillan in association with the Fabian Society, 1999), 167–77.

197   For Crosland's metropolitan world in the 1950s see Susan Crosland, *Tony Crosland* (London: Jonathan Cape, 1982), 50–114.

198   Rodney Garland [pseud. Adam Hegedüs], *The Heart in Exile* (London: Four Square Books, 1961), 43.

199   See Alcock, 1985, C456/003/01; Michael James, 1993, Hall Carpenter Oral History Project, British Library Sound Archive, C456/122/02.

200   For these contrasting views of the club see Roger Butler, 1990, Hall Carpenter Oral History Project, British Library Sound Archive, C456/091/01, and Tom Cullen, 1999, C456/031/01–02.

201   Mike, Manager of the A&B club, 1980, Hall Carpenter Oral History Project, British Library Sound Archive, C547/006/02; Peter Burton, *Parallel Lives* (London: GMP, 1985), 14.

202 Garland, *Heart in Exile*, 110. For other fictional accounts of the club see Lehmann, *In the Purely Pagan Sense*, 210–12.

203 Gordon Westwood [pseud. Michael Schofield], *A Minority: A Report of the Life of the Male Homosexual in Great Britain* (London: Longman, 1960), 130–1; Westwood, *Society and the Homosexual*, 131.

204 See Antony Grey, 1990, Hall Carpenter Oral History Project, British Library Sound Archive, C456/71/01–03.

205 'Vice Den Allegations Strongly Denied', *North London Press*, 1 July 1955, 5. See also '100 Men Found in Saloon Bar', *St Pancras Chronicle*, 9 December 1955, 3; 'Fitzroy Tavern Licensees are Cleared', *Marylebone Mercury*, 20 January 1956, 4; the Allchilds were finally cleared of the allegations on appeal. For details of the case see 21 June 1955, London Metropolitan Archives, Marlborough Street Magistrates Court, Court Register, Court no. 1, part 2, PS/MS/A2/165; 'Appeal Clears Licensee', *Daily Telegraph and Morning Post*, 13 January 1956, 11; Fiber, *Fitzroy*, 77–90.

206 On Bill's Snack Bar see Prostitutes, Coffee Stall Bouchin Street, 25 October 1949, London Metropolitan Archives, Public Morality Council, File of Patrolling Officer's Report and Correspondence, 1946–1957, A/PMC/43, p. 3.

207 Murray Llewellyn-Jones to Public Morality Council, 1 June 1955, London Metropolitan Archives, Public Morality Council, File Concerning Homosexuality, 1955–1959, A/PMC/80.

208 Ibid., and Public Morality Council, Patrolling Officer's Report, Prostitutes, Coffee Stall Bouchin Street, 27 September 1949, Public Morality Council, Patrolling Officer's Report, p. 3.

209 See John, Tony Dean Interviews, British Library Sound Archive, C547/06/01. For other recollections of the coffee bar culture in the mid- to late 1950s see Richard, 1980, Tony Dean Interviews, British Library Sound Archive, C547/43/01; Burton, *Parallel Lives*, 30–31.

210 See Platt, *London's Rock Routes*, 10–12. For queer clientele at the 2i's see John Chesterman, 1993, Hall Carpenter Oral History Project, British Library Sound Archive, C456/123/03; Betty Bourne, 1994, C456/126/01.

211 Michael James, 1993, Hall Carpenter Oral History Project, British Library Sound Archive, C456/122/02. For the Mousehole see Chesterman, C456/123/03.

212 James, 1993, C456/122/02.

213 Ina Zweiniger-Bargielowska, *Austerity in Britain: Rationing, Controls, and Consumption, 1939–1955* (Oxford: Oxford University Press, 2000). For the effects of the rationing debate on party politics see Stephen Brooke, 'Problems of "Socialist Planning": Evan Durbin and the Labour Government of 1945', *Historical Journal* 34, no. 3 (1991): 687–702; Nick Tiratsoo, 'Popular Politics, Affluence and the Labour Party in the 1950s', in Anthony Gorst, Lewis Johnman and W. Scott Lucas, eds, *Contemporary British History, 1931–1961: Politics and the Limits of Policy* (London: Pinter in association with the Institute of Contemporary British History, 1991), 44–61. On popular attitudes to rationing see Harry Hopkins, *The New Look: A Social History of the Forties and Fifties in Britain* (London: Secker & Warburg, 1963); Michael Sissons and Philip French, eds, *Age of Austerity* (London: Hodder & Stoughton, 1963); David Kynaston, *Austerity Britain 1945–51* (London: Bloomsbury, 2007).

214 Peter Noble, 'Eating Out in Soho', in Soho Association, *Soho Fair* (1956), 23.

215 See for example Karl Baedeker, *London and its Environs: A Handbook for Travellers by Karl Baedeker*, 20th revised edn (London: George Allen & Unwin, 1951), 26–32; Karl Baedeker, *London and its Environs: A Handbook for Travellers by Karl Baedeker*, 21st revised edn (London: George Allen & Unwin, 1955), 26–31. Baedeker's guide noted that 'in Soho are innumerable little restaurants, attractive by their foreignness', but these were listed at the end of a section that began with the prestigious Café Royal in Regent Street and Quaglino's in Bury Street: Baedeker, *London* (1951), 30.

216 Noble, 'Eating Out in Soho', 23.

217 'Foreword', in Eugene Fodor, ed., *The Men's Guide to Europe* (London: Newman Neame, 1955), unpaginated.

218 Eugene Fodor, ed., *The Men's Guide to Europe* (London: Newman Neame, 1957), 22; Fodor, *Men's Guide to Europe* (1955), 254–5.

219 John Mountjoy, 'Men About Soho', in Soho Association, *Soho Fair* (1956), 26–7. For other coverage of male consumption at the fairs see John Taylor, 'Sartorial Observations', ibid., 53, 63; Hugh Mackay, 'Tips for Wine Drinkers', in Soho Association, *Soho Annual*, 37.

220 Anne Worthington, 'Shopping in Soho', in Soho Association, *Soho Annual*, 60. For other coverage of the female consumer see Marjory Creed, 'Let's Be Natural' and Anthony Edwards, 'Soho and the Baby Doll', ibid., 57, 63.

221 Salvoni, *Elena*, 1–2.

222 See Cyril Aynsley, 'As I was Walking Up . . .', *Daily Express*, 1 December 1953, cutting in Windmill Theatre Collection, Victoria and Albert Museum Archive of Art and Design, Blythe House, London, Press Cuttings 1953, Box 55.

223 Margaret Pearson, 'Soho – Its Fascination and its Food', in Soho Association, *Soho Fair* (1956), 48–9.

224 Keith Williams, *British Writers and the Media, 1930–45* (London: Macmillan, 1996), 17. For different appropriations of this mood in the inter-war imagination see Paul Fussell, *Abroad: British Literary Traveling Between the Wars* (New York and Oxford: Oxford University Press, 1980); Mica Nava, 'Wider Horizons and Modern Desire: The Contradictions of America and Racial Difference in London 1935–45', *New Formations*, no. 37 (1999): 71–91.

225 See Fiona MacCarthy, *Last Curtsey: The End of the Debutantes* (London: Faber & Faber, 2006), 101.

226 Olivia Manning, 'London Letter', *Jerusalem Post*, 12 November 1954, quoted in Artemis Cooper, *Writing at the Kitchen Table: The Authorized Biography of Elizabeth David* (London: Michael Joseph, 1999), 179.

227 Elizabeth David, draft of a letter to Patricia Siddall, Penguin Books, February 1963, quoted in Cooper, *Writing at the Kitchen Table*, 153. As David put it, her aim was 'to give some idea of the lovely cookery of those regions to people who do not already know them, and to stir the memories of those who have eaten this food on its native shores, and who would like sometimes to bring a flavour of those blessed lands of sun and sea and olive trees into their kitchens': Elizabeth David, *A Book of Mediterranean Food* (London: John Lehmann, 1950), vii–viii.

228 Elizabeth David, *Italian Food* (London: Macdonald, 1954), 39, 91, 293. See also Cooper, *Writing at the Kitchen Table*, 175; Lisa Chaney, *Elizabeth David: A Biography* (London: Macmillan, 1998), 272.

229 Chaney, *Elizabeth David*, 215, 236.

230 MacCarthy, *Last Curtsey*, 102.

231 See for example David, *Book of Mediterranean Food*, 41, 97; Elizabeth David, *French Country Cooking* (London: John Lehmann, 1951), 50, 152. The Sicilian painter Renato Guttuso illustrated *Italian Food* and David preferred Guttuso's monumental images to Minton's decorative fantasies; see Chaney, *Elizabeth David*, 339–40; Cooper, *Writing at the Kitchen Table*, 169.

232 See 'Soho Fair Programme and Route of the Procession', in Soho Association, *Soho Annual*, 50–1.

233 Reformist politicians like Tony Crosland and Roy Jenkins drew extensively on these images of Continental gaiety and cultural sophistication in their blueprints for the social democratic future of Britain, where freedom from restraint and social tolerance would replace Victorian values. See Crosland, *Future of Socialism*, 520–9; Crosland, *Conservative Enemy*, 237–41; Roy Jenkins, *The Labour Case* (Harmondsworth: Penguin, 1959), 135–46.

234 For Britain's position in this wider process of European rapprochement see Derek Urwin, *Western Europe since 1945: A Short Political History*, 3rd edn (London: Longman, 1981); Michael Hogan, *The Marshall Plan: America, Britain, and the Reconstruction of Western Europe, 1947–1952* (Cambridge: Cambridge University Press, 1987), 293–335; Alan Milward, *The European Rescue of the Nation-State* (London: Routledge, 1992), 345–433; Anthony Sutcliffe, *An Economic and Social*

History of Western Europe since 1945 (London: Longman, 1996), 28–40; Till Geiger, 'Reconstruction and the Beginnings of European Integration', in Max-Stephan Schulze, ed., *Western Europe: Economic and Social Change since 1945* (London: Longman, 1999), 23–41.

235 For population decline across the inner London boroughs see J. H. Westergaard, 'The Structure of Greater London', in Centre for Urban Studies, ed., *London: Aspects of Change* (London: MacGibbon and Kee, 1964), 93–6. For population decrease in Soho, especially among foreign and migrant groups, see White, *London in the Twentieth Century*, 105. An earlier generation of social investigators also noted a substantial local population decline in the late nineteenth century; see Sherwell, *Life in West London*, 4.

236 For the presence of foreign service-sector workers in post-war Soho, especially in the restaurant trade, see Salvoni, *Elena*, 55–6, 67.

237 For later cultural transformations of Soho see Mort, *Cultures of Consumption*, 149–99.

CHAPTER 6 EROTICA

1 The following account is based on the witness statement of PS Derek Caiels, C Division, 22 November 1961, Raymond Revue Bar: Suspected Disorderly House (1961–1963), TNA PRO MEPO 2/10168.

2 'Taking a Look at Soho', *Municipal Journal*, 15 March 1963, cutting in St James's Parish Piccadilly, Prints and Cuttings, D138 Sc–Z, Westminster City Archives. For the local economy in and around Walker's Court see *The Post Office London Directory for 1958: Street Directory* (London: Kelly's Directories, 1958), 899, 113.

3 For the emphasis on luxury see Chief Superintendent C to Commander 1, Metropolitan Police, 18 April 1958, and for the club's 'Continental ambience' see Raymond Theatre Revuebar, publicity letter, n.d. (1958), Raymond's Review Club: Unlawful Gaming Unlawful Sale of Liquor and Unlicensed Music and Dancing (1958–1963), both TNA PRO MEPO 2/10232.

4 Raymond Revuebar, publicity letter, TNA PRO MEPO 2/10232.

5 *Paul Raymond's Raymond Revuebar*, programme, 1962, TNA PRO MEPO 2/10168, unpaginated.

6 Ibid.

7 Caiels, TNA PRO MEPO 2/10168, p. 2.

8 Ibid., p. 4.

9 Ibid., p. 6.

10 Ibid., p. 7.

11 Ibid.

12 For the reflections of one of the plain-clothes officers who covered the Revuebar case see 'The Night Sergeant Bobsin Went to a Club Show in Soho', *Daily Mail*, 24 September 1958, cutting in Greater London Council, Raymond Revuebar, Walker's Court, Brewer Street, London Metropolitan Archives, GLC/DG/EL2/58.

13 Caiels, TNA PRO MEPO 2/10168, p. 6.

14 Chief Superintendent C to Commander 1, Metropolitan Police, 29 November 1961, TNA PRO MEPO 2/10168.

15 Kenneth Allsop, 'Brave New Underworld', *Spectator*, 12 August 1960, 240–1.

16 Arthur Helliwell, 'Naughtiness in the Afternoon', *People*, 27 April 1958; Michael Hennessey, 'The Big Take-Off', *Tit-Bits*, 11 May 1959; Michael Hennessey, 'Used to Read Minds: Now He's Mr Striptease', *Tit-Bits*, 18 May 1959, cuttings in Windmill Theatre Collection, Victoria and Albert Museum Archive of Art and Design, Blythe House, London, Press Cuttings 1959–60, Box 62.

17 'Strip-Tease Clubs Sweeping Soho', *New York Herald Tribune* (Paris edn), 4–5 June 1960; see also Sam Wanamaker, 'Striptease: The Most Successful Theater in London', *London American*, 18–24 August 1960, cuttings in Windmill Theatre Collection, Press Cuttings 1960–2, Box 63.

18 See 'It's London's Latest Theatre Craze: My Bare Lady', *Adelaide News*, 16 May 1958, cutting in Windmill Theatre Collection, Press Cuttings 1958–9, Box 61; 'Strip-Tease in der Mittagspause', *Hamburger Echo*, 21 June 1958, cutting in Windmill Theatre Collection, Press Cuttings 1957–8, Box 60.

19 Allsop, 'Brave New Underworld', 241; 'Strip-Tease Clubs Sweeping Soho'.

20 Alfred Kinsey et al., *Sexual Behavior in the Human Female* (Philadelphia: W. B. Saunders, 1953), 663–4.

21 In a British context see Henry Havelock Ellis, *Psychology of Sex: A Manual for Students* (London: Heinemann, 1933), 63; Edward Glover, *The Roots of Crime.* (London: Imago, 1960), 246; Anthony Storr, *Sexual Deviation* (Harmondsworth: Penguin, 1964), 96–7; Ismond Rosen, 'The Male Response to Frigidity', *Journal of Psychosomatic Research* 10 (1966): 135–41.

22 See Michael Powell, *A Life in Movies: An Autobiography* (London: Methuen, 1987), 217, 656; Ian Christie, *Arrows of Desire: The Films of Michael Powell and Emeric Pressburger* (London: Waterstone, 1985), 102–5.

23 See British Vigilance Association, 76th Annual Report, 1963, The Women's Library, British Vigilance Association, Annual Reports, 4NVA/2/2; British Vigilance Association, Executive Committee Minutes, 31 July 1963, The Women's Library, British Vigilance Association, Executive Committee Minutes, 1963–1971, 4NVA/1/3/4, p. 2; James Riordan to Chief Superintendent, C Division, 18 January 1961, TNA PRO MEPO 2/10232, p. 2. For political debate over striptease see the Lord Chancellor, London Government Bill, 28 May 1963, *Parliamentary Debates (Hansard) House of Lords Official Report*, 5th ser., vol. 250, session 1962–3 (London: HMSO, 1963), col. 733.

24 Sheila Van Damm, *We Never Closed: The Windmill Story* (London: Robert Hale, 1967), 14.

25 Ibid.

26 There are three film versions of the Windmill story. The first was Hollywood's *Tonight and Every Night* (1945), directed by Victor Saville and starring Rita Hayworth. A British film of the story, *Murder at the Windmill* (1948), directed by Val Guest, was 'more authentic' according to Vivian Van Damm: *Tonight and Every Night* (London: Stanley Paul, 1952), 175. The most recent version, *Mrs Henderson Presents* (2005), was directed by Stephen Frears and starred Judi Dench as Laura Henderson and Bob Hoskins as Vivian Van Damm. The film again endorsed the theatre's national importance by highlighting its contribution to home front morale during the Second World War.

27 S. Van Damm, *We Never Closed*, 14.

28 In addition to the Windmill Theatre, Great Windmill Street included the Jardella Riccardo and Moustrides restaurants, Anglo-Israeli Club, Rena Wine Merchants, and Jack Solomon's, boxing promoter. Archer Street contained Sami Ziderman's Jewish ladies' tailor, London Theatrical Productions and the Conti Italian Stage School, as well as outlets for the metal manufacturing trades. See the entries for Archer Street and Great Windmill Street, *The Post Office London Directory for 1953* (London: Kelly's Directories, 1953), 53, 340.

29 See William Morris, *The Homeland Guide to London* (London: Homeland Association, 1947), 103; Francis Aldor, *The Good Time Guide to London* (London: Harrap, 1951), 134–8; Francis Marshall, *The London Week-End Book* (London: Seeley Service, 1953), 219–23.

30 Lydia Syson, *Doctor of Love: James Graham and his Celestial Bed* (London: Alma Books, 2008), 156–7. See also Peter Otto, 'The Regeneration of the Body: Sex, Religion and the Sublime in James Graham's *Temple of Health and Hymen*', *Romanticism on the Net* 23 (August 2001), http://users.ox.ac.uk/~scat@385/230otto.html (accessed 29 March 2009).

31 Edwin Beresford Chancellor, *The Romance of Soho: Being an Account of the District, its Past Distinguished Inhabitants, its Historic Houses, and its Place in the Social Annals of London* (London: Country Life, 1931), 9.

32 E. F. Rimbault, *Soho and its Associations, Historical, Literary and Artistic, Edited from the MSS. of E. F. Rimbault by George Clinch* (London: Dulau and Co., 1895), 50–3. See also Teresa Cornelys, *Mrs. Cornely's [sic] Entertainments at Carlisle House, Soho Square* (Blackburn: Bradford, 1840); Rev. J. H. Cardwell, *Men and Women of Soho: Famous and Infamous; Actors, Authors, Dramatists, Entertainers and Engravers* (London: Truslove &

Hanson, 1904), 267–9; Chancellor, *Romance of Soho*, 64–94; Margaret Goldsmith, *Soho Square* (London: Sampson Low, Marston & Co., 1947), 60–82; Judith Summers, *The Empress of Pleasure: The Life and Adventures of Teresa Cornelys – Queen of Masquerades and Casanova's Lover* (London: Viking, 2003).

33 For these styles of male and female impersonation see Terry Castle, *Masquerade and Civilization: The Carnivalesque in Eighteenth-Century English Culture and Fiction* (Stanford, CA: Stanford University Press, 1986), 34. For molly houses see Randolph Trumbach, *Sex and the Gender Revolution*, vol. 1, *Heterosexuality and the Third Gender in Enlightenment London* (Chicago: University of Chicago Press, 1998); Rictor Norton, *Mother Clap's Molly House: The Gay Subculture in England, 1700–1830* (London: Gay Men's Press, 1992).

34 See Brenda Assael, 'Art or Indecency? *Tableaux Vivants* on the London Stage and the Failure of Late Victorian Moral Reform', *Journal of British Studies* 45, no. 4 (October 2006): 744–58.

35 For the distinction between female nudity and nakedness see Lynda Nead, *The Female Nude: Art, Obscenity and Sexuality* (London: Routledge, 1992); Alison Smith, *The Victorian Nude: Sexuality, Morality and Art* (Manchester: Manchester University Press, 1996).

36 These confrontations culminated in the famous licensing case, the battle of the Empire, brought in 1894 before the London County Council by Laura Ormiston Chant and the National Vigilance Association against the management of the Empire Theatre in Leicester Square and the Palace Theatre of Varieties at Cambridge Circus; see Laura Ormiston Chant, *Why We Attacked the Empire* (London: Marshall & Son, 1895). Historians have cast the case as a formative event in modern sexual politics, highlighting the complex theatrical staging of the female body and the contested perspectives on sexual taste and urban vision that were generated by the affair; see Lucy Bland, *Banishing the Beast: English Feminism and Sexual Morality 1885–1914* (London: Penguin, 1995), 113–23; Erika Rappaport, *Shopping for Pleasure: Women in the Making of London's West*

End (Princeton, NJ: Princeton University Press, 2000), 182; Judith Walkowitz, 'Cosmopolitanism, Feminism, and the Moving Body', *Victorian Culture and Literature* 38, no. 2 (Fall 2010, forthcoming).

37 See Derek Parker and Julie Parker, *The Natural History of the Chorus Girl* (Newton Abbot: David & Charles, 1975), 81.

38 Ibid., 52. See also See also Kurt Gänzl, *Lydia Thompson, Queen of Burlesque* (London: Routledge, 2002).

39 Gänzl, *Lydia Thompson*, 101–65.

40 See Parker and Parker, *Natural History of the Chorus Girl*, 81–7, 102, 140; Robert Allen, *Horrible Prettiness: Burlesque and American Culture* (Chapel Hill: University of North Carolina Press, 1991), 26–7; Susan Glenn, *Female Spectacle: The Theatrical Roots of Modern Feminism* (Cambridge, MA: Harvard University Press, 2000), 158–85.

41 Glenn, *Female Spectacle*, 2.

42 'Woman Theatre Owner', *Hull Daily Mail*, 22 January 1932, cutting in Windmill Theatre Collection, Press Cuttings December 1931–May 1932, Box 23; 'At 80 She Lives in Youth and Beauty', *Daily Mail*, 4 December 1943, cutting in Windmill Theatre Archive, Theatre Museum, London; S. Van Damm, *We Never Closed*, 20.

43 Laura Henderson was patroness of the Hyde Park Babies' Club and on the committees of the Marie Stopes Clinic, the Musicians Benevolent Fund and the Docklands Settlement of Hulton House (a club for working women in the East End); see *South Wales Echo*, 7 May 1931, Windmill Theatre Collection, Press Cuttings December 1931–May 1932, Box 23. For Henderson's society connections see Ian Bevan, 'No Nudes Would Be Bad News', *Outspan* (Bloemfontein), 20 February 1953, Windmill Theatre Collection, Press Cuttings 1953, Box 55.

44 Laura Henderson, letter to the editor, *Daily Herald*, 17 May 1931, in Windmill Theatre Collection, Press Cuttings December 1931–May 1932, Box 23.

45 Ibid.

46 V. Van Damm, *Tonight and Every Night*, 40–58; S. Van Damm, *We Never Closed*, 34. Van Damm managed the Polytechnic Cinema

in Upper Regent Street and the Empire
Theatre, Leicester Square, during the 1920s.

47 S. Van Damm, *We Never Closed*, 21.

48 V. Van Damm, *Tonight and Every Night*, 86.

49 In Nigel Balchin's *Darkness Falls from the Air*
(London: Collins, 1942, 143–6) the narrator,
a high-profile civil servant, visited Liberty
Hall in Albemarle Street, a club with nude
exhibitions on the dance floor. Jack Glicco's
Madness After Midnight (London: Elek Books,
1952, 132–3) covered 'amateur strip tease' at
the Jigs Club in Wardour Street. Ex-
Detective Chief Superintendent Edward
Greeno's *War on the Underworld* (London:
Brown, Watson Ltd, 1961, 72–3) described a
raid on a brothel in Dover Street involving
naked public sex. All these accounts were
recollections of London in the 1930s. See
also Jerry White, *London in the Twentieth
Century: A City and its People* (London: Penguin, 2002), 343–4.

50 Judith Walkowitz, 'The Windmill Theatre:
Erotic Display, Middlebrow, and the Spirit
of the Blitz', unpublished paper to Centre
for Interdisciplinary Research in the Arts,
University of Manchester, October 2007.

51 S. Van Damm, *We Never Closed*, 21.

52 'The Windmill Throws a Party', *Picture Post*,
2 March 1946, 18.

53 S. Van Damm, *We Never Closed*, 63.

54 See V. Van Damm, *Tonight and Every Night*,
175.

55 For wartime attitudes to and representations
of female sexuality see Sonya Rose, *Which
People's War? National Identity and Citizenship
in Britain 1939–1945* (Oxford: Oxford Uni-
versity Press, 2003), 71–150; Pam Cook, ed.,
Gainsborough Pictures (London: Cassell, 1997);
Penny Summerfield, *Reconstructing Women's
Wartime Lives: Discourse and Subjectivity in
Oral Histories of the Second World War* (Manch-
ester: Manchester University Press, 1998),
142–3, 164; Sue Harper, *Women in British
Cinema: Mad, Bad and Dangerous to Know*
(London and New York: Continuum, 2000),
30–51.

56 Cover, *London Life*, 19 October 1940.

57 V. Van Damm, 'Introduction', *Revudeville Souvenir*, 18th edn, n.d. (1945?), British Library.

58 See *Revudeville* no. 251, 25 August 1952,
Report by the Assistant Comptroller, 28
August 1952, Lord Chamberlain's Plays,
Correspondence File 4482, British Library,
Manuscripts Department.

59 S. Van Damm, *We Never Closed*, 107.

60 V. Van Damm, *Tonight and Every Night*, 113–
14.

61 S. Van Damm, *We Never Closed*, 154.

62 Ibid., 65.

63 Ibid.

64 Michael Bentine, *The Long Banana Skin*
(London: Wolfe, 1975), 151.

65 'Top Hat', Revudeville no. 255, *Revudeville
27th Souvenir*, n.d. (February–March 1953),
unpaginated, Windmill Theatre, British
Library, playbills collection.

66 Revudeville no. 260, *Revudeville 29th
Souvenir*, n.d., unpaginated, Windmill Theatre,
British Library, playbills collection.

67 'On Parade', Revudeville no. 257, *Revudeville
27th Souvenir*, n.d. (May 1953), unpaginated,
Windmill Theatre, British Library, playbills
collection.

68 'Out of This World', *Revudeville*, no. 296,
n.d. (March 1958), unpaginated, Windmill
Theatre, British Library, playbills collection.

69 Allen, *Horrible Prettiness*, 264.

70 The Earl of Scarborough, Lord Chamberlain
between 1952 and 1963, was educated at
Sandhurst and Magdalen College, Oxford,
and served in the Eleventh Hussars during
the First World War. His senior assistants
were Lt-Col. Sir Terence Nugent, Comptroller of the Lord Chamberlain's Office
1936–60, who served in the Irish Guards and
who was subsequently Lord-in-Waiting to
Elizabeth II, and Sir Norman Gwatkin, Assistant Comptroller, educated at Eton and
Sandhurst. See Katherine Johnson, 'Apart
from "Look Back in Anger", What Else Was
Worrying the Lord Chamberlain's Office in
1956', in Dominic Shellard, ed., *British Theatre
in the 1950s* (Sheffield: Sheffield Academic
Press, 2000), 116–35.

71 For the Lord Chamberlain's regulation of the
English theatre see John Johnston, *The Lord
Chamberlain's Blue Pencil* (London: Hodder
& Stoughton, 1990); Anthony Aldgate, *Cens-*

orship and the Permissive Society: British Cinema and the Theatre 1955–1965 (Oxford: Clarendon Press, 1995); Nicholas de Jongh, *Politics, Prudery and Perversions: The Censoring of the English Stage, 1901–1968* (London: Methuen, 2000).

72 In April 1940 Lord Clarendon convened a conference at St James's Palace involving the police, the Home Office and representatives from the local authorities and the entertainment business to agree a policy to regulate the 'tendency which has become evident since the war of greater displays of nudity and impropriety of gesture and speech'; see Paul Ferris, *Sex and the British: A Twentieth Century History* (London: Michael Joseph, 1993), 143. See also Striptease, Revuebar Club, GLC/DG/EL2/58. This policy was a response partly to wartime demands, but also to the growth of unlicensed clubs with striptease acts during the 1930s.

73 See General Secretary, Public Morality Council, to Earl of Scarborough, 13 June 1956, Revuedeville no. 282, and N. W. Gwatkin, Assistant Comptroller, Lord Chamberlain's Department to the Manager, Windmill Theatre, 19 June 1956, Lord Chamberlain's Plays, Correspondence Files.

74 G. A. Titman to Anne Mitelle, Assistant Producer, Windmill Theatre, 18 October 1947; Reader's Report, Revudeville no. 207, 18 October 1947, Lord Chamberlain's Plays, Correspondence File 8423.

75 See the following observation: 'From my privileged position in the box I could see perhaps a little more than is visible to the audience below and in the circle, some people have all the luck': G. A. Titman, Reader's Report, Revudeville no. 229, 22 March 1950, Lord Chamberlain's Plays, Correspondence File 1301; also G. A. Titman, Reader's Report, Revudeville no. 205, 26 July 1947, Lord Chamberlain's Plays, Correspondence File 8251.

76 S. Van Damm, *We Never Closed*, 157.

77 'My Lady's Fan', Revudeville no. 223, *Revudeville 23rd Souvenir*, n.d., unpaginated, Windmill Theatre, British Library, playbills collection.

78 'My Lady's Fan', Revudeville no. 259, *Revudeville 27th Souvenir*, n.d., unpaginated, Windmill Theatre, British Library, playbills collection.

79 'It Pays to Advertise', Revudeville no. 269, *Revudeville 29th Souvenir*, n.d., unpaginated, Windmill Theatre, British Library, playbills collection.

80 See, for example, Lucinda Jarrett, *Stripping in Time: A History of Erotic Dancing* (London: Pandora, 1997); Richard Wortley, *A Pictorial History of Striptease* (London: Octopus, 1976).

81 Jimmy Edwards, *Six of the Best* (London: Robson, 1984), 219.

82 See Bentine, *Long Banana Skin*, 148–51; Alexander Walker, *Peter Sellers: The Authorized Biography* (London: Weidenfeld & Nicolson, 1981), 58; Harry Secombe, *Arias & Raspberries: The Autobiography of Harry Secombe*, vol. 1, *The Raspberry Years* (London: Robson, 1989), 132–5.

83 Secombe, *Arias & Raspberries*, 118–19.

84 Ibid., 146.

85 Bentine, *Long Banana Skin*, 206.

86 Ibid.

87 For the Goons see Walker, *Peter Sellers*, 62–6; Roger Lewis, *The Life and Death of Peter Sellers* (London: Century, 1994), 138–40.

88 See Phillip Purser and Jenny Wilkes, *The One and Only Phyllis Dixey* (London: Futura, 1978).

89 G. A. Titman, 28 August 1951, Revudeville no. 242, Lord Chamberlain's Plays, Correspondence Files.

90 Quoted in Bryan Bourne, 'Twenty-One Years of the Windmill', *Everybody's*, 7 February 1953, 12.

91 V. Van Damm, *Tonight and Every Night*, 125.

92 Ibid., 126.

93 Ibid., 127, 111. See also Sheila Van Damm, 'The Windmill and I', *Hackney Gazette*, 14 May 1958, Windmill Theatre Collection, Press Cuttings 1957–8, Box 60.

94 For Montague Burton as a Jewish entrepreneur see Eric Sigsworth, *Montague Burton: The Tailor of Taste* (Manchester: Manchester University Press, 1990); Frank Mort and Peter Thompson, 'Retailing, Commercial Culture and Masculinity in 1950s Britain:

The Case of Montague Burton, the "Tailor of Taste"', *History Workshop Journal*, no. 38 (1994): 106–27. For the Allchild family at the Fitzroy Tavern see Sally Fiber, *The Fitzroy: The Autobiography of a London Tavern; Sally Fiber's Story of the Fitzroy as Told to Clive Powell-Williams* (Lewes: Temple House, 1995).

95 See Brian Epstein, *A Cellarful of Noise* (London: New English Library, 1965); Ray Coleman, *Brian Epstein: The Man Who Made the Beatles* (London: Viking, 1989); Debbie Geller, *The Brian Epstein Story* (London: Faber & Faber, 2000).

96 'With Pictures of Cathedrals and Countryside', *Illustrated*, 3 December 1939; 'Pauline at Home', *Windmill Now*, 14th edn, 1950; 'The Windmill Came of Age', *Sketch*, 25 February 1953, cuttings in Windmill Theatre Archive, Theatre Museum.

97 Bevan, 'No Nudes Would Be Bad News'.

98 Daniel Farson, *Never A Normal Man* (London: HarperCollins, 1997), 98.

99 See the comments of the Lord Chamberlain's Office on the sketch 'Encore L'Amour', *Revudeville* no. 254, 15 December 1952, Lord Chamberlain's Office, Correspondence Files, British Library, Manuscript Department.

100 See Farson, *Never a Normal Man*, 98.

101 Cyril Aynsley, 'As I Was Walking Up . . .' *Daily Express*, 1 December 1953, Windmill Theatre Collection, Press Cuttings 1953, Box 55. See also Kenneth Bandy, 'A Diary of Success: The Windmill Story', in Soho Association, *Soho Fair*, Official Programme (London: Soho Association, 1957), 64–5.

102 Edwards, *Six of the Best*, 221.

103 Daniel Farson, *Soho in the Fifties* (London: Michael Joseph, 1987), 8.

104 'Non-Stop Peepshow', *Picture Post*, 21 July 1951, 28. See also 'London's Burlesque', *This Week Magazine: New York Herald Tribune*, 29 June 1952, Windmill Theatre Collection, Press Cuttings 1952–3, Box 54.

105 For comparative details of the Windmill's weekly wages see *Revudeville* no. 137, September–October 1940, and *Revudeville* no. 281, Windmill Theatre Collection, Accounts Books 1932–1964, Box 19.

106 'There's a Public for Nude Shows, Alright', *Show News*, 6 February 1954, Windmill Theatre Collection, Press Cuttings 1953, Box 55.

107 'Follow Her and Be a Good Trouper', *People*, 1 March 1953, Windmill Theatre Collection, Press Cuttings 1953, Box 55.

108 See 'Other People's Jobs – How It Feels to Be a Windmill Girl', *Weekly Post*, 19 March 1952, Windmill Theatre Collection, Press Cuttings 1952–3, Box 54.

109 S. Van Damm, 'The Windmill and I'.

110 Quoted in Purser and Wilkes, *One and Only Phyllis Dixey*, 88.

111 S. Van Damm, *We Never Closed*, 15, facing page 32.

112 See (among very many) 'Dancer's Son', *The Star*, 27 August 1953; 'Windmill Bride', *Evening News*, 31 August 1953, Windmill Theatre Collection, Press Cuttings 1953, Box 55.

113 See Robert Hounsome, *The Very Nearly Man: An Autobiography* (Leicester: Matador, 2006), 200.

114 Christopher Booker, *The Neophiliacs: A Study of the Revolution in English Life in the Fifties and Sixties* (London: Collins, 1969), 155.

115 'Jack's Ten Years', *New Statesman*, 2 January 1960, 1.

116 Nelson Algren, *Who Lost an American? Being a Guide to the Seamier Sides of New York City, Inner London, Paris, Dublin, Barcelona, Seville, Almeria, Istanbul, Crete and Chicago, Illinois* (London: Andre Deutsch, 1963), 79.

117 Daniel Farson, 'Raymond Reviewed', *Sunday Telegraph Magazine*, 13 July 1997, 12.

118 Bernard Levin, *The Pendulum Years: Britain and the Sixties* (London: Jonathan Cape, 1970), 69–71.

119 See Irma Kurtz, 'Raymond Reviewed', *Guardian*, 12 May 1976, cutting in Windmill Theatre Archive.

120 See 'How Paul Raymond Peeped Through a Loophole', *Sunday Telegraph Magazine*, 8 April 1979, cutting in Windmill Theatre Archive.

121 See *Soho Sex King: The Paul Raymond Story*, Channel 4, 15 March 2008; 'The Man Who Owned Seedy Soho', *The Times*, 4 March 2008, 3; 'Paul Raymond', *Guardian*, 4 March 2008, 3; 'Paul Raymond', *Daily Telegraph*, 4 March 2008, 25.

122 For analysis of London's changing labour market in the 1950s and early 1960s see J. H. Westergaard, 'The Structure of Greater London', in Centre for Urban Studies, ed., *London: Aspects of Change* (London: Mac-Gibbon and Kee, 1964), 91–156; General Register Office, *Census 1951: England and Wales; Report on Greater London and Five Other Conurbations* (London: HMSO, 1956), xliii.

123 Jonathon Green, *All Dressed Up: The Sixties and the Counterculture* (London: Pimlico, 1999), 69. See also Thomas Wolfe, *The Mid-Atlantic Man: And Other New Breeds in England and America* (London: Weidenfeld & Nicolson, 1969), 47. For contemporary emphasis on the importance of London's consumer industries see 'Living in Boom Time', *Queen*, 15 September 1959, 1, 97–107.

124 For La Rue see Danny La Rue, with Howard Elson, *From Drags to Riches: My Autobiography* (London: Viking, 1987); Peter Underwood, *Danny La Rue: Life's A Drag* (London: Star Books, 1975). For John Stephen see Nik Cohn, *Ball the Wall: Nik Cohn in the Age of Rock* (London: Picador, 1989), 280–8; Shaun Cole, *'Don We Now Our Gay Apparel': Gay Men's Dress in the Twentieth Century* (Oxford: Berg, 2000), 73, 75.

125 For Raymond's early career see Kurtz, 'Raymond Reviewed'; 'Pass Notes', *Guardian*, 1 December 1992, cuttings in Windmill Theatre Archive.

126 'Paul Raymond', *Daily Telegraph*.

127 Ibid.; 'Paul Raymond', *Guardian*.

128 La Rue, *From Drags to Riches*, 81. Raymond asked La Rue to teach the performers in his touring shows 'how to stand correctly and how to walk down a staircase'.

129 'Paul Raymond', *Guardian*.

130 Carol Sarler, 'The Girl Who Never Said No', *Sunday Times Magazine*, 10 January 1993, 22.

131 See Reader's Report, *The Brothel*, 9 November 1955, Lord Chamberlain's Plays, Correspondence File 205; Reader's Report, *Pyjama Tops*, 1956, Lord Chamberlain's Plays, Correspondence File 9088.

132 Leo Abse, 'Divorce and Reconciliation', *Spectator*, 8 February 1963, 156. Abse was commenting on the Matrimonial Causes and Reconciliation Bill currently being debated in Parliament. For the impact of privatized leisure on elite West End venues see Charles Graves, *Champagne and Chandeliers: The Story of the Café de Paris* (London: Odhams Press, 1958), 219.

133 'Bright Lights', *Stage and Television Today*, 3 March 1960, 8. See also Harold Davidson, 'Belief in Live Entertainment', *Stage and Television Today*, 14 January 1960, 5.

134 Finlater noted how the 'command points' of theatreland in Shaftesbury Avenue were bathed in a 'sunset glow': Richard Findlater, 'Spotlight on the Theatre', *Lilliput*, 30 October 1958, 12–17, Windmill Theatre Collection, Press Cuttings 1958–9, Box 61.

135 For the impact of naturalistic realism on British television during the late 1950s and early 1960s see Stuart Hall and Paddy Whannel, *The Popular Arts* (London: Hutchinson Educational, 1964), 227–8.

136 Jarrett, *Stripping in Time*, 179. See also Keith Sutton, 'Figures of Speech', *New Statesman and Nation*, 19 March 1960, 398.

137 For the sexual significance of *From Here To Eternity* see Gary Fishgall, *Against Type: The Biography of Burt Lancaster* (New York and London: Scribner, 1995), 112–17; Eric Braun, *Deborah Kerr* (London: W. H. Allen, 1977), 136–42.

138 See Tom Pendergast and Sara Pendergast, eds, *International Dictionary of Films and Filmmakers 3: Actors and Actresses* (Detroit: St James Press, 1986), 68–70.

139 Ibid, 177–8.

140 Kenneth Tynan, quoted in Damon Wise, *Come By Sunday: The Fabulous, Ruined Life of Diana Dors* (London: Pan, 1999), 63. See also Joan Flory and Damien Walne, *Diana Dors: Only a Whisper Away* (Wheathampstead: Lennard, 1987).

141 Geoffrey Gorer, *Exploring English Character* (London: Cresset Press, 1955), 117. Seven per cent of those interviewed in Gorer's sample said they thought that 'English people fall in love the way you see Americans doing it on the films'.

142 'A Run on Clubs', *Eastern Daily Press*, 1 May 1958, Windmill Theatre Collection, Press Cuttings 1957–8, Box 60.

143 S. Van Damm, *We Never Closed*, 177.

144 See Rules of Raymond Theatre Revuebar Club, n.d. (1958), and Raymond Revuebar Club, Amendation to Club Rules, 8 January 1959, TNA PRO MEPO 2/10232.

145 'Soho – So What?' *Queen*, July 1960, 45. See also Cyril Ray, 'Soho Night Out', *Punch*, 23 October 1968, 579–80; Nicholas Coleridge and Stephen Quinn, eds, *The Sixties in Queen* (London: Ebury, 1987).

146 'Soho – So What?', 45–6.

147 See advertisements for Trattoria La Belle [*sic*] Napoli, Frith Street, Black Angus Steakhouse, Great Newport Street, Mandarin Restaurant, Haymarket, and Alfred Harley, Bespoke Tailors, Berwick Street, in *Paul Raymond's Raymond Revuebar*, TNA PRO MEPO 2/10168.

148 'How Soho Residents See It', *Municipal Journal*, 15 March 1963, 751. Cultural and environmental critics of Soho's sex industry remained relatively isolated during the 1960s. By the early 1980s they were backed by the authority of Westminster Council and the Soho Society, an alliance which eventually led to a drastic reduction in the number of nude shows, sex clubs and pornographic bookshops. For the expansion and subsequent curtailment of Soho's sex industry see Martin Tomkinson, *Pornbrokers: The Rise of the Soho Sex Barons* (London: Virgin Books, 1982); Frank Mort, *Cultures of Consumption: Masculinities and Social Space in Late Twentieth-Century Britain* (London: Routledge, 1996), 156–7.

149 'Taking a Look at Soho'.

150 'How Soho Residents See It'.

151 'Few Mourners as Soho Buries the Past', *The Times*, 18 November 1963, 7.

152 Jack Isowitsky, or Isow, was a Russian Jewish émigré who ran a small cinema and a billiard club in the East End before opening his restaurant, which catered 'especially at lunchtime, to the Wardour Street film types': Lew Grade, *Still Dancing: My Story* (London: Collins, 1987), 20.

153 Kathy Brewis, 'Saint Paul', *Sunday Times Magazine*, 17 August 2008, 23.

154 See Paul Raymond to the author, 15 March 1999, letter in the author's collection. It is unclear why Raymond was hostile to the Wolfenden committee.

155 For the interior of the Revuebar see To Receive Evidence of Due Completion of Approved Alterations, 17 April 1962, County of London Sessions, Westminster Division, Justices Minute Book Licensing and Regulating Victuallers etc., 10 September 1959–25 September 1962, Westminster City Archives, 804/54.

156 Raymond Theatre Revuebar, publicity letter.

157 Farson, 'Raymond Reviewed', 12.

158 Visits to the Revuebar were cited by the pseudonymous 'Harry' in his sex diary. Born in 1928, 'Harry' was from a lower-middle-class provincial background; see Ferris, *Sex and the British*, 183, 121–2.

159 See *Paul Raymond's Raymond Revuebar*, TNA PRO MEPO 2/10168.

160 Ibid.

161 See Chief Superintendent C to Commander 1 and Police Inspector Hugh White, C Division, 30 October 1962, TNA PRO MEPO 2/10168.

162 Chief Superintendent C to Commander 1, ibid.

163 Raymond Theatre Revuebar, Execution of Warrant, 23 May 1958, TNA PRO MEPO 2/10232, pp. 20–1.

164 Chief Superintendent C, 28 May 1958, and Solicitor's Department, 29 May 1958, Raymond Theatre Revuebar, Execution of Warrant, TNA PRO MEPO 2/10232, p. 22 and unpaginated.

165 Membership Register, Raymond Theatre Revuebar, Execution of Warrant, 23 May 1958, TNA PRO MEPO 2/10232, p. 17.

166 Ibid.

167 See Aldgate, *Censorship and the Permissive Society*, 1–12; de Jongh, *Politics, Prudery and Perversions*, 136–64.

168 For police tactics against queer clubs in the 1930s see Matt Houlbrook, *Queer London: Perils and Pleasures in the Sexual Metropolis, 1918–1957* (Chicago: University of Chicago Press, 2005), 75–80. For surveillance of sexually and racially mixed venues see Judith Walkowitz, 'Tarts and the Prince of Wales' (unpublished paper to American Historical Association Annual Meeting, Seattle, 2005).

169 Raymond was prosecuted several times in the late 1950s for presenting new stage plays without a licence, for selling intoxicating liquor without a justice's licence, and for keeping premises for unlicensed music and dancing. See Detective Sergeant R. Clark to Superintendent, Metropolitan Police, Criminal Investigation Department, 16 December 1958, and Chief Superintendent C Division, Raymond Revuebar Club, Result of Proceedings, 28 November 1958, TNA PRO MEPO 2/10232; 'Soho Club on Six Months' "Probation"', *Daily Telegraph and Morning Post*, 28 November 1958, 19. Specific evidence of police bribery by club proprietors is extremely difficult to access, but see the comments of the London Public Morality Council's patrol officer in 1941, who noted that 'the Police are accepting bribes and giving the Clubs "protection"': Patrol Work, Public Morality Council: Patrolling Officer's Report, June 1941, File of Patrolling Officer Reports 1941–1945, London Metropolitan Archives A/PMC/41. There is no direct evidence of bribery by Raymond himself, but testimonies from showgirls who worked in the Soho club scene during the 1960s and 1970s indicated that many club owners paid the police; see Jarrett, *Stripping in Time*, 198–211.

170 See Statement of WPS M. Spalton, C Division, 14 May 1958, TNA PRO MEPO 2/10232.

171 See 'Darlene's' busy afternoon and evening work schedule, in 'Soho – Where Strip Makes a Million a Year', *People*, 5 May 1968, 14.

172 Patrick Marnham, *The Private Eye Story: The First 21 Years* (London: Andre Deutsch, 1982), 8.

173 'These Clubs', *Daily Express*, 6 June 1958, 10.

174 Ibid.

175 Monica Furlong, 'The Girl with the Most Attentive Audience in Town', *Daily Mail*, 9 February 1967, cutting in Greater London Council, Director-General's Department: Entertainment Licensing Group, Striptease – General – Employment of Young Persons, n.d., London Metropolitan Archives, GLC/DG/EL/7/50.

176 'We Regard This as an Art Form', *Daily Mail*, n.d., cutting in London Metropolitan Archives, GLC/DG/EL/7/50. See also Linzi Drew, *Try Everything Once – Except Incest & Morris Dancing* (London: Blake, 1993).

177 'We Regard This as an Art Form'.

178 For Raymond's conception of international glamour and his rejection of an older style of London's sex industry see David Taylor, 'Naked as Human Nature Intended', *Punch*, 11 June 1975, 1024; 'The World Made Flesh', *The Times*, 13 April 1988, cutting in Windmill Theatre Archive.

179 Tom Sutcliffe, 'High Priest of the Body Beautiful', *Guardian*, 24 May 1986, cutting in Windmill Theatre Archive.

180 *Paul Raymond's Raymond Revuebar*, TNA PRO MEPO 2/10168. For details of the performers' actual backgrounds see Statement of WPC M. Smith, C Division, 14 May 1958; Statement of Spalton, TNA PRO MEPO 2/10232.

181 Wanamaker, 'Striptease'.

182 Stage Plays Sub-Committee Meetings, 1 June 1963, Public Morality Council, File of Papers for Stage Plays, Radio and TV Sub-Committee Meetings January–June 1963, London Metropolitan Archives A/PMC/51.

183 Police evidence, based on witness statements from the artists at the Revuebar, revealed that many of the dancers trained at stage school or ballet school. Wages for dancers and showgirls ranged from between ten and fifteen pounds per week, with standard three-month or more occasionally year-long contracts. See Statement of WPC J. Peacock, C Division, 14 May 1958; Statement of WPC J. Cook, 15 May 1958; Statement of Smith, TNA PRO MEPO 2/10232.

184 For the parody element in striptease see Jarrett, *Stripping in Time*, 173.

185 Raymond Theatre Review Bar, advertising bill, TNA PRO MEPO 2/10232.

186 La Rue, *From Drags to Riches*, 72. La Rue appeared briefly in the successful all-male review *Soldiers in Skirts*, which ran from 1945 to 1952.

187 Superintendent, Clubs, to Chief Superintendent, Raymond Theatre Revuebar Club, Results of Police Observations, 29 April 1958, TNA PRO MEPO 2/10232.

188 Statement of PS A. Bobsin, C Division, 28 April 1958; see also Statement of PC M. McGinnes, 2 May 1958, TNA PRO MEPO 2/10232.

189 Raymond Revuebar, publicity letter.

190 Ibid.

191 In an American context Kinsey noted that while a decade earlier the audiences at burlesque shows were almost exclusively·male, 'today the audiences may include a more equal number of females and males'. He believed that most women were drawn to the performances 'because they are social functions about which they are curious, and which they may share with their male companions': Kinsey et al., *Sexual Behavior in the Human Female*, 661. For female audiences at the Revuebar see Statement of Peacock, TNA PRO MEPO 2/10232.

192 See Statement of Peacock.

193 See Chief Superintendent A. Walker, C Division, Raymond Revuebar Club, Amendment to Club Rules, 8 January 1959, TNA PRO MEPO 2/10232.

194 For the suggestion of sexual approaches made to plain-clothes police officers see Statement of PC C. Philips, C Division, 24 April 1958, TNA PRO MEPO 2/10232, p. 2.

195 'The Boy Who Went to the West End', *South London Press*, 22 August 1958, in Windmill Theatre Collection, Press Cuttings 1958–9, Box 61.

196 See Paul Raymond, 'Introducing King Magazine', *King: The Men's Magazine*, no. 1, 1964, 1; 'Night Clubs', *Nova*, June 1974, 47.

197 'Night Clubs', 47.

198 Peter Elliott, family friend, in *Soho Sex King*.

199 Kurtz, 'Raymond Reviewed'. For foreign and provincial tourism see Paul Raymond, Circular Letter to Proprietors and Customers, n.d. (April 1958), TNA PRO MEPO 2/10232; Hunter Davies, ed., *The New London Spy: A Discreet Guide to the City's Pleasures* (London: Anthony Blond, 1966), 174–5.

200 Davies, *New London Spy*, 174–5.

201 Statement of PS J. Baxter, C Division, 2 May 1958, TNA PRO MEPO 2/10232.

202 For this type of sexual customer see Hunter Davies, *The Other Half* (London: Heinemann, 1966), 140.

203 Statement of PC D. Keating, C Division, 2 May 1958, TNA PRO MEPO 2/10232.

204 Ibid.

205 Statement of PC E. Cooper, C Division, 2 May 1958, TNA PRO MEPO 2/10232.

206 See Raymond, 'Introducing King Magazine'. See also Marcus Collins, 'The Pornography of Permissiveness: Men's Sexuality and Women's Emancipation in Mid Twentieth-Century Britain', *History Workshop Journal*, no. 47 (1999): 99–120.

207 'King's Weekend – Copenhagen', *King*, no. 1, 1964, 39. See also 'King's Dublin', *King*, no. 2, March 1965, 22–5; 'The GT Game', *King*, no. 3, June 1965, 10–15.

208 'Pounds of Flesh', *Sunday Telegraph*, 6 December 1992, cutting in Windmill Theatre Archive.

209 'Paul Raymond', *Guardian*.

210 'Porn King Deposes Duke in Wealth Table', *Guardian*, 30 November 1992, cutting in Windmill Theatre Archive; 'Paul Raymond', *Guardian*.

211 See 'How Paul Raymond Peeped Through a Loophole'. Raymond's death in March 2008 attracted front-page press coverage and was a substantial item on national television news; see especially 'Battle Over Soho King's £650m "will"', *Evening Standard*, 3 March 2008, 1; BBC Television, *Ten O'Clock News*, 3 March 2008; Brewis, 'Saint Paul', 12–24.

CHAPTER 7 SCANDAL

1 Lord Denning, *The Denning Report: The Profumo Affair with a New Introduction by the Author* (London: Pimlico, 1992), 114. For accounts of the Profumo affair that have been drawn on here see Iain Crawford, *The Profumo Affair: A Crisis in Contemporary Society* (London: White Lodge Books, 1963); Clive Irving, Ron Hall and Jeremy Wallington, *Scandal '63: A Study of the Profumo Affair* (London: Heinemann, 1963); Ludovic Kennedy, *The Trial of Stephen Ward* (New York: Simon & Schuster, 1965); Phillip Knightley and Caroline Kennedy, *An Affair of*

State: The Profumo Case and the Framing of Stephen Ward (London: Jonathan Cape, 1987); Anthony Summers and Stephen Dorril, *Honeytrap: The Secret Worlds of Stephen Ward* (London: Weidenfeld & Nicolson, 1987); David Thurlow, *Profumo: The Hate Factor* (London: Robert Hale, 1992); Gillian Swanson, 'Good-Time Girls, Men of Truth and a Thoroughly Filthy Fellow: Sexual Pathology and National Character in the Profumo Affair', *New Formations*, no. 24 (1994): 122–54. For accounts from the principal actors in the scandal see Warwick Charlton and Gerald Sparrow, *Stephen Ward Speaks: Conversations with Warwick Charlton; Judge Gerald Sparrow Sums Up the Profumo Affair* (London: Today Magazine, 1963); Marilyn Rice-Davies, *The Mandy Report* (London: Confidential Publications, 1964); Christine Keeler, *Scandal* (New York: St Martin's Press, 1989); Yevgeny Ivanov, with Gennady Sokolov, *The Naked Spy* (London: Blake, 1992); Christine Keeler, with Douglas Thompson, *The Truth at Last: My Story* (London: Sidgwick & Jackson, 2001); John Edgecombe, *Black Scandal* (London: Westworld International, 2002); David Profumo, *Bringing the House Down: A Family Memoir* (London: John Murray, 2006).

2   Denning, *Denning Report*, v.

3   Fictional works dealing broadly with the events of the Profumo scandal have included the novel *The Last Temptation* (1984), a *roman-à-clef* by David Mure, an ex-naval intelligence colleague of Lord Astor's. It contained a thinly veiled portrait of 'Lord Bill Asterisk', who was very keen on being whipped by prostitutes. In 1989 Michael Caton-Jones's film *Scandal*, starring John Hurt as Ward, Ian McKellen as Profumo, and Joanne Whalley-Kilmer as Keeler, was launched to roughly coincide with the twenty-fifth anniversary of the affair. A box office hit, it reignited public debate over the case.

4   Profumo, *Bringing the House Down*, 8. David Profumo observed that his father's 'great fall' was invoked in later scandals associated with political figures such as Lord Lambton, Jeremy Thorpe and Cecil Parkinson.

5   Nigel West, *A Matter of Trust: MI5 1945–72* (London: Weidenfeld & Nicolson, 1982); Dominic Sandbrook, *Never Had It So Good: A History of Britain from Suez to the Beatles* (London: Abacus, 2006), 638–81.

6   See for example Alistair Horne, *Macmillan, 1957–1986: Volume II of the Official Biography* (London: Macmillan, 1988), 471–97; Ben Pimlott, *Harold Wilson* (London: Harper Collins, 1992), 285–99; Sandbrook, *Never Had It So Good*.

7   Denning, in his inquiry set up ostensibly to sift corroborated facts from rumour, was the first of many commentators to note that the case presented particular problems of evidence: Denning, *Denning Report*, 2–3.

8   Ibid., 7. See also Knightley and Kennedy, *Affair of State*, 251. The privileging of Ward's role has been disputed by many commentators as a deliberate official attempt to narrow the scandal's remit, thus occluding the culpability of others, especially a number of the Establishment figures who were compromised by the episode; see Knightley and Kennedy, *Affair of State*; Summers and Dorril, *Honeytrap*, 11; Swanson, 'Good-Time Girls'.

9   Summers and Dorril, *Honeytrap*, 13–14.

10   Charlton and Sparrow, *Stephen Ward Speaks*, 27. Osteopathy was established by a Virginian army doctor, Andrew Taylor Still, during the American Civil War. For discussion of osteopathy and its ambiguous medical status in relation to Ward's career see Brian Inglis, 'Stephen Ward Osteopath', *Queen*, 28 August 1963, 18.

11   Charlton and Sparrow, *Stephen Ward Speaks*, 86.

12   Ibid., 35. See also Kennedy, *Trial of Stephen Ward*, 11; Irving et al., *Scandal*, 27.

13   Journalist Ludovic Kennedy observed Ward's hands at his trial: 'Hands had always played an important part in his life. With them he had healed the sick, sketched the famous, excited women': Kennedy, *Trial of Stephen Ward*, 161.

14   Knightley and Kennedy, *Affair of State*, 19. Ward's patients included statesmen and politicians Anthony Eden, Hugh Gaitskell, Nancy Astor and Joseph Kennedy; Hollywood film stars Elizabeth Taylor, Danny Kaye, Douglas Fairbanks Jr, Frank Sinatra and

Ava Gardner; royalty, the Maharajahs of Jaipur, Cooch Behar, and Baroda, and King Peter of Jugoslavia; the conductors Sir Malcolm Sargent and Sir Thomas Beecham; and the press baron Lord Rothermere.

15 Knightley and Kennedy, *Affair of State*, 21; Summers and Dorril, *Honeytrap*, 19.

16 Knightley and Kennedy, *Affair of State*, 25.

17 Charlton and Sparrow, *Stephen Ward Speaks*, 56.

18 Profumo, *Bringing the House Down*, 156. See also Charlton and Sparrow, *Stephen Ward Speaks*, 27; 'Steps of Destiny in the Years of an Artist . . .' *Daily Express*, 1 August 1963, 1.

19 Peter Stanford, *Bronwen Astor: Her Life and Times* (London: HarperCollins, 1999), 155. See also Lucy Kavaler, *The Astors: A Family Chronicle* (London: Harrap, 1966); Virginia Cowles, *The Astors: The Story of a Transatlantic Family* (London: Weidenfeld & Nicolson, 1979); Derek Wilson, *The Astors: 1763–1992: Landscape with Millionaires* (London: Weidenfeld & Nicolson, 1993).

20 Knightly and Kennedy, *Affair of State*, 61–2.

21 'Through a Doctor's Eyes: Celebrities Drawn by a Gifted Amateur', *Illustrated London News*, 23 July 1960, 156.

22 See 'A Man with Four Faces', *Daily Express*, 1 August 1963, 8.

23 Irving et al., *Scandal*, 32.

24 Charlton and Sparrow, *Stephen Ward Speaks*, 44.

25 Ibid.

26 As Ward put it: 'Come with me along Oxford Street and I'll show you more beautiful girls in half an hour than at any debs' ball': Charlton and Sparrow, *Stephen Ward Speaks*, 47. Ward first met the prostitute Vickie Barrett while 'cruising' in his white Jaguar near Oxford Street underground station: Crawford, *Profumo Affair*, 145.

27 Knightley and Kennedy, *Affair of State*, 61.

28 Ibid. See also Charlton and Sparrow, *Stephen Ward Speaks*, 18.

29 Charlton and Sparrow, *Stephen Ward Speaks*, 78.

30 'A Man with Four Faces'. See also Charlton and Sparrow, *Stephen Ward Speaks*, 63.

31 Charlton and Sparrow, *Stephen Ward Speaks*, 71.

32 Ibid., 55.

33 Mr Wigg, Security (Mr Profumo's Resignation), 17 June 1963, *Parliamentary Debates (Hansard) House of Commons Official Report*, 5th ser., vol. 679, session 1962–3, (London: HMSO, 1963), col. 108.

34 Ronna Ricardo, quoted in Summers and Dorril, *Honeytrap*, 188. Ricardo was a prostitute who had known Ward since 1960; she was later to feature in Ward's trial. Johnny Edgecombe also remembered Ward's visits to the All Nighters club, noting that the 'attraction' for Ward 'was drugs': *Honeytrap*, 187.

35 Charlton and Sparrow, *Stephen Ward Speaks*, 55.

36 Peter Earle, 'The Hidden World of Stephen Ward', *News of the World*, 4 August 1963, 7.

37 Quoted in Ruth Glass, *Newcomers: The West Indians in London* (London: Centre for Urban Studies and George Allen & Unwin, 1960), 248. See also Edward Pilkington, *Beyond the Mother Country: West Indians and the Notting Hill White Riots* (London: Tauris, 1988), 66.

38 Pilkington, *Beyond the Mother Country*, 65; Charlie Phillips and Mike Phillips, *Notting Hill in the Sixties* (London: Lawrence & Wishart, 1991), 25; Mike Phillips and Trevor Phillips, *Windrush: The Irresistible Rise of Multi-Racial Britain* (London: HarperCollins, 1998), 108–9, 112–14.

39 For Notting Hill's shebeens see Phillips and Phillips, *Windrush*, 110–18; Edgecombe, *Black Scandal*, 56–8.

40 Tony Gould, *Inside Outsider: The Life and Times of Colin MacInnes* (London: Allison & Busby, 1993), 194. For further commentary on the El Rio Café see Keeler, *Truth at Last*, 124–5.

41 Keeler, *Truth at Last*, 89.

42 See 'The Evil Peter Rachman', *Sunday Mirror*, 14 July 1963, 8–9; 'The Technique of Rachmanism', *Sunday Times*, 21 July 1963, 8–9. For official debate see Ministry of Housing and Local Government, *Report of the Committee on Housing in Greater London*, Cmnd. 2605 (London: HMSO, 1965). Rice-Davies insisted that 'the name . . . Rachman conjures up a vision of squalid slums, overcrowded tene-

ments, and an evil . . . man growing fat on the misery of unfortunate tenants': Rice-Davies, *Mandy Report*, unpaginated.

43 See Christopher Booker, *The Neophiliacs: A Study of the Revolution in English Life in the Fifties and Sixties* (London: Collins, 1969), 199. John Davis has argued that Rachman's exposure at the height of the Profumo affair was 'largely accidental', but that with the emergence of a 'racy' scandal the London housing question became an even more politically sensitive issue than it would have been under normal circumstances: John Davis, 'Rents and Race in 1960s London: New Light on Rachmanism', *Twentieth Century British History* 12, no. 1 (2001): 69.

44 For Rachman's early life and career see Shirley Green, *Rachman* (London: Hamlyn Paperbacks, 1981); Summers and Dorril, *Honeytrap*, 57.

45 By the end of 1956 Rachman was in control of thirty houses in Shepherd's Bush, a similar number in Notting Hill, and twenty flats in Maida Vale: Green, *Rachman*, 55. For contrasting analysis of Rachman's property transactions see Irving et al., *Scandal*, 34–5; Summers and Dorril, *Honeytrap*, 57–8; Davis, 'Rents and Race', 69–70.

46 Phillips and Phillips, *Windrush*, 190.

47 Rev. Sybil Phoenix, quoted in ibid., 130.

48 Ivan Weekes, former tenant of Rachman, quoted ibid., 191. For Rachman's lavish lifestyle see also Crawford, *Profumo Affair*, 127.

49 Green, *Rachman*, 177. Rachman's other clubs included the 150 Club on Earl's Court Road and the New Court Club in Inverness Terrace, Bayswater.

50 For Rachman's relationship with Ward see Green, *Rachman*, 149.

51 Ibid., 76.

52 Rice-Davies, *Mandy Report*, unpaginated.

53 Charlton and Sparrow, *Stephen Ward Speaks*, 46.

54 Keeler, *Scandal*, 75.

55 Tory MP William Shepherd described Ward's voice as having a 'phoney, almost homosexual intonation': Irving et al., *Scandal*, 60.

56 Charlton and Sparrow, *Stephen Ward Speaks*, 66.

57 Swanson, 'Good-Time Girls', 148.

58 Charlton and Sparrow, *Stephen Ward Speaks*, 45.

59 Knightley and Kennedy, *An Affair of State*, 48. See also Charlton and Sparrow, *Stephen Ward Speaks*, 60.

60 Rice-Davies, *Mandy Report*, unpaginated.

61 Douglas Sutherland, *Portrait of a Decade: London Life 1945–1955* (London: Harrap, 1988), 121. For a different account of this event see Charlton and Sparrow, *Stephen Ward Speaks*, 41–2.

62 For speculation about Ward's homosexuality see Irving et al., *Scandal*, 60; Rice-Davies, *Mandy Report*, unpaginated.

63 Rice-Davies, *Mandy Report*, unpaginated.

64 Kennedy, *Trial of Stephen Ward*, 161; Charlton and Sparrow, *Stephen Ward Speaks*, 30, 60.

65 Irving et al., *Scandal*, 60.

66 Charlton and Sparrow, *Stephen Ward Speaks*, 98.

67 See Summers and Dorril, *Honeytrap*, 38.

68 Through his friendship with Bobbie Shaw, Ward was introduced to Sir Malcolm Bullock, Conservative MP and Chairman of the Sadler's Wells Society; controversial Cath-olic churchman, Monsignor Hugh Montgo-mery; and Sir Gilbert Laithwaite, Permanent Under-Secretary of State for Common-wealth Relations: Summers and Dorril, *Honeytrap*, 37–9; Stanford, *Bronwen Astor*, 223.

69 Profumo, *Bringing the House Down*, 157; Rebecca West, *The Meaning of Treason* (London: Virago, 1982), 403.

70 West, *Meaning of Treason*, 403.

71 Ivanov, *Naked Spy*, 172–3. Ivanov's autobiography was drafted by Gennady Sokolov, and based on lengthy taped interviews with Ivanov between 1988 and 1991. See also Charlton and Sparrow, *Stephen Ward Speaks*, 85.

72 Charlton and Sparrow, *Stephen Ward Speaks*, 85.

73 Ivanov, *Naked Spy*, 24.

74 Ibid.

75 For the Duke of Edinburgh's rumoured involvement see 'Prince Philip and the Profumo Scandal', *Daily Mirror*, 24 June 1963, 1.

76   Anthony Sampson, *Anatomy of Britain* (London: Hodder & Stoughton, 1962), xi.

77   Ibid., 624. Sampson argued that the contemporary intoxication with the whole idea of the Establishment was a convenient 'mirage' designed to mask the real economic power that defined Britain as a corporate state.

78   Ibid.

79   Colin Coote, *The Other Club* (London: Sidgwick & Jackson, 1971), 114.

80   See Ivanov, *Naked Spy*, 52–3.

81   Ibid., 80.

82   For the extended kinship and family networks connecting the Establishment in 1962 see the genealogical table in Sampson, *Anatomy of Britain*, between pages 34–5.

83   Of all post-war prime ministers, Macmillan was the one who paid most attention to the monarchy's residual rights and its social prestige: Horne, *Macmillan*, 168. According to Ben Pimlott, what this meant in practice was an appropriation of the royal aura for Macmillan's own brand of one-nation Conservatism: Ben Pimlott, *The Queen: A Biography of Elizabeth II* (London: HarperCollins, 1996), 275.

84   See Profumo, *Bringing the House Down*, 56–7.

85   Irving et al., *Scandal*, 15.

86   Ibid.

87   Profumo, *Bringing the House Down*, 66.

88   Irving et al., *Scandal*, 16; Profumo, *Bringing the House Down*, 61.

89   Profumo, *Bringing the House Down*, 65.

90   Irving et al., *Scandal*, 16–18.

91   Ibid., 18. For Profumo's aristocratic approach to politics see Charlton and Sparrow, *Stephen Ward Speaks*, 117–18.

92   Comments attributed to Mrs Fraser, East Fulham Conservative Association, quoted in Profumo, *Bringing the House Down*, 74.

93   For an assessment of Profumo's political status see Ian Gilmour, 'Dingy Quadrilaterals', *London Review of Books* 28, no. 20 (19 October 2006): 19–21; 'John Profumo', Obituaries, *Independent*, 11 March 2006, http://www.independent.co.uk/news/obituaries/john-profumo-469445.html (accessed 21 January 2009).

94   The undated photograph shows Profumo in a hybrid form of British court dress, a civil uniform that was rarely worn after the Second World War, except at the time of the coronation, which is when the photo may have been taken. The image is designed to project Profumo's patrician style and his intense traditionalism. I am grateful to Joanna Marschner for explaining this point. See also George Titman, ed., *Dress and Insignia Worn at His Majesty's Court, Issued with the Authority of the Lord Chamberlain* (London: Harrison, 1937).

95   Profumo, *Bringing the House Down*, 139. For MPs' hostility to Profumo see Andrew Roth, 'John Profumo', *Guardian Unlimited*, 10 March 2006, www.guardian.co.uk/print/0,,329431331-103684,00.html (accessed 20 October 2006).

96   Profumo, *Bringing the House Down*, 7.

97   Summers and Dorril, *Honeytrap*, 42.

98   Profumo, *Bringing the House Down*, 103, 270.

99   Ibid., 11–55. See also Anne Edwards, 'A Personal and Public Slap in the Face from her Husband', *Daily Express*, 7 June 1963, 8; Nancy Spain, 'Valerie Profumo', *News of the World*, 30 June 1963, 10.

100   Profumo, *Bringing the House Down*, 103.

101   Ibid.

102   When the Profumo's London home was refurbished in the early 1960s the couple demanded a temporary establishment on a similarly grand scale, including ample servants' quarters, a nursery, and state rooms for receptions and entertaining; see J. S. Hogg, Note for the Record, 1 June 1962, No. 3: Sub-lease to Mr. John Profumo M. P. (1961–1966), TNA PRO CRES 35/5177.

103   Profumo, *Bringing the House Down*, 157.

104   Ibid., 156.

105   Martin Francis, 'The Labour Party: Modernisation and the Politics of Restraint', in Becky Conekin, Frank Mort and Chris Waters, eds, *Moments of Modernity: Reconstructing Britain, 1945–1964* (London: Rivers Oram, 1999), 152–70. Francis has argued that this emotional economy was undercut by a new culture of sensation and emotional display within public and civic culture; see also his 'Tears, Tantrums, and Bared Teeth: The

Emotional Economy of Three Conservative Prime Ministers, 1951–63', *Journal of British Studies* 41, no. 3 (July 2002): 354–87.

106 Profumo, *Bringing the House Down*, 152. John Profumo's draft statement to the Denning inquiry contained his observations on the women at the centre of the affair: 'All the girls were very young, and very pretty, and very common': ibid., 159.

107 Knightley and Kennedy, *Affair of State*, 115.

108 Profumo, *Bringing the House Down*, 167.

109 Knightley and Kennedy, *Affair of State*, 116.

110 Cliveden was an original seventeenth-century mansion that had been remodelled by the Victorian architect Sir Charles Barry; see Norman Rose, *The Cliveden Set: Portrait of an Exclusive Fraternity* (London: Jonathan Cape, 2000), 11.

111 Claude Cockburn (Frank Pitcairn) first defined the Astors' network of 'concentrated political power' as 'one of the most important supports of German influence' in the news sheet *This Week* on 17 June 1936; see Rose, *Cliveden Set*, 154.

112 For social life at Cliveden under the third Viscount Astor and his wife see Stanforth, *Bronwen Astor*, 195–8, 218–47.

113 Charlton and Sparrow, *Stephen Ward Speaks*, 78.

114 22 March 1963, Diaries of Maurice Harold Macmillan, 1st Earl of Stockton (1894–1986), Second Series February 1957–October 1963, Diary 49, 20 March–18 July 1963, p. 9, Department of Special Collections and Western Manuscripts, Bodleian Library, University of Oxford.

115 Ivanov, *Naked Spy*, 69.

116 Ward did not believe that Keeler and Ivanov had a sexual relationship; see Charlton and Sparrow, *Stephen Ward Speaks*, 85; Knightley and Kennedy, *An Affair of State*, 86.

117 Keeler, *Scandal*, 110. Keeler, *Truth at Last*, 112. In the later, substantially revised version of her story, Keeler stated that the affair went on for much longer than she had originally admitted and that she became pregnant by Profumo: Keeler, *Truth at Last*, 116.

118 See especially the case of the prominent Liberal minister Sir Charles Dilke, whose career was ruined as a result of his being cited a co-respondent in the Crawford divorce case in 1886, and the Irish nationalist leader Charles Parnell, who was compromised as a result of his long-term affair with Mrs Katherine (Kitty) O'Shea in 1890: H. Montgomery Hyde, *A Tangled Web: Sex Scandals in British Politics and Society* (London: Constable, 1986), 111–45.

119 Christine Keeler, 'Foreword', in Ivanov, *Naked Spy*, 7.

120 Christine Keeler, *Sex Scandals* (London: Xanadu, 1985), 9.

121 Keeler, *Truth at Last*, 11–12. See also 'The Kind of Girl I Really Am', *News of the World*, 23 June 1963, 2–3.

122 Knightley and Kennedy, *Affair of State*, 54; Summers and Dorril, *Honeytrap*, 55.

123 Keeler, *Scandal*, 75.

124 Keeler, *Sex Scandals*, 10.

125 Ibid., 10.

126 Keeler, *Scandal*, 27.

127 *TitBits*, 22 March 1958, cited in Knightley and Kennedy, *An Affair of State*, 53.

128 Description by D Branch MI5 agent, officer 'Woods', in West, *Matter of Trust*, 92.

129 Ivanov, *Naked Spy*, 95–6.

130 Profumo, *Bringing the House Down*, 158.

131 Keeler, *Truth at Last*, 5.

132 Keeler, *Sex Scandals*, 10.

133 Summers and Dorril, *Honeytrap*, 55. For accounts of Murray's see Sydney Moseley, *The Night Haunts of London* (London: Stanley Paul, 1920), 14–18; Hunter Davies, ed., *The New London Spy: A Discreet Guide to the City's Pleasures* (London: Anthony Blond, 1966), 173.

134 See Knightley and Kennedy, *Affair of State*, 55.

135 Keeler, *Truth at Last*, 8.

136 Knightley and Kennedy, *Affair of State*, 55.

137 For Keeler's 'grand showgirl outfit' see the photograph in Keeler, *Truth at Last*, between pages 76–7. For the 'bird outfit' see Knightley and Kennedy, *Affair of State*, plate 18.

138 Keeler, *Truth at Last*, 1–2; Knightley and Kennedy, *Affair of State*, 55–6.

139 Rice-Davies, *Mandy Report*, unpaginated.

140 The actress Kay Kendall started out at Murray's before starring in films such as

Genevieve (1953) and marrying Rex Harrison: Keeler, *Truth at Last*, 8.

141 Ibid., 2.

142 Ibid., 8.

143 Knightley and Kennedy, *Affair of State*, 115. For Keeler and Profumo at Murray's see Keeler, *Truth at Last*, 122; Profumo, *Bringing the House Down*, 158.

144 See Keeler, *Truth at Last*, 5.

145 In 1962 Percy Murray successfully appealed against a condition of his licence that customers could not use the club for forty-eight hours after they joined. Murray insisted that his club was not in 'that category' of doorstep membership clubs, a veiled reference to the Raymond Revuebar; see 'London Night Clubs "The Best"', *The Times*, 6 October 1962, 12. In the late 1950s Murray's charged a membership fee of one guinea; see Knightley and Kennedy, *Affair of State*, 55.

146 Keeler, *Truth at Last*, 43–5; Keeler, *Sex Scandals*, 48–51.

147 Keeeler, *Sex Scandals*, 14.

148 Keeler, *Truth at Last*, 64. For details of the Twenty-One Club as a site of commercial sex see 'Hostess Denial by Club Owner', *The Times*, 26 January 1980, 3.

149 Irving et al., *Scandal*, 197.

150 Keeler, *Sex Scandals*, 15. See also 'The Men in My Life by Christine Keeler', *Daily Express*, 29 June 1963, 4–5; 'Love and Ivanov', *News of the World*, 16 June 1963, 2–3.

151 Rice-Davies, *Mandy Report*, unpaginated; Keeler, *Truth at Last*, 58.

152 Rice-Davies, *Mandy Report*, unpaginated.

153 For the All Nighters club see John Platt, *London's Rock Routes* (London: Fourth Estate, 1985), 42–5.

154 For the Caribbean and African American presence at the club see Edgecombe, *Black Scandal*, 73–4. For the Mod crowd see Platt, *London's Rock Routes*, 45.

155 Ronna Ricardo, quoted in Summers and Dorril, *Honeytrap*, 187–8.

156 Platt, *London's Rock Routes*, 45.

157 For Lucky Gordon's movements around central London see Witness Statement, Aloysius Gordon, 30 October 1962, Edgecombe, John: Attempted Murder of Christine Keeler on 14 December 1962 in Mayfair, London W1. Convicted of Being in Possession of Firearm (1962–1963), TNA PRO DPP 2/3591.

158 See 'Christine Told Me She Was a Call Girl', *Daily Express*, 7 June 1963, 6; 'Jazz Singer Given Three Years Gaol', *Sydney Morning Herald*, 8 June 1963, 3; Regina v John Arthur Edgecombe, 27 May 1963, TNA PRO DPP 2/3591; Edgecombe, *Black Scandal*, 57–8; Phillips and Phillips, *Windrush*, 193–4.

159 Keeler, *Truth at Last*, 94–5.

160 See Return of Convictions Recorded Against John A. A. Edgecombe, D Division, 19 December 1962, TNA PRO DPP 2/3591.

161 Edgecombe, *Black Scandal*, 50.

162 Edgecombe, interview in Phillips and Phillips, *Windrush*, 189.

163 Edgecombe, *Black Scandal*, 56–7.

164 Ibid., 56.

165 Ibid., 60.

166 Ibid.

167 For the extensive official concern about Caribbean pimps see Notes on the Proposed Bill to Provide for the Deportation of Undesirable British Immigrants (1958–1959), TNA PRO MEPO 2/9773. For the perceived aggression of Caribbean immigrants see Sheila Patterson, *Dark Strangers: A Sociological Study of the Absorption of a Recent West Indian Migrant Group in Brixton, South London* (London: Tavistock, 1963), 81; Anthony Richmond, *Colour Prejudice in Britain: A Study of West Indian Workers in Liverpool, 1941–1951* (London: Routledge & Kegan Paul, 1954), 117–21. Notting Hill social worker Pearl Jephcott offered a more measured explanation for these negative perceptions that focused on the intense competition among local young men for scarce material resources and sexual status 'in a society . . . when so many of the local-born boys have little . . . they attach even more importance than usual to sex. And the coloured boy is held to be a threat in this highly competitive field': Pearl Jephcott, *A Troubled Area: Notes on Notting Hill* (London: Faber & Faber, 1964), 90. See also Marcus Collins, 'Pride and Prejudice: West Indian Men in Mid-Twentieth-Century Britain', *Journal of British Studies* 40, no. 3 (July 2001): 391–418.

168 Robert Fabian, *London After Dark: An Intimate Record of Night Life in London, and a Selection of Crime Stories from the Case Book of Ex-Superintendent Robert Fabian* (London: Naldrett Press, 1954), 54, 26. Social research sponsored by the British Social Hygiene Council revealed that while public attitudes towards prostitutes had become somewhat more tolerant after the Second World War, they had hardened against the men who lived with them. The council acknowledged that part of the underlying reason for this hostility was the influx of coloured men from the Caribbean: C. H. Rolph, ed., *Women of the Streets: A Sociological Study of the Common Prostitute* (London: Secker & Warburg, 1955), 112, 240.

169 Edgecombe, *Black Scandal*, 34, 52.

170 Edgecombe's account paralleled the experience of many other West Indian settlers, one of whom argued: 'if it weren't for the sympathy and generosity of English women in their relations with black men, black men would find it virtually impossible to survive in England': Ken Pryce, *Endless Pressure: A Study of West Indian Life-Styles in Bristol* (Harmondsworth: Penguin, 1979), 84. See also the experience of Swedish prostitute Majbritt Morrison, who lived with Caribbean men in Notting Hill in the late 1950s and early 1960s, in her *Jungle West 11* (London: Tandem Books, 1964).

171 Keeeler, *Sex Scandals*, 19. For the cultural positioning of white women who were involved in inter-racial sex see Sonya Rose, *Which People's War? National Identity and Citizenship in Britain 1939–1945* (Oxford: Oxford University Press, 2003), 71–106; Chris Waters, '"Dark Strangers" in Our Midst: Discourses of Race and Nation in Britain, 1947–63', *Journal of British Studies* 36, no. 2 (April 1997): 230; Wendy Webster, *Englishness and Empire, 1939–1965* (Oxford: Oxford University Press, 2005), 157–9.

172 Statement of Christine Margaret Keeler, 14 December 1962, TNA PRO DPP 2/3591. See also Keeler, *Scandal*, 85–6. For publicly expressed miscegenation fears about white women who associated sexually with Caribbean men see 'Teenagers Give Their Views',

and 'Vice?: Housing?: Violence?' *Kensington News and West London Times*, 12 September 1958, 1, 12.

173 Keeler, *Truth at Last*, 132.

174 Witness Statement, Sydney Beresford, Chief Inspector, 15 December 1962, TNA PRO DPP 2/3591. See also Edgecombe's later account in his *Black Scandal*, 91–7.

175 'Six Shots Fired at Girls' West End Flat', *Evening Standard*, 14 December 1962, 1. See also 'Shooting: I Love Her Story', *Evening Standard*, 15 December 1962, 2.

176 Keeler, *Truth at Last*, 163.

177 The other cases were Lucky Gordon's trial for the assault of Keeler in June 1963, Ward's own trial in July and August, and Keeler's prosecution for perjury during the Gordon trial in December.

178 For the implications of Keeler's threatened disclosures see Kennedy, *Trial of Stephen Ward*, 12–13; Edgecombe, *Black Scandal*, 102–3.

179 Keeler, *Truth at Last*, 158.

180 See Knightley and Kennedy, *Affair of State*, 124; Summers and Dorril, *Honeytrap*, 147. In May 1963 Keeler replaced Mann with businessman Robin Drury as her manager.

181 Keeler, *Truth at Last*, 174. For coverage of the 'missing model' story see 'Girl in Shots Case Vanished', *Evening Standard*, 14 March 1963, 14; 'Missing Model "Still in England"', *Evening Standard*, 19 March 1963, 1. For Lord Denning's conclusions on Keeler's disappearance see his *Denning Report*, 49–50.

182 Profumo, *Bringing the House Down*, 163.

183 Keeler, *Truth at Last*, 163–4; Knightley and Kennedy, *Affair of State*, 130.

184 Keeler, *Truth at Last*, 164.

185 Colin Coote, *Editorial: The Memoirs of Colin R. Coote* (London: Eyre & Spottiswoode, 1965), 249.

186 Knightley and Kennedy, *Affair of State*, 130–1; Keeler, *Truth at Last*, 164.

187 Knightley and Kennedy, *Affair of State*, 130–1.

188 Ibid., 131.

189 Ibid., 131–2; Keeler, *Truth at Last*, 164.

190 Denning, *Denning Report*, 22. See also Knightley and Kennedy, *Affair of State*, 132.

191 For MI5's activities against Ward see West, *Matter of Trust*, 96–7.

192 Anna Clark, *Scandal: The Sexual Politics of the British Constitution* (Princeton, NJ: Princeton University Press, 2004), 208.

193 In July 1961 £100,000 damages were awarded against the *Daily Telegraph* in a libel action to John Lewis and his company, Rubber Improvement Ltd. The same month £117,000 were awarded against the *Daily Mail* in the same case. These awards marked a new severity in the handling of libel cases, a trend that worried both Fleet Street and the legal profession; see Irving et al., *Scandal*, 45–6.

194 Ibid., 90.

195 'Drink to Me Only with Thine Eyes', *Daily Express*, 13 May 1963, 5.

196 See Irving et al., *Scandal*, 90.

197 Lawyers acting for Mulholland and Foster argued that the long-standing freedom of the press and basic constitutional rights were at risk if they were forced to reveal their sources over the Vassall affair, but the High Court ruled that withholding information necessary to the administration of justice was not a privilege allowed to anyone, including the media. See Thurlow, *Profumo*, 125; Knightley and Kennedy, *Affair of State*, 150–1; Irving et al., *Scandal*, 73.

198 7 July 1963, Macmillan, Diaries, 49, p. 120. See also Harold Macmillan, *At the End of the Day, 1961–1963* (London: Macmillan, 1973), 442.

199 Robin Douglas-Home, 'Sentences I'd Like to Hear the End of', *Queen*, 31 July 1962, 52. There was a suggestion that Ward himself had planted the story; see Summers and Dorril, *Honeytrap*, 139–41.

200 Knightley and Kennedy, *Affair of State*, 126.

201 Irving et al., *Scandal*, 85.

202 Ibid.

203 Knightley and Kennedy, *Affair of State*, 152.

204 Mr. Wigg, Journalists (Imprisonment), 21 March 1963, *Parliamentary Debates (Hansard) House of Commons Official Report*, 5th ser., vol. 674, session 1962–3 (London: HMSO, 1963), col. 725.

205 Robert Shepherd, *Iain Macleod* (London: Hutchinson, 1994), 295; Nigel Fisher, *Iain Macleod* (London: Andre Deutsch, 1973), 229–30. Macleod's recollection is not corroborated by others who were present at the interview, but David Profumo suggests that a version of this question was put to his father; see Profumo, *Bringing the House Down*, 181.

206 Profumo, *Bringing the House Down*, 181.

207 Secretary of State for War (Mr. John Profumo), Personal Statement, 22 March 1963, *Parliamentary Debates (Hansard) Commons*, vol. 674, col. 810.

208 'Londoner's Diary: Profumo's Dinner-Dance', *Evening Standard*, 22 March 1963, 6. See also Coote, *Editorial*, 90.

209 'The Minister and the Missing Model', *Evening Standard*, 22 March 1963, 1.

210 Ibid; 'Londoner's Diary: Profumo's Dinner-Dance'.

211 Peter Earle, 'The Two Worlds of Christine Keeler', *News of the World*, 17 March 1963, 1, 11.

212 Peter Earle, 'Take a Girl Like Christine', *News of the World*, 7 April 1963, 6, and his 'The Two Worlds of Christine Keeler'. See also 'Confessions of Christine', *News of the World*, 9 June 1963, 1, 4, 5. All these stories were orchestrated by Keeler and her publicity managers.

213 'Take a Girl Like Christine'.

214 Knightley and Kennedy, *Affair of State*, 150.

215 Peter Earle, 'Mandy Talked – And It's Dynamite', *News of the World*, 5 May 1963, 4. For other similar coverage see 'Mandy in a Cell', *Daily Express*, 25 April 1963, 11; 'Jewels, Mink and a Jag', *Daily Express*, 2 May 1963, 11.

216 Rice-Davies, *Mandy Report*, unpaginated.

217 Ibid.

218 For this view of the official framing of Ward see Knightley and Kennedy, *Affair of State*; Summers and Dorrill, *Honeytrap*; Kennedy, *Trial of Stephen Ward*; Thurlow, *Profumo*; Swanson, 'Good-Time Girls'.

219 For MI5's tracking of Ward see West, *Matter of Trust*, 90–6; Summers and Dorril, *Honeytrap*, 72–91. For Roger Hollis's position on Ward see Thurlow, *Profumo*, 145; Knightley and Kennedy, *Affair of State* 165.

220 See Richard Davenport-Hines, 'Brooke, Henry, Baron Brooke of Cumnor', *Oxford Dictionary of National Biography* (Oxford: Oxford University Press, 2004), http://www.

oxforddnb.com/view/article/37227 (accessed 17 April 2008); David Frost and Christopher Booker, 'This is Your Life, Henry Brooke', in David Frost and Ned Sherrin, eds, *That Was The Week That Was* (London: W. H. Allen, 1963), 113–14; John Ramsden, *The Winds of Change: Macmillan to Heath, 1957–1975* (London: Longman, 1996), 115.

221 Mr. Brooke, Drugs (Prevention of), 30 April 1964, *Parliamentary Debates (Hansard) House of Commons Official Report*, 5th ser., vol. 694, session 1963–4, (London: HMSO, 1964), col. 605; Timothy Raison, 'Crime is the Priority: Mr Henry Brooke Talks to Timothy Raison', *New Society*, 4 October 1962, 20.

222 Senior civil servants counselled caution in prosecuting Ward, on account of the potential embarrassment it might cause ministers and other public figures if they were called to give evidence. See Sir Lawrence Helsby, Treasury, to Sir George Coldstream, Treasury Chambers, 17 June 1963, Lord Dilhorne's Examination of the Security Reports and Other Documents Referring to the Enquiries Carried Out into the Part Stephen Ward Played in the Activities of John Profumo (1963), TNA PRO LCO 2/8270.

223 Summers and Dorril, *Honeytrap*, 219. Herbert joined the Metropolitan Police in Paddington in 1946. He went to extraordinary lengths to collect evidence in a West End gaming case in 1958; see 'Inspector's Evidence of Seeing Gaming in Flat', *The Times*, 13 February 1958, 3.

224 The police interviewed between 125 and 140 witnesses in the Ward case. For Herbert's evidence at Ward's trial see Kennedy, *Trial of Stephen Ward*, 128–46. For Ward's own account of police tactics see Charlton and Sparrow, *Stephen Ward Speaks*, 101. For the surveillance tactics of the post-war state see Peter Hennessy, *The Secret State: Whitehall and the Cold War* (London: Allen Lane, 2002).

225 Pimlott, *Harold Wilson*, 291. See also Mr. Harold Wilson, Mr. Profumo's Resignation, 17 June 1963, *Parliamentary Debates Commons*, vol. 679, col. 39.

226 Macmillan, *At the End of the Day*, 441.

227 See Irving et al., *Scandal*, 135; Knightley and Kennedy, *Affair of State*, 184.

228 See 'Profumo Seeing the Queen', *Daily Express*, 7 June 1963, 1; 'The Profumo Dossier', *Sunday Mirror*, 9 June 1963, 2–3; 'Macmillan Takes the 9.30 to Biggest Crisis', *Daily Mirror*, 10 June 1963, 1.

229 William Sewell, 'Historical Events as Transformative Structures: Inventing Revolution at the Bastille', *Theory and Society* 25, no. 6 (December 1996): 865.

230 For the temporary slump in the stock market see 'Shares Wilt Along the Line', *Daily Express*, 11 June 1963, 1. For the weather see *Daily Express*, 10 June 1963, 1.

231 'The Long Queues for London's Most Significant Drama', *Daily Mirror*, 15 June 1963, 20.

232 See Irving et al., *Scandal*, 161.

233 14 June 1963, Tony Benn, *Out of the Wilderness: Diaries 1963–1967* (London: Hutchinson, 1987), 30–1; June 1963, R. H. S. Crossman, *The Backbench Diaries of Richard Crossman*, ed. Janet Morgan (London: Hamish Hamilton and Jonathan Cape, 1981), 996.

234 7 July 1963, Macmillan, *Diaries*, 49, p. 123.

235 Booker termed 1963 'The Year of the Death Wish', noting how local anxieties relating to changes in English society and culture were run together with a series of international disturbances, culminating with President Kennedy's assassination in November; see Booker, *Neophiliacs*, 183–214.

236 Ibid., 195. See also Pimlott, *Harold Wilson*, 293.

237 '5,000 Besiege Houses of Parliament', *The Times*, 27 March 1963, 10.

238 'Several Arrests as the Big Trek Nears End', *Evening Standard*, 15 April 1963, 1; 'Coaches at Whitehall Barricades', *The Times*, 16 April 1963, 10.

239 See 'Greek Prime Minister to See Mrs. Ambatielos', *The Times*, 11 July 1963, 10.

240 ' "Filthy Abuse", Says Home Secretary', *The Times*, 15 July 1963, 7.

241 See 'Angus Drives the Princess to Rehearsal', *Evening Standard*, 22 April 1963, 1; 'Wish Her Well', *Evening Standard*, 24 April 1963, 6.

242 Telstar, launched in July 1962, facilitated the international transmission of television pictures and improved the international telephone service. Though it failed in February

1963, it was followed by the launch of the Syncom satellites that year; see Helen Gavaghan, *Something New Under the Sun: Satellites and the Beginning of the Space Age* (New York: Copernicus, 1998); David Whalen, *The Origins of Satellite Communications 1945–1965* (Washington, DC, and London: Smithsonian Institution Press, 2002), 112–19, 129; Peter Jensen, *From the Wireless to the Web: The Evolution of Telecommunication 1901–2001* (Sydney: University of New South Wales Press, 2000), 233–4.

243　See 'British Scandal Mounts', *New York Post*, 7 June 1963, 1; 'Britain's Vice Scandal Widens', *New York Post*, 9 June 1963, 1; 'Speed Vice Probe for Macmillan', *New York Post*, 11 June 1963, 1. Gerald Sparrow noted that the 'American Press turned with gratitude from the unhappy contemplation of their own scandals' and 'the embarrassment of the Negro revolution' to 'fix on John Profumo and Stephen Ward': Charlton and Sparrow, *Stephen Ward Speaks*, 138–40.

244　'The New Pornocracy', *Newsweek*, 8 July 1963, 35. See also Knightley and Kennedy, *Affair of State*, 9.

245　Shortly after Profumo resigned, the anti-Kennedy, Hearst-owned *New York Journal-American* linked Kennedy to the scandal; see Michael O'Brien, *John F. Kennedy: A Biography* (New York: St Martin's Press, 2005), 709–10.

246　'Mother of Parliaments', *Sydney Morning Herald*, 15 June 1963, 2. See also 'Major Political Scandal in the UK', *Sydney Morning Herald*, 7 June 1963, 1; 'Will Macmillan Have to Go Over Profumo?' *Sun-Herald* (Sydney), 16 June 1963, 81.

247　Sir William Oliver, to Sir Saville Garner, Commonwealth Relations Office, London, 3 September 1963, Commonwealth Press Comments on the Denning Report About the Profumo Affair (1963), TNA PRO DO 194/22.

248　British High Commission, Wellington, to Mrs M. B. Chitty, Constitutional Department, Commonwealth Relations Office, 21 June 1963, TNA PRO DO 194/22.

249　The satirical Indian weekly *Blitz* published revelations that President Ayub Khan 'was a special friend . . . [of] Dr. Ward's who . . . carried home art-photo souvenirs of several models to Pakistan': *Blitz*, 15 June 1963, cutting preserved in Christine Keeler Affair: Allegations of President Ayub Khan Involvement (1963), TNA PRO DO 196/5. See also Draft Message from the Secretary of State to President Ayub [*sic*], undated, and Indian Press on Presidential Visit, Inward Telegram to Commonwealth Relations Office from Delhi, 13 June 1963, TNA PRO DO 196/5.

250　See Profumo Scandal, Extract from *The Star*, undated, extract preserved in TNA PRO DO 194/22.

251　7 July 1963, Macmillan, Diaries, 49, p. 119. Macmillan's diary revealed just how close he came to resigning after the parliamentary debate on the affair in June.

252　'At Christine's Screen Test', *Daily Express*, 27 June 1963, 11. See also 'Confessions of Christine'.

253　For details of Keeler's commercial contracts see Crawford, *Profumo Affair*, 129; Keeler, *Truth at Last*, 199–201.

254　There were five charges against Ward; two concerning abortion had been placed on a separate indictment. The first three were concerned with living wholly or in part on the earnings of prostitution, the fourth and fifth involved inciting Keeler to procure a girl under twenty-one to have intercourse with a third person; see Kennedy, *Trial of Stephen Ward*, 22.

255　For the effects of the Profumo affair on Macmillan and his administration see Horne, *Macmillan*, 453–568; Anthony Sampson, *Macmillan: A Study in Ambiguity* (London: Allen Lane, 1967), 243–6; George Hutchinson, *The Last Edwardian at No. 10: An Impression of Harold Macmillan* (London: Quartet, 1980), 116–18; Robert Blake, *The Conservative Party from Peel to Major* (London: Heinemann, 1997), 288–90.

256　Denning, *Denning Report*, 101–14.

257　Cassandra, 'Cherchez La Femme', *Daily Mirror*, 10 June 1963, 6.

258　For Connor's journalistic style see 'William Connor', http://www.answers.com/topic/william-connor (accessed 14 January 2009).

Two of Connor's most prominent campaigns denounced the novelist P. G. Wodehouse as a Nazi collaborator and Liberace, the American entertainer, as a homosexual; see Robert Connor, *Cassandra: Reflections in a Mirror* (London: Cassell, 1969), 105–10.

259 Cassandra, 'The Intimate Closed Shop', *Daily Mirror*, 14 June 1963, 6; Cassandra, 'It Has Made the Scandals of Britain's Past Seem Like the Sweet Tinklings of Snow White and the Seven Dwarfs', *Sunday Mirror*, 21 July 1963, 8–9. See also Cassandra, 'The George Wigg Story', *Daily Mirror*, 18 June 1963, 6.

260 Cassandra, 'The End of the Affair', *Sunday Mirror*, 4 August 1963, 4.

261 Malcolm Muggeridge, 'The Slow, Sure Death of the Upper Classes', *Sunday Mirror*, 23 June 1963, 7. For Muggeridge's attacks on the Establishment and the monarchy see Richard Ingrams, *Muggeridge: The Biography* (London: HarperCollins, 1995), 181–4; Pimlott, *Queen*, 276, 284–7.

262 Muggeridge, 'Slow, Sure Death'. See also Malcolm Muggeridge, 'Who Blushes Today at Painted Ladies', *Sunday Mirror*, 28 July 1963, 10–11.

263 See 'Viewpoint: Security', *Daily Mirror*, 14 June 1963, 8. For the modernization agenda championed by the Mirror group see 'The Toast is the Moderns', *Sunday Mirror and Sunday Pictorial*, 7 April 1963, 2.

264 21 July 1963, Graham Payn and Sheridan Morley, eds, *The Noël Coward Diaries*, (London: Phoenix, 1998), 538–9.

265 5 August 1963, ibid., 539.

266 9 June 1963, ibid., 536.

267 21 July 1963, ibid., 538.

268 Ibid. Coward had intimate personal insights into the sexual behaviour of the social elite via his own homosexual affair with George, Duke of Kent, the youngest surviving son of George V and Queen Mary.

269 Ibid., 538.

270 For Coward's invocation of the abdication crisis see ibid., 539. The drama of Edward VIII and Mrs Simpson involved heavy criticism of society because the principal characters moved within it.

271 Norah Docker, *Norah: The Autobiography of Lady Docker* (London: W. H. Allen, 1969), 13.

272 Lord Denning, *This Is My Life: A Public Lecture Delivered by The Rt. Hon. Lord Denning Master of the Rolls*, Child & Co. Lecture 5 (London: Inns of Court School of Law, 1979), 12. See also Lord Denning, *The Family Story* (London: Butterworths, 1981), 217–18.

273 June 1963, Crossman, *Backbench Diaries*, 997. See also Anthony Howard, *Crossman: The Pursuit of Power* (London: Jonathan Cape, 1990), 252–4.

274 June 1963, Crossman, *Backbench Diaries*, 1000.

275 5 June 1963, Benn, *Out of the Wilderness*, 29.

276 13 June 1963, ibid., 30.

277 Benn was busy announcing some important 'mood changing measures' that spring as part of an eye-catching preamble to Labour's election manifesto. They included postage stamps without the Queen's head on and Mini cars instead of Daimlers and Rolls-Royces for ministers: 3 May 1963, ibid., 14.

278 Mr. Harold Wilson, Security (Mr. Profumo's Resignation), 17 June 1963, *Parliamentary Debates Commons*, vol. 679, col. 35.

279 Macmillan, *At the End of the Day*, 438. Tony Benn's concern was that Wigg might be given the title Minister of Security: 3 July 1963, Benn *Out of the Wilderness*, 37. See also George Wigg, *George Wigg* (London: Michael Joseph, 1972), 154, 187, 290. In the 1940s Wigg had campaigned to get the Westminster bars closed at 10.00 pm to avoid drunken parliamentary behaviour.

280 Wilson, 17 June 1963, *Parliamentary Debates Commons*, vol. 679, col. 34.

281 Ibid., col. 38.

282 Ibid., cols 53–4.

283 See 'Jack's Ten Years', *New Statesman*, 2 January 1960, 1.

284 'The Evil Peter Rachman'. See also 'Why Did Rachman Get Away With It?' *Daily Mirror*, 15 July 1963, 1.

285 Wilson had already developed his critique of metropolitan life in a speech in May, when he suggested that part of the country's political problems lay with the forms of masculine behaviour represented by Tory public man. He played off the sleek, unmanly and 'effete crew' who dominated political society at Westminster against the 'virile leadership' Britain so urgently needed and that he was

prepared to give under Labour: 'Wilson: Put "Great" Back in Britain . . .' *Sunday Mirror*, 5 May 1963, 5.

286 For Wilson's efforts to construct this vision and its political and cultural consequences see Pimlott, *Harold Wilson*, 213–15, 264–8; Stuart Hall, 'Reformism and the Legislation of Consent', in National Deviancy Conference, eds, *Permissiveness and Control: The Fate of the Sixties Legislation* (London: Macmillan, 1980), 36–7.

287 John Freeman, 'A Time for Austerity', *Queen*, 25 September 1963, 67.

288 H. T., 'The Trial of Stephen Ward by Ludovic Kennedy', *Shield*, November 1964, 19.

289 'A Message from the Chairman', *Shield*, November 1963, 3. See also 'Courts and Parliament', *Shield*, November 1964, 14.

290 ' "These Farmyard Morals Can Corrupt Us All" ', *People*, 16 June 1963, 12.

291 See for example Rev. P. A. Kerridge, Hull, to Public Morality Council, Parliamentary, Patrol and Propaganda Sub-Committee, Minutes of Meeting held 18 September 1963, Public Morality Council, Parliamentary, Patrol and Propaganda Sub-Committee Minute Book January 1957–May 1964, London Metropolitan Archives A/PMC/12; G. M. Holsen, Neasden, to General Secretary, Public Morality Council, undated, Public Morality Council, File of Papers for Parliamentary, Patrol and Propaganda Sub-Committee Meetings 1962–64, London Metropolitan Archives A/PMC/38.

292 'We're Not Immoral at Heart Says Butler', *Daily Mirror*, 17 June 1963, 24. See also 'Britain is Still Decent . . . Lord Shawcross', *Daily Express*, 19 June 1963, 6.

293 Morality, Religion and Politics: An Address by the Rt. Hon. Viscount Hailsham Delivered at the Annual Public Meeting of the Public Morality Council, October 25 1962, Printed Reports of Addresses at Annual Public Meetings: Morality, Religion and Politics by Viscount Hailsham and the New Image of Morality by General Kitching, London Metropolitan Archives A/PMC/205.

294 For Hailsham's moral code see Lord Hailsham, *The Door Wherein I Went* (London: Collins, 1975), 18–19, 197–200, and his *A*

Sparrow's Flight: The Memoirs of Lord Hailsham of Marylebone (London: Collins, 1990), 32.

295 'Hailsham Blazes – "This Kick in the Stomach" ', *Daily Mirror*, 14 June 1963, 1. For the long-term impact of the scandal on Conservative Party politics see Lord Butler, *The Art of the Possible: The Memoirs of Lord Butler* (London: Hamish Hamilton, 1971), 237–50; Blake, *Conservative Party*, 288–90; Mark Jarvis, *Conservative Governments, Morality and Social Change in Affluent Britain, 1957–64* (Manchester: Manchester University Press, 2005), 101–4.

296 Hailsham, *Door Wherein I Went*, 197.

297 'Visitez-L'Angleterre: Le "Can-Can" Anglais', *Daily Express*, 8 June 1963, 7.

298 'Observations: Role of Two Cities', *New Society*, 27 June 1963, 5. See also James Cameron, 'Lies', *Queen*, 19 August 1963, 45–7.

299 'IT *IS* A MORAL ISSUE', *The Times*, 11 June 1963, 13.

300 'A Decent Reticence', *The Times*, 3 November 1960, 13. For Haley's career at *The Times* see Iverach McDonald, *The History of The Times, Volume V: Struggles in War and Peace 1939–1966* (London: Times Books, 1984), 203–18.

301 'IT *IS* A MORAL ISSUE'.

302 Ibid.

303 R. M. Blomfield, letter to the editor, *The Times*, 14 June 1963, 13. See also Geoffrey Johnson-Smith and N. J. Gell, letters to the editor, *The Times*, 13 June 1963, 13.

304 McDonald, *History of The Times*, 361.

305 'Constituency "Not Shocked" Over Morality Aspect', *Guardian*, 14 June 1963, 4.

306 Randolph Churchill, 'I'm Still for Mac', *News of the World*, 16 June 1963, 10; 7 July 1963, Macmillan, Diaries, 49, pp. 120, 128.

307 Shepherd, *Iain Macleod*, 296. See also Fisher, *Iain Macleod*, 229–30.

308 Macleod's parliamentary colleague Angus Maude threw down a direct challenge to the purity campaigners in the *Sunday Citizen* (formerly *Reynold's News*) in June with an article entitled 'Howl of Hate for Puritans!' parodying George Wigg as the nation's 'snooping' detective: Wigg, *George Wigg*, 289.

309 Mr Richard Crossman, Security (Mr. Profumo's Resignation), 17 June 1963, *Parlia-*

mentary *Debates Commons*, vol. 679, cols. 127–8. See also the speech of Jo Grimmond, Leader of the Liberal Party, in the same debate, cols. 81–4.

310 Barbara Castle, *Fighting All the Way* (London: Macmillan, 1993), 337.

311 Pimlott, *Harold Wilson*, 285. See also Bernard Levin, *The Pendulum Years: Britain and the Sixties* (London: Jonathan Cape, 1970), 49–88; Mark Donnelly, *Sixties Britain: Culture, Society, and Politics* (Harlow: Longman, 2005), 69.

312 Gerald Sparrow, *Confessions of an Eccentric* (London: Jarrods, 1965), 49, 56; Charlton and Sparrow, *Stephen Ward Speaks*, 109–11.

313 Sparrow, *Confessions*, 60.

314 Charlton and Sparrow, *Stephen Ward Speaks*, 111.

315 Ibid., 112.

316 7 July 1963, Macmillan, *Diaries*, 49, p. 120. For Macmillan's own later account of events see Macmillan, *At the End of the Day*, 434–46. Observing him at close quarters, Rab Butler believed that the Prime Minister was 'more worried about the continued revelation of moral disturbance than he was about his own future': Butler, *Art of the Possible*, 236.

317 22 March 1963, Macmillan, *Diaries*, 49, p. 10.

318 Ibid., pp. 10–11.

319 'It's Wonderful to be Premier, says Macmillan', *Daily Mirror*, 2 August 1963, 24. Macmillan was interviewed on ITV by Kenneth Harris on 1 August.

320 Alistair Horne has suggested that the 'Boothby factor' was a significant personal element in Macmillan's 'deafness' over the Profumo scandal. As a result of Dorothy Macmillan's affair with Boothby, Macmillan deliberately closed his mind to society gossip and to the 'sly innuendos' in the clubs: Horne, *Macmillan*, 495. See also Hutchinson, *Last Edwardian at No. 10*, 116–18; Sampson, *Macmillan*, 245; Sandbrook, *Never Had it So Good*, 658.

321 Horne, *Macmillan*, 495.

322 See Irving et al., *Scandal*, 124. For coverage of the case see Charles Castle, *The Duchess Who Dared: Margaret, Duchess of Argyll* (London: Sidgwick & Jackson, 1994), 98–115;

Margaret, Duchess of Argyll, *Forget Not: The Autobiography of Margaret, Duchess of Argyll* (London: W. H. Allen, 1975), 180–201. For press treatment see 'Duke Wins Divorce and Celebrates', *Daily Mirror*, 9 May 1963, 1; 'Duchess: It's Been Horrible for Me', *Daily Express*, 9 May 1963, 1.

323 For Sandys's rumoured role in both scandals see Castle, *Duchess Who Dared*, 102–3; Irving et al., *Scandal*, 124.

324 Denning, *Denning Report*, 111–12.

325 'Ward: Pimp or Rake?' *Daily Mirror*, 30 July 1963, 5.

326 See 'Ward Would Tell Me "Go and Get That Girl" Says Christine', *Daily Mirror*, 29 June 1963, 3–5; 'The Hidden World of Stephen Ward', *News of the World*, 4 August 1963, 6–7; 'The Shadow World of Stephen Ward', *People*, 11 August 1963, 10.

327 'Ward in TV Film', *Daily Mirror*, 22 July 1963, 1; 'Ward's Ten Sensational Hours', *Daily Mirror*, 1 August 1963, 11. See also 'Ward to Face New Charges', *Daily Mirror*, 11 June 1963, 7.

328 Swanson, 'Good-Time Girls', 145.

329 Kennedy, *Trial of Stephen Ward*, 20.

330 Cameron, 'Lies', 47.

331 June 1963, Crossman, *Backbench Diaries*, 1000.

332 Waugh to Ann Fleming, 28 March 1963, in Mark Amory, ed., *The Letters of Evelyn Waugh* (London: Phoenix, 1995), 603. See also Waugh to Lady Acton, 10 June 1963, ibid., 608.

333 Kennedy, *Trial of Stephen Ward*, 39. See also Swanson, 'Good-Time Girls', 130–1.

334 Kennedy, *Trial of Stephen Ward*, 151.

335 Earle, 'Two Worlds of Christine Keeler', 1.

336 Ibid.

337 Earle, 'Take a Girl Like Christine'.

338 Edgecombe, *Black Scandal*, 70–1.

339 Ibid., 70.

340 For the reactions of established women's organizations and the purity movement to the scandal see Broadcast and TV News, Sectional Committees: Moral Welfare, 19 July 1963, National Council of Women of Great Britain, Committee Minutes and Reports, London Metropolitan Archives ACC/3613/01/025, p. 8; 'Lord Denning's Report', *Shield*, November 1963, 11.

341   Anne Edwards, quoted in 'Femmes of Fleet Street', *Time*, 2 March 1959, http://www.time.com/magazine/article/0,9171,892277,00.htm (accessed 14 January 2009).

342   Spain, 'Valerie Profumo'.

343   Edwards, 'A Personal and Public Slap in the Face'. See also 'Valerie Hobson Yesterday', *Daily Express*, 8 July 1963, 5.

344   Mary Stott, 'Women Talking', *Guardian*, 1 July 1963, 4.

345   Stott consistently championed these aspects of modern feminism in her *Guardian* journalism. For Stott's role as editor of the paper's women's page between 1957 and 1972 see Mary Stott, *Before I Go . . . : Reflections on My Life and Times* (London: Virago, 1985), 64–85.

346   Stott, 'Women Talking'.

347   Dorothy Reich, letter to the editor, *Guardian*, 10 July 1963, 6. See also 'Women Talking', *Guardian*, 5 July 1963, 10. For letters supporting Stott's position see Pamela Norman, Monica Walker and VMD, letters to the editor, *Guardian*, 10 July 1963, 6.

348   'The Men in My Life, by Christine Keeler', *Daily Express*, 28 June 1963, 5.

349   Rice-Davies, *Mandy Report*, unpaginated.

350   Muggeridge, 'Who Blushes Today'.

351   Marjorie Proops, 'Naught Girls Don't Show a Profit', *Daily Mirror*, 8 May 1963, 9.

352   See 'The Startling Facts About the "Sweet Life" Set in London', *People*, 16 June 1963, 2–3; 'The Startling Facts About London's "Sweet Life" Set – From Mayfair', *People*, 23 June 1963, 2; 'The "Sweet Life" Set: Why the Big Gamblers Must Have Girls', *People*, 7 July 1963, 12.

353   See 'In London for a Week', *Nova*, July 1963, 39; 'The Pilgrim Honey', *Honey*, April 1963, 34; 'How to Leave Home and Like It', *Honey*, August 1963, 16. For analysis of the cultural significance of these new consumer magazines see Janice Winship, *Inside Women's Magazines* (London: Pandora, 1987), 45–51.

354   Helen Gurley Brown Papers, 1938–2001, Five College Archives and Manuscript Collections, Sophia Smith Collection, Smith College, Northampton, MA, http://asteria.fivecolleges.edu/findaids/sophiasmith/mnsss142_bioghist.html (accessed 8 July 2008).

355   Archbishop of Canterbury, quoted in 'With Prejudice', *British Medical Journal* 1 (23 February 1963): 532.

356   West, *Meaning of Treason*, 406.

357   Irving et al., *Scandal*, 222–3. See also D. E. Butler and Anthony King, *The British General Election of 1964* (London: Macmillan, 1965), 13–21.

358   'Stop This Witch-Hunt', *People*, 16 June 1963, 1. For other liberal views see 'A Matter of Quality', *New Society*, 20 June 1963, 3–4; 'Morals and Responsibility', *New Society*, 20 June 1963, 6–7.

359   'How the U.S. Sees Britain's "Barrage of Frankness" About Sex', *Evening Standard*, 21 March 1963, 7.

360   Ibid. For Carstairs's pronouncements see G. M. Carstairs, 'This Island Now: Vicissitudes of Adolescence, The Third Reith Lecture', *Listener*, 29 November 1962, 894.

361   The opinion poll survey was conducted by the Austrian sociologist Heinrich Blezinger, researching at King's College, Cambridge. Blezinger's sample was confined to men aged between twenty-five and thirty-five in middle-income groups, mostly in junior executive or white-collar jobs, and mostly living in the Cambridge area. His in-depth interviews were designed to map the formation of political beliefs, and he took reactions to the Profumo affair as the basis for his study. When pollsters asked which aspect of the scandal interviewees thought most significant, an overwhelming majority believed that Profumo's lie was very important, while only a small minority prioritized the fact that the minister had a mistress. Researchers concluded that the sample demonstrated a 'very limited concern for issues of sexual morality': Irving et al., *Scandal*, 226–7.

362   'Great Britain: The Shock of Today', *Time*, 25 January 1963, 18.

363   For analysis of these economic and political problems see Butler and King, *British General Election*, 13–21.

364   Michael Shanks, *The Stagnant Society: A Warning* (Harmondsworth: Penguin, 1961), 173–4, 29.

365   Ibid., 28–9.

366   Arthur Koestler, 'Introduction', in Arthur Koestler, ed., *Suicide of a Nation? An Enquiry into the State of Britain Today* (London: Hutchinson, 1963), 12.

367   Ibid., 13.

368   Marcus Cunliffe, 'The Comforts of the Sick-Bay', and Michael Shanks, 'The Comforts of Stagnation', in Koestler, *Suicide of a Nation?*, 196–203, 51–69.

369   David Frost, *An Autobiography, David Frost Part One: From Congregations to Audiences* (London: HarperCollins, 1993), 111.

370   Pimlott, *Harold Wilson*, 269. For commentary on the satire boom see Richard Ingrams, ed., *The Life and Times of Private Eye, 1961–1971* (Harmondsworth: Penguin, 1971); Roger Wilmut, *From Fringe to Flying Circus: Celebrating a Unique Generation of Comedy 1960–1980* (London: Eyre Methuen, 1980); Patrick Marnham, *The Private Eye Story: The First 21 Years* (London: Andre Deutsch, 1982); Harry Thompson, *Richard Ingrams: Lord of the Gnomes* (London: Mandarin, 1995).

371   'The Last Days of Macmillan', *Private Eye*, 5 April 1963, 8–9. See also the cover of this issue, which pictured Profumo in a bedroom scene.

372   See Ned Sherrin, 'Talking a TV Revolution', *Sunday Times*, 7 August 2005, 3.

373   'Britain Gets Wythe Itte, 1963', *Private Eye*, 31 May 1963, 9–10.

374   For the traditions of eighteenth-century satire see Diana Donald, *The Age of Caricature: Satirical Prints in the Reign of George III* (New Haven and London: Yale University Press, 1996); Mark Hallett, *The Spectacle of Difference: Graphic Satire in the Age of Hogarth* (New Haven and London: Yale University Press, 1999).

EPILOGUE

1   Piri Halasz, 'Great Britain', *Time*, 15 April 1966, 32.

2   Ibid., 41.

3   'A Letter from the Publisher', *Time*, 15 April 1966, 11.

4   Halasz, 'Great Britain', 41.

5   Ibid., 41B, 32.

6   Ibid., 41.

7   Piri Halasz, *A Memoir of Creativity: Abstract Painting, Politics and the Media, 1956–2008* (Bloomington, IN: iUniverse, 2009) 125.

8   Halasz, 'Great Britain', 32, 30.

9   Ibid., 41B and photo 'Oh, To Be In London', between pp. 32 and 41.

10   Ibid., 32, 41.

11   Ibid., 41A.

12   Earlier comments had appeared in *L'Express* in September 1964 and *Epoca* in November 1965, as well as in the *Weekend Telegraph* in April 1965; see Jerry White, *London in the Twentieth Century: A City and its People* (London: Penguin, 2002), 341.

13   Halasz, *Memoir of Creativity*.

14   See (for example) Sheila Rowbotham, *Promise of a Dream: Remembering the Sixties* (London: Allen Lane, 2000), 118; White, *London*, 341; Arthur Marwick, *The Sixties: Cultural Revolution in Britain, France, Italy, and the United States, c.1958–c.1974* (Oxford: Oxford University Press, 1998), 16; Christopher Breward, *Fashioning London: Clothing and the Modern Metropolis* (Oxford: Berg, 2004), 162–8.

15   Halasz, 'Great Britain', 32.

16   The term 'grand climacteric' is Christopher Booker's, which he used to describe the Profumo affair in *The Neophiliacs: A Study of the Revolution in English Life in the Fifties and Sixties* (London: Collins, 1969), 219.

17   See especially Jonathan Raban, *Soft City* (New York: E. P. Dutton, 1974).

18   Ibid., 179.

19   White, *London*, 405.

20   John Wolfenden, *Turning Points: The Memoirs of Lord Wolfenden* (London: Bodley Head, 1976), 146.

21   For Australia see Duncan Chappell and Paul Wilson, 'Public Attitudes to the Reform of the Law Relating to Abortion and Homosexuality', *Australian Law Journal* 42 (August 1968): 175–80; Robert French, *Camping by a Billabong* (Sydney: Black Wattle Press, 1993), 102. For Canada see Gary Kinsman, *The Regulation of Desire: Sexuality in Canada* (Montreal: Black Rose Books, 1987), 139–77. For commentary see Leslie Moran, *Homosexual(ity) of Law* (London: Routledge, 1996), 14.

22   Marwick, *Sixties*, 806.

23   See David Bell and Jon Binnie, *The Sexual Citizen: Queer Politics and Beyond* (Oxford: Polity, 2000), 2–3; Matt Houlbrook, *Queer London: Perils and Pleasures in the Sexual Metropolis, 1918–1957* (Chicago: University of Chicago Press, 2005), 262–3.

24   Co-ordinated by the Soho Society, a new alliance of conservationists, local resident, and businesses that paralleled many of the earlier aims of the Soho Association, the organization was dedicated to promoting a mixed local economy and preserving the area's cultural heritage; see my own *Cultures of Consumption: Masculinities and Social Space in Late Twentieth-Century Britain* (London: Routledge, 1996), 156–7.

25   'Paul Raymond, 82, Dies; Built an Erotic Empire', *New York Times*, 8 March 2008, 16.

26   White, *London*, 405–6.

27   Sexual sadism, the vulnerability of children and the elderly, together with issues of medical power and expert authority, were among the dominant themes covered by these cases, while the Yorkshire Ripper murders also acted as a catalyst for widespread women's protests about male violence and the emergence of prostitutes as political actors in their own right. See Fred Harrison, *Brady and Hindley: The Genesis of the Moors Murders* (Bath: Ashgrove, 1986); Nicole Jouve Ward, *'The Streetcleaner': The Yorkshire Ripper Case on Trial* (London: Boyars, 1986); Colin Wilson, *The Corpse Garden: The Crimes of Fred and Rose West* (London: True Crime Library, 1998); Shipman Inquiry, *Third Report, Death Certification and the Investigation of Deaths by Coroners* (Norwich: Stationery Office, 2003).

28   Closer in subject-matter and location to the Christie case were the London-based serial murders perpetrated in the 1970s by the quiet and self-effacing homosexual killer, civil service clerk Dennis Nilsen, who stalked the West End's gay pubs and clubs in search of sexually available and supposedly rootless young men; see Brian Masters, *Killing for Company: The Case of Dennis Nilsen* (London: Jonathan Cape, 1985).

29   See Peter Chippindale and David Leigh, *The Thorpe Committal* (London: Arrow Books, 1979); Auberon Waugh, *The Last Word: An Eye-Witness Account of the Trial of Jeremy Thorpe* (London: Michael Joseph, 1980).

30   See Sara Keays, *A Question of Judgement* (London: Quintessential, 1985); Cecil Parkinson, *Right at the Centre: An Autobiography* (London: Weidenfeld & Nicolson, 1992); Adam Raphael, *My Learned Friends* (London: W. H. Allen, 1989); Michael Crick, *Jeffrey Archer: Stranger than Fiction* (London: Hamish Hamilton, 1995).

31   H. Montgomery Hyde, *A Tangled Web: Sex Scandals in British Politics and Society* (London: Constable, 1986), 345.

32   For this analysis of the Diana episode see Ross McKibbin, 'Mass-Observation in the Mall', in Mandy Merck, ed., *After Diana: Irreverent Elegies* (London: Verso, 1998), 23.

Bibliography

I   UNPUBLISHED MANUSCRIPTS AND COLLECTIONS

Bodleian Library, University of Oxford, Department of Special Collections and Western Manuscripts

Diaries of Maurice Harold Macmillan, 1st Earl of Stockton.

British Library

Lord Chamberlain's Office. Correspondence Files. Manuscripts Department.
Lord Chamberlain's Plays. Correspondence Files 1900–1968. Manuscripts Department.
Windmill Theatre. Revudeville. Playbills collection.

The Kinsey Institute for Research in Sex, Gender, and Reproduction, Bloomington, Indiana

Alfred C. Kinsey Collection.

London Metropolitan Archives

Greater London Council Papers GLC/DG/EL/2/58, GLC/DG/EL/7/50.
London Council of Social Service Papers ACC 1888/53, ACC 1888/110.
Marlborough Street Magistrates Court. Court Registers PS/MS/A2/165.
National Council of Women of Great Britain Papers ACC/3613/01/025.
Public Morality Council Papers A/PMC/3, A/PMC/12, A/PMC/38, A/PMC/41, A/PMC/43, A/PMC/51, A/PMC/80, A/PMC/205.

Mass Observation Archive, University of Sussex

Topic Collection: Royalty.

The National Archives Public Record Office, Kew

Cabinet Papers TNA PRO CAB 128, CAB 129.
Central Criminal Court Papers TNA PRO CRIM 8.
Colonial Office Papers TNA PRO CO 1031.
Crown Estate Papers TNA PRO CRES 35.
Director of Public Prosecutions Papers TNA PRO DPP 2, DPP 6.
Dominions Office Papers TNA PRO DO 194, DO 196.
Home Office Papers TNA PRO HO 45, HO 291, HO 325, HO 345.
Lord Chancellor's Office Papers TNA PRO LCO 2.
Metropolitan Police Papers TNA PRO MEPO 2, MEPO 3.
Prison Commission Papers TNA PRO PCOM 9.

Theatre Museum, London

Windmill Theatre Archive.

University of Reading, Special Collections Service

Papers of John Frederick Wolfenden, MS 5311.

Victoria and Albert Museum Archive of Art and Design, Blythe House, London

Windmill Theatre Collection.

Westminster City Archives

City of Westminster. Town Planning and Improvements Committee. Minutes 1950–1957.
County of London Sessions, Westminster Division. Justices Minute Books 804/54.
Metropolitan Borough of Paddington. Minutes of Council 25th May 1950–26th April 1951.
St Anne Parish Soho. Parish Registers and Parish Records Acc 2288/33.
St Anne Parish Soho. Prints and Cuttings.
St James Parish Piccadilly. Prints and Cuttings.
Westminster City Council. Handbooks, 1946, 1950–1951.

The Women's Library, London

British Vigilance Association and National Vigilance Association Papers 4NVA/1/3/4, 4NVA/2/2, 4NVA/7/B/12.

Unpublished papers

Chauncey, George. 'The Child Molester, the Delinquent, and the Urban Jungle: Notes towards an Analysis of the Homosexual Specter Haunting Postwar New York and Postwar Urban Studies'. Paper to the Urban Atlantic Seminar, New York University, November 2005.

Pittam, Robert. Highlights (and some dark corners) of Home Office History: Lecture by R. R. Pittam, May 1982 at Lunar House. Home Office library.

Savage, Mike. 'Cultural Formation in England, 1939–1960'. 2006.

Walkowitz, Judith. 'Schleppers and Shoppers'. 2003.

———. 'Tarts and the Prince of Wales'. Unpublished paper to American Historical Association Annual Meeting. Seattle, 2005.

———. 'The Windmill Theatre: Erotic Display, Middlebrow and the Spirit of the Blitz'. Unpublished paper to Centre for Interdisciplinary Research in the Arts. University of Manchester, October 2007.

II   OFFICIAL PUBLICATIONS

Abercrombie, Patrick, and South East Regional Planning. *Greater London Plan 1944 . . . A Report Prepared on Behalf of the Standing Conference on London Regional Planning at the Request of the Minister of Town and Country Planning.* London: HMSO, 1945.

Colonial Office. *Historical Survey of the Origins and Growth of Mau Mau.* Cmnd. 1030. London: HMSO, 1960.

General Register Office. *Census 1951: England and Wales; Report on Greater London and Five Other Conurbations.* London: HMSO, 1956.

Home Office. 'Crime: Return to an Address of The House of Lords dated 23 March, 1950', *Papers Relating to the Large Number of Crimes Accompanied by Violence Occurring in Large Cities.* Great Britain Parliamentary Papers, House of Lords, Session 1950, no. 121.

———. *Report of the Commissioner of Police for the Metropolis for the Year 1945.* Cmnd. 6871. London: HMSO, 1946.

———. *Report . . . 1947.* Cmnd. 7406. London: HMSO, 1948.

———. *Report . . . 1951.* Cmnd. 8634. London: HMSO, 1952.

———. *Report of the Committee on Obscenity and Film Censorship.* Cmnd. 7772. London: HMSO, 1979.

———. *Report of the Royal Commission on Police Powers and Procedure.* Cmnd. 3297. London: HMSO, 1929.

———. *Report of the Street Offences Committee.* Cmnd. 3231. London: HMSO, 1928.

———. *Report of the Tribunal Appointed to Inquire into the Vassall Case and Related Matters.* Cmnd. 2009. London: HMSO, 1963.

Home Office, Scottish Home Department. *Report of the Committee on Homosexual Offences and Prostitution.* Cmnd. 247. London: HMSO, 1957.

Ministry of Health. *Mortality and Morbidity During the London Fog of December 1952: Reports on Public Heath and Medical Subjects No. 95*. London: HMSO, 1954.

Ministry of Housing and Local Government. *Report of the Committee on Housing in Greater London*. Cmnd. 2605. London: HMSO, 1965.

Parliamentary Debates (Hansard) House of Commons Official Reports, 5th ser. London: HMSO.

Parliamentary Debates (Hansard) House of Lords Official Reports, 5th ser. London: HMSO.

Report of the Royal Commission on the Distribution of the Industrial Population. Cmnd. 6153. London: HMSO, 1939.

Report of the Royal Commission on Marriage and Divorce, 1951–55. Cmnd. 9678. London: HMSO, 1955.

Statutes of the Realm, British Library.

III   RULES, REPORTS, AND PROCEEDINGS

City of Westminster. *Minutes and Proceedings of the Mayor, Aldermen and Councillors, 1922*. London: Harrison and Sons, 1926.

———. *Minutes and Proceedings of the Mayor, Aldermen and Councillors, 1926*. London: Harrison and Sons, 1927.

———. *Minutes and Proceedings of the Mayor, Aldermen and Councillors, 1927*. London: Harrison and Sons, 1928.

———. *Minutes and Proceedings of the Mayor, Aldermen and Councillors, 1950*. London: Harrison and Sons, 1951.

———. *Minutes and Proceedings of the Mayor, Aldermen and Councillors, 1951*. London: Harrison and Sons, 1952.

Corporation of London, Court of Common Council. *Report to the Right Honourable the Lord Mayor etc. on the Preliminary Draft Proposals for Post War Reconstruction in the City of London*. London: Batsford, 1944.

Family Welfare Association. *Eighty-First Annual Report . . . October 1 1946–September 30 1947*. London: Family Welfare Association, n.d.

Greater London Regional Planning Committee. *First Report of the Greater London Regional Planning Committee*. London: Knapp, Drewett, 1929.

———. *Second Report of the Greater London Regional Planning Committee*. London: Knapp, Drewett, 1933.

International Bureau for the Suppression of Traffic in Persons, British Vigilance Association, and the National Committee for the Suppression of Traffic in Persons. *Second Annual Report . . . for the Year Ending 1954*. London: International Bureau for the Suppression of Traffic in Persons, 1954.

London County Council. *Report of the County Medical Officer of Health and School Medical Officer for the Year 1952*. London: London County Council, 1953.

University College London, *University College Annual Report 1949–50*. London: University College, London, n.d.

IV NEWSPAPERS, PERIODICALS, JOURNALS, AND REFERENCE
WORKS

Architect and Building News
Architect's Journal
British Medical Journal
Cambrian News
Clapham Observer
Coles Classified Directories: The West End Directory Guide 1954–55
Country Life
Daily Express
Daily Gleaner (Jamaica)
Daily Mail
Daily Mirror
Daily Sketch
Daily Telegraph and Morning Post (Daily Telegraph from 1969*)*
Daily Worker
The Dictionary of National Biography 1951–1960
The Dictionary of National Biography 1961–1970
Evening News
Evening Standard
Illustrated London News
Independent
Journal of the Royal Statistical Society
Kensington News and West London Times
King
Listener
London American
London Review of Books
Man About Town
Manchester Guardian (Guardian from 1959*)*
Marylebone Mercury
Men's Wear
Motion Picture Herald
Municipal Journal
National and English Review
New Society
New Statesman and Nation (New Statesman from 1964*)*
New York Herald Tribune (Paris edn)
News of the World
Night and Day
North London Press
Nova
Observer
Official Architecture and Planning

Oxford Dictionary of National Biography
People
Picture Post
The Post Office London Directory for 1953
The Post Office London Directory for 1958: Street Directory
Practitioner
Punch
Queen
Radio Times
Reynold's News
Savelian Wakefield Grammar School Magazine
Shield
Spectator
Sphere
Stage and Television Today
Star
St Pancras Chronicle
Sunday Graphic
Sunday Herald (Sydney)
Sunday Mirror
Sunday Pictorial
Sunday Times
Sun-Herald (Sydney)
Sydney Morning Herald
Time (Atlantic Edition)
The Times
Times of India
Tit-Bits
Toronto Daily Star
Town Planning Review
Vogue
Western Mail and South Wales News
Westminster Chamber of Commerce Journal
Westminster and Pimlico News
Who's Who 1945
Who's Who 1960
Yorkshire Post

V   ORAL TESTIMONIES

Hall Carpenter Oral History Project, British Library Sound Archive

John Alcock, 1985, C456/003/01.
Betty Bourne, 1994, C456/126/01.

Roger Butler, 1990, C456/091/01.
Dudley Cave, 1987, C456/063/01.
John Chesterman, 1993, C456/123/03.
Tom Cullen, 1999, C456/031/01–02.
Tony Garrett, 1990, C456/090/01–02.
Antony Grey, 1990, C456/071/01–03.
Michael James, 1993, C456/122/02.
Mike, 1980, C547/006/02.
Patrick Trevor-Roper, 1990, C456/089/01.

Tony Dean Interviews, British Library Sound Archive

John, C547/06/01.
Richard, 1980, C547/43/01.

Interviews by the author

Michael Burn, June 1997.
Jean Graham Hall, August 1999.
Patrick Trevor-Roper, August 1999.

VI PUBLISHED BOOKS AND ARTICLES

Abercrombie, Patrick. 'The Preservation of Rural England'. *Town Planning Review* 12, no. 1 (May 1926): 5–56.
Abercrombie, Patrick, and Thomas Johnson. *The Doncaster Regional Planning Scheme*. London: University Press of Liverpool, 1922.
Abercrombie, Patrick, Sydney Kelly, and Thomas Johnson. *Sheffield and District Regional Planning Scheme*. London: Hodder & Stoughton, 1931.
Abrams, Mark. *The Teenage Consumer*. London: Press Exchange, 1959.
Abrams, Philip, and Paula Lewthwaite, eds. *Development and Diversity: British Sociology, 1950–1980; Transactions of the Annual Conference of the British Sociological Association . . . 1980*. London: British Sociological Association, 1980.
Abrams, Rebecca. *Woman in a Man's World: Pioneering Career Women of the Twentieth Century*. London: Methuen, 1993.
Ackroyd, Peter. *London: The Biography*. London: Vintage, 2001.
Adams, Thomas. 'Foreword'. In SERA, *Regional Survey of New York*, vol. 7, *Neighborhood and Community Planning Comprising Three Monographs . . .* New York: n.p., 1929.
———. *Outline of Town and City Planning: A Review of Past Efforts and Modern Aims*. London: J. & A. Churchill, 1935.
Adamson, David. *The Last Empire: Britain and the Commonwealth*. London: Tauris, 1989.
Adler, Larry, with Philip Judge. *Me and My Big Mouth*, edited by William Hall. London: Blake, 1994.

Aldgate, Anthony. *Censorship and the Permissive Society: British Cinema and the Theatre 1955–1965.* Oxford: Clarendon Press, 1995.

Aldor, Francis. *The Good Time Guide to London.* London: Harrap, 1951.

Alexander, Sally. 'Becoming a Woman in London in the 1920s and 1930s'. In *Metropolis – London: Histories and Representations since 1800,* edited by David Feldman and Gareth Stedman Jones, 245–71. London: Routledge, 1989.

Algren, Nelson. *Who Lost an American? Being a Guide to the Seamier Sides of New York City, Inner London, Paris, Dublin, Barcelona, Seville, Almeria, Istanbul, Crete and Chicago, Illinois.* London: Andre Deutsch, 1963.

Allen, Robert. *Horrible Prettiness: Burlesque and American Culture.* Chapel Hill: University of North Carolina Press, 1991.

Amies, Hardy. *Just So Far.* London: Collins, 1954.

Amory, Mark, ed. *The Letters of Ann Fleming.* London: Collins Harvill, 1985.

————, ed. *The Letters of Evelyn Waugh.* London: Phoenix, 1995.

Anderson, Amanda. *The Powers of Distance: Cosmopolitanism and the Culture of Detachment.* Princeton, NJ: Princeton University Press, 2001.

Anderson, Perry. 'Components of the National Culture'. In *Student Power: Problems, Diagnosis, Action,* edited by Alexander Cockburn and Robin Blackburn, 214–84. Harmondsworth: Penguin, 1970.

Annan, Noel. *Our Age: Portrait of a Generation.* London: Weidenfeld & Nicolson, 1990.

Anonymous. *London Pocket Guide.* London: Ernest Benn, 1962.

————. *The 1953 Guide to London Clubs.* London: Regency Press, 1953.

————. *The Post Office London Directory for 1958: Street Directory.* London: Kelly's Directories, 1958.

————. *Red Guide to London,* 61st edn. London: Ward Lock, 1957.

————. *Rillington Place.* London: The Stationery Office, 1999.

————. *The Sins of the Cities of the Plain; or, the Recollections of a Mary-Ann,* vol. 1. London, privately printed, 1881.

————. *Streetwalker.* London: Bodley Head, 1959.

————. *Wonderful London.* London: Associated Newspapers, 1961.

Anthony, Carl Sferrazza. *As We Remember Her: Jacqueline Kennedy Onassis in the Words of her Family and Friends.* New York: HarperCollins, 1997.

Armfelt, Count. 'Cosmopolitan London'. In *Living London,* vol. 1, edited by George Sims, 241–7. London: Cassell, n.d.

Aronson, Theo. *Princess Margaret: A Biography.* London: Michael O'Mara, 1997.

Ascoli, David. *The Queen's Peace: The Origins and Development of the Metropolitan Police, 1829–1979.* London: Hamish Hamilton, 1979.

Assael, Brenda. 'Art or Indecency? *Tableaux Vivants* on the London Stage and the Failure of Late Victorian Moral Reform'. *Journal of British Studies* 45, no. 4 (October 2006): 744–58.

Association of Royal Air Force Photographic Officers. *The History of Air Photography in the Royal Air Force.* England: Association of Royal Air Force Photographic Officers, 1987.

Baedeker, Karl. *London and its Environs: A Handbook for Travellers by Karl Baedeker*, 20th revised edn. London: George Allen & Unwin, 1951.

———. *London and its Environs: A Handbook for Travellers by Karl Baedeker*, 21st revised edn. London: George Allen & Unwin, 1955.

Bailey, Nick. *Fitzrovia*. London: Historical Publications in association with Camden History Society, 1981.

Bailey, Paul. *An English Madam: The Life and Work of Cynthia Payne*. London: Jonathan Cape, 1982.

Baker, Roger. *Drag: A History of Female Impersonation in the Performing Arts*. London: Cassell, 1994.

Bakewell, Michael. *Fitzrovia: London's Bohemia*. London: National Portrait Gallery, 1999.

Balchin, Nigel. *Darkness Falls from the Air*. London: Collins, 1942.

Banham, Mary, and Bevis Hillier, eds. *A Tonic to the Nation: The Festival of Britain 1951*. London: Thames & Hudson, 1976.

Banks, F. R. *The Penguin Guide to London*. Harmondsworth: Penguin, 1958.

Banton, Michael. *The Coloured Quarter: Negro Immigrants in an English City*. London: Jonathan Cape, 1955.

Barman, Christian. *The Man Who Built London Transport: A Biography of Frank Pick*. Newton Abbot: David & Charles, 1979.

Barnett, Donald. *Mau Mau from Within: Autobiography and Analysis of Kenya's Peasant Revolt*. London: MacGibbon and Kee, 1966.

Barty-King, Hugh. *The AA: A History of the First 75 Years of the Automobile Association 1905–1980*. Basingstoke: Automobile Association, 1980.

Bateson, David. *The Soho Jungle*. London: Robert Hale, 1957.

Bazley, Basil, and Frank Lambert. *Show Me London*. Tunbridge Wells: Graphic Studios, 1947.

Beaufoy, Helena. ' "Order Out of Chaos": The London Society and the Planning of London 1912–1920'. *Planning Perspectives* 12 (1997): 135–64.

Beck, Ulrich. *World Risk Society*. Cambridge: Polity, 1999.

Beer, Samuel. *British Politics in the Collectivist Age*. New York: Alfred Knopf, 1966.

Bell, David, and Jon Binnie, *The Sexual Citizen: Queer Politics and Beyond*. Oxford: Polity, 2000.

Benjamin, Walter. *Selected Writings, Volume 4: 1938–40*, edited by Howard Eiland and Michael Jennings, translated by Edmund Jephcott and others. Cambridge, MA, and London: Belknap Press of Harvard University Press, 2003.

Benn, Tony. *Out of the Wilderness: Diaries 1963–1967*. London: Hutchinson, 1987.

Bentine, Michael. *The Long Banana Skin*. London: Wolfe, 1975.

Bingham, Adrian. *Gender, Modernity, and the Popular Press in Inter-War Britain*. Oxford: Clarendon Press, 2004.

Binney, Cecil. *Crime and Abnormality*. London: Oxford University Press, 1949.

Bird, Peter. *The First Food Empire: A History of J. Lyons & Co*. Chichester: Phillimore, 2000.

Birmingham Feminist History Group. 'Feminism as Femininity in the Nineteen-Fifties?' *Feminist Review*, no. 3 (1979): 48–65.

Birnbaum, Norman. 'Monarchs and Sociologists: A Reply to Professor Shils and Mr. Young'. *Sociological Review*, n.s., 3, no. 1 (1955): 5–23.

Black, Gerry. *Living Up West: Jewish Life in London's West End*. London: London Museum of Jewish Life, 1994.

Black, Jeremy. *The Politics of James Bond: From Fleming's Novels to the Big Screen*. Westport, CT, and London: Praeger, 2001.

Black, Lawrence. *The Political Culture of the Left in Britain, 1951–64: Old Labour, New Britain?* Basingstoke: Palgrave Macmillan, 2003.

Blake, Robert. *The Conservative Party from Peel to Major*. London: Heinemann, 1997.

Bland, Lucy. *Banishing the Beast: English Feminism and Sexual Morality 1885–1914*. London: Penguin, 1995.

Bland, Lucy, Trisha McCabe, and Frank Mort. 'Sexuality and Reproduction: Three "Official" Instances'. In *Ideology and Cultural Production*, edited by Michèle Barrett, Philip Corrigan, and Janet Wolff, 78–111. London: Croom Helm, 1979.

Booker, Christopher. *The Neophiliacs: A Study of the Revolution in English Life in the Fifties and Sixties*. London: Collins, 1969.

Booth, Charles. *Life and Labour of the People in London, Third Series, Religious Influences 3: The City of London and the West End*. London: Macmillan, 1902.

———. *Life and Labour of the People in London, Third Series, Religious Influences 2: London North of the Thames; The Inner Ring*. London: Macmillan, 1902.

Borer, Mary Cathcart. *Two Villages: The Story of Chelsea and Kensington*. London: W. H. Allen, 1973.

Bradley, Simon, and Nikolaus Pevsner. *London 1: The City of London*, new edn. London: Penguin, 1997.

Brandon, David, and Alan Brooke, *Marylebone and Tyburn Past*. London: Historical Publications, 2007.

Braun, Eric. *Deborah Kerr*. London: W. H. Allen, 1977.

Brennan, Timothy. *At Home in the World: Cosmopolitanism Now*. Cambridge, MA: Harvard University Press, 1997.

Breward, Christopher. *Fashioning London: Clothing and the Modern Metropolis*. Oxford: Berg, 2004.

Breward, Christopher, Becky Conekin, and Caroline Cox, eds. *The Englishness of English Dress*. Oxford: Berg, 2002.

Breward, Christopher, and David Gilbert, eds. *Fashion's World Cities*. Oxford: Berg, 2006.

Briggs, Asa. *The History of Broadcasting in the United Kingdom*, vol. 4, *Sound and Vision*. Oxford: Oxford University Press, 1995.

———. *Victorian Cities*. Berkeley: University of California Press, 1993.

British Broadcasting Corporation. *The Year that Made the Day: How the BBC Planned and Prepared the Coronation Day Broadcasts*. London: British Broadcasting Corporation, 1953.

British Medical Association, Joint Committee on Psychiatry and the Law. *The Criminal Law and Sexual Offenders: A Report of the Joint Committee on Psychiatry and the Law Appointed by the British Medical Association and the Magistrates Association*. London: British Medical Association, 1949.

British Travel and Holidays Association. *Shopping in London*. London: British Travel and Holidays Association, 1953.

Brooke, Stephen. 'Problems of "Socialist Planning": Evan Durbin and the Labour Government of 1945'. *Historical Journal* 34, no. 3 (1991): 687–702.

Brown, James. *Techniques of Persuasion: From Propaganda to Brain-Washing*. Harmondsworth: Penguin, 1963.

Browne, Ray, and Michael Marsden. 'Introduction'. In *The Culture of Celebrations*, edited by Michael Marsden and Ray Browne, 1–8. Bowling Green, OH: Bowling Green State University Popular Press, 1994.

Brownlee, David. 'That "Regular Mongrel Affair": G. G. Scott's Design for the Government Offices'. *Architectural History* 28 (1985): 159–82.

Brunsdon, Charlotte. *London in Cinema: The Cinematic City since 1945*. London: British Film Institute, 2007.

———. 'Space and Place in the British Crime Film'. In *British Crime Cinema*, edited by Steve Chibnall and Robert Murphy, 148–59. London: Routledge, 1999.

Brunt, Rosalind. '"An Immense Verbosity": Permissive Sexual Advice in the 1970s'. In *Feminism, Culture and Politics*, edited by Rosalind Brunt and Caroline Rowan, 143–70. London: Lawrence & Wishart, 1982.

Buckle, Richard, ed. *Self Portrait with Friends: The Selected Diaries of Cecil Beaton*. New York: Times Books, 1979.

Bud, Robert. 'Penicillin and the New Elizabethans'. *British Journal for the History of Science* 31 (1988): 305–33.

Buijenhuijs, Robert. *Essays on Mau Mau*. Leiden: African Studies Centre, 1982.

Burford, James, and John Harvey. *Some Lesser Known Architecture of London*. London: Ernest Benn, 1925.

Burke, Thomas. *London in my Time*. London: Rich & Cowan, 1934.

Burn, Michael. *Turned Towards the Sun: An Autobiography*. Norwich: Michael Russell, 2003.

Burns, Wilfred. *New Towns for Old: The Technique for Urban Renewal*. London: Leonard Hill, 1963.

Burton, Peter. *Parallel Lives*. London: GMP, 1985.

Butler, D. E., and Anthony King. *The British General Election of 1964*. London: Macmillan, 1965.

Butler, Lord. *The Art of the Possible: The Memoirs of Lord Butler*. London: Hamish Hamilton, 1971.

Byrne, Gerald. *Borstal Boy: The Uncensored Story of Neville Heath*. London: John Hill Productions, 1954.

Cairncross, Alec. *The British Economy since 1945: Economic Policy and Performance 1945–1990*. Oxford: Blackwell, 1992.

Calder, Angus. *The Myth of the Blitz*. London: Jonathan Cape, 1991.

Callaghan, James. *Time and Chance*. London: Collins, 1987.

Cameron, Deborah, and Elizabeth Frazer. *Lust to Kill: A Feminist Investigation of Sexual Murder*. Cambridge: Polity, 1987.

Campbell, Beatrix. 'A Feminist Sexual Politics: Now You See It, Now You Don't'. *Feminist Review*, no. 5 (1980): 1–18.

Campbell, Duncan. *The Underworld*. London: BBC Books, 1994.

Camps, Francis. *Medical and Scientific Investigations in the Christie Case*. London: Medical Publications, 1953.

Camps, Francis, with Richard Barber. *The Investigation of Murder*. London: Michael Joseph, 1966.

Cannadine, David. 'The Context, Performance and Meaning of Ritual: The British Monarchy and the "Invention of Tradition", c.1820–1977'. In *The Invention of Tradition*, edited by Eric Hobsbawm and Terence Ranger, 101–64. Cambridge: Cambridge University Press, 1983.

———. *The Decline and Fall of the British Aristocracy*. New York: Anchor Books Doubleday, 1990.

———. 'James Bond and the Decline of England'. *Encounter* 53, no. 3 (September 1979): 46–55.

———. *Ornamentalism: How the British Saw their Empire*. London: Allen Lane, 2001.

Caputi, Jane. *The Age of Sex Crime*. Bowling Green, OH: Bowling Green University Popular Press, 1987.

Cardwell, Rev. J. H. *Men and Women of Soho: Famous and Infamous; Actors, Authors, Dramatists, Entertainers and Engravers*. London: Truslove & Hanson, 1904.

Carpenter, Edward. *Archbishop Fisher: His Life and Times*. Norwich: Canterbury Press, 1991.

Carpenter, Edward. *The Intermediate Sex: A Study of Some Transitional Types of Men and Women*. London: Allen & Unwin, 1908.

Carpenter, Humphrey. *Benjamin Britten: A Biography*. London: Faber & Faber, 1992.

Carter, Edward, and Erno Goldfinger. *The County of London Plan Explained*. West Drayton: Penguin, 1945.

Castle, Barbara. *Fighting All the Way*. London: Macmillan, 1993.

Castle, Charles. *The Duchess Who Dared: Margaret, Duchess of Argyll*. London: Sidgwick & Jackson, 1994.

Castle, Terry. *Masquerade and Civilization: The Carnivalesque in Eighteenth-Century English Culture and Fiction*. Stanford: Stanford University Press, 1986.

Centre for Urban Studies, ed. *London: Aspects of Change*. London: MacGibbon and Kee, 1964.

Chance, John. *The Crimes at Rillington Place: A Novelist's Reconstruction*. London: Hodder & Stoughton, 1961.

Chancellor, Edwin Beresford. *London's Old Latin Quarter, Being an Account of Tottenham Court Road and its Immediate Surroundings*. London: Jonathan Cape, 1930.

———. *The Romance of Soho: Being an Account of the District, its Past Distinguished Inhabitants, its Historic Houses, and its Place in the Social Annals of London*. London: Country Life, 1931.

Chaney, Lisa. *Elizabeth David: A Biography*. London: Macmillan, 1998.

Chant, Laura Ormiston. *Why We Attacked the Empire*. London: Marshall & Son, 1895.

Chapman, James. *Licence to Thrill: A Cultural History of the James Bond Films*. London: Tauris, 1999.

Chappell, Duncan, and Paul Wilson. 'Public Attitudes to the Reform of the Law Relating to Abortion and Homosexuality'. *Australian Law Journal* 42 (August 1968): 175–80.

Charlton, Warwick, and Gerald Sparrow. *Stephen Ward Speaks: Conversations with Warwick Charlton; Judge Gerald Sparrow Sums Up the Profumo Affair*. London: Today Magazine, 1963.

Cheah, Pheng, and Bruce Robbins, eds. *Cosmopolitics: Thinking and Feeling Beyond the Nation*. Minneapolis: University of Minnesota Press, 1998.

Cherry, Gordon. *The Evolution of British Town Planning: A History of Town Planning in the 20th Century and of the Royal Town Planning Institute, 1914–1974*. Leighton Buzzard: Leonard Hill Books, 1974.

———. *Town Planning in Britain since 1900: The Rise and Fall of the Planning Ideal*. Oxford: Blackwell, 1996.

Chibnall, Steve, and Robert Murphy. 'Parole Overdue: Releasing the British Crime Film into the Critical Community'. In *British Crime Cinema*, edited by Steve Chibnall and Robert Murphy, 1–15. London: Routledge, 1999.

Chippindale, Peter, and Chris Horrie. *Stick It Up Your Punter! The Rise and Fall of the Sun*. London: Heinemann, 1990.

Chippindale, Peter, and David Leigh. *The Thorpe Committal*. London: Arrow Books, 1979.

Christiansen, Arthur. *Headlines All My Life*. London: Heinemann, 1961.

Christie, Ian. *Arrows of Desire: The Films of Michael Powell and Emeric Pressburger*. London: Waterstone, 1985.

Churchill, Randolph. *The Story of the Coronation*. London: Derek Verschoyle, 1953.

Clark, Anna. *Scandal: The Sexual Politics of the British Constitution*. Princeton, NJ: Princeton University Press, 2004.

Clarke, Nick. *Alistair Cooke: The Biography*. London: Weidenfeld & Nicolson, 1999.

Clarkson, Wensley. *Hit 'Em Hard: Jack Spot, King of the Underworld*. London: HarperCollins, 2002.

Clay, Andrew. 'When the Gangs Came to Britain: The Postwar British Crime Film'. *Journal of Popular British Cinema*, no. 1 (1998): 76–86.

Cohen, Andrew. *British Policy in Changing Africa*. London: Routledge & Kegan Paul, 1959.

Cohen, Marek. *Dope Girls: The Birth of the British Drug Underground*. London: Lawrence & Wishart, 1992.

Cohn, Nik. *Ball the Wall: Nik Cohn in the Age of Rock*. London: Picador, 1989.

Cole, Shaun. *'Don We Now Our Gay Apparel': Gay Men's Dress in the Twentieth Century*. Oxford: Berg, 2000.

Coleman, Ray. *Brian Epstein: The Man Who Made the Beatles*. London: Viking, 1989.

Coleridge, Nicholas, and Stephen Quinn, eds. *The Sixties in Queen*. London: Ebury, 1987.

Collini, Stefan. *Absent Minds: Intellectuals in Britain*. Oxford: Oxford University Press, 2006.

Collins, Marcus. 'The Pornography of Permissiveness: Men's Sexuality and Women's Emancipation in Mid Twentieth-Century Britain'. *History Workshop Journal*, no. 47 (1999): 99–120.

———. 'Pride and Prejudice: West Indian Men in Mid-Twentieth-Century Britain'. *Journal of British Studies* 40, no. 3 (July 2001): 391–418.

Colomina, Beatriz. *Privacy and Publicity: Modern Architecture as Mass Media*. Cambridge, MA: MIT Press, 1994.

Commager, Henry Steele. *Britain Through American Eyes*. London: Bodley Head, 1974.

Conekin, Becky. *'The Autobiography of a Nation': The 1951 Festival of Britain*. Manchester: Manchester University Press, 2003.

Conekin, Becky, Frank Mort, and Chris Waters. 'Introduction'. In *Moments of Modernity: Reconstructing Britain 1945–1964*, edited by Becky Conekin, Frank Mort, and Chris Waters, 1–21. London: Rivers Oram, 1999.

Connolly, Cyril. *The Missing Diplomats*. London: Queen Anne Press, 1952.

Connor, Robert. *Cassandra: Reflections in a Mirror*. London: Cassell, 1969.

Constantine, Leary. *Colour Bar*. London: Stanley Paul, 1954.

Cook, Matt. *London and the Culture of Homosexuality, 1885–1914*. Cambridge: Cambridge University Press, 2003.

———. ' "A New City of Friends": London and Homosexuality in the 1890s'. *History Workshop Journal*, no. 56 (2003): 33–58.

Cook, Pam, ed. *Gainsborough Pictures*. London: Cassell, 1997.

Cooke, Alistair. *America Observed: The Newspaper Years of Alistair Cooke Selected and Introduced by Ronald A. Wells*. London: Reinhardt, 1988.

Cooper, Artemis. *Writing at the Kitchen Table: The Authorized Biography of Elizabeth David*. London: Michael Joseph, 1999.

Coote, Colin. *Editorial: The Memoirs of Colin R. Coote*. London: Eyre & Spottiswoode, 1965.

———. *The Other Club*. London: Sidgwick & Jackson, 1971.

Corbin, Alain. *The Foul and the Fragrant: Odor and the French Social Imagination*. Leamington Spa: Berg, 1986.

Cornelys, Teresa. *Mrs. Cornely's [sic] Entertainments at Carlisle House, Soho Square*. Blackburn: Bradford, 1840.

Cosgrove, Denis. 'Introduction: Mapping Meaning'. In *Mappings*, edited by Denis Cosgrove, 1–23. London: Reaktion, 1999.

Cowan, Peter. *The Office: A Facet of Urban Growth*. London: Heinemann, 1969.

Cowles, Virginia. *The Astors: The Story of a Transatlantic Family*. London: Weidenfeld & Nicolson, 1979.

Cox, Pamela. *Gender, Justice and Welfare: Bad Girls in Britain, 1900–1950*. Basingstoke: Palgrave Macmillan, 2003.

Crawford, Iain. *The Profumo Affair: A Crisis in Contemporary Society*. London: White Lodge Books, 1963.

Crawford, Marion. *The Little Princesses*. London: Cassell, 1950.

———. *Princess Margaret*. London: George Newnes, 1953.

Crick, Michael. *Jeffrey Archer: Stranger than Fiction*. London: Hamish Hamilton, 1995.

Crisp, Quentin. *The Naked Civil Servant*. London: Jonathan Cape, 1968.

Crosland, C. A. R. *The Conservative Enemy: A Programme of Radical Reform for the 1960s*. London: Jonathan Cape, 1962.

———. *The Future of Socialism*. London: Jonathan Cape, 1956.

Crosland, Susan. *Tony Crosland*. London: Jonathan Cape, 1982.

Crossman, R. H. S. *The Backbench Diaries of Richard Crossman*, edited by Janet Morgan. London: Hamish Hamilton and Jonathan Cape, 1981.

Cudlipp, Hugh. *At Your Peril: A Mid-Century View of the Exciting Changes of the Press in Britain, and a Press View of the Exciting Changes of Mid-Century*. London: Weidenfeld & Nicolson, 1962.

Cullingworth, John. *New Towns for Old: The Problem of Urban Renewal*. London: Fabian Society, 1962.

Cunliffe, Marcus. 'The Comforts of the Sick-Bay'. In *Suicide of a Nation? An Enquiry into the State of Britain Today*, edited by Arthur Koestler, 196–203. London: Hutchinson, 1963.

Cunningham, Valentine. *British Writers of the Thirties*. Oxford: Oxford University. Press, 1988.

Daley, Harry. *This Small Cloud: A Personal Memoir*. London: Weidenfeld & Nicolson, 1986.

David, Elizabeth. *A Book of Mediterranean Food*. London: John Lehmann, 1950.

———. *French Country Cooking*. London: John Lehmann, 1951.

———. *Italian Food*. London: Macdonald, 1954.

David, Hugh. *The Fitzrovians: A Portrait of Bohemian Society 1900–55*. London: Michael Joseph, 1988.

———. *Heroes, Mavericks and Bounders: The English Gentleman from Lord Curzon to James Bond*. London: Michael Joseph, 1991.

Davies, Hunter, ed. *The New London Spy: A Discreet Guide to the City's Pleasures*. London: Anthony Blond, 1966.

———. *The Other Half*. London: Heinemann, 1966.

Davies, Russell, ed. *The Kenneth Williams Diaries*. London: HarperCollins, 1994.

Davis, John. 'Rents and Race in 1960s London: New Light on Rachmanism'. *Twentieth Century British History* 12, no. 1 (2001): 69–92.

De Certeau, Michel. *The Practice of Everyday Life*, translated by Steven Rendall. Berkeley: University of California Press, 1988.

De Courcy, Anne. *Society's Queen: The Life of Edith, Marchioness of Londonderry*. London: Phoenix, 2004.

Deghy, Guy and Keith Waterhouse. *Café Royal: Ninety Years of Bohemia*. London: Hutchinson, 1955.

De Grazia, Victoria. *Irresistible Empire: America's Advance through Twentieth-Century Europe*. Cambridge, MA: Belknap Press of Harvard University Press, 2005.

De Jongh, Nicholas. *Politics, Prudery and Perversions: The Censoring of the English Stage, 1901–1968*. London: Methuen, 2000.

Delgado, Alan. *The Enormous File: A Social History of the Office*. London: John Murray, 1979.

Dempster, Nigel. *H.R.H. Princess Margaret: A Life Unfulfilled*. London: Quartet, 1981.

Denning, Lord. *The Denning Report: The Profumo Affair with a New Introduction by the Author*. London: Pimlico, 1992.

———. *The Family Story*. London: Butterworths, 1981.

———. *This Is My Life: A Public Lecture Delivered by The Rt. Hon. Lord Denning Master of the Rolls*, Child & Co. Lecture 5. London: Inns of Court School of Law, 1979.

Denny, Barbara. *Notting Hill & Holland Park Past: A Visual History*. London: Historical Publications, 1993.

Derrida, Jacques. *On Cosmopolitanism and Forgiveness*. London: Routledge, 2001.

Devlin, Patrick. *The Enforcement of Morals . . . Maccabaean Lecture in Jurisprudence of the British Academy, 1959*. London: Oxford University Press, 1959.

Dews, Simon. *Soho*. London: Rich and Cowan, 1952.

Dimbleby, Jonathan. *Richard Dimbleby: A Biography*. London: Hodder & Stoughton, 1975.

Dimbleby, Richard. *Elizabeth Our Queen*. London: Hodder & Stoughton, 1953.

Dix, Gerald. 'Patrick Abercrombie 1879–1957'. In *Pioneers in British Planning*, edited by Gordon Cherry, 103–30. London: Architectural Press, 1981.

Dixon, Piers. 'The Members'. In *Brooks's: A Social History*, edited by Philip Ziegler and Desmond Seward, 179–98. London: Constable, 1991.

Docker, Norah. *Norah: The Autobiography of Lady Docker*. London: W. H. Allen, 1969.

Dodd, Philip. 'The Arts of Life: Crosland's Culture'. In *Crosland and New Labour*, edited by Dick Leonard, 167–77. Basingstoke: Macmillan in association with the Fabian Society, 1999.

Doherty, Joe. 'The Distribution and Concentration of Immigrants in London'. *Race Today*, no. 1 (December 1966): 227–32.

Donald, Diana. *The Age of Caricature: Satirical Prints in the Reign of George III*. New Haven and London: Yale University Press, 1996.

Donnelly, Mark. *Sixties Britain: Culture, Society, and Politics*. Harlow: Longman, 2005.

Douglas-Home, Robin. *The Faint Aroma of Performing Seals*. London: Leslie Frewin, 1969.

Drew, Linzi. *Try Everything Once – Except Incest & Morris Dancing*. London: Blake, 1993.

Driberg, Tom. *Guy Burgess: A Portrait with Background*. London: Weidenfeld & Nicolson, 1956.

Driver, Felix, and David Gilbert. 'Heart of Empire? Landscape, Space and Performance in Imperial London'. *Environment and Planning D: Society and Space* 16 (1998): 11–28.

Durkheim, Émile. *Le suicide: Étude de sociologie*. Paris: Alcan, 1897.

Dyer, Richard. 'White'. *Screen* 29, no. 4 (1988): 44–64.

Dyos, H. J. 'The Growth of a Pre-Victorian Suburb: South London, 1580–1836'. *Town Planning Review* 25, no. 1 (April 1954): 59–78.

East, W. Norwood. *Medical Aspects of Crime*. London: J. & A. Churchill, 1936.

———. *Society and the Criminal*. London: HMSO, 1949.

Eddowes, John. *The Two Killers of Rillington Place*. London: Little, Brown, 1994.

Edge, Simon. 'Peter Wildeblood: Hero Without Applause'. *Soundings*, no. 3 (Summer 1996): 175–84.

Edgecombe, John. *Black Scandal*. London: Westworld International, 2002.

Edgerton, Robert. *Mau Mau: An African Crucible*. New York: Free Press, 1989.

Edward, Duke of Windsor. *A King's Story: The Memoirs of H.R.H. the Duke of Windsor*. London: Prion, 1998.

Edwards, Bronwen. 'Shaping the Fashion City: Master Plans and Pipe Dreams in the Post-War West End of London'. In *Fashion's World Cities*, edited by Christopher Breward and David Gilbert, 159–73. Oxford: Berg, 2006.

Edwards, Jimmy. *Six of the Best*. London: Robson, 1984.

Ehrman, Edwina. 'Broken Traditions'. In *The London Look: Fashion from Street to Catwalk*, edited by Christopher Breward, Edwina Ehrman, and Caroline Evans, 97–116. New Haven and London: Yale University Press in association with the Museum of London, 2004.

———. 'The Spirit of English Style: Hardy Amies, Royal Dressmaker and International Businessman'. In *The Englishness of English Dress*, edited by Christopher Breward, Becky Conekin, and Caroline Cox, 133–45. Oxford: Berg, 2002.

Ellis, Edward. *The University College of Wales Aberystwyth, 1872–1972*. Cardiff: University of Wales Press, 1972.

Ellis, Georgie, with Rod Taylor. *Ruth Ellis, My Mother: A Daughter's Memoir of the Last Woman To Be Hanged*. London: Smith Gryphon, 1995.

Ellis, Henry Havelock. *Psychology of Sex: A Manual for Students*. London: Heinemann, 1933.

Ellis, Henry Havelock, and John Addington Symonds. *Sexual Inversion*, vol. 1. London: Wilson and Macmillan, 1897.

Emsley, Clive. 'Sergeant Goddard: The Story of a Rotten Apple, or a Diseased Orchard?' In *Crime and Culture: An Historical Perspective*, edited by Amy Gilman Srebnick and René Lévy, 85–104. Aldershot: Ashgate, 2005.

Engel, Matthew. *Tickle the Public: One Hundred Years of the Popular Press*. London: Gollancz, 1996.

Epstein, Brian. *A Cellarful of Noise*. London: New English Library, 1965.

Erber, Nancy, and George Robb. 'Introduction'. In *Disorder in the Court: Trials and Sexual Conflict at the Turn of the Century*, edited by George Robb and Nancy Erber, 1–11. Basingstoke: Macmillan, 1999.

Evans, Caroline. 'Post-War Poses: 1955–75'. In *The London Look: Fashion from Street to Catwalk*, edited by Christopher Breward, Edwina Ehrman, and Caroline Evans, 117–37. New Haven and London: Yale University Press in Association with the Museum of London, 2004.

Fabian, Robert. *Fabian of the Yard: An Intimate Record by Ex-Superintendent Robert Fabian*. London: Naldrett Press, 1950.

———. *London After Dark: An Intimate Record of Night Life in London, and a Selection of Crime Stories from the Case Book of Ex-Superintendent Robert Fabian*. London: Naldrett Press, 1954.

Fairlie, Henry. *The Life of Politics*. London: Methuen, 1968.

Faris, Robert, and H. Warren Dunham. *Mental Disorders in Urban Areas: An Ecological Study of Schizophrenia and Other Psychoses*. Chicago: University of Chicago Press, 1939.

Farran, Denise. *The Trial of Ruth Ellis: A Descriptive Analysis*. Manchester: Sociology Department, University of Manchester, 1988.

Farson, Daniel. 'Muriel Belcher – Queen of Clubs'. In *Artists of the Colony Room Club: A Tribute to Muriel Belcher; November 11–December 4 1982*, unpaginated. London: Michael Parkin Fine Art, 1982.

———. *Never a Normal Man*. London: HarperCollins, 1997.

———. *Soho in the Fifties*. London: Michael Joseph, 1987.

Faulks, Sebastian. *The Fatal Englishman: Three Short Lives*. London: Hutchinson, 1996.

Feldman, David, and Gareth Stedman Jones, eds. *Metropolis – London: Histories and Representations since 1800*. London: Routledge, 1989.

Ferris, Paul. *Sex and the British: A Twentieth Century History*. London: Michael Joseph, 1993.

Fiber, Sally. *The Fitzroy: The Autobiography of a London Tavern; Sally Fiber's Story of the Fitzroy as Told to Clive Powell-Williams*. Lewes: Temple House, 1995.

Fielding, Daphne. *Emerald and Nancy: Lady Cunard and her Daughter*. London: Eyre & Spottiswoode, 1968.

Fisher, Geoffrey. *'I Here Present Unto You': Six Addresses Interpreting the Coronation of Her Majesty Queen Elizabeth II, Given on Various Occasions by His Grace the Archbishop of Canterbury*. London: S.P.C.K., 1953.

Fisher, Nigel. *Iain Macleod*. London: Andre Deutsch, 1973.

Fishgall, Gary. *Against Type: The Biography of Burt Lancaster*. New York and London: Scribner, 1995.

Fitzgibbon, Constantine. *The Life of Dylan Thomas*. London: J. M. Dent, 1965.

Flax, Jane. 'Postmodernism and Gender Relations in Feminist Theory'. *Signs* 12, no. 4 (Summer 1987): 621–43.

Fleming, Tom, ed. *Voices Out of the Air: The Royal Christmas Broadcasts 1932–1981*. London: Heinemann, 1981.

Flory, Joan, and Damien Walne. *Diana Dors: Only a Whisper Away*. Wheathampstead: Lennard, 1987.

Fodor, Eugene, ed. *The Men's Guide to Europe*. London: Newman Neame, 1955.

———, ed. *The Men's Guide to Europe*. London: Newman Neame, 1957.

———, ed. *Woman's Guide to Europe*. Continental edition. New York: Fodor's Modern Guides, 1953.

Foley, Donald. *Controlling London's Growth: Planning the Great Wen, 1940–1960*. Berkeley and Los Angeles: University of California Press, 1963.

Foner, Nancy. *Jamaica Farewell: Jamaican Migrants in London*. London: Routledge & Kegan Paul, 1979.

Foot, Michael. *Aneurin Bevan: A Biography Volume 2, 1945–1960*. London: Davis-Poynter, 1973.

Forshaw, J. H., and Patrick Abercrombie. *County of London Plan*. London: Macmillan, 1943.

Foucault, Michel. *The History of Sexuality Volume 1: An Introduction*, translated by Robert Hurley. New York: Pantheon, 1978.

Francis, Martin. 'The Labour Party: Modernisation and the Politics of Restraint'. In *Moments of Modernity: Reconstructing Britain 1945–1964*, edited by Becky Conekin, Frank Mort, and Chris Waters, 152–70. London: Rivers Oram, 1999.

———. 'Tears, Tantrums, and Bared Teeth: The Emotional Economy of Three Conservative Prime Ministers, 1951–63'. *Journal of British Studies* 41, no. 3 (July 2002): 354–87.

French, Robert. *Camping by a Billabong*. Sydney: Black Wattle Press, 1993.

Friedan, Betty. *The Feminine Mystique*. London: Penguin, 1965.

Frisby, David. *Fragments of Modernity: Theories of Modernity in the Work of Simmel, Kracauer and Benjamin*. Cambridge: Polity, 1985.

Frost, Conrad. *Coronation, June 2 1953*. London: Arthur Barker, 1978.

Frost, David. *An Autobiography, David Frost Part One: From Congregations to Audiences*. London: HarperCollins, 1993.

Frost, David, and Christopher Booker. 'This is Your Life, Henry Brooke'. In *That Was The Week That Was*, edited by David Frost and Ned Sherrin, 113–14. London: W. H. Allen, 1963.

Fryer, Jonathan. *Soho in the Fifties and Sixties*. London: National Portrait Gallery, 1998.

Furneaux, Rupert. *Michael John Davies*, crime documentaries no. 4. London: Stevens, 1962.

———. *The Two Stranglers of Rillington Place*. London: Panther: 1994.

Fussell, Paul. *Abroad: British Literary Traveling Between the Wars*. New York and Oxford: Oxford University Press, 1980.

Fyvel, T. R. *The Insecure Offenders: Rebellious Youth in the Welfare State*. London: Chatto & Windus, 1961.

Galsworthy, John. *The Forsyte Saga, Book II: In Chancery*. Oxford: Oxford University Press, 1995.

Gänzl, Kurt. *Lydia Thompson, Queen of Burlesque*. London: Routledge, 2002.

Garfitt, Alan. *The Book for Police*, vol. 1. London: Caxton, 1958.

Garland, Rodney [pseud. Adam Hegedüs]. *The Heart in Exile*. London: Four Square Books, 1961.

Gathorne-Hardy, Jonathan. *Alfred C. Kinsey: Sex and the Measure of Things; A Biography*. London: Chatto & Windus, 1998.

Gavaghan, Helen. *Something New Under the Sun: Satellites and the Beginning of the Space Age*. New York: Copernicus, 1998.

Geddes, Patrick. *Cities in Evolution: An Introduction to the Town Planning Movement and to the Study of Civics*. London: Williams & Norgate, 1915.

Geiger, Till. 'Reconstruction and the Beginnings of European Integration'. In *Western Europe: Economic and Social Change since 1945*, edited by Max-Stephan Schulze, 23–41. London: Longman, 1999.

Geller, Debbie. *The Brian Epstein Story*. London: Faber & Faber, 2000.

Gibbs, Philip. *Life's Adventure*. London: Angus and Robertson, 1957.

———. *The New Elizabethans*. London: Hutchinson, 1953.

Gilbert, David. 'Heart of Empire? Landscape, Space and Performance in Imperial London'. *Environment and Planning D. Society and Space* 16 (1998): 11–28.

———. 'London in All its Glory – Or How to Enjoy London: Guidebook Representations of Imperial London'. *Journal of Historical Geography* 25, no. 3 (1999): 279–97.

Glass, Ruth. 'Aspects of Change'. In *London: Aspects of Change*, edited by Centre for Urban Studies. London: MacGibbon and Kee, 1964.

———. *Newcomers: The West Indians in London*. London: Centre for Urban Studies and George Allen & Unwin, 1960.

Glenn, Susan. *Female Spectacle: The Theatrical Roots of Modern Feminism*. Cambridge, MA: Harvard University Press, 2000.

Glicco, Jack. *Madness After Midnight*. London: Elek Books, 1952.

Glover, Edward. *The Psychopathology of Prostitution*, 2nd edn. London: Institute for the Study and Treatment of Delinquency, 1957.

———. *The Roots of Crime*. London: Imago, 1960.

Goldsmith, Annabel. *Annabel: An Unconventional Life; The Memoirs of Lady Annabel Goldsmith*. London: Weidenfeld & Nicolson, 2004.

Goldsmith, Margaret. *Soho Square*. London: Sampson Low, Marston & Co., 1947.

Goldthorpe, John, David Lockwood, Frank Bechhofer, and Jennifer Platt. *The Affluent Worker in the Class Structure*. London: Cambridge University Press, 1969.

Gorer, Geoffrey. *Exploring English Character*. London: Cresset Press, 1955.

Gosling, John, and Douglas Warner. *The Shame of a City: An Inquiry into the Vice of London*. London: W. H. Allen, 1960.

Gottfried, Martin. *Nobody's Fool: The Lives of Danny Kaye*. New York and London: Simon & Schuster, 1994.

Gould, Tony. *Inside Outsider: The Life and Times of Colin MacInnes*. London: Allison & Busby, 1993.

Grade, Lew. *Still Dancing: My Story*. London: Collins, 1987.

Graham, Stephen. *Twice Round the London Clock and More London Nights*. London: Ernest Benn, 1933.

Graves, Charles. *Champagne and Chandeliers: The Story of the Café de Paris*. London: Odhams Press, 1958.

Green, Jonathon. *All Dressed Up: The Sixties and the Counterculture*. London: Pimlico, 1999.

Green, Shirley. *Rachman*. London: Hamlyn Paperbacks, 1981.

Greeno, Edward. *War on the Underworld*. London: Brown, Watson Ltd, 1961.

Grigg, John, and Ian Gilmour. *The Case of Timothy Evans: An Appeal to Reason*. London: Spectator, 1956.

Gruffudd, Pyrs. ' "Uncivil Engineering": Nature, Nationalism and Hydro-Electrics in North Wales'. In *Water, Engineering and Landscape: Water Control and Landscape Transformation in the Modern Period*, edited by Denis Cosgrove and Geoff Petts, 159–73. London: Belhaven Press, 1990.

Grünhut, M. 'Statistics in Criminology'. *Journal of the Royal Statistical Society*, series A (General) 114, no. 2 (1951): 139–62.

Grushow, Ira. 'Guidebooks'. In *Literature of Travel and Exploration: An Encyclopedia*, vol. 2, edited by Jennifer Speake, 519–23. New York and London: Fitzroy Dearborn, 2003.

Haigh, John. *The Trial of John George Haigh – The Acid Bath Murderer*, ed. Lord Dunboyne. London: William Hodge, 1953.

Hailsham, Lord. *The Door Wherein I Went*. London: Collins, 1975.

———. *A Sparrow's Flight: The Memoirs of Lord Hailsham of Marylebone*. London: Collins, 1990.

Halasz, Piri. *A Memoir of Creativity: Abstract Painting, Politics and the Media, 1956–2008*. Bloomington, IN: iUniverse, 2009.

Hall, Lesley. *Sex, Gender and Social Change in Britain since 1880*. Basingstoke: Macmillan, 2000.

Hall, Peter. *London 2001*. London: Unwin Hyman, 1989.

Hall, Stuart. 'Reformism and the Legislation of Consent'. In *Permissiveness and Control: The Fate of the Sixties Legislation*, edited by National Deviancy Conference, 1–43. London: Macmillan, 1980.

Hall, Stuart, and Tony Jefferson, eds. *Resistance through Rituals: Youth Sub-Cultures in Post-War Britain*. London: Hutchinson, 1976.

Hall, Stuart, and Paddy Whannel. *The Popular Arts*. London: Hutchinson Educational, 1964.

Hall Carpenter Archives, and Gay Men's Oral History Group. *Walking After Midnight: Gay Men's Life Stories*. London and New York: Routledge, 1989.

Hallett, Mark. *The Spectacle of Difference: Graphic Satire in the Age of Hogarth*. New Haven and London: Yale University Press, 1999.

Hamnett, Nina. *Is She a Lady?* London: Allan Wingate, 1955.

Hamrick, S. J. *Deceiving the Deceivers: Kim Philby, Donald Maclean and Guy Burgess*. New Haven and London: Yale University Press, 2004.

Hancock, Robert. *Ruth Ellis*. London: Arthur Barker, 1963.

Hansen, Peter. 'Coronation Everest: The Empire and Commonwealth in the "Second Elizabethan Age"'. In *British Culture and the End of Empire*, edited by Stuart Ward, 57–72. Manchester: Manchester University Press, 2001.

Harley, J. B. 'Maps, Knowledge and Power'. In *The Iconography of Landscape: Essays on the Symbolic Representation, Design and Use of Past Environments*, edited by Denis Cosgrove and Stephen Daniels, 277–312. Cambridge: Cambridge University Press, 1988.

Harper, Sue. *Women in British Cinema: Mad, Bad and Dangerous to Know*. London and New York: Continuum, 2000.

Harris, José. *William Beveridge: A Biography*. Oxford: Clarendon Press, 1997.

Harris, Kenneth. *The Queen*. London: Weidenfeld & Nicolson, 1994.

Harris, Ruth. *Murders and Madness: Medicine, Law and Society in the Fin de Siècle*. Oxford: Clarendon Press, 1989.

Harrison, Fred. *Brady and Hindley: The Genesis of the Moors Murders*. Bath: Ashgrove, 1986.

Harry, Lillian. *Corner House Girls*. London: Orion, 2000.

Hart, H. L. A. *Law, Liberty and Morality*. London: Oxford University Press, 1963.

Harvey, David. *The Urban Experience*. Oxford: Blackwell, 1989.

Harvey, Ian. *To Fall like Lucifer*. London: Sidgwick & Jackson, 1971.

Harvey, John. *Men in Black*. London: Reaktion, 1995.

Headington, Christopher. *Peter Pears: A Biography*. London: Faber & Faber, 1992.

Heald, Tim. *The Duke: A Portrait of Prince Philip*. London: Hodder & Stoughton, 1991.

Heath, Neville. *The Trial of Neville George Clevely Heath*, edited by MacDonald Critchley. London: William Hodge, 1951.

Hebdige, Dick. *Subculture: The Meaning of Style*. London: Methuen, 1979.

Hennessy, Peter. *The Great and the Good: An Inquiry into the British Establishment*. London: Policy Studies Institute, 1986.

———. *Having It So Good: Britain in the Fifties*. London: Allen Lane, 2006.

———. *The Secret State: Whitehall and the Cold War*. London: Allen Lane, 2002.

Hepworth, Mike, and Bryan Turner. *Confession: Studies in Deviance and Religion*. London: Routledge & Kegan Paul, 1982.

Hewison, Robert. *The Heritage Industry: Britain in a Climate of Decline*. London: Methuen, 1987.

———. *Under Siege: Literary Life in London, 1939–1945*. London: Weidenfeld & Nicolson, 1977.

Higgins, Patrick. *Heterosexual Dictatorship: Male Homosexuality in Post-War Britain*. London: Fourth Estate, 1996.

Hill, Clifford. *Black and White in Harmony: The Drama of West Indians in the Big City, from a London Minister's Notebook*. London: Hodder & Stoughton, 1958.

Hill, Paull. *Portrait of a Sadist*. London: Neville Spearman, 1960.

Hill, William. *Boss of Britain's Underworld*. London: Naldrett Press, 1955.

Hobsbawm, Eric. *Age of Extremes: The Short Twentieth Century, 1914–1991*. London: Abacus, 1995.

Hogan, Michael. *The Marshall Plan: America, Britain, and the Reconstruction of Western Europe, 1947–1952*. Cambridge: Cambridge University Press, 1987.

Hoggart, Richard. *The Uses of Literacy: Aspects of Working-Class Life, with Special Reference to Publications and Entertainments*. London: Chatto & Windus, 1957.

Home Office. *The Home Office 1782–1982: To Commemorate the Bicentenary of the Home Office*. London: Home Office, 1982.

Honeyman, Katrina. 'Montague Burton Ltd.: The Creators of Well-Dressed Men'. In *Leeds City Business 1893–1993: Essays Marking the Centenary of the Incorporation*, edited by John Chartres and Katrina Honeyman, 186–216. Leeds: Leeds University Press, 1993.

Hooker, Denise. *Nina Hamnett: Queen of Bohemia*. London: Constable, 1986.

Hopkins, Harry. *The New Look: A Social History of the Forties and Fifties in Britain*. London: Secker & Warburg, 1963.

Hopkins, Robert. *The Lure of London*. London: Cecil Palmer, 1929.

Horne, Alistair. *Macmillan, 1957–1986: Volume II of the Official Biography*. London: Macmillan, 1988.

Horwitz, Julius. *Can I Get There by Candlelight*. London: Panther, 1971.

Houlbrook, Matt. 'For Whose Convenience? Gay Guides, Cognitive Maps and the Construction of Homosexual London, 1917–67'. In *Identities in Space: Contested Terrains in the Western City since 1850*, edited by Simon Gunn and Robert Morris, 165–86. Aldershot: Ashgate, 2001.

———. 'The Private World of Public Urinals: London, 1918–57'. *London Journal* 25, no. 1 (2000): 52–70.

———. *Queer London: Perils and Pleasures in the Sexual Metropolis, 1918–1957*. Chicago and London: University of Chicago Press, 2005.

———. 'Soldier Heroes and Rent Boys: Homosex, Masculinities, and Britishness in the Brigade of Guards, c.1900–1960'. *Journal of British Studies* 42, no. 3 (2003): 351–88.

Houlbrook, Matt, and Chris Waters. '*The Heart in Exile*: Detachment and Desire in 1950s London'. *History Workshop Journal*, no. 62 (2006): 142–65.

Hounsome, Robert. *The Very Nearly Man: An Autobiography*. Leicester: Matador, 2006.

Howard, Anthony. *Crossman: The Pursuit of Power*. London: Jonathan Cape, 1990.

Humphreys, Laud. *Tearoom Trade: A Study of Homosexual Encounters in Public Places*. London: Duckworth, 1970.

Humphries, Steve, and John Taylor. *The Making of Modern London 1945–1985*. London: Sidgwick & Jackson, 1986.

Hunter, Leslie. *The Road to Brighton Pier*. London: Arthur Baker, 1959.

Hutchinson, George. *The Last Edwardian at No. 10: An Impression of Harold Macmillan*. London: Quartet, 1980.

Hutchinson, Harold. *Visitor's London*. London: London Transport Executive, 1954.

Hyde, H. Montgomery. *Londonderry House and its Pictures*. London: Cresset Press, 1937.

———. *The Londonderrys: A Family Portrait*. London: Hamish Hamilton, 1979.

———. *The Other Love: An Historical and Contemporary Survey of Homosexuality in Britain*. London: Heinemann, 1970.

———. *A Tangled Web: Sex Scandals in British Politics and Society*. London: Constable, 1986.

Ignatieff, Michael. *Isaiah Berlin: A Life*. London: Vintage, 2000.

Ingrams, Richard, ed. *The Life and Times of Private Eye, 1961–1971*. Harmondsworth: Penguin, 1971.

———. *Muggeridge: The Biography*. London: HarperCollins, 1995.

Inwood, Stephen. *A History of London*. London, Macmillan, 1998.

Irving, Clive, Ron Hall, and Jeremy Wallington. *Scandal '63: A Study of the Profumo Affair*. London: Heinemann, 1963.

Israel, Kali. 'French Vices and English Liberties: Gender, Class and Narrative Competition in a Late Victorian Sexual Scandal'. *Social History* 22, no. 1 (January 1997): 1–26.

Ivanov, Yevgeny, with Gennady Sokolov. *The Naked Spy*. London: Blake, 1992.

Ives, George. *The Continued Extension of the Criminal Law*. London: J. E. Francis, 1922.

Jackson, Kevin, ed. *The Humphrey Jennings Film Reader*. Manchester: Carcanet, 1993.

Jackson, Stanley. *An Indiscreet Guide to Soho*. London: Muse Arts, 1946.

James, Paul. *Margaret: A Woman of Conflict*. London: Sidgwick & Jackson, 1990.

James, Robert Rhodes, ed. *'Chips': The Diaries of Sir Henry Channon*. London: Weidenfeld & Nicolson, 1967.

James, Thomas. *Prostitution and the Law*. London: William Heinemann, 1951.

Jarrett, Lucinda. *Stripping in Time: A History of Erotic Dancing*. London: Pandora, 1997.

Jarvis, Mark. *Conservative Governments, Morality and Social Change in Affluent Britain, 1957–64*. Manchester: Manchester University Press, 2005.

Jefferson, Tony. 'Cultural Responses of the Teds: The Defence of Space'. In *Resistance Through Rituals: Youth Sub-Cultures in Post-War Britain*, edited by Stuart Hall and Tony Jefferson, 81–6. London: Hutchinson, 1976.

Jeffery-Poulter, Stephen. *Peers, Queers, and Commons: The Struggle for Gay Law Reform from 1950 to the Present*. London: Routledge, 1991.

Jenkins, Roy. *The Labour Case*. Harmondsworth: Penguin, 1959.

———. *A Life at the Centre*. London: Macmillan, 1991.

Jenkins, Simon. *Landlords to London: The Story of a Capital and its Growth*. London: Constable, 1975.

Jenkins, Tudor. *The Londoner*. London: MacGibbon and Kee, 1962.

Jennings, Mary-Lou, ed. *Humphrey Jennings: Film-Maker, Painter, Poet*. London: British Film Institute in Association with Riverside Studios, 1982.

Jensen, Peter. *From the Wireless to the Web: The Evolution of Telecommunication 1901–2001*. Sydney: University of New South Wales Press, 2000.

Jephcott, Pearl. *A Troubled Area: Notes on Notting Hill*. London: Faber & Faber, 1964.

Jesse, F. Tennyson, ed. *Trials of Timothy John Evans and John Reginald Halliday Christie*. London: William Hodge, 1957.

Johnson, Katherine. 'Apart from "Look Back in Anger", What Else Was Worrying the Lord Chamberlain's Office in 1956'. In *British Theatre in the 1950s*, edited by Dominic Shellard, 116–35. Sheffield: Sheffield Academic Press, 2000.

Johnston, John. *The Lord Chamberlain's Blue Pencil*. London: Hodder & Stoughton, 1990.

Jones, James. *Alfred C. Kinsey: A Public/Private Life*. New York: W. W. Norton, 1997.

Jones, Walter. *My Own Case*. Maidstone: Angley Books, 1966.

Joyce, Patrick. *The Rule of Freedom: Liberalism and the Modern City*. London: Verso, 2003.

Judt, Tony. *Postwar: A History of Europe since 1945*. London: Pimlico, 2007.

Kaplan, Morris. '"Did My Lord Gomorrah Smile?": Homosexuality, Class, and Prostitution in the Cleveland Street Affair'. In *Disorder in the Court: Trials and Sexual Conflict at the Turn of the Century*, edited by Nancy Erber and George Robb, 78–99. Basingstoke: Macmillan, 1999.

———. *Sodom on the Thames: Sex, Love, and Scandal in Wilde Times*. Ithaca, NY: Cornell University Press, 2005.

Kavaler, Lucy. *The Astors: A Family Chronicle*. London: Harrap, 1966.

Keays, Sara. *A Question of Judgement*. London: Quintessential, 1985.

Keeler, Christine. *Scandal*. New York: St Martin's Press, 1989.

———. *Sex Scandals*. London: Xanadu, 1985.

Keeler, Christine, with Douglas Thompson. *The Truth at Last: My Story*. London: Sidgwick & Jackson, 2001.

Keir, David, and Bryan Morgan, eds. *Golden Milestone: 50 Years of the AA*. London: Automobile Association, 1955.

Kemsley Newspapers. *The Kemsley Manual of Journalism*. London: Cassell, 1950.

Kennedy, Ludovic. *One Man's Meat*. London: Longmans, Green & Co., 1953.

———. *Ten Rillington Place*. London: Gollancz, 1961.

———. *The Trial of Stephen Ward*. New York: Simon & Schuster, 1965.

Kent, Susan Kingsley. *Sex and Suffrage in Britain, 1860–1914*. Princeton, NJ: Princeton University Press, 1987.

King, Stella. *Princess Marina: Her Life and Times*. London: Cassell, 1969.

Kinsey, Alfred, Wardell Pomeroy, Clyde Martin, and Paul Gebhard. *Sexual Behavior in the Human Female*. Philadelphia: W. B. Saunders, 1953.

Kinsman, Gary. *The Regulation of Desire: Sexuality in Canada*. Montreal: Black Rose Books, 1987.

Knightley, Phillip, and Caroline Kennedy. *An Affair of State: The Profumo Case and the Framing of Stephezn Ward*. London: Jonathan Cape, 1987.

Koestler, Arthur. 'Introduction'. In *Suicide of a Nation? An Enquiry into the State of Britain Today*, edited by Arthur Koestler, 7–14. London: Hutchinson, 1963.

Kuhn, Annette. *Family Secrets: Acts of Memory and Imagination*. London: Verso, 2002.

Kynaston, David. *Austerity Britain 1945–51*. London: Bloomsbury, 2007.

La Bern, Arthur. *Haigh: The Mind of a Murderer . . . Psychiatric Analysis by Nöel C. Browne*. London: W. H. Allen, 1973.

Lacey, Robert. *Majesty: Elizabeth II and the House of Windsor*. London: Hutchinson, 1977.

———. *Royal: Her Majesty Queen Elizabeth II*. London: Little, Brown, 2002.

Ladwick, Marty. *Soho Street Girl*. London: Kaye Publications, 1954.

Lal, Barbara Ballis. 'The "Chicago School" of American Sociology, Symbolic Interactionism, and Race Relations Theory'. In *Theories of Race and Ethnic Relations*, edited by John Rex and David Mason, 280–98. Cambridge: Cambridge University Press, 1986.

Lambert, Sam, ed. *London Night and Day: A Guide to Where the Other Books Don't Take You*, 6th edn. London: Architectural Press, 1958.

Lamond, Gaston. *Soho Lady*. Stone: Curzon Publishing, 1948.

La Rue, Danny, with Howard Elson. *From Drags to Riches: My Autobiography*. London: Viking, 1987.

Lee, Trevor. *Race and Residence: The Concentration and Dispersal of Immigrants in London*. Oxford: Clarendon Press, 1977.

Lees-Milne, James. *Diaries, 1946–1949: Caves of Ice and Midway on the Waves*. London: John Murray, 1996.

———. *Harold Nicolson: A Biography, Volume 2: 1930–1968*. London: Chatto & Windus, London, 1981.

———. *A Mingled Measure: Diaries 1953–1972*. London: John Murray, 1994.

———. 'The Second World War'. In *Brooks's: A Social History*, edited by Philip Ziegler and Desmond Seward, 93–102. London: Constable, 1991.

Lehmann, John. *In the Purely Pagan Sense*. London: GMP, 1985.

Levin, Bernard. *The Pendulum Years: Britain and the Sixties*. London: Jonathan Cape, 1970.

Levitt, Morton, and Michael Levitt. *A Tissue of Lies: Nixon vs Hiss*. New York: McGraw-Hill, 1979.

Lewis, Chaim. *A Soho Address*. London: Gollancz, 1965.

Lewis, Peter. *The Fifties: Portrait of an Age*. London: Herbert Press, 1989.

Lewis, Roger. *The Life and Death of Peter Sellers*. London: Century, 1994.

Little, Kenneth. *Negroes in Britain: A Study of Racial Relations in English Society*. London: Kegan Paul, Trench Trubner & Co., 1947.

Lodge, T. S. 'The Founding of the Home Office Research Unit'. In *Crime, Criminology and Public Policy: Essays in Honour of Sir Leon Radzinowicz*, edited by Roger Hood, 11–24. London: Heinemann, 1974.

London School of Economics and Political Science. *The New Survey of London Life and Labour*, vol. 1, *Forty Years of Change*. London: P. S. King, 1930.

———. *The New Survey of London Life and Labour*, vol. 6, *Survey of Social Conditions (2) The Western Area (Text)*. London: P. S. King, 1934.

Lycett, Andrew. *Ian Fleming*. London: Weidenfeld & Nicolson, 1995.

Mabell, Countess of Airlie. *Thatched with Gold: The Memoirs of Mabell Countess of Airlie*, edited by Jennifer Ellis. London: Hutchinson, 1962.

MacCarthy, Fiona. *Last Curtsey: The End of the Debutantes*. London: Faber & Faber, 2006.

McDonald, Iverach. *The History of The Times, Volume V: Struggles in War and Peace 1939–1966*. London: Times Books, 1984.

MacInnes, Colin. *Absolute Beginners*. Harmondsworth: Penguin, 1986.

———. ' "See You At Mabel's" '. *Encounter* 8 (March 1957): 21–6.

Mackenzie, Gordon. *Marylebone: Great City North of Oxford Street*. London: Macmillan, 1972.

McKibbin, Ross. *Classes and Cultures: England 1918–1951*. Oxford: Oxford University Press, 1998.

———. 'Mass-Observation in the Mall'. In *After Diana: Irreverent Elegies*, edited by Mandy Merck, 15–24. London: Verso, 1998.

McLaren, Angus. *The Trials of Masculinity: Policing Sexual Boundaries, 1870–1930*. Chicago: University of Chicago Press, 1997.

Maclaren-Ross, Julian. *Memoirs of the Forties*. Harmondsworth: Penguin, 1984.

Macmillan, Harold. *At the End of the Day, 1961–1963*. London: Macmillan, 1973.

———. *Riding the Storm, 1956–1959*. London: Macmillan, 1971.

———. *Tides of Fortune, 1945–1955*. London: Macmillan, 1969.

Maloba, Wunyabari. *Mau Mau and Kenya: An Analysis of a Peasant Revolt*. Bloomington: Indiana University Press, 1993.

Mander, Raymond, and Joe Mitcheson. *The Theatres of London*. London: Rupert Hart-Davis, 1961.

Mandler, Peter. *The Fall and Rise of the Stately Home*. New Haven and London: Yale University Press, 1997.

———. 'New Towns for Old: The Fate of the Town Centre'. In *Moments of Modernity: Reconstructing Britain 1945–64*, edited by Becky Conekin, Frank Mort, and Chris Waters, 208–27. London: Rivers Oram, 1999.

Mandler, Peter, and Susan Pedersen. 'The British Intelligentsia after the Victorians'. In *After the Victorians: Private Conscience and Public Duty in Modern Britain; Essays in Memory of John Clive*, edited by Susan Pedersen and Peter Mandler, 1–28. London: Routledge, 1994.

Manning, Frank. *The Celebration of Society: Perspectives on Contemporary Cultural Performance*. Bowling Green, OH: Bowling Green State University Popular Press, 1983.

Margaret, Duchess of Argyll. *Forget Not: The Autobiography of Margaret, Duchess of Argyll*. London: W. H. Allen, 1975.

Marks, Laurence. *Ruth Ellis: A Case of Diminished Responsibility?* Harmondsworth: Penguin, 1990.

Marnham, Patrick. *The Private Eye Story: The First 21 Years*. London: Andre Deutsch, 1982.

Marriott, Oliver. *The Property Boom*. London: Hamish Hamilton, 1967.

Marsden, Michael, and Ray Browne, eds. *The Culture of Celebrations*. Bowling Green, OH: Bowling Green State University Popular Press, 1994.

Marshall, Francis. *The London Week-End Book*. London: Seeley Service, 1953.

Martin, A. W. *Robert Menzies: A Life*, vol. 2, *1944–1978*. Carlton South, Vic.: Melbourne University Press, 1999.

Martin, Kingsley. *The Crown and the Establishment*. London: Hutchinson, 1962.

Marwick, Arthur. *British Society since 1945*. London: Allen Lane, 1982.

———. *The Sixties: Cultural Revolution in Britain, France, Italy, and the United States c.1958–c.1974*. Oxford: Oxford University Press, 1998.

Masters, Brian. *Great Hostesses*. London: Constable, 1982.

———. *Killing for Company: The Case of Dennis Nilsen*. London: Jonathan Cape, 1985.

Matless, David. ' "Appropriate Geography": Patrick Abercrombie and the Energy of the World'. *Journal of Design History* 6, no. 3 (1993): 167–78.

———. *Landscape and Englishness*. London: Reaktion, 1998.

Maxwell, Sir Alexander. *The Work of the Home Office: A Talk to the Staff by Sir Alexander Maxwell*. London: Home Office, 1944.

Maxwell Fyfe, David. *Political Adventure: The Memoirs of the Earl of Kilmuir*. London: Weidenfeld & Nicolson, 1964.

———. *Virtue, the State and the Family*. N.p.: Home Office Library collection, 1954.

May, Larry. *Aggression and Crimes Against Peace*. Cambridge: Cambridge University Press, 2008.

Melly, George. 'Introduction'. In Daniel Farson, *Soho in the Fifties*, xi–xv. London: Michael Joseph, 1987.

Metcalfe, John. *London A to Z*. London: Andre Deutsch, 1953.

Miller Peter, and Nikolas Rose, eds. *The Power of Psychiatry*. Cambridge: Polity, 1986.

Milward, Alan. *The European Rescue of the Nation-State*. London: Routledge, 1992.

Moran, Leslie. *Homosexual(ity) of Law*. London: Routledge, 1996.

Moran, Lord. *Winston Churchill: The Struggle for Survival 1940–1965*. London: Constable, 1966.

Moriarty, C. C. *Police Procedure and Administration*, 6th edn. London: Butterworth, 1955.

Morley, Sheridan. *John G: The Authorised Biography of John Gielgud*. London: Hodder & Stoughton, 2001.

Morris, William. *The Homeland Guide to London*. London: Homeland Association, 1947.

Morrison, Majbritt. *Jungle West 11*. London: Tandem Books, 1964.

Mort, Frank. *Cultures of Consumption: Masculinities and Social Space in Late Twentieth-Century Britain*. London: Routledge, 1996.

———. *Dangerous Sexualities: Medico-Moral Politics in England since 1830*, 2nd edn. London: Routledge, 2000.

————. 'Fantasies of Metropolitan Life: Planning London in the 1940s'. *Journal of British Studies* 42, no. 1 (January 2004): 120–51.

————. 'Mapping Sexual London: The Wolfenden Committee on Homosexual Offences and Prostitution 1954–57'. *New Formations*, no. 37 (Spring 1999): 92–113.

————. 'Scandalous Events: Metropolitan Culture and Moral Change in Post-Second World War London'. *Representations*, no. 93 (Winter 2006): 106–37.

————. 'Social and Symbolic Fathers and Sons in Postwar Britain'. *Journal of British Studies* 38, no. 3 (July 1999): 353–84.

————. 'Striptease, the Erotic Female Moving Body and Live Sexual Entertainment in Mid-Twentieth-Century London'. *Social History* 32, no. 1 (February 2007): 27–53.

Mort, Frank, and Lynda Nead. 'Introduction: Sexual Geographies'. *New Formations*, no. 37 (1999): 5–10.

Mort, Frank, and Miles Ogborn. 'Transforming Metropolitan London, 1750–1960'. *Journal of British Studies* 43, no. 1 (January 2004): 1–14.

Mort, Frank, and Peter Thompson. 'Retailing, Commercial Culture and Masculinity in 1950s Britain: The Case of Montague Burton, the "Tailor of Taste"'. *History Workshop Journal*, no. 38 (1994): 106–27.

Morton, H. V. *Ghosts of London*. London: Methuen, 1939.

————. *The Nights of London*. 3rd edn. London: Methuen, 1930.

————. *The Spell of London*. New York: Brentano's, 1926.

Moseley, Sydney. *The Night Haunts of London*. London: Stanley Paul, 1920.

Mosley, Nicholas. *Beyond the Pale: Sir Oswald Mosley and Family 1933–1980*. London: Secker & Warburg, 1983.

Mumford, Lewis. *The Culture of Cities*. London: Secker & Warburg, 1940.

————. *The Plan of the London County, etc.*, Rebuilding Britain series, no. 12. London: Faber & Faber, 1945.

Mungham, Geoff, and Geoff Pearson, eds. *Working Class Youth Culture*. London: Routledge & Kegan Paul, 1976.

Murger, Henri. *The Bohemians of the Latin Quarter*, translated by Ellen Marriage and John Selwyn. Philadelphia: University of Pennsylvania Press, 2004.

Murphy, Robert. *Realism and Tinsel: Cinema and Society in Britain 1939–1948*. London: Routledge, 1989.

————. 'Riff-Raff: British Cinema and the Underworld'. In *All Our Yesterdays: 90 Years of British Cinema*, edited by Charles Barr, 286–305. London: British Film Institute, 1986.

————. *Smash and Grab: Gangsters in the London Underworld 1920–60*. London: Faber & Faber: 1993.

Nahum, Baron. *Baron by Baron*. London: Frederick Muller, 1957.

Nairn, Ian. *Nairn's London*. Harmondsworth: Penguin, 1966.

Nairn, Tom. *The Enchanted Glass: Britain and its Monarchy*. London: Radius, 1988.

Nava, Mica. 'Modernity's Disavowal: Women, the City and the Department Store'.

In *Modern Times: Reflections on a Century of English Modernity*, edited by Mica Nava and Alan O'Shea, 38–76. London: Routledge, 1995.

———. *Visceral Cosmopolitanism: Gender, Culture and the Normalisation of Difference*. Oxford: Berg, 2007.

———. 'Wider Horizons and Modern Desire: The Contradictions of America and Racial Difference in London 1935–45'. *New Formations*, no. 37 (1999): 71–91.

Nead, Lynda. *The Female Nude: Art, Obscenity and Sexuality*. London: Routledge, 1992.

———. *Victorian Babylon: People, Streets and Images in Nineteenth-Century London*. New Haven and London: Yale University Press, 2000.

Neidpath, James. 'Brooks's Between the Wars'. In *Brooks's: A Social History*, edited by Philip Ziegler and Desmond Seward, 87–92. London: Constable, 1991.

Newsam, Frank. *The Home Office*. London: George Allen & Unwin, 1954.

Nicholson, Virginia. *Among the Bohemians: Experiments in Living 1900–1939*. London: Viking, 2002.

Nicolson, Harold. *Good Behaviour: Being a Study of Certain Types of Civility*. London: Constable, 1955.

———. *King George the Fifth: His Life and Reign*. London: Pan, 1967.

Nicolson, Nigel, ed. *Harold Nicolson: Diaries and Letters 1907–1964*. London: Weidenfeld & Nicolson, 2004.

Niven, David. *The Moon's A Balloon: Reminiscences*. London: Hodder & Stoughton, 1971.

Nixon, Sean. 'Apostles of Americanization? J. Walter Thompson Company Ltd, Advertising and Anglo-American Relations 1945–67'. *Contemporary British History* 22, no. 4 (2008): 477–99.

Norman, Frank. *Norman's London*. London: Secker & Warburg, 1969.

Norman, Frank, and Jeffrey Bernard. *Soho Night and Day*. Secker & Warburg, 1966.

Norton, Rictor. *Mother Clap's Molly House: The Gay Subculture in England, 1700–1830*. London: Gay Men's Press, 1992.

Nuttall, Jeremy. *Psychological Socialism: The Labour Party and Qualities of Mind and Character, 1931 to the Present*. Manchester: Manchester University Press, 2006.

O'Brien, Michael. *John F. Kennedy: A Biography*. New York: St Martin's Press, 2005.

Ogborn, Miles. *Spaces of Modernity: London's Geographies, 1680–1780*. New York and London: Guilford, 1998.

Otter, Christopher. 'Making Liberalism Durable: Vision and Civility in the Late Victorian City'. *Social History* 27, no.1 (January 2002): 1–15.

Paget, Reginald, and Sidney Silverman. *Hanged – And Innocent?* London: Gollancz, 1953.

Park, Robert, and Ezra Burgess. *The City*. Chicago: University of Chicago Press, 1925.

Parker, Derek, and Julie Parker. *The Natural History of the Chorus Girl*. Newton Abbot: David & Charles, 1975.

Parker, Eileen. *Step Aside for Royalty*. Maidstone: Bachman & Turner, 1982.

Parker, Peter. *Ackerley: A Life of J. R. Ackerley*. London: Constable, 1989.

Parker, Tony. *The Plough Boy*. London: Hutchinson, 1965.

Parkinson, Cecil. *Right at the Centre: An Autobiography*. London: Weidenfeld & Nicolson, 1992.

Parrott, E. V. *A Pocket History and Guide to Heathrow Airport, London*. Rickmansworth: EP Publications, 1977.

Patterson, Sheila. *Dark Strangers: A Sociological Study of the Absorption of a Recent West Indian Migrant Group in Brixton, South London*. London: Tavistock, 1963.

Payn, Graham, and Sheridan Morley, eds. *The Noël Coward Diaries*. London: Phoenix, 1998.

Pearson, John, and Graham Turner. *The Persuasion Industry*. London: Eyre & Spottiswoode, 1965.

Pendergast, Tom, and Sara Pendergast, eds. *International Dictionary of Films and Filmmakers 3: Actors and Actresses*. Detroit: St James Press, 1986.

Pentelow, Mike, and Marsha Rowe, *Characters of Fitzrovia*. London: Chatto & Windus, 2001.

Perkin, Harold. *The Rise of Professional Society: England since 1880*. London: Routledge, 1989.

Phillips, Charlie, and Mike Phillips. *Notting Hill in the Sixties*. London: Lawrence & Wishart, 1991.

Phillips, Conrad. *Murderer's Moon: Being Studies of Heath, Haigh, Christie & Chesney*. London: Arthur Barker, 1956.

Phillips, Mike, and Trevor Phillips. *Windrush: The Irresistible Rise of Multi-Racial Britain*. London: HarperCollins, 1998.

Phillips, Pearson. 'The New Look'. In *Age of Austerity*, edited by Michael Sissons and Philip French, 127–48. London: Hodder & Stoughton, 1963.

Pick, Daniel. *Svengali's Web: The Alien Enchanter in Modern Culture*. New Haven and London: Yale University Press, 2000.

Pierrepoint, Albert. *Executioner Pierrepoint*. London: Harrap, 1974.

Pilkington, Edward. *Beyond the Mother Country: West Indians and the Notting Hill White Riots*. London: Tauris, 1988.

Pimlott, Ben. *Harold Wilson*. London: HarperCollins, 1992.

———. *Hugh Dalton*. London: Jonathan Cape, 1985.

———. *The Queen: A Biography of Elizabeth II*. London: HarperCollins, 1996.

Platt, Jennifer. *Realities of Social Research: An Empirical Study of British Sociologists*. London: Chatto & Windus, 1976.

———. *Social Research in Bethnal Green: An Evaluation of the Work of the Institute of Community Studies*. London: Macmillan, 1971.

Platt, John. *London's Rock Routes*. London: Fourth Estate, 1985.

Pollock, Griselda. *Avant-Garde Gambits, 1883–93: Gender and the Colour of Art History*. London: Thames & Hudson, 1993.

Pomeroy, Wardell. *Dr. Kinsey and the Institute for Sex Research*. London: Thomas Nelson, 1972.

Poovey, Mary. *Making a Social Body: British Cultural Formation, 1830–1864*. Chicago: University of Chicago Press, 1995.

Pope-Hennessy, James. *Queen Mary 1867–1953*. London: George Allen & Unwin, 1959.

Port, Michael. *Imperial London: Civil Government Building in London 1850–1915*. New Haven and London: Yale University Press, 1995.

Porter, Roy. *London: A Social History*. London: Hamish Hamilton, 1994.

Powell, Michael. *A Life in Movies: An Autobiography*. London: Methuen, 1987.

Prakash, Gyan. 'Introduction'. In *The Spaces of the Modern City: Imaginaries, Politics, and Everyday Life*, edited by Gyan Prakash and Kevin Kruse, 1–18. Princeton, NJ: Princeton University Press, 2008.

Priestley, J. B. *Angel Pavement*. London: Heinemann, 1931.

Priestley, J. B., and Jacquetta Hawkes. *Journey Down a Rainbow*. London: Heinemann-Cresset, 1955.

Profumo, David. *Bringing the House Down: A Family Memoir*. London: John Murray, 2006.

Pry, Paul [pseud. Thomas Burke]. *For Your Convenience: A Learned Dialogue, Instructive to all Londoners and London Visitors Overheard in the Thélème Club and Taken Down Verbatim by Paul Pry*. London: George Routledge and Sons, 1937.

Pryce, Ken. *Endless Pressure: A Study of West Indian Life-Styles in Bristol*. Harmondsworth: Penguin, 1979.

Pugh, Martin. *Women and the Women's Movement in Britain, 1914–1959*. London: Macmillan, 1992.

Purser, Phillip, and Jenny Wilkes. *The One and Only Phyllis Dixey*. London: Futura, 1978.

Pyner, Alf. *Air Cameras: RAF & USAAF, 1915–1945*. Burnham-on-Crouch: Alf Pyner, 1988.

Quennell, Peter, ed. *Genius in the Drawing-Room: The Literary Salon in the Nineteenth and Twentieth Centuries*. London: Weidenfeld & Nicolson, 1980.

———. *The Wanton Chase: An Autobiography from 1939*. London: Collins, 1980.

Raban, Jonathan. *Soft City*. New York: E. P. Dutton, 1974.

Radosh, Ronald. *The Rosenberg File: A Search for the Truth*. London: Weidenfeld & Nicolson, 1983.

Radzinowicz, Leon. *Adventures in Criminology*. London: Routledge, 1999.

———. *Sexual Offences: A Report of the Cambridge Department of Criminal Science*. London: Macmillan, 1957.

Ramsden, John. *The Winds of Change: Macmillan to Heath, 1957–1975*. London: Longman, 1996.

Ramsey, Stanley, and John Harvey. *Small Georgian Houses and their Details 1750–1820*. London: Architectural Press, 1972.

Ransome, Arthur. *The Autobiography of Arthur Ransome*, edited by Rupert Hart-Davis. London: Jonathan Cape, 1976.

———. *Bohemia in London*. London: Chapman & Hall, 1907.

Raphael, Adam. *My Learned Friends*. London: W. H. Allen, 1989.

Rappaport, Erika. 'Art, Commerce, or Empire? The Rebuilding of Regent Street, 1880–1927'. *History Workshop Journal*, no. 53 (2002): 94–117.

———. *Shopping for Pleasure: Women in the Making of London's West End*. Princeton, NJ: Princeton University Press, 2000.

Rasmussen, Steen Eiler. *London: The Unique City*. London: Jonathan Cape, 1937.

Reed, Christopher, ed. *Not at Home: The Suppression of Domesticity in Modern Art and Architecture*. London: Thames & Hudson, 1996.

Rees, Goronwy. *Brief Encounters*. London: Chatto and Windus, 1974.

———. *A Bundle of Sensations: Sketches in Autobiography*. London: Chatto & Windus, 1960.

———. *A Chapter of Accidents*. London: Chatto & Windus, 1972.

Rees, Jenny. *Looking for Mr. Nobody: The Secret Life of Goronwy Rees*. London: Weidenfeld & Nicolson, 1994.

Rice-Davies, Marilyn. *The Mandy Report*. London: Confidential Publications, 1964.

Richardson, Anthony. *Nick of Notting Hill: The Bearded Policeman; The Story of Police Constable J. Nixon F.166, of the Metropolitan Police*. London: Harrap & Co., 1965.

Richmond, Anthony. *Colour Prejudice in Britain: A Study of West Indian Workers in Liverpool, 1941–1951*. London: Routledge & Kegan Paul, 1954.

Riley, Denise. 'Waiting'. In *Truth, Dare, or Promise: Girls Growing Up in the 1950s*, edited by Liz Heron, 237–48. London: Virago, 1985.

Rimbault, Edward. *Soho and its Associations, Historical, Literary and Artistic: Edited from the Mss. of E. F. Rimbault by George Clinch*. London: Dulau and Co., 1895.

Robbins, Bruce. *Feeling Global: Internationalism in Distress*. New York: New York University Press, 1999.

Robertson, James. 'The Censors and British Gangland, 1913–1990'. In *British Crime Cinema*, edited by Steve Chibnall and Robert Murphy, 16–26. London: Routledge, 1999.

Rock, Paul, and Stanley Cohen. 'The Teddy Boy'. In *The Age of Affluence 1951–1964*, edited by Vernon Bogdanor and Robert Skidelsky, 288–320. London: Macmillan, 1970.

Rodgers, Daniel. *Atlantic Crossings: Social Politics in a Progressive Age*. Cambridge, MA, and London: Belknap Press of Harvard University Press, 1998.

Rolph, C. H., ed. *Women of the Streets: A Sociological Study of the Common Prostitute*. London: Secker & Warburg, 1955.

Rose, Nikolas. *Governing the Soul: The Shaping of the Private Self*. London: Routledge, 1990.

Rose, Norman. *The Cliveden Set: Portrait of an Exclusive Fraternity*. London: Jonathan Cape, 2000.

Rose, Sonya. 'Girls and GI's: Race, Sex and Diplomacy in Second World War Britain'. *International History Review* 19, no. 1 (1997): 146–60.

———. 'Sex, Citizenship, and the Nation in World War II Britain'. *American Historical Review* 103, no. 4 (October 1998): 1147–76.

———. *Which People's War? National Identity and Citizenship in Britain 1939–1945*. Oxford: Oxford University Press, 2003.

Rosen, Ismond. 'The Male Response to Frigidity'. *Journal of Psychosomatic Research* 10 (1966): 135–41.

Ross, Alan. 'Introduction'. In Julian Maclaren-Ross, *Memoirs of the Forties*, vii–xiv. Harmondsworth: Penguin, 1984.

Ross, Alan, Nancy Mitford, Evelyn Waugh, 'Strix', Christopher Sykes, and John Betjeman. *Noblesse Oblige: An Enquiry into the Identifiable Characteristics of the English Aristocracy*. London: Hamish Hamilton, 1956.

Rowbotham, Sheila. *Promise of a Dream: Remembering the Sixties*. London: Allen Lane, 2000.

Rowse, A. L. *All Souls in My Time*. London: Duckworth, 1993.

Royal Academy Planning Committee. *London Replanned: The Royal Academy Planning Committee's Interim Report*. London: Country Life, 1942.

Royal Institute of Public Administration, *The Home Office: Perspectives on Policy and Administration: Bicentenary Lectures 1982*. London: Royal Institute of Public Administration, 1983.

Rubinstein, Ruth. *Dress Codes: Meanings and Messages in American Culture*. Boulder, CO: Westview Press, 1995.

Sainsbury, Peter. *Suicide in London: An Ecological Study*. London: Chapman & Hall, 1955.

Saint, Andrew. '"Spread the People": The LCC's Dispersal Policy 1889–1965'. In *Politics and the People of London: The London County Council 1889–1965*, edited by Andrew Saint, 215–36. London: Hambledon Press, 1986.

Saler, Michael. *The Avant-Garde in Interwar England: Medieval Modernism and the London Underground*. New York and Oxford: Oxford University Press, 1999.

Salvoni, Elena, with Sandy Fawkes, *Elena: A Life in Soho*. London: Quartet, 1990.

Sampson, Anthony. *Anatomy of Britain*. London: Hodder & Stoughton, 1962.

———. *Macmillan: A Study in Ambiguity*. London: Allen Lane, 1967.

Samuel, Raphael. *Theatres of Memory, Volume 1: Past and Present in Contemporary Culture*. London: Verso, 1994.

Sandbrook, Dominic. *Never Had It So Good: A History of Britain from Suez to the Beatles*. London: Abacus, 2006.

Sargant, William. *Battle for the Mind: A Physiology of Conversion and Brain-Washing*. London: Heinemann, 1957.

Sarto, Ben. *Soho Spivs*. London: Modern Fiction, 1949.

Schneer, Jonathan. *London 1900: The Imperial Metropolis*. New Haven and London: Yale University Press, 1999.

Schwarz, Bill. '"The Only White Man in There": The Re-Racialization of England 1956–1968'. *Race and Class* 38, no. 1 (1996): 65–78.

———. 'Reveries of Race: The Closing of the Imperial Moment'. In *Moments of Modernity: Reconstructing Britain 1945–1964*, edited by Becky Conekin, Frank Mort, and Chris Waters, 189–207. London: Rivers Oram, 1999.

Scott, Harold. *Scotland Yard*. London: Andre Deutsch, 1954.

Scott, James. *Seeing Like a State: How Certain Schemes to Improve the Human Condition Have Failed*. New Haven and London: Yale University Press, 1998.

Secombe, Harry. *Arias & Raspberries: The Autobiography of Harry Secombe*, vol. 1, *The Raspberry Years*. London: Robson, 1989.

Sekula, Allan. *Dismal Science Photo Works 1972–1996*. Normal, IL: University Galleries, Illinois State University, 1999.

———. *Photography Against the Grain: Essays and Photo Works 1973–1983*. Halifax, NS: Press of the Nova Scotia College of Art and Design, 1984.

Self, Helen. *Prostitution, Women and Misuse of the Law: The Fallen Daughters of Eve*. London: Frank Cass, 2003.

Sellin, Thorsten. 'The Significance of Records of Crime'. *Law Quarterly Review* 67 (1951): 489–504.

Selwyn, Francis. *Rotten to the Core? The Life and Death of Neville Heath*. London: Routledge, 1988.

Sennett, Richard. *The Fall of Public Man*. London: Faber & Faber, 1993.

Sewell, William. 'Historical Events as Transformative Structures: Inventing Revolution at the Bastille'. *Theory and Society* 25, no. 6 (December 1996): 841–81.

Shanks, Michael. 'The Comforts of Stagnation'. In *Suicide of a Nation? An Enquiry into the State of Britain Today*, edited by Arthur Koestler, 51–69. London: Hutchinson, 1963.

———. *The Stagnant Society: A Warning*. Harmondsworth: Penguin, 1961.

Shepherd, Robert. *Iain Macleod*. London: Hutchinson, 1994.

Sheppard, F. H. W., ed. *Survey of London*, vol. 33, *The Parish of St Anne Soho*. London: Athlone Press, University of London, 1966.

———, ed. *Survey of London*, vol. 37, *Northern Kensington*. London: Athlone Press, University of London, 1973.

———, *London: A History*. Oxford: Oxford University Press, 1998.

Sherwell, Arthur. *Life in West London: A Study and a Contrast*. London: Methuen, 1897.

Shils, Edward. *A Fragment of a Sociological Autobiography: The History of my Pursuit of a Few Ideas*, edited by Steven Grosby. Somerset, NJ: Transaction Publishers, 2006.

———. *The Intellectuals and the Powers, and Other Essays*. Chicago: University of Chicago Press, 1972.

———. 'The Intellectuals 1: Great Britain'. *Encounter* 4, no. 4 (April 1955): 5–16.

Shils, Edward, and Michael Young. 'The Meaning of the Coronation'. *Sociological Review*, n.s., 1, no. 2 (December 1953): 63–81.

Shipman Inquiry. *Third Report, Death Certification and the Investigation of Deaths by Coroners*. Norwich: Stationery Office, 2003.

Sigsworth, Eric. *Montague Burton: The Tailor of Taste*. Manchester: Manchester University Press, 1990.

Simmel, Georg. 'The Metropolis and Mental Life'. In *The Sociology of Georg Simmel*, edited by Kurt Wolff, 409–24. New York: Free Press of Glencoe, 1964.

Simpson, Colin, Lewis Chester, and David Leitch. *The Cleveland Street Affair*. Boston, MA: Little, Brown, 1976.

Sims, George. *Living London*, vol. 1. London: Cassell, n.d.

Sissons, Michael, and Philip French, eds. *Age of Austerity*. London: Hodder & Stoughton, 1963.

Skidelsky, Robert. *John Maynard Keynes: A Biography, Volume 2: The Economist as Saviour, 1920–1937*. London: Macmillan, 1992.

Smith, Alison. *The Victorian Nude: Sexuality, Morality and Art*. Manchester: Manchester University Press, 1996.

Smith, Bradley. *The Road to Nuremberg*. New York: Basic Books, 1981.

Soho Association. *Soho Annual*. London: Soho Association, 1958.

———. *Soho Fair*, Official Programme. London: Soho Association, 1956.

———. *Soho Fair*, Official Programme. London: Soho Association, 1957.

Soothill, Keith. *Criminal Conversations: An Anthology of the Work of Tony Parker*. London: Routledge, 1999.

Sorlin, Pierre. *European Cinemas, European Societies 1930–1990*. London: Routledge, 1991.

Sparrow, Gerald. *Confessions of an Eccentric*. London: Jarrods, 1965.

Spiegel, Gabrielle. 'History, Historicism, and the Social Logic of the Text'. *Speculum* 65, no. 1 (January 1990): 59–86.

Stallybrass, Peter, and Allon White. *The Politics and Poetics of Transgression*. London: Methuen, 1986.

Stanford, Peter. *Bronwen Astor: Her Life and Times*. London: HarperCollins, 1999.

Stansell, Christine. *American Moderns: Bohemian New York and the Creation of a New Century*. New York: Owl Books, 2000.

Steedman, Carolyn. *Dust*. Manchester: Manchester University Press, 2001.

———. *Landscape for a Good Woman: A Story of Two Lives*. London: Virago, 1985.

Steele-Perkins, Chris, and Richard Smith, *The Teds*. London: Travelling Light, 1979.

Storr, Anthony. *Sexual Deviation*. Harmondsworth: Penguin, 1964.

Stott, Mary. *Before I Go . . . : Reflections on My Life and Times*. London: Virago, 1985.

Summerfield, Penny. *Reconstructing Women's Wartime Lives: Discourse and Subjectivity in Oral Histories of the Second World War*. Manchester: Manchester University Press, 1998.

Summers, Anthony, and Stephen Dorril. *Honeytrap: The Secret Worlds of Stephen Ward*. London: Weidenfeld & Nicolson, 1987.

Summers, Judith. *The Empress of Pleasure: The Life and Adventures of Teresa Cornelys – Queen of Masquerades and Casanova's Lover*. London: Viking, 2003.

———. *Soho: A History of London's Most Colourful Neighbourhood*. London: Bloomsbury, 1989.

Sutcliffe, Anthony. *An Economic and Social History of Western Europe since 1945*. London: Longman, 1996.

Sutherland, Douglas. *Portrait of a Decade: London Life 1945–1955*. London: Harrap, 1988.

Swanson, Gillian. *Drunk with the Glitter: Space, Consumption and Sexual Instability in Modern Urban Culture*. Abingdon: Routledge, 2007.

———. 'Good-Time Girls, Men of Truth and a Thoroughly Filthy Fellow: Sexual Pathology and National Character in the Profumo Affair'. *New Formations*, no. 24 (1994): 122–54.

Symonds, John Addington. *A Problem in Modern Ethics: Being an Enquiry into the Phenomenon of Sexual Inversion, Addressed Especially to Medical Psychologists and Jurists*. London: privately printed, 1896.

Syson, Lydia. *Doctor of Love: James Graham and his Celestial Bed*. Richmond: Alma Books, 2008.

Tagg, John. *The Burden of Representation: Essays on Photographies and Histories*. Basingstoke: Macmillan Education, 1988.

Taki, and Jeffrey Bernard, *High Life, Low Life*. London: Unwin, 1982.

Thomas, Hugh, ed. *The Establishment: A Symposium*. London: Anthony Blond, 1959.

Thomas, Nick. 'Will the Real 1950s Please Stand Up?' *Cultural and Social History* 5, no. 2 (June 2008): 227–35.

Thompson, Edward. 'The Peculiarities of the English'. In *The Socialist Register 1965*, edited by Ralph Miliband and John Saville, 311–62. London: Merlin Press, 1965.

Thompson, F. M. L. 'Presidential Address: English Landed Society in the Twentieth Century: IV, Prestige without Power?' In *Transactions of the Royal Historical Society*, 6th ser., 3, edited by the Royal Historical Society, 1–23. London: Royal Historical Society, 1993.

Thompson, Harry. *Richard Ingrams: Lord of the Gnomes*. London: Mandarin, 1995.

Thurlow, David. *Profumo: The Hate Factor*. London, Robert Hale, 1992.

Timmermann, Brigitte. *The Third Man's Vienna: Celebrating a Film Classic*, translated by Penny Black. Vienna: Shippen Rock, 2005.

Tiratsoo, Nick. 'Popular Politics, Affluence and the Labour Party in the 1950s'. In *Contemporary British History, 1931–1961: Politics and the Limits of Policy*, edited by Anthony Gorst, Lewis Johnman, and W. Scott Lucas, 44–61. London: Pinter in association with the Institute of Contemporary British History, 1991.

Titman, George, ed. *Dress and Insignia Worn at His Majesty's Court, Issued with the Authority of the Lord Chamberlain*. London: Harrison, 1937.

Todd, Ruthven. *Fitzrovia & the Road to York Minster, or, Down Dean St.* London: Michael Parkin Gallery, 1973.

Tomkinson, Martin. *Pornbrokers: The Rise of the Soho Sex Barons*. London: Virgin Books, 1982.

Toplis, Ian. *The Foreign Office: An Architectural History*. London: Mansell, 1987.

Townsend, Peter. *The Family Life of Old People: An Inquiry in East London*. London: Routledge & Kegan Paul, 1957.

Townsend, Peter. *Time and Chance: An Autobiography*. London: Collins, 1978.

Trumbach, Randolph. 'London'. In *Queer Sites: Gay Urban Histories since 1600*, edited by David Higgs, 89–111. London: Routledge, 1999.

———. *Sex and the Gender Revolution*, vol. 1, *Heterosexuality and the Third Gender in Enlightenment London*. Chicago: University of Chicago Press, 1998.

Turner, Victor. *The Anthropology of Performance*. New York: PAJ Publications, 1986.

————. 'Social Dramas and Stories about Them'. *Critical Inquiry* 7, no. 1 (1980): 141–68.

Underwood, Peter. *Danny La Rue: Life's A Drag*. London: Star Books, 1975.

Unstead, R. J. *People in History*. London: Adam and Charles Black, 1955.

Urwin, Derek. *Western Europe since 1945: A Short Political History*, 3rd edn. London: Longman, 1981.

Van Damm, Sheila. *We Never Closed: The Windmill Story*. London: Robert Hale, 1967.

Van Damm, Vivian. *Tonight and Every Night*. London: Stanley Paul, 1952.

Vassall, William. *Vassall: The Autobiography of a Spy*. London: Sidgwick & Jackson, 1975.

Vernon, James. 'The Mirage of Modernity'. *Social History* 22, no. 2 (May 1997): 208–15.

Vincent, David. *The Culture of Secrecy: Britain, 1832–1998*. Oxford: Oxford University Press, 1998.

Walker, Alexander. *Peter Sellers: The Authorized Biography*. London: Weidenfeld & Nicolson, 1981.

Walkowitz, Judith. *City of Dreadful Delight: Narratives of Sexual Danger in Late-Victorian London*. London: Virago, 1992.

————. 'Cosmopolitanism, Feminism, and the Moving Body'. *Victorian Culture and Literature* 38, no. 2 (Fall 2010), forthcoming.

————. 'Male Vice and Feminist Virtue: Feminism and the Politics of Prostitution in Nineteenth-Century Britain'. *History Workshop Journal*, no. 13 (1982): 79–93.

————. *Prostitution and Victorian Society: Women, Class and the State*. Cambridge: Cambridge University Press, 1980.

————. 'The "Vision of Salome": Cosmopolitanism and Erotic Dancing in Central London, 1908–1918'. *American Historical Review* 102, no. 2 (2003): 337–76.

Ward, Christopher. 'Brooks's since the War'. In *Brooks's: A Social History*, edited by Philip Ziegler and Desmond Seward, 103–16. London: Constable, 1991.

Ward Jouve, Nicole. *'The Streetcleaner': The Yorkshire Ripper Case on Trial*. London: Boyars, 1986.

Warwick, Christopher. *Princess Margaret*. London: Weidenfeld & Nicolson, 1983.

Waters, Chris. '"Dark Strangers" in Our Midst: Discourses of Race and Nation in Britain, 1947–1964'. *Journal of British Studies* 36, no. 2 (April 1997): 207–38.

————. 'Disorders of the Mind, Disorders of the Body Social: Peter Wildeblood and the Making of the Modern Homosexual'. In *Moments of Modernity: Reconstructing Britain 1945–1964*, edited by Becky Conekin, Frank Mort, and Chris Waters, 134–51. London: Rivers Oram, 1999.

————. 'Havelock Ellis, Sigmund Freud and the State: Discourses of Homosexual Identity in Interwar Britain'. In *Sexology in Culture: Labelling Bodies and Desires*, edited by Lucy Bland and Laura Doan, 165–79. Cambridge: Polity, 1998.

Watson, Sophia. *Marina: The Story of a Princess*. London: Weidenfeld & Nicolson, 1994.

Waugh, Alec. 'Round About Soho'. In *Wonderful London*, vol. 1, edited by Arthur St John Adcock, 129–36. London: Fleetway House, n.d.

Waugh, Auberon. *The Last Word: An Eye-Witness Account of the Trial of Jeremy Thorpe*. London: Michael Joseph, 1980.

Waugh, Evelyn. *Brideshead Revisited: The Sacred and Profane Memories of Captain Charles Ryder*. New York: Little, Brown, 1999.

Webb, Aston, ed. *London of the Future*. London: London Society, 1921.

Webb, Duncan. *Crime Reporter*. London: Fleetway Colourbacks, 1963.

———. *Deadline for Crime*. London: Frederick Muller, 1955.

Webster, Wendy. *Englishness and Empire 1939–1965*. Oxford: Oxford University Press, 2005.

———. ' "There'll Always Be an England": Representations of Colonial Wars and Immigration, 1948–1968'. *Journal of British Studies* 40, no. 4 (October 2001): 557–84.

Weeks, Jeffrey. *Against Nature: Essays on History, Sexuality and Identity*. London: Rivers Oram, 1991.

———. *Coming Out: Homosexual Politics in Britain from the Nineteenth Century to the Present*, 2nd edn. London: Quartet, 1990.

———. *Sex, Politics and Society: The Regulation of Sexuality since 1800*. London: Longman, 1989.

Weeks, Jeffrey, and Kevin Porter, eds. *Between the Acts: Lives of Homosexual Men 1885–1967*, 2nd edn. London: Rivers Oram, 1998.

West, Nigel. *A Matter of Trust: MI5 1945–72*. London: Weidenfeld & Nicolson, 1982.

West, Rebecca. *The Meaning of Treason*. London: Virago, 1982.

———. *A Train of Powder*. London: Virago, 1984.

Westergaard, J. H. 'The Structure of Greater London'. In *London: Aspects of Change*, edited by Centre for Urban Studies, 91–156. London: MacGibbon and Kee, 1964.

Westwood, Gordon [pseud. Michael Schofield]. *A Minority: A Report of the Life of the Male Homosexual in Great Britain*. London: Longman, 1960.

———. *Society and the Homosexual*. London: Gollancz, 1952.

Whalen, David. *The Origins of Satellite Communications 1945–1965*. Washington, DC and London: Smithsonian Institution Press, 2002.

Wheeler-Bennett, John. *King George VI: His Life and Reign*. London: Pan, 1967.

White, Jerry. *London in the Twentieth Century: A City and its People*. London: Penguin, 2002.

Wickenden, James. *Colour in Britain . . . Issued Under the Auspices of the Institute of Race Relations*. London: Oxford University Press, 1958.

Wiebe, Heather. ' "Now and England": Britten's *Gloriana* and the "New Elizabethans" '. *Cambridge Opera Journal* 17, no. 2 (2005): 141–72.

Wigg, George. *George Wigg*. London: Michael Joseph, 1972.

Wigley, Mark. *White Walls, Designer Dresses: The Fashioning of Modern Architecture*. Cambridge, MA: MIT Press, 1995.

Wilcox, Claire, ed. *The Golden Age of Couture: Paris and London 1947–1957*. London: V&A Publications, 2007.

Wilde, Oscar. *The Picture of Dorian Gray*. London: Penguin, 1985.

Wildeblood, Peter. *Against the Law*. Harmondsworth: Penguin, 1957.

———. *The Main Chance*. London: Weidenfeld & Nicolson, 1957.

———. *West End People*. London: Weidenfeld & Nicolson, 1958.

Williams, Emlyn. *Emlyn: An Early Autobiography: 1927–1935*. London: Bodley Head, 1973.

Williams, Keith. *British Writers and the Media, 1930–45*. London: Macmillan, 1996.

Williams-Ellis, Clough. *England and the Octopus*. London: Geoffrey Bles, 1928.

Willmott, Peter, and Michael Young. *Family and Class in a London Suburb*. London: Routledge & Kegan Paul, 1960.

Wilmut, Roger. *From Fringe to Flying Circus: Celebrating a Unique Generation of Comedy 1960–1980*. London: Eyre Methuen, 1980.

Wilson, Colin. *The Corpse Garden: The Crimes of Fred and Rose West*. London: True Crime Library, 1998.

Wilson, Derek. *The Astors: 1763–1992: Landscape with Millionaires*. London: Weidenfeld & Nicolson, 1993.

Wilson, Elizabeth. *Bohemians: The Glamorous Outcasts*. London: Tauris, 2000.

———. *Only Halfway to Paradise: Women in Postwar Britain 1945–64*. London: Tavistock, 1980.

Wingrave, Josh. *Back Streets of Soho*. London: Kaye Publications, 1953.

———. *A Room in Soho*. London: Gaywood Press, 1953.

Winship, Janice, 'Culture of Restraint: The British Chain Store 1920–39'. In *Commercial Cultures: Economies, Practices and Spaces*, edited by Peter Jackson, Michelle Lowe, Daniel Miller, and Frank Mort, 15–34. Oxford: Berg, 2000.

———. *Inside Women's Magazines*. London: Pandora, 1987.

Winter, Jay. 'Paris, London, Berlin, 1914–1919: Capital Cities at War'. In *Capital Cities at War: Paris, London, Berlin, 1914–1919*, edited by Jay Winter and Jean-Louis Robert, 3–24. Cambridge: Cambridge University Press, 1997.

Wise, Damon. *Come By Sunday: The Fabulous, Ruined Life of Diana Dors*. London: Pan, 1999.

Wolfe, Thomas. *The Mid-Atlantic Man: And Other New Breeds in England and America*. London: Weidenfeld & Nicolson, 1969.

Wolfenden, John. *The Creation of a Public Conscience: The Twenty-First Shaftesbury Lecture*. London: Shaftesbury Society, 1961.

———. *Turning Points: The Memoirs of Lord Wolfenden*. London: Bodley Head, 1976.

Woolf, Virginia. 'The London Scene II: Oxford Street Tide'. In *Ragtime to Wartime: The Best of Good Housekeeping 1922–1939*, compiled by Brian Braithwaite, Nöelle Walsh, and Glyn Davies, 138–9. London: Ebury Press, 1986.

Worswick, G. D. N., and P. H. Ady, eds. *The British Economy in the Nineteen-Fifties*. Oxford: Clarendon Press, 1962.

Wortley, Richard. *A Pictorial History of Striptease*. London: Octopus, 1976.

Wright, Patrick. *On Living in an Old Country: The National Past in Contemporary Britain*. London: Verso, 1985.

Young, Ken, and Patricia Garside. *Metropolitan London: Politics and Urban Change 1837–1981*. London: Edward Arnold, 1982.

Young, Michael, and Peter Willmott, *Family and Kinship in East London*. London: Routledge & Kegan Paul, 1957.

Ziegler, Philip. *Crown and People*. London: Collins, 1978.

———. *King Edward VIII: The Official Biography*. London: Fontana, 1991.

Ziegler, Philip, and Desmond Seward, eds. *Brooks's: A Social History*. London: Constable, 1991.

Zorbaugh, Harvey. *Gold Coast and the Slum: A Sociological Study of Chicago's Near North Side*. Chicago: University of Chicago Press, 1929.

Zweig, Ferdynand. *The Worker in an Affluent Society: Family Life and Industry*. London: Heinemann, 1961.

Zweiniger-Bargielowska, Ina. *Austerity in Britain: Rationing, Controls, and Consumption, 1939–1955*. Oxford: Oxford University Press, 2000.

VII FILMOGRAPHY

The Blue Lamp, directed by Basil Dearden (Great Britain: Ealing Studios, 1950).

Mrs Henderson Presents, directed by Stephen Frears (Pathé Pictures International, 2005).

Murder at the Windmill, directed by Val Guest (Great Britain: Grand National Film Productions, 1948).

Night and the City, directed by Jules Dassin (Great Britain, United States: Twentieth Century Fox Film Corporation, 1950).

Noose, directed by Edmond Greville (Great Britain: Edward Dryhurst Productions, 1948).

Scandal, directed by Michael Caton-Jones (Great Britain: Palace Pictures, 1989).

They Made Me A Fugitive, directed by Alberto Cavalcanti (Great Britain: Alliance Film Studios, 1947).

The Third Man, directed by Carol Reed (Great Britain: London Film Productions, 1949).

Tonight and Every Night, directed by Victor Saville (United States: Columbia Pictures, 1945).

Index